Y0-BYW-322

monitoring the future

questionnaire responses from the nation's high school seniors

1976

Jerald G. Bachman, Lloyd D. Johnston, and
Patrick M. O'Malley

Survey Research Center • Institute for Social Research
The University of Michigan
Ann Arbor, Michigan

ISR Code Number 4156
ISSN 0190-9185
ISBN 0-87944-236-0

Copyright 1980 by The University of Michigan,
All Rights Reserved

Published in 1980 by:
Institute for Social Research,
The University of Michigan, Ann Arbor, Michigan

Printed in the United States of America

Table of Contents

Preface

This volume is the second in a series which presents descriptive statistical results from a national survey of young people entitled Monitoring the Future: A Continuing Study of the Lifestyles and Values of Youth. Each year the study surveys a large sample of high school seniors, located in approximately 125 schools nationwide, and drawn to be representative of all seniors in the coterminous United States. In 1976, the year covered by the present volume, 16,678 seniors in 108 public and 15 private high schools participated in the research.

The first four volumes in this series, dealing with the high school classes of 1975, 1976, 1977, and 1978, are being published simultaneously. Additional volumes are expected to appear on an annual basis. The most important contribution of this series is likely to be the opportunity it provides for the exploration of trends, a process that obviously involves the use of several different volumes. With that in mind, we have kept the format highly consistent from one volume to another, and we have developed an index (described below) which should facilitate the process of matching data across years. It should be noted that the volume presenting 1975 data is different from the others in several respects.*

Although we designed the volumes to fit together as a series, we also saw distinct advantages in having each volume able to stand alone — to be usable without reference to any of the others. For that reason, the introductory material on research design and questionnaire content, the instructions for accessing the data tables, and the appendices on

sampling errors are all included in each volume. Thus, the small price we pay for making each volume self-contained is that much of the text portion is repeated each year.

Purposes of this Series of Publications

Monitoring the Future, which is conducted by the University of Michigan's Institute for Social Research and receives its core funding from the National Institute on Drug Abuse, is an unusually comprehensive research project in several respects: surveys are conducted annually on an ongoing basis; the samples are large and nationally representative; and the subject matter is very broad, encompassing some 1,300 variables per year. Many people — scholars, policy makers, educators, and so on — will have an interest in the results.

The principal investigators are already writing for a number of these audiences and will continue to do so. Because of the limitations in our own time, interests, and expertise, however, there is an enormous amount of valuable information which may never be utilized if the initiative to digest and disseminate all of it must come from us alone. Further, since the project is in part a social indicators series, its value rests to a considerable degree on timely dissemination of the results. For these reasons, we wish to share the study's results with others in a number of fields on a rapid and regular basis. We have chosen to provide two major and complemen-

---

*The 1975 volume does not include comparison data for black and white subgroups, nor does it include data for the subgroups who did and did not plan to complete four years of college. Also, somewhat fewer questionnaire items appear than in the other volumes. These restrictions are the result primarily of missing data problems that occurred only in the 1975 survey. In most respects, however, those seeking to compare different classes of high school seniors will find the 1975 data useful.

tary vehicles for doing this: (a) these annual reference volumes of descriptive results, and (b) machine-readable data archives for direct analysis by others.

We believe that many potential users who would not mount the effort required to conduct computer analyses of archived data will be able to get most of what they want from these volumes of descriptive results. The user of any one of these volumes can estimate — usually with considerable accuracy — a wide variety of characteristics of the high school class described in that volume. To take just one example, the user of the present volume can ascertain that 44.5 percent of seniors in the high school class of 1976 reported using marijuana at least once during the preceding year. Further, by utilizing two or more of these volumes the reader can describe recent trends in any such characteristic. To continue with the same example, the volume describing the high school class of 1978 indicates that 50.2 percent of those seniors reported marijuana use during the preceding year; and when that is combined with the data from the present volume the reader is able to discern a shift of 5.7 percent over the two years between the classes of 1976 and 1978. And if all of the first four volumes in the series are used, one can observe a steady increase in the proportion of high school seniors who report having used marijuana at least once during the twelve months preceding the survey:

40.0 percent of seniors in 1975
44.5 percent of seniors in 1976
47.6 percent of seniors in 1977
50.2 percent of seniors in 1978

A similar examination of trends can be carried out for over 1,300 different variables dealing with a wide variety of subject areas (listed in Table 2 of the Introduction). A simple indexing system (described below) has been developed which makes it quite straightforward for the reader wishing to do trend analyses to locate the results for a given question for any year of the study. The index in the present volume lists the location of all items included in the surveys for 1976 through 1978 and most items included in 1975.

Analyses such as those illustrated above need not be limited to the total sample. The data provided in these volumes also permit examination of a variety of subgroups (e.g., males, females, those from different regions, those with different levels of drug use experience). The principal investigators have already conducted and reported some analyses in the area of drug use and related attitudes (Johnston, Bachman, and O'Malley, 1977, 1979), but many other areas have not yet been explored extensively.

We recognize that providing ready access to essentially undigested data carries certain risks, particularly the risk of mistaken interpretations based on inadequate controls, lack of awareness of sample limitations, etc. More than offsetting the risks, in our view, are the advantages of prompt and widespread dissemination of these nationally representative survey indicator data. Although we are unable to eliminate the risks, we hope to reduce them by providing the reader with an extensive list of caveats presented at the end of the Introduction section. We ask all who use the data to read these caveats carefully and take them seriously.

A Guide for the Reader

This volume is divided into three main parts: (1) the introductory section, (2) the section giving the descriptive results from the current year's survey, and (3) the cross-time item reference index.

Introductory Section. The introduction contains a description of the study — its purposes, major content areas, design, field procedures, response rates, and methods of publication and data dissemination. Since most of this material remains unchanged from year to year, anyone having read another of the volumes may wish to skim this section. We do, however, suggest reviewing the caveats, located at the end of the introductory section, which deal with interpreting and extrapolating from these data.

Descriptive Results Section. In this section all questions contained in this year's survey are presented along with percentagized frequency distributions of answers for the entire sample and for selected subgroups. The questions in this section are organized according to the number of the questionnaire form in which they were contained (forms one through five) and according to the order in which the questions occurred. There is one important exception, however. A major segment of questions common to all five forms of the questionnaire (dealing with drug use, background characteristics, and some other subjects) is presented only once, at the beginning of the Descriptive Results section, using the data from respondents on all five forms.

The first portion of the descriptive results section contains detailed definitions of all subgroups for whom data are presented. It also describes the statistical conventions used in generating the tables.

Cross-Time Index of Questionnaire Items. This index is intended to serve two purposes.

First it should be useful in locating items dealing with a subject area of interest. The subject area key at the beginning of the cross-time item index shows the alphabetical code assigned to various subject areas (e.g., "politics" or "work and leisure"). Having selected a subject area of interest, one can then scan the Subject Area column in the item index to locate all questions in any of the surveys (through 1978) which deal with that subject. To locate the results for any given question in the Descriptive Results section of this volume, simply look in column two of the item index for its page location.

The cross-time index can also be used to determine in which other years an item was used and where to locate it. If, in reviewing the Descriptive Results section, one locates an interesting item and would like to know in which of the other annual surveys of seniors it has appeared, it may be found in the cross-time index by its unique "item reference number." The index will indicate all years in which that same item appeared and show the questionnaire form, section, and item number for each year. This information thus can be used to decide which other volumes in this series might be of relevance; and the same item may be readily located by its reference number in the index of any other volume.

Sampling Appendices. Appendix A is provided for those wishing to determine the confidence limits around a percentage estimate, or to test the statistical significance of an observed difference between two groups, or to test the significance of a change from one year to another. It gives the necessary procedures and tables for such tests and provides the appropriate factors by which to correct for the fact that the study makes use of a multi-stage probability sample clustered in a limited number of schools (usually about 125). Appendix B provides further detail on sample design effects and the procedures which were used to derive the sampling error estimates.

Availability of Archived Data

As was mentioned earlier, this series of volumes will be complemented by an archiving of the raw data sets for direct analysis by others not associated with the project. The present volumes should be a considerable help to those wishing to access the archived data since they provide a verbatim statement of items and answer categories, and also because they include basic univariate and bivariate frequency distributions for all items, as well as the missing data rates. The cross-time index of items contained in each of these volumes also provides an efficient way to identify the relevant variables in various content areas, as well as to determine when they were measured and their

questionnaire locations. In fact, we hope that the availability of this series will not only facilitate the use of the archived data but actually stimulate interest in their use.

Two major social science archives will hold the individual level data which are summarized in this volume:

> The Interuniversity Consortium for Political and Social Research (ICPSR)
> Institute for Social Research
> P.O. Box 1248
> Ann Arbor, Michigan 48106

> The Drug Abuse Epidemiology Data Center (DAEDAC)
> Institute for Behavioral Research
> Texas Christian University
> Fort Worth, Texas 76129

The ICPSR archive will make individual-level data available on tape to interested investigators for analysis at their own facility. However, it is presently planned that these data sets will not contain the drug use or delinquency measures. Because of the sensitivity of the latter measures — that is, those describing the respondent's own use of illicit drugs and other delinquent behaviors — only the data set in the DAEDAC archive will contain those measures. The Monitoring the Future file at DAEDAC will be treated as a "restricted data set," meaning that all analyses must be carried out by the archive staff (under the instructions of the outside investigator). Individual level data will not be released by DAEDAC, thereby ensuring that the answers of an individual respondent cannot be located through pattern recognition (i.e., using various descriptor variables in combination to make a unique identification). While the probability of such identification may seem remote, we feel that the potential seriousness of the consequences is sufficient to justify this high level of caution.

Other Publications from the Study

A number of different forms of publications based on Monitoring the Future data have been developed or are being planned. One series of annual volumes, dealing with trends in drug use and drug-related attitudes and beliefs, is being published by the National Institute on Drug Abuse. The first volume in that series, *Drug Use Among American High School Students 1975-1977* (Johnston, Bachman, and O'Malley), was published in late 1977; and the second, *Drugs and the Class of '78* (Johnston, Bachman, and O'Malley), in 1979.*

---

*Either the full volumes, or abbreviated highlights versions of each, may be ordered without cost from the National Clearinghouse for Drug Abuse Information, National Institute on Drug Abuse, 5600 Fishers Lane, Rockville, Maryland 20857.

An Occasional Papers series has been launched by the project. It includes papers on design and methodological issues as well as special substantive analyses and early, and sometimes more detailed, drafts of articles planned for journal publication. The first occasional paper, "The Monitoring the Future Project Design and Procedures" (Bachman and Johnston, 1978), provides a detailed description of the study and its underlying rationale.

The present series of reference volumes is being published by the Institute for Social Research. A new volume will be added to this series each year.

Articles for academic journals, as well as for journals serving various professionals working with youths, are also being written. In addition, several integrative books based on the Monitoring the Future project are in the planning stages.

To request particular papers, reprints, or periodic notification of publications available from the study, write to Monitoring the Future, Room 2030, Institute for Social Research, The University of Michigan, Box 1248, Ann Arbor, Michigan 48106.

Acknowledgements

A great many people have contributed to the launching and development of this research effort. We are indebted to a number of officials of the National Institute on Drug Abuse and the Special Action Office for Drug Abuse Prevention for their encouragement and advice at the outset — in particular, Richard Bucher, Robert DuPont, William Pollin, and Louise Richards. To the members of our Advisory Panel we also express our thanks for their review and suggestions regarding instrumentation and design. In addition to Drs. Bucher and Richards, the committee members are John Ball, Donald Campbell, Ira Cisin, Wilbur Cohen, O. Dudley Duncan, Dorothy Gilford, Eric Josephson, Robert Kahn, Donald Michael, and Lee Robins.

Our colleagues at the Institute for Social Research and elsewhere who shared their insights, and often their most cherished instrumentation, are too numerous to mention; but their contributions are greatly appreciated. To the director of the Survey Research Center's Sampling Section, Irene Hess, we owe a particular debt for the creativity of her sampling design for the study. The contributions of the SRC Field Section also have been very valuable.

Major contributions to the production of this particular volume were made by staff members Dawn Bare, Deborah Poinier, Maria Sanchez, and Ann Taylor. We would also like to thank the staff of the Publishing Division of the Institute for Social Research for their work in arranging publication.

The present and former members of the project staff (listed below) have, of course, contributed greatly to the building of this large and complex research series.

Finally, we would like to acknowledge the tens of thousands of high school seniors, their teachers, and their principals, whose cooperation and generous contribution of time make the Monitoring the Future project possible.

JERALD G. BACHMAN
LLOYD D. JOHNSTON
PATRICK M. O'MALLEY

Present and Former Members of the Project Staff

Donna Ando	Walter Gruhn	Jim Neveaux
Margaret Bailey	James Hersey	Dorothy Paulette
Dawn Bare	A. Regula Herzog	Sharon Pietila
Ellen Berger	Mark Krell	Joseph Pleck
Mary Lou Bewley	Sally Lawson	Deborah Poinier
Katherine Blatt	Ludmilla Litus	Judith Redmond
Mary Lea Bonucchi	A. Kathryn Loker	Barbara Renaud
Marcy Breslow	Regina Lumbard	Maria Sanchez
Mary Lou Davis	Oksana Malanchuk	Ann Taylor
Mary Dempsy	Wayne McCulloch	Richard Taylor
William Diedrich	Joan McGraw	Lynda Tolen
Karen Donahue	John Miller	Sandra Wronski
Leslie Eveland	Marion Morse	Thelma Wurzelbacher
Halford Fairchild		

Introduction

The Monitoring the Future project is designed to explore changes in many important values, behaviors, and lifestyle orientations of contemporary American youth. Two general types of tasks may be distinguished. The first is to provide a systematic and accurate *description* of the youth population of interest in a given year, and to quantify the direction and rate of the changes taking place among them over time. The second task, more analytic than descriptive, involves the *explanation* of the relationships and trends observed to exist.

The task of description may be subdivided into three parts: (1) the description of static conditions (which may be accomplished through a single cross-sectional study); (2) the description of cross-cohort or, in longer time-spans, generational changes (usually accomplished using repeated cross sections of the same age groups); and (3) the description of changes with aging (usually accomplished by means of longitudinal studies). The Monitoring the Future project has the capacity to provide each of these three types of description, since it incorporates all three types of research design into a single study. (This complex design, in which multiple cohorts are followed longitudinally, has been referred to as a cohort-sequential design.)

The content of this volume exemplifies the first of these types of description in that it contains cross-sectional data on a single high school class. When the data in this volume are used in combination with data from other such volumes in the series, the nature, direction, and rates of change from one cohort of seniors to another also may be described — the type of reporting which is often labeled as the social indicator approach. The third class of description — dealing with the maturational changes which occur during the years after high school — will not be dealt with in this series of volumes but will be reported in other publications from the study.*

The accurate characterization of American young people and the description of important changes occurring among them is but one class of objectives for the study. The second class of objectives involves the development of a greater understanding of what causes these young people to be as they are, and why the changes being documented are occurring. Explanation will be sought through both the analysis of change at the aggregate level and at the individual level. The results of these explorations will be disseminated via the various publications discussed in the Preface.

The merging of the social indicator approach and the analysis of relationships (particularly longitudinal relationships) into a single cohort-sequential design is, in our view, synergistic: the effectiveness of the two approaches combined is greater than if the two were undertaken separately. Because the present series of volumes deals with senior year data only, our remarks here focus primarily on the project's social indicator contributions — the accurate description of high school seniors and the documentation of trends over time. It is worth not-

*Panels of students from each graduating class are being randomly selected and followed longitudinally for six years. Thus it soon will be possible to characterize the changes which seem to take place consistently with aging during the early adult years. Not only will longitudinal development in the years after high school be studied, but once enough of these longitudinal panels have accumulated, it will also be possible to characterize cross-sectionally most American young people aged 18 to 24, (at least the major segment of the population who completed high school — roughly 80-85 percent), and to describe the changing characteristics of that age group each year.

ing, however, that even the limited amount of bivariate data included in the present volumes will suggest promising directions for relational analyses, many of which can be carried out using the archived data tapes from the project.

The Need for Social Indicators

The fundamental argument for developing social indicators is that there are considerable scientific and practical benefits derived from having accurate information about current social realities and the way those realities have been changing. For the scientific community such indicators provide a rich set of information against which existing theory may be tested and from which new theory may be suggested. For the community at large, social indicators permit the "reality testing" of common perceptions and beliefs about the nation and its people. Past experience has demonstrated that widely held conceptions, which themselves may serve to create or exacerbate problems, can be most inaccurate. One example is the exaggerated popular conception of the size and nature of the "gap" between generations (see Adelson, 1970, 1979); another is the mistaken assumption that most young people condone the use of a variety of illegal drugs (Johnston, 1973; Johnston, Bachman, and O'Malley, 1977; 1979).

While deflating exaggerated perceptions, a continual monitoring of indicators on youth also can reveal the beginning of new problems and thus give rise to corrective efforts at a relatively early stage. For instance, most would view with concern the emergence of new types of drug use. Monitoring the Future has already documented and reported a sharp increase in regular marijuana use among high school seniors, and as a result more attention has been paid to the issue by policy makers, the media, and the general public. The discovery of such trends may trigger more intense efforts to discover the causes, consequences, and (when appropriate) preventatives of such behaviors.

Although social indicators seldom translate directly into specific policy decisions, the availability of descriptive information can substantially enhance the decision-making capabilities of policy makers. These data provide considerable insight into the size and nature of problems, the rate of change occurring nationally and in subgroups, and in some instances information about related factors and even the likely impacts of major social interventions (such as changed drug laws, or new incentives for recruitment into the military, to name but two). They also provide the possibility of feedback

on the consequences of some social interventions as well as major historical events.

The particular topics included in our monitoring system are summarized later in this introduction and, of course, they are presented fully in the complete set of data tables. For present purposes, it is enough to indicate that the range of topics is very broad. This breadth is partly due to the wide interests of the principal investigators; but it also reflects our conviction that the concurrent examination of trends in a variety of areas is not only much more cost efficient but also more scientifically productive.

Research Design and Procedures*

The basic research design involves annual data collections from high school seniors during the spring of each year, beginning with the class of 1975. Each data collection takes place in approximately 125 public and private high schools selected to provide an accurate cross section of high school seniors throughout the coterminous United States. The design also provides for the longitudinal study of a subsample from each class of participating seniors; but since the focus of this series of volumes is exclusively on the data collected annually from seniors, the follow-up procedures will not be discussed here.

Reasons for Focusing on High School Seniors. There are several reasons for choosing the senior year of high school as an optimal point for monitoring the behaviors and attitudes of youth. One is that the completion of high school represents the end of an important developmental stage in this society, since it demarcates both the end of universal public education and, for many, the end of living in the parental home. Therefore, it is a logical point at which to take stock of the accumulated influences of these two environments on American youth.

Further, the completion of high school represents the jumping-off point from which young people diverge into widely differing social environments, including college, business firms, military service, and homemaking. But these environmental transitions are not the only important changes which coincide with the end of high school. Most young men and women now reach the formal age of adulthood shortly before or after graduation; more significantly, they begin to assume adult roles, including financial self-support, marriage, and parenthood.

Finally, there are some important practical

---

*A more extensive description of the research design and procedures may be found in Bachman and Johnston (1978).

advantages to building a system of data collections around samples of high school seniors. The last year of high school constitutes the final point at which a reasonably good national sample of an age-specific cohort can be drawn and studied economically. The need for systematically repeated, large-scale samples from which to make reliable estimates of change requires that considerable stress be laid on efficiency and feasibility; the present design meets those requirements.

One limitation in the design is that it does not include in the target population those young men and women who drop out of high school before graduation (or before the last few months of the senior year, to be more precise). This excludes a relatively small proportion of each age cohort — between 15 and 20 percent (Golladay, 1976, 1977) — though not an unimportant segment, since we know that certain behaviors such as illicit drug use (Johnston, 1973) and delinquency (Bachman, O'Malley, and Johnston, 1978) tend to be higher than average in this group. However, the addition of a representative sample of dropouts would increase the cost of the present research enormously, because of their dispersion and generally higher level of resistance to being located and interviewed.

For the purposes of estimating characteristics of the entire age group, the omission of high school dropouts does introduce certain biases; however, their small proportion sets outer limits on the bias (Johnston, O'Malley, and Eveland, 1975, Appendix B). For the purposes of estimating *changes* from one cohort of high school seniors to another, the omission of dropouts represents a problem only if different cohorts have considerably different proportions who drop out. We have no reason to expect dramatic changes in those rates for the foreseeable future, and recently published government statistics indicate a great deal of stability in dropout rates since 1967 (Golladay, 1976, p. 62; 1977, p. 81).

Some may use our high school data to draw conclusions about changes for the entire age group. While we do not encourage such extrapolation, we suspect that the conclusions reached often would be valid, since over 80 percent of the age group is in the surveyed segment of the population *and* since we expect that change among those not in school are very likely to parallel the changes among those who are. Nevertheless, for purposes of characterizing the entire age group we would urge the user to check the results emanating from the present monitoring system against those emerging from other data collection systems using different methods, such as household interviews. (It is encouraging to note that when we have compared drug use data for this age group from the present study with those

from interview studies, the findings have shown a high degree of similarity.)

Sampling Procedures. The procedure for securing a nationwide sample of high school seniors is a multi-stage one. Stage 1 is the selection of particular geographic areas, Stage 2 is the selection of one or more high schools in each area, and Stage 3 is the selection of seniors within each high school.

Stage 1: Geographic Areas. The geographic areas used in this study are the primary sampling units (PSUs) developed by the Sampling Section of the Survey Research Center for use in the Center's nationwide interview studies. These consist of 74 primary areas throughout the coterminous United States — including the 12 largest metropolitan areas, which contain about 30 percent of the nation's population. Of the 62 other primary areas, 10 are in the Northeast, 18 in the North Central area, 24 in the South, and 10 in the West. Because these same PSUs are used for personal interview studies by the Survey Research Center (SRC), local field representatives can be assigned to administer the data collections in practically all schools.

Stage 2: Schools. In the major metropolitan areas more than one high school is often included in the sampling design; in most other sampling areas a single high school is sampled. In all cases, the selections of high schools are made such that the probability of drawing a school is proportionate to the size of its senior class. The larger the senior class (according to recent records), the higher the selection probability assigned to the high school. When a sampled school is unwilling to participate, a replacement school as similar to it as possible is selected from the same geographic area.

Stage 3: Students. Within each selected school, up to about 400 seniors may be included in the data collection. In schools with fewer than 400 seniors, the usual procedure is to include all of them in the data collection. In larger schools, a subset of seniors is selected either by randomly sampling classrooms or by some other random method that is convenient for the school and judged to be unbiased. Sample weights are assigned to each respondent so as to take account of variations in the sizes of samples from one school to another, as well as the (smaller) variations in selection probabilities occurring at the earlier stages of sampling.

The three-stage sampling procedure described above yielded the number of participating schools and students indicated in Table 1.

One other important feature of the base-year sampling procedure should be noted here. All schools (except for half of the initial 1975 sample) are asked to participate in two data collections, thereby permitting replacement of half of the total sample of schools each year. One motivation for

Table 1

Sample Sizes and Student Response Rates

	1975	1976	1977	1978
Number of Public Schools	111	108	108	111
Number of Private Schools	14	15	16	20
Total Number of Schools	125	123	124	131
Actual Number of Participating Students	15792	16678	18436	18924
Number of Weighted Cases (Total)*	15104	15299	15839	18924
Student Response Rate**	78%	77%	79%	83%

* Sample weights are assigned to each respondent to correct for unequal probablities of selection which arise in the multi-stage sampling procedure.

** The student response rate is derived by dividing the attained sample by the target sample (both based on weighted numbers of cases). The target sample is based upon listings provided by schools. Since such listings may fail to take account of recent student attrition, the actual response rate may be slightly underestimated.

requesting that schools participate for two years is administrative efficiency; it is a costly and time-consuming procedure to secure the cooperation of schools, and a two-year period of participation cuts down that effort substantially. Another important advantage is that whenever an appreciable shift in scores from one graduating class to the next is observed, it is possible to check whether the shift might be attributable to some differences in the newly sampled schools. This is done simply by repeating the analysis using only the 60 or so schools which participated both years. Thus far, the half-sample approach has worked quite well; an examination of drug prevalence data from the classes of 1975 and 1976 showed that the half sample of repeat schools yielded drug prevalence trends which were virtually identical to trends based on all schools.

School Recruiting Procedures. Early during the fall semester an initial contact is made with each sampled school. First a letter is sent to the principal describing the study and requesting permission to survey seniors. The letter is followed by a telephone call from a project staff member, who attempts to deal with any questions or problems and (when necessary) makes arrangements to contact and seek permission from other school district officials. Basically the same procedures are followed for schools asked to participate for the second year.

Once the school's agreement to participate is obtained, arrangements are made by phone for administering the questionnaires. A specific date for the survey is mutually agreed upon and a local SRC representative is assigned to carry out the administration.

Advance Contact with Teachers and Students. The local SRC representative is instructed to visit the school two weeks ahead of the actual date of administration. This visit serves as an occasion to meet the teachers whose classes will be affected and to provide them with a brochure describing the study, a brief set of guidelines about the questionnaire administration, and a supply of flyers to be distributed to the students a week to 10 days in advance of the questionnaire administration. The guidelines to the teachers include a suggested announcement to students at the time the flyers are distributed.

From the students' standpoint, the first information about the study usually consists of the teacher's announcement and the short descriptive flyer. In announcing the study, the teachers are asked to stress that the questionnaires used in the survey are not tests, and that there are no right or wrong answers. The flyer tells students that they will be invited to participate in the study, points out that their participation is strictly voluntary, and stresses confidentiality (including a reference to the fact that the Monitoring the Future project has a special government grant of confidentiality which allows their answers to be protected). The flyer also serves as an informative document which the students can show to their parents.

Questionnaire Administrations. The questionnaire administration in each school is carried out by the local SRC representatives and their assistants, following standardized procedures detailed in a project instruction manual. The questionnaires are administered in classrooms during normal class periods whenever possible, although circumstances in some schools require the use of larger group administrations. Teachers are not asked to do anything more than introduce the SRC staff members and (in most cases) remain in the classroom to help guarantee an orderly atmosphere for the survey. Teachers are urged to avoid walking around the room, so that students may feel free to write their answers without fear of being observed.

The actual process of completing the questionnaires is quite straightforward. Respondents are given sharpened pencils and asked to use them because the questionnaires are designed for automatic scanning. Most respondents can finish within a 45-minute class period; for those who cannot, an effort is made to provide a few minutes of additional time.

Procedures for Protecting Confidentiality. In any study that relies on voluntary reporting of drug use or other illegal acts, it is essential to develop procedures which guarantee the confidentiality of such reports. It is also desirable that these procedures be described adequately to respondents so that they are comfortable about providing honest answers.

We noted that the first information given to students about the survey consists of a descriptive flyer stressing confidentiality and voluntary participation. This theme is repeated at the start of the questionnaire administration. Each participating student is instructed to read the message on the cover of the questionnaire, which stresses the importance and value of the study, notes that

answers will be kept strictly confidential, states that the study is completely voluntary, and tells the student "If there is any question you or your parents would find objectionable for any reason, just leave it blank." The instructions then point out that in a few months a summary of nationwide results will be mailed to all participants and also that a follow-up questionnaire will be sent to some students after a year. The cover message explains that these are the reasons for asking that name and address be written on a special form which will be removed from the questionnaire and handed in separately. The message also points out that the two different code numbers (one on the questionnaire and one on the tear-out form) cannot be matched except by a special computer tape at The University of Michigan. (The content of the inside and outside of the standard questionnaire cover, including the tear-out form, may be found in Appendix C.)

Content Areas and Questionnaire Design

Drug use and related attitudes are the topics which receive the most extensive coverage in the Monitoring the Future project; but the questionnaires also deal with a wide range of other subject areas, including attitudes about government, social institutions, race relations, changing roles for women, educational aspirations, occupational aims, and marital and family plans, as well as a variety of background and demographic factors. (Table 2 provides an outline of the 19 general subject areas into which all items are categorized in the Question Index toward the end of this volume.) Given this breadth of content, the study is not presented to respondents as a "drug use study," nor do they tend to view it as such.

Table 2

Measurement Content Areas

A. **Drugs.** Drug use and related attitudes and beliefs, drug availability and exposure, surrounding conditions and social meaning of drug use. Views of significant others regarding drugs.

B. **Education.** Educational lifestyle, values, experiences, and environments. Media usage.

C. **Work and Leisure.** Vocational values, meaning of work and leisure, work and leisure activities, preferences regarding occupational characteristics and type of work setting.

Table 2 (continued)

D. **Sex Roles and Family.** Values, attitudes, and expectations about marriage, family structure, sex roles, and sex discrimination.

E. **Family Plans and Population Concerns.** Values, attitudes, and expectations about personal family plans. Views on sexual mores and concerns about overpopulation.

F. **Conservation, Materialism, Equity, etc.** Values, attitudes, and expectations related to conservation, pollution, materialism, equity, and the sharing of resources. Preferences regarding type of dwelling and urbanicity.

G. **Religion.** Religious affiliation, practices, and views.

H. **Politics.** Political affiliation, activities, and views.

I. **Social Change.** Values, attitudes, and expectations about social change.

J. **Social Problems.** Concern with various social problems facing the nation and the world.

K. **Major Social Institutions.** Confidence in and commitment to various major social institutions (business, unions, branches of government, press, organized religion, military, etc.).

L. **Military.** Views about the armed services and the use of military force. Personal plans for military service.

M. **Interpersonal Relationships.** Qualitative and quantitative characteristics of cross-age and peer relationships. Interpersonal conflict.

N. **Race Relations.** Attitudes toward and experiences with other racial groups.

O. **Concern for Others.** Radius of concern for others; voluntary and charitable activities.

P. **Happiness.** Happiness and life satisfaction, overall and in specific life domains.

Q. **Other Personality Variables.** Attitudes about self (including self-esteem), locus of control, loneliness, optimism, trust in others, somatic symptoms, importance placed on various life goals, counter-culture orientation.

R. **Background and School.** Demographic and family background characteristics, curriculum and grades in high school, victimization in school.

S. **Deviant Behavior and Victimization.** Delinquent behaviors, driving violations and accidents, violations and accidents under the influence of drugs, victimization experiences.

Because many questions are needed to cover all of these topic areas, much of the questionnaire content is divided into five different questionnaire forms which are distributed to participants in an ordered sequence that produces five virtually identical subsamples. About one-third of each questionnaire form consists of key or "core" variables which are common to all forms. All demographic variables and some measures of drug use are included in this "core" set of measures. This use of the full sample for drug and demographic measures provides a more accurate estimation on these dimensions and also makes it possible to link them statistically to all of the other measures which are included in a single form only.*

Representativeness and Validity

The samples for this study are intended to be representative of high school seniors throughout the 48 coterminous states. We have already discussed the fact that this definition of the sample excludes one important portion of the age cohort: those who have dropped out of high school before nearing the end of the senior year. But given the aim of representing high school seniors, it will now be useful to consider the extent to which the obtained samples of schools and students are likely to be representative of all seniors and the degree to which the data obtained are likely to be valid.

We can distinguish at least four ways in which survey data of this sort might fall short of being fully accurate. First, some sampled schools refuse to participate, which could introduce some bias. Second, the failure to obtain questionnaire data from 100 percent of the students sampled in participating schools could also introduce bias. Third, the answers provided by participating students are open to both conscious and unconscious distortions which could reduce validity. Finally, limitations in sample size and/or design could place limits on the accuracy of estimates. Each of these issues is treated extensively elsewhere (Johnston, Bachman, and O'Malley, 1979, especially Appendices A and B), so in this section we will present only the highlights of each of those discussions.

School Participation. As noted in the description of the sampling design, schools are invited to participate in the study for a two-year period. With very few exceptions, each school which has participated for one data collection has agreed to participate for a second. Thus far, from 66 percent to 80 percent of the schools initially invited to participate have agreed to do so each year; for each

school refusal, a similar school (in terms of size, geographic area, urbanicity, etc.) was recruited as a replacement. The selection of replacement schools almost entirely removes problems of bias in region, urbanicity, and the like that might result from certain schools refusing to participate. Other potential biases are more subtle, however. For example, if it turned out that most schools with "drug problems" refused to participate, that could seriously bias the drug estimates derived from the sample. And if any other single factor were dominant in most refusals, that also might suggest a source of serious bias. In fact, however, the reasons for schools' refusals to participate are varied and largely a function of happenstance events of the particular year. Thus, we feel fairly confident that school refusals have not seriously biased the surveys.

Student Participation. Completed questionnaires are obtained from three-fourths to four-fifths of all students sampled. The single most important reason that students are missed is that they are absent from class at the time of data collection, and in most cases it is not workable to schedule a special follow-up data collection for them. Students with fairly high rates of absenteeism also report above-average rates of drug use; therefore, there is some degree of bias introduced by missing the absentees. That bias could be largely corrected through the use of special weighting; however, this course was not chosen because the bias in estimates (for drug use, where the potential effect was hypothesized to be largest) was determined to be quite small and because the necessary weighting procedures would have introduced undesirable complications (see Johnston et al., 1977).

In addition to absenteeism, student nonparticipation occurs because of schedule conflicts with school trips and other activities which tend to be more frequent than usual during the final months of the senior year. Of course, some students refuse to complete or turn in a questionnaire. However, the SRC representatives in the field estimate this proportion to be only about one percent.

Validity of Self-Report Data. Survey measures of delinquency and of drug use depend upon respondents reporting what are, in many cases, illegal acts. Thus, a critical question is whether such self-reports are likely to be valid. Like most studies dealing with these areas, we have no direct, objective validation of the present measures; however, the considerable amount of inferential evidence which exists strongly suggests that the self-report questions produce largely valid data. A number of

---

*These core variables are the first ones on which data are presented in the Descriptive Results Section.

factors have given us reasonable confidence about the validity of the responses to what are presumably among the most sensitive questions in the study: a low nonresponse on the drug questions; a large proportion admitting to some illicit drug use; the consistency of findings across several years of the present study; strong evidence of construct validity (based on relationships observed between variables); a close match between our data and the findings from other studies using other methods; and the findings from several methodological studies which have used objective validation methods.*

As for others of the measures, a few have a long and venerable history — as scholars of the relevant literatures will recognize — though some of these measures have been modified to fit the present questionnaire format. Many (probably most) questions, however, have been developed specifically for this project through a careful process of question writing, pilot testing, pretesting, and question revision or elimination. Some already have been included in other publications from the study, but many have not; therefore, there currently exists little *empirical* evidence of their validity and reliability. On the other hand, the fact that virtually all results presented in this volume are based on individual items, rather than indexes or abstract concepts, should make it easy for the reader to judge the degree to which each item has "face validity" and also the degree to which there is some evidence of construct validity in the bivariate results.

Accuracy of the Sample. A sample survey never can provide the same level of accuracy as would be obtained if the entire target population were to participate in the survey — in the case of the present study, about three million seniors per year. But perfect accuracy of this sort would be extremely expensive and certainly not worthwhile considering the fact that a high level of accuracy can be provided by a carefully designed probability sample. The accuracy of the sample in this study is affected both by the size of the student sample and by the number of schools in which they are clustered. Appendix B presents a discussion of the ways in which this clustering and other aspects of the sampling design are taken into account in computing the precision or accuracy of the samples. For the purposes of this introduction, it is sufficient to note that virtually all estimates based on the total sample have confidence intervals of ±1.5 percentage points or smaller — sometimes considerably smaller. This means that, had we been able to invite all schools and all seniors in the 48 coterminous states to participate, the results from such a

massive survey would be within an estimated 1.5 percentage points of our present sample findings at least 95 times out of 100. We consider this to be a quite high level of accuracy, and one that permits the detection of fairly small trends from one year to the next.

Consistency and the Measurement of Trends. One other point is worth noting in a discussion of the validity of our findings. The Monitoring the Future project is, by intention, a study designed to be sensitive to changes from one time to another. Accordingly, the measures and procedures have been standardized and applied consistently across each data collection. To the extent that any biases remain because of limits in school and/or student participation, and to the extent that there are distortions (lack of validity) in the responses of some students, it seems very likely that such problems will exist in much the same way from one year to the next. In other words, biases in the survey estimates should tend to be consistent from one year to another, which means that the measurement of *trends* should be affected very little by any such biases.

Caveats to Users of the Data

In attempting to understand and interpret the statistical results contained in this volume, the reader should keep in mind the several considerations discussed below.

Estimation of Sampling Errors. Appendix A provides figures which allow the reader to determine the 95 percent confidence interval around any observed percentage for both the total sample and the several subgroups for which statistics are given. Appendix A also provides tables and guidelines for testing the statistical significance of observed differences between subgroups (e.g., males vs. females) and the significance of year-to-year changes for the entire sample and for the various subgroups on any given variable. Estimates based on subgroups containing relatively few cases (e.g., those who have used heroin) will have substantially larger margins of error than those subgroups with large numbers of cases.

Subgroup Definitions. At the beginning of the Descriptive Results section there is a careful definition of each of the subgroups analyzed in this series of volumes. It is important for the reader to read these definitions so as not to be misled by the

---

*A more detailed discussion of the evidence for validity of the measures of illicit drug use may be found in Johnston et al. (1977), Appendix A.

necessarily abbreviated descriptions given in the column headings of the data tables. For example, the column labeled "4-year college plans" includes data only for seniors who expect to be graduated from a four-year college, which is only a subset of all who expect to receive some college training. To take another example, several column headings in the lifetime illicit drug use index use the term "pills"; however, these categories contain people who indicate that they used any of a number of drugs — including some which usually are not taken in pill form (e.g., cocaine and narcotics other than heroin).

Missing Data Notes. Each column of percentages for a given variable adds to 100 percent (with slight variations due to rounding), whether based on the entire sample or any one of the subgroups being described. Missing data were not included in computing these percentages, so it is up to the reader to determine whether an exceptional level of missing data exists on any given question. This can be done by comparing the weighted number of cases on which those percentages were based (given in italics under each percentage distribution) with the total number of weighted cases who took the questionnaire (given at the top of the same column). As would be expected, the missing data rate tends to rise modestly toward the end of each questionnaire. Occasionally there is an exceptional level of nonresponse for some other reason, the most common being that the respondent has been branched around a question or set of questions which are inappropriate for him or her. In this case the percentages are based only on those for whom the question was appropriate *and* who answered. A footnote has been entered to help call attention to the fact that completing a particular question is contingent upon the answer on a prior question. Most such cases are contained in Form 1 of the questionnaire, which has several sets of detailed questions about drug use which are answered only by those respondents who have used a particular class of drug during the past year.

Characterizing Heroin Users. Because this project places a special emphasis on the study of drug use, one set of columns distinguishes respondents according to the extent to which they have been involved with illicit drugs. The five drug use categories are based on an index of seriousness of involvement. The index has Guttman-like properties — that is, anyone classified at a given level is also very likely to have exhibited any drug-using behaviors which are associated with the lower levels in the index.

The most extreme category in the index is defined in terms of the respondent's ever having used heroin during his or her lifetime. However, any interpretations made about heroin users from these data must be tempered with extreme caution, not only because the small number of cases makes estimation in a given year relatively unreliable, but also because heroin users are probably the most selectively represented of all of the subgroups presented here. Heroin users — especially continuing users — are among those most likely to drop out of high school (Johnston, 1973). Therefore, we feel that heroin users are particularly under-represented in a sample of high school seniors. Furthermore, most of those included in the study report only very occasional heroin use. Frequent users — addicts, if you will — are not well represented in these data.

Given these problems with the representation of heroin users, the reader may wonder why it was decided to present them as a separate category of drug users. There are two reasons for doing so. First, because even occasional heroin use represents such an extreme point on the continuum of drug involvement, it seems preferable that the heroin users not be mixed in with the next highest category of use (the "more pills" category). It remains quite possible, of course, for anyone to *combine* any two or more categories in the drug use continuum (by computing means of percentages weighted by the number of cases in each category); therefore, those wishing to incorporate heroin users with the next category can do so whenever they wish. The second reason for keeping them separate is that we suspect the data based on high school seniors provide some indication of the characteristics which might be found among heavier heroin users who dropped out of school. Some variables in the study are strongly correlated with the drug use continuum, and the present heroin user category provides both an end point for that continuum and an indication of the direction (further out on the continuum) in which heavier heroin users are likely to lie.

In sum, the reporting of separate percentages for heroin users among high school seniors permits greater clarity in analyzing other levels of drug use and provides data which may be suggestive about the larger population of young heroin users. But the particular data are clearly limited and should be interpreted with these cautions in mind.

Interpreting Racial Differences. Data are given for the two largest racial/ethnic subgroups in the population — those who identify themselves as white or Caucasian and those who identify themselves as black or Afro-American. Data are not given for the other ethnic categories (American Indians, Asian Americans, Mexican Americans, Puerto Ricans, or other Latin Americans) since

each of these groups comprises less than three percent of the sample in any given year, which means
that their small Ns (in combination with their clustered groupings in a limited number of schools)
would yield estimates which would be too unreliable. In fact, even blacks — who constitute approximately 12 percent of each year's sample — are
represented by only 350 to 425 respondents per
year on any single questionnaire form. Further,
because our sample is a stratified clustered sample, it yields less accuracy than would be yielded
by a pure random sample of equal size (see Appendix B for details). Therefore, because of the limited
number of cases, the margin of sampling error
around any statistic describing blacks is larger than
for most other subgroups described in this volume.

There exists, however, a quick way to determine
the replicability of any finding involving racial
comparisons. Since most questions are repeated
from year to year, one can readily establish the
degree to which a finding is replicated by looking
at the results for the same question in prior or subsequent years. Given the relatively small Ns for
blacks, the reader is urged to seek such replication
before putting much faith in the reliability of any
particular racial comparison.

There are factors in addition to unreliability,
however, which could be misleading in the interpretation of racial differences. Given the social
importance which has been placed on various
racial differences reported in the social science lit-
erature, we would like to caution the reader to consider the various factors which could account for
differences. These factors fall into three categories: differential representation in the sample, differential response tendencies, and the confounding
of race with a number of other background and
demographic characteristics.

Differential Representation. Census data characterizing American young people in the approximate age range of those in our sample show that
somewhat lower proportions of blacks than whites
remain in school through the end of twelfth grade
(Golladay, 1977, p. 197). Therefore, a slightly different segment of the black population than of the
white population resides in our target population
of high school seniors. Further, our samples appear
to underrepresent slightly those black males who,
according to census figures, are in high school at
the twelfth grade level. Identified black males
comprise about 6 percent of our sample, whereas
census data suggest that they should comprise
around 7 percent (U.S. Bureau of the Census, 1978).
Therefore, it appears that we are losing more black
males from our target population than white males
or females of either race. This may be due to generally poorer attendance rates on the part of some
black males and/or an unwillingness on the part of

some to participate in data collections of this sort.

In sum, a smaller segment of the black population than of the white population of high school age
is represented by the data contained here. Insofar
as any characteristic is associated with being a
school dropout or absentee, it is likely to be somewhat disproportionately underrepresented among
blacks in our sample.

Differential Response Tendencies. In examining
our full range of variables, we have noted certain
racial differences in response tendencies. First, the
tendency to state agreement in response to agree-
disagree questions is generally somewhat greater
among blacks than among whites. For example,
blacks tend to agree more with the positively
worded items in our index of self-esteem, but they
also tend to agree more with the negatively worded
items. As it happens, that particular index has an
equal number of positively and negatively worded
items, so that any overall "agreement bias" should
be self-cancelling when the index score is computed. Since all data in this volume are based on single
items, however, group differences in agreement
bias are likely to affect results on questions
employing the agree-disagree format. Fortunately,
most of our questions are not of that type.

We have also observed a somewhat greater than
average tendency for black respondents to select
extreme answer categories on attitudinal scales.
For example, even if the same proportion of blacks
as whites felt positively (or negatively) about some
subject, fewer of the whites are likely to say they
feel *very* positively (or *very* negatively). We do not
have any ready explanations for these differences
in response styles, but what seems important for
our present purposes is that, in the process of interpreting racial differences, the reader should be
aware that differences in responses to particular
questions may be related to these more general
tendencies.

A somewhat separate issue in response tendency
is a respondent's willingness to answer particular
questions. The missing data rate, which can be
determined by dividing the number responding to
a question by the number taking the questionnaire
(given at the top of each page), may reflect willingness to answer particular questions. If a particular
question or set of questions has a missing data rate
higher than is true for the prior or subsequent
questions, then presumably more respondents than
usual were unwilling (or perhaps unable) to
answer it. We have observed such an exaggerated
missing data rate for black males on the set of questions dealing with the respondent's own use of
illicit drugs. Clearly a respondent's willingness to
be candid on such questions depends on his or her
trust of the research process and of the researchers
themselves. We interpret the exaggerated missing

data rates for black males in these sections as possibly reflecting, at least in part, less trust. The reader is advised to check for exceptional levels of missing data when making comparisons on any variable in which candor is likely to be reduced by lower system trust.

Covariance with Other Factors. Some characteristics such as race are highly confounded (correlated) with other variables — variables which may in fact explain some observed racial differences. Put another way, at the aggregate level we might observe a considerable racial difference on some characteristic, but once we control for some background characteristics such as socioeconomic level or region of the country — that is, once we compare the black respondents with whites who come from similar backgrounds — there may be no racial difference at all.

Race happens to be correlated with important background and demographic variables much more than some of the other variables dealt with here (like the respondent's sex). When we compare males and females in this sample we know that observed differences between them are not likely to be explained by differences in their family background (such as the socioeconomic level of their families, the region of the country, or the size of the cities in which they grew up) because males and females on the average come from extremely similar backgrounds. A perusal of Section C of Questionnaire Forms 1 through 5, however, will illustrate that on the average the black subgroup in this sample is quite different from the white subgroup in a number of such respects. A higher proportion of blacks live in the South and a higher proportion grew up in large cities. Blacks are more likely to report low levels of parental education (an indication of a lower socioeconomic background more generally). A greater than average proportion of blacks grew up in families with the father and/or mother absent, and more had mothers who worked while they were growing up. A substantially higher proportion of blacks are Baptists, and blacks tend to attribute more importance to religion in their lives than do whites. Fewer are enrolled in a college-preparatory curriculum (though a higher proportion say they plan to attend some type of college). A slightly higher proportion of black respondents are married and have children, and on the average they are slightly older than the white sample. As was mentioned earlier, black males are more underrepresented in our sample than black females, with the result that each year roughly 58 percent of our black sample is female versus roughly 51 percent of the white sample.

We note these differences in demographic, background, and ascriptive characteristics because, in any attempt to understand *why* a racial difference exists, one would want to be able to examine the role of these covarying characteristics. It is not possible, given the amount of data contained in this volume, to "factor out" the contribution of most of these covarying characteristics when interpreting racial differences. Therefore, while the data here may provide a relatively accurate *description* of racial differences (keeping in mind our earlier cautions about representativeness and response style), they do not by themselves yield a great deal by way of explanation. However, since the full data sets now reside in two archives, described in the Preface, it is possible for the reader to conduct a more in depth exploration of observed differences — or nondifferences, for that matter. We particularly encourage readers interested in racial comparisons to make further explorations in the data in order to determine the possible role of the other variables discussed here. Users of the data are also encouraged to contact the principal investigators for information on the most recent analyses of racial differences, some of which are already underway.

Given the long list of caveats about interpreting racial differences, one might ask why we chose to publish the statistics for racial subgroups at all. After considerable deliberation among ourselves as well as with colleagues more knowledgeable in the field of race relations, we concluded that the expected benefits of making these data available (along with this cautionary discussion) outweigh the potential costs of having them misused. Unfortunately, because blacks constitute a relatively small proportion of the American population, they constitute too small a number in most surveys to be characterized separately. Because the sample sizes in the present survey are large in comparison to most, we have at least sufficient numbers of cases to consider publishing data on blacks separately. Further, given the iterative nature of the series, we are also able to provide checks for replication of findings on different samples each year. While there may be some risk that findings will be taken out of context or used carelessly in ways that might tend to increase racial misunderstandings, there is substantially greater risk that valuable information concerning the races (and relevant to their well-being) will be lost if it were not included here.

Descriptive Results: 1976

Introduction to the Table Format and Conventions

Univariate and selected bivariate percentage distributions are given in this section for all questions asked of this year's senior class. The definitions of column headings and the source of the standard contents for each table are given below under the numbers indicated in Figure 1.

Definitions of Column Headings

① **Questionnaire Form.** The form from which all data on the page were derived is given here. When the designation "Forms 1-5" is used, it indicates that responses from students completing all five questionnaires have been combined; accordingly, the numbers of respondents in each column are five times as large for questions contained in a single form only.

② **Total Sample.** Univariate percentage distributions based on the total sample of respondents are given in this column.

③ **Sex.** Percentage distributions are given separately for males (M) and females (F). Respondents with missing data on the question asking the respondent's sex (Question C03) are omitted from both groupings.

④ **Race.** Percentage distributions are given separately for those describing themselves as "White or Caucasian" (W) and "Black or Afro-American" (B) in answer to Question C04. Comparable columns for the other racial or ethnic groups (Mexican Americans, Asian Americans, American Indians, etc.) are not shown because of the low number of cases in each group. *Note:* See the caveats regarding the interpretation of racial differences in the Introduction section of this volume.

⑤ **Region.** Percentage distributions are given separately for respondents living in each of four mutually exclusive regions of the country. The regional classifications are based on Census categories and are defined as follows:

Northeast (NE): Census classifications of New England and Middle Atlantic states; includes Maine, New Hampshire, Vermont, Massachusetts, Rhode Island, Connecticut, New York, New Jersey, and Pennsylvania.

North Central (NC): Census classifications of East North Central and West North Central states; includes Ohio, Indiana, Illinois, Michigan, Wisconsin, Minnesota, Iowa, Missouri, North Dakota, South Dakota, Nebraska, and Kansas.

South (S): Census classifications of South Atlantic, East South Central, and West South Central states; includes Delaware, Maryland, District of Columbia, Virginia, West Virginia, North Carolina, South Carolina, Georgia, Florida, Kentucky, Tennessee, Alabama, Mississippi, Arkansas, Louisiana, Oklahoma, and Texas.

West (W): Census classifications of Mountain and Pacific states; includes Montana, Idaho, Wyoming, Colorado, New Mexico, Arizona, Utah, Nevada, Washington, Oregon, and California.

⑥ **Four-Year College Plans.** Percentage distributions are given separately for (1) respondents who indicate that they "definitely will" or "probably will" graduate from a four-year college program and (2) those who say that they "definitely won't" or "probably won't" graduate from a four-year college program, based on responses to Question C21d. Respondents not answering question C21d are omitted from both columns. (A number of those who do not expect to complete a four-year college program *do* expect to get some post-secondary education, as may be seen in the tables for questions

C21a and c.)

⑦ **Illicit Drug Use: Lifetime.** Percentage distributions are given separately for five mutually exclusive subgroups differentiated by their degree of involvement with illicit drugs. Eligibility for each category is defined below.

None. This column contains data from those respondents who indicated that they had not used marijuana at any time and did not report use of any of the following illicit drugs in their lifetime: LSD, other psychedelics, cocaine, amphetamines, tranquilizers, methaqualone, barbiturates, heroin, or other narcotics.

Marijuana Only. This column contains data from those respondents who indicated that they had used marijuana (or hashish) but had never used any of the other illicit drugs just listed.

Few Pills. This column contains data from those respondents who indicated having used one or more of the above listed drugs (other than marijuana) but who had not used any one class of them on more than three occasions *and* who had not used heroin at all.

More Pills. This column contains data from respondents who had used any of the above listed drugs (other than marijuana) on more than three occasions but who had never used heroin.

Any Heroin. This column contains data from those respondents who indicated having used heroin on one or more occasions in their lifetime.

⑧ **Weighted Number of Cases.** This row contains the number of students who turned in questionnaires in each of the categories indicated by the column headings. The number of cases is stated in terms of the weighted number of respondents rather than the actual number, since all percentages in the tables have been calculated using weighted cases. The actual number of respondents generally is about 15 percent higher than the weighted number for data collected in 1975, 1976, and 1977. (A comparison of weighted and unweighted numbers is provided in Tables B-1 and B-2 in Appendix B.) For data collected in 1978 or later, the actual number of respondents is roughly equal to the weighted number. Weighting is used to improve the accuracy of estimates by correcting for unequal probabilities of selection which arise in the multi-stage sampling procedures.

⑨ **Percentage of Weighted Total.** This row indicates the percentage of the total number of respondents who fall into the category indicated by each column heading. Unlike all other percentages on the page, which can be summed vertically, these percentages sum horizontally. To the extent that the subcategories in a column (e.g., Males and Females) fail to sum to 100 percent, cases have been eliminated because of missing data on the variable in question (e.g., Sex), or, in the case of Race, because several subcategories have been omitted intentionally.

Table Contents

⑩ **Questions and Answers.** Each question along with its accompanying answer alternatives is presented verbatim. The alphanumeric prefix to the question indicates the section of the questionnaire in which it is located and its sequence within that section. So, for example, a prefix of B12c indicates that the item was question 12c in the B Section of the questionnaire.

⑪ **Item Reference Number.** This is a unique identification number permanently assigned to each question. Any question may be located in the cross-time item index of this volume (or any other volume in this series) by using this reference number.

⑫ **Percentage Distribution.** Each column of numbers beside a question gives the percentage of each group (defined by the column heading) who chose each answer alternative, rounded to the nearest tenth of a percent. These figures add vertically to 100 percent (with some rounding error). Nonrespondents to the question are excluded from the percentage calculations.

⑬ **Number of Weighted Cases Answering (N Wtd.).** The number of students in the relevant group (defined by the column heading) who answered the question is given just below the percentage distribution. The number of nonrespondents may be determined by subtracting this weighted number answering from the weighted number taking the questionnaire, shown at the top of the same column. Nonresponse may be due to the subject not answering the question, even though it pertains to him or her, or to the subject skipping inappropriate questions as instructed on a prior item.

Figure 1
Guide to Table Format

Column guide markers: (1) (2) (3) (4) (5) (6) (7)

QUESTIONNAIRE FORM 1-5 1976	TOTAL	SEX		RACE		REGION				4YR COLLEGE PLANS		ILLICIT DRUG USE: LIFETIME				
		M	F	White	Black	NE	NC	S	W	Yes	No	None	Marijuana Only	Few Pills	More Pills	Any Heroin
(8) Weighted No. of Cases:	15138	7241	7257	11796	1716	3570	4687	4597	2284	6994	6877	6091	3457	1736	2987	268
(9) % of Weighted Total:	100.0	47.8	47.9	77.9	11.3	23.6	31.0	30.4	15.1	46.2	45.4	40.2	22.8	11.5	19.7	1.8

These next questions ask for some background information about yourself.

C01: In what year were you born? (10)

	TOTAL	M	F	White	Black	NE	NC	S	W	Yes	No	None	Mari-juana Only	Few Pills	More Pills	Any Heroin
1. Before '56	.3	.3	.3	.1	.9	.2	.1	.6	.1	.2	.5	.4	.1	.3	.2	1.1
2. 1956	2.2	2.8	1.6	1.5	4.7	2.0	1.9	3.3	.9	1.3	2.9	2.2	2.0	2.0	1.6	5.3
3. 1957	22.4	26.4	18.3	21.2	26.2	15.9	24.8	24.4	23.4	18.6	25.6	22.6	21.6	23.0	20.9	27.9
4. 1958	72.5	69.0	76.0	75.1	63.1	76.8	72.1	69.1	73.3	76.7	69.1	72.3	73.8	72.3	74.3	63.8
5. 1959	2.5	1.4	3.6	2.1	4.7	4.9	.9	2.3	2.2	3.0	1.8	2.4	2.4	2.2	2.9	1.9
6. 1960	.1	.1	.1	.1	.3	.1	.1	.1	*	.1	.1	.1	.1	.1	*	-
7. 1961	*	-	*	-	.1	-	-	*	-	-	*	-	-	-	-	-
8. After 1961	.1	.1	*	-	.1	*	.1	*	*	*	.1	*	*	-	.1	-
(11) Item 10 N(Wtd)	14767	7232	7256	11786	1715	3437	4600	4509	2221	6955	6827	6023	3399	1720	2925	265

C02: (12) In what month were you born?

	TOTAL	M	F	White	Black	NE	NC	S	W	Yes	No	None	Mari-juana Only	Few Pills	More Pills	Any Heroin
01. January	7.9	7.7	8.1	7.9	7.8	7.9	7.7	8.2	7.6	7.8	7.8	8.3	7.2	7.7	7.2	10.4
02. February	7.5	7.5	7.6	7.4	7.8	7.4	7.7	7.9	6.6	7.7	7.4	7.4	7.7	7.6	7.4	8.8
03. March	8.7	8.8	8.6	8.8	7.8	9.0	9.4	7.7	8.7	9.2	8.2	8.8	8.5	8.7	8.6	9.6
04. April	7.5	7.6	7.5	7.7	6.5	7.6	7.5	7.3	7.9	7.7	7.5	7.0	7.6	7.2	8.7	7.3
05. May	8.1	8.1	8.3	8.3	7.5	8.5	8.5	7.4	8.1	8.2	8.2	8.4	8.0	8.1	8.2	8.5
06. June	8.2	8.0	8.5	8.0	9.3	7.8	8.5	8.5	7.4	8.0	8.2	8.1	8.5	7.7	8.6	5.8
07. July	8.9	9.0	8.8	8.8	9.3	8.5	9.0	8.8	9.9	9.0	8.8	9.0	8.8	9.7	8.7	7.3
08. August	8.9	8.9	8.8	8.8	10.1	8.4	9.0	9.2	8.6	8.6	9.1	8.8	8.7	9.5	9.1	6.9
09. September	8.9	9.2	8.8	8.9	8.8	9.1	7.8	9.8	8.8	8.7	9.1	9.6	9.4	6.9	8.4	8.5
10. October	8.9	8.7	8.7	8.9	8.5	9.1	8.9	8.3	9.6	8.7	8.8	8.7	9.0	8.9	8.5	9.6
11. November	8.0	7.7	7.7	8.1	6.9	8.1	7.5	8.4	7.9	7.7	8.3	7.3	8.1	9.6	8.1	8.8
12. December	8.6	8.8	8.5	8.3	9.6	8.6	8.4	8.6	8.8	8.7	8.5	8.7	8.5	8.3	8.6	8.1
Item 20 N(Wtd)	14708	7190	7243	11742	1715	3418	4578	4498	2215	6931	6807	6010	3384	1714	2911	260

C03: What is your sex?

	TOTAL	M	F	White	Black	NE	NC	S	W	Yes	No	None	Mari-juana Only	Few Pills	More Pills	Any Heroin
1. Male	49.9	100.0	-	50.6	42.1	48.8	49.8	49.5	52.8	51.3	47.2	44.5	59.2	48.7	49.1	66.9
2. Female	50.1	-	100.0	49.4	57.9	51.2	50.2	50.4	47.2	48.7	52.8	55.5	40.7	51.3	50.9	33.1
(13) Item 30 N(Wtd)	14498	7241	7257	11605	1669	3374	4514	4433	2178	6837	6716	5943	3334	1681	2874	257

C04: How do you describe yourself?

	TOTAL	M	F	White	Black	NE	NC	S	W	Yes	No	None	Mari-juana Only	Few Pills	More Pills	Any Heroin
1. American Indian	1.1	1.2	.9	-	-	.5	1.2	1.3	1.0	.5	1.5	.8	.7	1.4	1.8	1.2
2. Black or Afro-American	11.7	9.8	13.4	-	100.0	10.7	4.9	22.2	5.7	12.5	9.2	12.6	13.1	11.2	5.1	11.7
3. Mexican American or Chicano	1.9	2.0	1.7	-	-	.1	1.0	1.3	7.5	1.8	1.7	1.8	2.2	2.0	1.5	2.0
4. Puerto Rican or other Latin American	1.3	1.4	1.2	-	-	4.3	.3	.3	.9	1.6	1.0	1.2	1.1	1.6	1.2	3.5
5. Oriental or Asian American	.7	.8	.7	-	-	.6	.3	.2	3.0	1.1	.4	1.0	.6	.8	.4	.8
6. White or Caucasian	80.4	81.8	79.4	100.0	-	79.9	89.2	73.4	77.3	80.2	82.9	80.0	80.2	80.3	86.7	75.0
7. Other	2.9	3.1	2.6	-	-	3.9	3.1	1.2	4.6	2.2	3.4	2.8	2.2	2.9	3.3	5.5
Item 40 N(Wtd)	14670	7183	7217	11796	1716	3396	4568	4502	2203	6922	6787	5990	3388	1713	2901	256

C05: Where did you grow up mostly?

	TOTAL	M	F	White	Black	NE	NC	S	W	Yes	No	None	Mari-juana Only	Few Pills	More Pills	Any Heroin
1. On a farm	10.5	11.7	9.2	11.4	5.9	4.3	14.9	11.4	9.1	7.5	13.6	12.6	9.7	8.5	7.5	6.9
2. In the country, not …			…4.6	14.2	15.8	13.4	12.3	19.9	8.1	10.0	18.7	15.8	13.0	13.8	12.6	11.0
3. In a sma…				…5	31.3	31.9	29.1	24.0	29.5	30.3	30.3	29.2	30.4	30.3	24…
							12.1	12.3	23.3	14.0	11.9	12.4	12.6	13.4…		
							…6	9.4	8.5	9.0	7.4	7.1	8.7			
							…5	7.5	8.1	7.3	6.9					

QUESTIONNAIRE FORM 1-5 1976	TOTAL	SEX		RACE		REGION				4YR COLLEGE PLANS		ILLICIT DRUG USE: LIFETIME				
		M	F	White	Black	NE	NC	S	W	Yes	No	None	Mari-juana Only	Few Pills	More Pills	Any Her-oin
Weighted No. of Cases:	15138	7241	7257	11796	1716	3570	4687	4597	2284	6994	6877	6091	3457	1736	2987	268
% of Weighted Total:	100.0	47.8	47.9	77.9	11.3	23.6	31.0	30.4	15.1	46.2	45.4	40.2	22.8	11.5	19.7	1.8

These next questions ask for some background information about yourself.

C01: In what year were you born?

	TOTAL	M	F	White	Black	NE	NC	S	W	Yes	No	None	Mari-juana Only	Few Pills	More Pills	Any Her-oin
1. Before '56	.3	.3	.3	.1	.9	.2	.1	.6	.1	.2	.5	.4	.1	.3	.2	1.1
2. 1956	2.2	2.8	1.6	1.5	4.7	2.0	1.9	3.3	.9	1.3	2.9	2.2	2.0	2.0	1.6	5.3
3. 1957	22.4	26.4	18.3	21.2	26.2	15.9	24.8	24.4	23.4	18.6	25.6	22.6	21.6	23.0	20.9	27.9
4. 1958	72.5	69.0	76.0	75.1	63.1	76.8	72.1	69.1	73.3	76.7	69.1	72.3	73.8	72.3	74.3	63.8
5. 1959	2.5	1.4	3.6	2.1	4.7	4.9	.9	2.3	2.2	3.0	1.8	2.4	2.4	2.2	2.9	1.9
6. 1960	.1	.1	.1	.1	.3	.1	.1	.1	*	.1	.1	.1	.1	.1	*	-
7. 1961	*	-	*	-	.1	-	-	-	*	-	*	-	-	-	-	-
8. After 1961	.1	.1	*	-	.1	*	.1	*	*	*	.1	*	*	-	.1	-
Item 10 N(Wtd)	14767	7232	7256	11786	1715	3437	4600	4509	2221	6955	6827	6023	3399	1720	2925	265

C02: In what month were you born?

	TOTAL	M	F	White	Black	NE	NC	S	W	Yes	No	None	Mari-juana Only	Few Pills	More Pills	Any Her-oin
01. January	7.9	7.7	8.1	7.9	7.8	7.9	7.7	8.2	7.6	7.8	7.8	8.3	7.2	7.7	7.2	10.4
02. February	7.5	7.5	7.6	7.4	7.8	7.4	7.7	7.9	6.6	7.7	7.4	7.4	7.7	7.6	7.4	8.8
03. March	8.7	8.8	8.6	8.8	7.8	9.0	9.4	7.7	8.7	9.2	8.2	8.8	8.5	8.7	8.6	9.6
04. April	7.5	7.6	7.5	7.7	6.5	7.6	7.5	7.3	7.9	7.7	7.5	7.0	7.6	7.2	8.7	7.3
05. May	8.1	8.1	8.3	8.3	7.5	8.5	8.5	7.4	8.1	8.2	8.2	8.4	8.0	8.1	8.2	8.5
06. June	8.2	8.0	8.5	8.0	9.3	7.8	8.5	8.5	7.4	8.0	8.2	8.1	8.5	7.7	8.6	5.8
07. July	8.9	9.0	8.8	8.8	9.3	8.5	9.0	8.8	9.9	9.0	8.8	9.0	8.8	9.7	8.7	7.3
08. August	8.9	8.9	8.8	8.8	10.1	8.4	9.0	9.2	9.6	8.6	9.1	8.8	8.7	9.5	9.1	6.9
09. September	8.9	9.2	8.8	8.9	8.8	9.1	7.8	9.8	8.8	8.7	9.1	9.6	9.4	6.9	8.4	8.5
10. October	8.9	8.7	8.7	8.9	8.5	9.1	8.9	8.3	9.6	8.7	8.8	8.7	9.0	8.9	8.5	9.6
11. November	8.0	7.7	7.7	8.1	6.9	8.1	7.5	8.4	7.9	7.7	8.3	7.3	8.1	9.6	8.1	8.8
12. December	8.6	8.8	8.5	8.3	9.6	8.6	8.4	8.6	8.8	8.7	8.5	8.7	8.5	8.3	8.6	8.1
Item 20 N(Wtd)	14708	7190	7243	11742	1715	3418	4578	4498	2215	6931	6807	6010	3384	1714	2911	260

C03: What is your sex?

	TOTAL	M	F	White	Black	NE	NC	S	W	Yes	No	None	Mari-juana Only	Few Pills	More Pills	Any Her-oin
1. Male	49.9	100.0	-	50.6	42.1	48.8	49.8	49.5	52.8	51.3	47.2	44.5	59.2	48.7	49.1	66.9
2. Female	50.1	-	100.0	49.4	57.9	51.2	50.2	50.4	47.2	48.7	52.8	55.5	40.7	51.3	50.9	33.1
Item 30 N(Wtd)	14498	7241	7257	11605	1669	3374	4514	4433	2178	6837	6716	5943	3334	1681	2874	257

C04: How do you describe yourself?

	TOTAL	M	F	White	Black	NE	NC	S	W	Yes	No	None	Mari-juana Only	Few Pills	More Pills	Any Her-oin
1. American Indian	1.1	1.2	.9	-	-	.5	1.2	1.3	1.0	.5	1.5	.8	.7	1.4	1.8	1.2
2. Black or Afro-American	11.7	9.8	13.4	-	100.0	10.7	4.9	22.2	5.7	12.5	9.2	12.6	13.1	11.2	5.1	11.7
3. Mexican American or Chicano	1.9	2.0	1.7	-	-	.1	1.0	1.3	7.5	1.8	1.7	1.8	2.2	2.0	1.5	2.0
4. Puerto Rican or other Latin American	1.3	1.4	1.2	-	-	4.3	.3	.3	.9	1.6	1.0	1.2	1.1	1.6	1.2	3.5
5. Oriental or Asian American	.7	.8	.7	-	-	.6	.3	.2	3.0	1.1	.4	1.0	.6	.8	.4	.8
6. White or Caucasian	80.4	81.8	79.4	100.0	-	79.9	89.2	73.4	77.3	80.2	82.9	80.0	80.2	80.3	86.7	75.0
7. Other	2.9	3.1	2.6	-	-	3.9	3.1	1.2	4.6	2.2	3.4	2.8	2.2	2.9	3.3	5.5
Item 40 N(Wtd)	14670	7183	7217	11796	1716	3396	4568	4502	2203	6922	6787	5990	3388	1713	2901	256

C05: Where did you grow up mostly?

	TOTAL	M	F	White	Black	NE	NC	S	W	Yes	No	None	Mari-juana Only	Few Pills	More Pills	Any Her-oin
1. On a farm	10.5	11.7	9.2	11.4	5.9	4.3	14.9	11.4	9.1	7.5	13.6	12.6	9.7	8.5	7.5	6.9
2. In the country, not on a farm	14.2	13.9	14.6	14.2	15.8	13.4	12.3	19.9	8.1	10.0	18.7	15.8	13.0	13.8	12.6	11.0
3. In a small city or town (under 50,000 people)	29.7	28.2	31.4	30.7	29.5	31.3	31.9	29.1	24.0	29.5	30.3	30.3	29.2	30.4	30.3	24.1
4. In a medium-sized city (50,000 - 100,000)	13.0	12.3	13.4	12.4	13.2	8.3	12.1	12.3	23.3	14.0	11.9	12.4	12.6	13.4	13.9	13.9
5. In a suburb of a medium-sized city	8.2	8.2	8.3	8.8	5.1	8.8	6.6	9.4	8.5	9.0	7.4	7.1	8.7	9.2	9.9	8.2
6. In a large city (100,000 - 500,000)	7.9	7.6	8.2	6.3	15.5	11.6	6.9	6.5	7.5	8.1	7.3	6.9	9.0	7.9	8.2	8.2
7. In a suburb of a large city	7.5	7.4	7.7	8.7	1.3	8.4	7.4	5.9	9.6	9.4	5.7	7.0	7.6	7.9	8.7	9.4
8. In a very large city (over 500,000)	4.8	5.3	4.2	2.8	13.1	7.5	4.8	2.9	3.9	6.3	2.9	3.9	5.5	4.8	4.6	10.6
9. In a suburb of a very large city	4.2	5.3	3.1	4.7	.6	6.3	3.3	2.6	5.9	6.1	2.2	3.8	4.8	4.1	4.3	8.2
Item 50 N(Wtd)	13600	6691	6613	10867	1581	3207	4288	4069	2036	6431	6288	5556	3165	1574	2670	245

* = less than .05 per cent.

QUESTIONNAIRE FORM 1-5 1976	TOTAL	SEX		RACE		REGION				4YR COLLEGE PLANS		ILLICIT DRUG USE: LIFETIME				
		M	F	White	Black	NE	NC	S	W	Yes	No	None	Marijuana Only	Few Pills	More Pills	Any Heroin
Weighted No. of Cases:	15138	7241	7257	11796	1716	3570	4687	4597	2284	6994	6877	6091	3457	1736	2987	268
% of Weighted Total:	100.0	47.8	47.9	77.9	11.3	23.6	31.0	30.4	15.1	46.2	45.4	40.2	22.8	11.5	19.7	1.8
C06: What is your present marital status?																
1. Married	2.5	2.3	2.7	2.2	4.0	1.1	2.4	4.1	2.0	1.1	3.9	2.4	2.7	2.0	2.1	5.3
2. Engaged	7.3	4.2	10.5	7.3	6.8	5.1	7.7	9.4	5.8	3.2	11.5	6.7	6.0	7.9	9.2	11.5
3. Separated/divorced	.5	.5	.4	.3	1.0	.5	.4	.5	.5	.3	.6	.3	.4	.1	.7	1.1
4. Single	89.7	93.1	86.4	90.3	88.1	93.4	89.5	86.0	91.7	95.4	83.9	90.6	90.9	89.9	88.0	82.1
Item 60 N(Wtd)	14728	7171	7237	11759	1685	3423	4598	4494	2214	6947	6832	6000	3397	1716	2924	262
C07: Which of the following people live in the same household with you? (Mark ALL that apply.)																
A. I live alone	.6	.8	.4	.5	.8	.6	.5	.6	.8	.3	.8	.4	.4	.5	.7	1.9
B. Father (or male guardian)	81.7	83.2	80.4	86.1	54.6	81.4	86.2	76.9	82.2	83.6	80.5	83.8	82.3	80.1	80.7	71.9
C. Mother (or female guardian)	92.0	92.0	92.3	93.7	83.9	93.2	93.3	89.7	91.8	94.2	90.2	93.9	92.0	92.9	90.9	78.8
D. Brother(s) and/or sister(s)	77.7	77.5	78.0	78.5	71.8	80.1	79.7	74.3	76.6	79.3	76.4	80.0	79.1	77.0	73.7	69.6
E. Grandparent(s)	5.4	5.9	4.8	4.9	9.2	7.8	3.5	6.5	3.5	5.6	5.1	5.6	5.8	5.3	4.6	2.3
F. My husband/wife	1.4	.7	2.1	1.4	1.5	.4	1.5	2.4	.8	.4	2.5	1.4	1.5	.9	1.4	3.5
G. My children	1.0	.3	1.6	.5	3.5	.6	.9	1.5	.5	.4	1.5	.8	1.1	1.1	1.0	1.2
H. Other relative(s)	4.3	3.4	5.2	2.9	11.8	4.4	3.1	5.9	3.2	3.7	4.7	3.6	4.5	5.4	4.4	3.8
I. Non-relative(s)	2.2	1.8	2.6	2.2	1.4	2.5	2.0	1.9	2.9	1.9	2.6	1.4	1.9	2.2	3.9	4.6
Item 80-160 N(Wtd)	14692	7153	7225	11728	1685	3408	4584	4494	2206	6937	6823	5997	3391	1711	2910	260

If you were raised mostly by foster parents, step-parents, or others, answer the next three questions for them. For example, if you have both a step-father and a natural father, answer for the one that was most important in raising you.

	TOTAL	M	F	White	Black	NE	NC	S	W	Yes	No	None	Marijuana Only	Few Pills	More Pills	Any Heroin
C08: What is the highest level of schooling your father completed?																
1. Completed grade school or less	9.8	8.3	11.3	8.3	16.2	7.9	9.4	12.9	7.2	6.1	13.5	10.7	9.4	8.6	8.8	8.2
2. Some high school	17.5	17.8	17.1	16.5	23.0	17.9	16.3	20.8	12.9	11.6	23.5	16.3	18.2	18.5	18.4	19.5
3. Completed high school	31.3	32.5	30.2	32.9	24.6	31.6	36.2	27.8	27.9	28.5	34.3	31.9	31.5	32.4	30.1	27.7
4. Some college	11.9	12.1	11.7	12.9	6.8	9.6	12.9	10.3	16.4	14.6	9.2	11.6	11.6	12.0	12.9	12.6
5. Completed college	13.7	13.6	13.9	15.2	5.9	15.0	12.4	12.1	17.6	19.7	7.9	13.5	14.3	13.7	13.8	16.5
6. Graduate or professional school after college	8.6	8.7	8.5	9.6	3.8	11.2	7.4	6.9	10.7	14.0	3.3	8.1	9.4	7.2	9.9	7.8
7. Don't know, or does not apply	7.1	7.0	7.3	4.7	19.6	6.8	5.4	9.1	7.2	5.6	8.3	7.8	5.7	7.6	5.9	7.4
Item 310 N(Wtd)	12056	5953	5834	9588	1406	2754	3792	3695	1814	5732	5590	4835	2816	1413	2402	231
C09: What is the highest level of schooling your mother completed?																
1. Completed grade school or less	5.7	4.8	6.6	4.2	9.4	4.9	5.1	7.6	4.4	3.7	7.8	6.8	4.8	5.9	3.9	5.2
2. Some high school	17.6	16.6	18.7	15.5	28.5	17.0	14.7	23.3	13.0	11.4	23.9	17.3	16.0	18.5	18.6	23.8
3. Completed high school	43.1	45.1	41.2	45.7	32.6	43.6	48.7	39.0	38.9	40.5	46.0	42.9	44.5	43.8	43.3	37.2
4. Some college	12.8	12.2	13.4	13.8	9.7	10.6	12.8	12.2	17.3	16.7	9.2	12.4	11.9	13.3	14.4	13.4
5. Completed college	11.9	12.3	11.6	13.1	7.8	14.2	11.2	9.4	15.3	17.4	6.5	11.9	13.8	10.1	11.8	10.4
6. Graduate or professional school after college	4.6	4.1	5.1	4.6	4.1	5.7	3.9	3.8	6.0	7.0	1.9	4.3	4.7	4.8	4.9	5.2
7. Don't know, or does not apply	4.2	4.8	3.5	3.0	8.1	4.0	3.5	4.7	5.1	3.2	4.8	4.4	4.4	3.6	3.0	4.8
Item 320 N(Wtd)	12119	5974	5874	9625	1428	2770	3802	3727	1820	5763	5620	4864	2827	1416	2414	231
C10: Did your mother have a paid job (half-time or more) during the time you were growing up?																
1. No	37.2	38.0	36.5	40.0	17.5	38.0	41.0	32.5	37.8	38.9	35.8	39.9	36.7	34.4	34.7	42.3
2. Yes, some of the time when I was growing up	31.3	31.7	30.9	32.3	27.0	31.9	32.4	29.4	31.7	30.7	32.1	30.8	30.8	34.1	31.4	29.1
3. Yes, most of the time	14.4	14.4	14.2	13.2	20.9	14.6	12.7	16.1	14.2	13.1	15.7	12.7	14.7	15.4	16.1	13.7
4. Yes, all or nearly all of the time	17.2	15.8	18.5	14.5	34.7	15.5	13.9	22.1	16.4	17.4	16.4	16.6	17.8	16.2	17.7	15.4
Item 330 N(Wtd)	12088	5959	5862	9636	1398	2785	3775	3713	1815	5769	5604	4858	2832	1419	2398	227

QUESTIONNAIRE FORM 1-5 1976	TOTAL	SEX		RACE		REGION				4YR COLLEGE PLANS		ILLICIT DRUG USE: LIFETIME				
		M	F	White	Black	NE	NC	S	W	Yes	No	None	Marijuana Only	Few Pills	More Pills	Any Heroin
Weighted No. of Cases:	15138	7241	7257	11796	1716	3570	4687	4597	2284	6994	6877	6091	3457	1736	2987	268
% of Weighted Total:	100.0	47.8	47.9	77.9	11.3	23.6	31.0	30.4	15.1	46.2	45.4	40.2	22.8	11.5	19.7	1.8
C11: How would you describe your political preference?																
1. Strongly Republican	4.2	5.6	2.7	4.4	3.6	3.7	4.5	4.1	4.1	4.1	4.2	5.1	3.4	2.5	3.6	5.4
2. Mildly Republican	12.3	13.4	11.3	14.0	4.6	10.1	13.9	11.2	14.9	14.5	10.6	14.3	11.8	12.8	9.6	8.9
3. Mildly Democrat	15.8	16.4	15.2	15.7	17.5	13.7	15.9	17.9	14.5	16.8	14.8	15.4	16.8	16.9	15.0	15.1
4. Strongly Democrat	9.9	10.4	9.4	8.2	21.4	8.9	9.1	12.3	8.5	10.1	9.5	9.4	10.2	11.5	9.2	10.5
5. American Independent Party	1.7	1.6	1.7	1.6	2.5	2.6	1.2	1.7	1.5	1.4	1.9	1.6	1.3	2.5	1.6	3.1
6. No preference, independent	30.2	30.1	30.3	32.3	18.1	33.7	32.2	26.2	28.6	31.5	29.2	28.8	29.7	28.8	35.9	33.3
7. Other	1.7	2.0	1.3	1.3	1.9	2.1	1.5	1.3	2.3	1.4	1.8	1.0	1.4	1.6	1.8	8.5
8. Don't know, haven't decided	24.2	20.6	28.1	22.5	30.5	25.2	21.8	25.4	25.6	20.1	28.1	24.4	25.3	23.4	23.2	15.5
Item 340 N(Wtd)	14429	7038	7085	11571	1624	3331	4519	4410	2169	6892	6717	5903	3327	1689	2864	258
C12: How would you describe your political beliefs?																
1. Very conservative	2.5	3.1	1.9	2.2	4.2	2.5	1.6	3.4	2.8	2.2	2.6	2.8	2.3	2.0	1.9	4.6
2. Conservative	11.6	13.8	9.4	11.8	12.4	9.3	11.2	13.1	12.6	12.3	11.0	14.1	11.0	11.6	7.6	6.2
3. Moderate	33.4	33.2	33.5	35.7	24.6	30.9	35.5	34.1	31.3	36.4	31.1	36.9	33.6	34.2	27.5	22.7
4. Liberal	19.7	20.3	19.1	20.2	16.2	22.0	21.2	16.6	19.4	22.9	16.6	14.8	21.4	22.4	27.0	21.2
5. Very liberal	4.4	4.7	4.1	4.0	6.2	5.8	4.0	3.7	4.6	5.3	3.4	2.6	4.4	4.3	7.9	10.8
6. Radical	2.9	3.8	2.0	2.4	4.7	3.9	2.2	2.5	3.7	2.6	3.0	1.5	1.9	2.9	5.1	14.2
8. None of the above, or don't know	25.5	21.2	29.9	23.7	31.9	25.7	24.2	26.5	25.6	18.4	32.3	27.2	25.2	22.6	23.0	20.4
Item 350 N(Wtd)	14403	7026	7075	11565	1609	3316	4504	4420	2163	6896	6706	5909	3320	1689	2840	260
C13: The next three questions are about religion.																
C13A: What is your religious preference?																
01. Baptist	21.9	19.9	23.8	17.3	62.4	7.6	13.0	47.9	9.6	19.3	24.2	25.0	19.5	22.8	17.0	16.3
02. Churches of Christ	4.6	5.0	4.1	4.4	4.4	4.1	3.7	5.6	4.9	3.4	5.7	4.4	4.0	5.2	4.4	7.0
03. Disciples of Christ	.5	.4	.6	.2	1.8	.2	.3	.9	.4	.6	.4	.5	.5	.6	.2	.4
04. Episcopal	1.8	1.6	1.9	2.0	.9	2.1	.9	2.3	1.8	2.5	1.0	1.5	1.8	2.4	1.9	3.1
05. Lutheran	7.0	6.9	7.1	8.2	.5	3.8	15.3	1.6	5.5	6.7	7.7	7.6	6.5	6.5	7.0	3.9
06. Methodist	8.6	8.0	9.2	9.0	8.6	4.9	9.8	11.2	6.1	8.9	8.1	9.6	8.5	8.0	7.1	8.9
07. Presbyterian	3.5	3.4	3.7	4.1	1.1	3.2	4.1	3.0	4.0	4.0	3.1	3.5	3.8	3.0	3.9	2.7
08. United Church of Christ	1.5	1.7	1.4	1.8	.1	2.1	2.5	.2	1.2	1.5	1.5	1.6	1.8	1.2	1.2	1.2
09. Other Protestant	5.0	4.9	5.1	5.4	2.1	5.9	6.0	2.7	6.2	4.9	5.1	5.8	4.1	4.6	4.8	5.1
10. Unitarian	.3	.2	.4	.4	.1	.8	.2	.2	.2	.5	.2	.2	.5	.3	.4	-
11. Roman Catholic	25.6	26.4	24.8	26.8	5.5	42.9	27.0	11.4	24.9	26.8	24.4	23.7	30.2	25.4	25.6	21.8
12. Eastern Orthodox	.3	.3	.3	.3	-	.9	.2	.1	.2	.4	.2	.3	.3	.5	.3	.4
13. Jewish	1.6	1.5	1.6	1.8	.1	3.8	1.2	.5	1.0	2.8	.4	1.2	1.9	1.5	1.8	1.9
14. Other religion	6.5	6.0	6.9	6.3	5.1	4.6	4.9	4.9	15.7	6.1	6.9	7.4	4.5	6.6	6.7	9.3
15. None	11.4	13.7	9.0	11.7	7.2	13.1	11.0	7.4	18.1	11.6	11.2	7.7	12.1	11.4	17.6	17.5
Item 360 N(Wtd)	14444	7026	7120	11579	1631	3333	4517	4439	2156	6883	6743	5931	3327	1686	2848	257
C13B: How often do you attend religious services?																
1. Never	11.0	13.3	8.6	11.0	7.0	13.6	10.0	7.1	17.0	9.4	12.5	7.3	11.1	11.1	16.9	19.4
2. Rarely	32.0	34.7	29.2	31.7	29.4	34.3	30.9	30.1	34.5	28.1	35.3	23.6	35.9	34.0	42.8	42.2
3. Once or twice a month	16.3	16.4	16.2	15.1	27.0	14.1	16.5	20.2	11.3	17.0	15.5	14.9	17.5	19.0	15.0	21.7
4. About once a week or more	40.7	35.7	46.0	42.2	36.5	38.1	42.7	42.6	37.1	45.5	36.7	54.1	35.5	36.0	25.2	16.7
Item 370 N(Wtd)	14589	7093	7191	11682	1650	3368	4558	4469	2194	6940	6821	5968	3364	1699	2888	263
C13C: How important is religion in your life?																
1. Not important	12.9	16.5	9.2	14.0	4.7	17.6	12.3	7.1	19.1	12.9	12.8	8.0	14.5	13.0	20.3	24.3
2. A little important	27.8	31.4	24.3	29.2	16.6	31.4	30.2	22.1	29.0	24.9	31.1	20.9	31.6	31.8	35.1	33.5
3. Pretty important	30.5	28.6	32.5	31.0	27.5	29.9	32.8	31.2	24.8	30.2	30.9	30.7	33.1	31.3	27.4	24.0
4. Very important	28.8	23.5	34.0	25.8	51.1	21.1	24.6	39.6	27.0	31.9	25.3	40.4	20.7	24.0	17.1	17.9
Item 380 N(Wtd)	14572	7082	7180	11673	1643	3363	4552	4467	2190	6939	6807	5962	3361	1697	2882	263

QUESTIONNAIRE FORM 1-5 1976	TOTAL	SEX		RACE		REGION				4YR COLLEGE PLANS		ILLICIT DRUG USE: LIFETIME				
		M	F	White	Black	NE	NC	S	W	Yes	No	None	Mari-juana Only	Few Pills	More Pills	Any Her-oin
Weighted No. of Cases:	15138	7241	7257	11796	1716	3570	4687	4597	2284	6994	6877	6091	3457	1736	2987	268
% of Weighted Total:	100.0	47.8	47.9	77.9	11.3	23.6	31.0	30.4	15.1	46.2	45.4	40.2	22.8	11.5	19.7	1.8

C14: When are you most likely to graduate from high school?

	TOTAL	M	F	White	Black	NE	NC	S	W	Yes	No	None	Mari-juana Only	Few Pills	More Pills	Any Her-oin
1. By this June	98.3	97.8	98.8	98.8	96.9	98.8	98.4	98.0	97.7	99.1	97.5	99.0	99.0	98.6	96.9	94.2
2. July to January	1.3	1.6	1.0	1.0	2.0	1.0	1.3	1.5	1.6	.7	1.7	.7	.8	1.2	2.6	3.5
3. After next January	-	-	-	-	-	-	-	-	-	-	-	-	-	-	-	-
6. Don't expect to graduate	.4	.6	.3	.2	1.0	.3	.3	.5	.7	.1	.8	.3	.2	.2	.5	2.3
Item 390 N(Wtd)	14601	7080	7171	11660	1639	3364	4565	4472	2199	6985	6857	5980	3372	1694	2883	260

C15: Which of the following best describes your present high school program?

	TOTAL	M	F	White	Black	NE	NC	S	W	Yes	No	None	Mari-juana Only	Few Pills	More Pills	Any Her-oin
1. Academic or college prep	42.2	42.4	42.3	43.7	36.8	61.1	35.8	36.4	38.2	68.3	16.5	46.3	45.8	40.4	34.6	23.2
2. General	32.1	31.0	32.9	32.5	30.9	18.2	34.9	36.1	39.6	22.6	41.7	29.8	30.5	33.2	37.5	35.1
3. Vocation, technical, or commercial	16.3	17.2	15.2	16.3	15.2	14.7	20.3	15.5	11.8	5.0	27.5	15.1	15.9	16.9	17.9	26.6
4. Other, or don't know	9.4	9.3	9.6	7.5	17.2	6.0	8.9	12.0	10.4	4.1	14.4	8.8	7.8	9.5	10.0	15.1
Item 400 N(Wtd)	14502	7041	7117	11594	1623	3343	4547	4437	2175	6964	6816	5951	3345	1680	2862	259

C16: Compared with others your age throughout the country, how do you rate yourself on school ability?

	TOTAL	M	F	White	Black	NE	NC	S	W	Yes	No	None	Mari-juana Only	Few Pills	More Pills	Any Her-oin
1. Far below average	.6	.7	.4	.4	1.1	.4	.5	.6	.9	.3	.9	.5	.2	.7	.4	2.0
2. Below average	1.7	2.2	1.0	1.4	2.0	2.0	1.4	1.5	2.0	.8	2.4	1.2	1.6	1.7	2.2	3.7
3. Slightly below average	4.8	5.8	3.9	4.4	6.7	4.5	5.4	4.8	4.3	2.8	6.7	3.5	5.2	5.3	6.3	7.7
4. Average	37.9	37.1	38.4	35.4	50.2	35.7	36.9	42.8	33.6	24.4	51.1	35.0	38.9	40.0	39.2	44.3
5. Slightly above average	23.2	22.5	24.2	24.0	20.2	22.9	23.4	23.1	23.4	25.2	21.2	23.4	23.5	23.5	23.8	19.5
6. Above average	26.9	25.9	28.3	29.2	17.0	28.3	28.1	23.2	29.9	38.6	16.0	30.8	26.3	24.4	24.0	16.7
7. Far above average	4.9	5.9	3.8	5.1	2.8	6.3	4.2	4.0	5.9	7.9	1.7	5.6	4.3	4.3	4.1	6.1
Item 410 N(Wtd)	14064	6877	6860	11297	1522	3214	4422	4310	2119	6798	6593	5770	3259	1627	2773	246

C17: How intelligent do you think you are compared with others your age?

	TOTAL	M	F	White	Black	NE	NC	S	W	Yes	No	None	Mari-juana Only	Few Pills	More Pills	Any Her-oin
1. Far below average	.4	.6	.3	.3	1.0	.3	.5	.5	.6	.3	.6	.4	.2	.4	.4	2.0
2. Below average	1.2	1.3	1.1	1.1	.9	1.1	1.3	1.2	1.3	.6	1.8	1.1	1.0	.8	1.5	1.6
3. Slightly below average	3.6	3.7	3.5	3.5	3.4	3.5	3.8	3.7	3.5	1.8	5.5	3.2	3.1	4.4	4.4	5.2
4. Average	39.5	36.7	42.1	38.4	41.9	36.5	39.3	43.1	37.0	24.7	53.7	37.0	40.5	40.8	41.5	44.4
5. Slightly above average	22.5	22.5	22.6	22.8	22.1	22.6	23.4	21.4	22.8	25.4	19.6	23.1	23.5	22.4	22.1	13.5
6. Above average	27.3	28.7	26.3	28.8	23.4	29.3	27.1	25.4	28.6	38.9	16.4	29.5	26.9	26.6	25.3	24.2
7. Far above average	5.4	6.6	4.2	5.1	7.4	6.8	4.6	4.8	6.3	8.3	2.4	5.8	4.8	4.5	4.8	9.5
Item 420 N(Wtd)	14327	6942	7045	11491	1578	3297	4489	4388	2152	6888	6771	5887	3314	1660	2822	252

C18: During the LAST FOUR WEEKS, how many whole days of school have you missed...

C18A: Because of illness

	TOTAL	M	F	White	Black	NE	NC	S	W	Yes	No	None	Mari-juana Only	Few Pills	More Pills	Any Her-oin
1. None	57.1	62.2	52.2	58.0	53.5	54.2	59.2	56.6	57.9	61.2	53.8	63.7	58.6	50.9	48.1	42.0
2. 1 day	15.9	14.3	17.2	16.1	15.0	16.9	15.4	16.0	14.7	16.2	15.6	14.7	15.5	17.8	17.2	18.5
3. 2 days	10.7	9.1	12.2	10.7	11.3	11.4	10.4	11.0	9.8	9.5	12.0	9.2	10.2	12.8	12.6	14.0
4. 3 days	6.5	5.8	7.2	6.1	7.6	6.5	6.4	6.4	6.7	5.7	6.9	5.2	6.0	7.5	8.8	7.4
5. 4-5 days	5.8	5.1	6.5	5.4	7.0	6.3	5.1	6.1	5.8	4.5	6.8	4.4	6.1	7.1	7.3	7.8
6. 6-10 days	2.8	2.2	3.3	2.5	3.6	2.9	2.3	2.8	3.7	2.2	3.3	2.1	2.5	2.6	4.0	6.6
7. 11 or more	1.3	1.1	1.4	1.1	1.9	1.7	1.2	1.0	1.3	.8	1.6	.7	1.1	1.3	2.1	3.3
Item 430 N(Wtd)	14008	6756	6921	11220	1562	3210	4423	4296	2079	6778	6633	5754	3231	1632	2758	243

C18B: Because you skipped or "cut"

	TOTAL	M	F	White	Black	NE	NC	S	W	Yes	No	None	Mari-juana Only	Few Pills	More Pills	Any Her-oin
1. None	69.1	67.5	71.0	68.2	80.4	65.6	69.4	72.9	66.6	74.0	64.9	83.9	68.0	62.3	48.3	38.0
2. 1 day	12.5	12.4	12.5	13.4	7.4	12.7	13.4	11.3	12.5	11.9	13.1	8.7	13.6	15.2	16.9	16.1
3. 2 days	6.9	7.6	6.1	7.1	4.3	8.4	6.4	5.9	7.7	6.2	7.4	3.5	8.3	8.9	10.2	16.5
4. 3 days	4.5	4.7	4.5	4.6	3.2	5.5	4.4	3.9	4.5	3.3	5.7	1.9	4.1	5.2	9.1	7.0
5. 4-5 days	4.1	4.4	3.8	4.1	2.7	4.5	3.6	3.8	5.1	3.0	5.0	1.3	3.3	6.2	8.9	12.4
6. 6-10 days	1.7	2.0	1.4	1.6	.9	2.1	1.7	1.3	1.8	1.1	2.3	.4	1.7	1.3	4.2	5.4
7. 11 or more	1.1	1.4	.9	1.0	1.1	1.3	1.1	.8	1.7	.6	1.7	.3	1.0	1.0	2.4	4.1
Item 440 N(Wtd)	13423	6542	6574	10820	1428	3101	4265	4053	2003	6521	6373	5457	3114	1577	2687	242

QUESTIONNAIRE FORM 1-5 1976	TOTAL	SEX		RACE		REGION				4YR COLLEGE PLANS		ILLICIT DRUG USE: LIFETIME				
		M	F	White	Black	NE	NC	S	W	Yes	No	None	Mari-juana Only	Few Pills	More Pills	Any Her-oin
Weighted No. of Cases:	15138	7241	7257	11796	1716	3570	4687	4597	2284	6994	6877	6091	3457	1736	2987	268
% of Weighted Total:	100.0	47.8	47.9	77.9	11.3	23.6	31.0	30.4	15.1	46.2	45.4	40.2	22.8	11.5	19.7	1.8

C18C: For other reasons

	TOTAL	M	F	White	Black	NE	NC	S	W	Yes	No	None	Mari-juana Only	Few Pills	More Pills	Any Her-oin
1. None	58.5	59.1	58.0	57.9	64.6	57.2	60.1	58.9	56.6	58.9	59.0	62.3	58.8	56.4	52.8	48.5
2. 1 day	18.9	18.3	19.5	19.7	14.7	20.1	19.2	18.3	17.5	19.5	18.1	18.2	18.4	20.3	20.3	20.6
3. 2 days	10.3	10.3	10.2	10.4	9.9	11.5	10.0	9.8	10.0	10.8	9.6	9.6	10.0	10.9	11.4	15.5
4. 3 days	5.8	5.7	5.9	5.9	4.6	4.6	5.2	6.4	7.6	5.6	5.8	5.0	5.7	6.4	7.1	6.4
5. 4-5 days	4.0	4.0	4.0	3.9	3.8	4.4	2.9	4.3	5.2	3.3	4.6	3.4	4.2	3.9	5.1	4.3
6. 6-10 days	1.6	1.6	1.5	1.5	1.2	1.3	1.7	1.4	2.0	1.4	1.8	1.2	1.9	1.1	1.9	2.6
7. 11 or more	.9	.9	.8	.7	1.2	.8	.8	.9	1.2	.6	1.0	.3	.8	1.0	1.4	2.6
Item 450 N(Wtd)	13534	6528	6693	10877	1459	3106	4280	4113	2035	6604	6381	5625	3122	1574	2631	233

C19: During the last four weeks, how often have you gone to school, but skipped a class when you weren't supposed to?

	TOTAL	M	F	White	Black	NE	NC	S	W	Yes	No	None	Mari-juana Only	Few Pills	More Pills	Any Her-oin
1. Not at all	60.4	56.4	64.6	60.0	67.2	54.9	60.0	70.6	48.8	61.0	60.0	75.5	54.7	54.1	42.9	30.7
2. 1 or 2 times	22.3	23.5	21.3	22.4	20.9	24.5	22.9	17.6	27.3	23.0	21.7	17.0	26.0	27.3	25.4	29.5
3. 3-5 times	10.1	11.6	8.4	10.4	6.2	11.4	10.2	6.6	14.9	9.7	10.5	4.7	11.9	11.2	17.6	19.3
4. 6-10 times	4.2	4.9	3.4	4.4	2.4	5.3	4.1	2.9	5.7	3.8	4.5	1.2	5.0	4.8	8.3	12.6
5. 11-20 times	1.5	1.8	1.2	1.6	.8	1.9	1.5	1.2	1.7	1.3	1.8	.7	1.3	1.7	3.1	3.1
6. More than 20 times	1.4	1.7	1.1	1.2	2.6	2.0	1.3	1.1	1.6	1.2	1.6	.8	1.1	.8	2.6	4.3
Item 460 N(Wtd)	14452	7004	7109	11584	1596	3310	4541	4431	2170	6968	6847	5943	3333	1682	2841	254

C20: Which of the following best describes your average grade so far in high school?

	TOTAL	M	F	White	Black	NE	NC	S	W	Yes	No	None	Mari-juana Only	Few Pills	More Pills	Any Her-oin
9. A (93-100)	7.7	6.0	9.4	8.4	3.5	7.4	6.5	9.5	7.1	12.2	3.3	10.5	5.9	7.3	4.3	5.3
8. A- (90-92)	11.7	8.0	15.5	12.4	9.2	11.5	10.7	11.7	13.8	16.2	7.3	15.2	10.1	9.6	8.3	4.1
7. B+ (87-89)	18.6	15.8	21.6	19.2	17.7	19.3	16.4	19.9	19.6	22.7	15.0	21.2	18.2	17.5	16.4	10.2
6. B (83-86)	21.0	21.3	20.8	21.8	17.8	22.8	21.0	19.5	21.4	21.5	20.7	20.6	22.1	21.9	20.7	18.9
5. B- (80-82)	15.3	16.9	13.8	14.7	18.4	15.4	15.5	15.0	15.1	13.5	16.9	13.4	16.7	16.2	17.1	12.7
4. C+ (77-79)	12.4	14.2	10.1	11.1	18.1	11.4	13.6	11.9	12.1	8.1	16.4	9.9	13.5	12.7	15.0	14.8
3. C (73-76)	8.7	11.0	6.3	8.3	9.1	7.7	10.4	8.2	7.4	4.2	12.9	6.2	9.1	9.4	11.7	18.9
2. C- (70-72)	3.7	5.0	2.2	3.2	5.2	3.4	4.6	3.4	2.5	1.4	5.7	2.4	3.6	4.4	5.1	7.4
1. D (69 or below)	1.0	1.8	.3	.8	1.0	1.1	1.3	.7	1.0	.2	1.8	.6	.9	1.0	1.4	7.4
Item 470 N(Wtd)	14392	6961	7094	11535	1587	3292	4523	4411	2166	6954	6818	5924	3322	1676	2824	244

C21: How likely is it that you will do each of the following things after high school?

C21A: Attend a technical or vocational school

	TOTAL	M	F	White	Black	NE	NC	S	W	Yes	No	None	Mari-juana Only	Few Pills	More Pills	Any Her-oin
1. Definitely won't	40.4	35.7	45.3	41.2	35.2	54.1	38.7	36.0	32.4	53.9	27.9	42.8	41.0	38.6	36.9	36.5
2. Probably won't	32.8	35.6	30.1	33.7	29.4	26.6	33.8	33.2	38.8	34.3	31.7	33.1	33.9	33.4	31.8	22.8
3. Probably will	18.6	20.1	16.8	17.2	25.5	12.3	18.5	21.8	21.9	9.1	27.4	16.4	17.6	18.9	22.4	26.1
4. Definitely will	8.2	8.6	7.8	8.0	9.9	6.9	9.0	9.0	6.9	2.8	12.9	7.7	7.5	9.1	8.9	14.9
Item 480 N(Wtd)	13682	6566	6807	11042	1448	3099	4336	4194	2053	6666	6795	5689	3119	1587	2683	241

C21B: Serve in the armed forces

	TOTAL	M	F	White	Black	NE	NC	S	W	Yes	No	None	Mari-juana Only	Few Pills	More Pills	Any Her-oin
1. Definitely won't	56.6	39.6	73.3	57.8	47.2	59.2	58.8	51.7	58.3	59.2	54.8	57.6	53.3	57.9	59.1	54.3
2. Probably won't	28.9	38.4	19.7	30.0	23.6	27.2	29.5	29.7	28.7	30.4	27.8	28.9	30.5	27.8	27.8	27.6
3. Probably will	9.7	14.4	5.0	8.5	16.8	8.8	7.9	12.4	9.1	7.6	11.3	8.7	10.7	10.7	8.9	12.5
4. Definitely will	4.8	7.6	2.0	3.7	12.5	4.9	3.8	6.3	4.0	2.8	6.0	4.8	5.6	3.6	4.2	5.2
Item 490 N(Wtd)	13338	6404	6644	10853	1370	3026	4227	4086	2000	6548	6591	5543	3072	1545	2623	232

C21C: Graduate from a two-year college program

	TOTAL	M	F	White	Black	NE	NC	S	W	Yes	No	None	Mari-juana Only	Few Pills	More Pills	Any Her-oin
1. Definitely won't	37.6	36.8	38.8	38.2	34.1	44.9	40.2	36.8	23.1	38.7	37.6	40.7	36.0	35.9	34.2	37.1
2. Probably won't	30.9	33.6	28.0	31.5	31.2	25.0	33.9	33.2	28.3	33.5	29.0	30.4	32.5	28.0	31.4	31.3
3. Probably will	20.4	19.8	20.6	19.1	25.5	17.0	17.6	20.1	31.7	16.7	23.1	18.2	20.5	23.4	22.5	24.2
4. Definitely will	11.2	9.8	12.6	11.2	9.2	13.1	8.3	9.8	17.0	11.1	10.3	10.7	11.0	12.7	11.9	7.1
Item 500 N(Wtd)	13669	6550	6809	11043	1438	3097	4330	4173	2069	6619	6810	5659	3120	1595	2692	240

QUESTIONNAIRE FORM 1-5 1976	TOTAL	SEX		RACE		REGION				4YR COLLEGE PLANS		ILLICIT DRUG USE: LIFETIME				
		M	F	White	Black	NE	NC	S	W	Yes	No	None	Mari-juana Only	Few Pills	More Pills	Any Her-oin
Weighted No. of Cases:	15138	7241	7257	11796	1716	3570	4687	4597	2284	6994	6877	6091	3457	1736	2987	268
% of Weighted Total:	100.0	47.8	47.9	77.9	11.3	23.6	31.0	30.4	15.1	46.2	45.4	40.2	22.8	11.5	19.7	1.8
C21D: Graduate from a four-year college program																
1. Definitely won't	29.6	27.1	32.2	30.3	22.6	27.9	34.5	30.1	21.2	-	59.8	27.5	26.3	31.2	35.1	37.8
2. Probably won't	19.9	20.4	19.3	20.0	19.3	14.9	20.4	21.4	23.7	-	40.2	18.0	20.2	19.6	22.8	26.6
3. Probably will	23.1	25.4	20.7	22.7	25.6	21.9	21.8	22.3	29.0	45.8	-	22.6	25.4	23.8	22.1	17.4
4. Definitely will	27.4	27.1	27.7	26.9	32.5	35.3	23.3	26.2	26.1	54.2	-	31.9	28.1	25.4	19.9	18.3
Item 510 N(Wtd)	13871	6678	6875	11178	1488	3160	4390	4248	2073	6994	6877	5750	3186	1617	2707	241
C21E: Attend graduate or professional school after college																
1. Definitely won't	38.3	35.7	40.8	39.6	28.1	35.2	43.3	39.1	30.9	10.8	65.6	36.1	36.1	38.2	43.9	41.9
2. Probably won't	33.1	34.3	32.0	33.7	31.8	28.5	32.6	34.1	38.7	38.2	28.5	34.0	33.9	32.8	31.2	33.2
3. Probably will	20.4	21.3	19.5	19.4	26.7	26.2	17.3	18.9	21.0	36.5	4.5	21.0	21.7	21.5	17.6	16.2
4. Definitely will	8.2	8.7	7.7	7.3	13.5	10.1	6.7	7.9	9.4	14.5	1.4	8.8	8.3	7.5	7.4	8.3
Item 520 N(Wtd)	13622	6559	6754	11003	1436	3079	4330	4167	2047	6646	6825	5653	3117	1591	2665	241
C22: Suppose you could do just what you'd like and nothing stood in your way. How many of the following things would you WANT to do? (Mark ALL that apply)																
A. Attend a technical or vocational school	27.0	29.1	24.8	27.1	26.0	20.6	29.1	29.3	27.8	12.3	42.3	25.2	25.5	28.1	31.3	34.6
B. Serve in the armed forces	15.6	19.7	11.4	14.1	24.7	15.5	13.5	19.4	12.1	12.9	17.9	16.6	15.7	15.5	12.8	17.7
C. Graduate from a two-year college program	24.5	20.1	28.8	24.4	22.8	22.8	22.3	23.3	33.9	16.5	32.3	23.2	23.5	26.2	27.7	18.9
D. Graduate from college (four year program)	53.3	54.3	52.6	53.3	58.0	56.1	50.4	51.6	58.7	87.7	20.1	57.3	55.1	51.9	47.5	40.7
E. Attend graduate or professional school after college	33.5	34.8	32.4	32.9	38.0	38.1	30.5	32.1	36.0	53.8	13.2	35.3	35.6	32.4	30.2	27.2
F. None of the above	13.0	12.6	13.4	13.5	6.5	12.8	15.1	12.2	10.4	3.5	22.7	11.3	12.1	14.6	15.1	17.7
Item 530-580 N(Wtd)	14247	6890	7024	11456	1546	3255	4480	4374	2138	6940	6781	5887	3282	1663	2787	243
C23: On the average over the school year, how many hours per week do you work in a paid or unpaid job?																
1. None	26.0	21.2	30.7	22.6	48.0	29.0	21.0	29.8	24.5	26.9	25.2	29.4	24.0	22.5	22.9	22.5
2. 5 or less hours	11.3	11.1	11.6	11.2	13.1	12.0	10.1	12.0	11.6	13.2	9.5	12.1	11.0	11.5	9.7	11.2
3. 6 to 10 hours	10.1	9.6	10.5	10.3	9.9	11.8	10.1	8.8	9.8	11.1	8.9	10.6	9.5	11.2	8.7	9.6
4. 11 to 15 hours	9.4	9.5	9.3	10.0	5.3	11.3	8.9	8.3	9.6	10.6	8.2	9.3	9.5	10.3	9.3	10.4
5. 16 to 20 hours	14.0	13.6	14.2	15.0	7.2	12.8	15.9	12.0	15.8	14.6	13.4	13.8	14.7	14.6	13.8	8.4
6. 21 to 25 hours	10.7	11.5	10.0	11.8	4.2	9.6	13.7	8.5	10.9	10.4	11.1	9.4	11.5	11.4	13.1	9.2
7. 26 to 30 hours	7.6	8.9	6.5	8.2	4.1	6.2	8.6	7.7	7.6	6.2	8.9	6.7	7.9	7.3	9.7	9.6
8. More than 30 hours	10.9	14.6	7.2	11.1	8.2	7.5	11.7	13.0	10.2	7.0	14.8	8.8	11.9	11.3	12.8	18.5
Item 590 N(Wtd)	14227	6882	7013	11473	1518	3242	4490	4357	2138	6938	6766	5877	3281	1655	2790	249
C24: During an average week, how much money do you get from...																
C24A: A job or other work																
1. None	29.3	24.3	34.1	26.8	45.8	30.7	25.7	32.4	28.6	31.1	28.0	33.5	26.3	25.8	26.0	25.0
2. $1-5	6.8	5.6	8.2	7.2	6.2	6.8	6.6	6.7	7.9	7.6	6.1	7.6	6.1	7.0	5.8	3.9
3. $6-10	5.7	6.1	5.4	5.8	5.7	6.1	5.6	5.9	5.2	6.0	5.5	6.2	5.6	5.0	5.0	5.7
4. $11-20	9.2	9.4	9.2	9.4	9.0	10.2	8.9	8.8	9.3	9.7	8.7	9.5	9.4	10.2	8.3	8.8
5. $21-35	14.8	13.3	16.3	15.7	9.9	16.5	16.6	12.0	14.3	15.8	14.0	14.0	14.1	17.3	15.0	11.8
6. $36-50	16.4	17.5	15.4	17.2	10.1	16.0	18.5	14.0	17.3	16.1	16.5	15.5	17.5	16.0	18.0	15.4
7. $51 +	17.7	23.8	11.5	17.8	13.2	13.8	18.1	20.2	17.5	13.7	21.2	13.7	19.6	18.6	21.8	28.9
Item 600 N(Wtd)	13470	6589	6579	10934	1379	3039	4316	4099	2016	6580	6426	5598	3133	1568	2603	228

QUESTIONNAIRE FORM 1-5 1976	TOTAL	SEX		RACE		REGION				4YR COLLEGE PLANS		ILLICIT DRUG USE: LIFETIME				
		M	F	White	Black	NE	NC	S	W	Yes	No	None	Mari-juana Only	Few Pills	More Pills	Any Her-oin
Weighted No. of Cases:	15138	7241	7257	11796	1716	3570	4687	4597	2284	6994	6877	6091	3457	1736	2987	268
% of Weighted Total:	100.0	47.8	47.9	77.9	11.3	23.6	31.0	30.4	15.1	46.2	45.4	40.2	22.8	11.5	19.7	1.8
C24B: Other sources (allowances, etc.)																
1. None	38.4	40.7	36.4	39.8	28.4	39.3	40.6	35.4	38.4	36.4	40.4	39.4	39.8	39.1	35.5	38.4
2. $1-5	32.3	29.3	35.4	33.8	25.9	31.8	32.7	31.1	34.8	34.4	30.4	35.2	31.8	32.7	28.7	21.8
3. $6-10	16.2	15.8	16.4	15.4	21.3	15.9	14.5	18.7	15.0	16.8	15.5	15.2	15.6	13.8	19.3	14.4
4. $11-20	7.3	7.3	7.2	6.4	13.0	8.0	6.4	8.6	5.9	7.2	7.3	6.0	7.8	7.9	8.7	13.1
5. $21-35	2.6	2.9	2.3	2.1	5.2	2.4	2.5	2.9	2.4	2.7	2.5	2.2	2.3	3.0	3.1	3.9
6. $36-50	1.1	1.3	.8	.8	2.5	.8	1.1	1.3	1.0	.9	1.3	.8	1.0	1.3	1.4	1.7
7. $51 +	2.1	2.7	1.5	1.6	3.8	1.8	2.3	1.9	2.5	1.5	2.6	1.3	1.8	2.1	3.2	6.1
Item 610 N(Wtd)	13036	6286	6469	10563	1372	2951	4166	3978	1941	6466	6171	5422	2993	1513	2565	229
C25: During a typical week, on how many evenings do you go out for fun and recreation?																
1. Less than one	8.1	6.7	9.3	7.1	12.5	8.3	6.7	8.9	9.0	8.0	8.1	12.2	5.2	6.4	3.8	4.5
2. One	12.7	11.2	14.4	12.4	14.9	10.1	12.8	12.6	16.8	13.5	12.1	17.8	10.4	11.5	6.4	4.9
3. Two	26.4	25.3	27.5	26.2	28.2	26.8	25.4	26.7	27.1	29.8	23.0	29.3	28.4	25.7	19.8	12.6
4. Three	25.8	25.7	25.8	26.6	22.7	24.0	27.6	25.5	25.4	26.5	24.9	23.9	28.2	27.4	26.8	17.4
5. Four or five	17.8	18.8	16.8	18.9	11.7	18.1	18.6	18.0	15.0	15.6	19.9	12.4	18.9	19.2	26.7	31.2
6. Six or seven	9.2	12.2	6.2	8.9	10.0	12.6	8.9	8.2	6.8	6.5	12.0	4.5	8.9	9.7	16.5	29.1
Item 620 N(Wtd)	14216	6880	7006	11463	1518	3232	4490	4361	2133	6923	6768	5870	3281	1652	2783	247
C26: On the average, how often do you go out with a date (or your spouse, if you are married)?																
1. Never	15.1	14.8	15.5	14.3	17.0	17.8	15.2	12.0	17.4	15.1	15.2	22.0	10.5	10.6	9.4	4.6
2. Once a month or less	19.0	20.8	17.0	19.6	16.2	19.4	18.6	17.2	22.8	21.8	16.1	21.1	17.9	19.0	16.4	14.5
3. 2 or 3 times a month	17.1	19.5	14.8	16.5	21.8	14.9	16.5	18.3	19.3	18.7	15.5	14.9	20.0	18.8	18.2	15.8
4. Once a week	15.7	17.0	14.3	15.3	18.0	14.9	15.3	16.8	15.6	16.7	14.7	15.2	16.8	16.1	15.4	15.4
5. 2 or 3 times a week	21.9	19.4	24.5	22.4	21.0	20.2	22.5	25.2	16.4	20.3	23.5	19.3	23.8	22.7	24.3	27.0
6. Over 3 times a week	11.2	8.4	14.0	11.8	6.0	12.9	11.8	10.5	8.4	7.4	14.9	7.6	11.0	12.9	16.4	23.2
Item 630 N(Wtd)	14040	6794	6926	11343	1486	3171	4456	4311	2101	6818	6663	5788	3245	1642	2757	241
C27: During an average week, how much do you usually drive a car, truck, or motorcycle?																
1. Not at all	14.1	8.6	19.4	9.7	38.8	22.1	10.2	13.1	12.4	14.1	13.7	16.6	12.4	11.8	12.0	9.3
2. 1 to 10 miles	14.2	10.1	18.1	12.9	23.2	16.3	13.1	13.4	14.8	14.1	14.4	16.2	12.5	12.9	12.2	11.0
3. 11 to 50 miles	30.4	25.4	35.5	32.2	21.6	31.1	32.2	28.3	29.6	32.7	28.2	32.5	30.7	31.2	26.8	18.3
4. 51 to 100 miles	19.8	24.3	15.3	21.5	10.0	15.0	21.6	20.1	22.6	20.5	19.3	18.4	21.1	21.4	20.8	23.2
5. 100 to 200 miles	13.7	19.3	8.2	15.4	3.7	9.8	15.3	14.8	13.7	12.4	14.8	10.7	15.3	15.2	16.7	23.6
6. More than 200 miles	7.8	12.3	3.5	8.3	2.8	5.5	7.6	10.3	6.8	6.1	9.5	5.7	8.0	7.5	11.6	14.6
Item 640 N(Wtd)	14195	6870	6997	11437	1520	3231	4472	4359	2134	6896	6721	5862	3282	1647	2783	246
C28: Within the LAST 12 MONTHS how many times, if any, have you received a ticket (OR been stopped and warned) for moving violations, such as speeding, running a stop light, or improper passing?																
0. None--GO TO Q.C30	74.4	62.8	85.7	72.7	87.6	81.9	71.5	73.9	70.3	76.0	72.9	82.6	70.3	70.9	64.8	55.6
1. Once	16.2	21.4	11.1	17.2	8.7	11.7	17.8	16.7	18.5	15.8	16.5	13.3	18.2	16.7	19.9	19.7
2. Twice	5.2	8.1	2.3	5.5	2.4	3.1	5.7	5.8	5.8	4.6	5.7	2.3	6.7	6.6	7.8	14.1
3. Three times	2.5	4.5	.6	2.7	1.0	2.2	2.5	2.3	3.4	2.2	2.7	1.0	3.0	3.3	4.3	7.7
4. Four or more times	1.8	3.3	.3	1.9	.3	1.3	2.4	1.4	2.1	1.3	2.2	.8	1.8	2.5	3.2	3.4
Item 650 N(Wtd)	13820	6656	6847	11254	1402	3119	4404	4212	2085	6772	6485	5767	3193	1616	2724	234
C29: How many of these tickets or warnings occurred after you were...																

QUESTIONNAIRE FORM 1-5 1976	TOTAL	M	F	White	Black	NE	NC	S	W	Yes	No	None	Marijuana Only	Few Pills	More Pills	Any Heroin
		SEX		RACE		REGION				4YR COLLEGE PLANS		ILLICIT DRUG USE: LIFETIME				
Weighted No. of Cases:	15138	7241	7257	11796	1716	3570	4687	4597	2284	6994	6877	6091	3457	1736	2987	268
% of Weighted Total:	100.0	47.8	47.9	77.9	11.3	23.6	31.0	30.4	15.1	46.2	45.4	40.2	22.8	11.5	19.7	1.8
C29A: Drinking alcoholic beverages?																
0. None	84.2	81.3	91.7	83.9	92.5	79.1	83.7	86.9	85.5	87.3	81.5	94.3	85.4	83.8	73.7	68.7
1. One	11.6	13.2	7.3	11.7	6.9	14.4	11.4	10.8	10.6	9.6	13.6	4.4	11.6	11.9	18.0	23.2
2. Two	2.6	3.4	.6	2.7	1.2	5.0	2.7	1.4	2.5	2.1	2.9	.5	2.0	2.6	5.1	6.1
3. Three	.8	1.0	.4	.9	-	.4	1.3	.5	1.0	.6	1.1	.4	.6	.9	1.5	1.0
4. Four or more	.7	1.0	-	.8	-	1.1	.9	.5	.5	.5	.9	.3	.3	.6	1.5	1.0
Item 660 N(Wtd) ★	3492	2437	972	3040	173	556	1241	1089	606	1600	1737	1000	945	462	935	99
C29B: Smoking marijuana or hashish?																
0. None	90.4	88.9	94.5	90.6	88.9	86.4	90.7	92.2	90.2	91.5	89.4	100.0	96.3	87.9	78.6	60.4
1. One	7.1	7.9	4.8	7.1	8.8	9.4	6.7	6.2	7.2	6.6	7.6	-	3.0	9.4	16.0	23.6
2. Two	1.5	1.9	.5	1.4	1.2	2.4	1.6	1.1	1.3	1.1	1.8	-	.3	1.8	3.5	8.5
3. Three	.6	.7	.2	.5	1.2	.9	.6	.4	.7	.6	.6	-	.1	.2	1.2	6.6
4. Four or more	.5	.6	-	.4	-	1.1	.5	.1	.7	.2	.6	-	.3	.7	1.0	1.9
Item 670 N(Wtd) ★	3449	2400	968	3004	171	551	1218	1080	600	1591	1708	987	930	456	920	106
C29C: Using other illegal drugs?																
0. None	97.9	97.6	99.2	98.0	98.8	96.5	97.7	98.5	98.7	98.4	97.5	99.9	99.6	99.3	94.9	83.0
1. One	1.5	1.6	.8	1.4	1.8	2.2	1.7	1.1	.8	1.3	1.5	.1	-	.7	3.7	12.0
2. Two	.3	.5	.1	.3	-	.9	.2	.3	.2	.1	.6	-	.2	-	.9	1.0
3. Three	.1	.1	-	.1	-	-	.2	-	-	.1	.1	-	-	-	.2	1.0
4. Four or more	.2	.3	-	.2	-	.4	.2	.1	.3	.1	.4	-	.1	-	.3	3.0
Item 680 N(Wtd) ★	3410	2366	961	2968	168	539	1210	1066	594	1574	1691	990	920	450	900	100
C30: We are interested in any accidents which occurred while you were driving a car, truck, or motorcycle. ("Accidents" means a collision involving property damage or personal injury-- not bumps or scratches in parking lots.) During the LAST 12 MONTHS, how many accidents have you had while you were driving (whether or not you were responsible)?																
0. None--GO TO Q.C32	75.8	69.5	81.9	73.9	90.3	78.8	72.9	76.0	77.1	76.8	74.8	82.5	74.5	70.8	67.4	57.6
1. One	18.3	22.6	14.3	19.8	7.5	15.5	20.5	18.0	18.5	17.9	18.8	14.5	19.5	20.9	22.6	32.6
2. Two	4.3	5.8	2.8	4.6	1.8	3.9	4.8	4.5	3.5	4.0	4.5	2.4	4.4	6.8	6.7	4.5
3. Three	1.1	1.5	.7	1.2	.3	1.4	1.0	1.2	.6	.9	1.3	.4	1.0	1.2	2.6	2.7
4. Four or more	.5	.6	.3	.5	.1	.4	.7	.3	.3	.3	.6	.2	.7	.4	.8	2.2
Item 690 N(Wtd)	13549	6521	6716	11064	1345	3046	4312	4144	2048	6668	6343	5674	3120	1595	2663	224
C31: How many of these accidents occurred after you were...																
C31A: Drinking alcoholic beverages?																
0. None	88.7	86.6	92.9	88.5	93.4	84.3	88.4	91.5	89.8	91.1	86.7	96.5	90.3	89.3	79.2	74.7
1. One	9.4	11.2	6.1	9.7	5.1	12.7	9.7	7.2	8.9	8.0	10.8	2.9	8.6	9.0	17.4	18.9
2. Two	1.4	1.7	.7	1.3	.7	2.6	1.4	.9	.9	.8	1.8	.4	1.0	2.0	2.4	3.2
3. Three	.2	.3	.1	.2	-	.5	-	.2	.2	.2	.2	-	.1	-	.4	2.1
4. Four or more	.2	.3	.2	.3	-	-	.4	.2	.2	-	.5	.1	.3	-	.6	1.1
Item 700 N(Wtd) ★	3249	1973	1205	2864	136	645	1162	980	463	1543	1577	1004	791	458	850	95
C31B: Smoking marijuana or hashish?																
0. None	93.3	92.1	95.4	93.3	94.0	91.0	93.2	94.9	93.9	95.0	91.5	100.0	97.2	95.3	82.3	75.8
1. One	5.5	6.4	3.9	5.5	4.5	7.0	5.4	4.7	5.0	4.5	6.6	-	2.4	3.8	14.8	15.4
2. Two	.8	1.1	.3	.8	-	1.4	1.0	.2	.7	.4	1.2	-	.3	.9	1.9	3.3
3. Three	.2	.3	.1	.2	-	.5	-	-	.4	.1	.3	-	-	-	.4	2.2
4. Four or more	.3	.2	.3	.2	.7	-	.4	.2	.2	-	.4	-	.1	-	.6	2.2
Item 710 N(Wtd) ★	3191	1927	1196	2812	134	630	1140	964	457	1521	1549	995	778	447	830	91

★ = excludes respondents for whom question was inappropriate.

QUESTIONNAIRE FORM 1-5 1976	TOTAL	SEX		RACE		REGION				4YR COLLEGE PLANS		ILLICIT DRUG USE: LIFETIME				
		M	F	White	Black	NE	NC	S	W	Yes	No	None	Marijuana Only	Few Pills	More Pills	Any Heroin
Weighted No. of Cases:	15138	7241	7257	11796	1716	3570	4687	4597	2284	6994	6877	6091	3457	1736	2987	268
% of Weighted Total:	100.0	47.8	47.9	77.9	11.3	23.6	31.0	30.4	15.1	46.2	45.4	40.2	22.8	11.5	19.7	1.8

C31C: Using other illegal drugs?

	TOTAL	M	F	White	Black	NE	NC	S	W	Yes	No	None	Marijuana Only	Few Pills	More Pills	Any Heroin
0. None	98.3	97.8	99.2	98.2	99.3	97.6	97.8	99.3	98.7	99.0	97.8	99.8	99.5	99.5	95.9	87.4
1. One	1.2	1.5	.6	1.3	-	1.8	1.7	.5	.7	.8	1.5	.1	-	-	3.6	8.0
2. Two	.4	.5	.2	.4	.7	.5	.4	.2	.4	.3	.5	.1	.4	.5	.4	3.4
3. Three	*	-	.1	-	-	.2	-	-	-	.1	-	-	-	-	.1	-
4. Four or more	.1	.1	-	.1	-	-	.1	-	.2	-	.1	-	.1	-	-	-
Item 720 N(Wtd) ★	3150	1893	1191	2777	134	616	1127	960	447	1508	1521	999	775	441	799	87

C32: If you have not entered military service, and do not expect to enter, GO TO PART D.

What is, or will be, your branch of service?

	TOTAL	M	F	White	Black	NE	NC	S	W	Yes	No	None	Marijuana Only	Few Pills	More Pills	Any Heroin
1. Army	21.2	20.3	23.8	18.4	34.5	20.4	19.4	26.5	11.9	20.3	22.5	23.7	18.7	21.8	18.6	16.7
2. Navy	19.8	19.4	20.5	21.7	10.6	21.3	19.4	16.9	25.8	18.8	20.1	18.5	19.6	20.4	24.3	18.5
3. Marine Corps	10.8	13.4	3.4	10.7	9.0	12.9	13.2	8.1	10.7	8.2	12.1	9.6	11.6	11.2	10.8	9.3
4. Air Force	28.7	27.1	33.1	28.9	30.0	23.7	31.0	29.9	28.4	32.3	26.8	30.8	30.0	27.4	24.1	31.5
5. Coast Guard	4.0	4.7	1.7	4.2	2.1	4.9	2.4	4.1	5.2	4.1	3.6	3.1	4.5	3.5	4.6	13.0
6. Uncertain	15.5	15.1	17.4	16.1	13.7	16.8	14.7	14.5	18.0	16.4	14.9	14.2	15.6	16.1	17.4	11.1
Item 730 N(Wtd) ★	2369	1720	580	1704	423	511	613	901	345	895	1311	892	603	285	436	54

C33: Do you expect to be an officer?

	TOTAL	M	F	White	Black	NE	NC	S	W	Yes	No	None	Marijuana Only	Few Pills	More Pills	Any Heroin
1. No	17.9	16.8	21.1	17.6	14.9	18.0	19.3	16.6	18.8	10.1	22.2	17.1	13.6	18.8	21.7	24.5
2. Uncertain	47.2	45.9	52.3	49.0	43.5	49.3	50.2	44.0	46.5	37.3	54.8	43.7	51.2	48.1	50.2	41.5
3. Yes	34.9	37.4	26.6	33.5	41.6	32.4	30.6	39.3	34.4	52.6	23.0	39.2	35.3	33.1	28.1	34.0
Item 740 N(Wtd) ★	2393	1744	579	1718	430	521	618	909	346	910	1322	899	609	287	442	53

C34: Do you expect to have a career in the Armed Forces?

	TOTAL	M	F	White	Black	NE	NC	S	W	Yes	No	None	Marijuana Only	Few Pills	More Pills	Any Heroin
1. No	30.1	30.8	28.7	31.5	23.0	32.6	32.0	25.6	34.6	31.8	28.3	29.0	26.3	31.0	35.7	30.2
2. Uncertain	49.4	50.0	49.1	51.9	43.4	46.4	52.3	49.7	48.0	48.8	50.7	47.4	53.2	50.0	50.7	47.2
3. Yes	20.5	19.2	22.1	16.6	33.6	20.8	15.8	24.8	17.4	19.4	20.9	23.6	20.6	19.0	13.7	22.6
Item 750 N(Wtd) ★	2409	1754	585	1731	431	528	622	909	350	912	1330	903	613	290	446	53

The following questions are about cigarette smoking.

B01: Have you ever smoked cigarettes?

	TOTAL	M	F	White	Black	NE	NC	S	W	Yes	No	None	Marijuana Only	Few Pills	More Pills	Any Heroin
1. Never	24.6	24.3	25.2	24.8	23.6	21.8	23.7	24.4	31.2	30.9	19.2	44.3	11.3	15.1	8.0	7.2
2. Once or twice	25.8	27.5	24.4	25.1	32.8	24.1	24.8	27.1	27.7	28.6	23.5	32.0	28.3	23.5	13.4	8.4
3. Occasionally but not regularly	16.9	16.4	17.3	17.0	16.6	17.2	17.9	15.8	16.5	17.4	16.4	12.6	23.8	21.2	15.5	9.5
4. Regularly in the past	9.2	9.4	9.0	9.2	6.4	10.6	8.4	9.0	9.2	7.6	10.5	4.5	10.5	12.0	15.0	18.6
5. Regularly now	23.5	22.5	24.1	23.9	20.7	26.3	25.2	23.6	15.4	15.5	30.4	6.6	26.2	28.2	48.2	56.7
Item 760 N(Wtd)	14642	7023	7107	11567	1613	3444	4563	4429	2206	6848	6675	5963	3402	1705	2942	263

B02: How frequently have you smoked cigarettes in the past 30 days?

	TOTAL	M	F	White	Black	NE	NC	S	W	Yes	No	None	Marijuana Only	Few Pills	More Pills	Any Heroin
1. Not at all - incl. (1) in b01	61.2	62.3	60.9	61.7	60.3	58.2	58.7	60.9	71.7	70.2	53.7	83.7	53.4	52.6	34.4	26.9
2. Less than one cigarette per day	10.0	9.7	10.3	9.5	12.9	9.5	11.1	9.9	8.9	10.0	10.0	7.2	13.7	12.2	10.1	6.1
3. One to five cigarettes per day	9.5	8.1	10.8	8.7	15.0	9.8	10.0	10.1	7.0	7.9	10.7	4.4	13.5	12.0	13.2	13.6
4. About one-half pack per day	9.3	9.1	9.2	9.4	9.0	11.1	9.4	9.2	6.5	6.5	11.7	2.7	10.7	12.9	17.8	18.2
5. About one pack per day	7.9	8.7	7.1	8.6	2.0	9.3	8.7	7.5	5.0	4.5	10.9	1.5	7.2	8.6	19.7	23.1
6. About one and one-half packs per day	1.6	1.7	1.4	1.8	.4	1.7	1.9	1.8	.7	.7	2.5	.2	1.4	1.5	4.2	10.2
7. Two packs or more per day	.3	.4	.3	.3	.3	.3	.2	.5	.2	.1	.4	.2	.3	.2	.6	1.5
Item 780 N(Wtd)	14608	7010	7092	11540	1614	3437	4554	4419	2199	6831	6661	5949	3395	1703	2939	264

* = less than .05 per cent.　　★ = excludes respondents for whom question was inappropriate.

QUESTIONNAIRE FORM 1-5 1976	TOTAL	SEX		RACE		REGION				4YR COLLEGE PLANS		ILLICIT DRUG USE: LIFETIME				
		M	F	White	Black	NE	NC	S	W	Yes	No	None	Marijuana Only	Few Pills	More Pills	Any Heroin
Weighted No. of Cases:	15138	7241	7257	11796	1716	3570	4687	4597	2284	6994	6877	6091	3457	1736	2987	268
% of Weighted Total:	100.0	47.8	47.9	77.9	11.3	23.6	31.0	30.4	15.1	46.2	45.4	40.2	22.8	11.5	19.7	1.8

B03: Next we want to ask you about drinking alcoholic beverages, including beer, wine, and liquor.

Have you ever had any beer, wine, or liquor to drink?

	TOTAL	M	F	White	Black	NE	NC	S	W	Yes	No	None	Marijuana Only	Few Pills	More Pills	Any Heroin
1. No	7.6	6.5	8.7	7.0	10.6	4.3	6.2	10.2	10.4	8.2	7.0	16.2	.7	2.7	1.0	.5
2. Yes	92.4	93.5	91.3	93.0	89.4	95.7	93.8	89.8	89.6	91.8	93.0	83.8	99.3	97.2	99.0	99.0
Item 790 N(Wtd)	11424	5534	5541	9140	1193	2672	3587	3427	1738	5417	5255	4704	2695	1343	2296	207

On how many occasions have you had alcoholic beverages to drink...

B04A: ...in your lifetime?

	TOTAL	M	F	White	Black	NE	NC	S	W	Yes	No	None	Marijuana Only	Few Pills	More Pills	Any Heroin
1. 0 occasions - incl. (1) in b03	8.1	6.8	9.4	7.4	12.4	4.6	6.5	11.2	10.7	8.6	7.6	17.3	.9	2.9	1.0	.4
2. 1-2	8.0	6.3	9.8	6.8	18.0	4.7	6.4	12.0	8.4	8.2	7.8	15.1	3.0	5.4	1.1	.8
3. 3-5	8.3	6.6	10.1	7.6	13.1	6.4	7.2	10.9	8.3	8.9	7.9	14.1	4.7	6.1	2.1	.8
4. 6-9	8.5	6.6	10.4	7.8	14.9	7.8	8.1	9.9	7.6	8.5	8.3	12.3	7.1	8.1	3.2	1.2
5. 10-19	11.9	9.8	14.0	11.7	13.5	12.3	11.7	11.8	11.9	12.9	11.3	13.7	13.6	12.1	7.1	4.5
6. 20-39	13.5	12.9	14.2	14.0	9.4	14.8	14.3	11.5	13.9	14.1	13.2	11.1	18.5	16.7	11.6	6.6
7. 40 or more	41.7	51.0	32.1	44.6	18.6	49.3	45.8	32.7	39.1	38.8	44.0	16.3	52.2	48.7	74.0	85.1
Item 810 N(Wtd)	13939	6746	6735	11218	1405	3273	4393	4134	2139	6662	6291	5725	3247	1624	2842	242

B04B: ...during the last 12 months?

	TOTAL	M	F	White	Black	NE	NC	S	W	Yes	No	None	Marijuana Only	Few Pills	More Pills	Any Heroin
1. 0 occasions - incl. (1) in b03	14.3	11.7	16.8	12.7	25.4	8.4	11.3	19.8	18.8	15.1	13.3	28.0	4.1	7.0	2.7	2.0
2. 1-2	13.3	10.8	16.0	11.9	24.5	10.5	11.0	18.1	13.3	13.5	13.3	21.4	8.5	12.4	4.2	3.2
3. 3-5	12.3	9.9	14.7	11.6	17.4	12.6	12.1	12.6	11.6	13.3	11.5	16.7	11.1	10.8	6.2	4.9
4. 6-9	11.1	10.0	12.2	10.9	11.2	12.2	11.2	10.1	11.3	11.5	10.9	11.6	13.4	12.2	7.4	4.0
5. 10-19	16.5	17.0	16.2	17.6	10.0	17.9	17.7	14.1	16.4	17.0	16.2	11.8	22.4	19.7	17.7	11.3
6. 20-39	12.6	13.4	12.0	13.8	6.0	14.6	13.7	10.4	11.5	12.8	12.4	5.7	18.2	16.3	18.1	16.6
7. 40 or more	19.9	27.2	12.1	21.5	5.4	23.7	23.0	14.8	17.1	16.8	22.4	4.9	22.2	21.7	43.6	57.9
Item 820 N(Wtd)	13894	6712	6724	11180	1394	3281	4402	4098	2113	6655	6265	5698	3240	1618	2834	247

B04C: ...during the last 30 days?

	TOTAL	M	F	White	Black	NE	NC	S	W	Yes	No	None	Marijuana Only	Few Pills	More Pills	Any Heroin
1. 0 occasions - incl. (1) in b03	31.7	25.5	38.2	28.8	51.8	24.3	26.8	39.8	37.8	33.5	30.1	53.9	17.1	23.6	10.9	6.9
2. 1-2	22.0	20.1	24.2	21.8	25.5	21.2	21.6	22.6	23.0	23.3	21.1	24.7	24.2	21.7	15.4	9.3
3. 3-5	18.4	19.7	17.2	19.6	11.8	21.2	19.6	15.2	18.2	19.6	17.3	12.4	25.3	22.0	21.5	13.0
4. 6-9	12.6	14.7	10.5	13.8	4.9	15.6	14.3	9.8	10.1	12.3	12.9	5.4	18.0	15.2	18.8	18.7
5. 10-19	9.6	12.0	7.2	10.3	3.9	11.5	10.8	7.9	7.1	7.7	11.4	2.7	10.8	11.1	20.0	21.5
6. 20-39	3.3	4.6	1.8	3.4	.9	3.9	4.0	2.7	2.0	2.2	4.2	.6	2.3	4.0	8.3	15.4
7. 40 or more	2.3	3.5	.9	2.2	1.1	2.4	2.9	1.9	1.8	1.3	3.0	.4	2.4	2.3	5.1	15.0
Item 830 N(Wtd)	13930	6737	6737	11222	1393	3286	4409	4113	2123	6659	6298	5679	3263	1633	2853	246

B05: On the occasions that you drink alcoholic beverages, how often do you drink enough to feel pretty high?

	TOTAL	M	F	White	Black	NE	NC	S	W	Yes	No	None	Marijuana Only	Few Pills	More Pills	Any Heroin
1. On none of the occasions	25.6	19.8	32.0	23.7	40.8	21.6	23.8	31.0	25.5	29.6	22.0	50.6	12.7	16.5	6.0	6.1
2. On few of the occasions	31.5	30.8	32.3	30.7	36.8	32.5	30.3	32.7	30.2	31.3	31.7	31.8	35.4	34.6	24.6	22.5
3. On about half of the occasions	16.0	18.1	13.8	16.9	10.2	17.0	17.6	13.5	15.8	16.0	16.2	7.8	21.0	19.5	22.2	16.5
4. On most of the occasions	17.3	20.0	14.3	18.7	8.0	19.0	19.0	14.3	17.0	15.8	18.6	6.4	20.7	21.2	28.4	31.2
5. On nearly all of the occasions	9.5	11.3	7.6	10.0	4.3	9.9	9.3	8.5	11.4	7.3	11.5	3.4	10.3	8.2	18.8	23.4
Item 840 N(Wtd)	10704	5261	5119	8592	1112	2616	3376	3122	1590	5026	4977	3959	2686	1325	2325	231

B06: Think back over the LAST TWO WEEKS. How many times have you had five or more drinks in a row? (A "drink" is a glass of wine, a bottle of beer, a shot glass of liquor, or a mixed drink.)

	TOTAL	M	F	White	Black	NE	NC	S	W	Yes	No	None	Marijuana Only	Few Pills	More Pills	Any Heroin
1. None - incl. (1) in b03	62.9	52.1	74.1	60.8	81.2	59.2	57.7	69.2	67.2	68.4	58.2	85.4	52.7	55.3	37.4	18.2
2. Once	11.4	12.7	10.2	12.2	7.1	11.9	12.3	9.8	11.9	11.3	11.2	6.9	15.5	13.3	14.7	8.7
3. Twice	10.0	12.9	7.2	10.4	6.3	11.5	10.8	8.5	8.9	9.0	10.9	3.6	14.3	14.9	14.5	13.5
4. Three to five times	10.5	14.6	6.2	11.3	3.4	11.7	12.8	8.3	8.4	8.4	12.5	3.1	12.9	11.6	21.0	27.4
5. Six to nine times	3.1	4.5	1.5	3.4	1.1	3.5	4.2	2.0	2.1	1.9	4.1	0.6	2.9	3.1	7.4	15.4
6. Ten or more times	2.1	3.2	0.8	1.9	0.8	2.2	2.3	2.1	1.5	1.1	2.9	0.4	1.6	1.8	5.0	16.8
Item 850 N(Wtd)	13945	6707	6786	11240	1393	3280	4404	4134	2126	6678	6264	5737	3263	1613	2832	238

QUESTIONNAIRE FORM 1-5 1976	TOTAL	SEX		RACE		REGION				4YR COLLEGE PLANS		ILLICIT DRUG USE: LIFETIME				
		M	F	White	Black	NE	NC	S	W	Yes	No	None	Mari-juana Only	Few Pills	More Pills	Any Her-oin
Weighted No. of Cases:	15138	7241	7257	11796	1716	3570	4687	4597	2284	6994	6877	6091	3457	1736	2987	268
% of Weighted Total:	100.0	47.8	47.9	77.9	11.3	23.6	31.0	30.4	15.1	46.2	45.4	40.2	22.8	11.5	19.7	1.8

The next major section of the questionnaire deals with various other drugs. There is a lot of talk these days about this subject, but very little accurate information. Therefore, we still have a lot to learn about the actual experiences and attitudes of people your age.

We hope that you can answer all questions; but if you find one which you feel you cannot answer honestly, we would prefer that you leave it blank.

Remember that your answers will be kept strictly confidential: they are never connected with you name or your class.

B07: On how many occasions (if any) have you used marijuana (grass, pot) or hashish (hash, hash oil)...

B07A: ...in your lifetime?

	TOTAL	M	F	White	Black	NE	NC	S	W	Yes	No	None	Mari-juana Only	Few Pills	More Pills	Any Her-oin
1. 0 occasions	47.2	41.1	53.9	46.6	54.6	39.3	47.9	54.3	44.1	51.3	44.7	100.0	-	26.1	9.0	2.4
2. 1-2	9.0	10.0	8.0	8.8	12.0	8.0	9.7	9.0	9.2	9.1	9.0	-	30.4	10.5	2.4	2.0
3. 3-5	5.4	5.7	5.1	5.4	5.6	6.0	5.8	4.6	5.2	5.4	5.2	-	16.3	7.1	2.8	2.4
4. 6-9	4.0	4.1	4.0	4.1	4.1	4.6	4.0	3.2	4.8	4.0	3.9	-	11.3	5.2	3.2	2.0
5. 10-19	5.9	6.3	5.5	5.9	5.5	6.4	5.7	5.3	6.6	5.5	6.5	-	13.4	10.1	6.8	4.3
6. 20-39	5.6	5.2	5.9	5.7	4.1	7.3	5.4	4.0	6.3	5.5	5.7	-	10.4	10.8	8.7	3.6
7. 40 or more	22.9	27.7	17.6	23.5	14.2	28.4	21.5	19.7	23.8	19.2	25.0	-	18.1	30.3	67.1	83.4
Item 860 N(Wtd)	14387	6933	6997	11483	1529	3370	4493	4340	2184	6821	6538	6091	3421	1679	2898	253

B07B: ...during the last 12 months?

	TOTAL	M	F	White	Black	NE	NC	S	W	Yes	No	None	Mari-juana Only	Few Pills	More Pills	Any Her-oin
1. 0 occasions	55.5	49.4	62.2	54.8	64.8	47.3	56.0	62.1	54.2	59.2	53.2	100.0	23.6	36.9	14.4	6.1
2. 1-2	8.6	9.2	8.0	8.7	9.1	9.4	9.3	7.4	8.5	8.9	8.4	-	26.4	10.8	5.2	3.6
3. 3-5	5.9	6.3	5.7	6.1	4.8	6.9	6.4	4.6	6.2	5.8	6.1	-	14.9	8.6	6.7	2.0
4. 6-9	4.7	4.8	4.5	4.6	4.4	5.4	4.3	4.1	5.3	4.6	4.9	-	10.3	6.8	6.3	8.1
5. 10-19	5.8	6.0	5.7	5.8	5.3	6.7	5.8	4.9	6.4	5.7	6.0	-	10.2	12.1	9.3	6.5
6. 20-39	5.1	5.4	4.7	5.2	3.8	6.7	4.4	4.2	5.9	4.7	5.4	-	6.6	9.0	11.5	10.1
7. 40 or more	14.3	18.8	9.2	14.7	8.0	17.6	13.9	12.5	13.5	11.2	16.1	-	8.0	15.9	46.6	63.6
Item 870 N(Wtd)	14295	6882	6960	11421	1510	3340	4476	4313	2166	6795	6499	6091	3380	1663	2869	247

B07C: ...during the last 30 days?

	TOTAL	M	F	White	Black	NE	NC	S	W	Yes	No	None	Mari-juana Only	Few Pills	More Pills	Any Her-oin
1. 0 occasions	67.8	62.3	74.0	67.8	72.8	61.4	68.6	72.3	67.3	71.6	65.6	100.0	55.7	53.9	26.8	14.1
2. 1-2	8.3	8.8	7.9	8.3	8.4	8.5	8.4	7.4	9.7	8.7	7.8	-	20.0	12.4	10.0	4.8
3. 3-5	5.4	6.0	4.7	5.4	5.4	6.6	5.1	4.7	5.4	5.1	5.8	-	10.1	9.3	8.5	10.0
4. 6-9	4.7	5.2	4.1	4.7	4.1	6.1	4.6	4.0	3.9	4.3	4.9	-	6.4	8.0	10.5	7.2
5. 10-19	5.7	6.9	4.3	5.7	3.8	7.3	5.2	4.9	5.7	4.8	6.2	-	4.8	8.7	15.9	17.3
6. 20-39	4.3	5.3	3.0	4.3	3.0	5.5	4.1	3.6	4.4	3.0	5.2	-	1.6	4.8	14.8	20.9
7. 40 or more	3.9	5.5	2.0	3.8	2.4	4.8	4.1	3.1	3.6	2.5	4.7	-	1.5	2.9	13.6	26.1
Item 880 N(Wtd)	14277	6873	6959	11412	1513	3333	4469	4316	2159	6793	6491	6091	3362	1665	2862	249

B08: On how many occasions (if any) have you used LSD ("acid")...

B08A: ...during lifetime?

	TOTAL	M	F	White	Black	NE	NC	S	W	Yes	No	None	Mari-juana Only	Few Pills	More Pills	Any Her-oin
1. 0 occasions	89.0	87.4	91.0	88.5	95.9	87.4	88.4	91.0	88.7	91.6	87.2	100.0	100.0	90.2	57.9	23.0
2. 1-2	5.0	5.4	4.4	5.3	2.2	5.1	5.3	4.3	5.4	3.8	5.8	-	-	9.8	17.4	18.0
3. 3-5	2.4	2.7	2.0	2.4	1.2	3.2	2.3	1.8	2.4	2.1	2.5	-	-	-	10.6	13.4
4. 6-9	1.3	1.4	1.0	1.3	.2	1.5	1.4	1.0	1.3	1.1	1.4	-	-	-	5.6	7.7
5. 10-19	1.3	1.6	.9	1.4	.5	1.6	1.5	1.0	1.0	.7	1.6	-	-	-	4.8	17.2
6. 20-39	.6	.8	.3	.6	.1	.7	.7	.4	.6	.3	.8	-	-	-	2.1	8.4
7. 40 or more	.6	.7	.3	.5	.1	.6	.6	.5	.6	.3	.8	-	-	-	1.7	12.6
Item 890 N(Wtd)	14576	7032	7090	11574	1611	3401	4548	4429	2197	6870	6662	6071	3440	1708	2936	261

QUESTIONNAIRE FORM 1-5 1976	TOTAL	SEX		RACE		REGION				4YR COLLEGE PLANS		ILLICIT DRUG USE: LIFETIME				
		M	F	White	Black	NE	NC	S	W	Yes	No	None	Marijuana Only	Few Pills	More Pills	Any Heroin
Weighted No. of Cases:	15138	7241	7257	11796	1716	3570	4687	4597	2284	6994	6877	6091	3457	1736	2987	268
% of Weighted Total:	100.0	47.8	47.9	77.9	11.3	23.6	31.0	30.4	15.1	46.2	45.4	40.2	22.8	11.5	19.7	1.8
B08B: ...during the last 12 months?																
1. 0 occasions	93.6	92.1	95.4	93.2	98.4	92.0	93.0	95.3	94.1	95.3	92.5	100.0	100.0	96.1	75.0	48.6
2. 1-2	3.8	4.6	2.9	4.1	.9	4.7	3.9	3.0	3.8	3.0	4.2	-	-	3.9	15.2	16.2
3. 3-5	1.4	1.7	1.0	1.5	.5	1.8	1.6	1.0	1.3	1.0	1.7	-	-	-	5.4	17.8
4. 6-9	.7	.8	.5	.7	.1	.8	.9	.5	.2	.4	.9	-	-	-	2.4	11.6
5. 10-19	.3	.5	.1	.3	.1	.5	.4	.1	.3	.1	.4	-	-	-	1.2	2.7
6. 20-39	.1	.1	.1	.1	.1	.1	.1	*	.2	*	.2	-	-	-	.4	1.5
7. 40 or more	.1	.1	*	.1	-	.1	.2	*	*	.1	.1	-	-	-	.3	1.2
Item 900 N(Wtd)	14562	7023	7087	11567	1609	3402	4541	4428	2191	6875	6652	6076	3444	1702	2921	259
B08C: ...during the last 30 days?																
1. 0 occasions	98.1	97.4	98.8	98.0	99.3	97.4	97.5	98.8	99.0	98.6	97.7	100.0	100.0	98.9	92.9	79.4
2. 1-2	1.4	1.9	1.0	1.5	.4	1.9	1.9	1.0	.7	1.1	1.7	-	-	1.0	5.5	12.6
3. 3-5	.3	.4	.2	.3	.2	.5	.5	.1	.1	.2	.4	-	-	-	1.2	4.6
4. 6-9	.1	.1	*	.1	.1	.1	.1	*	.1	*	.1	-	-	-	.2	1.5
5. 10-19	*	.1	*	*	-	.1	.1	-	.1	*	.1	-	-	-	.2	.4
6. 20-39	*	*	-	*	-	-	-	-	-	*	*	-	-	-	*	.4
7. 40 or more	*	*	-	*	-	*	*	*	-	*	*	-	-	-	-	.8
Item 910 N(Wtd)	14561	7019	7090	11565	1612	3398	4542	4432	2189	6877	6651	6077	3444	1704	2913	262
B09: On how many occasions (if any) have you used psychedelics other than LSD (like mescaline, peyote, psilocybin, PCP)...																
B09A: ...in your lifetime?																
1. 0 occasions	87.9	86.2	90.1	87.0	96.4	86.6	87.1	89.8	87.8	90.8	85.7	100.0	100.0	87.9	53.7	22.6
2. 1-2	5.3	5.7	4.9	5.7	2.3	6.1	5.1	4.3	6.6	4.3	6.2	-	-	12.1	18.1	16.3
3. 3-5	2.3	2.6	2.0	2.5	.4	2.5	2.5	2.0	2.3	1.9	2.5	-	-	-	10.6	10.1
4. 6-9	1.5	1.9	1.0	1.6	.5	1.4	1.5	1.5	1.3	1.3	1.6	-	-	-	6.4	10.1
5. 10-19	1.3	1.6	1.0	1.4	.3	1.3	1.6	1.0	1.0	.7	1.7	-	-	-	5.0	14.8
6. 20-39	.8	.8	.6	.8	.1	.9	1.1	.5	.5	.5	1.0	-	-	-	2.7	12.1
7. 40 or more	.9	1.3	.4	.9	-	1.1	1.1	.9	.3	.5	1.2	-	-	-	3.4	14.0
Item 920 N(Wtd)	14498	6993	7066	11526	1598	3369	4524	4417	2188	6846	6629	6066	3410	1697	2913	257
B09B: ...during the last 12 months?																
1. 0 occasions	93.0	91.2	95.0	92.3	98.6	92.2	92.1	94.3	93.3	94.8	91.7	100.0	100.0	95.5	71.9	47.2
2. 1-2	3.7	4.6	2.9	4.1	.8	3.8	4.0	3.0	4.4	3.1	4.2	-	-	4.5	15.0	13.4
3. 3-5	1.4	1.9	1.0	1.6	.3	1.8	1.9	.9	1.2	1.1	1.6	-	-	-	6.1	13.4
4. 6-9	.9	1.0	.8	1.0	.2	1.0	.9	.8	.7	.4	1.3	-	-	-	3.5	10.2
5. 10-19	.5	.7	.2	.4	.1	.6	.5	.4	.3	.3	.5	-	-	-	1.6	8.3
6. 20-39	.3	.5	.1	.4	-	.4	.4	.3	.1	.3	.4	-	-	-	1.2	5.1
7. 40 or more	.2	.2	.1	.2	-	.3	.1	.2	-	*	.3	-	-	-	.7	2.4
Item 930 N(Wtd)	14449	6963	7049	11484	1598	3361	4503	4404	2180	6841	6592	6069	3414	1694	2863	254
B09C: ...during the last 30 days?																
1. 0 occasions	97.7	96.9	98.6	97.5	99.5	97.1	97.3	98.1	98.3	98.6	97.1	100.0	100.0	99.4	91.1	71.2
2. 1-2	1.5	1.9	1.1	1.6	.3	1.7	1.9	1.1	1.3	1.1	1.8	-	-	.6	6.0	15.2
3. 3-5	.5	.7	.2	.5	.1	.8	.5	.3	.2	.3	.7	-	-	-	1.9	5.8
4. 6-9	.2	.3	.1	.2	.1	.3	.2	.2	*	.1	.3	-	-	-	.6	5.1
5. 10-19	.1	.1	*	.1	-	.1	.1	.1	*	*	.1	-	-	-	.2	1.2
6. 20-39	*	.1	-	*	-	*	*	.1	-	-	.1	-	-	-	.1	1.2
7. 40 or more	*	*	-	*	-	-	-	*	-	-	*	-	-	-	.1	-
Item 940 N(Wtd)	14469	6978	7050	11501	1599	3365	4514	4410	2180	6842	6610	6070	3414	1697	2877	257
B10: On how many occasions (if any) have you used cocaine (sometimes called "coke")...																

*=less than .05 per cent.

QUESTIONNAIRE FORM 1-5 1976	TOTAL	SEX		RACE		REGION				4YR COLLEGE PLANS		ILLICIT DRUG USE: LIFETIME				
		M	F	White	Black	NE	NC	S	W	Yes	No	None	Mari- juana Only	Few Pills	More Pills	Any Her- oin
Weighted No. of Cases:	15138	7241	7257	11796	1716	3570	4687	4597	2284	6994	6877	6091	3457	1736	2987	268
% of Weighted Total:	100.0	47.8	47.9	77.9	11.3	23.6	31.0	30.4	15.1	46.2	45.4	40.2	22.8	11.5	19.7	1.8
B10A: ...in your lifetime?																
1. 0 occasions	90.3	88.1	92.6	90.5	91.3	89.7	91.0	91.1	87.9	92.2	89.2	100.0	100.0	88.6	65.6	19.8
2. 1-2	5.1	6.0	4.1	5.1	4.5	5.5	4.8	4.4	6.4	4.3	5.5	-	-	11.4	17.2	15.6
3. 3-5	2.0	2.5	1.6	1.9	2.3	2.2	1.9	2.1	2.0	1.7	2.2	-	-	-	8.3	20.2
4. 6-9	1.0	1.3	.7	1.0	1.0	1.1	.9	.9	1.4	.7	1.2	-	-	-	3.9	13.4
5. 10-19	.7	1.0	.4	.7	.6	.7	.7	.5	1.1	.5	.9	-	-	-	2.6	11.1
6. 20-39	.5	.5	.4	.5	.3	.4	.4	.5	.6	.5	.4	-	-	-	1.4	10.7
7. 40 or more	.4	.5	.2	.3	.1	.3	.3	.4	.6	.2	.5	-	-	-	1.1	9.5
Item 950 N(Wtd)	14491	7001	7074	11545	1591	3378	4521	4405	2188	6847	6643	6050	3412	1687	2926	262
B10B: ...during the last 12 months?																
1. 0 occasions	94.0	92.5	95.6	94.1	94.8	93.4	94.5	94.9	92.1	95.0	93.4	100.0	100.0	94.8	78.5	40.2
2. 1-2	3.5	4.3	2.8	3.6	3.1	4.0	3.5	2.8	4.2	3.0	3.9	-	-	5.2	12.2	26.1
3. 3-5	1.2	1.6	.7	1.1	.9	1.2	1.0	1.1	1.6	.9	1.3	-	-	-	4.6	12.6
4. 6-9	.6	.7	.4	.5	.6	.8	.4	.5	.7	.5	.6	-	-	-	2.3	6.9
5. 10-19	.4	.5	.2	.3	.4	.4	.2	.3	.7	.3	.4	-	-	-	1.1	7.3
6. 20-39	.2	.2	.2	.2	.1	.1	.2	.2	.3	.2	.2	-	-	-	.7	4.2
7. 40 or more	.1	.2	.1	.1	-	.1	.1	.1	.4	.1	.2	-	-	-	.5	2.3
Item 960 N(Wtd)	14469	6989	7066	11533	1589	3373	4515	4399	2183	6847	6630	6051	3415	1682	2905	261
B10C: ...during the last 30 days?																
1. 0 occasions	98.0	97.5	98.6	98.2	97.6	97.6	98.4	98.4	96.7	98.4	97.8	100.0	100.0	98.4	92.7	78.2
2. 1-2	1.4	1.7	.9	1.3	1.8	1.8	1.2	1.0	2.1	1.1	1.4	-	-	1.5	5.1	10.3
3. 3-5	.3	.4	.2	.3	.3	.3	.2	.3	.5	.3	.3	-	-	-	1.1	5.0
4. 6-9	.2	.3	.1	.2	.3	.1	.1	.2	.4	.1	.2	-	-	-	.6	4.6
5. 10-19	.1	.1	.1	.1	.1	.1	*	.1	.1	*	.1	-	-	-	.3	1.1
6. 20-39	*	.1	*	*	-	.1	*	*	*	*	*	-	-	-	.1	1.1
7. 40 or more	*	*	*	*	-	-	*	-	.2	-	*	-	-	-	.2	-
Item 970 N(Wtd)	14466	6988	7064	11528	1591	3371	4512	4402	2181	6845	6630	6051	3415	1684	2900	261
B11: Amphetamines are sometimes prescribed by doctors to help people lose weight or to give people more energy. They are sometimes called uppers, ups, speed, bennies, dexies, pep pills, and diet pills. On how many occasions (if any) have you taken amphetamines on your own--that is, without a doctor telling you to take them...																
B11A: ...in your lifetime?																
1. 0 occasions	77.4	77.7	77.3	76.1	90.1	78.1	76.2	79.8	73.7	82.3	73.0	100.0	100.0	58.6	20.1	14.2
2. 1-2	7.1	7.1	7.1	7.2	5.7	7.9	5.9	7.5	7.5	6.2	7.9	-	-	41.4	10.2	9.6
3. 3-5	3.8	3.9	3.7	3.9	1.9	3.5	4.0	3.2	5.1	3.1	4.4	-	-	-	18.1	7.3
4. 6-9	2.8	2.7	2.8	2.9	.9	2.5	2.8	2.7	3.2	2.4	3.2	-	-	-	12.9	8.0
5. 10-19	3.2	3.0	3.3	3.5	.9	3.0	4.0	2.5	3.3	2.2	4.1	-	-	-	14.4	13.8
6. 20-39	2.0	1.9	2.0	2.2	.4	1.8	2.3	1.7	2.4	1.3	2.5	-	-	-	8.9	11.5
7. 40 or more	3.8	3.6	3.8	4.2	.2	3.1	4.9	2.7	4.8	2.5	5.0	-	-	-	15.5	35.6
Item 980 N(Wtd)	14458	7010	7064	11540	1600	3381	4504	4398	2175	6836	6613	6012	3370	1690	2937	261
B11B: ...during the last 12 months?																
1. 0 occasions	84.2	84.2	84.6	83.1	94.8	85.3	82.2	86.3	82.7	88.1	80.7	100.0	100.0	80.8	38.8	31.3
2. 1-2	5.7	5.9	5.5	6.0	3.3	5.9	5.6	5.4	6.4	4.6	6.8	-	-	19.2	16.3	13.1
3. 3-5	2.9	2.9	2.8	3.1	.9	2.3	2.9	2.9	3.4	2.4	3.4	-	-	-	13.3	11.2
4. 6-9	2.3	2.4	2.1	2.4	.6	2.3	2.6	2.0	2.2	1.7	2.7	-	-	-	10.6	10.0
5. 10-19	2.2	2.1	2.2	2.4	.3	1.8	2.9	1.6	2.4	1.3	2.9	-	-	-	10.0	10.4
6. 20-39	1.3	1.2	1.4	1.5	.1	1.1	1.7	1.1	1.3	.9	1.6	-	-	-	5.5	11.6
7. 40 or more	1.4	1.3	1.4	1.5	.1	1.2	2.1	.6	1.5	.9	1.9	-	-	-	5.7	12.4
Item 990 N(Wtd)	14420	6991	7049	11513	1593	3373	4496	4383	2168	6829	6595	6020	3378	1681	2894	259

* = less than .05 per cent.

QUESTIONNAIRE FORM 1-5 1976	TOTAL	SEX		RACE		REGION				4YR COLLEGE PLANS		ILLICIT DRUG USE: LIFETIME				
		M	F	White	Black	NE	NC	S	W	Yes	No	None	Marijuana Only	Few Pills	More Pills	Any Heroin
Weighted No. of Cases:	15138	7241	7257	11796	1716	3570	4687	4597	2284	6994	6877	6091	3457	1736	2987	268
% of Weighted Total:	100.0	47.8	47.9	77.9	11.3	23.6	31.0	30.4	15.1	46.2	45.4	40.2	22.8	11.5	19.7	1.8
B11C: ...during the last 30 days?																
1. 0 occasions	92.3	92.2	92.4	91.4	98.7	93.0	90.3	93.8	92.2	94.3	90.4	100.0	100.0	96.4	67.5	55.8
2. 1-2	3.9	4.0	3.7	4.3	.8	3.6	4.5	3.5	3.9	3.2	4.5	-	-	3.6	15.7	16.5
3. 3-5	1.7	1.8	1.4	1.8	.3	1.5	2.0	1.3	1.8	1.2	2.0	-	-	-	7.2	11.2
4. 6-9	1.0	1.0	1.1	1.1	.2	.9	1.3	.8	.9	.5	1.6	-	-	-	4.4	8.5
5. 10-19	.7	.7	.8	.8	-	.6	1.2	.4	.8	.6	.8	-	-	-	3.3	4.2
6. 20-39	.3	.2	.5	.4	.1	.4	.5	.1	.3	.2	.5	-	-	-	1.3	3.5
7. 40 or more	.1	.1	.1	.1	-	.1	.2	*	.1	.1	.1	-	-	-	.5	.8
Item 1000 N(Wtd)	14421	6996	7045	11510	1595	3373	4495	4386	2167	6834	6596	6022	3380	1676	2896	260
B12: On how many occasions (if any) have you used quaaludes (quads, soapers, methaqualone) on you own--that is, without a doctor telling you to take them...																
B12A: ...in your lifetime?																
1. 0 occasions	92.2	91.4	93.3	91.6	97.5	91.4	92.3	90.9	96.0	93.7	91.2	100.0	100.0	93.7	70.2	37.6
2. 1-2	3.2	3.4	3.1	3.4	1.6	3.6	3.1	3.8	1.9	3.0	3.4	-	-	6.3	11.6	11.6
3. 3-5	1.4	1.7	1.1	1.6	.2	1.6	1.3	1.7	1.0	1.2	1.6	-	-	-	6.3	9.7
4. 6-9	1.0	1.1	.9	1.1	.4	1.2	1.2	1.0	.3	.7	1.2	-	-	-	4.0	12.8
5. 10-19	.9	1.3	.6	1.0	.1	1.0	.9	1.2	.3	.6	1.2	-	-	-	3.9	9.7
6. 20-39	.5	.5	.5	.5	.1	.6	.5	.6	.2	.3	.6	-	-	-	2.0	7.0
7. 40 or more	.6	.8	.5	.7	.1	.5	.7	.9	.3	.5	.8	-	-	-	2.1	12.4
Item 1010 N(Wtd)	14433	6996	7066	11519	1607	3371	4486	4411	2165	6835	6607	6021	3385	1698	2873	258
B12B: ...during the last 12 months?																
1. 0 occasions	95.3	94.5	96.3	94.9	98.9	94.9	95.0	94.6	97.9	96.5	94.5	100.0	100.0	97.9	81.8	53.5
2. 1-2	2.3	2.8	1.7	2.5	.7	2.5	2.5	2.5	1.1	1.8	2.7	-	-	2.1	8.8	16.9
3. 3-5	1.1	1.1	.9	1.1	.2	1.2	1.0	1.2	.5	.8	1.3	-	-	-	4.3	11.8
4. 6-9	.6	.7	.5	.7	.1	.7	.6	.7	.2	.4	.6	-	-	-	2.5	6.3
5. 10-19	.4	.5	.3	.4	.1	.4	.5	.5	.1	.2	.5	-	-	-	1.5	6.3
6. 20-39	.1	.1	.1	.1	-	.1	.2	.2	*	.1	.2	-	-	-	.4	3.1
7. 40 or more	.2	.2	.2	.2	-	.1	.2	.3	*	.2	.2	-	-	-	.7	2.4
Item 1020 N(Wtd)	14419	6989	7061	11510	1604	3370	4482	4405	2164	6834	6601	6022	3385	1697	2864	254
B12C: ...during the last 30 days?																
1. 0 occasions	98.4	98.0	98.8	98.2	99.8	98.7	97.9	98.2	99.3	98.9	98.0	100.0	100.0	99.6	93.8	79.7
2. 1-2	1.0	1.2	.8	1.1	.2	.9	1.4	1.0	.6	.7	1.2	-	-	.4	3.9	11.3
3. 3-5	.3	.4	.2	.3	.1	.3	.3	.4	.1	.2	.4	-	-	-	1.1	5.5
4. 6-9	.2	.2	.1	.2	-	.1	.2	.2	*	.1	.2	-	-	-	.8	.8
5. 10-19	.1	*	.1	.1	-	-	.1	.1	*	*	.1	-	-	-	.2	.8
6. 20-39	*	*	*	*	-	*	*	*	-	-	*	-	-	-	*	1.2
7. 40 or more	*	*	*	*	-	*	.1	*	-	-	.1	-	-	-	.1	.4
Item 1030 N(Wtd)	14417	6989	7058	11510	1604	3368	4479	4407	2163	6834	6599	6022	3386	1698	2857	256
B13: Barbiturates are sometimes prescribed by doctors to help people relax or get to sleep. They are sometimes called downs, downers, goofballs, yellows, reds, blues, rainbows. On how many occasions (if any) have you taken barbiturates on your own-- that is, without a doctor telling you to take them...																
B13A: ...in your lifetime?																
1. 0 occasions	83.8	83.7	84.0	82.7	92.6	82.6	83.7	83.6	86.0	87.3	80.9	100.0	100.0	74.9	40.9	20.2
2. 1-2	6.5	6.4	6.6	6.8	4.3	7.0	6.1	6.6	6.6	5.8	7.1	-	-	25.1	16.8	11.1
3. 3-5	2.9	2.8	2.9	3.0	1.4	3.1	2.7	3.1	2.2	2.0	3.5	-	-	-	13.6	7.6
4. 6-9	2.1	2.1	2.1	2.4	.8	2.3	2.3	1.9	2.0	1.4	2.8	-	-	-	9.4	14.5
5. 10-19	1.9	2.0	1.8	2.1	.3	2.1	2.2	1.7	1.3	1.4	2.3	-	-	-	8.5	10.3
6. 20-39	1.3	1.3	1.2	1.3	.3	1.4	1.4	1.3	.9	.9	1.5	-	-	-	5.1	12.6
7. 40 or more	1.6	1.8	1.3	1.7	.4	1.4	1.8	1.8	.9	1.1	1.9	-	-	-	5.7	23.7
Item 1040 N(Wtd)	14443	7014	7066	11543	1599	3371	4511	4392	2169	6832	6627	6015	3381	1694	2894	262

*=less than .05 per cent.

QUESTIONNAIRE FORM 1-5 1976	TOTAL	SEX		RACE		REGION				4YR COLLEGE PLANS		ILLICIT DRUG USE: LIFETIME				
		M	F	White	Black	NE	NC	S	W	Yes	No	None	Mari- juana Only	Few Pills	More Pills	Any Her- oin
Weighted No. of Cases:	15138	7241	7257	11796	1716	3570	4687	4597	2284	6994	6877	6091	3457	1736	2987	268
% of Weighted Total:	100.0	47.8	47.9	77.9	11.3	23.6	31.0	30.4	15.1	46.2	45.4	40.2	22.8	11.5	19.7	1.8
B13B: ...during the last 12 months?																
1. 0 occasions	90.4	90.1	90.8	89.6	97.0	89.6	89.6	90.3	93.3	92.7	88.4	100.0	100.0	91.5	61.9	40.1
2. 1-2	4.6	4.6	4.5	5.0	1.8	5.0	4.8	4.5	3.3	3.5	5.4	-	-	8.5	16.7	13.6
3. 3-5	2.0	2.1	1.9	2.2	.6	2.3	2.0	2.0	1.7	1.5	2.5	-	-	-	9.0	11.3
4. 6-9	1.3	1.2	1.3	1.3	.2	1.4	1.4	1.2	.7	.9	1.5	-	-	-	5.2	12.1
5. 10-19	1.0	1.1	.9	1.1	.4	1.0	1.4	1.0	.5	.9	1.1	-	-	-	4.1	12.5
6. 20-39	.5	.5	.4	.5	.1	.5	.4	.5	.2	.2	.6	-	-	-	1.7	6.6
7. 40 or more	.4	.4	.3	.4	-	.2	.4	.5	.2	.3	.4	-	-	-	1.4	4.3
Item 1050 N(Wtd)	14398	6989	7052	11514	1591	3359	4503	4376	2161	6823	6606	6015	3383	1687	2858	257
B13C: ...during the last 30 days?																
1. 0 occasions	96.1	96.3	96.1	95.8	99.0	96.2	95.4	95.9	97.7	97.2	95.2	100.0	100.0	98.2	84.6	65.9
2. 1-2	2.2	2.2	2.2	2.5	.6	2.4	2.5	2.1	1.6	1.7	2.7	-	-	1.8	9.0	13.2
3. 3-5	.8	.8	.8	.9	.2	.8	1.2	.8	.3	.5	1.1	-	-	-	3.3	11.2
4. 6-9	.4	.3	.5	.4	.1	.3	.5	.6	.1	.3	.5	-	-	-	1.7	5.4
5. 10-19	.3	.3	.2	.3	.1	.1	.2	.4	.1	.1	.3	-	-	-	1.1	2.3
6. 20-39	.1	*	.1	.1	-	*	.1	.1	.1	.1	.1	-	-	-	.2	1.6
7. 40 or more	*	*	.1	.1	-	.1		.1	*	*	*	-	-	-	.2	-
Item 1060 N(Wtd)	14397	6987	7053	11515	1591	3358	4502	4378	2160	6822	6607	6015	3383	1687	2857	258
B14: Tranquilizers are sometimes prescribed by doctors to calm people down, quiet their nerves, or relax their muscles. Librium, Valium, and Miltown are all tranquilizers. On how many occasions (if any) have you taken tranquilizers on your own--that is, without a doctor telling you to take them...																
B14A: ...in your lifetime?																
1. 0 occasions	83.2	84.5	82.0	82.0	91.7	83.8	84.2	81.3	83.8	85.3	81.4	100.0	100.0	63.4	44.0	29.3
2. 1-2	7.5	7.0	8.0	7.8	4.8	7.3	6.8	8.4	7.7	7.2	7.8	-	-	36.6	15.0	12.5
3. 3-5	3.4	3.0	3.8	3.8	1.4	3.0	3.4	3.6	3.8	2.8	3.8	-	-	-	15.8	13.3
4. 6-9	2.0	1.6	2.4	2.2	.6	2.4	1.8	2.3	1.5	1.8	2.3	-	-	-	9.1	11.0
5. 10-19	1.7	1.7	1.6	1.8	.8	1.7	1.6	1.7	1.6	1.3	2.0	-	-	-	7.3	10.6
6. 20-39	1.0	1.2	.9	1.1	.3	1.0	.9	1.3	.9	.8	1.3	-	-	-	4.2	9.5
7. 40 or more	1.2	1.2	1.1	1.3	.4	.9	1.3	1.5	.6	1.0	1.3	-	-	-	4.6	13.3
Item 1070 N(Wtd)	14414	7000	7064	11532	1595	3357	4495	4388	2173	6835	6611	5999	3370	1687	2900	263
B14B: ...during the last 12 months?																
1. 0 occasions	89.7	90.6	89.0	88.8	96.0	90.3	89.9	88.3	91.5	91.1	88.6	100.0	100.0	86.2	61.4	48.7
2. 1-2	5.2	4.9	5.5	5.7	2.2	5.0	5.1	5.8	4.7	4.6	5.9	-	-	13.8	16.3	21.1
3. 3-5	2.2	2.0	2.4	2.4	.8	2.0	2.2	2.5	1.7	1.8	2.5	-	-	-	10.1	8.4
4. 6-9	1.3	1.2	1.4	1.4	.4	1.4	1.2	1.5	.9	1.3	1.3	-	-	-	5.7	7.7
5. 10-19	.8	.6	.9	.9	.4	.8	.9	.8	.6	.6	1.0	-	-	-	3.6	3.4
6. 20-39	.4	.3	.5	.4	.2	.3	.5	.4	.2	.3	.5	-	-	-	1.7	4.2
7. 40 or more	.4	.4	.3	.4	.1	.2	.3	.6	.3	.3	.4	-	-	-	1.3	5.7
Item 1080 N(Wtd)	14370	6987	7040	11499	1590	3351	4492	4362	2165	6826	6588	6002	3371	1665	2875	261
B14C: ...during the last 30 days?																
1. 0 occasions	96.0	96.3	95.8	95.7	98.4	96.4	95.9	95.3	97.0	96.7	95.6	100.0	100.0	96.7	84.0	77.9
2. 1-2	2.5	2.5	2.4	2.7	.9	2.3	2.5	2.9	1.8	2.1	2.7	-	-	3.3	9.5	9.9
3. 3-5	.8	.7	.9	.9	.3	.9	.9	.8	.6	.7	.8	-	-	-	3.8	3.1
4. 6-9	.4	.2	.5	.4	.2	.1	.4	.5	.3	.2	.5	-	-	-	1.3	5.3
5. 10-19	.2	.1	.3	.2	.2	.1	.2	.3	.1	.2	.2	-	-	-	.7	1.9
6. 20-39	.1	.1	.1	.1	.1	.1	.1	.1	.1	.1	.1	-	-	-	.2	1.5
7. 40 or more	.1	.1	.1	.1	-	.1	.1	.1	*	.1	*	-	-	-	.3	.4
Item 1090 N(Wtd)	14365	6987	7034	11493	1591	3349	4488	4362	2165	6821	6590	6002	3373	1661	2871	262

* = less than .05 per cent.

QUESTIONNAIRE FORM 1-5 1976	TOTAL	SEX		RACE		REGION				4YR COLLEGE PLANS		ILLICIT DRUG USE: LIFETIME				
		M	F	White	Black	NE	NC	S	W	Yes	No	None	Mari- juana Only	Few Pills	More Pills	Any Her- oin
Weighted No. of Cases:	15138	7241	7257	11796	1716	3570	4687	4597	2284	6994	6877	6091	3457	1736	2987	268
% of Weighted Total:	100.0	47.8	47.9	77.9	11.3	23.6	31.0	30.4	15.1	46.2	45.4	40.2	22.8	11.5	19.7	1.8

B15: On how many occasions (if any) have you used heroin (smack, horse, skag)...

B15A: ...in your lifetime?

	TOTAL	M	F	White	Black	NE	NC	S	W	Yes	No	None	Mari- juana Only	Few Pills	More Pills	Any Her- oin
1. 0 occasions	98.2	97.6	98.8	98.4	98.1	98.3	98.0	98.0	98.6	98.7	97.7	100.0	100.0	100.0	100.0	-
2. 1-2	1.2	1.6	.8	1.1	1.2	1.0	1.4	1.4	1.0	.8	1.5	-	-	-	-	67.4
3. 3-5	.2	.3	.2	.2	.1	.3	.3	.2	.2	.1	.4	-	-	-	-	12.7
4. 6-9	.1	.1	.1	.1	.2	.1	.1	.2	-	.1	.2	-	-	-	-	7.5
5. 10-19	.1	.2	*	.1	.1	*	.1	.2	*	*	.1	-	-	-	-	5.2
6. 20-39	*	.1	*	*	.1	.1	.1	-	-	*	*	-	-	-	-	1.9
7. 40 or more	.1	.2	*	.1	.1	.2	.1	.1	.1	.1	.1	-	-	-	-	5.6
Item 1100 N(Wtd)	14469	7027	7100	11580	1605	3367	4520	4408	2174	6851	6653	6021	3380	1697	2906	267

B15B: ...during the last 12 months?

	TOTAL	M	F	White	Black	NE	NC	S	W	Yes	No	None	Mari- juana Only	Few Pills	More Pills	Any Her- oin
1. 0 occasions	99.2	99.0	99.5	99.3	99.4	99.3	99.0	99.3	99.4	99.4	99.1	100.0	100.0	100.0	100.0	56.7
2. 1-2	.5	.7	.4	.5	.4	.4	.7	.5	.4	.3	.7	-	-	-	-	28.7
3. 3-5	.1	.1	.1	.1	-	.1	.2	*	*	.1	.1	-	-	-	-	5.0
4. 6-9	.1	.1	*	.1	.1	.1	*	.1	*	*	.1	-	-	-	-	3.8
5. 10-19	*	.1	*	*	.1	.1	*	-	*	*	*	-	-	-	-	1.9
6. 20-39	*	*	*	*	.1	.1	*	-	*	*	*	-	-	-	-	1.5
7. 40 or more	*	*	*	*	-	.1	*	*	*	.1	*	-	-	-	-	2.3
Item 1110 N(Wtd)	14467	7025	7101	11581	1603	3368	4518	4407	2174	6851	6650	6023	3382	1697	2906	261

B15C: ...during the last 30 days?

	TOTAL	M	F	White	Black	NE	NC	S	W	Yes	No	None	Mari- juana Only	Few Pills	More Pills	Any Her- oin
1. 0 occasions	99.8	99.7	99.9	99.9	99.6	99.7	99.8	99.8	99.9	99.8	99.8	100.0	100.0	100.0	100.0	88.6
2. 1-2	.1	.1	.1	.1	.2	.1	.2	.1	*	.1	.1	-	-	-	-	5.3
3. 3-5	*	.1	*	*	.1	.1	*	*	*	.1	-	-	-	-	-	2.3
4. 6-9	-	-	-	-	-	-	-	-	-	-	-	-	-	-	-	-
5. 10-19	*	*	*	*	.1	.1	*	-	-	*	-	-	-	-	-	1.5
6. 20-39	*	-	*	*	-	-	-	-	*	-	*	-	-	-	-	.4
7. 40 or more	*	*	*	*	-	.1	*	*	*	*	*	-	-	-	-	1.9
Item 1120 N(Wtd)	14469	7026	7101	11582	1604	3368	4519	4409	2173	6851	6653	6023	3381	1698	2906	263

B16: There are a number of narcotics other than heroin, such as methadone, opium, morphine, codeine, demerol, paregoric, talwin, and laudanum. These are sometimes prescribed by doctors. On how many occasions (if any) have you taken narcotics other than heroin on your own--that is, without a doctor telling you to take them...

B16A: ...in your lifetime?

	TOTAL	M	F	White	Black	NE	NC	S	W	Yes	No	None	Mari- juana Only	Few Pills	More Pills	Any Her- oin
1. 0 occasions	90.4	89.0	91.9	89.9	94.9	88.8	90.3	91.5	91.2	92.2	88.9	100.0	100.0	87.7	65.8	23.9
2. 1-2	4.6	5.2	3.9	4.7	3.2	5.7	4.2	4.1	4.5	4.0	4.9	-	-	12.3	13.5	24.7
3. 3-5	2.0	2.3	1.6	2.1	.7	2.2	2.2	1.6	1.9	1.8	2.1	-	-	-	8.8	13.1
4. 6-9	.9	1.0	.8	1.0	.5	1.1	.9	.8	.9	.7	1.1	-	-	-	3.9	8.8
5. 10-19	.9	1.1	.7	1.0	.1	.7	1.0	.9	.8	.5	1.3	-	-	-	3.5	11.2
6. 20-39	.4	.4	.5	.5	.2	.6	.4	.5	.2	.3	.6	-	-	-	1.8	5.2
7. 40 or more	.8	1.0	.5	.8	.2	.8	.9	.7	.7	.4	1.1	-	-	-	2.7	13.1
Item 1130 N(Wtd)	14324	6971	7051	11492	1604	3322	4480	4370	2152	6804	6590	5992	3360	1685	2843	251

B16B: ...during the last 12 months?

	TOTAL	M	F	White	Black	NE	NC	S	W	Yes	No	None	Mari- juana Only	Few Pills	More Pills	Any Her- oin
1. 0 occasions	94.3	93.2	95.3	93.8	97.8	93.5	93.8	95.0	95.0	95.4	93.2	100.0	100.0	95.8	78.2	47.0
2. 1-2	3.2	3.7	2.6	3.4	1.4	3.6	3.3	2.7	3.0	2.8	3.3	-	-	4.2	11.5	22.5
3. 3-5	1.1	1.3	.9	1.3	.2	1.4	1.3	.9	.8	.8	1.4	-	-	-	4.8	9.1
4. 6-9	.6	.6	.6	.7	.3	.6	.7	.6	.4	.4	.8	-	-	-	2.3	8.7
5. 10-19	.4	.5	.3	.4	.1	.3	.3	.3	.5	.2	.5	-	-	-	1.4	5.5
6. 20-39	.3	.4	.2	.3	.2	.4	.4	.1	.1	.2	.3	-	-	-	1.0	4.7
7. 40 or more	.2	.3	.1	.2	.1	.2	.2	.3	.2	.1	.4	-	-	-	.8	2.4
Item 1140 N(Wtd)	14323	6971	7051	11487	1605	3317	4482	4375	2150	6801	6597	6000	3367	1680	2831	253

* = less than .05 per cent.

QUESTIONNAIRE FORM 1-5 1976	TOTAL	SEX		RACE		REGION				4YR COLLEGE PLANS		ILLICIT DRUG USE: LIFETIME				
		M	F	White	Black	NE	NC	S	W	Yes	No	None	Mari- juana Only	Few Pills	More Pills	Any Her- oin
Weighted No. of Cases:	15138	7241	7257	11796	1716	3570	4687	4597	2284	6994	6877	6091	3457	1736	2987	268
% of Weighted Total:	100.0	47.8	47.9	77.9	11.3	23.6	31.0	30.4	15.1	46.2	45.4	40.2	22.8	11.5	19.7	1.8
B16C: ...during the last 30 days?																
1. 0 occasions	98.0	97.6	98.4	97.8	99.3	97.9	97.5	98.4	98.2	98.5	97.4	100.0	100.0	99.0	92.4	74.8
2. 1-2	1.2	1.5	.9	1.3	.4	1.3	1.4	1.0	1.2	1.0	1.4	-	-	1.0	4.2	14.8
3. 3-5	.4	.5	.4	.4	.1	.4	.5	.4	.4	.3	.5	-	-	-	1.8	4.4
4. 6-9	.2	.2	.2	.2	.1	.1	.3	.2	.1	.1	.3	-	-	-	.7	3.6
5. 10-19	.1	.1	.1	.1	-	.1	.2	*	.1	*	.2	-	-	-	.4	1.2
6. 20-39	*	*	*	*	.1	.1	*	-	*	*	.1	-	-	-	.2	.4
7. 40 or more	.1	.1	*	.1	-	.1	.1	.1	*	*	.1	-	-	-	.3	.8
Item 1150 N(Wtd)	14324	6969	7051	11488	1604	3317	4483	4374	2149	6802	6599	6001	3369	1680	2831	250
B17: On how many occasions (if any) have you sniffed glue, or breathed the contents of aerosol spray cans, or inhaled any other gases or sprays in order to get high...																
B17A: ...in your lifetime?																
1. 0 occasions	89.7	87.4	92.1	89.4	93.2	89.1	91.1	88.7	89.9	92.0	87.6	98.0	93.1	85.9	74.2	55.7
2. 1-2	6.4	7.6	5.0	6.5	4.4	7.1	5.5	6.5	6.7	5.1	7.5	1.6	5.3	10.1	13.8	22.4
3. 3-5	1.7	2.1	1.5	1.8	.8	1.4	1.4	2.4	1.6	1.4	2.0	.3	.6	1.7	5.6	8.2
4. 6-9	.8	1.0	.6	.8	.5	.7	.6	1.0	.6	.6	1.0	.1	.3	.9	2.3	2.3
5. 10-19	.7	.9	.5	.7	.2	.7	.7	.5	.7	.5	.8	*	.4	.9	2.0	3.2
6. 20-39	.3	.4	.2	.3	.3	.5	.2	.3	.1	.2	.4	-	*	.2	.9	4.1
7. 40 or more	.4	.7	.2	.4	.5	.4	.4	.6	.3	.3	.6	-	.2	.4	1.3	4.1
Item 1160 N(Wtd)	11669	5704	5728	9353	1315	2716	3633	3565	1756	5535	5422	4810	2743	1393	2341	219
B17B: ...during the last 12 months?																
1. 0 occasions	97.0	96.2	98.0	97.0	97.9	96.8	97.4	96.2	98.3	97.8	96.4	99.6	98.4	95.9	92.1	83.6
2. 1-2	1.8	2.3	1.3	1.9	1.0	1.9	1.6	2.5	1.0	1.4	2.2	.3	1.1	3.1	4.3	9.6
3. 3-5	.6	.8	.4	.6	.4	.6	.6	.6	.4	.4	.7	*	.3	.7	1.8	2.3
4. 6-9	.2	.3	.1	.2	.1	.3	.1	.3	.1	.1	.3	-	*	.1	.9	1.8
5. 10-19	.2	.2	.1	.1	.3	.1	.1	.3	.2	.1	.2	-	.2	.1	.4	.9
6. 20-39	.1	.1	*	.1	.1	.1	.1	*	-	.1	.1	-	-	-	.1	1.8
7. 40 or more	.1	.2	*	.1	.2	.2	.1	.1	.1	.1	.2	-	*	.1	.4	.5
Item 1170 N(Wtd)	11651	5692	5721	9337	1313	2715	3628	3558	1750	5530	5411	4807	2736	1392	2333	219
B17C: ...during the last 30 days?																
1. 0 occasions	99.1	98.7	99.5	99.2	98.9	98.8	99.2	99.1	99.4	99.3	98.9	99.9	99.5	98.8	97.8	94.5
2. 1-2	.6	.9	.4	.6	.7	.8	.5	.6	.5	.5	.8	.1	.5	1.1	1.4	3.2
3. 3-5	.1	.2	.1	.1	.2	.2	.1	.1	.1	.1	.1	-	.1	.1	.4	1.4
4. 6-9	*	*	*	*	.1	-	-	.1	.1	*	*	-	-	-	.1	.5
5. 10-19	.1	.1	-	.1	-	*	.1	*	.1	.1	.1	*	-	-	.1	.9
6. 20-39	*	*	*	*	-	*	-	-	-	-	*	-	-	-	-	-
7. 40 or more	*	.1	-	*	-	.1	.1	-	-	.1	*	-	-	-	.1	-
Item 1180 N(Wtd)	11644	5687	5719	9333	1312	2711	3627	3556	1749	5528	5408	4808	2735	1392	2328	217

*=less than .05 per cent.

QUESTIONNAIRE FORM 1 1976	TOTAL	SEX		RACE		REGION				4YR COLLEGE PLANS		ILLICIT DRUG USE: LIFETIME				
		M	F	White	Black	NE	NC	S	W	Yes	No	None	Mari-juana Only	Few Pills	More Pills	Any Her-oin
Weighted No. of Cases: % of Weighted Total:	3039 100.0	1426 46.9	1466 48.2	2356 77.5	338 11.1	715 23.5	950 31.3	919 30.2	454 15.0	1384 45.5	1321 43.5	1219 40.1	669 22.0	329 10.8	605 19.9	47 1.6
A001: Taking all things together, how would you say things are these days-would you say you're very happy, pretty happy, or not too happy these days?																
3. Very happy	17.6	14.8	20.9	18.5	13.7	14.9	17.8	17.6	21.5	19.9	16.2	20.4	16.4	11.5	16.1	18.2
2. Pretty happy	68.7	71.5	66.2	70.4	61.2	69.2	68.9	69.1	67.0	67.3	70.8	67.3	69.7	74.5	68.4	72.6
1. Not too happy	13.7	13.7	12.9	11.1	25.0	15.9	13.4	13.3	11.6	12.8	13.0	12.3	13.9	14.1	15.4	9.2
Item 1190 N(Wtd)	3023	1417	1462	2344	337	709	945	918	451	1379	1313	1216	665	328	603	47
A002: How much do you agree or disagree with each of the following statements?																
A002A: The nation needs much more long-range planning and coordination to be prepared for the future																
1. Disagree	2.1	2.4	1.7	1.7	3.8	2.7	1.6	2.5	1.3	1.4	2.3	2.2	1.7	2.6	1.6	1.9
2. Mostly disagree	3.0	3.0	2.9	3.0	3.6	3.2	3.4	2.6	2.8	2.7	3.2	3.1	2.8	2.7	3.1	6.5
3. Neither	8.5	9.5	7.2	8.6	7.1	7.0	10.2	6.6	11.1	7.3	9.9	8.5	7.8	8.9	9.4	4.3
4. Mostly agree	42.7	40.2	45.8	45.9	27.7	41.9	45.4	40.0	44.0	43.3	44.0	45.8	41.3	45.1	40.8	34.1
5. Agree	43.7	45.0	42.4	40.8	57.7	45.1	39.5	48.4	40.7	45.4	40.6	40.4	46.5	40.7	45.1	53.2
Item 1200 N(Wtd)	2996	1414	1440	2328	331	699	941	908	448	1373	1301	1201	661	328	596	47
A002B: I enjoy the fast pace and changes of today's world																
1. Disagree	18.6	18.6	18.0	17.0	22.9	17.1	17.1	20.9	19.2	14.5	20.5	18.0	16.2	19.8	19.0	26.0
2. Mostly disagree	19.2	18.9	19.7	20.5	15.1	16.4	21.8	17.6	21.2	20.4	18.6	20.8	19.3	18.6	16.9	10.4
3. Neither	18.7	20.3	16.9	19.7	13.5	18.2	21.7	15.1	20.6	20.3	16.8	21.0	19.6	16.4	16.0	12.5
4. Mostly agree	29.3	26.7	32.3	30.2	24.9	32.7	27.5	28.8	28.6	32.2	28.4	28.9	29.8	30.0	30.5	27.2
5. Agree	14.3	15.4	13.1	12.7	23.6	15.6	11.9	17.6	10.4	12.5	15.7	11.3	15.2	15.3	17.5	23.9
Item 1210 N(Wtd)	2999	1412	1445	2331	330	701	941	908	449	1372	1303	1205	658	329	598	47
A002C: Things change too quickly in today's world																
1. Disagree	11.9	11.9	12.1	10.9	17.9	12.8	11.4	12.7	10.2	11.2	13.0	10.9	13.0	9.9	14.5	16.3
2. Mostly disagree	19.5	19.4	19.6	21.4	11.8	20.1	19.6	19.2	19.3	22.5	17.5	18.2	21.1	22.0	20.9	20.3
3. Neither	15.8	17.8	14.4	17.2	9.8	17.2	17.9	11.7	17.6	17.6	13.5	15.2	17.6	15.4	16.5	15.8
4. Mostly agree	25.4	24.7	25.9	26.2	20.8	23.3	27.1	24.4	27.1	26.1	25.4	29.1	23.8	22.9	23.0	14.2
5. Agree	27.3	26.1	28.1	24.3	39.7	26.6	24.0	32.0	25.8	22.7	30.7	26.6	24.4	29.9	25.0	33.4
Item 1220 N(Wtd)	3008	1413	1452	2335	334	706	942	910	450	1374	1310	1206	665	328	597	47
A002D: I think the times ahead for me will be tougher and less fun than things are now																
1. Disagree	19.0	17.7	20.0	18.3	23.4	19.7	17.4	20.0	19.7	17.3	19.7	17.9	20.8	17.6	19.2	31.5
2. Mostly disagree	18.1	16.2	20.8	20.2	10.9	19.4	19.4	15.8	18.1	19.9	17.3	19.3	17.9	16.3	13.1	11.3
3. Neither	13.3	14.4	11.9	14.4	6.5	14.6	15.0	10.8	12.9	14.9	12.2	13.0	13.1	16.3	13.1	12.5
4. Mostly agree	23.4	23.6	23.6	24.7	19.1	23.1	25.6	21.9	22.4	23.1	23.7	24.7	21.1	21.5	25.0	19.6
5. Agree	26.1	28.1	23.7	22.4	40.1	23.2	22.7	31.5	26.9	24.8	27.0	25.2	27.2	27.0	25.0	25.1
Item 1230 N(Wtd)	3003	1411	1447	2331	331	702	943	909	449	1371	1305	1210	661	327	596	47
A003: Of all the time you spend with other people, about how much is spent with people over 30?																
1. Very little	21.4	23.2	19.4	19.0	32.9	24.4	20.5	20.5	20.5	17.7	23.1	17.0	24.3	21.1	24.8	25.9
2. Some	40.7	44.5	37.3	43.2	32.0	42.8	42.4	36.4	42.6	45.0	36.7	39.2	41.6	42.5	42.7	46.1
3. About half	31.3	26.5	36.5	32.0	27.2	27.1	30.1	36.2	30.3	32.2	32.4	35.3	28.3	30.8	28.7	23.7
4. Most	5.2	4.8	5.6	5.0	4.8	4.6	6.1	5.0	4.6	4.7	6.2	6.8	4.5	4.7	3.0	2.2
5. Nearly all	1.4	1.0	1.3	.9	3.0	1.1	.9	1.8	2.0	.5	1.7	1.7	1.2	1.0	.8	2.1
Item 1240 N(Wtd)	3034	1424	1465	2355	337	712	950	918	453	1383	1317	1219	668	329	605	47

QUESTIONNAIRE FORM 1 1976	TOTAL	SEX		RACE		REGION				4YR COLLEGE PLANS		ILLICIT DRUG USE: LIFETIME				
		M	F	White	Black	NE	NC	S	W	Yes	No	None	Mari-juana Only	Few Pills	More Pills	Any Her-oin
Weighted No. of Cases:	3039	1426	1466	2356	338	715	950	919	454	1384	1321	1219	669	329	605	47
% of Weighted Total:	100.0	46.9	48.2	77.5	11.1	23.5	31.3	30.2	15.0	45.5	43.5	40.1	22.0	10.8	19.9	1.6

A004: Would you like to spend more time, or less time, with people over 30 if you could?

1. Much less time	3.0	3.0	2.7	2.2	6.7	4.6	1.6	3.4	2.7	2.6	2.8	2.1	4.2	3.4	2.3	10.8
2. Somewhat less time	8.2	9.3	7.1	7.7	8.1	8.3	9.6	8.1	5.5	6.7	9.9	7.2	7.1	9.9	10.4	10.4
3. About the same as now	70.0	71.3	69.2	72.6	63.5	70.0	72.1	67.8	70.3	72.0	69.3	70.8	69.4	69.4	70.9	64.0
4. Somewhat more time	15.9	14.7	17.3	15.7	14.8	14.2	15.1	16.8	18.4	16.3	15.4	16.9	16.2	15.7	14.1	11.7
5. Much more time	2.8	1.7	3.7	1.9	6.9	2.9	1.6	3.9	3.1	2.4	2.6	2.9	3.1	1.7	2.2	3.1
Item 1250 N(Wtd)	3028	1419	1464	2350	337	712	948	917	451	1381	1316	1217	668	329	601	47

A005: Would you like to spend more time, or less time, working with or helping younger children?

1. Much less time	4.7	7.4	1.7	4.6	3.3	4.0	5.2	4.2	5.5	3.5	5.3	3.8	4.4	4.4	5.5	8.1
2. Somewhat less time	5.7	8.5	3.2	6.0	3.3	6.2	5.9	4.5	6.9	5.1	5.5	4.1	6.1	5.9	7.6	7.7
3. About the same as now	33.3	44.8	22.3	36.1	16.0	33.5	36.2	29.4	34.9	33.1	33.8	30.8	37.2	35.1	35.4	35.4
4. Somewhat more time	31.9	27.4	36.8	32.3	32.2	31.8	32.9	31.8	29.9	33.5	31.3	34.1	28.2	36.7	32.4	26.9
5. Much more time	24.4	12.0	36.0	21.0	45.1	24.5	19.8	30.0	22.7	24.7	24.1	27.2	24.2	17.8	19.1	21.9
Item 1260 N(Wtd)	3026	1416	1464	2348	337	709	946	918	452	1380	1313	1214	667	328	603	47

A006: The next questions ask how satisfied or dissatisfied you are with several aspects of your life. For each question, mark the circle that shows best how you feel. If you are neutral about something, or are just as satisfied as you are dissatisfied, mark the middle answer.

How satisfied are you with...

A006A: Your job? (If you have no job, leave blank)

7. Completely satisfied	20.7	19.1	22.5	19.8	25.6	18.2	17.7	24.0	25.1	19.6	21.6	23.0	18.2	17.1	17.7	35.3
6.	18.5	19.5	18.3	20.1	11.0	18.2	19.9	16.9	19.0	21.1	17.2	19.1	15.0	23.2	21.3	13.2
5.	14.8	15.9	13.7	16.2	6.6	11.5	18.2	12.4	16.2	16.7	13.7	17.0	14.8	13.4	13.4	10.1
4. Neutral	25.4	24.1	25.4	22.7	38.5	28.0	23.8	27.5	21.1	22.0	27.6	23.4	29.8	22.3	24.2	29.0
3.	9.0	9.7	8.6	9.5	6.6	10.9	7.9	8.3	9.9	10.2	7.7	6.9	8.5	15.1	11.0	2.0
2.	5.2	5.0	5.5	5.6	3.8	5.9	5.6	4.1	5.1	5.7	5.0	4.9	6.0	3.7	5.8	4.9
1. Completely dissatisfied	6.4	6.7	5.9	6.2	8.0	7.3	6.8	6.8	3.6	4.7	7.2	5.7	7.8	5.3	6.6	5.5
Item 1270 N(Wtd)	1856	962	814	1509	145	416	632	520	288	829	827	692	434	214	390	29

A006B: The neighborhood where you live?

7. Completely satisfied	34.0	33.0	35.4	34.1	38.6	28.9	33.3	38.2	34.8	30.8	38.7	37.7	31.9	28.2	30.2	32.4
6.	18.4	20.9	16.1	21.2	5.3	18.5	22.5	13.5	19.3	20.8	15.9	18.0	20.3	23.3	16.3	10.0
5.	10.3	11.3	9.2	11.3	4.6	9.8	9.9	10.1	12.2	13.7	7.0	9.6	9.0	11.9	12.7	6.1
4. Neutral	21.0	19.6	22.0	18.7	28.7	21.9	20.5	21.6	19.3	17.5	23.8	19.5	22.2	20.3	21.9	28.3
3.	6.2	7.0	5.5	6.5	3.9	6.9	6.7	5.2	5.8	7.4	5.0	6.4	7.0	6.8	5.9	6.3
2.	3.8	3.1	4.5	3.6	3.6	5.0	3.6	2.6	4.6	4.3	3.3	3.0	3.7	2.8	5.4	8.1
1. Completely dissatisfied	6.4	5.0	7.4	4.5	15.3	9.1	3.4	8.8	3.8	5.5	6.4	5.8	5.8	6.7	7.5	8.8
Item 1280 N(Wtd)	3024	1420	1461	2350	336	710	948	912	454	1380	1315	1216	667	326	605	47

A006C: Your personal safety in your neighborhood, on your job, and in your school--safety from being attacked and injured in some way?

7. Completely satisfied	36.3	40.0	33.1	37.8	30.3	36.9	37.2	35.0	36.1	37.0	37.0	36.3	38.7	35.3	34.1	34.4
6.	20.4	23.1	18.2	22.6	11.0	17.7	24.0	17.8	22.5	23.1	18.4	21.6	22.0	20.7	19.2	15.8
5.	10.4	9.4	11.3	11.1	6.3	9.1	10.7	9.7	13.2	11.9	9.6	12.2	7.3	11.5	9.4	11.8
4. Neutral	21.3	18.4	23.1	18.5	35.0	23.6	17.8	24.9	17.4	15.9	23.9	19.0	20.7	21.7	25.5	11.2
3.	4.7	3.4	6.1	4.6	4.4	5.8	4.0	4.9	4.1	5.3	4.6	5.1	4.4	4.9	4.7	.9
2.	2.3	2.0	2.6	2.1	2.5	1.8	2.3	2.3	3.0	2.7	1.9	2.2	2.3	2.5	2.0	4.2
1. Completely dissatisfied	4.6	3.7	5.5	3.3	10.4	5.1	4.0	5.3	3.8	4.1	4.5	3.4	4.5	3.4	5.1	21.8
Item 1290 N(Wtd)	3024	1419	1461	2354	334	707	945	918	454	1381	1314	1217	665	329	602	47

QUESTIONNAIRE FORM 1 1976	TOTAL	SEX		RACE		REGION				4YR COLLEGE PLANS		ILLICIT DRUG USE: LIFETIME				
		M	F	White	Black	NE	NC	S	W	Yes	No	None	Marijuana Only	Few Pills	More Pills	Any Heroin
Weighted No. of Cases:	3039	1426	1466	2356	338	715	950	919	454	1384	1321	1219	669	329	605	47
% of Weighted Total:	100.0	46.9	48.2	77.5	11.1	23.5	31.3	30.2	15.0	45.5	43.5	40.1	22.0	10.8	19.9	1.6

A006D: The safety of things you own from being stolen or destroyed in your neighborhood, on your job, and in your school?

7. Completely satisfied	17.2	17.0	18.0	16.9	20.5	18.9	13.7	20.2	15.7	14.5	20.1	17.2	15.4	17.5	17.1	17.1
6.	18.6	19.4	18.4	20.0	12.3	16.8	23.3	15.1	18.7	21.4	17.0	20.5	18.5	19.2	16.8	8.1
5.	14.1	14.9	13.4	15.8	6.6	11.3	19.0	10.8	14.8	14.9	14.0	14.6	14.5	16.0	12.5	16.5
4. Neutral	20.3	18.0	21.6	18.1	28.6	23.9	18.3	20.7	17.6	17.9	21.7	19.2	22.0	17.1	21.5	21.9
3.	10.8	12.3	9.9	12.3	3.7	10.4	12.0	9.5	11.7	12.9	9.3	10.5	11.4	12.4	11.2	14.6
2.	6.7	6.9	6.5	6.9	5.3	6.6	5.6	6.3	10.2	8.6	4.2	6.5	7.6	6.6	7.4	.8
1. Completely dissatisfied	12.3	11.6	12.2	10.0	23.0	12.0	8.2	17.4	11.3	9.7	13.8	11.5	10.7	11.3	13.5	21.0
Item 1300 N(Wtd)	3011	1411	1457	2344	333	702	941	916	451	1375	1311	1212	661	327	602	47

A006E: Your educational experiences?

7. Completely satisfied	19.4	18.0	20.8	17.6	30.6	19.9	14.8	26.0	14.5	17.8	21.3	21.9	19.1	18.7	12.1	24.5
6.	23.0	23.2	23.8	25.4	14.4	23.1	26.0	19.1	24.8	29.5	18.0	26.8	22.5	21.0	19.8	13.2
5.	16.6	18.1	15.0	18.5	9.1	16.2	18.6	13.3	19.3	17.7	16.4	17.9	17.8	16.0	14.9	15.6
4. Neutral	23.9	22.6	24.6	22.7	25.9	23.8	23.1	24.6	24.1	18.3	28.4	20.7	23.5	26.1	28.6	23.1
3.	7.3	8.2	6.3	7.5	7.6	5.4	9.1	7.3	7.0	7.2	7.3	6.3	7.8	6.5	9.8	8.1
2.	4.3	4.2	4.4	4.2	3.1	5.1	3.9	4.0	4.4	4.7	3.9	2.8	4.2	4.6	7.6	5.3
1. Completely dissatisfied	5.5	5.7	5.0	4.2	9.3	6.4	4.5	5.6	5.8	4.8	4.7	3.7	5.2	7.2	7.3	10.1
Item 1310 N(Wtd)	3016	1416	1458	2349	331	707	941	914	454	1379	1310	1213	662	327	602	47

A006F: Your friends and other people you spend time with?

7. Completely satisfied	45.2	40.4	50.6	43.9	53.1	42.6	39.4	53.8	43.9	42.8	48.6	45.7	42.9	44.2	43.4	56.5
6.	27.2	28.7	26.1	29.9	15.3	27.0	30.7	21.0	32.7	30.2	25.4	27.8	27.9	30.6	26.6	11.4
5.	10.9	14.1	7.7	11.7	6.8	9.4	13.0	10.2	10.2	12.0	9.7	11.3	12.0	11.9	9.5	5.2
4. Neutral	10.8	10.7	10.5	9.1	20.1	13.3	9.6	11.1	8.7	8.5	12.0	10.2	10.9	8.0	12.9	7.6
3.	3.2	3.6	2.5	3.2	1.8	4.8	3.5	1.9	2.6	3.7	2.3	2.7	3.1	3.5	4.0	10.0
2.	1.5	1.5	1.5	1.5	1.3	1.5	2.6	.7	.6	1.9	1.2	1.3	1.4	.7	2.4	3.3
1. Completely dissatisfied	1.2	1.0	1.1	.8	1.6	1.3	1.1	1.2	1.2	.9	.9	.9	1.7	1.0	1.2	6.1
Item 1320 N(Wtd)	3020	1417	1459	2344	335	709	946	913	453	1379	1310	1213	660	329	604	47

A006G: The way you get along with your parents?

7. Completely satisfied	33.7	30.2	36.9	31.7	47.6	33.7	29.8	37.6	33.9	32.4	33.0	37.3	30.5	31.8	26.3	31.6
6.	22.1	24.6	20.1	23.9	12.5	22.6	25.2	17.1	24.8	27.1	18.8	25.3	22.1	21.8	19.5	13.5
5.	12.3	14.9	9.8	13.6	7.9	11.3	14.3	10.4	13.4	13.3	12.5	11.3	11.3	14.3	16.0	8.5
4. Neutral	17.1	16.7	17.2	16.3	19.7	17.9	15.7	19.3	14.2	14.1	19.7	15.1	19.2	19.1	17.3	20.5
3.	5.8	6.5	5.3	5.9	4.7	5.2	5.6	6.2	6.6	5.8	6.3	4.1	7.7	6.3	7.4	9.3
2.	3.3	2.9	3.5	3.3	2.1	4.7	3.5	2.4	2.5	3.2	3.0	1.9	3.5	3.0	6.1	7.5
1. Completely dissatisfied	5.7	4.3	7.1	5.3	5.4	4.6	5.9	6.9	4.5	4.1	6.7	5.1	5.8	3.7	7.4	9.2
Item 1330 N(Wtd)	3024	1420	1462	2352	334	710	945	917	453	1379	1318	1215	666	328	602	47

A006H: Yourself?

7. Completely satisfied	27.0	27.8	25.5	22.1	53.5	27.9	22.2	31.3	27.0	24.5	27.9	27.3	28.0	24.7	21.8	30.1
6.	25.5	26.8	25.1	27.9	16.7	24.8	27.3	21.6	30.9	29.5	22.6	26.8	26.6	24.1	26.0	17.5
5.	15.2	15.5	15.4	17.4	5.6	14.5	17.1	13.8	15.3	17.1	13.9	17.0	14.4	14.7	14.4	15.8
4. Neutral	21.7	20.4	22.4	21.7	15.5	21.1	21.3	24.2	18.5	16.7	26.4	19.1	21.3	23.6	25.6	21.4
3.	5.3	5.0	5.7	6.0	2.4	5.3	6.2	4.2	5.8	6.5	4.5	5.3	3.7	7.5	6.2	5.3
2.	2.3	1.7	2.9	2.4	2.1	3.3	2.7	1.6	1.5	2.6	2.3	2.1	2.4	2.1	3.3	3.3
1. Completely dissatisfied	2.9	2.8	3.0	2.5	4.0	3.1	3.1	3.3	1.1	3.0	2.4	2.4	3.5	3.3	2.8	6.6
Item 1340 N(Wtd)	3025	1422	1460	2353	333	708	948	916	453	1381	1316	1214	665	329	602	47

A006I: Your standard of living--the things you have like housing, car, furniture, recreation, and the like?

7. Completely satisfied	34.8	32.1	37.5	34.0	37.3	33.4	32.3	37.0	38.0	35.8	35.1	35.7	37.3	34.2	27.9	36.1
6.	26.5	27.6	25.8	29.0	17.0	24.6	29.5	25.1	25.8	30.1	22.9	27.9	25.6	29.3	25.9	11.4
5.	13.1	15.3	10.8	14.2	8.3	14.2	14.3	9.2	16.6	13.0	13.9	12.5	12.2	13.2	16.2	21.9
4. Neutral	15.3	15.0	15.5	13.2	25.1	17.9	13.0	18.1	10.5	11.4	18.0	14.6	15.1	13.7	16.4	15.9
3.	4.6	4.7	4.4	4.7	2.4	5.5	4.6	3.9	4.6	4.3	4.6	4.2	4.0	4.9	5.3	6.3
2.	2.1	2.4	2.0	2.4	.7	1.6	3.3	1.3	2.3	2.6	1.6	2.0	1.6	2.7	3.0	4.1
1. Completely dissatisfied	3.6	3.0	3.9	2.5	9.3	2.8	3.0	5.4	2.3	2.9	3.7	3.1	4.1	2.0	5.2	4.4
Item 1350 N(Wtd)	3027	1422	1463	2354	336	709	948	916	453	1382	1317	1214	666	329	605	47

QUESTIONNAIRE FORM 1 1976	TOTAL	SEX		RACE		REGION				4YR COLLEGE PLANS		ILLICIT DRUG USE: LIFETIME				
		M	F	White	Black	NE	NC	S	W	Yes	No	None	Marijuana Only	Few Pills	More Pills	Any Heroin
Weighted No. of Cases:	3039	1426	1466	2356	338	715	950	919	454	1384	1321	1219	669	329	605	47
% of Weighted Total:	100.0	46.9	48.2	77.5	11.1	23.5	31.3	30.2	15.0	45.5	43.5	40.1	22.0	10.8	19.9	1.6

A006J: The amount of time you have for doing things you want to do?

7. Completely satisfied	17.4	17.8	17.0	16.0	27.9	19.3	14.3	19.0	17.8	16.4	17.3	19.2	14.7	17.3	16.4	12.7
6.	16.1	17.1	15.9	17.4	12.4	15.9	18.6	12.4	18.8	17.0	15.9	15.6	16.6	19.3	16.5	11.1
5.	15.7	17.5	14.2	17.4	7.8	13.9	20.2	11.4	17.9	18.3	14.3	16.8	17.5	14.5	13.5	16.3
4. Neutral	16.3	14.3	17.5	14.0	26.7	18.1	13.2	19.2	13.9	13.4	18.3	15.7	17.1	15.1	13.4	15.3
3.	12.9	13.0	13.3	14.2	6.2	11.8	14.4	12.0	13.6	15.2	11.5	14.0	13.1	9.4	14.6	13.7
2.	7.4	6.7	8.0	8.2	3.1	6.4	9.1	6.2	7.7	8.6	6.3	7.4	6.6	9.3	7.8	7.6
1. Completely dissatisfied	14.1	13.6	14.2	12.8	15.9	14.5	10.1	19.8	10.2	11.2	16.4	11.3	14.3	15.2	17.7	23.3
Item 1360 N(Wtd)	3024	1420	1463	2350	336	708	945	918	453	1378	1319	1211	668	329	603	47

A006K: The way you spend your leisure time--recreation, relaxation, and so on?

7. Completely satisfied	29.9	29.6	30.1	27.8	42.3	28.4	24.7	36.2	30.3	27.8	31.8	30.5	27.7	29.0	28.0	42.8
6.	21.0	24.5	18.2	23.0	11.6	22.3	23.4	15.0	26.1	24.0	18.4	20.4	23.8	21.4	21.3	8.7
5.	15.4	16.9	14.5	17.3	6.6	15.1	20.1	11.2	14.7	17.8	13.9	16.4	16.3	16.8	13.6	11.6
4. Neutral	15.5	13.5	16.7	14.1	19.3	16.0	14.4	17.6	12.4	12.1	18.3	14.8	13.4	18.7	16.0	19.0
3.	8.4	7.6	9.4	9.2	4.9	8.0	9.8	7.2	8.7	9.6	7.6	8.4	8.7	7.0	10.0	6.7
2.	4.0	3.2	4.6	3.9	3.9	5.0	4.1	3.6	3.2	4.6	3.8	4.2	4.3	2.1	4.9	5.6
1. Completely dissatisfied	5.8	4.7	6.5	4.7	11.5	5.1	3.6	9.2	4.6	4.1	6.2	5.2	5.8	5.1	6.2	5.5
Item 1370 N(Wtd)	3021	1420	1461	2348	335	709	946	914	453	1381	1313	1211	665	329	605	47

A006L: Your life as a whole these days?

7. Completely satisfied	18.6	17.0	20.2	17.2	28.1	19.9	14.1	22.9	17.3	17.3	20.0	18.7	19.2	17.8	14.3	21.6
6.	27.9	29.1	27.5	31.2	14.5	25.3	30.9	24.3	32.9	33.4	23.8	30.8	30.2	25.7	24.3	12.4
5.	17.6	20.0	15.5	18.6	13.0	15.7	19.7	15.4	20.4	18.3	16.7	16.7	16.4	20.9	20.4	18.2
4. Neutral	24.0	22.5	24.7	21.9	30.0	24.8	23.6	25.8	20.3	18.7	28.1	23.4	21.2	20.7	28.0	36.1
3.	5.7	5.5	5.7	5.8	6.1	7.2	5.4	5.4	4.8	6.0	5.3	5.3	5.3	8.2	6.1	2.4
2.	2.9	3.1	2.7	3.0	1.5	3.0	3.6	2.4	2.6	3.4	2.6	2.4	3.0	4.4	3.4	3.6
1. Completely dissatisfied	3.2	2.7	3.6	2.4	6.8	4.1	2.7	3.9	1.5	2.9	3.4	2.8	4.7	2.1	3.4	5.9
Item 1380 N(Wtd)	3018	1420	1460	2349	334	708	947	912	451	1379	1317	1210	665	329	601	47

A006M: The way our national government is operating?

7. Completely satisfied	1.4	1.6	.5	.8	3.3	.9	.9	2.0	1.8	1.4	1.3	1.1	2.0	.8	1.2	1.8
6.	3.1	3.3	2.8	3.1	3.9	2.6	3.4	3.3	2.6	3.4	2.8	3.5	3.3	3.1	2.2	2.6
5.	8.6	10.2	7.3	10.0	1.9	6.2	10.7	7.5	10.3	10.5	7.3	9.1	10.0	9.6	6.3	3.8
4. Neutral	33.6	28.2	38.8	32.8	37.0	34.5	34.4	33.7	30.5	32.2	35.3	36.4	34.4	32.2	28.8	17.3
3.	16.6	19.4	14.3	18.5	9.7	15.8	18.7	13.8	19.2	20.1	14.3	17.3	16.7	15.1	19.0	7.1
2.	14.3	13.4	15.3	15.0	9.7	15.4	14.2	12.5	16.3	16.0	12.2	13.7	14.8	15.4	14.5	17.8
1. Completely dissatisfied	22.5	23.9	20.9	19.7	34.6	24.6	17.8	27.2	19.3	16.4	26.7	18.9	18.7	23.6	27.9	49.5
Item 1390 N(Wtd)	3022	1422	1459	2350	334	708	948	914	452	1380	1317	1210	667	328	604	47

A006N: The amount of fun you are having?

7. Completely satisfied	25.7	21.8	29.6	25.1	31.8	24.3	20.9	30.7	28.0	22.3	29.4	26.1	24.2	24.9	23.2	34.4
6.	24.5	26.2	23.4	26.4	15.4	25.0	26.5	20.5	27.7	28.0	21.7	26.8	23.8	27.1	21.8	13.5
5.	17.5	20.1	15.1	19.2	9.0	17.5	21.9	12.9	17.4	19.0	16.5	16.4	18.9	18.5	19.5	15.8
4. Neutral	19.3	18.5	19.3	17.2	25.8	19.4	17.5	22.7	15.9	16.0	21.6	17.9	20.7	15.5	21.0	24.5
3.	6.1	6.7	5.6	6.4	5.2	6.8	6.9	4.8	5.9	7.2	4.6	6.3	4.7	7.1	7.3	5.3
2.	3.4	3.5	3.1	3.2	4.2	4.6	2.7	3.4	3.0	4.0	3.0	2.7	4.4	4.7	3.3	1.0
1. Completely dissatisfied	3.6	3.2	3.8	2.4	8.4	2.5	3.7	5.0	2.0	3.5	3.2	3.7	3.3	2.3	4.0	5.5
Item 1400 N(Wtd)	3026	1423	1463	2355	335	708	949	916	454	1381	1319	1215	667	329	604	47

A007: How important is each of the following to you in your life?

A007A: Being successful in my line of work

1. Not important	1.8	2.2	1.3	1.7	2.2	1.3	2.0	2.0	1.6	1.1	2.3	1.1	1.3	1.5	2.6	8.0
2. Somewhat important	10.6	11.7	9.7	11.3	7.6	11.5	12.2	9.5	8.2	7.0	14.6	9.7	11.0	12.1	10.7	9.3
3. Quite important	35.1	32.8	37.3	37.3	23.3	34.0	36.3	32.3	40.3	34.0	37.2	36.9	32.9	35.6	34.6	33.9
4. Extremely important	52.5	53.2	51.7	49.7	66.9	53.2	49.6	56.2	49.9	57.9	45.8	52.3	54.9	50.8	52.1	48.8
Item 1410 N(Wtd)	3001	1409	1450	2332	332	703	936	910	453	1373	1303	1210	663	324	593	46

QUESTIONNAIRE FORM 1 1976	TOTAL	SEX		RACE		REGION				4YR COLLEGE PLANS		ILLICIT DRUG USE: LIFETIME				
		M	F	White	Black	NE	NC	S	W	Yes	No	None	Marijuana Only	Few Pills	More Pills	Any Heroin
Weighted No. of Cases:	3039	1426	1466	2356	338	715	950	919	454	1384	1321	1219	669	329	605	47
% of Weighted Total:	100.0	46.9	48.2	77.5	11.1	23.5	31.3	30.2	15.0	45.5	43.5	40.1	22.0	10.8	19.9	1.6

A007B: Having a good marriage and family life

	TOTAL	M	F	White	Black	NE	NC	S	W	Yes	No	None	Marijuana Only	Few Pills	More Pills	Any Heroin
1. Not important	5.1	6.6	3.5	4.9	5.1	5.6	4.6	5.1	5.6	4.0	5.9	3.6	4.4	4.6	8.6	5.4
2. Somewhat important	7.4	9.0	5.7	7.6	5.7	8.0	8.2	6.7	6.4	6.5	8.3	5.4	7.4	8.0	11.5	12.8
3. Quite important	15.0	18.7	11.2	15.3	14.2	17.0	15.3	13.3	14.6	14.9	14.8	13.9	13.5	16.8	16.8	23.7
4. Extremely important	72.5	65.7	79.5	72.2	75.0	69.3	72.0	75.0	73.5	74.6	71.0	77.2	74.8	70.6	63.0	58.1
Item 1420 N(Wtd)	2996	1405	1453	2336	327	697	943	909	447	1370	1303	1206	664	321	597	47

A007C: Having lots of money

	TOTAL	M	F	White	Black	NE	NC	S	W	Yes	No	None	Marijuana Only	Few Pills	More Pills	Any Heroin
1. Not important	11.0	8.2	14.4	12.2	7.1	11.2	12.1	10.2	10.0	12.1	11.0	13.5	7.2	7.2	12.8	9.8
2. Somewhat important	43.1	36.8	50.2	46.5	26.7	39.7	45.5	41.9	46.0	44.8	44.0	47.5	42.2	42.5	39.2	29.7
3. Quite important	30.4	35.2	24.7	29.2	33.4	32.2	30.1	29.8	29.5	29.1	29.9	27.1	33.8	32.6	31.7	34.9
4. Extremely important	15.4	19.8	10.7	12.2	32.7	16.9	12.3	18.0	14.5	14.0	15.1	11.9	16.8	17.8	16.3	25.6
Item 1430 N(Wtd)	3009	1413	1453	2341	330	706	945	907	451	1375	1307	1207	666	324	599	47

A007D: Having plenty of time for recreation and hobbies

	TOTAL	M	F	White	Black	NE	NC	S	W	Yes	No	None	Marijuana Only	Few Pills	More Pills	Any Heroin
1. Not important	2.9	2.6	3.0	2.3	6.8	3.3	1.4	4.2	3.0	3.0	2.6	3.3	2.1	1.9	3.1	2.7
2. Somewhat important	33.2	28.8	37.3	32.1	39.1	30.9	35.1	34.4	30.4	29.0	36.8	37.6	29.1	30.0	28.9	22.8
3. Quite important	40.5	41.7	39.4	42.3	31.4	41.6	40.9	38.6	42.0	42.4	39.9	39.9	43.0	45.8	39.5	43.9
4. Extremely important	23.3	26.9	20.2	23.3	22.6	24.2	22.7	22.8	24.6	25.5	20.7	19.2	25.9	22.4	28.5	30.6
Item 1440 N(Wtd)	3015	1418	1455	2343	334	706	943	915	450	1379	1311	1215	666	325	598	47

A007E: Having strong friendships

	TOTAL	M	F	White	Black	NE	NC	S	W	Yes	No	None	Marijuana Only	Few Pills	More Pills	Any Heroin
1. Not important	1.5	1.4	1.6	.9	4.7	2.0	1.0	1.5	1.5	1.2	1.5	1.6	.9	1.6	1.2	3.2
2. Somewhat important	9.7	8.4	10.4	7.4	22.3	10.9	8.7	10.6	8.1	6.9	11.9	9.4	10.6	8.4	8.1	3.3
3. Quite important	30.9	33.6	28.0	30.9	28.9	27.5	36.5	27.8	30.9	27.3	34.1	32.0	30.3	27.2	31.8	21.0
4. Extremely important	57.9	56.6	60.1	60.8	44.2	59.6	53.8	60.0	59.5	64.5	52.5	57.0	58.1	62.7	58.9	72.5
Item 1450 N(Wtd)	3015	1417	1455	2345	330	705	946	912	452	1378	1311	1214	665	326	597	47

A007F: Being able to find steady work

	TOTAL	M	F	White	Black	NE	NC	S	W	Yes	No	None	Marijuana Only	Few Pills	More Pills	Any Heroin
1. Not important	1.4	1.4	1.5	1.2	2.0	2.1	1.5	.9	1.4	1.2	1.7	1.2	.7	1.0	1.9	3.6
2. Somewhat important	6.6	5.9	7.2	6.7	5.9	6.7	6.5	7.2	5.4	6.4	7.1	7.7	5.2	6.7	6.5	5.2
3. Quite important	28.7	26.8	30.6	31.0	18.4	31.3	29.4	23.9	32.6	29.8	28.5	31.6	29.6	25.3	26.9	18.8
4. Extremely important	63.3	65.9	60.7	61.0	73.6	59.9	62.5	68.0	60.6	62.5	62.7	59.5	64.4	67.1	64.7	72.3
Item 1460 N(Wtd)	3015	1417	1457	2343	334	704	944	915	452	1376	1314	1214	665	325	598	47

A007G: Making a contribution to society

	TOTAL	M	F	White	Black	NE	NC	S	W	Yes	No	None	Marijuana Only	Few Pills	More Pills	Any Heroin
1. Not important	8.0	9.7	6.0	7.6	10.4	7.0	8.8	7.5	8.7	5.1	10.1	6.6	7.7	6.9	9.9	13.6
2. Somewhat important	39.4	39.9	39.3	39.7	36.1	40.5	40.2	37.6	39.8	33.9	44.7	39.0	39.5	39.3	40.6	36.7
3. Quite important	34.7	34.3	34.5	35.1	31.0	33.7	33.7	36.2	35.4	36.9	32.7	34.9	36.7	36.1	32.0	35.4
4. Extremely important	17.9	16.2	20.2	17.6	22.5	18.7	17.3	18.7	16.2	24.1	12.4	19.6	16.1	17.8	17.4	14.3
Item 1470 N(Wtd)	3010	1412	1459	2341	333	701	945	912	452	1376	1310	1215	661	325	598	47

A007H: Being a leader in my community

	TOTAL	M	F	White	Black	NE	NC	S	W	Yes	No	None	Marijuana Only	Few Pills	More Pills	Any Heroin
1. Not important	39.4	36.8	42.1	40.7	30.1	42.2	42.6	32.7	41.7	33.1	45.4	35.5	39.7	35.9	49.3	37.2
2. Somewhat important	39.6	39.5	39.2	39.9	38.5	36.9	38.9	42.3	39.7	40.1	39.0	41.7	39.7	41.6	34.5	42.5
3. Quite important	14.3	15.9	13.0	13.8	17.5	14.2	13.2	15.9	13.8	18.0	10.9	15.0	15.0	18.3	10.3	14.1
4. Extremely important	6.7	7.7	5.7	5.6	13.9	6.7	5.3	9.1	4.8	8.8	4.7	7.7	5.5	4.2	6.0	6.2
Item 1480 N(Wtd)	3013	1412	1460	2345	331	704	943	914	453	1376	1312	1216	663	325	597	47

A007I: Being able to give my children better opportunities than I've had

	TOTAL	M	F	White	Black	NE	NC	S	W	Yes	No	None	Marijuana Only	Few Pills	More Pills	Any Heroin
1. Not important	3.7	3.9	3.7	4.2	1.0	4.3	5.5	1.5	3.7	4.1	3.5	3.6	3.8	3.2	4.2	2.7
2. Somewhat important	12.9	13.1	13.0	14.6	3.9	12.2	16.1	9.3	14.8	15.3	11.4	12.6	12.0	12.6	16.6	7.0
3. Quite important	33.8	35.2	32.5	37.6	14.5	35.0	38.8	28.2	32.9	34.2	34.6	35.4	31.1	29.9	36.9	36.8
4. Extremely important	49.6	47.8	50.8	43.7	80.6	48.6	39.6	61.0	48.7	46.4	50.5	48.4	53.0	54.3	42.3	53.5
Item 1490 N(Wtd)	2981	1401	1439	2316	330	694	937	906	444	1358	1300	1198	663	323	588	47

QUESTIONNAIRE FORM 1 1976	TOTAL	SEX		RACE		REGION				4YR COLLEGE PLANS		ILLICIT DRUG USE: LIFETIME				
		M	F	White	Black	NE	NC	S	W	Yes	No	None	Marijuana Only	Few Pills	More Pills	Any Heroin
Weighted No. of Cases:	3039	1426	1466	2356	338	715	950	919	454	1384	1321	1219	669	329	605	47
% of Weighted Total:	100.0	46.9	48.2	77.5	11.1	23.5	31.3	30.2	15.0	45.5	43.5	40.1	22.0	10.8	19.9	1.6

A007J: Living close to parents and relatives

	TOTAL	M	F	White	Black	NE	NC	S	W	Yes	No	None	Marijuana Only	Few Pills	More Pills	Any Heroin
1. Not important	33.6	36.1	31.1	32.9	38.1	34.4	32.4	34.1	33.7	33.5	32.8	29.8	33.5	34.3	42.3	37.2
2. Somewhat important	40.8	39.1	41.9	42.1	33.8	39.6	43.4	39.5	39.9	41.3	40.7	42.2	40.8	42.4	38.1	39.9
3. Quite important	17.6	17.8	17.9	18.0	15.8	18.3	18.9	16.6	16.0	16.8	18.9	19.2	18.5	15.8	14.1	12.9
4. Extremely important	8.0	7.0	9.2	7.0	12.4	7.8	5.2	9.8	10.3	8.3	7.6	8.7	7.2	7.4	5.4	10.0
Item 1500 N(Wtd)	3011	1411	1458	2340	333	706	944	912	449	1372	1313	1211	665	324	598	47

A007K: Getting away from this area of the country

	TOTAL	M	F	White	Black	NE	NC	S	W	Yes	No	None	Marijuana Only	Few Pills	More Pills	Any Heroin
1. Not important	54.9	56.0	54.3	58.1	41.0	49.8	52.6	58.4	60.9	55.4	56.4	62.1	52.8	51.4	46.0	34.0
2. Somewhat important	22.6	22.4	22.7	21.9	26.0	22.3	25.5	20.5	21.2	22.9	21.1	20.8	24.3	23.0	23.9	23.4
3. Quite important	10.6	10.3	10.8	10.0	11.1	12.3	12.2	8.5	9.0	10.6	10.5	8.8	9.3	13.1	14.1	19.9
4. Extremely important	11.8	11.3	12.2	10.0	21.9	15.5	9.7	12.6	8.9	11.1	12.0	8.3	13.6	12.5	16.0	22.7
Item 1510 N(Wtd)	3017	1415	1460	2344	333	707	944	913	453	1377	1313	1214	666	326	599	47

A007L: Working to correct social and economic inequalities

	TOTAL	M	F	White	Black	NE	NC	S	W	Yes	No	None	Marijuana Only	Few Pills	More Pills	Any Heroin
1. Not important	21.0	24.9	17.2	22.5	14.2	21.1	25.0	17.0	20.7	17.1	25.0	20.2	21.1	19.9	23.4	20.4
2. Somewhat important	46.1	46.6	45.4	48.1	35.0	45.3	47.5	44.1	48.5	46.3	47.0	47.6	48.0	44.3	44.5	31.5
3. Quite important	22.6	20.8	24.7	21.1	31.0	23.8	19.8	25.7	20.4	25.0	19.6	22.0	20.6	26.4	21.7	34.9
4. Extremely important	10.3	7.8	12.7	8.3	19.7	9.8	7.8	13.1	10.4	11.5	8.4	10.1	10.4	9.4	10.3	13.1
Item 1520 N(Wtd)	2999	1408	1449	2330	331	702	936	912	449	1372	1302	1203	663	324	598	46

A007M: Discovering new ways to experience things

	TOTAL	M	F	White	Black	NE	NC	S	W	Yes	No	None	Marijuana Only	Few Pills	More Pills	Any Heroin
1. Not important	8.9	10.1	7.9	9.2	10.0	5.7	9.9	10.7	8.1	9.4	8.5	12.4	7.6	5.3	6.0	3.4
2. Somewhat important	34.7	37.8	32.0	36.3	29.8	32.9	37.5	34.5	32.0	31.8	39.0	39.4	34.3	33.5	29.4	24.8
3. Quite important	36.0	34.1	36.9	34.9	37.7	37.8	32.3	36.3	40.4	36.9	34.0	32.6	36.0	40.9	38.2	32.0
4. Extremely important	20.4	18.0	23.2	19.6	22.5	23.6	20.3	18.6	19.5	21.9	18.5	15.6	22.1	20.3	26.5	39.8
Item 1530 N(Wtd)	3007	1412	1456	2337	334	701	944	911	451	1375	1311	1212	664	325	597	47

A007N: Finding purpose and meaning in my life

	TOTAL	M	F	White	Black	NE	NC	S	W	Yes	No	None	Marijuana Only	Few Pills	More Pills	Any Heroin
1. Not important	2.4	3.9	.9	2.4	1.4	2.1	3.2	1.4	3.0	2.0	2.6	2.5	2.7	1.2	1.7	6.8
2. Somewhat important	8.8	12.0	5.7	9.1	5.7	8.5	10.2	7.8	8.7	7.7	9.5	9.1	10.6	6.8	6.8	8.8
3. Quite important	24.9	30.6	18.9	26.4	15.8	23.2	27.9	22.9	25.0	22.4	27.7	24.0	28.0	23.8	25.6	28.9
4. Extremely important	63.9	53.5	74.5	62.0	77.1	66.2	58.7	67.9	63.4	67.8	60.1	64.4	58.7	68.1	65.9	55.5
Item 1540 N(Wtd)	3012	1411	1460	2340	334	703	943	913	453	1374	1313	1216	661	325	599	47

A008: Generally speaking, would you say that most people can be trusted or that you can't be too careful in dealing with people?

	TOTAL	M	F	White	Black	NE	NC	S	W	Yes	No	None	Marijuana Only	Few Pills	More Pills	Any Heroin
3. Most people can be trusted	31.5	31.6	32.6	35.4	14.5	32.6	33.5	28.0	32.7	37.0	28.2	35.6	35.1	27.5	25.8	27.2
2. Don't know, undecided	30.7	33.1	27.9	29.9	30.1	31.5	30.5	30.1	31.2	28.7	32.3	31.5	27.4	30.2	33.1	23.7
1. Can't be too careful	37.8	35.3	39.5	34.7	55.4	35.8	36.0	41.9	36.1	34.3	39.4	32.9	37.5	42.3	41.2	49.0
Item 1550 N(Wtd)	2953	1384	1438	2315	313	686	935	893	440	1361	1281	1199	647	317	588	45

A009: Would you say that most of the time people try to be helpful or that they are mostly just looking out for themselves?

	TOTAL	M	F	White	Black	NE	NC	S	W	Yes	No	None	Marijuana Only	Few Pills	More Pills	Any Heroin
3. Try to be helpful	31.7	29.3	35.5	33.5	26.9	32.3	33.3	29.2	32.5	34.7	31.5	34.6	33.7	29.1	25.0	37.4
2. Don't know, undecided	31.0	31.1	29.7	31.3	26.4	30.0	32.4	29.5	32.7	29.7	31.0	32.3	28.9	26.3	34.2	19.8
1. Just looking out for themselves	37.3	39.6	34.8	35.2	46.7	37.7	34.4	41.4	34.8	35.6	37.5	33.1	37.4	44.7	40.8	42.9
Item 1560 N(Wtd)	3010	1409	1457	2336	333	700	943	915	451	1374	1311	1217	662	323	597	47

QUESTIONNAIRE FORM 1 1976	TOTAL	SEX		RACE		REGION				4YR COLLEGE PLANS		ILLICIT DRUG USE: LIFETIME				
		M	F	White	Black	NE	NC	S	W	Yes	No	None	Mari-juana Only	Few Pills	More Pills	Any Her-oin
Weighted No. of Cases:	3039	1426	1466	2356	338	715	950	919	454	1384	1321	1219	669	329	605	47
% of Weighted Total:	100.0	46.9	48.2	77.5	11.1	23.5	31.3	30.2	15.0	45.5	43.5	40.1	22.0	10.8	19.9	1.6

A010: Do you think most people would try to take advantage of you if they got a chance or would they try to be fair?

3. Would try to be fair	27.9	24.7	31.5	31.3	11.9	29.6	28.5	24.5	31.0	31.2	26.1	32.1	26.5	24.8	23.9	24.4
2. Don't know, undecided	34.0	35.4	32.6	36.2	21.5	33.6	35.9	31.5	35.4	33.3	34.3	33.8	35.7	34.7	32.4	34.5
1. Would try to take advantage of you	38.1	40.0	35.9	32.6	66.6	36.8	35.6	44.0	33.7	35.4	39.6	34.1	37.8	40.5	43.8	41.1
Item 1570 N(Wtd)	3004	1406	1456	2333	333	696	944	914	450	1372	1309	1215	659	324	596	47

A011: These next questions ask your opinions about a number of different topics. How much do you agree or disagree with each statement below?

A011A: I feel that you can't be a good citizen unless you always obey the law

1. Disagree	17.8	19.7	15.9	15.8	28.6	21.4	17.2	17.0	15.6	17.3	17.9	11.4	19.3	21.7	25.1	40.3
2. Mostly disagree	16.7	16.9	17.0	18.0	13.5	21.1	17.2	13.5	15.6	15.7	17.8	13.5	18.4	16.4	22.0	19.5
3. Neither	17.2	18.5	16.0	18.1	11.3	18.7	18.9	13.9	17.8	16.3	18.1	15.8	18.9	15.8	20.1	14.4
4. Mostly agree	35.1	32.8	37.8	37.1	23.8	28.6	36.7	36.4	39.1	39.0	32.9	41.7	34.3	35.4	24.8	16.7
5. Agree	13.1	12.1	13.3	11.0	22.8	10.2	9.9	19.2	11.9	11.7	13.4	17.6	9.0	10.7	7.9	9.1
Item 1580 N(Wtd)	3011	1414	1456	2341	331	701	944	913	453	1376	1311	1215	662	326	599	47

A011B: I feel a good citizen should go along with whatever the government does even if he disagrees with it

1. Disagree	42.0	41.8	41.9	40.6	47.1	48.9	39.3	42.1	36.5	43.9	40.0	35.4	45.0	46.7	48.9	58.6
2. Mostly disagree	24.1	23.6	25.3	26.4	14.8	24.4	26.6	19.8	26.8	26.0	23.4	25.4	24.7	22.2	22.5	23.0
3. Neither	16.0	15.7	15.9	16.2	12.7	13.6	17.7	14.9	18.0	12.4	18.7	16.7	13.8	18.9	15.8	4.8
4. Mostly agree	13.0	14.1	11.7	13.0	13.9	9.6	12.7	14.9	14.8	12.9	12.9	16.9	12.0	7.9	9.0	7.5
5. Agree	5.0	4.8	5.2	3.8	11.5	3.4	3.7	8.2	3.8	4.7	4.9	5.6	4.4	4.3	3.9	6.1
Item 1590 N(Wtd)	3007	1411	1456	2340	330	703	941	913	451	1375	1309	1211	664	326	599	47

A011C: I feel a good citizen tries to change the government policies he disagrees with

1. Disagree	5.0	4.6	5.2	3.3	16.0	5.6	3.4	7.0	3.1	4.4	4.6	4.6	5.8	3.7	4.6	3.8
2. Mostly disagree	7.3	6.9	7.8	7.0	9.8	8.0	6.8	7.6	6.7	5.5	9.2	6.8	7.1	9.6	6.4	2.8
3. Neither	21.4	20.3	22.4	21.0	22.0	19.0	24.0	19.8	24.9	18.8	24.2	22.4	20.5	23.5	19.4	15.1
4. Mostly agree	32.5	32.4	33.1	34.7	21.6	30.2	35.0	30.9	33.9	32.3	33.0	33.3	31.8	30.3	34.6	29.0
5. Agree	33.8	35.9	31.5	34.0	30.6	37.2	30.8	35.7	31.3	39.0	29.0	33.0	34.7	32.8	35.0	49.2
Item 1600 N(Wtd)	3000	1408	1453	2334	331	695	940	912	452	1371	1307	1212	659	323	598	47

A011D: The way people vote has a major impact on how things are run in this country

1. Disagree	9.8	10.1	9.6	9.8	9.4	13.3	8.6	9.1	8.7	10.2	9.3	7.6	9.6	13.5	13.1	15.5
2. Mostly disagree	14.4	14.4	14.2	15.2	9.1	15.4	16.2	12.6	12.9	16.5	12.8	14.5	15.1	12.3	15.0	14.1
3. Neither	15.4	16.4	14.7	16.7	7.6	17.0	17.3	11.2	17.7	16.3	14.0	14.8	17.1	15.1	16.1	15.0
4. Mostly agree	28.2	27.1	29.9	28.9	25.4	25.9	29.3	27.3	31.4	28.5	28.3	28.9	27.7	28.2	27.4	21.3
5. Agree	32.1	32.0	31.6	29.3	48.4	28.4	28.5	39.9	29.3	28.5	35.7	34.2	30.4	30.9	28.4	34.1
Item 1610 N(Wtd)	3003	1411	1453	2339	327	698	942	912	451	1374	1306	1210	660	325	599	47

A011E: People who get together in citizen action groups to influence government policies can have a real effect

1. Disagree	4.4	4.9	3.8	3.7	7.0	5.8	4.2	4.6	2.5	3.9	4.6	3.6	4.2	6.2	4.5	8.9
2. Mostly disagree	10.5	10.9	10.1	11.0	8.1	13.0	10.2	9.8	8.8	10.1	10.7	9.6	11.0	10.3	12.7	8.5
3. Neither	27.1	24.5	29.7	28.0	21.5	26.4	29.6	23.1	30.8	24.0	30.3	27.6	24.2	21.4	32.4	23.5
4. Mostly agree	36.8	38.2	35.5	37.9	30.1	36.0	38.3	35.2	38.5	39.8	34.1	37.9	37.4	40.4	32.8	38.5
5. Agree	21.1	21.5	20.9	19.4	33.3	18.8	17.7	27.3	19.4	22.3	20.3	21.4	23.2	21.7	17.6	20.5
Item 1620 N(Wtd)	2992	1407	1451	2332	327	697	936	912	448	1368	1304	1207	660	324	597	47

QUESTIONNAIRE FORM 1 1976	TOTAL	SEX		RACE		REGION				4YR COLLEGE PLANS		ILLICIT DRUG USE: LIFETIME				
		M	F	White	Black	NE	NC	S	W	Yes	No	None	Mari-juana Only	Few Pills	More Pills	Any Her-oin
Weighted No. of Cases:	3039	1426	1466	2356	338	715	950	919	454	1384	1321	1219	669	329	605	47
% of Weighted Total:	100.0	46.9	48.2	77.5	11.1	23.5	31.3	30.2	15.0	45.5	43.5	40.1	22.0	10.8	19.9	1.6
A011F: Despite its many faults, our system of doing things is still the best in the world																
1. Disagree	6.5	5.5	7.4	4.4	18.7	8.0	5.0	7.3	6.0	5.9	6.2	5.7	6.3	7.3	6.8	9.4
2. Mostly disagree	7.4	6.9	7.9	6.4	10.5	9.1	7.6	6.2	6.9	5.5	8.4	5.5	7.7	9.0	8.2	10.5
3. Neither	22.1	19.9	24.1	21.6	21.1	25.9	23.7	17.9	21.4	19.6	24.3	21.0	22.3	19.8	25.6	19.9
4. Mostly agree	32.0	33.1	31.7	34.5	20.2	32.3	32.4	29.9	34.9	32.8	32.8	34.0	33.3	33.7	28.2	28.6
5. Agree	31.9	34.7	28.9	33.1	29.5	24.7	31.3	38.6	30.8	36.2	28.2	33.9	30.4	30.1	31.2	31.6
Item 1630 N(Wtd)	2993	1407	1449	2332	332	700	937	907	449	1373	1305	1209	663	321	594	47
A011G: America needs growth to survive, and that is going to require some increase in pollution																
1. Disagree	38.1	37.3	39.0	39.6	30.6	41.2	35.1	37.8	39.7	40.4	35.8	36.3	37.0	37.4	44.9	37.4
2. Mostly disagree	23.0	22.9	23.5	24.6	15.1	21.4	25.7	22.1	21.4	25.2	21.9	25.2	22.9	25.1	19.7	16.6
3. Neither	18.6	18.0	18.8	18.4	19.0	16.6	21.4	17.0	18.9	16.5	20.7	19.3	18.2	18.7	16.6	20.1
4. Mostly agree	11.6	13.8	9.7	11.1	14.9	12.0	11.3	11.2	12.6	10.5	12.4	12.0	12.5	7.8	11.0	6.9
5. Agree	8.7	8.0	9.0	6.3	20.4	8.7	6.4	11.8	7.4	7.5	9.2	7.1	9.4	11.0	7.7	18.9
Item 1640 N(Wtd)	2993	1409	1448	2332	330	695	938	911	449	1366	1307	1208	660	324	596	47
A011H: If we just leave things to God, they will turn out for the best																
1. Disagree	22.8	25.3	20.6	23.4	14.1	29.8	22.7	15.3	27.2	25.6	19.0	17.5	24.8	24.9	29.5	33.3
2. Mostly disagree	15.1	16.2	14.4	16.1	7.7	16.3	16.4	11.4	18.3	15.2	15.9	14.5	16.1	16.6	16.1	18.8
3. Neither	25.2	26.3	23.8	26.1	16.9	29.6	27.3	19.8	24.8	23.1	26.9	22.7	26.4	24.4	28.5	24.5
4. Mostly agree	15.4	13.6	17.0	15.4	17.7	13.5	16.4	17.5	11.7	15.3	16.1	18.0	15.7	14.2	12.0	7.2
5. Agree	21.6	18.5	24.3	18.9	43.6	10.8	17.2	35.9	18.0	20.8	22.1	27.3	17.0	19.8	13.8	16.3
Item 1650 N(Wtd)	2970	1397	1437	2319	322	688	933	905	443	1364	1295	1201	656	323	591	47
A011I: Going to school has been an enjoyable experience for me																
1. Disagree	6.3	7.5	4.8	5.9	6.3	8.0	6.0	5.6	5.9	3.7	7.7	4.1	6.4	8.6	9.4	11.4
2. Mostly disagree	7.7	8.9	6.8	7.8	6.5	8.0	9.7	4.5	9.5	5.2	10.5	4.9	7.6	6.8	14.0	7.8
3. Neither	13.7	15.2	12.2	14.3	9.0	14.3	14.7	13.1	13.1	11.9	15.3	12.3	13.7	13.2	16.9	25.5
4. Mostly agree	38.1	38.3	37.9	39.9	27.8	38.6	42.7	32.1	39.9	41.4	35.4	38.8	39.3	38.0	36.3	37.5
5. Agree	34.1	30.2	38.3	32.1	50.4	31.1	26.9	45.0	31.7	37.7	31.1	39.9	33.0	33.4	23.4	17.8
Item 1660 N(Wtd)	3002	1407	1457	2340	328	699	940	911	452	1372	1307	1214	661	324	598	47
A011J: Doing well in school is important for getting a good job																
1. Disagree	3.2	4.8	1.6	3.0	3.3	3.4	2.8	2.9	3.9	1.9	4.3	1.7	3.3	2.7	5.6	8.9
2. Mostly disagree	4.2	5.7	2.5	4.1	1.9	4.5	4.8	3.3	4.6	2.8	5.5	2.7	4.4	4.9	6.5	3.1
3. Neither	9.6	10.5	8.4	10.1	5.3	12.0	9.4	8.1	9.1	8.2	10.5	7.9	9.7	11.4	12.4	9.0
4. Mostly agree	34.6	35.2	34.1	36.0	29.4	36.3	35.5	31.1	37.3	36.3	33.3	35.0	35.1	31.8	36.6	35.7
5. Agree	48.4	43.8	53.4	46.9	60.2	43.7	47.5	54.7	45.0	50.7	46.5	52.7	47.5	49.2	38.9	43.3
Item 1670 N(Wtd)	3010	1412	1460	2341	332	703	942	913	451	1377	1312	1216	664	324	599	47
The following questions are about CIGARETTE SMOKING.																
B001: Have you ever smoked cigarettes?																
1. Never--GO TO Q.B006	24.7	24.1	26.1	25.8	24.6	22.1	25.8	23.5	29.3	31.6	19.2	45.5	11.4	18.5	7.1	8.8
2. Once or twice	24.5	26.5	22.9	23.9	33.0	23.5	22.3	26.1	27.6	27.3	23.4	30.0	29.0	20.5	12.2	7.5
3. Occasionally but not regularly	17.8	18.1	17.8	17.5	17.7	18.7	18.4	16.7	17.8	19.1	17.1	13.6	24.8	22.3	15.9	5.8
4. Regularly in the past	8.8	8.6	8.5	8.9	3.3	10.9	8.0	8.6	7.7	7.2	10.2	3.8	8.8	12.0	16.4	13.6
5. Regularly now	24.1	22.6	24.7	23.8	21.3	24.9	25.6	25.1	17.6	14.9	30.2	7.1	26.0	26.7	48.5	64.3
Item 760 N(Wtd)	2949	1385	1428	2301	320	696	929	885	440	1342	1289	1174	659	320	598	46

QUESTIONNAIRE FORM 1 1976	TOTAL	SEX		RACE		REGION				4YR COLLEGE PLANS		ILLICIT DRUG USE: LIFETIME				
		M	F	White	Black	NE	NC	S	W	Yes	No	None	Mari-juana Only	Few Pills	More Pills	Any Her-oin
Weighted No. of Cases:	3039	1426	1466	2356	338	715	950	919	454	1384	1321	1219	669	329	605	47
% of Weighted Total:	100.0	46.9	48.2	77.5	11.1	23.5	31.3	30.2	15.0	45.5	43.5	40.1	22.0	10.8	19.9	1.6
B002: When did you first smoke cigarettes on a regular daily basis?																
0. Never smoked daily	40.1	43.2	39.1	41.8	39.2	38.7	40.5	36.0	50.2	51.8	34.3	61.1	43.9	33.7	19.6	9.7
1. Grade 6 or earlier	4.5	5.8	3.1	4.5	3.8	3.6	5.2	4.6	4.6	3.8	4.9	4.3	3.0	4.9	6.1	11.5
2. Grade 7 or 8	13.6	13.9	12.4	14.4	6.9	16.5	14.3	11.4	12.0	9.7	16.0	8.6	10.9	12.6	22.5	21.4
3. Grade 9 (Freshman)	15.0	14.3	14.7	14.3	14.1	16.2	13.6	17.2	11.5	11.4	16.3	8.5	13.0	14.9	21.3	35.4
4. Grade 10 (Sophomore)	10.8	10.1	11.3	10.7	9.6	11.4	11.1	11.2	7.9	8.1	12.4	4.5	10.7	15.2	16.3	7.5
5. Grade 11 (Junior)	10.7	9.2	12.1	9.8	15.2	10.0	11.3	11.2	9.4	10.7	10.5	7.6	12.4	15.4	9.9	13.0
6. Grade 12 (Senior)	5.3	3.5	7.3	4.5	11.2	3.5	3.9	8.5	4.4	4.5	5.6	5.3	6.1	3.3	4.4	1.4
Item 1680 N(Wtd) ★	2189	1033	1045	1681	241	531	683	667	308	903	1026	633	577	259	545	42
B003: How frequently have you smoked cigarettes during the past 30 days?																
1. Not at all	48.1	48.9	48.5	49.4	48.4	47.9	45.4	46.8	57.2	56.2	44.5	73.0	47.6	43.7	27.5	19.0
2. Less than one cigarette per day	13.1	14.1	12.3	12.0	18.0	13.9	13.5	12.4	12.4	16.6	10.7	10.3	15.0	14.6	12.8	6.1
3. One to five cigarettes per day	13.5	11.3	15.2	12.6	18.5	12.4	14.6	14.0	11.8	11.4	14.7	8.3	16.0	17.2	14.8	3.8
4. About one-half pack per day	12.7	12.0	12.8	12.2	12.4	12.4	11.9	15.5	8.6	8.4	15.1	5.7	12.1	13.3	19.5	28.6
5. About one pack per day	10.4	11.6	8.9	11.3	2.2	10.2	12.4	9.7	8.0	5.9	12.3	2.2	8.3	8.9	19.9	35.3
6. About one and one-half packs per day	2.0	2.0	2.1	2.2	.5	3.0	2.0	1.5	1.1	1.4	2.5	.4	.9	1.7	5.1	3.2
7. Two packs or more per day	.3	.2	.3	.2	-	.2	.1	.2	.9	.1	.3	-	.1	.6	.3	4.0
Item 780 N(Wtd) ★	2203	1044	1047	1694	242	536	687	671	309	909	1034	632	580	262	551	43
B004: Have you ever tried to stop smoking and found that you could not?																
1. Yes	19.2	19.0	18.8	18.5	16.1	20.8	20.1	19.3	14.5	13.5	21.9	8.5	18.3	15.9	30.4	25.1
2. No	80.8	81.0	81.2	81.5	83.9	79.2	79.9	80.7	85.5	86.5	78.1	91.5	81.7	84.1	69.6	74.9
Item 1690 N(Wtd) ★	2068	972	990	1595	220	509	642	630	286	836	981	569	555	246	534	42
B005: Do you want to stop smoking now?																
1. Yes	19.4	19.8	18.3	18.8	20.3	18.6	19.9	20.9	16.2	13.4	22.6	9.5	21.2	18.9	26.4	35.2
2. No	25.1	23.7	25.8	24.8	22.2	24.1	26.7	26.1	21.3	19.8	28.1	12.9	23.6	28.8	35.4	40.8
8. Don't smoke now	55.5	56.5	55.9	56.3	57.5	57.3	53.4	53.0	62.5	66.8	49.3	77.7	55.2	52.3	38.2	24.0
Item 1700 N(Wtd) ★	2126	999	1021	1645	225	520	666	644	296	874	1001	603	555	254	541	43
B006: Do you think you will be smoking cigarettes five years from now?																
1. I definitely will	1.2	1.2	1.1	.9	.8	1.9	1.0	.7	1.8	1.2	1.0	.5	1.2	1.9	2.1	3.4
2. I probably will	20.5	19.0	21.8	20.3	18.5	21.2	22.0	23.3	11.0	12.5	27.5	8.8	21.7	23.8	37.4	52.2
3. I probably will not	28.1	27.9	27.5	26.6	32.7	28.2	29.7	27.1	26.6	27.7	27.5	22.0	31.7	35.5	31.7	18.1
4. I definitely will not	50.1	51.8	49.6	52.2	48.0	48.6	47.4	49.0	60.6	58.7	43.9	68.7	45.4	38.8	28.7	26.3
Item 1710 N(Wtd)	2978	1399	1448	2318	330	694	935	903	446	1358	1299	1203	658	325	589	46

The different questionnaire forms used in this study tend to emphasize somewhat different topics. The next major section in this form deals with alcohol and various other drugs. There is a lot of talk these days about these subjects, but very little accurate information. Therefore, we still have a lot to learn about the actual experiences and attitudes of people your age.

We hope that you can answer all questions; but if you find one which you feel you cannot answer honestly, we would prefer that you leave it blank.

★=excludes respondents for whom question was inappropriate.

QUESTIONNAIRE FORM 1 1976	TOTAL	SEX		RACE		REGION				4YR COLLEGE PLANS		ILLICIT DRUG USE: LIFETIME				
		M	F	White	Black	NE	NC	S	W	Yes	No	None	Mari-juana Only	Few Pills	More Pills	Any Her-oin
Weighted No. of Cases:	3039	1426	1466	2356	338	715	950	919	454	1384	1321	1219	669	329	605	47
% of Weighted Total:	100.0	46.9	48.2	77.5	11.1	23.5	31.3	30.2	15.0	45.5	43.5	40.1	22.0	10.8	19.9	1.6

Remember that your answers will be strictly confidential. We never connect them with your name or your class.

The next questions are about ALCOHOLIC BEVERAGES, including beer, wine, and liquor.

B007: On how many occasions (if any) have you had alcohol to drink...

B007A: ...in your lifetime?

	TOTAL	M	F	White	Black	NE	NC	S	W	Yes	No	None	Mari-juana Only	Few Pills	More Pills	Any Her-oin
1. 0 occasions	9.1	7.2	10.8	8.4	15.9	5.3	6.8	13.6	11.2	9.6	9.0	19.3	1.3	3.2	.6	-
2. 1-2	9.8	8.6	11.5	8.5	23.4	5.6	9.1	14.0	9.9	10.4	9.7	17.8	3.9	7.8	.9	2.3
3. 3-5	8.2	6.2	10.3	7.7	10.2	6.5	7.6	9.4	9.3	9.7	7.3	13.5	4.8	7.7	1.4	-
4. 6-9	8.4	5.7	10.8	7.4	16.2	8.3	7.6	9.9	7.3	7.8	8.7	11.2	8.2	6.9	3.5	3.6
5. 10-19	12.4	9.2	15.4	12.6	11.4	13.9	10.9	14.2	10.2	13.2	12.4	13.9	14.2	12.8	8.4	6.4
6. 20-39	13.0	13.3	13.0	13.8	6.8	14.7	13.3	10.4	14.8	11.7	14.3	9.5	18.8	14.6	13.0	14.6
7. 40 or more	39.0	49.7	28.0	41.6	16.1	45.7	44.7	28.5	37.3	37.5	38.5	14.8	48.8	46.9	72.1	73.1
Item 810 N(Wtd)	2831	1346	1358	2236	292	662	900	834	435	1316	1224	1162	621	309	576	45

B007B: ...during the last 12 months?

	TOTAL	M	F	White	Black	NE	NC	S	W	Yes	No	None	Mari-juana Only	Few Pills	More Pills	Any Her-oin
1. 0 occasions	17.5	13.6	21.8	15.8	34.5	10.1	13.5	26.2	21.0	18.8	17.3	34.5	5.7	8.6	1.6	1.5
2. 1-2	13.4	11.4	15.2	11.9	23.9	10.7	12.4	17.7	11.1	13.5	13.2	19.3	9.2	13.6	6.1	2.3
3. 3-5	11.9	8.3	15.2	11.5	14.8	15.5	11.4	10.6	10.1	12.7	11.4	15.4	11.6	10.8	5.7	6.5
4. 6-9	11.2	10.3	12.1	11.6	8.3	9.6	12.3	10.4	12.8	11.1	11.4	10.4	14.5	11.6	9.7	9.9
5. 10-19	16.0	15.9	16.5	17.0	9.5	18.2	15.7	13.9	17.2	16.1	16.1	11.2	20.3	18.5	19.7	17.9
6. 20-39	12.0	14.5	9.9	13.2	4.3	14.1	13.2	8.9	12.3	12.2	11.2	3.9	21.1	13.1	18.3	14.3
7. 40 or more	18.0	25.9	9.2	19.0	4.7	21.9	21.5	12.3	15.5	15.5	19.0	5.3	17.6	23.7	39.1	47.6
Item 820 N(Wtd)	2815	1338	1351	2228	283	665	902	819	429	1319	1210	1152	619	309	572	46

B007C: ...during the last 30 days?

	TOTAL	M	F	White	Black	NE	NC	S	W	Yes	No	None	Mari-juana Only	Few Pills	More Pills	Any Her-oin
1. 0 occasions	35.0	27.4	42.8	32.6	58.1	27.1	30.9	45.1	36.6	37.7	33.6	59.5	20.1	24.2	11.4	8.0
2. 1-2	21.1	19.0	23.4	21.0	23.3	21.3	19.8	20.3	25.2	22.0	21.4	20.6	25.6	21.6	17.0	16.0
3. 3-5	18.4	20.4	17.0	19.7	10.8	20.4	19.7	14.7	19.7	19.0	16.8	11.8	24.5	22.7	23.1	14.6
4. 6-9	11.9	14.3	9.7	13.0	4.7	14.7	12.8	10.0	9.4	11.2	12.7	4.3	16.8	15.1	18.8	20.4
5. 10-19	8.1	10.8	5.2	8.5	1.3	9.9	10.3	5.7	5.0	7.0	9.0	2.7	8.3	7.8	18.1	15.4
6. 20-39	3.3	4.8	1.3	3.3	1.6	4.1	4.3	2.3	1.9	1.9	4.4	.6	2.2	5.0	8.3	13.6
7. 40 or more	2.1	3.3	.6	1.9	.3	2.5	2.1	1.7	2.2	1.2	2.2	.4	2.5	3.7	3.3	11.9
Item 830 N(Wtd)	2842	1347	1367	2244	290	671	912	828	431	1322	1230	1148	629	318	579	45

IF YOU HAVE NOT HAD ANY BEER, WINE, OR LIQUOR IN THE LAST TWELVE MONTHS, GO TO Q.B017.

B008: When you used alcohol during the last year, how often did you use it in each of the following situations?

B008A: When you were alone

	TOTAL	M	F	White	Black	NE	NC	S	W	Yes	No	None	Mari-juana Only	Few Pills	More Pills	Any Her-oin
1. Not at all	68.3	58.4	80.5	68.8	73.9	69.8	66.1	67.9	71.9	74.1	64.3	78.3	73.4	65.4	55.5	45.5
2. A few of the times	25.0	32.9	16.4	25.4	19.1	22.9	28.1	24.4	22.4	22.2	27.2	18.0	22.0	25.4	34.3	34.4
3. Some of the times	5.3	7.1	2.1	4.7	3.2	6.1	4.5	5.9	4.9	2.6	7.2	1.9	3.4	7.4	9.3	20.1
4. Most of the times	1.1	1.5	.7	.9	3.8	1.0	1.1	1.2	.6	1.0	1.1	1.4	.6	1.7	.6	-
5. Every time	.3	.2	.3	.2	-	.1	.2	.6	.2	.1	.2	.3	.5	-	.2	-
Item 1720 N(Wtd) ★	2385	1178	1096	1916	199	612	793	637	343	1089	1032	760	604	288	579	45

B008B: With just 1 or 2 other people

	TOTAL	M	F	White	Black	NE	NC	S	W	Yes	No	None	Mari-juana Only	Few Pills	More Pills	Any Her-oin
1. Not at all	13.0	8.7	18.3	12.2	20.1	14.5	12.3	12.2	13.2	16.0	10.5	23.6	9.4	10.3	5.7	.9
2. A few of the times	32.7	29.5	36.5	32.1	39.3	35.3	29.4	34.5	32.7	34.8	32.1	39.1	33.8	34.2	23.6	20.7
3. Some of the times	24.4	26.4	21.2	24.9	14.8	27.9	26.2	19.8	24.5	22.8	24.4	22.8	25.5	25.4	34.8	35.2
4. Most of the times	23.7	29.4	17.8	24.7	18.7	18.9	26.7	26.3	20.8	21.4	26.3	15.2	26.7	24.0	30.8	35.1
5. Every time	6.1	6.0	6.3	6.1	7.0	3.4	5.5	8.2	8.8	5.0	6.6	7.8	4.5	6.2	5.0	8.1
Item 1730 N(Wtd) ★	2381	1175	1092	1907	202	610	795	636	341	1088	1026	754	603	289	580	45

★ = excludes respondents for whom question was inappropriate.

QUESTIONNAIRE FORM 1 1976	TOTAL	SEX		RACE		REGION				4YR COLLEGE PLANS		ILLICIT DRUG USE: LIFETIME				
		M	F	White	Black	NE	NC	S	W	Yes	No	None	Marijuana Only	Few Pills	More Pills	Any Heroin
Weighted No. of Cases:	3039	1426	1466	2356	338	715	950	919	454	1384	1321	1219	669	329	605	47
% of Weighted Total:	100.0	46.9	48.2	77.5	11.1	23.5	31.3	30.2	15.0	45.5	43.5	40.1	22.0	10.8	19.9	1.6
B008C: At a party																
1. Not at all	12.5	10.7	14.8	12.6	17.1	9.1	12.3	15.8	13.1	12.6	13.6	24.6	7.3	8.8	5.2	5.9
2. A few of the times	19.3	17.7	22.0	18.9	30.0	17.8	17.4	24.8	16.5	20.3	19.3	24.0	17.2	21.5	14.8	14.2
3. Some of the times	18.1	18.8	17.5	18.1	18.0	16.5	20.1	17.8	17.2	19.0	17.2	14.8	19.4	17.2	20.9	14.7
4. Most of the times	31.8	32.4	30.7	32.6	22.6	35.8	33.1	24.4	35.3	33.0	30.1	26.1	37.1	31.9	35.5	28.0
5. Every time	18.2	20.4	15.1	17.9	12.4	20.9	17.0	17.2	17.9	15.0	19.9	10.6	19.0	20.6	23.6	37.1
Item 1740 N(Wtd) ★	2387	1179	1093	1910	203	611	794	640	342	1087	1034	759	603	289	579	45
B008D: When your date or spouse was present																
1. Not at all	32.4	36.1	28.6	31.1	52.3	29.8	29.7	37.2	34.4	38.0	27.9	51.9	26.5	29.5	16.9	20.1
2. A few of the times	27.8	28.4	28.1	27.9	22.7	27.3	29.0	28.4	24.9	29.3	27.4	24.1	31.6	31.4	26.1	25.4
3. Some of the times	17.4	19.0	15.3	17.0	14.4	20.9	16.9	14.2	18.4	14.9	18.5	7.7	20.8	19.7	25.4	23.9
4. Most of the times	15.2	12.8	17.3	16.6	6.9	15.6	17.3	12.9	14.2	13.4	16.8	11.7	15.4	11.1	21.6	17.7
5. Every time	7.1	3.7	10.7	7.5	3.7	6.4	7.0	7.3	8.1	4.4	9.4	4.7	5.7	8.2	10.0	13.0
Item 1750 N(Wtd) ★	2351	1163	1076	1880	202	594	787	638	332	1072	1015	746	596	286	572	44
B008E: When people over age 30 were present																
1. Not at all	27.4	25.5	29.1	25.6	49.4	20.0	24.1	38.5	27.3	27.4	28.1	33.8	29.3	26.4	17.4	15.8
2. A few of the times	38.7	40.4	37.5	39.8	32.4	42.6	39.6	34.7	37.5	39.4	37.6	32.6	41.3	38.0	46.3	30.4
3. Some of the times	19.0	21.5	16.1	19.7	11.1	21.4	21.9	13.5	18.0	17.1	20.3	12.1	19.1	24.4	23.9	28.2
4. Most of the times	9.4	8.1	10.7	9.4	4.8	10.6	8.9	8.4	10.4	8.9	10.2	11.1	7.2	7.0	9.9	18.5
5. Every time	5.5	4.5	6.6	5.6	2.2	5.4	5.4	4.9	6.8	7.2	3.9	10.4	3.1	4.2	2.5	7.2
Item 1760 N(Wtd) ★	2390	1183	1093	1915	200	611	796	642	342	1092	1032	763	603	290	580	45
B008F: During the daytime (before 4:00 p.m.)																
1. Not at all	58.2	47.2	72.0	56.5	80.9	57.8	54.8	63.4	57.1	64.0	55.4	74.1	58.5	57.3	39.1	29.9
2. A few of the times	29.9	36.8	21.6	31.4	15.7	29.8	33.2	26.4	29.2	27.7	31.3	16.7	33.2	34.5	40.5	39.7
3. Some of the times	9.7	13.5	4.9	10.3	2.1	10.4	10.0	8.0	11.4	6.2	11.6	5.8	6.9	7.8	18.6	23.2
4. Most of the times	1.5	1.6	1.1	1.3	.8	1.1	1.7	1.7	1.6	1.6	1.0	2.5	.9	.4	1.4	3.4
5. Every time	.6	.9	.3	.5	.5	.9	.4	.6	.7	.5	.7	.9	.5	-	.3	3.8
Item 1770 N(Wtd) ★	2383	1181	1090	1911	199	610	794	638	341	1088	1030	759	605	287	580	45
B008G: At your home (or apartment or dorm)																
1. Not at all	35.3	31.7	39.4	34.2	46.1	32.3	33.8	41.7	32.1	37.5	33.6	43.4	40.5	34.3	20.4	18.7
2. A few of the times	36.0	38.0	34.3	37.9	28.5	35.0	38.7	33.9	35.7	33.8	38.2	29.8	36.3	40.0	41.9	40.5
3. Some of the times	16.9	19.6	13.5	17.0	11.1	20.2	15.8	14.5	18.3	16.2	16.5	11.6	13.9	16.1	27.9	13.0
4. Most of the times	8.7	8.1	8.8	7.9	10.7	10.0	9.3	6.3	9.3	8.2	9.3	9.6	7.7	6.7	8.7	22.7
5. Every time	3.1	2.6	3.9	3.0	3.7	2.6	2.4	3.6	4.5	4.2	2.3	5.6	1.6	2.9	1.1	5.1
Item 1780 N(Wtd) ★	2392	1183	1095	1918	202	614	795	643	341	1089	1034	763	604	291	581	45
B008H: At school																
1. Not at all	84.8	78.2	92.8	84.9	91.6	83.3	86.6	87.0	79.4	88.4	83.5	95.8	85.7	82.4	73.6	53.1
2. A few of the times	12.0	16.4	6.3	12.0	5.9	13.8	10.8	11.0	13.3	9.2	12.9	3.8	11.5	15.0	19.9	34.9
3. Some of the times	2.7	4.5	.8	2.7	1.6	2.5	2.0	1.7	6.5	2.2	2.7	.3	2.6	2.2	5.7	10.3
4. Most of the times	.2	.4	-	.2	.3	.4	.3	.1	-	.1	.2	-	.3	-	.4	-
5. Every time	.3	.4	.1	.2	.5	-	.3	.2	.8	-	.6	.2	-	.5	.4	1.7
Item 1790 N(Wtd) ★	2383	1182	1090	1911	202	611	793	637	341	1091	1030	758	603	288	580	45
B008I: In a car																
1. Not at all	33.9	25.2	43.5	31.8	49.8	40.6	29.3	31.6	36.6	38.9	29.7	53.8	26.5	33.0	17.2	20.5
2. A few of the times	25.1	23.1	27.3	24.8	26.1	24.9	24.0	26.6	25.4	26.8	24.3	23.0	27.3	25.3	26.9	17.4
3. Some of the times	22.8	27.4	17.7	23.6	15.5	18.5	28.0	20.7	22.4	19.8	24.2	14.2	26.1	22.7	29.5	28.0
4. Most of the times	16.4	21.7	10.2	17.9	7.0	14.1	17.3	19.0	13.2	13.3	19.1	7.6	18.8	17.3	23.9	30.6
5. Every time	1.9	2.6	1.2	1.9	1.6	2.0	1.3	2.1	2.4	1.2	2.6	1.3	1.3	1.8	2.5	3.6
Item 1810 N(Wtd) ★	2387	1185	1091	1914	202	612	795	638	342	1089	1034	758	604	289	581	45

★=excludes respondents for whom question was inappropriate.

QUESTIONNAIRE FORM 1 1976	TOTAL	SEX		RACE		REGION				4YR COLLEGE PLANS		ILLICIT DRUG USE: LIFETIME				
		M	F	White	Black	NE	NC	S	W	Yes	No	None	Mari- juana Only	Few Pills	More Pills	Any Her- oin
Weighted No. of Cases:	3039	1426	1466	2356	338	715	950	919	454	1384	1321	1219	669	329	605	47
% of Weighted Total:	100.0	46.9	48.2	77.5	11.1	23.5	31.3	30.2	15.0	45.5	43.5	40.1	22.0	10.8	19.9	1.6

B009: What have been the most important reasons for your drinking alcoholic beverages? (Mark all that apply.)

	TOTAL	M	F	White	Black	NE	NC	S	W	Yes	No	None	Mari juana Only	Few Pills	More Pills	Any Heroin
A. To experiment--to see what it's like	37.5	34.0	40.9	36.3	51.5	31.0	37.0	44.3	37.2	38.0	36.3	47.6	36.4	35.6	28.0	22.9
B. To relax or relieve tension	33.5	31.9	35.2	34.4	22.3	36.5	32.4	33.0	32.1	31.4	36.1	23.7	30.3	35.9	46.2	48.5
C. To feel good or get high	52.0	56.0	46.3	52.9	34.5	56.9	53.2	44.7	54.6	50.4	50.8	27.0	58.6	49.7	75.1	78.5
D. To seek deeper insights and understanding	3.4	3.3	2.6	2.8	2.8	3.6	3.5	2.7	4.4	2.6	3.2	2.9	2.9	4.1	3.6	11.8
E. To have a good time with my friends	66.0	69.8	61.6	67.4	47.6	68.5	70.7	55.4	70.4	66.8	63.6	53.2	75.3	65.8	72.1	66.3
F. To fit in with a group I like	13.9	15.5	11.3	14.4	8.9	11.5	14.8	14.5	14.4	14.9	12.7	15.1	16.2	14.6	10.6	9.2
G. To get away from my problems or troubles	14.6	13.2	15.4	14.1	9.2	16.7	14.6	14.0	12.4	11.4	17.4	10.6	13.2	16.3	19.8	22.4
H. Because of boredom, nothing else to do	21.4	23.4	18.7	22.0	14.5	18.9	23.7	20.0	23.4	19.2	22.9	13.1	22.8	22.9	28.7	30.6
I. Because of anger or frustration	12.9	12.7	12.7	13.1	8.3	13.9	12.6	13.2	11.7	10.6	15.3	9.0	11.7	13.0	17.8	21.5
J. To get through the day	1.1	1.0	.7	.8	1.3	1.0	.8	1.3	1.4	.4	1.2	.9	1.0	.8	1.1	5.8
K. To increase the effects of some other drug(s)	7.3	8.0	5.1	6.7	4.9	7.0	8.3	6.9	6.4	4.9	7.8	.4	2.1	6.6	20.8	27.0
L. To decrease (offset) the effects of some other drug(s)	.9	1.0	.3	.8	-	1.0	.9	.9	.5	.4	.8	.4	.3	-	2.4	2.5
M. To get to sleep	5.0	5.1	4.6	4.6	6.8	4.3	5.6	4.7	5.4	4.3	5.5	3.5	3.9	5.0	7.5	15.1
N. Because it tastes good	46.8	49.4	43.6	48.3	30.4	48.5	50.8	40.6	46.2	48.3	46.1	42.3	48.1	45.6	51.8	67.8
O. Because I am "hooked"--I feel I have to drink	.7	.9	.1	.6	-	1.2	.5	.3	.8	.5	.6	.5	.3	.6	.6	5.5
Item 1820-1960 N(Wtd) ★	2307	1154	1048	1856	194	575	777	624	331	1043	1007	699	593	284	580	44

B010: When you drink alcoholic beverages, how high do you usually get?

	TOTAL	M	F	White	Black	NE	NC	S	W	Yes	No	None	Mari juana Only	Few Pills	More Pills	Any Heroin
1. Not at all high	21.6	17.1	27.3	20.8	32.7	19.8	21.2	24.2	20.9	25.8	19.6	45.3	12.0	13.5	6.4	2.6
2. A little high	32.3	29.3	35.6	31.9	36.8	30.9	31.5	37.4	27.0	34.9	30.6	32.9	36.6	35.7	25.1	28.1
3. Moderately high	38.0	44.8	30.6	39.0	24.1	41.7	38.5	31.6	42.4	33.5	40.8	18.9	42.9	42.3	55.1	53.7
4. Very high	8.1	8.9	6.5	8.3	6.3	7.6	8.7	6.8	9.7	5.9	9.0	2.9	8.6	8.4	13.4	15.6
Item 1970 N(Wtd) ★	2368	1166	1092	1900	199	606	782	641	339	1082	1021	755	597	288	576	45

B011: When you drink alcoholic beverages, how long do you usually stay high?

	TOTAL	M	F	White	Black	NE	NC	S	W	Yes	No	None	Mari juana Only	Few Pills	More Pills	Any Heroin
1. Usually don't get high	24.6	20.1	30.3	23.3	40.8	23.2	23.8	28.3	21.6	29.6	22.0	49.8	15.3	16.3	8.4	2.6
2. One to two hours	38.5	37.6	40.3	38.8	39.1	38.4	39.3	39.3	34.9	40.4	37.8	34.3	46.2	44.5	33.2	25.8
3. Three to six hours	33.8	38.4	27.5	34.8	17.3	34.6	33.2	30.1	40.3	28.4	36.4	14.5	34.8	34.9	54.7	61.2
4. Seven to 24 hours	3.0	3.7	1.8	2.8	2.7	3.4	3.3	2.2	3.1	1.6	3.7	1.3	3.6	3.8	3.8	8.4
5. More than 24 hours	.2	.2	.1	.2	-	.3	.3	-	.1	.1	.2	.1	.1	.5	-	2.0
Item 1980 N(Wtd) ★	2358	1164	1080	1888	200	601	782	638	338	1079	1016	739	601	290	575	45

The following questions ask about how much you have to drink on the occasions when you drink alcoholic beverages. For these questions, a "drink" means any of the following: A 12-ounce can (or bottle) of beer, a 4-ounce glass of wine, a mixed drink or shot glass of liquor.

B012: Think back over the LAST TWO WEEKS. how many times have you had five or more drinks in a row?

	TOTAL	M	F	White	Black	NE	NC	S	W	Yes	No	None	Mari juana Only	Few Pills	More Pills	Any Heroin
1. None	61.1	48.8	74.8	59.5	84.2	60.8	55.9	67.3	61.9	67.4	57.7	83.3	57.0	57.1	42.4	24.7
2. Once	12.5	13.4	11.9	13.5	6.4	12.9	12.6	11.2	13.6	11.9	12.0	7.6	15.5	15.5	13.2	9.4
3. Twice	11.1	14.9	7.2	11.5	4.7	9.3	13.4	9.7	11.3	10.6	11.4	4.2	12.3	13.1	16.0	20.7
4. 3 to 5 times	11.0	16.3	4.8	11.1	4.2	12.6	12.9	7.7	9.9	7.8	13.3	3.9	12.2	8.2	20.2	21.7
5. 6 to 9 times	2.6	3.8	.9	2.8	-	2.9	3.3	2.1	1.3	1.5	3.3	.6	1.8	3.7	5.1	10.3
6. 10 or more times	1.8	2.8	.4	1.6	.5	1.4	1.8	1.9	2.0	.8	2.2	.4	1.2	2.2	3.1	13.2
Item 850 N(Wtd) ★	2346	1146	1090	1882	198	598	780	633	335	1074	1009	750	595	281	573	44

★ = excludes respondents for whom question was inappropriate.

QUESTIONNAIRE FORM 1 1976	TOTAL	SEX		RACE		REGION				4YR COLLEGE PLANS		ILLICIT DRUG USE: LIFETIME				
		M	F	White	Black	NE	NC	S	W	Yes	No	None	Mari-juana Only	Few Pills	More Pills	Any Her-oin
Weighted No. of Cases:	3039	1426	1466	2356	338	715	950	919	454	1384	1321	1219	669	329	605	47
% of Weighted Total:	100.0	46.9	48.2	77.5	11.1	23.5	31.3	30.2	15.0	45.5	43.5	40.1	22.0	10.8	19.9	1.6

B013: During the last two weeks, how many times have you had 3 or 4 drinks in a row?

	TOTAL	M	F	White	Black	NE	NC	S	W	Yes	No	None	Mari-juana Only	Few Pills	More Pills	Any Her-oin
1. None	53.5	43.1	64.6	50.6	82.6	52.3	48.2	59.5	56.8	57.5	51.3	76.2	49.1	45.7	33.4	32.6
2. Once	16.8	16.2	18.1	18.5	6.1	17.1	17.9	16.1	14.8	18.0	15.3	13.2	17.8	21.1	19.6	8.4
3. Twice	11.9	15.8	8.2	12.6	6.7	11.1	14.0	9.1	13.7	11.2	13.0	5.5	15.6	12.8	14.4	12.8
4. 3 to 5 times	12.4	16.5	7.6	12.7	3.1	13.6	13.9	10.2	11.1	10.0	13.5	4.0	13.5	11.1	23.0	25.9
5. 6 to 9 times	3.8	5.7	1.3	4.0	.9	4.8	3.7	3.7	2.4	2.7	4.5	.7	3.2	7.2	6.5	12.3
6. 10 or more times	1.6	2.8	.2	1.6	.5	1.1	2.3	1.4	1.2	.7	2.4	.4	.8	2.0	3.2	7.9
Item 1990 N(Wtd) ★	2340	1139	1088	1870	199	596	775	632	338	1069	1007	747	593	281	572	43

B014: During the last two weeks, how many times have you had two drinks in a row?

	TOTAL	M	F	White	Black	NE	NC	S	W	Yes	No	None	Mari-juana Only	Few Pills	More Pills	Any Her-oin
1. None	45.9	37.1	54.9	43.9	68.5	46.5	40.1	51.4	47.5	49.0	44.3	68.7	39.5	38.4	26.5	34.6
2. Once	17.8	17.3	18.9	18.4	15.6	14.3	21.6	16.5	17.6	17.9	18.3	16.3	19.6	18.8	17.4	12.6
3. Twice	14.1	14.7	13.2	13.9	9.8	14.0	13.8	13.0	16.8	14.7	12.3	7.7	17.8	16.8	18.1	9.3
4. 3 to 5 times	13.4	17.8	9.1	14.6	4.3	15.8	14.1	10.7	12.7	12.7	14.1	5.2	16.4	16.1	19.5	13.7
5. 6 to 9 times	5.8	8.2	3.0	5.9	1.5	6.7	6.1	5.5	4.0	4.5	7.0	1.7	5.1	6.2	11.7	10.0
6. 10 to 19 times	2.3	3.6	.8	2.6	-	2.1	3.5	2.0	.8	.8	3.1	.2	1.2	3.0	5.7	11.4
7. 20 or more times	.7	1.3	*	.7	.3	.6	.8	.8	.6	.4	1.0	.2	.4	.6	1.2	8.3
Item 2000 N(Wtd) ★	2289	1109	1070	1837	191	585	754	620	330	1049	987	729	584	271	565	42

B015: During the last two weeks, how many times have you had just one drink?

	TOTAL	M	F	White	Black	NE	NC	S	W	Yes	No	None	Mari-juana Only	Few Pills	More Pills	Any Her-oin
1. None	49.2	44.6	54.9	49.5	55.6	45.3	48.0	54.9	48.0	50.8	48.5	64.3	46.8	35.8	39.3	42.3
2. Once	24.4	23.4	25.2	23.7	27.9	22.3	26.0	23.5	25.8	23.9	25.3	20.7	24.3	30.6	25.1	25.9
3. Twice	10.9	9.9	11.6	10.8	10.1	13.3	10.3	8.8	12.0	10.8	10.4	7.9	12.1	11.5	13.9	7.1
4. 3 to 5 times	10.0	13.5	6.4	10.5	5.2	10.9	9.6	9.2	10.4	10.3	9.7	5.9	12.2	12.5	12.2	10.2
5. 6 to 9 times	3.3	5.0	1.3	3.4	.4	5.3	2.9	2.7	1.9	2.7	3.5	.7	3.5	7.2	4.4	3.9
6. 10 to 19 times	1.8	3.1	.3	1.8	.7	2.5	2.6	.4	1.5	1.4	2.1	.3	.9	1.9	4.4	6.6
7. 20 or more times	.4	.5	.2	.4	-	.2	.5	.6	.3	.1	.6	.2	.1	.5	.7	4.0
Item 2010 N(Wtd) ★	2238	1102	1034	1804	181	563	740	608	325	1024	960	707	566	270	553	42

B016: Have you ever tried to stop using alcoholic beverages and found that you couldn't stop?

	TOTAL	M	F	White	Black	NE	NC	S	W	Yes	No	None	Mari-juana Only	Few Pills	More Pills	Any Her-oin
1. Yes	2.7	2.3	2.8	2.2	5.2	2.8	2.7	2.9	2.3	1.8	3.1	3.5	2.4	2.4	1.9	7.7
2. No	97.3	97.7	97.2	97.8	94.8	97.2	97.3	97.1	97.7	98.2	96.9	96.5	97.6	97.6	98.1	92.3
Item 2020 N(Wtd) ★	2331	1159	1064	1878	189	595	779	625	333	1061	1012	721	599	287	577	45

B017: Do you think you will be drinking alcoholic beverages five years from now?

	TOTAL	M	F	White	Black	NE	NC	S	W	Yes	No	None	Mari-juana Only	Few Pills	More Pills	Any Her-oin
1. I definitely will	13.0	17.0	9.4	14.2	3.4	17.7	16.1	6.1	12.9	13.4	12.4	6.8	13.8	16.7	22.9	19.8
2. I probably will	53.2	54.2	52.1	56.4	33.1	58.1	56.9	45.3	54.0	52.3	53.8	41.9	63.0	58.6	61.1	68.5
3. I probably will not	15.7	13.9	16.9	13.8	27.1	12.7	13.5	22.1	12.1	15.8	15.6	21.0	12.0	16.2	8.9	7.5
4. I definitely will not	18.1	14.9	21.6	15.5	36.4	11.5	13.5	26.5	21.0	18.5	18.2	30.2	11.2	8.5	7.0	4.3
Item 2030 N(Wtd)	2970	1394	1447	2310	334	695	932	899	444	1363	1299	1196	658	326	596	46

The next questions are about MARIJUANA and HASHISH.

Marijuana is sometimes called: grass, pot, dope.

Hashish is sometimes called: hash, hash oil.

B018: On how many occasions (if any) have you used hashish...

★ = excludes respondents for whom question was inappropriate.   * = less than .05 per cent.

QUESTIONNAIRE FORM 1 1976	TOTAL	SEX		RACE		REGION				4YR COLLEGE PLANS		ILLICIT DRUG USE: LIFETIME				
		M	F	White	Black	NE	NC	S	W	Yes	No	None	Marijuana Only	Few Pills	More Pills	Any Heroin
Weighted No. of Cases:	3039	1426	1466	2356	338	715	950	919	454	1384	1321	1219	669	329	605	47
% of Weighted Total:	100.0	46.9	48.2	77.5	11.1	23.5	31.3	30.2	15.0	45.5	43.5	40.1	22.0	10.8	19.9	1.6

B018A: ...in your lifetime?

1. 0 occasions	71.0	66.4	76.9	70.3	87.2	61.5	71.6	78.3	69.9	77.0	68.2	100.0	71.7	55.0	23.0	9.9
2. 1-2	10.7	11.6	10.1	11.2	5.9	13.8	9.3	9.1	11.5	9.5	12.0	-	17.9	22.7	18.3	9.3
3. 3-5	5.3	5.9	4.9	5.7	3.5	6.1	5.8	4.8	4.4	4.4	5.9	-	4.9	10.8	13.7	13.8
4. 6-9	3.5	4.3	2.3	3.4	1.3	5.6	3.5	2.4	2.5	2.5	3.9	-	2.6	4.7	11.0	4.4
5. 10-19	3.5	4.1	2.6	3.6	.8	4.6	3.9	1.5	4.8	2.5	3.8	-	1.4	3.0	11.9	19.7
6. 20-39	2.1	2.4	1.4	2.1	.3	3.1	1.9	.9	2.9	1.6	2.0	-	.9	1.2	8.0	6.4
7. 40 or more	4.0	5.3	1.8	3.7	1.1	5.2	4.0	3.1	4.0	2.4	4.1	-	.7	2.6	14.1	36.5
Item 2040 N(Wtd)	2898	1376	1397	2277	312	683	908	869	438	1348	1254	1219	667	320	589	45

B018B: ...during the last 12 months?

1. 0 occasions	78.9	73.7	85.6	78.4	91.9	71.9	77.8	86.1	77.7	83.3	77.7	100.0	82.7	70.7	38.8	26.1
2. 1-2	9.0	10.0	7.5	9.4	4.9	11.2	9.2	7.0	9.0	8.0	9.7	-	11.2	15.8	21.5	6.7
3. 3-5	4.4	6.1	2.6	4.8	.7	6.8	5.0	2.0	4.2	3.3	4.4	-	3.4	7.9	12.2	17.4
4. 6-9	2.8	3.8	1.3	2.6	.3	3.3	2.8	1.6	4.0	2.2	3.2	-	1.3	1.6	10.1	13.6
5. 10-19	2.2	2.4	1.8	2.0	.9	3.5	2.2	1.1	2.3	1.5	2.1	-	.6	1.4	7.8	12.9
6. 20-39	1.4	2.0	.7	1.3	1.2	1.4	1.6	1.3	1.1	.8	1.7	-	.5	.4	5.3	11.1
7. 40 or more	1.4	1.9	.5	1.4	-	1.9	1.4	.9	1.6	.9	1.3	-	.3	2.0	4.3	12.2
Item 2050 N(Wtd)	2883	1369	1389	2261	313	683	905	858	438	1346	1243	1219	666	316	578	45

B018C: ...during the last 30 days?

1. 0 occasions	90.3	86.8	95.0	90.9	96.0	85.7	90.3	94.1	90.2	93.5	89.7	100.0	94.4	87.7	70.1	50.8
2. 1-2	5.4	7.3	3.3	5.2	2.8	8.7	4.9	3.8	4.7	4.0	6.2	-	4.3	9.2	15.4	17.8
3. 3-5	1.5	2.2	.6	1.4	-	1.8	1.9	.6	1.9	1.1	1.4	-	.5	.7	6.0	5.9
4. 6-9	1.1	1.4	.5	1.0	.5	1.8	1.4	.3	1.3	.5	1.0	-	.1	.3	4.1	7.9
5. 10-19	.6	.9	.3	.6	.5	.6	.6	.6	.9	.3	.7	-	.3	-	2.3	6.7
6. 20-39	.6	1.0	.2	.6	.2	1.0	.5	.5	.2	.4	.8	-	.1	1.6	1.4	6.0
7. 40 or more	.4	.4	*	.2	-	.5	.3	.1	.7	.1	.2	-	.3	.4	.7	4.9
Item 2060 N(Wtd)	2878	1367	1385	2258	310	680	904	856	437	1344	1239	1219	665	315	577	46

B019: On how many occasions (if any) have you used marijuana...

B019A: ...in your lifetime?

1. 0 occasions	47.5	40.6	55.6	47.7	56.9	38.3	50.0	54.5	42.8	52.1	46.0	100.0	-	29.3	7.8	2.3
2. 1-2	9.2	10.9	7.9	9.2	13.1	7.1	9.2	10.0	10.7	9.8	9.1	-	31.1	7.9	3.5	5.6
3. 3-5	4.6	4.9	4.2	4.7	3.6	6.2	4.4	3.0	5.6	5.1	4.1	-	14.0	6.6	1.8	2.7
4. 6-9	4.3	4.4	4.3	4.5	4.0	5.7	3.9	3.5	4.7	4.5	4.3	-	13.1	4.0	3.3	1.2
5. 10-19	5.4	5.8	5.0	5.3	4.3	7.4	4.1	5.0	6.0	5.3	5.9	-	13.6	9.0	4.8	1.0
6. 20-39	5.3	4.9	5.6	5.1	4.0	5.6	5.1	4.6	6.6	5.0	5.3	-	9.5	10.8	8.3	1.9
7. 40 or more	23.7	28.4	17.4	23.4	14.1	29.7	23.3	19.6	23.6	18.3	25.3	-	18.0	32.4	70.5	85.3
Item 2070 N(Wtd)	2882	1361	1392	2275	300	684	899	860	440	1343	1246	1219	668	322	583	45

B019B: ...during the last 12 months?

1. 0 occasions	55.8	49.0	63.9	56.2	66.5	46.6	57.8	62.4	53.2	60.1	55.1	100.0	26.1	37.9	13.3	7.4
2. 1-2	7.8	8.6	7.4	7.8	8.5	8.8	6.4	8.1	8.6	8.8	6.6	-	24.6	9.0	4.1	3.9
3. 3-5	5.6	5.5	5.7	5.9	2.4	7.3	5.8	3.4	6.8	6.2	5.1	-	12.7	7.7	7.2	2.3
4. 6-9	4.4	4.9	3.7	4.1	4.6	5.3	4.3	3.8	4.8	4.2	4.8	-	12.1	5.4	4.1	6.7
5. 10-19	5.7	5.7	5.4	5.3	5.7	7.2	4.7	4.8	6.9	5.1	5.9	-	10.1	11.0	8.3	10.2
6. 20-39	5.0	5.4	4.4	5.3	3.5	6.6	4.2	4.3	5.7	4.5	4.9	-	5.4	10.2	11.7	11.6
7. 40 or more	15.6	20.8	9.6	15.4	8.8	18.3	16.8	13.2	14.0	11.0	17.5	-	9.0	18.8	51.3	58.0
Item 2080 N(Wtd)	2867	1353	1388	2263	299	677	900	855	435	1344	1238	1219	658	318	580	45

B019C: ...during the last 30 days?

1. 0 occasions	67.0	61.0	74.5	67.8	71.9	60.0	67.3	71.4	68.3	72.7	64.6	100.0	54.8	52.2	24.5	22.5
2. 1-2	8.0	8.1	7.8	7.8	9.7	8.6	7.3	8.2	8.3	8.3	7.7	-	20.8	10.5	8.7	4.1
3. 3-5	5.0	5.4	4.3	4.9	4.6	6.6	4.7	4.3	4.5	4.5	5.5	-	9.2	7.6	9.2	4.6
4. 6-9	4.9	5.7	4.2	5.0	4.0	7.0	4.8	4.0	3.5	4.5	5.3	-	7.4	8.1	10.0	7.2
5. 10-19	6.1	8.6	3.7	6.0	4.0	7.8	6.5	4.9	4.6	4.9	6.5	-	4.7	9.9	17.6	16.4
6. 20-39	4.7	5.4	3.5	4.7	2.4	4.8	4.9	3.7	6.3	2.6	5.8	-	1.3	8.7	15.9	10.8
7. 40 or more	4.3	5.6	2.1	3.7	3.5	5.1	4.4	3.4	4.4	2.6	4.6	-	1.9	3.0	14.1	34.3
Item 2090 N(Wtd)	2863	1351	1388	2258	303	674	897	858	434	1338	1239	1219	651	318	581	45

* = less than .05 per cent.

QUESTIONNAIRE FORM 1 1976	TOTAL	SEX		RACE		REGION				4YR COLLEGE PLANS		ILLICIT DRUG USE: LIFETIME				
		M	F	White	Black	NE	NC	S	W	Yes	No	None	Mari-juana Only	Few Pills	More Pills	Any Her-oin
Weighted No. of Cases:	3039	1426	1466	2356	338	715	950	919	454	1384	1321	1219	669	329	605	47
% of Weighted Total:	100.0	46.9	48.2	77.5	11.1	23.5	31.3	30.2	15.0	45.5	43.5	40.1	22.0	10.8	19.9	1.6

IF YOU HAVE NOT USED MARIJUANA OR HASHISH IN THE LAST TWELVE MONTHS, GO TO Q.B028.

B020: When you used marijuana or hashish during the last year, how often did you use it in each of the following situations?

B020A: When you were alone

	TOTAL	M	F	White	Black	NE	NC	S	W	Yes	No	None	Mari Only	Few Pills	More Pills	Any Heroin
1. Not at all	58.1	55.5	64.7	60.1	52.7	58.0	57.2	57.8	60.4	65.9	54.7	-	80.0	57.8	40.0	23.7
2. A few of the times	27.5	28.3	25.2	26.7	31.4	27.6	27.5	28.8	25.6	22.6	29.7	-	11.8	34.1	39.0	43.9
3. Some of the times	12.0	13.7	7.7	11.3	10.7	11.3	13.2	11.3	11.7	9.0	13.3	-	6.3	6.4	18.6	21.7
4. Most of the times	1.8	1.9	1.9	1.6	3.9	2.0	1.5	2.1	1.1	2.1	1.8	-	1.3	1.7	1.7	6.4
5. Every time	.6	.6	.6	.3	1.3	1.0	.5	-	1.1	.5	.5	-	.6	-	.7	4.3
Item 2100 N(Wtd) ★	1265	689	498	989	103	365	382	317	201	533	551	-	480	198	503	42

B020B: With just 1 or 2 other people

	TOTAL	M	F	White	Black	NE	NC	S	W	Yes	No	None	Mari Only	Few Pills	More Pills	Any Heroin
1. Not at all	5.9	6.9	4.7	6.2	5.2	4.8	7.4	4.0	8.3	8.9	4.1	-	9.6	5.5	2.7	2.0
2. A few of the times	25.3	23.4	29.7	24.9	35.3	24.6	24.2	28.2	24.2	27.4	23.6	-	34.3	27.4	16.0	21.4
3. Some of the times	24.9	25.1	22.7	23.8	23.1	28.9	26.7	19.5	22.7	19.6	29.2	-	18.7	23.0	31.2	27.9
4. Most of the times	34.5	36.0	32.3	35.8	24.3	31.9	32.0	39.2	36.4	34.6	33.3	-	23.5	38.1	43.8	37.7
5. Every time	9.4	8.6	10.6	9.3	12.1	9.8	9.6	9.1	8.5	9.4	9.9	-	13.9	5.9	6.2	11.0
Item 2110 N(Wtd) ★	1269	690	500	991	103	365	383	318	202	534	553	-	480	199	504	42

B020C: At a party

	TOTAL	M	F	White	Black	NE	NC	S	W	Yes	No	None	Mari Only	Few Pills	More Pills	Any Heroin
1. Not at all	18.8	17.6	22.2	20.1	20.2	18.3	14.6	26.6	15.2	21.8	17.4	-	31.8	14.3	9.5	5.0
2. A few of the times	19.7	20.4	19.2	19.4	28.4	19.6	18.6	21.4	19.6	23.3	17.7	-	22.8	22.7	15.0	16.7
3. Some of the times	22.3	23.6	19.5	22.8	15.6	21.5	23.9	19.7	25.2	24.1	19.9	-	20.1	16.6	27.8	13.7
4. Most of the times	21.2	18.6	24.1	20.6	21.4	22.3	23.3	15.8	23.9	17.1	24.5	-	17.2	23.1	23.9	25.4
5. Every time	17.9	19.8	15.0	17.1	14.4	18.3	19.6	16.4	16.1	13.7	20.5	-	8.1	23.3	23.8	39.1
Item 2120 N(Wtd) ★	1269	692	498	990	105	365	382	320	202	532	554	-	481	200	504	42

B020D: When your date or spouse was present

	TOTAL	M	F	White	Black	NE	NC	S	W	Yes	No	None	Mari Only	Few Pills	More Pills	Any Heroin
1. Not at all	39.2	47.6	30.0	40.7	40.4	36.5	36.4	44.4	41.2	48.1	34.2	-	56.7	45.1	22.5	13.8
2. A few of the times	21.5	20.7	22.1	19.8	26.6	21.2	24.6	17.9	22.0	21.7	20.2	-	19.1	19.5	23.5	25.8
3. Some of the times	17.4	16.7	17.5	17.1	17.3	21.5	16.6	14.1	16.5	14.7	19.0	-	12.5	18.0	21.4	23.8
4. Most of the times	15.1	11.7	19.0	15.6	9.3	16.0	15.3	15.3	12.8	11.1	18.4	-	6.3	14.9	23.7	16.1
5. Every time	6.8	3.2	11.4	6.9	6.4	4.8	7.1	8.1	7.4	4.4	8.1	-	5.4	2.5	9.0	20.5
Item 2130 N(Wtd) ★	1247	674	497	975	102	359	380	311	196	526	541	-	475	195	494	42

B020E: When people over age 30 were present

	TOTAL	M	F	White	Black	NE	NC	S	W	Yes	No	None	Mari Only	Few Pills	More Pills	Any Heroin
1. Not at all	67.1	67.6	69.5	68.7	65.5	67.4	69.9	64.4	65.7	74.3	64.3	-	82.8	71.2	53.0	36.4
2. A few of the times	21.3	23.0	18.1	20.6	19.9	20.6	21.3	22.9	20.4	16.1	23.4	-	10.4	18.2	33.3	22.7
3. Some of the times	8.8	7.3	9.2	8.1	10.4	9.2	7.5	9.0	10.2	7.3	9.2	-	4.5	7.5	11.1	34.8
4. Most of the times	1.8	1.3	2.3	1.7	2.7	1.8	.7	3.4	1.6	1.4	2.1	-	1.2	2.4	2.0	3.5
5. Every time	.9	.9	1.0	.8	1.5	1.0	.6	.4	2.0	.8	.9	-	1.1	.7	.6	2.6
Item 2140 N(Wtd) ★	1263	687	498	989	102	364	380	317	202	535	550	-	479	198	502	41

B020F: During the daytime (before 4:00 p.m.)

	TOTAL	M	F	White	Black	NE	NC	S	W	Yes	No	None	Mari Only	Few Pills	More Pills	Any Heroin
1. Not at all	28.9	29.3	30.6	30.5	27.5	28.2	29.7	28.4	29.4	35.9	25.8	-	45.8	30.1	12.5	9.5
2. A few of the times	28.0	27.4	30.2	27.3	36.5	25.4	29.8	27.9	29.4	29.0	28.4	-	32.6	30.2	24.2	17.7
3. Some of the times	31.1	30.4	29.8	30.8	25.2	32.0	31.3	32.5	26.8	25.3	34.1	-	15.4	29.6	46.2	44.9
4. Most of the times	8.4	8.3	7.1	8.1	7.6	10.5	6.6	7.3	9.9	6.8	7.7	-	3.4	7.7	12.5	19.3
5. Every time	3.6	4.7	2.2	3.4	3.2	3.8	2.5	3.9	4.5	3.1	4.0	-	2.8	2.3	4.5	8.6
Item 2150 N(Wtd) ★	1265	688	499	988	103	365	380	319	201	534	550	-	479	199	503	40

★ = excludes respondents for whom question was inappropriate.

QUESTIONNAIRE FORM 1 1976	TOTAL	SEX		RACE		REGION				4YR COLLEGE PLANS		ILLICIT DRUG USE: LIFETIME				
		M	F	White	Black	NE	NC	S	W	Yes	No	None	Marijuana Only	Few Pills	More Pills	Any Heroin
Weighted No. of Cases:	3039	1426	1466	2356	338	715	950	919	454	1384	1321	1219	669	329	605	47
% of Weighted Total:	100.0	46.9	48.2	77.5	11.1	23.5	31.3	30.2	15.0	45.5	43.5	40.1	22.0	10.8	19.9	1.6

B020G: At your home (or apartment or dorm)

1. Not at all	50.9	52.1	52.1	53.3	50.2	48.8	50.8	53.7	50.5	58.6	47.7	-	71.6	56.7	31.2	21.6
2. A few of the times	24.5	23.6	25.0	24.0	23.2	22.2	25.2	25.0	26.4	20.9	26.5	-	14.8	25.5	33.4	26.5
3. Some of the times	14.8	13.9	14.2	13.7	14.4	17.1	16.0	11.8	13.1	11.6	16.0	-	7.6	9.0	23.1	28.1
4. Most of the times	7.3	8.2	5.9	6.7	9.4	9.2	5.4	7.7	7.2	7.1	7.1	-	4.2	5.2	10.0	15.4
5. Every time	2.5	2.2	2.8	2.2	2.7	2.8	2.6	1.8	2.8	1.8	2.7	-	1.7	3.6	2.4	8.4
Item 2160 N(Wtd) ★	1268	690	499	990	104	366	381	319	202	535	552	-	481	199	504	42

B020H: At school

1. Not at all	52.4	48.5	60.8	54.6	54.1	50.4	53.5	53.8	51.8	61.5	49.1	-	74.4	53.1	32.9	23.9
2. A few of the times	20.7	21.0	21.0	21.0	16.9	16.8	23.7	23.2	18.2	18.8	22.7	-	14.0	23.6	26.4	18.3
3. Some of the times	16.8	18.5	11.8	15.3	18.3	20.9	15.3	12.6	18.9	11.7	18.4	-	7.8	13.4	25.1	36.7
4. Most of the times	7.9	9.5	4.8	7.3	7.9	8.5	5.6	9.4	8.6	6.0	7.7	-	2.6	7.7	13.0	13.0
5. Every time	2.3	2.5	1.6	1.8	2.9	3.5	1.9	1.1	2.6	1.9	2.2	-	1.2	2.2	2.6	8.0
Item 2170 N(Wtd) ★	1267	689	499	989	104	366	380	318	202	535	551	-	480	199	502	42

B020I: In a car

1. Not at all	13.9	14.1	14.5	14.1	15.9	15.3	13.2	9.6	19.5	18.5	11.1	-	22.9	15.4	4.9	11.1
2. A few of the times	21.6	20.5	24.5	20.7	34.4	21.6	18.6	25.1	22.1	23.9	22.2	-	29.9	23.8	13.5	12.5
3. Some of the times	27.2	26.3	26.4	25.4	29.5	31.7	29.8	19.0	27.1	25.4	25.5	-	22.8	21.9	34.3	15.9
4. Most of the times	30.1	30.4	30.1	32.4	14.3	26.6	31.6	34.4	26.6	26.8	33.7	-	16.6	33.3	40.9	43.2
5. Every time	7.2	8.7	4.5	7.4	5.9	4.9	6.8	11.8	4.6	5.4	8.4	-	7.9	5.6	6.5	17.2
Item 2190 N(Wtd) ★	1265	687	500	987	105	365	379	319	202	534	550	-	479	199	503	41

B021: How many of the times when you used marijuana or hashish during the last year did you use it along with alcohol--that is, so that their effects overlapped?

1. Not at all	28.7	26.1	33.9	26.7	48.2	29.0	26.6	33.9	23.8	31.3	28.3	-	44.0	28.1	15.1	14.9
2. A few of the times	25.7	24.0	27.6	26.4	25.0	29.0	22.9	25.1	25.9	28.6	22.8	-	28.7	26.2	22.7	12.7
3. Some of the times	24.4	25.9	21.2	24.3	12.9	24.4	26.7	20.0	27.1	21.8	25.5	-	13.6	22.0	35.1	38.1
4. Most of the times	16.6	18.1	14.2	17.8	10.9	12.7	19.0	16.7	18.6	12.3	19.8	-	8.2	19.3	22.9	31.6
5. Every time	4.6	5.9	3.1	4.8	3.0	4.9	4.8	4.2	4.6	5.9	3.6	-	5.5	4.4	4.2	2.7
Item 2200 N(Wtd) ★	1254	682	499	980	104	358	380	319	197	528	551	-	474	199	498	42

B022: What have been the most important reasons for your using marijuana or hashish? (Mark all that apply.)

A. To experiment--to see what it's like	63.6	60.6	68.5	63.7	66.0	66.3	65.5	62.2	57.0	66.4	62.7	-	76.4	62.5	52.7	39.0
B. To relax or relieve tension	39.2	39.4	38.0	40.0	25.6	36.5	40.7	38.6	42.2	35.5	42.3	-	24.0	37.0	54.9	50.8
C. To feel good or get high	77.9	79.9	74.5	78.7	63.8	77.1	81.8	73.2	79.2	75.8	79.2	-	67.5	78.3	89.0	89.2
D. To seek deeper insights and understanding	14.1	12.9	14.5	12.9	10.2	18.1	13.1	12.5	11.5	11.8	15.9	-	7.0	11.4	21.3	20.6
E. To have a good time with my friends	62.6	65.5	57.6	63.1	46.0	57.3	68.8	57.9	67.9	59.8	65.0	-	55.1	57.5	71.1	74.1
F. To fit in with a group I like	13.4	16.4	9.2	13.7	10.0	12.6	14.0	12.9	14.6	14.5	13.0	-	14.9	13.1	11.7	11.0
G. To get away from my problems or troubles	18.3	17.6	18.7	18.6	10.4	18.4	21.1	17.9	13.6	14.9	21.4	-	14.1	17.6	22.3	23.0
H. Because of boredom, nothing else to do	25.8	26.7	22.6	25.6	22.8	22.8	26.7	27.7	26.7	23.9	26.3	-	16.6	23.5	34.8	42.5
I. Because of anger or frustration	12.4	10.9	13.8	12.5	8.1	11.9	11.2	14.9	11.4	9.7	15.2	-	7.9	9.9	16.9	17.7
J. To get through the day	5.6	5.5	5.0	5.1	5.1	6.9	3.7	5.8	6.4	2.9	7.0	-	2.3	3.2	8.8	18.1
K. To increase the effects of some other drug(s)	10.9	11.7	7.9	10.6	6.5	10.3	12.7	9.0	11.6	9.9	10.9	-	3.7	6.4	18.6	29.2
L. To decrease (offset) the effects of some other drug(s)	1.5	1.9	.7	1.4	-	1.3	2.5	.2	2.1	1.4	1.4	-	.3	-	2.8	7.3
M. Because I am "hooked"--I have to have it	1.3	1.4	1.1	1.0	1.7	2.3	.6	.6	2.2	.6	1.6	-	-	2.0	1.7	7.4
Item 2210-2330 N(Wtd) ★	1265	693	498	989	106	363	382	320	200	532	554	-	480	199	502	41

★=excludes respondents for whom question was inappropriate.

QUESTIONNAIRE FORM 1 1976	TOTAL	SEX		RACE		REGION				4YR COLLEGE PLANS		ILLICIT DRUG USE: LIFETIME				
		M	F	White	Black	NE	NC	S	W	Yes	No	None	Mari- juana Only	Few Pills	More Pills	Any Her- oin
Weighted No. of Cases:	3039	1426	1466	2356	338	715	950	919	454	1384	1321	1219	669	329	605	47
% of Weighted Total:	100.0	46.9	48.2	77.5	11.1	23.5	31.3	30.2	15.0	45.5	43.5	40.1	22.0	10.8	19.9	1.6

B023: When you use marijuana or hashish how high do you usually get?

1. Not at all high	5.7	5.3	6.4	6.1	6.3	5.1	5.6	7.0	4.7	8.2	3.8	-	10.5	6.9	1.1	2.1
2. A little high	20.9	20.2	23.8	21.2	29.6	19.7	21.2	17.8	27.5	24.4	19.1	-	34.5	15.3	11.0	10.0
3. Moderately high	47.7	50.7	41.8	46.7	41.1	46.2	47.8	48.2	49.8	46.7	47.4	-	40.5	55.6	51.8	37.4
4. Very high	25.7	23.8	28.0	26.0	23.1	28.9	25.4	27.1	18.0	20.7	29.7	-	14.6	22.2	36.2	50.6
Item 2340 N(Wtd) ★	1266	690	502	992	103	366	380	321	199	535	551	-	479	202	501	41

B024: When you use marijuana or hashish how long do you usually stay high?

1. Usually don't get high	8.0	7.3	9.1	8.2	10.2	8.1	8.0	8.6	6.7	11.5	5.2	-	14.7	8.1	1.5	3.3
2. One to two hours	43.2	44.3	43.3	44.0	48.1	41.9	43.7	39.8	50.4	44.5	42.3	-	50.5	43.8	36.4	32.0
3. Three to six hours	43.7	43.1	42.6	42.9	35.6	46.7	43.6	44.2	37.4	40.6	46.3	-	32.4	43.7	54.7	49.4
4. Seven to 24 hours	4.9	5.1	4.7	4.7	6.1	3.2	4.7	7.1	4.7	3.3	5.7	-	2.1	4.4	7.2	13.2
5. More than 24 hours	.2	.2	.3	.2	-	.1	-	.3	.7	.1	.4	-	.3		.1	2.1
Item 2350 N(Wtd) ★	1261	691	495	984	106	363	376	324	199	532	549	-	479	199	498	42

B025: During the LAST MONTH, about how many marijuana cigarettes (joints, reefers), or the equivalent, did you smoke a day, on the average? (If you shared them with other people, count only the amount YOU smoked.)

1. None	30.4	26.8	37.8	32.8	20.6	29.7	27.5	30.6	37.3	37.8	26.6	-	45.8	30.6	16.4	17.7
2. Less than 1 a day	34.4	35.9	32.9	35.6	34.8	36.5	35.7	32.6	30.7	37.4	33.0	-	40.8	28.7	31.9	22.8
3. 1 a day	10.1	11.8	7.8	10.5	4.7	9.4	10.8	9.1	12.0	9.2	11.1	-	4.2	13.2	14.8	7.8
4. 2 - 3 a day	15.3	14.7	15.1	13.8	21.8	13.5	17.9	17.4	10.2	10.3	17.6	-	6.3	17.3	22.3	26.5
5. 4 - 6 a day	6.4	6.9	4.8	4.9	11.8	7.8	6.6	5.3	5.6	3.5	7.9	-	2.4	6.4	9.7	14.1
6. 7 - 10 a day	1.4	1.7	.5	1.0	2.2	1.3	1.0	1.7	1.5	.7	1.7	-	.4	.3	2.5	1.7
7. 11 or more a day	1.9	2.1	1.0	1.3	4.1	1.8	.5	3.3	2.6	1.1	2.1	-	.2	3.5	2.3	9.3
Item 2360 N(Wtd) ★	1213	658	482	954	98	353	362	310	188	508	531	-	454	189	487	43

B026: Do you know how much marijuana you have used (in ounces) during the LAST MONTH?

8. Don't know	20.9	15.0	28.5	19.4	31.9	20.9	20.0	23.8	18.0	18.6	24.0	-	20.9	17.6	22.0	14.3
1. None	27.7	25.3	32.6	29.4	18.9	28.3	24.1	27.5	33.4	32.2	25.1	-	42.5	26.5	14.7	16.2
2. Less than 1/2 ounce	16.0	17.7	14.3	17.5	14.8	20.3	15.4	14.4	11.5	20.5	13.4	-	19.8	18.6	12.3	8.3
3. About 1/2 ounce	8.4	9.7	6.7	8.3	12.3	8.2	8.1	11.0	5.1	9.2	7.6	-	7.2	10.6	9.4	2.1
4. About 1 ounce	10.0	12.3	7.6	9.5	6.1	10.3	9.6	8.4	12.9	8.7	10.0	-	3.8	9.8	15.7	16.7
5. About 2 ounces	9.2	11.7	5.1	9.1	5.3	7.0	13.3	7.0	9.4	6.0	11.3	-	3.3	11.5	13.9	15.2
6. 3 to 5 ounces	5.5	6.3	3.0	4.7	7.2	3.8	6.8	4.6	7.7	3.9	5.1	-	2.4	4.2	7.8	17.3
7. 6 or more ounces	2.3	2.0	2.1	2.1	3.6	1.1	2.7	3.3	1.9	.9	3.5	-	.1	1.1	4.1	9.9
Item 2370 N(Wtd) ★	1215	659	485	957	99	355	361	312	187	507	535	-	454	186	492	43

B027: Have you ever tried to stop using marijuana or hashish and found that you couldn't stop?

1. Yes	3.4	3.8	2.2	2.9	5.4	2.4	3.3	4.3	4.2	2.5	4.0	-	3.4	3.7	3.3	5.5
2. No	96.6	96.2	97.8	97.0	94.6	97.6	96.7	95.7	95.8	97.5	96.0	-	96.6	96.3	96.7	94.5
Item 2380 N(Wtd) ★	1259	687	502	992	105	363	380	319	197	529	556	-	479	195	502	42

B028: Do you think you will be using marijuana or hashish five years from now?

1. I definitely will	5.1	6.7	3.0	5.1	2.1	6.8	5.5	3.6	4.6	3.8	5.6	.3	2.4	8.2	15.2	24.5
2. I probably will	20.5	23.7	16.4	19.9	18.8	25.4	18.6	18.4	21.0	17.5	21.1	1.2	24.0	32.6	47.3	47.3
3. I probably will not	21.3	23.2	19.2	21.5	17.8	26.0	21.6	17.0	21.7	22.0	20.4	13.0	35.5	24.1	19.9	14.5
4. I definitely will not	53.2	46.5	61.4	53.5	61.3	41.8	54.2	60.9	52.7	56.8	52.9	85.4	38.1	35.1	17.7	13.7
Item 2390 N(Wtd)	2932	1392	1423	2291	331	679	921	889	443	1346	1292	1179	657	319	591	47

★ = excludes respondents for whom question was inappropriate.

QUESTIONNAIRE FORM 1 1976	TOTAL	SEX		RACE		REGION				4YR COLLEGE PLANS		ILLICIT DRUG USE: LIFETIME				
		M	F	White	Black	NE	NC	S	W	Yes	No	None	Mari-juana Only	Few Pills	More Pills	Any Her-oin
Weighted No. of Cases:	3039	1426	1466	2356	338	715	950	919	454	1384	1321	1219	669	329	605	47
% of Weighted Total:	100.0	46.9	48.2	77.5	11.1	23.5	31.3	30.2	15.0	45.5	43.5	40.1	22.0	10.8	19.9	1.6

The next questions are about LSD, the psychedelic drug which is sometimes called "acid".

B029: On how many occasions (if any) have you taken LSD...

B029A: ...in your lifetime?

	TOTAL	M	F	White	Black	NE	NC	S	W	Yes	No	None	Mari-juana Only	Few Pills	More Pills	Any Her-oin
1. 0 occasions	88.7	87.7	91.3	88.8	97.7	87.0	87.9	91.1	88.1	92.2	87.9	100.0	100.0	90.1	55.7	30.9
2. 1-2	5.0	5.2	4.3	5.1	.7	5.5	4.6	4.5	6.1	3.5	5.6	-	-	9.9	17.9	16.4
3. 3-5	2.5	3.3	1.6	2.5	1.5	3.4	3.2	1.7	1.0	2.1	2.4	-	-	-	11.2	11.8
4. 6-9	1.4	1.5	1.3	1.6	-	1.4	1.3	1.4	1.7	1.2	1.5	-	-	-	6.5	4.6
5. 10-19	1.0	1.0	.7	.9	.2	1.3	1.2	.5	1.6	.5	1.1	-	-	-	4.0	14.3
6. 20-39	.7	.7	.4	.5	-	.8	1.0	.2	.7	.3	.6	-	-	-	2.6	8.8
7. 40 or more	.6	.6	.4	.6	-	.6	.7	.6	.7	.1	.9	-	-	-	2.1	13.2
Item 890　N(Wtd)	2874	1360	1397	2265	311	672	908	864	430	1340	1249	1210	662	321	588	47

B029B: ...during the last 12 months?

	TOTAL	M	F	White	Black	NE	NC	S	W	Yes	No	None	Mari-juana Only	Few Pills	More Pills	Any Her-oin
1. 0 occasions	93.1	91.9	95.7	93.5	98.9	92.0	91.3	96.0	93.0	95.4	93.3	100.0	100.0	96.5	71.8	54.5
2. 1-2	4.5	5.4	2.8	4.3	.6	5.2	5.5	3.1	3.9	3.4	3.7	-	-	3.5	18.5	20.4
3. 3-5	1.3	1.5	1.0	1.3	.4	1.5	1.4	.8	2.0	.8	1.8	-	-	-	5.5	13.3
4. 6-9	.7	.7	.4	.6	-	.9	1.3	.1	.2	.3	.8	-	-	-	2.8	7.6
5. 10-19	.2	.2	.1	.2	-	.2	.2	*	.4	.1	.2	-	-	-	.9	-
6. 20-39	.1	*	.1	.1	-	.1	.1	-	.2	-	.1	-	-	-	.3	1.3
7. 40 or more	.1	.2	-	.1	-	.1	.1	-	.2	.1	.2	-	-	-	.2	3.0
Item 900　N(Wtd)	2867	1356	1394	2260	311	670	903	863	430	1339	1245	1210	662	320	582	47

B029C: ...during the last 30 days?

	TOTAL	M	F	White	Black	NE	NC	S	W	Yes	No	None	Mari-juana Only	Few Pills	More Pills	Any Her-oin
1. 0 occasions	98.3	97.7	99.1	98.3	99.1	98.0	97.4	99.3	98.4	98.8	98.1	100.0	100.0	98.8	93.6	80.3
2. 1-2	1.3	1.6	.9	1.3	.9	1.6	1.9	.6	.9	.9	1.6	-	-	1.2	4.8	13.0
3. 3-5	.3	.4	*	.2	-	.2	.6	*	.3	.2	*	-	-	-	1.2	2.5
4. 6-9	-	-	-	-	-	-	-	-	-	-	-	-	-	-	-	-
5. 10-19	.1	.1	*	.1	-	.2	-	-	.2	.1	.1	-	-	-	.3	2.1
6. 20-39	-	-	-	-	-	-	-	-	-	-	-	-	-	-	-	-
7. 40 or more	.1	.1	-	*	-	-	.1	-	.2	-	.1	-	-	-	.1	2.1
Item 910　N(Wtd)	2864	1354	1393	2257	311	668	903	863	429	1339	1242	1210	662	320	578	47

If you have not taken LSD in the last TWELVE MONTHS, GO TO Q.B037.

B030: When you used LSD during the last year, how often did you use it in each of the following situations?

B030A: When you were alone

	TOTAL	M	F	White	Black	NE	NC	S	W	Yes	No	None	Mari-juana Only	Few Pills	More Pills	Any Her-oin
1. Not at all	84.3	84.0	88.7	89.4	100.0	77.5	84.5	90.2	88.7	87.4	84.2	-	-	100.0	84.7	70.7
2. A few of the times	11.0	10.3	9.3	7.1	-	16.3	9.7	9.8	6.4	12.6	9.0	-	-	-	12.2	9.5
3. Some of the times	1.6	1.6	1.0	.4	-	1.8	2.0	-	2.1	-	1.6	-	-	-	.5	11.2
4. Most of the times	2.5	3.0	1.1	2.7	-	4.4	2.3	-	2.7	-	3.8	-	-	-	2.3	5.6
5. Every time	.6	1.1	-	.4	-	-	1.5	-	-	-	1.4	-	-	-	.3	3.1
Item 2400　N(Wtd) ★	196	110	62	148	3	53	79	36	28	61	85	-	-	12	161	21

B030B: With just 1 or 2 other people

	TOTAL	M	F	White	Black	NE	NC	S	W	Yes	No	None	Mari-juana Only	Few Pills	More Pills	Any Her-oin
1. Not at all	18.9	19.1	23.5	19.9	29.0	21.8	24.3	13.0	5.9	17.9	21.7	-	-	24.1	19.8	2.7
2. A few of the times	34.5	31.6	41.2	34.6	27.4	39.3	30.3	38.0	32.7	38.3	31.1	-	-	29.7	34.8	37.1
3. Some of the times	13.4	14.5	8.4	9.6	26.7	15.1	12.6	11.3	15.1	5.0	17.1	-	-	13.3	11.5	29.7
4. Most of the times	11.0	10.5	8.7	11.2	-	6.4	10.1	10.4	23.3	10.0	9.8	-	-	-	12.0	11.0
5. Every time	22.2	24.3	18.2	24.7	16.9	17.4	22.7	27.3	23.0	28.8	20.4	-	-	32.9	22.0	19.4
Item 2410　N(Wtd) ★	199	112	62	151	3	53	80	37	28	63	85	-	-	12	164	21

* = less than .05 per cent.　　★ = excludes respondents for whom question was inappropriate.

QUESTIONNAIRE FORM 1 1976	TOTAL	SEX		RACE		REGION				4YR COLLEGE PLANS		ILLICIT DRUG USE: LIFETIME				
		M	F	White	Black	NE	NC	S	W	Yes	No	None	Marijuana Only	Few Pills	More Pills	Any Heroin
Weighted No. of Cases:	3039	1426	1466	2356	338	715	950	919	454	1384	1321	1219	669	329	605	47
% of Weighted Total:	100.0	46.9	48.2	77.5	11.1	23.5	31.3	30.2	15.0	45.5	43.5	40.1	22.0	10.8	19.9	1.6
B030C: At a party																
1. Not at all	43.2	47.7	38.4	48.0	45.9	44.1	37.1	52.1	46.8	54.9	37.5	-	-	80.4	43.1	17.5
2. A few of the times	26.3	18.9	33.8	20.3	27.4	32.0	22.2	22.3	31.9	25.9	20.5	-	-	6.7	27.2	32.8
3. Some of the times	15.1	16.2	11.5	15.2	-	10.7	17.2	20.9	10.7	8.0	21.2	-	-	-	15.1	25.2
4. Most of the times	7.5	9.1	7.5	8.5	-	6.9	9.9	2.0	8.7	7.5	8.3	-	-	6.1	6.2	18.8
5. Every time	7.9	8.2	8.9	8.0	26.7	6.3	13.6	2.7	1.9	3.6	12.5	-	-	6.8	8.3	5.8
Item 2420 N(Wtd) ★	195	110	61	147	3	53	78	36	29	62	83	-	-	12	161	21
B030D: When your date or spouse was present																
1. Not at all	55.4	67.9	37.0	57.1	45.9	65.2	48.9	57.9	52.4	57.3	49.0	-	-	86.5	53.3	49.7
2. A few of the times	22.5	19.0	27.6	21.4	27.4	18.1	22.5	26.2	25.7	20.8	23.2	-	-	6.7	24.4	19.5
3. Some of the times	8.1	6.3	10.9	7.7	-	4.6	12.3	4.3	7.1	9.3	8.6	-	-	-	6.7	23.8
4. Most of the times	4.9	2.8	5.2	2.8	26.7	5.9	5.2	2.0	5.9	2.1	5.3	-	-	6.8	4.7	5.2
5. Every time	9.2	3.9	19.3	11.0	-	6.2	11.0	9.5	8.9	10.4	13.8	-	-	-	11.0	1.7
Item 2430 N(Wtd) ★	191	107	59	143	3	51	78	35	28	62	80	-	-	12	157	21
B030E: When people over age 30 were present																
1. Not at all	72.9	75.8	71.9	74.2	45.9	74.0	76.3	69.5	65.7	73.4	74.3	-	-	88.1	72.3	66.3
2. A few of the times	19.1	16.4	22.1	18.1	54.1	17.3	16.7	22.7	24.6	17.5	17.9	-	-	11.9	20.0	18.1
3. Some of the times	4.5	4.4	5.1	4.7	-	6.4	4.1	2.0	5.3	4.6	4.8	-	-	-	4.5	7.5
4. Most of the times	2.0	1.7	.9	1.8	-	1.0	1.7	5.9	-	3.1	1.5	-	-	-	1.8	5.4
5. Every time	1.5	1.6	-	1.2	-	1.3	1.1	-	4.5	1.4	1.5	-	-	-	1.4	2.7
Item 2440 N(Wtd) ★	195	110	60	147	3	53	78	36	28	62	83	-	-	12	160	21
B030F: During the daytime (before 4:00 p.m.)																
1. Not at all	40.1	44.8	36.4	39.4	55.8	46.0	41.2	48.9	16.0	40.2	44.8	-	-	93.2	37.5	25.2
2. A few of the times	33.5	30.8	35.7	35.3	-	33.2	39.1	19.4	35.6	33.8	27.8	-	-	6.8	34.4	44.5
3. Some of the times	12.2	11.1	11.3	9.6	44.2	9.6	9.7	11.4	24.2	8.1	13.8	-	-	-	11.4	26.0
4. Most of the times	8.3	7.0	10.3	9.2	-	9.0	6.6	8.2	12.1	10.3	7.0	-	-	-	10.1	-
5. Every time	5.9	6.3	6.3	6.4	-	2.2	3.4	12.1	12.1	7.7	6.5	-	-	-	6.7	4.3
Item 2450 N(Wtd) ★	197	110	62	148	3	53	79	36	29	62	85	-	-	12	163	21
B030G: At your home (or apartment or dorm)																
1. Not at all	54.8	57.3	57.7	55.7	72.6	56.7	60.2	48.1	45.1	55.1	54.4	-	-	83.4	54.8	36.2
2. A few of the times	29.3	26.0	29.5	27.7	27.4	29.6	24.3	39.6	29.6	31.7	27.3	-	-	16.6	29.9	33.9
3. Some of the times	10.0	9.5	8.9	10.7	-	9.5	8.4	7.7	18.2	10.0	9.7	-	-	-	9.8	17.2
4. Most of the times	3.2	3.6	2.4	2.7	-	2.5	4.3	2.3	2.5	1.0	5.0	-	-	-	2.6	10.0
5. Every time	2.7	3.6	1.4	3.3	-	1.7	2.7	2.4	4.6	2.2	3.6	-	-	-	2.8	2.8
Item 2460 N(Wtd) ★	192	109	59	145	3	52	77	36	27	63	81	-	-	11	160	20
B030H: At school																
1. Not at all	64.6	66.9	67.3	68.1	55.8	63.6	63.9	76.3	53.1	62.8	66.8	-	-	93.2	64.8	47.8
2. A few of the times	25.0	24.9	20.5	22.5	44.2	33.8	22.6	14.9	28.1	25.9	21.5	-	-	6.8	26.7	25.8
3. Some of the times	8.3	6.1	9.8	7.7	-	2.5	10.5	4.8	17.5	10.6	7.3	-	-	-	7.3	21.6
4. Most of the times	.3	.5	-	.4	-	-	.7	-	-	-	.6	-	-	-	.3	-
5. Every time	1.9	1.6	2.4	1.3	-	-	2.3	4.0	1.3	.7	3.8	-	-	-	.7	4.8
Item 2470 N(Wtd) ★	195	110	61	148	3	53	78	37	28	62	84	-	-	12	160	21
B030I: In a car																
1. Not at all	52.9	55.3	55.7	52.2	55.8	69.7	45.5	46.1	49.8	54.0	55.5	-	-	84.5	50.7	47.0
2. A few of the times	26.9	25.7	25.3	27.6	44.2	21.6	27.2	34.5	26.8	26.9	23.9	-	-	6.5	28.9	26.3
3. Some of the times	12.3	10.4	11.5	11.9	-	7.3	15.4	9.5	16.1	8.6	11.9	-	-	-	12.3	20.3
4. Most of the times	4.3	3.1	6.3	4.2	-	1.3	7.0	1.8	5.3	1.3	7.1	-	-	-	4.7	3.8
5. Every time	3.7	5.4	1.3	4.1	-	-	4.8	8.1	2.0	9.2	1.6	-	-	9.0	3.4	2.7
Item 2490 N(Wtd) ★	191	107	60	144	3	52	78	33	28	61	83	-	-	12	157	21

★ = excludes respondents for whom question was inappropriate.

QUESTIONNAIRE FORM 1 1976	TOTAL	SEX		RACE		REGION				4YR COLLEGE PLANS		ILLICIT DRUG USE: LIFETIME				
		M	F	White	Black	NE	NC	S	W	Yes	No	None	Mari-juana Only	Few Pills	More Pills	Any Her-oin
Weighted No. of Cases:	3039	1426	1466	2356	338	715	950	919	454	1384	1321	1219	669	329	605	47
% of Weighted Total:	100.0	46.9	48.2	77.5	11.1	23.5	31.3	30.2	15.0	45.5	43.5	40.1	22.0	10.8	19.9	1.6

B031: How many of the times when you used LSD during the last year did you use it along with each of the following drugs--that is, so that their effects overlapped?

B031A: With alcohol

	TOTAL	M	F	White	Black	NE	NC	S	W	Yes	No	None	Mari Only	Few Pills	More Pills	Heroin
1. Not at all	47.9	43.8	58.9	46.9	100.0	44.1	43.6	60.6	51.2	56.1	43.1	-	-	74.5	49.7	13.0
2. A few of the times	22.2	22.4	23.7	22.7	-	31.4	15.7	19.8	25.8	17.7	25.4	-	-	-	23.2	28.9
3. Some of the times	9.8	10.3	9.4	10.1	-	3.7	15.9	4.4	11.2	9.3	12.6	-	-	6.5	6.8	37.9
4. Most of the times	7.0	8.0	2.3	5.9	-	11.6	7.1	3.7	2.0	2.7	7.1	-	-	-	7.4	7.7
5. Every time	13.1	15.5	5.7	14.4	-	9.3	17.7	11.5	9.8	14.1	11.8	-	-	19.1	12.9	12.5
Item 2500　N(Wtd) ★	191	108	59	146	2	52	77	34	29	62	80	-	-	11	159	19

B031B: With marijuana

	TOTAL	M	F	White	Black	NE	NC	S	W	Yes	No	None	Mari Only	Few Pills	More Pills	Heroin
1. Not at all	21.3	21.6	22.4	20.9	83.1	25.1	16.4	29.3	16.9	18.7	25.1	-	-	47.1	19.3	16.2
2. A few of the times	30.2	26.8	38.7	29.2	-	39.3	29.6	23.5	23.2	38.8	21.9	-	-	15.0	33.0	18.1
3. Some of the times	9.5	11.1	8.0	10.2	-	4.6	10.8	4.2	21.6	6.4	10.2	-	-	6.6	9.1	14.9
4. Most of the times	13.3	12.3	11.4	12.5	-	16.1	17.1	-	15.0	10.0	14.8	-	-	-	13.0	24.4
5. Every time	25.8	28.2	19.6	27.1	16.9	14.8	26.1	42.9	23.4	26.0	28.1	-	-	31.3	25.6	26.4
Item 2510　N(Wtd) ★	197	112	61	150	3	53	78	37	29	63	83	-	-	11	163	21

B032: What have been the most important reasons for your taking LSD? (Mark all that apply.)

	TOTAL	M	F	White	Black	NE	NC	S	W	Yes	No	None	Mari Only	Few Pills	More Pills	Heroin
A. To experiment--to see what it's like	83.7	84.4	88.5	86.6	37.7	87.3	83.1	71.9	92.4	92.1	84.4	-	-	90.1	83.4	80.2
B. To relax or relieve tension	6.3	6.5	6.8	6.1	-	6.0	4.2	7.5	11.1	6.6	7.1	-	-	-	4.5	21.5
C. To feel good or get high	64.6	62.0	69.1	65.1	76.3	65.8	68.2	66.7	50.3	59.7	65.8	-	-	56.6	64.7	74.8
D. To seek deeper insights and understanding	25.3	21.2	24.5	23.9	23.7	34.4	20.0	18.7	30.8	29.7	20.7	-	-	9.9	24.9	39.6
E. To have a good time with my friends	40.9	34.2	50.1	41.0	37.7	37.3	46.6	38.1	35.8	39.0	47.6	-	-	34.1	40.3	54.3
F. To fit in with a group I like	4.8	7.1	1.9	4.6	-	4.1	8.8	-	1.2	5.0	5.1	-	-	-	4.7	9.1
G. To get away from my problems or troubles	10.9	11.6	13.7	10.2	-	11.6	11.7	11.0	7.6	14.1	10.6	-	-	-	9.4	30.3
H. Because of boredom, nothing else to do	15.9	20.3	9.5	17.2	23.7	17.1	11.2	19.2	22.3	16.5	17.1	-	-	9.9	14.4	32.9
I. Because of anger or frustration	8.6	7.1	11.2	9.5	-	9.9	6.2	11.1	9.5	9.9	10.8	-	-	9.9	7.8	15.1
J. To get through the day	3.3	3.1	4.3	3.1	-	4.3	2.4	-	7.5	.9	5.9	-	-	-	2.1	15.0
K. To increase the effects of some other drug(s)	7.2	7.6	7.3	6.5	-	8.6	5.9	3.1	13.0	9.1	9.1	-	-	9.9	5.8	18.2
L. To decrease (offset) the effects of some other drug(s)	1.5	2.1	.9	.5	-	2.8	.9	-	2.3	.9	1.7	-	-	-	.9	7.3
M. Because I am "hooked"--I have to have it	1.9	1.5	1.9	.9	-	2.8	.8	-	5.5	.9	2.0	-	-	-	.8	12.0
Item 2520-2640　N(Wtd) ★	196	110	60	149	2	53	78	35	30	61	84	-	-	11	163	20

B033: When you take LSD how high do you usually get?

	TOTAL	M	F	White	Black	NE	NC	S	W	Yes	No	None	Mari Only	Few Pills	More Pills	Heroin
1. Not at all high	1.7	.9	3.1	2.0	-	.8	2.6	2.8	-	-	2.3	-	-	-	2.1	-
2. A little high	1.9	3.0	-	1.8	-	3.0	1.6	-	3.2	-	1.9	-	-	20.2	.9	-
3. Moderately high	22.4	19.9	28.0	20.6	37.7	20.8	24.4	22.2	20.2	25.0	23.4	-	-	44.9	21.0	21.2
4. Very high	73.9	76.3	68.9	75.6	62.3	75.4	71.5	75.0	76.5	75.0	72.4	-	-	34.9	76.0	78.8
Item 2650　N(Wtd) ★	193	107	63	147	2	53	77	34	29	61	84	-	-	11	161	21

B034: When you take LSD how long do you usually stay high?

	TOTAL	M	F	White	Black	NE	NC	S	W	Yes	No	None	Mari Only	Few Pills	More Pills	Heroin
1. Usually don't get high	2.3	1.4	3.1	2.0	-	.8	3.3	2.8	1.9	-	3.0	-	-	-	2.7	-
2. One to two hours	1.7	2.4	1.0	2.0	-	4.1	.8	-	1.3	-	1.2	-	-	25.9	.2	-
3. Three to six hours	30.7	35.7	22.9	27.5	23.7	34.0	29.2	24.9	35.3	33.4	26.3	-	-	25.0	31.5	26.9
4. Seven to 24 hours	59.9	55.0	68.2	64.0	76.3	55.5	61.6	64.9	57.4	61.4	64.5	-	-	49.1	61.5	53.2
5. More than 24 hours	5.5	5.4	4.8	4.6	-	5.5	5.1	7.4	4.2	5.2	5.0	-	-	-	4.0	19.9
Item 2660　N(Wtd) ★	193	106	63	146	2	54	77	34	28	62	82	-	-	11	161	21

★=excludes respondents for whom question was inappropriate.

QUESTIONNAIRE FORM 1 1976	TOTAL	SEX		RACE		REGION				4YR COLLEGE PLANS		ILLICIT DRUG USE: LIFETIME				
		M	F	White	Black	NE	NC	S	W	Yes	No	None	Mari-juana Only	Few Pills	More Pills	Any Her-oin
Weighted No. of Cases:	3039	1426	1466	2356	338	715	950	919	454	1384	1321	1219	669	329	605	47
% of Weighted Total:	100.0	46.9	48.2	77.5	11.1	23.5	31.3	30.2	15.0	45.5	43.5	40.1	22.0	10.8	19.9	1.6
B035: Have you ever had a "bad trip" on LSD?																
1. No	70.4	68.7	73.3	71.5	56.4	69.0	74.0	69.3	64.8	72.5	71.6	-	-	83.6	71.5	51.5
2. Yes, once	21.3	24.6	13.9	20.7	16.9	19.6	17.2	29.5	24.9	21.9	15.4	-	-	9.9	21.5	27.9
3. Yes, more than once	8.3	6.6	12.8	7.9	26.7	11.4	8.8	1.2	10.4	5.6	12.9	-	-	6.6	7.0	20.7
Item 2670 N(Wtd) ★	199	112	63	152	3	54	78	37	30	63	85	-	-	13	164	21
B036: Have you ever tried to stop using LSD and found that you couldn't stop?																
1. Yes	2.8	1.7	4.2	1.6	-	2.5	3.1	2.0	3.3	3.2	3.3	-	-	-	1.5	14.3
2. No	97.2	98.3	95.8	98.4	100.0	97.5	96.9	98.0	96.7	96.8	96.7	-	-	100.0	98.5	85.7
Item 2680 N(Wtd) ★	194	107	63	147	2	54	77	35	29	63	83	-	-	13	160	21
B037: Do you think you will be using LSD five years from now?																
1. I definitely will	.7	.7	.6	.6	.8	.8	1.0	.2	.8	.6	.7	.6	.6	.2	.9	4.6
2. I probably will	2.0	2.5	1.4	2.1	.5	2.9	2.0	1.4	2.0	1.2	2.3	-	1.0	1.1	7.6	11.7
3. I probably will not	10.9	12.3	8.3	10.6	8.3	12.8	10.3	11.4	8.6	9.6	10.7	4.1	6.8	15.2	27.5	29.7
4. I definitely will not	86.4	84.6	89.7	86.7	90.4	83.5	86.7	87.0	88.6	88.5	86.3	95.3	91.6	83.5	64.0	54.0
Item 2690 N(Wtd)	2797	1311	1379	2189	321	632	880	857	428	1292	1238	1178	606	302	550	45

The next questions are about PSYCHEDELICS OTHER THAN LSD.

This group would include the following drugs: mescaline, peyote, psilocybin, PCP.

B038: On how many occasions (if any) have you taken psychedelics other than LSD...

B038A: ...in your lifetime?

	TOTAL	M	F	White	Black	NE	NC	S	W	Yes	No	None	Mari-juana Only	Few Pills	More Pills	Any Her-oin
1. 0 occasions	86.3	84.3	89.4	86.5	95.1	84.2	86.0	88.4	85.8	91.1	83.4	100.0	100.0	85.7	46.2	26.6
2. 1-2	5.4	6.1	4.6	5.6	2.1	7.9	4.7	3.9	6.4	4.1	6.7	-	-	14.3	18.1	9.8
3. 3-5	2.7	2.7	2.5	2.6	.7	2.5	2.5	2.8	3.2	1.8	3.2	-	-	-	12.3	10.7
4. 6-9	1.4	2.0	.8	1.4	1.5	1.6	1.1	1.7	1.4	1.0	1.7	-	-	-	6.8	2.8
5. 10-19	1.5	1.8	1.2	1.6	.3	1.4	2.3	1.0	1.2	.6	2.0	-	-	-	6.6	12.5
6. 20-39	1.1	1.2	.8	.9	.2	1.3	1.1	.8	1.3	1.0	.7	-	-	-	3.8	19.7
7. 40 or more	1.5	1.9	.8	1.4	.2	1.2	2.2	1.4	.8	.3	2.3	-	-	-	6.1	18.0
Item 920 N(Wtd)	2800	1328	1366	2217	301	644	885	851	420	1319	1214	1202	634	310	572	43

B038B: ...during the last 12 months?

	TOTAL	M	F	White	Black	NE	NC	S	W	Yes	No	None	Mari-juana Only	Few Pills	More Pills	Any Her-oin
1. 0 occasions	91.7	89.5	94.7	91.9	97.4	91.8	90.7	93.0	90.9	95.0	89.8	100.0	100.0	94.9	65.2	46.4
2. 1-2	4.3	5.4	2.9	4.3	1.4	4.6	4.2	3.4	5.8	3.0	5.3	-	-	5.1	17.8	9.0
3. 3-5	1.6	1.9	1.1	1.5	1.0	1.7	2.2	.9	1.4	.8	1.9	-	-	-	6.7	14.2
4. 6-9	1.1	1.1	.9	1.1	-	.9	1.3	1.1	.9	.5	1.5	-	-	-	4.6	10.0
5. 10-19	.8	1.1	.1	.5	-	.4	1.0	.9	.3	.6	.3	-	-	-	2.6	14.3
6. 20-39	.3	.5	.1	.3	-	.1	.3	.4	.4	.1	.5	-	-	-	1.4	1.3
7. 40 or more	.4	.5	.2	.3	.2	.5	.4	.4	.3	*	.7	-	-	-	1.7	4.8
Item 930 N(Wtd)	2781	1318	1357	2202	300	638	878	844	420	1314	1204	1202	634	306	556	43

B038C: ...during the last 30 days?

	TOTAL	M	F	White	Black	NE	NC	S	W	Yes	No	None	Mari-juana Only	Few Pills	More Pills	Any Her-oin
1. 0 occasions	96.7	95.7	98.3	97.1	98.3	97.4	96.0	96.6	97.3	98.5	95.9	100.0	100.0	99.6	86.5	65.0
2. 1-2	2.3	3.1	1.2	2.1	1.5	1.6	3.0	2.3	1.8	1.1	2.9	-	-	.4	9.8	19.9
3. 3-5	.4	.4	.2	.3	-	.3	.5	.3	.4	.2	.4	-	-	-	1.3	6.7
4. 6-9	.3	.5	.1	.3	-	.4	.2	.4	.2	.1	.3	-	-	-	1.1	4.0
5. 10-19	.1	.1	.2	.2	-	.2	.1	.2	-	*	.2	-	-	-	.6	1.2
6. 20-39	.1	.1	*	*	.2	.1	-	.2	.1	*	.1	-	-	-	.4	.9
7. 40 or more	.1	.1	-	*	-	-	.1	-	.3	-	.1	-	-	-	.2	2.3
Item 940 N(Wtd)	2781	1319	1357	2203	300	638	879	844	420	1314	1204	1202	634	306	557	43

★ = excludes respondents for whom question was inappropriate.   * = less than .05 per cent.

QUESTIONNAIRE FORM 1 1976	TOTAL	SEX		RACE		REGION				4YR COLLEGE PLANS		ILLICIT DRUG USE: LIFETIME				
		M	F	White	Black	NE	NC	S	W	Yes	No	None	Marijuana Only	Few Pills	More Pills	Any Heroin
Weighted No. of Cases:	3039	1426	1466	2356	338	715	950	919	454	1384	1321	1219	669	329	605	47
% of Weighted Total:	100.0	46.9	48.2	77.5	11.1	23.5	31.3	30.2	15.0	45.5	43.5	40.1	22.0	10.8	19.9	1.6

IF YOU HAVE NOT TAKEN ANY PSYCHEDELICS OTHER THAN LSD IN THE LAST TWELVE MONTHS, GO TO Q.B042.

B039: When you take psychedelics other than LSD how high do you usually get?

	TOTAL	M	F	White	Black	NE	NC	S	W	Yes	No	None	Mar	Few	More	Any
1. Not at all high	1.2	1.2	.9	1.3	-	1.9	1.3	-	1.6	-	1.9	-	-	-	1.1	-
2. A little high	9.6	8.9	11.7	11.2	-	11.0	7.2	6.3	17.8	8.8	10.6	-	-	42.7	7.6	2.7
3. Moderately high	39.6	37.6	44.7	40.6	37.8	36.4	44.7	40.0	32.4	42.8	41.7	-	-	14.3	41.7	41.1
4. Very high	49.7	52.4	42.7	47.0	62.2	50.7	46.9	53.7	48.1	48.4	45.8	-	-	43.0	49.6	56.2
Item 2700 N(Wtd) ★	237	142	72	183	8	55	83	60	38	69	120	-	-	17	196	23

B040: When you take psychedelics other than LSD how long do you usually stay high?

	TOTAL	M	F	White	Black	NE	NC	S	W	Yes	No	None	Mar	Few	More	Any
1. Usually don't get high	1.2	1.2	.8	1.2	-	1.9	1.3	-	1.6	-	1.9	-	-	-	1.1	-
2. One to two hours	9.4	9.9	11.5	11.9	-	8.1	8.8	10.4	11.2	10.1	10.6	-	-	27.9	8.9	-
3. Three to six hours	46.1	46.5	45.4	47.5	51.3	50.1	41.5	52.3	40.8	52.8	44.4	-	-	33.0	46.7	51.8
4. Seven to 24 hours	39.9	39.2	39.9	37.5	38.8	36.0	46.7	33.3	40.9	34.8	40.3	-	-	39.1	40.5	36.1
5. More than 24 hours	3.4	3.2	2.3	1.8	9.9	3.9	1.7	4.1	5.5	2.3	2.8	-	-	-	2.8	12.1
Item 2710 N(Wtd) ★	238	141	73	185	8	55	84	60	38	68	121	-	-	17	198	22

B041: What psychedelics other than LSD have you taken during the last year? (Mark all that apply.)

	TOTAL	M	F	White	Black	NE	NC	S	W	Yes	No	None	Mar	Few	More	Any
A. Mescaline	60.5	58.5	65.9	61.7	77.5	52.2	69.1	59.8	54.7	52.0	64.3	-	-	35.2	60.7	77.2
B. Peyote	22.4	20.2	22.8	21.8	13.5	15.1	27.8	18.7	26.3	20.4	22.0	-	-	23.0	23.0	33.0
C. Psilocybin	19.9	19.3	19.3	19.6	-	13.9	13.4	25.6	34.2	28.7	12.9	-	-	23.4	19.3	22.6
D. PCP	34.4	35.2	25.7	30.4	54.5	40.4	26.1	43.1	31.0	28.9	31.9	-	-	12.3	37.2	26.9
E. Concentrated THC	65.3	67.0	61.7	67.6	45.5	83.8	67.9	64.1	34.6	60.7	64.6	-	-	56.6	64.5	78.2
F. Other	39.8	39.8	36.7	40.4	7.2	34.5	50.2	38.9	25.6	35.9	40.6	-	-	10.3	41.2	49.5
G. Don't know the names of some I have used	14.6	10.9	20.2	13.1	6.3	12.9	15.2	15.8	13.5	10.1	15.4	-	-	9.1	12.3	37.8
Item 2720-2780 N(Wtd) ★	239	143	73	185	8	55	86	60	38	69	122	-	-	17	199	23

The next questions are about AMPHETAMINES, which doctors sometimes prescribe to help people lose weight or to give people more energy. Drugstores are not supposed to sell them without a prescription.

Amphetamines are sometimes called: uppers, ups, speed, bennies, dexies, pep pills, diet pills. They include the following drugs: Benzedrine, Dexedrine, Methedrine, Ritalin, Preludin, Dexamyl, Methamphetamine.

B042: Have you ever taken amphetamines because a doctor told you to use them?

	TOTAL	M	F	White	Black	NE	NC	S	W	Yes	No	None	Mar	Few	More	Any
1. No	84.9	84.6	85.1	83.9	90.8	87.2	86.0	82.6	83.3	86.9	83.4	91.1	87.5	75.6	76.0	67.7
2. Yes, but I had already tried them on my own.	3.5	3.8	2.9	3.5	.9	3.9	3.2	3.2	3.8	2.6	3.7	-	-	3.1	13.0	19.7
3. Yes, and it was the first time I took any	11.7	11.6	12.0	12.6	8.3	8.9	10.8	14.2	12.9	10.5	12.9	8.9	12.5	21.3	11.0	12.6
Item 2790 N(Wtd)	2837	1335	1396	2251	302	658	894	856	428	1328	1236	1185	626	316	589	47

B043: On how many occasions (if any) have you taken amphetamines on your own--that is, without a doctor telling you to take them...

★=excludes respondents for whom question was inappropriate.

QUESTIONNAIRE FORM 1 1976	TOTAL	SEX		RACE		REGION				4YR COLLEGE PLANS		ILLICIT DRUG USE: LIFETIME				
		M	F	White	Black	NE	NC	S	W	Yes	No	None	Mari- juana Only	Few Pills	More Pills	Any Her- oin
Weighted No. of Cases:	3039	1426	1466	2356	338	715	950	919	454	1384	1321	1219	669	329	605	47
% of Weighted Total:	100.0	46.9	48.2	77.5	11.1	23.5	31.3	30.2	15.0	45.5	43.5	40.1	22.0	10.8	19.9	1.6
B043A: ...in your lifetime?																
1. 0 occasions	77.6	78.8	77.9	77.1	91.6	77.3	77.1	79.7	74.9	84.6	72.9	100.0	100.0	61.7	20.2	20.1
2. 1-2	7.0	6.7	7.1	6.9	5.7	9.4	4.7	7.2	7.8	5.7	7.8	-	-	38.3	12.4	10.3
3. 3-5	3.5	4.0	3.0	3.6	1.0	2.8	4.1	3.0	4.4	2.8	3.9	-	-	-	16.0	7.9
4. 6-9	2.9	2.8	2.9	3.1	.9	2.2	2.9	3.4	2.6	2.1	3.6	-	-	-	13.1	6.0
5. 10-19	3.5	2.7	3.6	3.7	.3	3.6	3.9	2.9	3.5	1.9	4.5	-	-	-	15.6	11.6
6. 20-39	1.9	1.6	1.8	1.8	.2	2.0	2.0	1.6	1.8	.7	2.6	-	-	-	7.9	10.9
7. 40 or more	3.7	3.3	3.5	3.7	.4	2.6	5.3	2.1	5.0	2.2	4.8	-	-	-	14.8	33.1
Item 980 N(Wtd)	2793	1321	1370	2225	295	649	884	839	420	1314	1211	1190	622	310	589	46
B043B: ...during the last 12 months?																
1. 0 occasions	84.4	85.0	85.4	84.0	95.2	86.9	81.8	86.2	82.7	89.8	81.4	100.0	100.0	81.1	39.5	40.6
2. 1-2	5.7	5.4	5.8	5.7	3.8	5.5	5.2	5.8	7.0	4.9	5.7	-	-	18.9	16.5	14.1
3. 3-5	2.6	2.4	2.6	2.8	.3	2.5	2.3	2.9	2.8	1.7	3.3	-	-	-	12.5	2.7
4. 6-9	2.3	2.7	1.3	2.1	.3	1.7	3.7	1.5	2.1	1.4	2.7	-	-	-	10.6	8.5
5. 10-19	2.4	2.6	2.1	2.5	.2	1.6	3.3	2.1	2.2	.9	3.6	-	-	-	10.4	15.2
6. 20-39	1.4	.7	1.9	1.6	-	1.0	1.6	1.0	2.1	.9	1.6	-	-	-	5.8	10.2
7. 40 or more	1.1	1.3	.9	1.2	.2	.8	2.1	.4	1.0	.5	1.6	-	-	-	4.6	8.7
Item 990 N(Wtd)	2770	1311	1359	2205	291	643	876	832	419	1304	1201	1190	622	303	573	45
B043C: ...during the last 30 days?																
1. 0 occasions	92.4	92.4	93.4	92.3	98.8	94.9	89.6	93.6	92.1	95.8	90.2	100.0	100.0	96.3	68.4	57.9
2. 1-2	3.9	3.6	3.6	4.0	.7	2.7	5.0	3.2	4.6	2.3	4.7	-	-	3.7	15.6	16.6
3. 3-5	1.5	1.7	1.1	1.3	.2	.8	2.0	1.5	1.6	.7	1.9	-	-	-	6.4	12.7
4. 6-9	1.0	1.1	.8	1.1	.1	.7	1.2	1.0	.9	.5	1.4	-	-	-	4.4	5.2
5. 10-19	.7	.9	.6	.8	-	.4	1.4	.4	.6	.4	.9	-	-	-	3.4	1.8
6. 20-39	.3	.2	.5	.4	-	.5	.6	-	.1	.1	.6	-	-	-	1.5	1.2
7. 40 or more	.1	.2	*	.1	.2	.1	.1	.2	.1	*	.2	-	-	-	.3	4.8
Item 1000 N(Wtd)	2763	1310	1354	2199	291	643	872	830	418	1304	1197	1190	622	301	569	45

IF YOU HAVE NOT TAKEN AMPHETAMINES IN THE LAST TWELVE MONTHS, GO TO Q.B052.

THE FOLLOWING QUESTIONS REFER ONLY TO TAKING AMPHETAMINES WITHOUT A DOCTOR'S ORDERS. IF YOU HAVE NOT DONE THIS IN THE LAST TWELVE MONTHS, GO TO Q.B052.

B044: When you used amphetamines during the last year, how often did you use them in each of the following situations?

	TOTAL	M	F	White	Black	NE	NC	S	W	Yes	No	None	Mari- juana Only	Few Pills	More Pills	Any Her- oin
B044A: When you were alone																
1. Not at all	43.8	51.0	37.2	45.3	3.4	43.3	46.3	40.5	44.0	50.6	38.5	-	-	75.6	40.0	30.8
2. A few of the times	35.3	33.1	37.6	33.9	82.3	36.7	34.0	35.3	36.8	32.0	37.2	-	-	23.0	36.9	40.5
3. Some of the times	9.4	8.5	8.9	8.5	10.0	7.4	10.1	10.0	9.1	8.2	9.5	-	-	1.4	9.5	22.5
4. Most of the times	7.9	5.7	10.1	8.3	-	7.5	6.8	9.3	8.7	4.9	10.4	-	-	-	9.5	2.9
5. Every time	3.6	1.6	6.2	4.1	4.3	5.2	2.7	4.9	1.5	4.3	4.4	-	-	-	4.1	3.4
Item 2800 N(Wtd) ★	419	192	190	345	11	82	156	110	70	130	214	-	-	49	342	27
B044B: With just 1 or 2 other people																
1. Not at all	17.4	15.3	20.0	18.1	44.7	26.5	11.5	20.5	15.1	26.1	15.2	-	-	25.9	17.3	.8
2. A few of the times	37.1	33.8	43.1	35.8	26.3	46.8	37.7	31.0	34.1	35.5	38.9	-	-	45.6	37.1	20.9
3. Some of the times	23.4	25.7	19.6	22.8	29.0	12.9	30.2	19.3	26.9	16.7	27.1	-	-	3.8	25.0	40.7
4. Most of the times	14.8	17.0	11.6	15.7	-	9.9	14.2	18.6	15.5	15.4	12.8	-	-	-	15.6	32.2
5. Every time	7.4	8.1	5.7	7.6	-	3.9	6.4	10.6	8.3	6.3	6.0	-	-	24.7	5.0	5.4
Item 2810 N(Wtd) ★	415	191	188	342	11	81	153	112	69	128	212	-	-	49	337	27

* = less than .05 per cent.   ★ = excludes respondents for whom question was inappropriate.

QUESTIONNAIRE FORM 1 1976	TOTAL	SEX		RACE		REGION				4YR COLLEGE PLANS		ILLICIT DRUG USE: LIFETIME				
		M	F	White	Black	NE	NC	S	W	Yes	No	None	Marijuana Only	Few Pills	More Pills	Any Heroin
Weighted No. of Cases:	3039	1426	1466	2356	338	715	950	919	454	1384	1321	1219	669	329	605	47
% of Weighted Total:	100.0	46.9	48.2	77.5	11.1	23.5	31.3	30.2	15.0	45.5	43.5	40.1	22.0	10.8	19.9	1.6

B044C: At a party

	TOTAL	M	F	White	Black	NE	NC	S	W	Yes	No	None	Marij. Only	Few Pills	More Pills	Any Heroin
1. Not at all	41.5	37.2	46.0	42.1	76.9	42.6	31.5	51.5	46.9	47.4	39.8	-	-	82.5	37.7	11.8
2. A few of the times	20.4	19.9	21.8	21.3	4.6	25.1	17.1	19.5	23.7	17.8	21.1	-	-	14.7	22.0	11.8
3. Some of the times	21.5	23.6	18.1	20.6	5.3	15.4	28.0	16.9	21.2	21.6	20.1	-	-	1.1	23.4	36.3
4. Most of the times	10.7	10.8	11.1	10.3	13.1	12.7	17.0	3.2	6.5	7.9	12.7	-	-	-	10.8	30.3
5. Every time	5.8	8.5	2.9	5.7	-	4.2	6.4	8.8	1.7	5.3	6.4	-	-	1.7	6.1	9.9
Item 2820 N(Wtd) ★	413	189	187	340	11	81	154	109	69	127	211	-	-	48	336	27

B044D: When your date or spouse was present

	TOTAL	M	F	White	Black	NE	NC	S	W	Yes	No	None	Marij. Only	Few Pills	More Pills	Any Heroin
1. Not at all	52.5	57.2	48.2	51.9	77.9	64.2	43.5	55.5	54.3	66.6	45.9	-	-	71.9	51.7	24.5
2. A few of the times	24.5	24.5	24.8	24.7	13.4	26.4	23.7	24.7	23.7	17.0	26.4	-	-	22.5	25.5	17.0
3. Some of the times	13.7	13.5	12.3	13.2	5.3	6.4	17.3	12.0	17.0	12.0	14.9	-	-	-	13.8	38.1
4. Most of the times	6.4	2.1	11.0	7.0	3.4	1.8	11.5	3.4	5.0	2.0	9.9	-	-	-	6.8	13.7
5. Every time	2.9	2.6	3.7	3.1	-	1.1	4.0	4.4	-	2.4	2.9	-	-	5.7	2.2	6.8
Item 2830 N(Wtd) ★	410	187	188	338	11	79	153	111	68	128	209	-	-	49	333	27

B044E: When people over age 30 were present

	TOTAL	M	F	White	Black	NE	NC	S	W	Yes	No	None	Marij. Only	Few Pills	More Pills	Any Heroin
1. Not at all	62.1	63.9	60.7	60.7	92.0	64.7	56.3	66.9	64.6	60.9	63.1	-	-	88.3	60.4	33.3
2. A few of the times	19.6	19.0	20.9	21.1	3.4	24.2	21.6	15.1	16.6	15.8	22.7	-	-	7.8	20.8	27.4
3. Some of the times	12.1	11.7	12.8	12.1	4.6	5.1	16.4	10.0	14.1	13.8	10.8	-	-	-	12.5	30.4
4. Most of the times	3.8	3.7	3.0	3.6	-	4.0	3.7	4.1	3.6	6.6	1.1	-	-	-	4.2	5.7
5. Every time	2.4	1.6	2.7	2.5	-	2.0	2.1	3.9	1.1	2.8	2.2	-	-	3.9	2.1	3.2
Item 2840 N(Wtd) ★	418	191	191	344	11	81	156	111	70	129	213	-	-	49	341	27

B044F: During the daytime (before 4:00 p.m.)

	TOTAL	M	F	White	Black	NE	NC	S	W	Yes	No	None	Marij. Only	Few Pills	More Pills	Any Heroin
1. Not at all	27.9	34.8	21.5	27.3	22.8	31.0	19.8	38.4	26.0	34.5	24.3	-	-	66.4	23.0	16.0
2. A few of the times	25.6	25.9	25.1	23.8	40.9	27.9	29.0	23.9	18.3	21.1	26.0	-	-	23.4	25.8	29.3
3. Some of the times	22.2	20.8	23.8	23.0	24.0	14.9	28.8	19.4	20.6	20.3	22.9	-	-	4.3	23.8	36.8
4. Most of the times	15.6	12.4	18.6	16.5	12.3	15.2	16.4	9.7	23.8	14.1	17.9	-	-	1.2	18.0	12.6
5. Every time	8.5	6.0	11.0	9.3	-	11.0	6.0	8.6	11.3	10.0	8.9	-	-	4.6	9.4	5.3
Item 2850 N(Wtd) ★	419	190	192	345	11	81	157	111	70	129	213	-	-	49	341	27

B044G: At your home (or apartment or dorm)

	TOTAL	M	F	White	Black	NE	NC	S	W	Yes	No	None	Marij. Only	Few Pills	More Pills	Any Heroin
1. Not at all	37.3	44.5	31.2	38.0	30.6	39.0	30.6	44.8	38.2	40.7	34.1	-	-	69.1	33.9	17.5
2. A few of the times	29.9	28.0	31.6	28.2	55.2	29.5	33.8	24.7	29.8	31.5	27.7	-	-	26.7	29.8	39.0
3. Some of the times	19.2	19.1	18.5	20.4	10.0	17.1	24.0	15.7	16.6	15.9	22.4	-	-	-	21.3	29.8
4. Most of the times	8.5	5.3	11.4	8.0	4.3	10.8	7.1	7.8	10.0	6.9	9.3	-	-	-	9.7	9.4
5. Every time	5.2	3.1	7.3	5.5	-	3.6	4.5	7.1	5.5	4.9	6.5	-	-	4.2	5.4	4.4
Item 2860 N(Wtd) ★	417	190	191	344	11	81	156	111	69	129	213	-	-	49	339	27

B044H: At school

	TOTAL	M	F	White	Black	NE	NC	S	W	Yes	No	None	Marij. Only	Few Pills	More Pills	Any Heroin
1. Not at all	39.9	37.6	42.7	39.6	35.4	47.4	31.5	47.9	37.1	48.4	33.5	-	-	77.1	36.0	18.1
2. A few of the times	27.6	31.7	21.9	25.8	50.3	19.4	36.0	24.1	23.8	24.6	29.9	-	-	13.3	29.6	29.5
3. Some of the times	18.5	15.7	20.8	19.5	4.3	16.6	18.5	18.6	20.5	15.2	19.8	-	-	3.2	19.9	29.9
4. Most of the times	9.6	8.9	10.9	10.3	10.0	13.1	10.3	4.7	12.0	9.2	10.7	-	-	1.2	10.6	13.6
5. Every time	4.4	6.0	3.7	4.8	-	3.5	3.7	4.7	6.6	2.6	6.1	-	-	5.2	4.0	8.8
Item 2880 N(Wtd) ★	418	191	190	344	11	82	156	112	69	129	214	-	-	49	341	27

B044I: In a car

	TOTAL	M	F	White	Black	NE	NC	S	W	Yes	No	None	Marij. Only	Few Pills	More Pills	Any Heroin
1. Not at all	42.2	41.7	43.9	42.0	56.3	57.4	32.2	46.9	39.1	54.2	37.5	-	-	73.1	38.9	23.1
2. A few of the times	26.6	23.2	26.7	24.5	33.7	24.1	30.5	22.5	27.2	21.1	25.8	-	-	26.9	27.1	21.4
3. Some of the times	19.1	20.3	18.6	20.1	4.6	10.0	21.5	20.2	22.1	16.6	21.3	-	-	-	20.9	32.2
4. Most of the times	9.6	11.7	8.2	10.5	5.3	7.7	14.1	5.2	9.0	5.4	12.4	-	-	-	10.5	16.6
5. Every time	2.6	3.1	2.6	2.9	-	.8	1.7	5.1	2.6	2.6	3.1	-	-	-	2.7	6.7
Item 2890 N(Wtd) ★	416	191	189	343	11	80	155	112	69	128	213	-	-	49	339	27

★ = excludes respondents for whom question was inappropriate.

QUESTIONNAIRE FORM 1 1976	TOTAL	SEX		RACE		REGION				4YR COLLEGE PLANS		ILLICIT DRUG USE: LIFETIME				
		M	F	White	Black	NE	NC	S	W	Yes	No	None	Mari-juana Only	Few Pills	More Pills	Any Her-oin
Weighted No. of Cases:	3039	1426	1466	2356	338	715	950	919	454	1384	1321	1219	669	329	605	47
% of Weighted Total:	100.0	46.9	48.2	77.5	11.1	23.5	31.3	30.2	15.0	45.5	43.5	40.1	22.0	10.8	19.9	1.6

B045: How many of the times when you used amphetamines during the last year did you use them along with each of the following drugs--that is, so that their effects overlapped?

B045A: With alcohol

1. Not at all	43.0	40.8	44.6	40.7	77.9	43.3	35.6	48.7	49.8	54.6	37.9	-	-	56.8	42.7	20.7
2. A few of the times	29.5	27.2	32.5	30.8	16.8	33.9	25.9	28.0	34.9	24.6	30.5	-	-	34.1	28.8	29.8
3. Some of the times	12.3	13.8	11.3	12.9	5.3	13.3	16.6	9.1	6.6	9.4	14.8	-	-	-	13.8	16.1
4. Most of the times	10.1	11.6	8.4	10.4	-	5.8	16.4	8.1	4.4	7.0	12.1	-	-	-	10.4	25.0
5. Every time	5.1	6.6	3.2	5.2	-	3.6	5.5	6.1	4.2	4.4	4.7	-	-	9.2	4.3	8.2
Item 2900 N(Wtd) ★	415	189	192	344	11	81	154	110	70	132	212	-	-	49	339	27

B045B: With marijuana

1. Not at all	28.4	16.5	38.6	27.9	54.2	35.5	17.0	36.8	31.5	39.1	23.8	-	-	54.3	26.0	8.7
2. A few of the times	24.6	26.3	24.2	25.7	18.1	24.7	28.0	17.1	28.7	20.0	26.8	-	-	26.4	25.6	8.3
3. Some of the times	18.7	18.9	19.1	17.6	9.3	16.3	22.5	13.2	21.5	14.5	19.5	-	-	-	20.0	36.5
4. Most of the times	17.1	21.6	13.5	17.8	9.8	13.9	24.2	14.7	9.2	16.6	19.4	-	-	3.3	17.7	35.2
5. Every time	11.3	16.7	4.6	10.9	8.7	9.6	8.3	18.1	9.0	9.8	10.5	-	-	16.0	10.6	11.3
Item 2910 N(Wtd) ★	419	190	193	346	11	83	155	111	70	132	213	-	-	49	343	27

B045C: With LSD

1. Not at all	96.4	95.7	97.7	96.7	100.0	95.2	95.0	98.2	98.0	96.2	95.6	-	-	97.5	97.4	81.5
2. A few of the times	2.3	2.7	1.9	2.0	-	3.0	4.1	-	1.1	2.0	3.0	-	-	-	1.9	10.8
3. Some of the times	.6	1.0	.4	.6	-	1.8	-	.8	.3	1.8	.1	-	-	-	.3	6.3
4. Most of the times	.4	.7	-	.4	-	-	.8	-	.5	-	.8	-	-	-	.4	1.4
5. Every time	.3	-	-	.3	-	-	-	1.0	-	-	.5	-	-	2.5	-	-
Item 2920 N(Wtd) ★	400	184	182	329	13	78	146	108	68	130	205	-	-	44	329	26

B045D: With psychedelics other than LSD

1. Not at all	90.4	86.2	94.9	91.9	90.0	90.2	85.2	95.2	93.7	90.7	90.1	-	-	98.1	90.6	73.5
2. A few of the times	6.3	7.7	4.1	5.8	10.0	8.3	8.5	3.4	3.9	7.4	5.7	-	-	-	6.2	18.9
3. Some of the times	2.5	5.3	.2	2.4	-	.9	5.3	1.4	.6	1.5	3.2	-	-	-	3.0	1.8
4. Most of the times	.3	.4	-	-	-	-	.5	-	.5	-	.2	-	-	-	.2	1.4
5. Every time	.5	.3	.8	-	-	.7	.4	-	1.2	.4	.7	-	-	1.9	-	4.5
Item 2930 N(Wtd) ★	395	181	181	324	11	79	141	106	69	128	201	-	-	45	323	26

B046: What have been the most important reasons for your taking amphetamines without a doctor's orders? (Mark all that apply.)

A. To experiment--to see what it's like	54.8	58.0	53.2	56.2	45.4	61.0	56.4	50.9	50.1	57.6	55.2	-	-	64.1	54.3	42.5
B. To relax or relieve tension	21.4	15.1	26.0	21.4	32.1	22.9	17.7	31.5	11.9	16.2	26.2	-	-	18.5	20.7	35.0
C. To feel good or get high	62.4	64.0	61.4	63.0	45.3	62.6	71.2	55.4	54.0	57.1	64.6	-	-	31.8	65.3	82.5
D. To seek deeper insights and understanding	5.9	3.4	6.6	4.7	5.0	4.6	5.5	8.6	3.7	2.0	7.3	-	-	2.3	5.9	12.5
E. To have a good time with my friends	32.2	36.8	28.1	33.6	14.9	34.5	43.8	15.8	29.2	27.8	36.8	-	-	18.9	33.1	45.1
F. To fit in with a group I like	4.0	6.9	1.7	4.2	5.0	5.0	5.4	3.0	1.3	3.1	5.0	-	-	1.5	4.1	7.7
G. To get away from my problems or troubles	15.2	10.9	18.6	14.4	23.0	12.4	15.1	19.6	11.9	9.7	20.2	-	-	10.6	15.6	19.7
H. Because of boredom, nothing else to do	15.1	15.4	13.5	15.6	8.1	11.1	13.7	18.3	17.9	13.2	18.0	-	-	12.6	15.4	16.0
I. Because of anger or frustration	9.5	6.1	11.6	9.4	5.0	5.7	8.1	16.2	6.8	7.7	11.2	-	-	7.1	9.8	10.8
J. To get through the day	22.3	16.7	28.6	23.2	9.0	17.4	30.0	11.3	28.0	17.8	25.4	-	-	2.7	24.7	28.1
K. To increase the effects of some other drug(s)	9.1	12.3	6.1	10.1	5.0	8.6	12.0	5.3	9.4	9.0	11.2	-	-	8.5	8.2	22.5
L. To decrease (offset) the effects of some other drug(s)	3.7	6.9	1.1	4.1	5.0	4.5	7.0	.5	-	4.2	3.8	-	-	-	4.0	5.9
M. To stay awake	51.5	51.5	53.1	53.5	30.6	47.1	57.0	40.4	61.8	50.3	53.6	-	-	27.4	53.5	70.6
N. To get more energy	56.2	48.4	65.9	58.8	47.4	53.7	60.3	48.0	63.0	55.2	56.1	-	-	32.4	60.5	45.6
O. To help me lose weight	26.4	11.8	42.0	28.3	21.4	23.2	33.7	16.7	29.2	27.4	26.7	-	-	12.3	27.5	38.4
P. Because I am "hooked"--I feel I have to have them	.7	.3	1.1	.3	5.0	.6	.4	.5	1.9	.7	1.0	-	-	-	.5	4.8
Item 2940-3090 N(Wtd) ★	418	191	193	346	12	82	155	110	70	133	213	-	-	49	342	27

★=excludes respondents for whom question was inappropriate.

QUESTIONNAIRE FORM 1 1976	TOTAL	SEX		RACE		REGION				4YR COLLEGE PLANS		ILLICIT DRUG USE: LIFETIME				
		M	F	White	Black	NE	NC	S	W	Yes	No	None	Mari- juana Only	Few Pills	More Pills	Any Her- oin
Weighted No. of Cases:	3039	1426	1466	2356	338	715	950	919	454	1384	1321	1219	669	329	605	47
% of Weighted Total:	100.0	46.9	48.2	77.5	11.1	23.5	31.3	30.2	15.0	45.5	43.5	40.1	22.0	10.8	19.9	1.6

B047: When you take amphetamines, how high do you usually get?

	TOTAL	M	F	White	Black	NE	NC	S	W	Yes	No	None	Mari- juana Only	Few Pills	More Pills	Any Her- oin
1. Not at all high	5.0	2.9	6.2	4.3	37.0	8.7	2.4	5.8	5.3	6.0	4.3	-	-	18.6	3.4	-
2. A little high	26.1	27.4	24.9	27.7	17.4	28.5	25.2	22.0	31.8	26.5	27.3	-	-	42.8	24.2	20.2
3. Moderately high	43.8	42.5	44.7	42.4	31.3	32.4	46.7	49.8	40.9	38.7	44.6	-	-	20.4	45.9	58.9
4. Very high	14.4	14.9	14.1	14.4	5.3	17.5	16.7	13.9	6.3	14.1	14.2	-	-	2.4	16.2	12.2
5. I don't take them to get high	10.7	12.2	10.0	11.1	8.9	13.0	9.0	8.4	15.6	14.6	9.5	-	-	15.8	10.2	8.8
Item 3100　N(Wtd) ★	406	185	188	336	11	79	152	107	68	126	208	-	-	45	334	25

B048: When you take amphetamines how long do you usually stay high?

	TOTAL	M	F	White	Black	NE	NC	S	W	Yes	No	None	Mari- juana Only	Few Pills	More Pills	Any Her- oin
1. Usually don't get high	11.2	9.3	13.4	10.1	41.3	10.9	9.8	14.4	9.6	13.8	10.7	-	-	38.0	7.9	4.4
2. One to two hours	12.1	12.7	11.6	13.1	16.1	12.9	8.5	13.8	16.8	11.9	12.9	-	-	12.9	12.4	7.4
3. Three to six hours	48.4	48.4	49.4	48.7	22.8	47.6	47.1	46.8	55.0	49.4	45.9	-	-	41.9	49.3	49.6
4. Seven to 24 hours	26.1	28.5	22.5	26.5	14.4	25.3	32.0	23.8	17.2	23.5	27.4	-	-	7.1	28.4	30.4
5. More than 24 hours	2.1	1.0	3.0	1.7	5.3	3.2	2.6	1.1	1.4	1.3	3.0	-	-	-	1.9	8.1
Item 3110　N(Wtd) ★	413	188	192	343	11	81	155	110	68	132	209	-	-	47	339	27

B049: What amphetamines have you taken during the last year without a doctor's orders? (Mark all that apply.)

	TOTAL	M	F	White	Black	NE	NC	S	W	Yes	No	None	Mari- juana Only	Few Pills	More Pills	Any Her- oin
A. Benzedrine	24.1	26.3	19.8	21.9	14.6	14.2	24.6	26.9	29.6	22.4	24.1	-	-	2.7	24.4	57.9
B. Dexedrine	20.2	22.1	17.6	19.6	18.8	25.2	19.4	19.5	17.0	21.9	18.0	-	-	3.6	20.4	47.1
C. Methedrine	23.4	22.8	22.4	23.5	10.0	18.6	27.9	19.8	24.7	17.8	28.9	-	-	27.0	21.5	41.8
D. Ritalin	3.4	3.3	3.1	2.7	8.0	4.1	2.5	.6	9.1	4.6	1.5	-	-	1.2	3.3	9.2
E. Preludin	4.0	4.8	2.7	3.7	-	1.5	4.6	6.3	2.3	4.0	3.9	-	-	2.0	3.6	12.9
F. Dexamyl	9.5	10.4	9.3	8.0	8.7	5.5	8.9	15.9	5.5	11.7	8.6	-	-	1.2	9.3	27.2
G. Methamphetamine	13.5	11.9	14.7	12.4	22.6	10.8	14.3	16.1	10.8	11.1	14.4	-	-	-	14.7	21.6
H. Other	32.0	30.9	33.2	32.2	17.6	38.9	31.2	32.5	25.1	32.0	32.1	-	-	34.5	30.2	50.9
I. Don't know the names of some amphetamines I have used	47.1	43.7	49.0	48.0	56.3	47.9	50.3	44.5	43.1	49.1	45.9	-	-	33.6	49.7	35.0
Item 3120-3200　N(Wtd) ★	401	184	186	334	11	78	148	107	68	128	203	-	-	45	330	26

B050: What methods have you used for taking amphetamines? (Mark all that apply.)

	TOTAL	M	F	White	Black	NE	NC	S	W	Yes	No	None	Mari- juana Only	Few Pills	More Pills	Any Her- oin
A. By mouth	98.5	98.7	98.4	98.7	100.0	99.2	98.0	99.4	97.6	98.2	99.1	-	-	98.7	98.8	95.3
B. Injection	2.5	3.2	1.1	2.0	-	.7	2.0	3.9	3.8	1.5	2.6	-	-	-	1.7	16.9
C. Other	12.3	16.0	7.9	12.2	-	9.3	14.7	8.8	15.7	10.3	12.6	-	-	1.3	11.9	36.5
Item 3210-3230　N(Wtd) ★	413	188	192	342	11	81	155	106	71	128	213	-	-	45	340	27

B051: Have you ever tried to stop using amphetamines and found that you couldn't stop?

	TOTAL	M	F	White	Black	NE	NC	S	W	Yes	No	None	Mari- juana Only	Few Pills	More Pills	Any Her- oin
1. Yes	2.1	2.6	1.4	1.6	-	.7	1.7	2.4	3.9	2.9	2.0	-	-	7.6	.6	11.2
2. No	97.9	97.3	98.6	98.4	100.0	99.3	98.3	97.6	96.1	97.1	98.0	-	-	92.4	99.4	88.8
Item 3240　N(Wtd) ★	412	188	191	343	10	79	155	109	69	131	211	-	-	47	338	27

B052: Do you think you will be using amphetamines without a doctor's orders five years from now?

	TOTAL	M	F	White	Black	NE	NC	S	W	Yes	No	None	Mari- juana Only	Few Pills	More Pills	Any Her- oin
1. I definitely will	.8	.9	.6	.8	.3	.9	1.0	.4	1.1	.7	.8	.4	.6	.2	1.8	6.2
2. I probably will	5.5	5.5	5.3	6.1	2.2	5.0	6.9	4.4	5.6	3.5	7.4	.1	.7	4.1	22.1	24.3
3. I probably will not	21.5	22.7	19.7	21.2	17.5	23.4	19.7	21.0	23.1	18.7	22.0	10.9	17.6	33.3	41.9	39.1
4. I definitely will not	72.2	70.8	74.4	71.9	80.0	70.6	72.4	74.2	70.2	77.1	69.8	88.7	81.0	62.3	34.2	30.4
Item 3250　N(Wtd)	2802	1315	1392	2208	316	636	877	860	428	1299	1236	1166	605	299	569	44

★=excludes respondents for whom question was inappropriate.

QUESTIONNAIRE FORM 1 1976	TOTAL	SEX		RACE		REGION				4YR COLLEGE PLANS		ILLICIT DRUG USE: LIFETIME				
		M	F	White	Black	NE	NC	S	W	Yes	No	None	Marijuana Only	Few Pills	More Pills	Any Heroin
Weighted No. of Cases:	3039	1426	1466	2356	338	715	950	919	454	1384	1321	1219	669	329	605	47
% of Weighted Total:	100.0	46.9	48.2	77.5	11.1	23.5	31.3	30.2	15.0	45.5	43.5	40.1	22.0	10.8	19.9	1.6

The next questions are about QUAALUDES (Methaqualone), which are sometimes prescribed by doctors. Drugstores are not supposed to sell them without a prescription.

Quaaludes are sometimes called: soapers, quads.

B053: On how many occasions (if any) have you taken quaaludes on your own--that is, without a doctor telling you to take them...

B053A: ...in your lifetime?

	TOTAL	M	F	White	Black	NE	NC	S	W	Yes	No	None	Marijuana Only	Few Pills	More Pills	Any Heroin
1. 0 occasions	92.7	91.8	94.6	92.8	98.4	92.7	92.7	91.0	96.1	95.4	91.9	100.0	100.0	95.4	70.5	41.9
2. 1-2	3.1	3.3	2.6	3.1	1.4	3.1	2.9	3.8	2.0	2.6	3.1	-	-	4.6	11.8	14.5
3. 3-5	1.6	1.9	1.0	1.6	-	1.6	1.4	2.3	.8	1.0	1.9	-	-	-	7.3	12.4
4. 6-9	.7	.9	.4	.7	.2	.6	.9	.9	.1	*	1.0	-	-	-	3.1	5.5
5. 10-19	.8	1.0	.5	.8	-	1.2	.5	1.0	-	.5	.7	-	-	-	3.2	7.4
6. 20-39	.5	.5	.5	.6	-	.5	.6	.6	.4	.2	.6	-	-	-	2.2	5.3
7. 40 or more	.6	.5	.4	.5	-	.3	1.0	.3	.6	.2	.8	-	-	-	1.8	13.2
Item 1010 N(Wtd)	2769	1317	1359	2206	295	647	865	842	416	1317	1199	1195	630	307	556	41

B053B: ...during the last 12 months?

	TOTAL	M	F	White	Black	NE	NC	S	W	Yes	No	None	Marijuana Only	Few Pills	More Pills	Any Heroin
1. 0 occasions	95.8	94.9	97.5	95.9	99.3	97.0	95.5	94.1	98.2	97.4	95.6	100.0	100.0	96.3	84.0	61.6
2. 1-2	2.0	2.3	1.3	2.0	.5	1.5	2.2	2.7	1.0	1.8	1.6	-	-	3.7	7.0	13.3
3. 3-5	1.0	1.4	.6	1.0	.2	.5	.9	1.8	.3	.2	1.6	-	-	-	4.6	5.5
4. 6-9	.6	.9	.2	.6	-	.6	.6	.8	.1	.3	.4	-	-	-	2.5	7.4
5. 10-19	.3	.3	.2	.3	-	.1	.5	.3	.2	.1	.5	-	-	-	1.3	3.2
6. 20-39	.2	.3	.1	.2	-	.2	.3	.2	.1	.1	.2	-	-	-	.5	6.6
7. 40 or more	.1	-	*	*	-	-	.1	-	.2	-	.1	-	-	-	.1	2.4
Item 1020 N(Wtd)	2767	1316	1358	2203	295	645	865	841	416	1317	1197	1195	630	307	554	41

B053C: ...during the last 30 days?

	TOTAL	M	F	White	Black	NE	NC	S	W	Yes	No	None	Marijuana Only	Few Pills	More Pills	Any Heroin
1. 0 occasions	98.4	97.8	99.3	98.6	99.8	98.9	98.5	97.6	99.0	99.5	97.8	100.0	100.0	99.3	93.8	80.2
2. 1-2	1.1	1.6	.4	1.0	.2	.9	.9	1.8	.6	.3	1.5	-	-	.7	4.7	5.5
3. 3-5	.3	.4	.1	.3	-	.1	.3	.4	.2	.1	.3	-	-	-	.8	7.3
4. 6-9	.2	.2	*	.1	-	-	.3	.2	-	*	.2	-	-	-	.6	1.9
5. 10-19	*	*	-	*	-	-	-	.1	-	-	*	-	-	-	-	1.5
6. 20-39	*	-	*	-	-	.1	-	-	.1	*	-	-	-	-	-	2.8
7. 40 or more	*	-	-	-	-	-	-	-	.1	-	*	-	-	-	-	.9
Item 1030 N(Wtd)	2763	1315	1355	2199	295	644	862	841	416	1317	1193	1195	630	307	550	41

IF YOU HAVE NOT TAKEN QUAALUDES IN THE LAST TWELVE MONTHS, GO TO Q.B056.

THE FOLLOWING QUESTIONS REFER ONLY TO TAKING QUAALUDES WITHOUT A DOCTOR'S ORDERS. IF YOU HAVE NOT DONE THIS IN THE LAST TWELVE MONTHS, GO TO Q.B056.

B054: When you take quaaludes how high do you usually get?

	TOTAL	M	F	White	Black	NE	NC	S	W	Yes	No	None	Marijuana Only	Few Pills	More Pills	Any Heroin
1. Not at all high	.6	1.1	-	.8	-	-	-	-	10.5	-	1.3	-	-	-	.8	-
2. A little high	8.2	7.2	4.4	9.0	-	4.9	9.8	7.6	12.4	12.8	7.7	-	-	18.6	7.1	9.0
3. Moderately high	39.2	33.5	52.5	40.2	73.9	29.1	48.2	39.1	12.0	40.5	40.8	-	-	28.8	40.5	37.3
4. Very high	49.7	54.5	42.3	47.1	26.1	64.5	37.9	51.8	65.1	43.5	49.4	-	-	52.6	48.6	53.6
5. I don't take them to get high	2.3	3.6	.8	2.9	-	1.5	4.0	1.4	-	3.2	.9	-	-	-	3.0	-
Item 3260 N(Wtd) ★	114	64	36	89	2	19	41	47	7	30	55	-	-	9	87	18

* = less than .05 per cent.   ★ = excludes respondents for whom question was inappropriate.

QUESTIONNAIRE FORM 1 1976	TOTAL	SEX		RACE		REGION				4YR COLLEGE PLANS		ILLICIT DRUG USE: LIFETIME				
		M	F	White	Black	NE	NC	S	W	Yes	No	None	Marijuana Only	Few Pills	More Pills	Any Heroin
Weighted No. of Cases:	3039	1426	1466	2356	338	715	950	919	454	1384	1321	1219	669	329	605	47
% of Weighted Total:	100.0	46.9	48.2	77.5	11.1	23.5	31.3	30.2	15.0	45.5	43.5	40.1	22.0	10.8	19.9	1.6
B055: When you take quaaludes how long do you usually stay high?																
1. Usually don't get high	5.2	7.7	1.3	5.7	24.3	2.3	4.0	6.7	10.6	10.3	1.3	-	-	23.8	4.0	-
2. One to two hours	15.8	14.8	18.8	19.4	-	5.2	22.5	15.8	3.1	21.1	17.9	-	-	14.2	17.8	6.7
3. Three to six hours	52.2	48.5	55.0	50.3	49.6	61.1	52.3	47.8	59.5	49.1	52.0	-	-	35.6	52.7	60.4
4. Seven to 24 hours	25.3	27.7	23.4	23.6	26.1	28.7	21.2	27.9	21.5	15.2	28.2	-	-	26.5	25.5	23.2
5. More than 24 hours	1.5	1.3	1.5	1.0	-	2.8	-	1.8	5.4	4.3	.7	-	-	-	-	9.7
Item 3270 N(Wtd) ★	118	68	36	92	2	19	42	50	7	33	55	-	-	11	88	18

The next questions are about BARBITURATES, which doctors sometimes prescribe to help people relax or get to sleep. Drugstores are not supposed to sell them without a prescription.

Barbiturates are sometimes called: downs, downers, goofballs, yellows, reds, blues, rainbows.

They include the following drugs: Phenobarbitol, Seconal, Tuinal, Nembutal, Luminal, Desbutal, Amytal.

	TOTAL	M	F	White	Black	NE	NC	S	W	Yes	No	None	Marijuana Only	Few Pills	More Pills	Any Heroin
B056: Have you ever taken barbiturates because a doctor told you to use them?																
1. No	86.7	85.9	87.4	86.3	92.6	87.1	88.3	85.1	86.0	87.5	86.2	94.6	90.9	78.3	71.8	65.8
2. Yes, but I had already tried them on my own.	3.0	3.0	2.7	3.1	.8	3.1	3.1	3.2	2.1	1.6	3.8	-	-	3.7	10.7	25.2
3. Yes, and it was the first time I took any	10.3	11.1	9.9	10.6	6.5	9.8	8.6	11.7	11.9	10.8	10.0	5.4	9.1	18.0	17.5	9.0
Item 3280 N(Wtd)	2777	1309	1382	2220	299	644	878	842	413	1318	1210	1171	620	310	563	47
B057: On how many occasions (if any) have you taken barbiturates on your own--that is, without a doctor telling you to take them...																
B057A: ...in your lifetime?																
1. 0 occasions	84.9	85.8	85.5	84.5	94.2	83.6	85.0	83.3	89.6	89.0	83.2	100.0	100.0	80.4	42.4	25.5
2. 1-2	5.5	5.6	5.1	5.6	3.4	6.4	4.3	6.9	3.7	4.8	5.5	-	-	19.6	15.2	13.6
3. 3-5	3.0	2.0	3.8	3.1	.8	3.3	2.8	3.5	1.7	2.0	3.4	-	-	-	14.2	5.3
4. 6-9	1.7	1.3	1.7	1.9	.3	1.5	1.6	2.0	1.6	1.1	2.0	-	-	-	7.8	6.3
5. 10-19	1.6	2.0	1.1	1.8	-	2.1	2.4	.9	.8	1.2	1.6	-	-	-	7.4	7.7
6. 20-39	1.3	1.1	1.3	1.3	.2	1.6	.8	1.7	1.3	.9	1.5	-	-	-	6.0	6.1
7. 40 or more	2.0	2.2	1.5	1.8	1.0	1.5	3.1	1.7	1.2	.9	2.7	-	-	-	7.0	35.6
Item 1040 N(Wtd)	2766	1318	1360	2212	293	640	879	836	411	1303	1213	1186	626	304	564	45
B057B: ...during the last 12 months?																
1. 0 occasions	91.1	91.5	92.0	91.1	97.7	91.3	90.4	90.4	94.2	94.2	89.9	100.0	100.0	92.7	63.9	51.5
2. 1-2	3.8	3.5	3.5	4.0	1.3	4.2	3.3	4.4	3.0	2.7	4.1	-	-	7.3	14.5	5.8
3. 3-5	1.9	1.6	2.3	1.9	-	1.8	2.4	1.9	1.2	1.5	2.2	-	-	-	9.2	4.1
4. 6-9	1.0	1.1	.8	1.0	.2	1.4	1.2	.8	.4	.4	1.1	-	-	-	4.0	11.0
5. 10-19	1.0	1.3	.5	.9	.6	.5	1.3	1.4	.5	.6	1.1	-	-	-	4.7	4.7
6. 20-39	.5	.4	.5	.5	-	.4	.5	.6	.3	.3	.6	-	-	-	1.8	8.8
7. 40 or more	.6	.7	.5	.5	.2	.5	.9	.6	.3	.3	.9	-	-	-	1.9	14.1
Item 1050 N(Wtd)	2749	1308	1355	2199	292	635	874	831	409	1299	1205	1186	626	300	552	45
B057C: ...during the last 30 days?																
1. 0 occasions	96.2	96.8	96.3	96.4	99.2	97.7	95.5	95.1	97.8	98.2	95.2	100.0	100.0	98.1	85.1	64.6
2. 1-2	1.8	1.3	1.9	1.9	-	1.0	2.3	2.1	1.4	1.0	2.1	-	-	1.9	7.3	7.5
3. 3-5	.9	.9	.8	.8	.6	.8	.8	1.4	.3	.3	1.1	-	-	-	3.7	11.3
4. 6-9	.5	.5	.4	.5	-	.3	.7	.6	.2	.2	.8	-	-	-	2.2	5.0
5. 10-19	.3	.3	.2	.2	-	-	.3	.6	-	.2	.4	-	-	-	1.1	2.6
6. 20-39	.2	.1	.3	.2	.2	.2	.3	.2	.2	.1	.3	-	-	-	.6	6.9
7. 40 or more	*	*	-	-	-	-	.1	-	.1	-	.1	-	-	-	-	2.2
Item 1060 N(Wtd)	2747	1307	1355	2198	292	635	872	830	409	1297	1205	1186	626	300	549	45

★ = excludes respondents for whom question was inappropriate.   * = less than .05 per cent.

QUESTIONNAIRE FORM 1 1976	TOTAL	SEX		RACE		REGION				4YR COLLEGE PLANS		ILLICIT DRUG USE: LIFETIME				
		M	F	White	Black	NE	NC	S	W	Yes	No	None	Mari-juana Only	Few Pills	More Pills	Any Her-oin
Weighted No. of Cases:	3039	1426	1466	2356	338	715	950	919	454	1384	1321	1219	669	329	605	47
% of Weighted Total:	100.0	46.9	48.2	77.5	11.1	23.5	31.3	30.2	15.0	45.5	43.5	40.1	22.0	10.8	19.9	1.6

IF YOU HAVE NOT TAKEN BARBITURATES IN THE LAST TWELVE MONTHS, GO TO Q.B065.

THE FOLLOWING QUESTIONS REFER ONLY TO TAKING BARBITURATES WITHOUT A DOCTOR'S ORDERS. IF YOU HAVE NOT DONE THIS IN THE LAST TWELVE MONTHS, GO TO Q.B065.

B058: When you used barbiturates during the last year, how often did you use them in each of the following situations?

B058A: When you were alone

	TOTAL	M	F	White	Black	NE	NC	S	W	Yes	No	None	Mari-juana Only	Few Pills	More Pills	Any Heroin
1. Not at all	51.5	57.5	45.6	50.9	57.3	48.5	53.7	48.6	62.3	50.6	52.5	–	–	76.7	50.8	23.9
2. A few of the times	31.8	27.9	39.1	33.8	33.8	34.5	30.5	34.6	19.0	29.7	34.9	–	–	12.0	33.3	44.3
3. Some of the times	7.5	5.1	8.3	5.9	8.9	5.3	8.2	7.6	10.1	9.1	5.7	–	–		7.9	13.2
4. Most of the times	2.9	3.0	2.7	2.8	–	3.2	2.3	3.5	2.3	3.2	2.5	–	–		1.9	15.7
5. Every time	6.3	6.5	4.3	6.6	–	8.5	5.3	5.7	6.3	7.5	4.4	–	–	11.2	6.1	2.8
Item 3290 N(Wtd) ★	241	115	103	199	7	56	83	82	21	76	123	–	–	24	193	22

B058B: With just 1 or 2 other people

	TOTAL	M	F	White	Black	NE	NC	S	W	Yes	No	None	Mari-juana Only	Few Pills	More Pills	Any Heroin
1. Not at all	18.1	14.0	22.7	19.2	–	19.5	13.9	23.6	10.0	22.4	14.1	–	–	24.0	17.9	4.0
2. A few of the times	39.8	41.1	39.2	39.7	57.3	57.2	38.3	33.0	25.8	44.8	36.3	–	–	56.6	41.1	15.1
3. Some of the times	22.2	20.6	25.1	22.4	35.0	14.9	23.8	22.6	33.2	15.2	27.1	–	–		22.1	49.9
4. Most of the times	11.9	14.2	8.0	10.9	–	3.7	14.4	13.1	18.9	8.1	15.2	–	–		12.2	23.3
5. Every time	8.0	10.1	5.0	7.8	7.7	4.7	9.6	7.6	12.0	9.5	7.2	–	–	19.5	6.8	7.5
Item 3300 N(Wtd) ★	242	113	105	199	7	57	84	80	22	75	122	–	–	24	194	22

B058C: At a party

	TOTAL	M	F	White	Black	NE	NC	S	W	Yes	No	None	Mari-juana Only	Few Pills	More Pills	Any Heroin
1. Not at all	41.7	37.7	47.7	43.8	83.5	51.6	29.2	50.4	33.9	47.6	38.6	–	–	86.3	39.9	11.6
2. A few of the times	15.0	16.4	14.9	16.7	–	17.0	18.2	11.8	8.8	16.2	17.8	–	–	10.8	16.7	4.5
3. Some of the times	24.2	19.7	26.9	23.0	16.5	15.3	30.0	19.2	42.5	21.8	24.8	–	–		25.3	39.4
4. Most of the times	12.7	19.1	5.9	11.1	–	11.3	16.3	12.1	4.9	7.0	13.5	–	–		12.4	28.7
5. Every time	6.4	7.1	4.6	5.3	–	4.8	6.3	6.5	9.8	7.4	5.3	–	–	2.9	5.7	15.8
Item 3310 N(Wtd) ★	235	113	99	193	7	55	82	77	22	71	121	–	–	22	191	22

B058D: When your date or spouse was present

	TOTAL	M	F	White	Black	NE	NC	S	W	Yes	No	None	Mari-juana Only	Few Pills	More Pills	Any Heroin
1. Not at all	53.8	56.1	51.7	53.9	65.0	70.8	47.2	52.0	41.9	65.1	46.5	–	–	82.0	52.4	29.9
2. A few of the times	20.4	19.4	20.4	20.1	–	18.7	17.1	23.1	27.2	19.6	20.2	–	–	15.4	21.0	23.3
3. Some of the times	14.8	15.3	14.5	14.7	35.0	2.2	18.1	18.8	19.4	6.4	21.7	–	–		15.8	23.7
4. Most of the times	4.5	4.9	4.3	4.4	–	6.9	7.0	1.6	–	2.4	4.0	–	–		4.0	13.9
5. Every time	6.5	4.3	9.1	6.9	–	1.5	10.6	4.5	11.5	6.5	7.6	–	–	2.6	6.8	9.1
Item 3320 N(Wtd) ★	239	114	103	198	7	55	82	80	22	75	121	–	–	24	191	22

B058E: When people over age 30 were present

	TOTAL	M	F	White	Black	NE	NC	S	W	Yes	No	None	Mari-juana Only	Few Pills	More Pills	Any Heroin
1. Not at all	62.4	66.2	56.9	63.5	71.7	69.1	59.4	62.6	55.6	61.3	58.8	–	–	79.1	62.2	42.0
2. A few of the times	21.5	22.2	23.4	23.0	–	15.9	26.0	20.2	23.7	17.0	27.4	–	–	6.7	23.4	23.7
3. Some of the times	9.9	7.7	11.7	8.6	–	9.5	11.7	8.1	10.5	12.6	9.2	–	–	6.5	9.0	22.2
4. Most of the times	2.6	2.3	2.7	2.3	–	2.6	1.4	4.0	1.7	2.8	2.4	–	–		2.5	6.5
5. Every time	3.6	1.6	5.3	2.6	28.3	2.9	1.4	5.1	8.5	6.3	2.2	–	–	7.8	2.9	5.6
Item 3330 N(Wtd) ★	241	113	104	199	6	56	84	80	21	75	123	–	–	24	193	22

B058F: During the daytime (before 4:00 p.m.)

	TOTAL	M	F	White	Black	NE	NC	S	W	Yes	No	None	Mari-juana Only	Few Pills	More Pills	Any Heroin
1. Not at all	41.4	42.3	43.7	43.9	50.2	37.2	40.4	47.3	34.5	45.0	41.5	–	–	84.2	37.6	22.6
2. A few of the times	32.4	35.3	26.5	31.3	26.1	44.6	27.8	30.7	25.1	34.7	29.3	–	–	12.3	35.4	31.2
3. Some of the times	18.7	16.4	21.2	18.0	–	6.8	28.9	15.3	22.4	12.2	22.1	–	–		19.3	35.6
4. Most of the times	4.8	3.7	6.4	4.4	23.6	6.7	2.2	3.9	13.5	6.5	4.9	–	–		5.2	7.7
5. Every time	2.6	2.3	2.2	2.5	–	4.6	.7	2.8	4.5	1.7	2.3	–	–	3.5	2.5	2.8
Item 3340 N(Wtd) ★	241	114	105	199	7	56	83	80	22	75	123	–	–	24	193	22

★=excludes respondents for whom question was inappropriate.

QUESTIONNAIRE FORM 1 1976	TOTAL	SEX		RACE		REGION				4YR COLLEGE PLANS		ILLICIT DRUG USE: LIFETIME				
		M	F	White	Black	NE	NC	S	W	Yes	No	None	Mari- juana Only	Few Pills	More Pills	Any Her- oin
Weighted No. of Cases:	3039	1426	1466	2356	338	715	950	919	454	1384	1321	1219	669	329	605	47
% of Weighted Total:	100.0	46.9	48.2	77.5	11.1	23.5	31.3	30.2	15.0	45.5	43.5	40.1	22.0	10.8	19.9	1.6
B058G: At your home (or apartment or dorm)																
1. Not at all	42.0	47.5	39.3	43.1	40.5	40.7	41.1	41.9	49.2	35.5	46.5	-	-	53.1	43.3	15.0
2. A few of the times	24.6	24.9	21.3	24.6	24.5	26.7	28.2	21.1	17.7	22.9	26.0	-	-	14.5	24.9	33.8
3. Some of the times	14.5	12.8	15.8	12.9	-	18.3	13.0	12.5	18.3	19.1	10.1	-	-	6.5	13.6	31.7
4. Most of the times	8.4	6.8	9.5	8.6	8.9	5.0	8.8	10.6	7.6	4.2	10.0	-	-	7.4	7.9	14.8
5. Every time	10.5	7.9	14.1	10.8	26.1	9.3	8.9	13.8	7.2	18.3	7.4	-	-	18.6	10.2	4.6
Item 3350 N(Wtd) ★	241	114	105	200	7	54	84	80	22	75	123	-	-	24	193	22
B058H: At school																
1. Not at all	54.3	53.7	58.6	55.7	83.5	57.3	49.2	58.3	51.7	57.6	54.8	-	-	88.0	53.0	25.2
2. A few of the times	23.9	24.0	21.9	23.1	7.7	30.0	25.1	20.8	15.1	21.8	23.5	-	-	8.3	26.2	22.3
3. Some of the times	15.1	15.8	12.7	14.5	-	5.5	20.3	13.6	25.5	15.1	15.0	-	-	-	15.1	32.5
4. Most of the times	5.3	5.0	5.9	5.3	8.9	4.1	4.7	7.4	3.1	4.8	5.7	-	-	-	4.7	17.1
5. Every time	1.4	1.5	.9	1.3	-	3.1	.7	-	4.5	.7	1.0	-	-	3.7	1.0	2.8
Item 3360 N(Wtd) ★	240	114	105	199	7	56	84	79	22	75	122	-	-	23	193	22
B058I: In a car																
1. Not at all	49.6	45.2	55.0	50.3	73.1	67.1	38.2	45.9	61.9	65.6	39.3	-	-	89.4	46.4	28.6
2. A few of the times	24.1	28.1	17.6	21.7	18.1	17.7	26.9	28.9	12.6	21.3	25.7	-	-	6.0	26.7	23.8
3. Some of the times	16.2	15.9	17.8	17.0	-	8.0	19.9	17.1	19.4	6.4	21.1	-	-	-	17.6	22.7
4. Most of the times	4.9	5.0	5.6	5.3	8.9	4.2	6.6	4.2	3.3	3.1	7.8	-	-	-	4.0	19.1
5. Every time	5.2	5.8	4.0	5.6	-	3.0	8.4	4.0	2.9	3.7	6.1	-	-	4.6	5.2	5.7
Item 3380 N(Wtd) ★	241	113	105	199	7	56	83	80	22	75	122	-	-	24	193	22
B059: How many of the times when you used barbiturates during the last year did you use them along with each of the following drugs--that is, so that their effects overlapped?																
B059A: With alcohol																
1. Not at all	47.0	41.0	55.9	47.4	73.1	56.9	39.7	47.9	47.5	58.6	41.5	-	-	90.3	42.6	28.9
2. A few of the times	20.1	24.0	18.8	21.3	18.1	18.0	22.2	21.9	10.4	18.0	23.9	-	-	2.8	23.2	15.0
3. Some of the times	12.9	11.6	10.9	12.1	-	10.8	16.8	10.0	13.9	11.5	13.2	-	-	-	14.3	17.6
4. Most of the times	11.0	13.5	7.9	10.7	-	8.5	13.0	11.2	8.7	7.3	14.5	-	-	-	11.0	25.2
5. Every time	9.0	9.9	6.5	8.4	8.9	5.8	8.3	9.0	19.4	4.6	7.0	-	-	6.9	8.9	13.3
Item 3390 N(Wtd) ★	240	114	103	198	7	53	84	81	22	77	121	-	-	25	191	22
B059B: With marijuana																
1. Not at all	31.2	21.2	41.7	33.4	26.1	45.7	25.4	28.1	29.4	44.5	24.3	-	-	75.8	27.2	6.6
2. A few of the times	16.9	18.8	17.9	18.7	40.5	19.3	14.7	17.2	18.4	10.0	19.6	-	-	2.8	20.7	2.6
3. Some of the times	19.1	23.2	15.6	17.3	33.3	12.6	25.3	17.4	17.8	21.1	18.5	-	-	6.6	18.5	41.6
4. Most of the times	18.0	23.0	10.5	16.1	-	15.0	18.3	20.9	13.2	18.2	19.6	-	-	-	20.1	22.6
5. Every time	14.8	13.8	14.2	14.5	-	7.4	16.2	16.4	21.2	6.2	18.1	-	-	14.8	13.6	26.7
Item 3400 N(Wtd) ★	240	114	102	197	7	53	84	80	22	76	121	-	-	25	190	22
B059C: With LSD																
1. Not at all	97.5	97.0	99.3	98.8	100.0	99.0	96.3	98.8	93.5	96.9	98.3	-	-	100.0	99.6	76.3
2. A few of the times	1.8	2.4	.2	1.2	-	-	2.9	1.2	4.7	2.4	.9	-	-	-	.4	16.3
3. Some of the times	.2	-	.5	-	-	1.0	-	-	-	.7	-	-	-	-	-	2.6
4. Most of the times	.4	.6	-	-	-	-	.8	-	1.8	-	.9	-	-	-	-	4.8
5. Every time	-	-	-	-	-	-	-	-	-	-	-	-	-	-	-	-
Item 3410 N(Wtd) ★	226	105	100	187	6	53	80	73	20	74	114	-	-	24	179	21
B059D: With psychedelics other than LSD																
1. Not at all	92.3	89.2	95.7	92.6	91.1	94.6	87.2	94.9	96.2	92.9	91.1	-	-	100.0	93.6	70.4
2. A few of the times	4.8	7.1	1.9	4.7	8.9	1.3	10.0	2.9	1.0	3.0	5.8	-	-	-	4.5	13.4
3. Some of the times	2.2	2.4	2.3	2.3	-	4.2	1.1	2.2	1.0	4.1	1.6	-	-	-	1.4	11.3
4. Most of the times	.2	-	-	-	-	-	-	-	1.8	-	.3	-	-	-	-	1.7
5. Every time	.6	1.3	-	.4	-	-	1.8	-	-	-	1.2	-	-	-	.4	3.1
Item 3420 N(Wtd) ★	225	105	100	187	7	53	78	74	20	74	114	-	-	24	178	21

★=excludes respondents for whom question was inappropriate.

QUESTIONNAIRE FORM 1 1976	TOTAL	SEX		RACE		REGION				4YR COLLEGE PLANS		ILLICIT DRUG USE: LIFETIME				
		M	F	White	Black	NE	NC	S	W	Yes	No	None	Mari- juana Only	Few Pills	More Pills	Any Her- oin
Weighted No. of Cases:	3039	1426	1466	2356	338	715	950	919	454	1384	1321	1219	669	329	605	47
% of Weighted Total:	100.0	46.9	48.2	77.5	11.1	23.5	31.3	30.2	15.0	45.5	43.5	40.1	22.0	10.8	19.9	1.6
B059E: With amphetamines																
1. Not at all	89.3	89.5	90.8	90.7	91.1	94.2	87.8	86.1	94.1	91.2	87.1	–	–	100.0	89.6	72.6
2. A few of the times	5.4	6.1	3.7	5.5	–	4.8	8.9	3.5	–	3.4	7.3	–	–	–	6.1	6.1
3. Some of the times	4.7	4.4	4.9	3.7	8.9	–	3.3	10.4	1.0	4.7	5.3	–	–	–	4.3	14.0
4. Most of the times	.2	–	–	–	–	–	–	–	1.8	–	.3	–	–	–	–	1.7
5. Every time	.5	–	.5	–	–	1.0	–	–	3.1	.7	–	–	–	–	–	5.6
Item 3430 N(Wtd) ★	228	105	101	188	7	53	79	75	20	74	115	–	–	24	180	21
B059F: With quaaludes																
1. Not at all	92.2	89.6	96.4	92.8	100.0	95.6	93.7	88.3	91.6	92.9	92.0	–	–	100.0	93.7	69.7
2. A few of the times	3.1	5.0	1.8	3.6	–	2.1	1.6	6.4	–	3.6	3.4	–	–	–	2.8	10.2
3. Some of the times	2.9	4.9	.2	2.9	–	1.3	3.7	3.5	2.0	2.7	3.2	–	–	–	2.5	10.1
4. Most of the times	.5	–	.7	.4	–	–	–	.9	1.7	–	.9	–	–	–	.4	1.7
5. Every time	1.3	.6	.9	.3	–	1.0	1.0	.8	4.7	.7	.5	–	–	–	.6	8.3
Item 3440 N(Wtd) ★	226	107	98	187	7	53	78	75	21	74	115	–	–	24	179	21
B060: What are the most important reasons for your taking barbiturates without a doctor's orders? (Mark all that apply.)																
A. To experiment--to see what it's like	48.2	51.2	46.0	46.2	89.6	46.8	50.8	44.7	53.1	42.6	57.2	–	–	43.4	50.0	36.7
B. To relax or relieve tension	57.4	52.3	63.0	57.4	22.4	57.3	62.7	55.5	44.6	57.9	59.0	–	–	39.2	60.2	50.8
C. To feel good or get high	60.6	65.4	52.2	58.2	56.5	60.2	64.4	55.9	63.0	50.2	66.1	–	–	17.2	63.5	78.9
D. To seek deeper insights and understanding	6.6	6.9	4.0	5.8	12.0	3.7	12.0	3.2	4.4	2.2	8.5	–	–	7.0	5.7	13.9
E. To have a good time with my friends	37.7	43.0	30.1	35.4	59.2	35.1	47.2	30.2	33.4	26.1	44.4	–	–	18.8	39.6	39.8
F. To fit in with a group I like	2.2	3.9	.5	1.5	12.0	2.4	2.7	1.7	1.6	2.4	2.2	–	–	–	1.9	6.7
G. To get away from my problems or troubles	20.7	12.6	28.2	21.2	12.0	18.6	22.0	21.8	17.4	18.2	23.1	–	–	11.5	21.9	19.4
H. Because of boredom, nothing else to do	16.1	16.7	11.4	16.3	45.1	10.6	15.4	18.1	25.5	8.6	21.7	–	–	20.6	16.0	12.9
I. Because of anger or frustration	16.1	8.1	21.5	16.6	12.0	14.3	13.3	22.0	11.0	14.6	16.9	–	–	16.5	16.4	13.1
J. To get through the day	7.1	4.6	9.7	7.4	12.0	4.5	9.4	5.2	10.8	4.6	9.6	–	–	2.6	7.5	7.9
K. To increase the effects of some other drug(s)	11.4	16.4	5.5	11.2	12.0	11.4	13.2	9.0	13.0	10.3	12.3	–	–	5.0	10.4	26.9
L. To decrease (offset) the effects of some other drug(s)	4.9	8.1	1.0	3.8	12.0	4.2	7.8	1.9	6.3	7.8	3.4	–	–	–	5.5	4.5
M. To get to sleep	36.8	33.2	43.0	37.0	75.5	29.1	46.5	32.5	33.9	45.6	32.3	–	–	28.6	38.0	34.5
N. Because I am "hooked"--I have to have them	1.0	.8	1.1	.8	–	1.0	.9	–	5.2	.7	1.0	–	–	–	.4	7.7
Item 3450-3580 N(Wtd) ★	234	109	102	195	5	54	83	75	22	75	117	–	–	22	190	22
B061: When you take barbiturates how high do you usually get?																
1. Not at all high	4.6	3.6	6.0	4.0	24.4	8.6	2.6	4.9	1.6	5.8	4.4	–	–	19.4	3.1	–
2. A little high	22.6	21.8	23.2	25.2	7.2	20.9	30.6	13.9	27.5	23.1	24.9	–	–	26.0	23.8	8.1
3. Moderately high	46.3	45.9	49.6	45.2	53.5	41.8	45.3	50.4	46.7	37.0	54.4	–	–	24.0	47.3	65.5
4. Very high	14.7	17.2	9.4	12.6	8.3	15.8	9.6	19.5	14.1	13.7	11.0	–	–	–	15.9	21.8
5. I don't take them to get high	11.7	11.5	11.8	13.0	6.7	12.8	11.8	11.2	10.2	20.4	5.3	–	–	30.6	9.9	4.7
Item 3590 N(Wtd) ★	242	115	105	201	7	55	84	80	23	78	121	–	–	25	195	21
B062: When you take barbiturates how long do you usually stay high?																
1. Usually don't get high	13.8	13.5	14.5	14.2	26.1	19.5	15.7	8.3	11.9	19.6	9.2	–	–	35.1	12.8	1.8
2. One to two hours	26.0	22.4	31.1	27.2	32.9	25.7	29.0	25.9	16.7	22.2	32.0	–	–	24.9	27.4	14.9
3. Three to six hours	44.6	49.8	39.3	43.7	32.1	41.6	43.0	44.6	57.1	36.3	48.7	–	–	31.7	45.2	51.7
4. Seven to 24 hours	14.7	13.7	14.0	14.6	–	12.4	12.2	19.6	12.9	20.3	9.3	–	–	8.4	13.9	27.5
5. More than 24 hours	.9	.6	1.1	.3	8.9	1.0	–	1.6	1.6	1.5	.8	–	–	–	.6	4.1
Item 3600 N(Wtd) ★	234	107	105	194	7	55	81	75	23	73	121	–	–	20	192	22

★=excludes respondents for whom question was inappropriate.

QUESTIONNAIRE FORM 1 1976	TOTAL	SEX		RACE		REGION				4YR COLLEGE PLANS		ILLICIT DRUG USE: LIFETIME				
		M	F	White	Black	NE	NC	S	W	Yes	No	None	Marijuana Only	Few Pills	More Pills	Any Heroin
Weighted No. of Cases:	3039	1426	1466	2356	338	715	950	919	454	1384	1321	1219	669	329	605	47
% of Weighted Total:	100.0	46.9	48.2	77.5	11.1	23.5	31.3	30.2	15.0	45.5	43.5	40.1	22.0	10.8	19.9	1.6

B063: What barbiturates have you taken during the last year without a doctor's orders? (Mark all that apply.)

	TOTAL	M	F	White	Black	NE	NC	S	W	Yes	No	None	Marijuana Only	Few Pills	More Pills	Any Heroin
A. Phenobarbital	32.2	33.8	29.7	32.3	9.9	31.4	38.9	24.9	34.3	35.6	28.5	-	-	18.1	31.0	58.3
B. Seconal	38.0	40.9	34.5	37.6	18.4	25.0	42.0	40.7	45.1	40.0	35.7	-	-	11.6	37.9	65.8
C. Tuinal	21.2	23.5	14.9	18.2	-	20.9	20.4	24.7	13.1	13.0	19.3	-	-	4.0	20.8	43.5
D. Nembutal	10.8	12.8	9.0	8.3	18.4	4.4	9.9	14.5	17.1	10.7	10.8	-	-	-	11.3	17.8
E. Luminal	8.1	7.6	7.3	7.5	18.4	4.2	9.9	8.3	10.2	14.9	4.5	-	-	2.9	7.8	16.5
F. Desbutal	3.2	3.1	1.5	3.0	-	5.2	2.7	2.0	4.2	4.0	3.2	-	-	-	2.3	14.5
G. Amytal	7.4	8.0	7.2	5.9	9.9	1.8	10.0	8.9	6.8	11.1	6.0	-	-	2.9	6.6	19.7
H. Adrenocal	4.0	3.1	2.7	2.3	9.9	1.0	5.9	3.9	4.2	3.5	2.7	-	-	-	3.3	14.3
I. Other	37.5	41.5	33.3	36.8	-	30.9	44.2	34.3	40.3	34.5	41.2	-	-	6.4	39.7	50.0
J. Don't know the names of some that I have used	45.6	37.1	53.6	45.9	73.0	41.5	49.9	46.2	38.2	44.2	48.4	-	-	60.0	45.3	33.1
Item 3610-3700 N(Wtd) ★	236	109	105	197	6	54	82	77	23	75	119	-	-	21	194	21

B064: Have you ever tried to stop using barbiturates and found that you couldn't stop?

	TOTAL	M	F	White	Black	NE	NC	S	W	Yes	No	None	Marijuana Only	Few Pills	More Pills	Any Heroin
1. Yes	2.2	1.3	2.7	1.6	-	2.1	1.3	1.0	9.6	.7	3.4	-	-	-	1.3	12.7
2. No	97.8	98.7	97.3	98.4	100.0	97.9	98.7	99.0	90.4	99.3	96.6	-	-	100.0	98.7	87.3
Item 3710 N(Wtd) ★	238	110	106	198	7	54	84	77	24	75	121	-	-	22	194	22

B065: Do you think you will be using barbiturates without a doctor's prescription five years from now?

	TOTAL	M	F	White	Black	NE	NC	S	W	Yes	No	None	Marijuana Only	Few Pills	More Pills	Any Heroin
1. I definitely will	.6	.4	.6	.4	.9	.7	.6	.4	.6	.5	.6	.4	.3	-	.9	7.1
2. I probably will	3.2	3.8	2.5	3.5	.8	2.6	3.5	3.9	2.4	1.9	4.5	*	.2	2.0	13.3	21.3
3. I probably will not	19.2	21.8	16.1	19.5	13.3	20.4	18.8	19.0	18.8	17.0	19.7	8.9	15.9	30.3	39.7	38.3
4. I definitely will not	77.0	73.9	80.7	76.6	85.0	76.3	77.2	76.6	78.2	80.5	75.2	90.7	83.6	67.7	46.1	33.3
Item 3720 N(Wtd)	2811	1335	1394	2232	316	633	892	862	424	1311	1250	1181	614	302	554	45

The next questions are about TRANQUILIZERS, which doctors sometimes prescribe to calm people down, quiet their nerves, or relax their muscles.

They include the following drugs: Librium, Valium, Miltown, Equanil, Meprobamate, Serax, Atarax, Tranxene, Vistaril.

B066: Have you ever taken tranquilizers because a doctor told you to use them?

	TOTAL	M	F	White	Black	NE	NC	S	W	Yes	No	None	Marijuana Only	Few Pills	More Pills	Any Heroin
1. No	83.7	84.7	82.7	82.9	89.1	87.8	85.5	79.7	81.1	83.7	83.8	90.2	88.2	70.4	73.4	71.5
2. Yes, but I had already tried them on my own.	2.4	2.2	2.4	2.4	1.4	2.2	2.1	3.0	2.3	1.9	2.3	.2	.4	1.6	7.9	23.9
3. Yes, and it was the first time I took any	13.9	13.0	14.9	14.6	9.4	9.9	12.4	17.2	16.6	14.4	13.9	9.6	11.4	28.0	18.7	4.6
Item 3730 N(Wtd)	2795	1322	1395	2242	298	650	884	842	419	1333	1222	1178	625	309	567	45

B067: On how many occasions (if any) have you taken tranquilizers on your own--that is, without a doctor telling you to take them...

B067A: ...in your lifetime?

	TOTAL	M	F	White	Black	NE	NC	S	W	Yes	No	None	Marijuana Only	Few Pills	More Pills	Any Heroin
1. 0 occasions	84.3	86.5	82.9	83.2	94.4	86.5	85.7	80.8	84.8	86.7	83.7	100.0	100.0	60.9	49.1	33.6
2. 1-2	7.5	7.1	7.6	7.8	3.5	6.5	5.9	10.2	7.1	7.4	6.6	-	-	39.1	14.6	13.9
3. 3-5	3.5	2.5	4.3	3.9	1.1	3.3	3.4	3.9	3.0	2.4	4.4	-	-	-	16.4	8.0
4. 6-9	1.4	1.0	1.6	1.5	.3	1.7	1.0	1.2	2.1	1.4	1.1	-	-	-	6.6	3.0
5. 10-19	1.4	1.4	1.4	1.6	.2	.9	1.6	1.5	1.6	1.0	1.7	-	-	-	6.0	12.9
6. 20-39	.8	.4	1.1	.8	.4	.7	1.0	1.0	.4	.5	1.0	-	-	-	3.4	7.5
7. 40 or more	1.1	1.0	1.1	1.1	.2	.5	1.4	1.4	1.0	.6	1.4	-	-	-	3.8	21.1
Item 1070 N(Wtd)	2756	1314	1363	2215	288	632	874	837	413	1314	1202	1186	623	304	563	43

★=excludes respondents for whom question was inappropriate.   * =less than .05 per cent.

QUESTIONNAIRE FORM 1 1976	TOTAL	SEX		RACE		REGION				4YR COLLEGE PLANS		ILLICIT DRUG USE: LIFETIME				
		M	F	White	Black	NE	NC	S	W	Yes	No	None	Mari-juana Only	Few Pills	More Pills	Any Her-oin
Weighted No. of Cases:	3039	1426	1466	2356	338	715	950	919	454	1384	1321	1219	669	329	605	47
% of Weighted Total:	100.0	46.9	48.2	77.5	11.1	23.5	31.3	30.2	15.0	45.5	43.5	40.1	22.0	10.8	19.9	1.6
B067B: ...during the last 12 months?																
1. 0 occasions	91.2	92.4	90.6	90.8	97.4	93.5	91.3	89.1	91.9	92.3	91.4	100.0	100.0	88.0	66.5	55.7
2. 1-2	4.3	4.0	4.2	4.5	1.3	3.9	3.3	5.3	4.6	4.4	3.6	-	-	12.0	14.2	6.0
3. 3-5	2.1	1.9	2.2	2.3	.7	1.3	2.4	2.8	1.3	1.4	2.5	-	-	-	10.0	6.7
4. 6-9	.7	.4	.9	.7	.3	.4	.8	.7	.7	.5	.7	-	-	-	2.5	9.7
5. 10-19	.9	.7	1.0	1.0	.2	.3	1.2	1.1	.6	.7	.7	-	-	-	4.0	3.0
6. 20-39	.3	.2	.3	.2	.2	.4	.5	.1	.2	.2	.3	-	-	-	1.2	4.5
7. 40 or more	.6	.4	.7	.5	-	.2	.5	.9	.7	.4	.8	-	-	-	1.7	14.3
Item 1080 N(Wtd)	2740	1310	1354	2201	287	631	872	825	412	1307	1198	1187	624	293	556	43
B067C: ...during the last 30 days?																
1. 0 occasions	96.5	96.8	96.4	96.6	98.7	97.3	96.2	95.7	97.5	97.4	96.5	100.0	100.0	96.5	86.9	72.2
2. 1-2	1.9	2.0	1.7	2.0	.8	2.2	1.9	1.9	1.7	1.5	1.8	-	-	3.5	7.1	9.5
3. 3-5	.7	.6	.8	.6	.3	.3	.8	1.2	.2	.7	.5	-	-	-	3.2	1.4
4. 6-9	.4	.1	.7	.4	-	-	.7	.6	.1	.1	.6	-	-	-	1.3	8.6
5. 10-19	.1	.1	.2	.1	.2	*	.1	.2	.2	.1	.2	-	-	-	.5	1.8
6. 20-39	.1	-	.2	.1	-	.1	-	.3	-	*	.2	-	-	-	.5	1.2
7. 40 or more	.2	.3	-	.1	-	.1	.2	.1	.3	.2	.2	-	-	-	.5	5.2
Item 1090 N(Wtd)	2733	1307	1350	2194	288	630	867	823	412	1304	1194	1187	624	291	551	43

IF YOU HAVE NOT TAKEN TRANQUILIZERS IN THE LAST TWELVE MONTHS, GO TO Q.B075.

THE FOLLOWING QUESTIONS REFER ONLY TO TAKING TRANQUILIZERS WITHOUT A DOCTOR'S ORDERS. IF YOU HAVE NOT DONE THIS IN THE LAST TWELVE MONTHS, GO TO Q.B075.

B068: When you used tranquilizers during the last year, how often did you use them in each of the following situations?

B068A: When you were alone	TOTAL	M	F	White	Black	NE	NC	S	W	Yes	No	None	Mari-juana Only	Few Pills	More Pills	Any Her-oin
1. Not at all	51.3	57.2	45.9	52.5	49.1	51.8	51.6	51.8	48.4	50.6	47.5	-	-	63.4	51.4	22.3
2. A few of the times	30.2	31.2	29.5	28.2	32.2	31.4	34.8	25.4	33.5	28.2	32.7	-	-	23.9	29.5	56.9
3. Some of the times	6.0	3.0	8.8	6.1	4.7	3.4	2.9	9.2	6.4	7.4	5.8	-	-	5.0	6.2	7.4
4. Most of the times	7.4	6.3	9.3	8.6	7.7	5.2	7.6	9.2	4.1	6.9	10.9	-	-	6.0	7.5	6.3
5. Every time	5.0	2.4	6.5	4.5	6.3	8.2	3.1	4.3	7.5	6.9	3.1	-	-	1.7	5.4	7.2
Item 3740 N(Wtd) ★	228	92	120	186	13	39	67	93	28	89	100	-	-	27	177	18
B068B: With just 1 or 2 other people																
1. Not at all	29.3	24.0	33.0	27.1	61.5	29.0	21.4	35.8	27.1	39.5	24.2	-	-	52.8	25.1	15.4
2. A few of the times	33.2	34.1	34.4	35.2	17.5	38.7	37.4	28.0	32.5	29.9	33.0	-	-	19.1	37.8	22.1
3. Some of the times	19.6	19.4	20.4	21.0	4.9	14.1	31.5	15.7	11.4	12.3	28.2	-	-	-	21.1	40.7
4. Most of the times	7.4	7.6	5.7	7.2	8.0	6.7	5.9	7.4	12.1	7.7	6.3	-	-	-	7.1	18.4
5. Every time	10.5	14.9	6.4	9.5	8.1	11.4	3.8	13.0	16.9	10.6	8.4	-	-	28.1	8.9	3.4
Item 3750 N(Wtd) ★	226	90	119	184	12	38	67	92	28	87	100	-	-	27	174	18
B068C: At a party																
1. Not at all	59.8	49.5	70.1	62.6	91.6	66.8	42.0	67.5	66.9	70.1	53.4	-	-	94.4	57.5	16.5
2. A few of the times	10.9	16.5	6.7	10.5	-	5.2	11.2	12.0	14.9	12.2	11.4	-	-	2.1	10.7	29.2
3. Some of the times	15.6	15.5	15.3	14.8	4.9	17.3	24.4	10.2	9.9	11.6	18.0	-	-	-	17.0	30.6
4. Most of the times	9.2	12.3	5.8	7.8	3.6	6.3	16.7	5.8	6.1	4.0	12.4	-	-	-	10.7	11.0
5. Every time	4.6	6.2	2.2	4.2	-	4.5	5.7	4.6	2.2	2.1	4.8	-	-	3.5	4.1	12.7
Item 3760 N(Wtd) ★	226	91	119	184	12	39	67	92	28	88	100	-	-	27	174	18

* = less than .05 per cent.   ★ = excludes respondents for whom question was inappropriate.

QUESTIONNAIRE FORM 1 1976	TOTAL	SEX		RACE		REGION				4YR COLLEGE PLANS		ILLICIT DRUG USE: LIFETIME				
		M	F	White	Black	NE	NC	S	W	Yes	No	None	Mari-juana Only	Few Pills	More Pills	Any Her-oin
Weighted No. of Cases:	3039	1426	1466	2356	338	715	950	919	454	1384	1321	1219	669	329	605	47
% of Weighted Total:	100.0	46.9	48.2	77.5	11.1	23.5	31.3	30.2	15.0	45.5	43.5	40.1	22.0	10.8	19.9	1.6
B068D: When your date or spouse was present																
1. Not at all	67.2	72.6	65.7	67.9	91.6	75.5	62.5	66.5	69.4	79.4	57.3	-	-	100.0	63.0	47.2
2. A few of the times	15.9	11.1	18.4	17.9	-	13.6	13.2	19.8	12.7	12.4	21.3	-	-	-	19.3	13.2
3. Some of the times	10.6	13.1	8.6	8.7	8.4	5.0	15.4	9.3	10.4	3.8	14.4	-	-	-	11.3	23.0
4. Most of the times	3.0	.9	4.5	3.0	-	1.4	8.0	1.0	-	1.4	4.9	-	-	-	3.3	5.9
5. Every time	3.3	2.3	2.7	2.5	-	4.4	.9	3.3	7.5	3.0	2.1	-	-	-	3.1	10.8
Item 3770 N(Wtd) ★	224	90	118	182	13	38	67	92	28	87	98	-	-	27	172	18
B068E: When people over age 30 were present																
1. Not at all	53.1	58.8	48.1	51.0	85.8	69.6	54.2	46.5	48.9	50.8	58.3	-	-	50.5	54.7	25.4
2. A few of the times	17.4	15.3	20.3	18.4	5.8	6.8	23.7	16.3	20.7	14.5	18.3	-	-	6.6	17.6	37.1
3. Some of the times	9.2	12.7	6.0	8.5	-	7.6	10.0	10.0	6.8	7.0	11.5	-	-	-	9.3	24.5
4. Most of the times	5.9	4.1	8.1	6.7	-	3.7	4.1	7.6	7.6	7.7	4.0	-	-	6.1	6.1	5.7
5. Every time	14.4	9.1	17.5	15.4	8.5	12.2	7.9	19.6	16.0	20.0	7.9	-	-	36.9	12.3	7.3
Item 3780 N(Wtd) ★	224	92	116	183	12	38	68	91	28	87	99	-	-	26	173	18
B068F: During the daytime (before 4:00 p.m.)																
1. Not at all	40.0	48.4	34.7	39.7	69.2	45.0	28.6	44.3	46.7	40.0	38.1	-	-	60.3	35.6	31.1
2. A few of the times	28.9	26.8	30.7	26.6	26.0	21.1	41.2	26.4	18.1	27.5	28.4	-	-	23.2	31.0	27.2
3. Some of the times	17.2	11.0	20.1	18.6	-	10.8	20.8	17.4	17.1	11.3	24.2	-	-	-	19.4	28.4
4. Most of the times	5.9	5.1	7.3	6.4	4.9	9.4	2.4	5.8	9.6	9.2	3.3	-	-	7.7	5.8	6.1
5. Every time	8.0	8.8	7.2	8.6	-	13.7	7.1	6.0	8.5	12.0	6.0	-	-	8.8	8.2	7.2
Item 3790 N(Wtd) ★	228	92	119	186	12	39	68	92	28	88	101	-	-	28	175	18
B068G: At your home (or apartment or dorm																
1. Not at all	34.8	51.6	23.5	34.1	45.9	54.0	34.4	26.4	37.5	33.9	36.1	-	-	34.1	35.7	10.9
2. A few of the times	25.5	18.6	29.4	24.0	26.7	18.3	34.1	25.7	14.8	18.1	28.2	-	-	17.5	24.5	55.3
3. Some of the times	8.7	8.9	8.5	7.2	4.9	5.5	8.9	9.7	9.6	9.0	8.8	-	-	-	9.9	13.3
4. Most of the times	9.7	9.3	10.2	10.8	8.0	7.8	7.0	11.0	13.9	9.5	11.3	-	-	6.0	9.6	13.3
5. Every time	21.3	11.6	28.4	24.0	14.6	14.4	15.7	27.2	24.3	29.5	15.6	-	-	42.4	20.3	7.2
Item 3800 N(Wtd) ★	223	91	118	181	12	38	66	91	29	86	99	-	-	26	172	18
B068H: At school																
1. Not at all	63.3	56.9	70.8	64.4	65.6	62.3	51.7	69.8	70.8	64.2	61.1	-	-	81.7	63.3	23.8
2. A few of the times	15.8	16.3	13.6	14.6	26.0	13.6	16.3	17.3	12.2	14.4	16.4	-	-	18.3	15.0	24.4
3. Some of the times	15.0	19.8	11.8	15.4	3.6	14.1	26.7	7.0	14.9	13.1	18.7	-	-	-	15.7	35.0
4. Most of the times	3.0	4.8	1.3	2.9	4.9	2.4	.7	5.9	-	2.4	3.7	-	-	-	2.9	9.5
5. Every time	2.9	2.3	2.6	2.8	-	7.7	4.6	-	2.2	5.9	-	-	-	-	3.0	7.2
Item 3810 N(Wtd) ★	225	91	119	183	12	38	66	92	28	87	100	-	-	27	173	18
B068I: In a car																
1. Not at all	62.2	52.9	72.1	63.5	77.6	70.4	48.6	67.9	64.7	74.4	48.3	-	-	86.1	60.3	32.6
2. A few of the times	18.3	24.4	11.1	16.0	17.6	19.3	19.6	17.4	17.0	13.1	22.8	-	-	13.9	19.4	21.0
3. Some of the times	14.1	15.3	13.7	15.2	4.9	6.2	25.6	9.5	12.4	10.2	20.1	-	-	-	15.2	28.9
4. Most of the times	3.2	5.8	1.3	3.7	-	-	6.2	2.9	1.3	1.5	5.9	-	-	-	3.0	10.4
5. Every time	2.2	1.5	1.8	1.6	-	4.1	-	2.3	4.6	.8	2.9	-	-	-	2.1	7.2
Item 3830 N(Wtd) ★	225	91	119	183	12	38	66	92	28	87	100	-	-	27	173	18
B069: How many of the times when you used tranquilizers during the last year did you use them along with each of the following drugs--that is, so that their effects overlapped?																

★ = excludes respondents for whom question was inappropriate.

QUESTIONNAIRE FORM 1 1976	TOTAL	SEX		RACE		REGION				4YR COLLEGE PLANS		ILLICIT DRUG USE: LIFETIME				
		M	F	White	Black	NE	NC	S	W	Yes	No	None	Marijuana Only	Few Pills	More Pills	Any Heroin
Weighted No. of Cases:	3039	1426	1466	2356	338	715	950	919	454	1384	1321	1219	669	329	605	47
% of Weighted Total:	100.0	46.9	48.2	77.5	11.1	23.5	31.3	30.2	15.0	45.5	43.5	40.1	22.0	10.8	19.9	1.6
B069A: With alcohol																
1. Not at all	60.6	49.2	71.1	57.9	83.1	60.5	45.6	72.1	58.0	69.0	53.0	-	-	96.6	55.5	41.4
2. A few of the times	17.1	23.0	14.0	19.4	13.3	11.8	27.7	10.3	21.3	14.4	22.0	-	-	-	21.2	8.2
3. Some of the times	10.0	9.8	8.6	9.9	3.6	8.7	14.9	7.8	7.2	8.9	11.2	-	-	-	10.5	23.5
4. Most of the times	6.9	8.5	4.2	7.3	-	7.8	7.4	5.4	9.3	3.6	10.3	-	-	-	7.0	18.9
5. Every time	5.5	9.6	2.1	5.4	-	11.1	4.4	4.4	4.2	4.2	3.6	-	-	3.4	5.7	7.9
Item 3840 N(Wtd) ★	224	88	119	182	12	37	66	92	28	89	97	-	-	28	173	18
B069B: With marijuana																
1. Not at all	49.1	30.7	63.6	51.7	87.4	48.9	36.8	58.8	47.2	61.4	43.7	-	-	96.6	44.7	4.4
2. A few of the times	17.6	26.2	11.4	17.1	-	20.6	28.9	7.6	19.5	15.1	17.6	-	-	-	21.3	15.2
3. Some of the times	14.3	18.4	12.2	13.6	12.6	11.2	12.9	14.9	20.1	9.0	17.7	-	-	-	16.3	21.7
4. Most of the times	11.9	13.1	9.9	10.5	-	8.4	16.0	10.6	11.0	8.1	14.2	-	-	-	11.2	39.6
5. Every time	7.1	11.7	2.9	7.1	-	10.8	5.4	8.1	2.2	6.4	6.8	-	-	3.4	6.6	19.1
Item 3850 N(Wtd) ★	224	88	119	183	12	38	66	92	28	89	97	-	-	28	172	18
B069C: With LSD																
1. Not at all	98.7	98.6	99.4	99.2	100.0	98.5	97.6	99.9	97.2	98.9	98.6	-	-	100.0	100.0	82.8
2. A few of the times	.7	1.2	-	.6	-	-	2.4	-	-	.5	.6	-	-	-	-	9.3
3. Some of the times	.2	.2	.2	.2	-	-	-	-	1.5	-	.4	-	-	-	-	2.5
4. Most of the times	.4	-	.4	-	-	1.5	-	-	1.3	.6	.4	-	-	-	-	5.4
5. Every time	-	-	-	-	-	-	-	-	-	-	-	-	-	-	-	-
Item 3860 N(Wtd) ★	216	82	119	175	12	36	63	90	28	85	94	-	-	28	166	16
B069D: With psychedelics other than LSD																
1. Not at all	96.5	93.0	99.4	96.8	100.0	98.6	91.4	99.2	96.5	97.6	95.2	-	-	100.0	97.8	77.0
2. A few of the times	2.7	6.2	.2	2.8	-	-	8.6	-	2.2	1.0	4.4	-	-	-	2.2	13.3
3. Some of the times	.6	.8	.4	.4	-	1.4	-	.8	-	1.4	-	-	-	-	-	7.5
4. Most of the times	.2	-	-	-	-	-	-	-	1.3	-	.4	-	-	-	-	2.2
5. Every time	-	-	-	-	-	-	-	-	-	-	-	-	-	-	-	-
Item 3870 N(Wtd) ★	215	83	117	175	12	37	62	88	28	86	92	-	-	28	166	16
B069E: With amphetamines																
1. Not at all	93.9	91.3	97.2	95.7	95.1	94.5	94.1	94.8	89.5	93.7	94.3	-	-	100.0	95.0	71.0
2. A few of the times	2.3	3.1	1.1	1.9	-	1.7	1.7	1.5	7.0	1.5	1.8	-	-	-	1.6	13.4
3. Some of the times	2.7	4.5	1.3	1.9	4.9	-	4.2	3.7	-	3.1	3.5	-	-	-	2.8	6.8
4. Most of the times	.8	1.1	.4	.5	-	3.8	-	-	1.3	1.7	.4	-	-	-	.6	5.2
5. Every time	.3	-	-	-	-	-	-	-	2.2	-	-	-	-	-	-	3.6
Item 3880 N(Wtd) ★	217	83	118	175	12	37	63	89	28	86	94	-	-	28	167	17
B069F: With quaaludes																
1. Not at all	95.9	94.6	97.7	96.4	100.0	98.6	96.0	95.4	93.6	97.7	95.1	-	-	100.0	97.3	74.5
2. A few of the times	1.6	2.4	1.3	1.6	-	-	2.1	2.5	-	-	2.3	-	-	-	1.8	3.3
3. Some of the times	1.5	2.8	.2	1.9	-	-	1.9	2.1	.8	1.7	2.0	-	-	-	.7	12.1
4. Most of the times	.7	.3	.8	.1	-	1.4	-	-	3.4	.6	.6	-	-	-	.2	6.4
5. Every time	.3	-	-	-	-	-	-	-	2.3	-	-	-	-	-	-	3.7
Item 3890 N(Wtd) ★	214	83	115	173	12	37	62	87	27	83	94	-	-	28	164	17
B069G: With barbiturates																
1. Not at all	86.6	81.6	90.3	86.9	95.1	96.7	70.0	92.5	92.3	87.1	83.4	-	-	100.0	88.1	45.6
2. A few of the times	9.0	13.9	6.7	9.4	-	-	25.5	3.1	2.2	10.0	11.2	-	-	-	8.7	30.1
3. Some of the times	3.7	3.7	2.6	3.3	4.9	1.9	3.8	4.4	3.5	2.4	4.8	-	-	-	3.0	17.9
4. Most of the times	.7	.8	.4	.4	-	1.4	.7	-	2.0	.6	.6	-	-	-	.3	6.4
5. Every time	-	-	-	-	-	-	-	-	-	-	-	-	-	-	-	-
Item 3900 N(Wtd) ★	220	86	118	178	12	37	64	90	28	89	93	-	-	28	169	17

★ = excludes respondents for whom question was inappropriate.

QUESTIONNAIRE FORM 1 1976	TOTAL	SEX		RACE		REGION				4YR COLLEGE PLANS		ILLICIT DRUG USE: LIFETIME				
		M	F	White	Black	NE	NC	S	W	Yes	No	None	Marijuana Only	Few Pills	More Pills	Any Heroin
Weighted No. of Cases:	3039	1426	1466	2356	338	715	950	919	454	1384	1321	1219	669	329	605	47
% of Weighted Total:	100.0	46.9	48.2	77.5	11.1	23.5	31.3	30.2	15.0	45.5	43.5	40.1	22.0	10.8	19.9	1.6

B070: What have been the most important reasons for your taking tranquilizers without a doctor's orders? (Mark all that apply.)

	TOTAL	M	F	White	Black	NE	NC	S	W	Yes	No	None	Marijuana Only	Few Pills	More Pills	Any Heroin
A. To experiment--to see what it's like	34.4	47.9	25.0	32.9	13.5	47.7	33.4	30.7	29.5	28.9	38.6	-	-	14.9	37.5	36.1
B. To relax or relieve tension	70.3	54.4	82.5	70.7	94.3	57.9	78.9	72.0	62.9	74.9	74.9	-	-	77.0	70.1	60.7
C. To feel good or get high	40.2	56.5	28.1	38.8	22.3	55.4	47.5	26.8	42.2	29.6	49.7	-	-	8.9	42.2	68.7
D. To seek deeper insights and understanding	5.6	8.0	3.5	4.5	7.8	9.8	7.8	1.7	6.8	6.5	6.1	-	-	3.9	4.9	15.1
E. To have a good time with my friends	24.4	40.2	11.6	23.2	7.8	38.9	31.0	11.3	28.5	19.1	31.2	-	-	1.6	25.2	51.5
F. To fit in with a group I like	3.3	5.8	1.5	2.3	7.8	3.3	4.2	1.6	6.4	4.1	2.3	-	-	-	3.7	4.8
G. To get away from my problems or troubles	22.6	15.0	26.6	23.0	35.8	29.8	24.8	17.7	22.5	19.8	27.5	-	-	19.7	23.7	18.7
H. Because of boredom, nothing else to do	10.3	16.2	5.6	10.1	7.8	7.3	9.4	7.8	23.7	5.7	15.5	-	-	-	11.2	17.3
I. Because of anger or frustration	18.1	11.2	24.8	18.5	12.8	26.4	18.5	14.3	17.3	19.5	18.5	-	-	3.9	19.7	19.4
J. To get through the day	7.1	6.0	8.6	6.8	8.8	10.8	10.7	2.2	8.7	8.3	8.8	-	-	7.1	7.5	4.8
K. To increase the effects of some other drug(s)	9.3	15.8	4.1	8.0	7.8	9.7	12.4	5.4	13.6	9.7	9.5	-	-	-	10.5	12.2
L. To decrease (offset) the effects of some other drug(s)	5.9	9.3	3.5	5.2	-	4.8	13.1	1.9	3.1	5.4	7.2	-	-	-	6.8	6.7
M. To get to sleep	42.6	38.1	46.2	42.6	72.0	31.8	48.1	39.6	54.3	40.0	42.4	-	-	38.0	43.6	37.7
N. Because I am "hooked"--I feel I have to have them	1.1	1.8	.5	.4	-	3.2	-	-	4.4	2.4	.4	-	-	-	.5	8.6
Item 3910-4040 N(Wtd) ★	213	86	113	178	8	39	64	83	28	88	90	-	-	27	167	18

B071: When you take tranquilizers how high do you usually get?

	TOTAL	M	F	White	Black	NE	NC	S	W	Yes	No	None	Marijuana Only	Few Pills	More Pills	Any Heroin
1. Not at all high	16.2	10.2	18.3	16.3	40.7	18.1	4.3	22.2	23.4	19.2	11.9	-	-	32.7	14.7	3.9
2. A little high	24.1	23.8	26.4	24.0	16.5	21.3	27.3	25.4	15.0	20.2	26.5	-	-	19.4	24.7	26.7
3. Moderately high	31.4	41.0	22.8	30.5	16.4	44.5	29.7	25.0	38.5	27.0	34.8	-	-	5.9	35.9	34.2
4. Very high	9.8	12.1	7.2	8.7	6.6	7.0	13.6	9.3	5.9	10.1	9.8	-	-	3.3	9.0	28.3
5. I don't take them to get high	18.5	12.9	25.3	20.5	19.8	9.2	25.1	18.0	17.1	23.4	17.0	-	-	38.8	15.6	7.0
Item 4050 N(Wtd) ★	213	87	111	177	9	38	64	86	25	85	93	-	-	29	164	18

B072: When you take tranquilizers how long do you usually stay high?

	TOTAL	M	F	White	Black	NE	NC	S	W	Yes	No	None	Marijuana Only	Few Pills	More Pills	Any Heroin
1. Usually don't get high	33.0	26.3	37.9	35.6	49.6	24.2	26.8	38.7	43.2	44.5	23.3	-	-	72.6	29.1	10.9
2. One to two hours	24.1	22.7	27.3	23.5	23.3	20.4	28.4	24.6	17.0	19.1	28.0	-	-	16.1	25.2	20.9
3. Three to six hours	35.6	43.7	27.6	33.4	20.5	46.8	36.5	31.3	31.0	30.6	39.2	-	-	11.2	37.7	55.7
4. Seven to 24 hours	6.5	6.4	6.7	7.0	6.6	5.4	8.3	5.3	7.5	4.3	9.1	-	-	-	7.9	3.5
5. More than 24 hours	.7	.8	.5	.4	-	3.2	-	-	1.3	1.4	.4	-	-	-	-	8.9
Item 4060 N(Wtd) ★	214	86	113	178	9	39	65	84	27	88	93	-	-	27	167	18

B073: What tranquilizers have you taken during the last year without a doctor's orders? (Mark all that apply.)

	TOTAL	M	F	White	Black	NE	NC	S	W	Yes	No	None	Marijuana Only	Few Pills	More Pills	Any Heroin
A. Librium	34.2	40.0	32.1	35.1	17.2	24.9	44.8	35.2	19.6	35.5	33.2	-	-	11.9	34.3	67.0
B. Valium	67.8	63.1	72.3	66.1	48.0	61.9	73.6	64.7	72.4	58.9	72.8	-	-	40.4	71.4	77.4
C. Miltown	3.4	4.4	2.1	3.1	-	5.9	3.1	1.7	5.9	6.9	1.4	-	-	-	2.3	18.5
D. Equanil	5.6	9.6	2.3	4.3	-	8.9	7.4	2.4	7.7	7.7	4.7	-	-	-	5.8	12.2
E. Meprobamate	7.5	5.1	9.5	7.2	-	3.4	6.6	9.3	9.1	7.3	8.3	-	-	-	6.2	31.7
F. Serax	3.4	3.7	3.3	3.1	-	5.3	-	3.8	7.4	6.5	2.0	-	-	-	2.4	18.6
G. Atarax	2.8	3.1	2.6	2.4	-	3.4	1.5	2.1	7.0	2.5	3.5	-	-	-	2.5	10.2
H. Tranxene	3.5	4.9	2.0	2.9	-	3.4	1.7	3.6	7.4	3.6	4.1	-	-	-	2.1	21.9
I. Vistaril	2.5	2.9	1.5	1.7	6.6	3.4	3.7	.7	4.4	3.8	2.2	-	-	-	2.0	11.2
J. Don't know the names of some tranquilizers I have used	39.7	42.8	33.9	38.8	41.4	49.8	44.4	31.7	41.7	44.1	41.7	-	-	57.2	35.8	48.0
Item 4070-4160 N(Wtd) ★	212	88	110	177	9	36	61	87	28	84	95	-	-	26	168	18

★ = excludes respondents for whom question was inappropriate.

QUESTIONNAIRE FORM 1 1976	TOTAL	SEX		RACE		REGION				4YR COLLEGE PLANS		ILLICIT DRUG USE: LIFETIME				
		M	F	White	Black	NE	NC	S	W	Yes	No	None	Marijuana Only	Few Pills	More Pills	Any Heroin
Weighted No. of Cases:	3039	1426	1466	2356	338	715	950	919	454	1384	1321	1219	669	329	605	47
% of Weighted Total:	100.0	46.9	48.2	77.5	11.1	23.5	31.3	30.2	15.0	45.5	43.5	40.1	22.0	10.8	19.9	1.6

B074: Have you ever tried to stop using tranquilizers and found that you couldn't stop?

1. Yes	2.3	1.5	2.0	1.4	13.6	3.3	1.7	.7	7.9	2.2	2.7	-	-	-	1.7	12.0
2. No	97.7	98.5	98.0	98.6	86.4	96.7	98.3	99.3	92.1	97.8	97.3	-	-	100.0	98.3	88.0
Item 4170 N(Wtd) ★	218	85	119	184	8	38	66	87	28	87	98	-	-	26	173	18

B075: Do you think you will be using tranquilizers without a doctor's orders five years from now?

1. I definitely will	.5	.6	.4	.5	.3	.5	.8	.2	.6	.6	.4	.4	.4	-	.5	8.8
2. I probably will	3.9	3.7	3.9	3.9	3.2	4.2	3.0	4.9	3.3	3.0	4.7	.9	1.3	3.1	13.5	14.9
3. I probably will not	25.9	27.0	24.8	26.5	19.3	26.7	27.1	24.2	25.9	24.0	26.6	15.6	21.8	40.0	46.6	44.6
4. I definitely will not	69.6	68.7	70.9	69.1	77.2	68.6	69.0	70.6	70.2	72.3	68.2	83.1	76.5	56.9	39.3	31.7
Item 4180 N(Wtd)	2791	1325	1391	2221	315	621	891	862	418	1310	1249	1175	619	301	540	42

The next questions are about COCAINE, which is sometimes called "coke".

B076: On how many occasions (if any) have you taken cocaine...

B076A: ...in your lifetime?

1. 0 occasions	89.8	87.3	92.8	90.3	92.1	90.0	90.4	91.0	86.0	93.7	88.0	100.0	100.0	86.9	63.0	25.1
2. 1-2	5.1	6.0	4.1	4.9	4.7	4.9	4.8	4.8	6.4	3.3	6.1	-	-	13.1	16.7	15.0
3. 3-5	1.8	2.8	.9	1.7	2.0	2.3	1.8	1.6	1.8	1.2	2.0	-	-	-	8.2	10.7
4. 6-9	1.2	1.5	.6	1.2	.3	1.1	1.1	1.2	1.7	.4	1.6	-	-	-	4.8	14.4
5. 10-19	.7	.9	.4	.6	.4	.6	.7	.4	1.2	.5	.8	-	-	-	2.6	8.1
6. 20-39	.7	.6	.7	.7	.4	.6	.4	.5	1.7	.6	.6	-	-	-	2.6	8.7
7. 40 or more	.7	.9	.4	.6	-	.5	.8	.5	1.2	.3	1.0	-	-	-	2.1	17.9
Item 950 N(Wtd)	2778	1321	1376	2221	298	645	875	839	418	1313	1220	1189	632	307	566	44

B076B: ...during the last 12 months?

1. 0 occasions	93.9	91.9	96.1	94.3	95.8	93.7	94.5	95.3	89.8	96.1	92.7	100.0	100.0	94.5	77.1	45.6
2. 1-2	3.1	4.1	2.2	3.1	2.9	3.5	2.9	2.9	3.7	2.2	3.8	-	-	5.5	10.5	24.8
3. 3-5	1.1	1.6	.6	1.2	.4	.9	1.1	.4	2.9	.5	1.5	-	-	-	5.1	5.1
4. 6-9	.7	1.1	.2	.5	.5	1.1	.6	.6	.6	.5	.8	-	-	-	3.3	2.0
5. 10-19	.4	.5	.3	.5	-	.2	.1	.3	1.5	.3	.4	-	-	-	1.4	8.4
6. 20-39	.4	.3	.4	.3	.4	.3	.4	.2	.6	.2	.4	-	-	-	1.4	5.1
7. 40 or more	.4	.6	.1	.3	-	.2	.3	.3	.9	.2	.4	-	-	-	1.1	9.0
Item 960 N(Wtd)	2773	1319	1372	2218	296	644	873	838	418	1313	1218	1189	632	304	563	44

B076C: ...during the last 30 days?

1. 0 occasions	97.1	96.3	98.4	97.3	98.2	96.9	97.7	98.4	93.7	98.1	96.9	100.0	100.0	96.5	89.6	76.0
2. 1-2	1.7	2.3	1.0	1.7	1.5	1.7	1.5	.9	4.0	1.2	1.8	-	-	3.5	6.4	3.5
3. 3-5	.4	.6	.2	.3	.3	.6	.4	.2	.5	.2	.6	-	-	-	1.3	10.4
4. 6-9	.3	.3	.1	.2	-	.2	.1	.1	1.1	.3	.1	-	-	-	1.0	3.7
5. 10-19	.2	.3	.2	.2	-	.3	-	.3	.5	.1	.2	-	-	-	.9	3.0
6. 20-39	*	.1	-	.1	-	.1	.1	-	-	*	.1	-	-	-	.2	-
7. 40 or more	.2	.2	*	.1	-	-	.2	.1	.3	-	.3	-	-	-	.5	3.4
Item 970 N(Wtd)	2770	1317	1372	2216	296	642	872	838	418	1313	1216	1189	632	303	562	44

IF YOU HAVE NOT TAKEN COCAINE IN THE LAST TWELVE MONTHS, GO TO Q.B084.

B077: When you used cocaine during the last year, how often did you use it in each of the following situations?

★ = excludes respondents for whom question was inappropriate.   * = less than .05 per cent.

QUESTIONNAIRE FORM 1 1976	TOTAL	SEX		RACE		REGION				4YR COLLEGE PLANS		ILLICIT DRUG USE: LIFETIME				
		M	F	White	Black	NE	NC	S	W	Yes	No	None	Mari-juana Only	Few Pills	More Pills	Any Her-oin
Weighted No. of Cases:	3039	1426	1466	2356	338	715	950	919	454	1384	1321	1219	669	329	605	47
% of Weighted Total:	100.0	46.9	48.2	77.5	11.1	23.5	31.3	30.2	15.0	45.5	43.5	40.1	22.0	10.8	19.9	1.6
B077A: When you were alone																
1. Not at all	77.0	72.1	89.3	80.1	67.5	73.2	81.4	76.3	75.9	81.2	75.7	-	-	92.2	77.6	56.3
2. A few of the times	14.4	16.5	8.3	12.0	21.1	16.7	13.7	10.8	16.6	13.3	15.0	-	-	7.8	14.9	20.0
3. Some of the times	4.6	5.7	2.4	4.8	-	6.3	3.4	5.9	3.1	3.0	3.6	-	-	-	4.4	10.3
4. Most of the times	2.0	3.1	-	.9	11.4	-	-	7.0	1.2	1.0	3.2	-	-	-	1.4	7.5
5. Every time	2.0	2.6	-	2.2	-	3.8	1.5	-	3.2	1.4	2.4	-	-	-	1.7	5.9
Item 4190 N(Wtd) ★	167	106	52	124	15	36	48	40	42	50	87	-	-	19	121	22
B077B: With just 1 or 2 other people																
1. Not at all	9.7	8.7	11.9	10.1	8.2	11.3	12.6	6.7	7.7	13.2	8.1	-	-	29.2	4.1	7.8
2. A few of the times	35.9	37.0	33.1	36.6	43.3	43.6	28.5	40.9	32.6	27.8	40.8	-	-	48.2	38.9	16.4
3. Some of the times	18.7	19.9	17.8	16.9	20.8	20.5	22.2	22.9	9.2	25.3	17.4	-	-	4.4	16.0	47.6
4. Most of the times	18.7	19.7	16.8	18.1	13.3	16.2	20.1	20.4	17.6	14.2	19.1	-	-	-	23.0	13.5
5. Every time	17.1	14.7	20.4	18.3	14.4	8.4	16.6	9.0	32.9	19.5	14.7	-	-	18.2	17.9	14.8
Item 4200 N(Wtd) ★	173	110	54	129	16	39	50	40	44	53	88	-	-	18	127	24
B077C: At a party																
1. Not at all	29.8	28.2	34.9	31.4	47.0	37.2	22.8	29.2	32.0	29.6	32.7	-	-	36.5	30.2	9.7
2. A few of the times	28.4	28.7	26.3	28.7	34.2	21.5	33.2	35.4	22.7	24.7	29.4	-	-	37.8	29.7	19.6
3. Some of the times	20.0	21.0	19.0	18.5	10.2	19.2	21.2	16.0	23.1	19.0	19.5	-	-	-	19.7	41.2
4. Most of the times	13.5	14.5	9.7	12.2	5.2	20.2	14.2	11.9	8.1	14.0	13.1	-	-	7.5	13.8	18.5
5. Every time	8.2	7.5	10.1	9.3	3.3	1.8	8.7	7.5	14.1	12.7	5.2	-	-	18.2	6.6	11.0
Item 4210 N(Wtd) ★	174	110	54	130	16	39	51	40	44	52	90	-	-	18	128	24
B077D: When your date or spouse was present																
1. Not at all	51.4	64.4	29.7	52.9	61.3	55.8	44.7	57.7	49.2	54.0	53.0	-	-	62.8	51.2	34.5
2. A few of the times	18.7	18.8	16.2	17.5	12.8	14.7	24.1	16.9	17.8	17.3	18.6	-	-	7.2	20.5	21.3
3. Some of the times	11.2	10.2	13.4	11.0	14.0	17.5	11.9	8.9	6.8	14.1	9.5	-	-	6.5	10.8	18.9
4. Most of the times	8.9	3.2	19.2	8.2	5.7	7.4	11.0	6.3	10.3	5.8	9.0	-	-	-	8.9	17.7
5. Every time	9.8	3.4	21.5	10.5	6.3	4.6	8.2	10.2	15.9	8.9	9.9	-	-	23.5	8.6	7.6
Item 4220 N(Wtd) ★	173	110	54	130	16	39	50	40	44	52	89	-	-	18	127	24
B077E: When people over age 30 were present																
1. Not at all	69.9	67.6	76.2	71.6	75.1	68.5	78.6	65.6	64.9	63.4	71.7	-	-	95.6	66.6	61.7
2. A few of the times	16.8	19.7	10.8	15.9	24.9	20.0	9.0	20.7	19.2	16.7	19.6	-	-	4.4	21.1	6.4
3. Some of the times	7.7	8.3	7.2	6.3	-	7.9	9.3	7.4	6.0	12.7	4.3	-	-	-	8.0	13.6
4. Most of the times	1.4	.9	1.9	1.2	-	-	-	1.9	3.6	1.9	1.1	-	-	-	.9	5.2
5. Every time	4.3	3.5	4.0	5.0	-	3.5	3.1	4.3	6.3	5.3	3.3	-	-	-	3.4	13.1
Item 4230 N(Wtd) ★	173	110	54	130	16	39	50	40	44	52	89	-	-	18	127	24
B077F: During the daytime (before 4:00 p.m.)																
1. Not at all	49.5	52.1	46.1	50.7	63.8	43.6	58.5	41.9	51.5	47.9	50.3	-	-	76.1	46.6	35.9
2. A few of the times	27.5	27.1	29.7	27.9	20.0	33.7	21.0	36.0	21.2	23.7	32.6	-	-	23.9	29.8	23.4
3. Some of the times	14.9	14.2	12.9	12.8	13.0	17.2	15.2	15.5	12.2	18.3	9.7	-	-	-	16.3	20.5
4. Most of the times	4.3	3.0	7.3	3.9	3.2	3.7	3.9	1.9	7.3	7.6	2.1	-	-	-	4.0	9.6
5. Every time	3.9	3.5	4.0	4.7	-	1.8	1.4	4.6	7.8	2.5	5.3	-	-	-	3.3	10.5
Item 4240 N(Wtd) ★	173	110	54	130	16	39	49	40	44	52	89	-	-	18	126	24
B077G: At your home (or apartment or dorm)																
1. Not at all	61.0	60.7	68.3	61.7	78.2	61.8	67.0	55.8	58.2	57.4	65.7	-	-	83.5	60.2	41.9
2. A few of the times	17.7	20.1	11.7	16.1	21.8	13.8	14.2	22.0	21.4	18.3	18.3	-	-	13.2	19.0	17.8
3. Some of the times	11.1	10.0	12.2	10.9	-	16.3	10.0	12.1	6.8	12.7	8.0	-	-	3.2	11.3	17.7
4. Most of the times	4.7	3.5	4.6	5.2	-	4.0	5.3	5.8	3.8	6.1	2.4	-	-	-	4.2	12.0
5. Every time	5.4	5.7	3.1	6.2	-	4.1	3.4	4.4	9.7	5.5	5.7	-	-	-	5.4	10.5
Item 4250 N(Wtd) ★	172	110	53	130	15	39	50	40	44	53	89	-	-	17	127	24

★ = excludes respondents for whom question was inappropriate.

QUESTIONNAIRE FORM 1 1976	TOTAL	SEX		RACE		REGION				4YR COLLEGE PLANS		ILLICIT DRUG USE: LIFETIME				
		M	F	White	Black	NE	NC	S	W	Yes	No	None	Mari- juana Only	Few Pills	More Pills	Any Her- oin
Weighted No. of Cases:	3039	1426	1466	2356	338	715	950	919	454	1384	1321	1219	669	329	605	47
% of Weighted Total:	100.0	46.9	48.2	77.5	11.1	23.5	31.3	30.2	15.0	45.5	43.5	40.1	22.0	10.8	19.9	1.6
B077H: At school																
1. Not at all	67.1	69.6	65.5	70.5	63.7	65.3	68.5	66.4	67.8	72.3	65.3	-	-	68.3	69.9	46.8
2. A few of the times	17.4	19.1	12.8	15.0	30.1	29.5	13.5	13.8	14.3	21.1	14.6	-	-	31.7	16.8	13.0
3. Some of the times	11.6	7.8	17.7	11.2	6.2	3.4	12.9	18.0	11.5	5.2	15.1	-	-	-	9.5	32.2
4. Most of the times	1.6	1.6	2.0	1.3	-	-	3.4	1.7	.8	-	2.1	-	-	-	1.8	2.4
5. Every time	2.3	2.0	2.0	1.9	-	1.8	1.6	-	5.5	1.3	2.9	-	-	-	2.1	5.6
Item 4260 N(Wtd) ★	173	110	54	130	16	39	50	40	44	52	89	-	-	18	127	24
B077I: In a car																
1. Not at all	52.6	48.8	61.4	54.5	56.6	62.4	43.3	53.5	53.6	64.5	46.6	-	-	89.6	48.3	36.3
2. A few of the times	22.3	29.9	9.0	21.2	33.9	28.2	17.3	21.9	22.8	22.0	21.4	-	-	8.4	25.9	18.0
3. Some of the times	16.0	14.7	17.7	15.9	6.2	5.7	27.2	14.2	14.1	10.0	20.1	-	-	2.0	16.1	29.7
4. Most of the times	5.1	3.4	6.6	4.1	3.3	-	8.2	2.9	8.1	-	7.6	-	-	-	5.1	10.1
5. Every time	4.1	3.2	5.3	4.3	-	3.6	4.0	7.5	1.4	3.5	4.2	-	-	-	4.5	5.8
Item 4280 N(Wtd) ★	173	110	54	130	16	39	49	40	44	53	88	-	-	18	127	23
B078: How many of the times when you used cocaine during the last year did you use it along with each of the following drugs-- that is, so that their effects overlapped?																
B078A: With alcohol																
1. Not at all	43.7	38.3	55.4	40.6	62.0	58.8	28.4	60.8	30.9	45.8	45.5	-	-	59.7	41.0	34.2
2. A few of the times	27.2	31.2	21.0	28.0	23.8	19.5	29.5	26.1	33.1	29.4	26.5	-	-	31.1	29.7	14.5
3. Some of the times	13.2	12.4	13.4	14.5	5.7	6.5	21.6	7.5	14.9	12.2	11.6	-	-	2.0	12.9	28.0
4. Most of the times	8.1	8.9	6.3	9.3	3.3	9.0	11.2	-	11.7	7.6	9.4	-	-	3.0	8.2	14.4
5. Every time	7.8	9.2	3.8	7.7	5.2	6.1	9.4	5.6	9.5	4.9	7.0	-	-	4.3	8.3	9.0
Item 4290 N(Wtd) ★	170	105	54	125	16	39	50	40	40	53	84	-	-	19	125	21
B078B: With marijuana																
1. Not at all	19.0	15.7	26.7	18.2	28.6	21.0	17.6	25.9	12.3	14.1	23.0	-	-	25.8	16.6	12.0
2. A few of the times	24.2	27.2	20.4	26.6	30.4	35.7	14.2	22.0	27.7	23.5	23.1	-	-	37.6	25.2	12.1
3. Some of the times	17.1	20.9	8.6	16.0	14.5	12.2	18.0	18.9	18.9	17.5	17.1	-	-	17.9	30.2
4. Most of the times	19.0	15.8	25.8	19.8	26.5	21.4	29.8	4.9	17.5	20.6	19.6	-	-	15.1	17.7	33.5
5. Every time	20.6	20.4	18.4	19.4	-	9.6	20.4	28.2	23.6	24.3	17.2	-	-	21.5	22.6	12.3
Item 4300 N(Wtd) ★	173	110	53	129	15	39	50	40	43	53	87	-	-	18	128	22
B078C: With LSD																
1. Not at all	96.7	98.4	95.4	97.5	100.0	98.6	99.1	97.8	91.0	97.3	96.3	-	-	100.0	97.4	87.4
2. A few of the times	2.3	.4	4.6	1.5	-	1.4	.8	2.2	5.0	2.7	1.7	-	-	-	2.0	7.3
3. Some of the times	.2	.4	-	.3	-	-	-	-	1.0	-	.5	-	-	-	-	2.2
4. Most of the times	.8	.9	-	.7	-	-	-	-	3.1	-	1.5	-	-	-	.6	3.1
5. Every time	-	-	-	-	-	-	-	-	-	-	-	-	-	-	-	-
Item 4310 N(Wtd) ★	163	103	51	122	14	38	46	38	41	49	84	-	-	18	123	18
B078D: With psychedelics other than LSD																
1. Not at all	96.0	97.2	96.3	97.2	100.0	96.9	97.8	93.7	95.3	95.9	96.7	-	-	100.0	97.1	83.8
2. A few of the times	2.6	2.1	1.1	1.5	-	3.1	2.2	4.1	1.0	3.3	.9	-	-	-	1.6	12.1
3. Some of the times	.8	-	2.6	.7	-	-	-	2.2	1.0	.8	1.1	-	-	-	.7	2.2
4. Most of the times	.2	-	-	-	-	-	-	-	.9	-	.5	-	-	-	-	2.0
5. Every time	.4	.7	-	.6	-	-	-	-	1.8	-	.9	-	-	-	.6	-
Item 4320 N(Wtd) ★	159	102	48	117	13	38	43	38	39	50	79	-	-	18	119	18
B078E: With amphetamines																
1. Not at all	92.7	93.7	93.4	94.1	100.0	92.7	91.6	98.8	88.7	93.2	92.5	-	-	100.0	93.8	77.4
2. A few of the times	4.1	3.4	4.2	3.2	-	5.2	4.7	1.2	5.1	4.3	3.8	-	-	-	3.3	14.4
3. Some of the times	1.8	2.2	1.5	1.7	-	2.1	2.7	-	2.1	1.6	2.4	-	-	-	1.9	3.0
4. Most of the times	.7	.7	-	.6	-	-	-	-	2.6	-	1.3	-	-	-	.6	1.9
5. Every time	.7	-	.9	.4	-	-	1.0	-	1.5	.9	-	-	-	-	.4	3.3
Item 4330 N(Wtd) ★	163	102	51	120	14	38	46	36	42	50	82	-	-	16	123	19

★=excludes respondents for whom question was inappropriate.

QUESTIONNAIRE FORM 1 1976	TOTAL	SEX		RACE		REGION				4YR COLLEGE PLANS		ILLICIT DRUG USE: LIFETIME				
		M	F	White	Black	NE	NC	S	W	Yes	No	None	Mari-juana Only	Few Pills	More Pills	Any Her-oin
Weighted No. of Cases:	3039	1426	1466	2356	338	715	950	919	454	1384	1321	1219	669	329	605	47
% of Weighted Total:	100.0	46.9	48.2	77.5	11.1	23.5	31.3	30.2	15.0	45.5	43.5	40.1	22.0	10.8	19.9	1.6
B078F: With quaaludes																
1. Not at all	96.3	98.6	95.5	97.9	96.2	95.9	95.8	99.9	93.8	98.9	96.6	-	-	100.0	97.4	84.8
2. A few of the times	1.7	.5	3.1	1.3	-	4.1	2.5	-	-	1.1	1.3	-	-	-	.8	8.9
3. Some of the times	.4	-	1.4	-	3.8	-	-	-	1.7	-	.6	-	-	-	.6	-
4. Most of the times	.8	.2	-	.2	-	-	1.7	-	1.3	-	.7	-	-	-	.6	3.0
5. Every time	.8	.7	-	.6	-	-	-	-	3.2	-	.8	-	-	-	.6	3.3
Item 4340 N(Wtd) ★	165	104	51	122	14	38	46	38	42	50	84	-	-	18	124	19
B078G: With barbiturates																
1. Not at all	95.4	94.9	98.6	96.6	100.0	95.0	95.2	96.5	95.0	94.9	96.3	-	-	100.0	97.2	77.9
2. A few of the times	3.0	3.7	1.0	2.2	-	3.1	4.8	3.5	.5	3.7	2.4	-	-	-	1.5	16.9
3. Some of the times	.6	.7	.4	.6	-	1.8	-	-	.5	1.4	-	-	-	-	.7	-
4. Most of the times	.6	.7	-	.6	-	-	-	-	2.5	-	1.3	-	-	-	.6	1.9
5. Every time	.4	-	-	-	-	-	-	-	1.5	-	-	-	-	-	-	3.3
Item 4350 N(Wtd) ★	165	104	51	122	14	38	46	38	42	50	84	-	-	18	124	19
B078H: With tranquilizers																
1. Not at all	96.0	96.0	98.5	96.5	100.0	95.0	97.9	98.2	92.8	94.0	97.5	-	-	100.0	98.1	78.4
2. A few of the times	2.0	2.0	1.1	1.7	-	1.4	2.1	1.8	2.5	3.2	1.2	-	-	-	.6	13.0
3. Some of the times	.6	.7	.4	.6	-	1.8	-	-	.5	1.4	-	-	-	-	.7	-
4. Most of the times	.7	.7	-	.6	-	1.8	-	-	.9	1.4	.4	-	-	-	-	5.5
5. Every time	.8	.7	-	.6	-	-	-	-	3.3	-	.9	-	-	-	.6	3.2
Item 4360 N(Wtd) ★	163	105	49	122	13	39	46	38	41	50	82	-	-	18	122	19
B079: What have been the most important reasons for your taking cocaine? (Mark all that apply.)																
A. To experiment--to see what it's like	64.5	65.4	62.0	63.9	52.0	77.1	55.7	58.5	69.1	67.5	67.1	-	-	73.9	68.7	35.5
B. To relax or relieve tension	19.6	20.7	17.2	20.5	26.0	18.4	20.4	23.0	20.5	22.7	20.5	-	-	8.8	20.6	23.4
C. To feel good or get high	77.6	77.6	76.4	79.3	53.6	70.1	84.3	70.2	83.7	75.5	77.9	-	-	59.6	76.5	97.5
D. To seek deeper insights and understanding	10.6	10.2	10.0	10.2	17.9	21.3	5.7	6.0	10.7	10.8	9.3	-	-	12.2	10.7	8.7
E. To have a good time with my friends	44.4	47.2	38.3	46.1	21.7	35.6	59.4	35.7	42.8	41.4	49.2	-	-	20.3	46.9	50.9
F. To fit in with a group I like	4.7	4.8	2.1	3.9	-	9.5	2.4	1.8	5.6	3.8	1.9	-	-	7.4	3.9	6.4
G. To get away from my problems or troubles	7.3	6.5	9.6	6.4	11.5	9.3	8.6	5.5	5.8	5.0	10.7	-	-	-	7.6	11.9
H. Because of boredom, nothing else to do	10.6	12.8	7.5	10.4	6.2	10.1	9.5	6.1	16.7	15.5	10.4	-	-	-	12.5	9.8
I. Because of anger or frustration	5.0	3.3	8.5	5.4	-	8.1	6.9	3.3	1.4	5.8	6.1	-	-	-	5.4	6.8
J. To get through the day	2.5	1.7	3.9	2.7	-	1.4	1.5	5.7	1.9	3.9	2.6	-	-	-	2.4	5.4
K. To increase the effects of some other drug(s)	8.1	10.6	2.8	6.4	2.6	5.7	10.4	3.7	11.9	17.1	3.7	-	-	-	7.7	17.0
L. To decrease (offset) the effects of some other drug(s)	.5	-	1.0	-	-	1.4	-	-	.9	1.0	.4	-	-	-	-	3.8
M. To stay awake	11.7	8.7	18.2	11.3	18.8	5.9	17.9	5.1	16.1	11.0	12.3	-	-	10.0	11.0	16.7
N. To get more energy	13.9	11.1	18.3	14.2	6.2	3.8	15.1	8.5	27.3	10.9	15.3	-	-	10.0	15.3	10.3
O. Because I am "hooked"--I have to have it	1.3	1.2	1.0	1.0	-	3.3	-	-	2.3	2.4	1.1	-	-	-	.5	6.8
Item 4370-4510 N(Wtd) ★	164	103	52	123	14	38	48	38	40	51	82	-	-	19	121	24
B080: When you take cocaine how high do you usually get?																
1. Not at all high	2.9	1.0	3.5	1.1	-	-	3.9	-	7.0	2.7	.8	-	-	3.9	3.0	-
2. A little high	11.8	13.1	8.9	12.2	10.0	14.0	5.1	12.0	17.6	14.3	12.0	-	-	16.6	12.6	4.3
3. Moderately high	45.1	38.7	60.5	46.9	54.7	43.8	42.3	48.7	46.1	45.0	49.3	-	-	55.9	46.1	31.8
4. Very high	39.5	46.4	26.4	39.1	32.5	39.9	48.6	39.3	28.3	35.6	38.0	-	-	23.7	37.3	63.9
5. I don't take it to get high	.8	.9	.7	.7	2.8	2.4	-	-	.9	2.5	-	-	-	-	1.0	-
Item 4520 N(Wtd) ★	166	104	53	125	14	38	49	39	40	51	83	-	-	18	124	24

★ = excludes respondents for whom question was inappropriate.

QUESTIONNAIRE FORM 1 1976	TOTAL	SEX		RACE		REGION				4YR COLLEGE PLANS		ILLICIT DRUG USE: LIFETIME				
		M	F	White	Black	NE	NC	S	W	Yes	No	None	Marijuana Only	Few Pills	More Pills	Any Heroin
Weighted No. of Cases:	3039	1426	1466	2356	338	715	950	919	454	1384	1321	1219	669	329	605	47
% of Weighted Total:	100.0	46.9	48.2	77.5	11.1	23.5	31.3	30.2	15.0	45.5	43.5	40.1	22.0	10.8	19.9	1.6

B081: When you take cocaine how long do you usually stay high?

1. Usually don't get high	2.8	2.1	2.6	2.9	-	2.4	1.6	-	7.8	5.5	.8	-	-	3.7	3.0	-
2. One to two hours	27.6	30.5	21.6	28.6	29.3	41.1	12.7	30.7	29.8	37.4	22.8	-	-	39.5	28.6	13.7
3. Three to six hours	46.8	40.5	62.3	46.8	55.6	26.9	61.3	45.3	50.0	37.1	58.6	-	-	45.9	46.5	50.2
4. Seven to 24 hours	19.6	22.9	12.5	18.4	15.1	24.6	24.4	18.7	9.6	14.4	15.0	-	-	10.9	20.8	20.6
5. More than 24 hours	3.1	4.1	1.0	3.4	-	5.1	-	5.2	2.8	5.5	2.7	-	-	-	1.1	15.5
Item 4530 N(Wtd) ★	165	103	53	123	14	38	49	39	38	51	82	-	-	18	122	24

B082: Have you ever tried to stop using cocaine and found that you couldn't stop?

1. Yes	4.0	4.1	2.6	3.3	5.6	3.2	4.4	2.2	6.1	5.2	3.0	-	-	3.5	2.5	12.0
2. No	96.0	95.9	97.4	96.7	94.4	96.8	95.6	97.8	93.9	94.8	97.0	-	-	96.5	97.5	88.0
Item 4540 N(Wtd) ★	165	103	53	122	14	38	50	38	38	51	82	-	-	18	122	24

B083: What methods have you used for taking cocaine? (Mark all that apply.)

A. Sniffing or "snorting"	90.8	92.7	85.2	89.5	100.0	92.5	89.8	89.9	91.3	92.3	89.3	-	-	86.2	92.1	93.8
B. Smoking	24.5	25.7	22.5	23.4	18.1	13.1	34.7	21.4	25.9	26.3	22.9	-	-	10.2	25.4	33.0
C. Injection	7.3	8.1	6.4	7.5	-	8.5	8.3	6.8	5.4	6.3	9.2	-	-	7.3	2.3	34.6
D. By mouth	27.8	26.8	28.1	24.9	28.7	30.8	25.0	26.7	29.7	23.1	28.1	-	-	9.2	27.4	46.5
E. Other	5.4	6.7	3.1	5.1	-	3.2	10.6	2.9	3.5	2.3	7.2	-	-	3.5	2.1	18.4
Item 4550-4590 N(Wtd) ★	169	107	53	126	14	39	51	40	39	53	85	-	-	18	126	24

B084: Do you think you will be using cocaine five years from now?

1. I definitely will	1.1	1.3	.8	1.1	.4	1.5	1.1	.9	1.3	1.0	1.0	.4	1.1	-	2.3	14.1
2. I probably will	4.1	5.7	2.2	3.8	3.2	5.4	4.1	2.8	4.6	3.1	4.9	.1	.7	3.0	16.5	17.9
3. I probably will not	15.6	19.0	12.0	15.7	13.1	17.1	15.9	14.4	15.3	14.6	15.1	5.5	14.1	25.1	33.3	41.7
4. I definitely will not	79.2	73.9	85.0	79.4	83.4	76.1	78.9	81.9	78.8	81.4	79.0	94.0	84.1	71.9	47.9	26.4
Item 4600 N(Wtd)	2815	1339	1398	2241	318	630	899	862	424	1327	1250	1180	622	306	546	45

The next questions are about HEROIN.

Heroin is sometimes called: smack, horse, skag.

B085: On how many occasions (if any) have you taken heroin...

B085A: ...in your lifetime?

1. 0 occasions	98.3	98.0	98.7	98.3	100.0	98.7	97.8	98.9	97.5	98.8	97.9	100.0	100.0	100.0	100.0	-
2. 1-2	1.2	1.4	.9	1.3	-	.8	1.4	.9	1.6	.9	1.4	-	-	-	-	67.9
3. 3-5	.1	.1	.2	.2	-	-	.2	.1	.3	*	.3	-	-	-	-	7.4
4. 6-9	*	-	*	*	-	*	.1	-	-	-	*	-	-	-	-	1.8
5. 10-19	.1	.1	*	.1	-	-	.2	-	.1	-	.2	-	-	-	-	5.3
6. 20-39	*	*	-	*	-	-	.1	-	-	-	*	-	-	-	-	1.2
7. 40 or more	.3	.3	.1	.1	-	.5	.2	.1	.4	.3	.2	-	-	-	-	16.4
Item 1100 N(Wtd)	2770	1325	1374	2226	295	641	880	835	414	1317	1217	1196	627	304	552	47

B085B: ...during the last 12 months?

1. 0 occasions	99.3	99.0	99.6	99.4	100.0	99.5	99.2	99.5	98.5	99.5	99.3	100.0	100.0	100.0	100.0	55.9
2. 1-2	.3	.4	.3	.4	-	-	.2	.4	.9	.3	.3	-	-	-	-	19.4
3. 3-5	.1	.2	-	.1	-	-	.3	-	-	-	.1	-	-	-	-	5.6
4. 6-9	.1	.1	-	.1	-	.1	.1	-	.1	.1	.1	-	-	-	-	3.2
5. 10-19	*	*	-	*	-	-	-	-	.1	-	*	-	-	-	-	.8
6. 20-39	.1	.2	*	*	-	.2	.1	-	.1	.1	*	-	-	-	-	5.8
7. 40 or more	.2	.1	.1	.1	-	.1	.2	.1	.2	.1	.2	-	-	-	-	9.3
Item 1110 N(Wtd)	2770	1325	1374	2226	295	641	881	835	414	1317	1216	1196	627	305	552	47

★ = excludes respondents for whom question was inappropriate.　　* = less than .05 per cent.

QUESTIONNAIRE FORM 1 1976	TOTAL	SEX		RACE		REGION				4YR COLLEGE PLANS		ILLICIT DRUG USE: LIFETIME				
		M	F	White	Black	NE	NC	S	W	Yes	No	None	Marijuana Only	Few Pills	More Pills	Any Heroin
Weighted No. of Cases: % of Weighted Total:	3039 100.0	1426 46.9	1466 48.2	2356 77.5	338 11.1	715 23.5	950 31.3	919 30.2	454 15.0	1384 45.5	1321 43.5	1219 40.1	669 22.0	329 10.8	605 19.9	47 1.6
B085C: ...during the last 30 days?																
1. 0 occasions	99.7	99.6	99.9	99.9	100.0	99.6	99.6	99.8	99.7	99.8	99.6	100.0	100.0	100.0	100.0	81.9
2. 1-2	.1	.1	-	*	-	-	.2	-	.1	-	.1	-	-	-	-	4.6
3. 3-5	.1	.1	-	*	-	-	.1	.1	.1	.1	.1	-	-	-	-	2.1
4. 6-9	-	-	-	-	-	-	-	-	-	-	-	-	-	-	-	-
5. 10-19	.1	.1	*	-	-	.2	-	-	-	*	-	-	-	-	-	3.2
6. 20-39	*	*	-	-	-	-	.1	-	-	-	*	-	-	-	-	1.4
7. 40 or more	.1	.1	.1	.1	-	.1	.1	.1	.1	.1	.1	-	-	-	-	6.9
Item 1120 N(Wtd)	2770	1325	1374	2225	295	641	880	836	414	1318	1216	1196	627	305	552	46

IF YOU HAVE NOT TAKEN HEROIN IN THE LAST TWELVE MONTHS, GO TO Q.B093.

B086: When you used heroin during the last year, how often did you use it in each of the following situations?

	TOTAL	M	F	White	Black	NE	NC	S	W	Yes	No	None	Marijuana Only	Few Pills	More Pills	Any Heroin
B086A: When you were alone																
1. Not at all	58.8	58.9	50.6	60.5	-	55.1	70.5	36.3	62.2	67.1	51.9	-	-	-	-	57.0
2. A few of the times	15.9	14.1	32.0	21.9	-	17.9	13.1	36.4	3.6	12.9	13.0	-	-	-	-	16.6
3. Some of the times	13.3	12.4	17.4	12.5	-	27.1	-	27.3	12.9	11.2	21.5	-	-	-	-	13.9
4. Most of the times	2.8	4.5	-	-	-	-	7.7	-	-	-	6.4	-	-	-	-	2.9
5. Every time	9.2	10.0	-	5.0	-	-	8.7	-	21.3	8.7	7.2	-	-	-	-	9.6
Item 4610 N(Wtd) ★	20	13	5	12	-	3	7	4	6	7	9	-	-	-	-	20
B086B: With just 1 or 2 other people																
1. Not at all	18.2	15.2	-	16.3	-	-	17.0	36.3	15.7	42.7	9.2	-	-	-	-	14.6
2. A few of the times	29.2	20.9	65.0	32.0	-	49.2	30.7	36.4	9.9	8.1	23.3	-	-	-	-	30.5
3. Some of the times	17.8	18.8	20.1	20.0	-	27.1	7.7	27.3	18.8	21.9	23.5	-	-	-	-	18.6
4. Most of the times	19.6	30.9	-	16.0	-	-	44.6	-	11.5	-	37.2	-	-	-	-	20.5
5. Every time	15.2	14.2	14.9	15.8	-	23.7	-	-	44.0	27.3	6.7	-	-	-	-	15.9
Item 4620 N(Wtd) ★	20	13	4	12	-	3	7	4	5	7	9	-	-	-	-	19
B086C: At a party																
1. Not at all	37.6	39.9	57.7	51.3	-	-	33.8	36.4	62.2	23.8	48.2	-	-	-	-	39.2
2. A few of the times	16.6	17.9	24.9	15.6	-	49.2	9.6	-	21.0	16.1	14.7	-	-	-	-	17.3
3. Some of the times	16.7	9.6	17.4	4.6	-	27.1	24.1	19.8	-	23.0	13.5	-	-	-	-	13.2
4. Most of the times	9.2	12.2	-	7.8	-	-	20.8	-	6.1	5.5	10.4	-	-	-	-	9.6
5. Every time	19.8	20.5	-	20.7	-	23.7	11.6	43.7	10.7	31.5	13.1	-	-	-	-	20.6
Item 4630 N(Wtd) ★	20	13	5	12	-	3	7	4	6	7	9	-	-	-	-	20
B086D: When your date or spouse was present																
1. Not at all	49.1	60.9	42.5	52.9	-	58.4	41.3	17.6	72.5	46.0	46.0	-	-	-	-	49.1
2. A few of the times	17.3	15.2	32.0	17.9	-	17.9	16.4	48.4	-	19.5	17.9	-	-	-	-	17.3
3. Some of the times	7.6	4.5	-	4.6	-	-	15.5	-	6.1	-	10.4	-	-	-	-	7.6
4. Most of the times	-	-	-	-	-	-	-	-	-	-	-	-	-	-	-	-
5. Every time	26.0	19.4	25.5	24.6	-	23.7	26.9	34.0	21.3	34.6	25.7	-	-	-	-	26.0
Item 4640 N(Wtd) ★	20	13	5	12	-	3	7	3	6	6	9	-	-	-	-	20
B086E: When people over age 30 were present																
1. Not at all	66.0	79.2	76.5	74.4	-	58.4	57.7	80.2	70.0	51.2	81.0	-	-	-	-	68.8
2. A few of the times	10.9	4.5	23.5	9.1	-	17.9	23.0	-	-	7.4	6.3	-	-	-	-	11.3
3. Some of the times	4.5	4.5	-	4.6	-	-	7.7	-	6.1	-	10.4	-	-	-	-	4.7
4. Most of the times	5.1	1.7	-	1.7	-	-	-	19.8	3.6	11.8	2.3	-	-	-	-	1.1
5. Every time	13.4	10.1	-	10.2	-	23.7	11.6	-	20.3	29.6	-	-	-	-	-	14.0
Item 4650 N(Wtd) ★	20	13	5	12	-	3	7	4	6	7	9	-	-	-	-	20

*=less than .05 per cent.   ★=excludes respondents for whom question was inappropriate.

QUESTIONNAIRE FORM 1 1976	TOTAL	SEX		RACE		REGION				4YR COLLEGE PLANS		ILLICIT DRUG USE: LIFETIME				
		M	F	White	Black	NE	NC	S	W	Yes	No	None	Mari-juana Only	Few Pills	More Pills	Any Her-oin
Weighted No. of Cases:	3039	1426	1466	2356	338	715	950	919	454	1384	1321	1219	669	329	605	47
% of Weighted Total:	100.0	46.9	48.2	77.5	11.1	23.5	31.3	30.2	15.0	45.5	43.5	40.1	22.0	10.8	19.9	1.6

B086F: During the daytime (before 4:00 p.m.)

1. Not at all	56.5	61.2	46.9	65.6	-	31.3	45.1	83.6	64.0	54.5	56.6	-	-	-	-	54.7
2. A few of the times	17.5	15.2	23.7	14.8	-	17.9	31.8	16.4	-	17.2	13.5	-	-	-	-	18.2
3. Some of the times	10.2	9.3	12.0	13.9	-	-	15.3	-	16.4	-	23.5	-	-	-	-	10.6
4. Most of the times	9.3	8.7	17.4	-	-	27.1	7.7	-	8.9	18.5	6.4	-	-	-	-	9.7
5. Every time	6.5	5.6	-	5.7	-	23.7	-	-	10.7	9.9	-	-	-	-	-	6.8
Item 4660 N(Wtd) ★	20	13	5	12	-	3	7	4	6	7	9	-	-	-	-	20

B086G: At your home (or apartment or dorm)

1. Not at all	46.5	40.0	59.2	59.6	-	-	34.3	67.3	72.9	68.4	41.0	-	-	-	-	44.1
2. A few of the times	13.2	12.7	11.5	4.9	-	49.2	15.5	-	-	8.2	-	-	-	-	-	13.8
3. Some of the times	20.0	23.4	17.4	11.5	-	27.1	34.9	-	9.7	12.5	28.9	-	-	-	-	20.9
4. Most of the times	2.8	-	12.0	4.8	-	-	7.6	-	-	-	6.3	-	-	-	-	2.9
5. Every time	17.5	23.9	-	19.3	-	23.7	7.7	32.7	17.4	10.9	23.9	-	-	-	-	18.3
Item 4670 N(Wtd) ★	20	12	5	12	-	3	7	4	6	6	9	-	-	-	-	19

B086H: At school

1. Not at all	71.1	76.0	58.9	76.2	-	31.3	66.2	99.9	76.5	71.5	63.6	-	-	-	-	69.9
2. A few of the times	7.3	3.1	23.7	7.8	-	17.9	7.7	-	6.7	7.4	10.8	-	-	-	-	7.6
3. Some of the times	10.2	10.2	17.4	10.3	-	27.1	17.4	-	-	11.2	14.4	-	-	-	-	10.6
4. Most of the times	4.9	5.1	-	-	-	-	8.7	-	6.1	-	11.2	-	-	-	-	5.1
5. Every time	6.5	5.6	-	5.7	-	23.7	-	-	10.7	9.9	-	-	-	-	-	6.8
Item 4680 N(Wtd) ★	20	13	5	12	-	3	7	4	6	7	9	-	-	-	-	20

B086I: In a car

1. Not at all	60.4	69.8	59.1	70.1	-	31.3	39.4	99.9	72.9	59.6	61.4	-	-	-	-	58.7
2. A few of the times	4.5	3.1	11.5	3.2	-	17.9	-	-	6.7	7.4	4.4	-	-	-	-	4.7
3. Some of the times	16.0	10.7	29.4	15.3	-	27.1	30.7	-	3.6	11.2	15.0	-	-	-	-	16.7
4. Most of the times	9.4	5.7	-	5.7	-	-	21.2	-	6.1	11.9	12.0	-	-	-	-	9.8
5. Every time	9.7	10.7	-	5.7	-	23.7	8.7	-	10.7	9.9	7.2	-	-	-	-	10.1
Item 4700 N(Wtd) ★	20	13	5	12	-	3	7	4	6	7	9	-	-	-	-	20

B087: How many of the times when you used heroin during the last year did you use it along with each of the following drugs--that is, so that their effects overlapped?

B087A: With alcohol

1. Not at all	51.8	46.8	86.8	64.6	-	35.5	55.0	36.4	67.3	55.5	56.2	-	-	-	-	54.3
2. A few of the times	17.9	24.8	13.2	16.8	-	64.5	-	43.7	-	21.1	13.9	-	-	-	-	18.8
3. Some of the times	17.2	15.3	-	5.1	-	-	17.8	19.8	21.9	23.4	14.5	-	-	-	-	13.3
4. Most of the times	13.0	13.2	-	13.4	-	-	27.2	-	10.9	-	15.3	-	-	-	-	13.6
5. Every time	-	-	-	-	-	-	-	-	-	-	-	-	-	-	-	-
Item 4710 N(Wtd) ★	18	11	4	11	-	2	7	4	5	6	8	-	-	-	-	18

B087B: With marijuana

1. Not at all	36.6	26.1	52.8	44.6	-	-	29.3	45.5	60.9	25.9	35.3	-	-	-	-	36.6
2. A few of the times	18.6	28.6	-	15.8	-	31.3	9.4	54.5	-	12.3	21.6	-	-	-	-	18.6
3. Some of the times	12.7	8.4	33.3	1.8	-	44.9	11.7	-	4.0	23.5	12.0	-	-	-	-	12.7
4. Most of the times	17.9	15.1	13.9	20.1	-	23.8	32.8	-	6.9	19.3	19.5	-	-	-	-	17.9
5. Every time	14.2	21.8	-	17.7	-	-	16.8	-	28.2	19.0	11.6	-	-	-	-	14.2
Item 4720 N(Wtd) ★	18	12	4	12	-	3	7	3	5	6	8	-	-	-	-	18

★ = excludes respondents for whom question was inappropriate.

QUESTIONNAIRE FORM 1 1976	TOTAL	SEX		RACE		REGION				4YR COLLEGE PLANS		ILLICIT DRUG USE: LIFETIME				
		M	F	White	Black	NE	NC	S	W	Yes	No	None	Mari- juana Only	Few Pills	More Pills	Any Her- oin
Weighted No. of Cases:	3039	1426	1466	2356	338	715	950	919	454	1384	1321	1219	669	329	605	47
% of Weighted Total:	100.0	46.9	48.2	77.5	11.1	23.5	31.3	30.2	15.0	45.5	43.5	40.1	22.0	10.8	19.9	1.6

B087C: With LSD

	TOTAL	M	F	White	Black	NE	NC	S	W	Yes	No	None	Mari- juana Only	Few Pills	More Pills	Any Her- oin
1. Not at all	94.8	100.0	86.8	100.0	-	76.6	99.9	99.9	92.2	90.9	95.3	-	-	-	-	94.6
2. A few of the times	3.1	-	13.2	-	-	23.4	-	-	-	9.1	-	-	-	-	-	3.2
3. Some of the times	-	-	-	-	-	-	-	-	-	-	-	-	-	-	-	-
4. Most of the times	2.1	-	-	-	-	-	-	-	7.8	-	4.7	-	-	-	-	2.2
5. Every time	-	-	-	-	-	-	-	-	-	-	-	-	-	-	-	-
Item 4730 N(Wtd) ★	17	11	4	10	-	2	6	4	5	6	8	-	-	-	-	16

B087D: With psychedelics other than LSD

	TOTAL	M	F	White	Black	NE	NC	S	W	Yes	No	None	Mari- juana Only	Few Pills	More Pills	Any Her- oin
1. Not at all	79.2	83.6	63.0	80.3	-	76.6	83.0	61.2	92.2	72.1	74.4	-	-	-	-	78.2
2. A few of the times	15.0	10.3	37.0	19.7	-	23.4	6.5	38.8	-	27.9	12.5	-	-	-	-	15.7
3. Some of the times	-	-	-	-	-	-	-	-	-	-	-	-	-	-	-	-
4. Most of the times	2.1	-	-	-	-	-	-	-	7.8	-	4.7	-	-	-	-	2.2
5. Every time	3.7	6.0	-	-	-	-	10.5	-	-	-	8.4	-	-	-	-	3.9
Item 4740 N(Wtd) ★	17	11	4	10	-	2	6	4	5	6	8	-	-	-	-	16

B087E: With amphetamines

	TOTAL	M	F	White	Black	NE	NC	S	W	Yes	No	None	Mari- juana Only	Few Pills	More Pills	Any Her- oin
1. Not at all	73.6	83.0	72.9	83.4	-	76.6	80.4	52.9	81.2	76.4	64.4	-	-	-	-	77.2
2. A few of the times	9.6	11.0	13.9	16.6	-	-	9.2	27.3	-	-	22.5	-	-	-	-	10.1
3. Some of the times	3.0	-	13.2	-	-	23.4	-	-	-	9.1	-	-	-	-	-	3.1
4. Most of the times	10.3	6.0	-	-	-	-	10.5	19.8	6.9	14.5	13.1	-	-	-	-	5.9
5. Every time	3.5	-	-	-	-	-	-	-	11.9	-	-	-	-	-	-	3.7
Item 4750 N(Wtd) ★	18	11	4	10	-	2	6	4	5	6	8	-	-	-	-	17

B087F: With quaaludes

	TOTAL	M	F	White	Black	NE	NC	S	W	Yes	No	None	Mari- juana Only	Few Pills	More Pills	Any Her- oin
1. Not at all	81.0	82.2	86.8	87.6	-	82.1	89.5	72.7	77.2	91.9	68.9	-	-	-	-	80.1
2. A few of the times	10.8	17.8	-	12.4	-	-	10.5	27.3	4.0	-	26.3	-	-	-	-	11.3
3. Some of the times	-	-	-	-	-	-	-	-	-	-	-	-	-	-	-	-
4. Most of the times	4.8	-	13.2	-	-	17.9	-	-	6.9	8.1	4.7	-	-	-	-	5.0
5. Every time	3.4	-	-	-	-	-	-	-	11.9	-	-	-	-	-	-	3.5
Item 4760 N(Wtd) ★	18	11	4	11	-	3	6	4	5	7	8	-	-	-	-	18

B087G: With barbiturates

	TOTAL	M	F	White	Black	NE	NC	S	W	Yes	No	None	Mari- juana Only	Few Pills	More Pills	Any Her- oin
1. Not at all	72.4	70.1	86.8	78.6	-	69.7	83.0	38.8	89.1	72.9	64.4	-	-	-	-	78.0
2. A few of the times	15.7	25.4	-	21.4	-	-	17.0	41.4	4.0	6.0	24.6	-	-	-	-	17.0
3. Some of the times	10.0	4.5	13.2	-	-	30.3	-	19.8	-	21.0	6.5	-	-	-	-	3.0
4. Most of the times	1.9	-	-	-	-	-	-	-	6.9	-	4.4	-	-	-	-	2.0
5. Every time	-	-	-	-	-	-	-	-	-	-	-	-	-	-	-	-
Item 4770 N(Wtd) ★	19	12	4	11	-	3	6	4	5	7	8	-	-	-	-	18

B087H: With tranquilizers

	TOTAL	M	F	White	Black	NE	NC	S	W	Yes	No	None	Mari- juana Only	Few Pills	More Pills	Any Her- oin
1. Not at all	80.2	76.9	86.8	85.9	-	69.7	83.0	66.0	93.1	83.8	67.0	-	-	-	-	82.6
2. A few of the times	12.0	18.6	-	14.1	-	-	17.0	34.0	-	6.9	22.1	-	-	-	-	12.4
3. Some of the times	5.8	4.5	13.2	-	-	30.3	-	-	-	9.3	6.5	-	-	-	-	3.0
4. Most of the times	2.0	-	-	-	-	-	-	-	6.9	-	4.4	-	-	-	-	2.0
5. Every time	-	-	-	-	-	-	-	-	-	-	-	-	-	-	-	-
Item 4780 N(Wtd) ★	18	12	4	11	-	3	6	3	5	6	8	-	-	-	-	18

B087I: With cocaine

	TOTAL	M	F	White	Black	NE	NC	S	W	Yes	No	None	Mari- juana Only	Few Pills	More Pills	Any Her- oin
1. Not at all	70.3	83.1	52.8	87.4	-	46.7	71.0	80.2	77.2	57.1	71.9	-	-	-	-	75.8
2. A few of the times	13.5	9.9	13.9	5.0	-	15.1	19.6	19.8	-	12.9	21.2	-	-	-	-	6.7
3. Some of the times	7.2	-	20.1	-	-	23.0	9.4	-	-	12.3	-	-	-	-	-	7.8
4. Most of the times	5.8	1.8	13.2	1.9	-	15.1	-	-	10.9	8.1	7.0	-	-	-	-	6.2
5. Every time	3.3	5.3	-	5.6	-	-	-	-	11.9	9.5	-	-	-	-	-	3.5
Item 4790 N(Wtd) ★	19	12	4	11	-	3	6	4	5	7	8	-	-	-	-	18

★ = excludes respondents for whom question was inappropriate.

QUESTIONNAIRE FORM 1 1976	TOTAL	SEX		RACE		REGION				4YR COLLEGE PLANS		ILLICIT DRUG USE: LIFETIME				
		M	F	White	Black	NE	NC	S	W	Yes	No	None	Mari-juana Only	Few Pills	More Pills	Any Her-oin
Weighted No. of Cases:	3039	1426	1466	2356	338	715	950	919	454	1384	1321	1219	669	329	605	47
% of Weighted Total:	100.0	46.9	48.2	77.5	11.1	23.5	31.3	30.2	15.0	45.5	43.5	40.1	22.0	10.8	19.9	1.6

B088: What have been the most important reasons for your taking heroin? (Mark all that apply.)

	TOTAL	M	F	White	Black	NE	NC	S	W	Yes	No	None	Mari-juana Only	Few Pills	More Pills	Any Her-oin
A. To experiment--to see what it's like	53.8	55.5	41.1	37.4	-	64.7	64.6	14.1	64.7	51.2	42.7	-	-	-	-	57.8
B. To relax or relieve tension	17.2	13.7	28.8	7.4	-	58.3	11.7	-	10.9	28.5	15.4	-	-	-	-	18.5
C. To feel good or get high	49.4	43.9	53.7	47.2	-	38.1	73.9	43.7	29.8	45.8	60.4	-	-	-	-	53.1
D. To seek deeper insights and understanding	18.2	15.1	28.8	8.9	-	58.3	17.5	-	6.9	34.0	13.0	-	-	-	-	19.5
E. To have a good time with my friends	18.8	15.7	11.5	9.4	-	15.1	38.5	-	10.9	24.8	21.8	-	-	-	-	20.2
F. To fit in with a group I like	12.4	5.6	11.5	5.7	-	35.3	12.6	-	6.9	29.2	4.1	-	-	-	-	13.3
G. To get away from my problems or troubles	16.6	-	62.9	12.7	-	38.1	-	22.4	18.8	27.4	14.8	-	-	-	-	17.8
H. Because of boredom, nothing else to do	13.2	13.8	11.5	13.9	-	35.3	-	-	26.4	26.0	8.5	-	-	-	-	14.2
I. Because of anger or frustration	8.8	-	11.5	-	-	15.1	-	19.8	6.9	19.2	4.1	-	-	-	-	4.8
J. To get through the day	10.1	8.8	11.5	8.9	-	35.3	-	-	14.4	17.3	8.5	-	-	-	-	10.8
K. To increase the effects of some other drug(s)	5.6	1.7	11.5	1.7	-	15.1	-	-	10.9	7.4	6.4	-	-	-	-	6.0
L. To decrease (offset) the effects of some other drug(s)	6.3	5.6	11.5	5.7	-	35.3	-	-	-	17.3	-	-	-	-	-	6.7
M. Because I am "hooked"--I have to have it	15.8	4.2	11.5	-	-	30.3	12.6	19.8	6.9	31.1	10.1	-	-	-	-	9.5
Item 4800-4920 N(Wtd) ★	20	12	5	12	-	3	7	4	5	7	9	-	-	-	-	18

B089: When you take heroin how high do you usually get?

	TOTAL	M	F	White	Black	NE	NC	S	W	Yes	No	None	Mari-juana Only	Few Pills	More Pills	Any Her-oin
1. Not at all high	-	-	-	-	-	-	-	-	-	-	-	-	-	-	-	-
2. A little high	7.9	12.2	-	6.6	-	-	9.4	-	15.7	-	17.5	-	-	-	-	7.9
3. Moderately high	20.9	22.5	24.9	26.9	-	-	8.2	17.6	51.6	27.0	18.6	-	-	-	-	20.9
4. Very high	71.2	65.3	75.1	66.5	-	100.0	82.4	82.4	32.7	73.0	63.9	-	-	-	-	71.2
5. I don't take it to get high	-	-	-	-	-	-	-	-	-	-	-	-	-	-	-	-
Item 4930 N(Wtd) ★	18	12	5	12	-	3	7	3	5	6	8	-	-	-	-	18

B090: When you take heroin how long do you usually stay high?

	TOTAL	M	F	White	Black	NE	NC	S	W	Yes	No	None	Mari-juana Only	Few Pills	More Pills	Any Her-oin
1. Usually don't get high	-	-	-	-	-	-	-	-	-	-	-	-	-	-	-	-
2. One to two hours	20.0	19.9	13.5	11.7	-	31.3	9.4	19.8	27.6	20.5	17.5	-	-	-	-	16.4
3. Three to six hours	43.3	45.2	50.8	45.6	-	27.1	53.1	38.8	43.6	41.6	50.7	-	-	-	-	45.3
4. Seven to 24 hours	22.3	19.3	24.3	27.7	-	-	37.5	14.1	21.9	20.6	13.5	-	-	-	-	23.3
5. More than 24 hours	14.3	15.6	11.5	15.1	-	41.6	-	27.3	6.9	17.3	18.3	-	-	-	-	15.0
Item 4940 N(Wtd) ★	19	12	5	12	-	3	7	4	5	7	8	-	-	-	-	18

B091: Have you ever tried to stop using heroin and found that you couldn't stop?

	TOTAL	M	F	White	Black	NE	NC	S	W	Yes	No	None	Mari-juana Only	Few Pills	More Pills	Any Her-oin
1. Yes	22.3	16.4	24.3	15.5	-	41.6	9.4	19.8	30.2	37.8	19.1	-	-	-	-	18.8
2. No	77.7	83.6	75.7	84.5	-	58.4	90.6	80.2	69.8	62.2	80.9	-	-	-	-	81.2
Item 4950 N(Wtd) ★	19	12	5	12	-	3	7	4	5	7	8	-	-	-	-	18

B092: What methods have you used for taking heroin? (Mark all that apply.)

	TOTAL	M	F	White	Black	NE	NC	S	W	Yes	No	None	Mari-juana Only	Few Pills	More Pills	Any Her-oin
A. Sniffing or "snorting"	62.2	52.3	67.5	47.2	-	100.0	68.2	19.8	66.7	84.7	47.1	-	-	-	-	60.5
B. Smoking	21.1	21.7	11.5	17.0	-	41.6	8.4	16.4	28.9	34.3	13.1	-	-	-	-	22.1
C. Injection	66.2	67.4	74.3	63.2	-	100.0	67.0	63.7	49.8	40.4	79.0	-	-	-	-	69.1
D. By mouth	15.5	12.9	11.5	8.5	-	41.6	14.2	-	15.1	30.0	4.0	-	-	-	-	16.2
E. Other	12.3	5.6	11.5	5.4	-	41.6	12.6	-	6.2	29.2	4.0	-	-	-	-	12.9
Item 4960-5000 N(Wtd) ★	20	13	5	13	-	3	7	4	6	7	9	-	-	-	-	19

★ = excludes respondents for whom question was inappropriate.

QUESTIONNAIRE FORM 1 1976	TOTAL	SEX		RACE		REGION				4YR COLLEGE PLANS		ILLICIT DRUG USE: LIFETIME				
		M	F	White	Black	NE	NC	S	W	Yes	No	None	Mari-juana Only	Few Pills	More Pills	Any Her-oin
Weighted No. of Cases:	3039	1426	1466	2356	338	715	950	919	454	1384	1321	1219	669	329	605	47
% of Weighted Total:	100.0	46.9	48.2	77.5	11.1	23.5	31.3	30.2	15.0	45.5	43.5	40.1	22.0	10.8	19.9	1.6

B093: Do you think you will be using heroin five years from now?

1. I definitely will	.6	.5	.6	.6	.7	1.7	.4	*	.3	.5	.6	.3	1.0	.2	.6	2.6
2. I probably will	.4	.6	.2	.4	.5	-	.5	.6	.5	.2	.6	*	.3	.2	.9	8.4
3. I probably will not	7.4	9.5	5.0	7.4	7.0	7.0	7.4	8.2	6.4	6.2	8.5	4.5	6.3	9.9	12.4	30.5
4. I definitely will not	91.6	89.4	94.1	91.7	91.8	91.2	91.7	91.1	92.8	93.2	90.3	95.1	92.4	89.7	86.1	58.6
Item 5010 N(Wtd)	2736	1302	1366	2183	310	618	867	842	409	1287	1222	1166	608	290	518	43

The next questions are about NARCOTICS OTHER THAN HEROIN, which are sometimes prescribed by doctors. Drugstores are not supposed to sell them without a prescription.

These include: Methadone, Opium, Morphine, Codeine, Demorol, Paregoric, Talwin, Laudanum.

B094: Have you ever taken any narcotics other than heroin because a doctor told you to use them?

1. No	83.9	83.8	83.5	82.4	94.6	84.1	84.2	84.9	80.8	82.7	85.1	89.9	87.8	69.1	75.8	61.0
2. Yes, but I had already tried them on my own.	2.1	2.2	2.0	2.1	.9	1.9	2.0	2.3	2.0	1.4	2.6	-	-	.5	7.5	24.4
3. Yes, and it was the first time I took any	14.0	14.0	14.5	15.5	4.4	14.0	13.8	12.8	17.1	15.9	12.4	9.9	12.1	30.4	16.7	14.6
Item 5020 N(Wtd)	2731	1301	1366	2200	295	633	873	818	407	1312	1197	1164	617	303	536	45

B095: On how many occasions (if any) have you taken narcotics other than heroin on your own--that is, without a doctor telling you to take them...

B095A: ...in your lifetime?

1. 0 occasions	89.7	87.9	91.5	89.1	96.5	87.6	89.1	91.6	90.2	91.8	88.7	100.0	100.0	82.8	62.9	31.3
2. 1-2	5.2	6.1	4.4	5.6	1.6	7.3	4.3	4.7	5.1	4.6	5.3	-	-	17.2	15.5	16.3
3. 3-5	2.3	2.6	1.9	2.4	.7	2.2	3.4	1.5	1.4	1.9	2.5	-	-	11.0	6.6
4. 6-9	.9	1.2	.5	.9	.4	.7	1.0	.6	1.6	.7	.9	-	-	-	3.8	9.8
5. 10-19	.6	.7	.5	.6	.4	.8	.7	.4	.7	.3	.6	-	-	-	2.6	7.8
6. 20-39	.5	.3	.6	.5	.4	.7	.2	.6	.4	.5	.4	-	-	-	1.8	6.4
7. 40 or more	.8	1.2	.5	.9	-	.8	1.3	.6	.5	.2	1.4	-	-	-	2.5	21.8
Item 1130 N(Wtd)	2724	1308	1353	2192	295	622	868	827	407	1300	1202	1185	620	302	538	43

B095B: ...during the last 12 months?

1. 0 occasions	94.5	93.7	95.5	94.3	98.6	93.9	93.3	96.4	94.5	96.0	93.9	100.0	100.0	95.2	77.9	61.3
2. 1-2	3.1	3.7	2.4	3.0	1.0	3.8	3.8	1.9	3.2	2.5	3.1	-	-	4.8	12.5	8.9
3. 3-5	1.3	1.2	1.5	1.5	-	1.5	1.6	1.1	.8	1.0	1.4	-	-	-	6.1	8.2
4. 6-9	.3	.4	.3	.3	.3	.2	.3	.3	.7	.3	.4	-	-	-	1.1	7.6
5. 10-19	.2	.4	.1	.3	-	.4	.2	-	.6	*	.3	-	-	-	1.0	3.3
6. 20-39	.2	.4	.1	.2	-	.2	.4	.1	.1	.2	.3	-	-	-	.8	4.3
7. 40 or more	.2	.3	.1	.2	-	.1	.4	.2	.1	-	.5	-	-	-	.6	6.4
Item 1140 N(Wtd)	2716	1304	1348	2184	295	621	867	821	406	1293	1202	1186	620	298	533	42

B095C: ...during the last 30 days?

1. 0 occasions	98.4	97.7	99.1	98.3	99.5	98.7	97.8	99.2	97.5	98.9	98.2	100.0	100.0	98.7	94.5	74.4
2. 1-2	.9	1.4	.5	1.0	.3	1.0	1.0	.5	1.6	.8	.8	-	-	1.3	3.2	10.1
3. 3-5	.4	.5	.3	.4	-	*	.7	.1	.7	.2	.5	-	-	-	1.4	6.1
4. 6-9	.1	.2	.1	.1	.2	-	.3	.1	.1	*	.3	-	-	-	.6	1.7
5. 10-19	.1	*	.1	.1	-	.2	.1	-	-	*	.1	-	-	-	.2	1.2
6. 20-39	-	-	-	-	-	-	-	-	-	-	-	-	-	-	-	-
7. 40 or more	.1	.2	-	.1	-	-	.1	.1	.1	-	.2	-	-	-	-	6.4
Item 1150 N(Wtd)	2713	1302	1347	2181	295	619	866	821	406	1292	1200	1186	620	297	531	42

* = less than .05 per cent.

QUESTIONNAIRE FORM 1 1976	TOTAL	SEX		RACE		REGION				4YR COLLEGE PLANS		ILLICIT DRUG USE: LIFETIME				
		M	F	White	Black	NE	NC	S	W	Yes	No	None	Mari-juana Only	Few Pills	More Pills	Any Her-oin
Weighted No. of Cases:	3039	1426	1466	2356	338	715	950	919	454	1384	1321	1219	669	329	605	47
% of Weighted Total:	100.0	46.9	48.2	77.5	11.1	23.5	31.3	30.2	15.0	45.5	43.5	40.1	22.0	10.8	19.9	1.6

IF YOU HAVE NOT TAKEN NARCOTICS OTHER THAN HEROIN IN THE LAST TWELVE MONTHS, GO TO Q.B104.

THE FOLLOWING QUESTIONS REFER ONLY TO TAKING NARCOTICS OTHER THAN HEROIN WITHOUT A DOCTOR'S ORDERS. IF YOU HAVE NOT DONE THIS IN THE LAST TWELVE MONTHS, GO TO Q.B104.

B096: When you used narcotics other than heroin during the last year, how often did you use them in each of the following situations?

B096A: When you were alone

	TOTAL	M	F	White	Black	NE	NC	S	W	Yes	No	None	Mari-juana Only	Few Pills	More Pills	Any Heroin
1. Not at all	60.4	59.6	60.1	58.6	67.1	64.0	66.2	49.1	54.7	63.6	53.5	-	-	73.8	65.0	21.9
2. A few of the times	18.3	18.4	20.2	20.2	-	11.9	20.0	15.7	28.5	18.3	24.8	-	-	7.4	15.6	42.8
3. Some of the times	11.9	12.6	9.4	10.0	32.9	15.2	10.5	14.9	5.5	10.3	9.9	-	-	11.4	20.5
4. Most of the times	6.4	5.3	8.4	7.7	-	6.6	1.4	17.1	4.7	2.7	11.9	-	-	-	6.3	10.1
5. Every time	2.9	4.0	1.8	3.5	-	2.2	1.9	3.1	6.6	5.2	-	-	-	18.8	1.7	4.6
Item 5030 N(Wtd) ★	126	68	52	104	5	32	50	26	19	45	58	-	-	7	103	15

B096B: With just 1 or 2 other people

	TOTAL	M	F	White	Black	NE	NC	S	W	Yes	No	None	Mari-juana Only	Few Pills	More Pills	Any Heroin
1. Not at all	19.0	14.8	24.5	14.6	48.9	19.0	14.5	18.5	32.0	30.6	10.0	-	-	22.1	19.6	8.0
2. A few of the times	40.8	38.8	46.1	44.2	19.1	45.6	44.5	38.9	24.2	40.8	43.6	-	-	54.6	43.0	21.0
3. Some of the times	14.8	19.6	7.8	15.8	13.0	13.7	13.9	13.2	21.8	16.9	11.2	-	-	-	13.4	33.5
4. Most of the times	13.1	15.9	7.4	13.0	-	6.7	14.8	16.4	15.6	6.2	18.4	-	-	6.0	10.8	32.9
5. Every time	12.3	10.9	14.2	12.5	19.1	15.0	12.4	13.0	6.4	5.4	16.9	-	-	17.3	13.2	4.6
Item 5040 N(Wtd) ★	130	73	52	109	5	35	51	26	19	46	61	-	-	8	106	15

B096C: At a party

	TOTAL	M	F	White	Black	NE	NC	S	W	Yes	No	None	Mari-juana Only	Few Pills	More Pills	Any Heroin
1. Not at all	39.5	36.0	44.8	37.7	67.9	53.5	24.1	37.8	56.8	40.9	40.3	-	-	60.0	41.8	9.9
2. A few of the times	19.5	22.5	15.9	20.6	19.1	18.3	22.3	15.4	20.2	31.1	13.6	-	-	32.0	17.3	30.6
3. Some of the times	19.2	18.5	19.9	19.4	13.0	17.0	19.7	23.2	17.1	18.6	20.1	-	-	-	20.1	23.7
4. Most of the times	7.4	11.4	1.9	7.5	-	5.9	10.1	5.2	5.9	5.7	8.0	-	-	8.0	5.0	24.1
5. Every time	14.3	11.6	17.5	14.7	-	5.4	23.9	18.4	-	3.7	18.1	-	-	-	15.7	11.7
Item 5050 N(Wtd) ★	130	72	52	108	5	36	50	25	18	45	62	-	-	7	106	15

B096D: When your date or spouse was present

	TOTAL	M	F	White	Black	NE	NC	S	W	Yes	No	None	Mari-juana Only	Few Pills	More Pills	Any Heroin
1. Not at all	61.6	71.8	48.7	58.2	100.0	76.3	57.2	46.4	67.5	77.6	51.0	-	-	64.4	63.8	42.7
2. A few of the times	14.1	14.2	15.6	16.4	-	11.7	13.2	14.5	21.0	7.8	17.2	-	-	24.5	12.0	25.0
3. Some of the times	10.1	9.6	7.7	9.7	-	5.1	9.4	16.9	11.5	9.2	9.5	-	-	11.1	8.5	21.1
4. Most of the times	4.2	1.8	8.1	4.4	-	6.9	6.1	-	-	3.6	6.3	-	-	-	4.6	3.6
5. Every time	10.0	2.6	20.0	11.3	-	-	14.1	22.1	-	1.8	16.0	-	-	-	11.1	7.6
Item 5060 N(Wtd) ★	128	71	51	106	5	34	50	26	18	44	60	-	-	7	104	15

B096E: When people over age 30 were present

	TOTAL	M	F	White	Black	NE	NC	S	W	Yes	No	None	Mari-juana Only	Few Pills	More Pills	Any Heroin
1. Not at all	67.2	76.8	55.2	67.5	67.1	72.4	71.9	55.1	61.6	71.2	62.7	-	-	82.3	66.5	63.2
2. A few of the times	12.4	12.3	13.9	12.7	-	10.1	14.8	11.5	11.8	13.2	13.6	-	-	-	12.1	21.4
3. Some of the times	10.7	8.2	12.6	10.2	13.0	4.4	7.9	20.3	17.4	9.5	9.8	-	-	-	10.9	15.3
4. Most of the times	2.1	1.8	2.6	2.1	-	1.9	1.1	4.2	1.9	-	3.7	-	-	-	2.5	-
5. Every time	7.5	1.0	15.7	7.4	19.9	11.1	4.3	8.9	7.3	6.1	10.2	-	-	17.7	8.0	-
Item 5070 N(Wtd) ★	131	71	54	109	5	36	50	26	19	45	62	-	-	7	107	15

★=excludes respondents for whom question was inappropriate.

QUESTIONNAIRE FORM 1 1976	TOTAL	SEX		RACE		REGION				4YR COLLEGE PLANS		ILLICIT DRUG USE: LIFETIME				
		M	F	White	Black	NE	NC	S	W	Yes	No	None	Mari-juana Only	Few Pills	More Pills	Any Her-oin
Weighted No. of Cases:	3039	1426	1466	2356	338	715	950	919	454	1384	1321	1219	669	329	605	47
% of Weighted Total:	100.0	46.9	48.2	77.5	11.1	23.5	31.3	30.2	15.0	45.5	43.5	40.1	22.0	10.8	19.9	1.6
B096F: During the daytime (before 4:00 p.m.)																
1. Not at all	41.9	42.7	42.8	41.0	29.0	43.2	49.8	30.6	35.1	47.5	38.3	-	-	55.3	42.2	28.8
2. A few of the times	29.1	30.2	24.7	31.0	19.1	32.7	24.0	29.6	34.9	28.1	28.0	-	-	15.3	31.1	24.2
3. Some of the times	18.9	17.1	22.7	19.3	32.9	14.7	20.9	22.9	16.2	17.8	22.0	-	-	8.8	18.1	31.2
4. Most of the times	3.3	4.2	2.4	3.2	-	-	2.5	6.9	6.1	2.5	4.5	-	-	10.1	2.1	7.9
5. Every time	6.8	5.8	7.4	5.4	19.1	9.4	2.8	10.1	7.8	4.1	7.2	-	-	10.6	6.4	7.9
Item 5080 N(Wtd) ★	125	68	52	103	5	33	47	26	19	42	59	-	-	8	101	15
B096G: At your home (or apartment or dorm)																
1. Not at all	43.3	46.4	40.3	39.4	67.1	49.9	46.4	32.6	38.3	47.8	38.7	-	-	45.2	44.1	33.4
2. A few of the times	24.0	26.9	17.7	26.0	-	19.1	27.1	26.6	20.9	26.9	24.0	-	-	12.9	24.2	28.9
3. Some of the times	11.1	12.5	9.6	11.9	-	9.5	12.9	10.6	9.6	7.4	11.5	-	-	9.7	10.7	15.1
4. Most of the times	4.5	4.9	4.4	3.7	13.0	4.0	3.4	2.7	10.7	5.2	4.7	-	-	6.8	3.7	9.2
5. Every time	17.2	9.3	28.1	19.0	19.9	17.5	10.3	27.6	20.7	12.7	21.1	-	-	25.5	17.3	13.4
Item 5090 N(Wtd) ★	127	70	52	106	5	33	50	26	19	45	59	-	-	7	104	15
B096H: At school																
1. Not at all	61.6	50.8	76.3	60.4	67.9	66.2	62.8	56.4	57.5	63.0	61.6	-	-	80.3	65.3	24.7
2. A few of the times	21.5	28.5	10.8	23.2	32.1	21.0	18.4	22.6	29.0	28.7	15.6	-	-	9.1	21.9	26.0
3. Some of the times	11.8	15.3	8.3	12.5	-	8.8	11.8	15.9	11.6	1.6	17.8	-	-	10.6	9.5	29.1
4. Most of the times	3.6	4.3	2.4	2.6	-	2.4	5.5	2.7	1.9	4.3	3.8	-	-	-	2.0	16.8
5. Every time	1.4	1.0	2.2	1.2	-	1.6	1.4	2.3	-	2.5	1.2	-	-	-	1.3	3.5
Item 5100 N(Wtd) ★	128	71	52	107	5	33	51	26	19	45	59	-	-	8	104	15
B096I: In a car																
1. Not at all	57.4	50.9	66.2	53.6	87.0	76.0	39.6	49.0	82.9	68.9	49.2	-	-	83.6	59.2	29.2
2. A few of the times	16.7	13.9	18.9	18.3	-	12.8	22.3	17.1	7.6	14.7	16.5	-	-	9.1	16.6	22.2
3. Some of the times	14.7	22.6	5.3	15.6	-	2.2	24.1	19.0	6.5	8.4	19.0	-	-	-	12.9	35.6
4. Most of the times	7.0	8.2	5.2	7.4	13.0	4.4	11.1	5.0	3.0	8.0	8.9	-	-	7.3	6.1	12.9
5. Every time	4.3	4.5	4.5	5.1	-	4.6	2.8	9.9	-	-	6.4	-	-	-	5.3	-
Item 5120 N(Wtd) ★	130	73	52	109	5	35	51	26	19	46	61	-	-	8	106	15
B097: How many of the times when you used narcotics other than heroin during the last year did you use them along with each of the following drugs--that is, so that their effects overlapped?																
B097A: With alcohol																
1. Not at all	51.9	51.2	55.1	50.3	87.0	59.5	43.6	53.8	57.9	62.3	49.2	-	-	77.7	51.1	40.2
2. A few of the times	26.3	21.5	30.4	26.3	-	33.2	20.4	25.9	29.9	22.0	29.0	-	-	22.3	26.4	29.4
3. Some of the times	9.1	9.3	8.4	10.2	13.0	7.4	12.7	5.7	7.3	12.3	7.4	-	-	-	11.1	-
4. Most of the times	6.2	9.3	2.0	6.7	-	-	11.6	4.8	4.9	2.0	11.0	-	-	-	4.6	21.7
5. Every time	6.5	8.7	4.2	6.5	-	-	11.8	9.8	-	1.3	3.4	-	-	-	6.8	8.7
Item 5130 N(Wtd) ★	127	69	53	107	5	34	50	24	19	45	60	-	-	8	104	14
B097B: With marijuana																
1. Not at all	31.7	25.3	40.8	30.9	48.9	47.4	18.2	23.7	48.5	39.1	28.9	-	-	56.7	31.8	13.6
2. A few of the times	16.5	14.1	18.7	17.0	19.0	17.0	17.5	12.2	18.6	15.9	16.8	-	-	25.4	16.9	10.3
3. Some of the times	14.9	17.7	12.3	17.1	13.0	10.7	19.0	19.0	6.4	17.3	12.9	-	-	-	14.8	23.9
4. Most of the times	16.4	17.1	14.4	15.4	-	13.0	21.3	14.3	12.6	13.1	21.4	-	-	-	15.0	36.1
5. Every time	20.5	25.8	13.8	19.6	19.1	11.9	24.0	30.8	13.9	14.6	20.0	-	-	17.9	21.5	16.1
Item 5140 N(Wtd) ★	131	73	54	110	5	36	51	25	19	46	62	-	-	8	107	15

★ = excludes respondents for whom question was inappropriate.

QUESTIONNAIRE FORM 1 1976	TOTAL	SEX		RACE		REGION				4YR COLLEGE PLANS		ILLICIT DRUG USE: LIFETIME				
		M	F	White	Black	NE	NC	S	W	Yes	No	None	Mari-juana Only	Few Pills	More Pills	Any Her-oin
Weighted No. of Cases:	3039	1426	1466	2356	338	715	950	919	454	1384	1321	1219	669	329	605	47
% of Weighted Total:	100.0	46.9	48.2	77.5	11.1	23.5	31.3	30.2	15.0	45.5	43.5	40.1	22.0	10.8	19.9	1.6
B097C: With LSD																
1. Not at all	97.6	98.0	97.6	98.7	100.0	98.3	96.1	99.9	96.9	96.5	97.7	-	-	100.0	100.0	75.6
2. A few of the times	1.1	1.0	1.3	1.3	-	-	2.4	-	1.1	2.3	.4	-	-	-	-	10.9
3. Some of the times	-	-	-	-	-	-	-	-	-	-	-	-	-	-	-	7.9
4. Most of the times	.8	-	1.1	-	-	1.7	-	-	2.0	1.2	.7	-	-	-	-	5.6
5. Every time	.5	1.0	-	-	-	-	1.5	-	-	-	1.2	-	-	-	-	5.6
Item 5150 N(Wtd) ★	116	62	49	96	5	32	42	23	18	45	53	-	-	8	95	11
B097D: With psychedelics other than LSD																
1. Not at all	96.7	96.6	97.4	97.6	100.0	93.9	96.5	99.9	98.1	97.9	94.7	-	-	100.0	98.0	84.6
2. A few of the times	2.4	2.4	2.6	2.4	-	6.1	2.0	-	-	2.1	3.5	-	-	-	2.0	7.4
3. Some of the times	-	-	-	-	-	-	-	-	-	-	-	-	-	-	-	-
4. Most of the times	.9	1.0	-	-	-	-	1.5	-	1.9	-	1.8	-	-	-	-	8.0
5. Every time	-	-	-	-	-	-	-	-	-	-	-	-	-	-	-	-
Item 5160 N(Wtd) ★	117	64	49	97	5	32	43	23	19	44	55	-	-	8	96	12
B097E: With amphetamines																
1. Not at all	90.6	91.2	93.1	90.6	91.6	97.8	85.3	88.7	93.7	94.9	86.8	-	-	100.0	91.2	79.8
2. A few of the times	5.4	5.5	2.3	5.0	8.4	2.2	8.6	4.4	4.4	5.1	4.9	-	-	-	4.3	17.5
3. Some of the times	.6	-	1.3	.7	-	-	1.4	-	-	1.1	-	-	-	-	.7	-
4. Most of the times	2.1	3.3	-	2.1	-	-	4.7	-	1.9	-	4.4	-	-	-	2.2	2.7
5. Every time	1.3	-	3.3	1.6	-	-	-	6.9	-	-	2.8	-	-	-	1.6	-
Item 5170 N(Wtd) ★	118	65	49	99	6	31	46	23	19	43	57	-	-	8	96	13
B097F: With quaaludes																
1. Not at all	97.9	97.3	99.3	98.8	100.0	100.0	96.5	99.9	95.1	100.0	97.0	-	-	100.0	98.6	90.8
2. A few of the times	.4	.7	-	.5	-	-	1.1	-	-	-	.8	-	-	-	.5	-
3. Some of the times	1.1	2.0	-	.7	-	-	2.4	-	1.1	-	1.5	-	-	-	.5	6.4
4. Most of the times	.6	-	.7	-	-	-	-	-	3.8	-	.7	-	-	-	.4	2.8
5. Every time	-	-	-	-	-	-	-	-	-	-	-	-	-	-	-	-
Item 5180 N(Wtd) ★	119	64	50	99	5	32	45	23	19	45	56	-	-	8	97	13
B097G: With barbiturates																
1. Not at all	94.7	91.5	99.3	95.0	100.0	97.9	94.8	92.7	91.6	97.1	94.1	-	-	100.0	96.1	81.0
2. A few of the times	3.0	5.4	-	3.6	-	2.1	2.8	7.3	-	2.9	2.5	-	-	-	2.4	9.8
3. Some of the times	1.4	2.0	.7	.7	-	-	2.4	-	2.9	-	1.5	-	-	-	.8	6.4
4. Most of the times	.9	1.1	-	.7	-	-	-	-	5.5	-	1.9	-	-	-	.7	2.8
5. Every time	-	-	-	-	-	-	-	-	-	-	-	-	-	-	-	-
Item 5190 N(Wtd) ★	120	66	50	100	5	32	45	23	19	45	57	-	-	8	98	13
B097H: With tranquilizers																
1. Not at all	96.2	94.2	99.3	96.8	100.0	97.9	96.7	99.9	87.4	97.6	95.3	-	-	100.0	98.5	77.4
2. A few of the times	1.0	1.8	-	1.2	-	-	.9	-	4.2	.9	1.4	-	-	-	-	8.8
3. Some of the times	1.4	1.9	.7	.6	-	-	2.4	-	2.9	-	1.5	-	-	-	.8	6.1
4. Most of the times	1.4	2.1	-	1.4	-	2.1	-	-	5.5	1.5	1.8	-	-	-	.7	7.7
5. Every time	-	-	-	-	-	-	-	-	-	-	-	-	-	-	-	-
Item 5200 N(Wtd) ★	122	67	50	102	5	33	46	23	19	45	58	-	-	8	99	14
B097I: With cocaine																
1. Not at all	90.7	86.7	95.8	93.3	87.0	87.4	94.6	92.0	85.8	90.7	90.4	-	-	100.0	95.0	54.1
2. A few of the times	3.0	5.4	-	2.2	13.0	4.3	2.4	3.0	1.8	2.4	2.4	-	-	-	2.5	8.3
3. Some of the times	3.2	4.7	1.6	2.4	-	4.6	1.4	5.0	3.1	3.3	4.1	-	-	-	.7	23.2
4. Most of the times	1.3	-	2.6	-	-	1.6	-	-	5.7	2.0	.6	-	-	-	.4	9.3
5. Every time	1.8	3.2	-	2.1	-	2.1	1.6	-	3.6	1.6	2.5	-	-	-	1.4	5.1
Item 5210 N(Wtd) ★	121	66	50	101	5	33	45	23	19	45	58	-	-	8	98	14

★=excludes respondents for whom question was inappropriate.

QUESTIONNAIRE FORM 1 1976	TOTAL	SEX		RACE		REGION				4YR COLLEGE PLANS		ILLICIT DRUG USE: LIFETIME				
		M	F	White	Black	NE	NC	S	W	Yes	No	None	Mari- juana Only	Few Pills	More Pills	Any Her- oin
Weighted No. of Cases:	3039	1426	1466	2356	338	715	950	919	454	1384	1321	1219	669	329	605	47
% of Weighted Total:	100.0	46.9	48.2	77.5	11.1	23.5	31.3	30.2	15.0	45.5	43.5	40.1	22.0	10.8	19.9	1.6

B097J: With heroin

	TOTAL	M	F	White	Black	NE	NC	S	W	Yes	No	None	Mari- juana Only	Few Pills	More Pills	Any Her- oin
1. Not at all	96.1	94.3	98.9	96.9	100.0	96.3	98.6	95.0	91.2	97.3	94.0	-	-	100.0	99.3	70.0
2. A few of the times	.2	.3	-	.2	-	-	-	-	1.1	-	.4	-	-	-	-	1.6
3. Some of the times	1.8	3.3	-	1.5	-	-	1.4	5.0	2.1	-	3.8	-	-	-	-	16.4
4. Most of the times	1.3	1.0	1.1	.7	-	3.7	-	-	1.9	2.7	.6	-	-	-	-	12.0
5. Every time	.6	1.1	-	.7	-	-	-	-	3.7	-	1.2	-	-	-	.7	-
Item 5220 N(Wtd) ★	121	67	49	101	5	33	46	23	19	45	57	-	-	8	99	13

B098: What have been the most important reasons for your using narcotics other than heroin without a doctor's orders? (Mark all that apply.)

	TOTAL	M	F	White	Black	NE	NC	S	W	Yes	No	None	Mari- juana Only	Few Pills	More Pills	Any Her- oin
A. To experiment--to see what it's like	62.9	64.3	58.6	60.2	78.7	59.7	66.6	61.8	59.0	62.6	62.2	-	-	75.5	63.2	54.5
B. To relax or relieve tension	36.8	30.4	44.8	37.8	31.2	37.2	35.0	32.5	48.8	30.3	44.2	-	-	38.5	36.6	37.2
C. To feel good or get high	66.2	73.7	58.2	66.5	52.5	68.3	66.9	55.5	76.5	65.1	64.8	-	-	50.1	64.0	87.8
D. To seek deeper insights and understanding	11.3	12.1	10.5	9.9	31.2	14.2	7.3	14.7	12.8	9.2	15.2	-	-	-	11.0	18.8
E. To have a good time with my friends	29.6	36.8	19.6	30.8	31.2	35.3	30.8	14.3	38.4	32.1	29.3	-	-	42.4	26.5	44.3
F. To fit in with a group I like	6.8	9.9	2.1	6.4	-	8.6	7.9	2.8	5.5	3.4	9.6	-	-	-	6.9	9.0
G. To get away from my problems or troubles	12.0	12.9	11.0	13.0	-	11.7	15.2	6.0	11.4	9.5	17.1	-	-	-	12.2	15.8
H. Because of boredom, nothing else to do	10.7	12.2	7.7	10.2	31.2	12.0	3.1	8.4	37.1	9.5	10.6	-	-	-	9.1	26.1
I. Because of anger or frustration	8.8	5.4	14.1	9.4	-	11.1	8.6	2.8	14.4	7.7	11.9	-	-	6.6	8.2	14.3
J. To get through the day	6.0	4.6	7.8	5.4	-	5.7	5.6	2.8	13.1	2.9	9.3	-	-	-	6.0	8.4
K. To increase the effects of some other drug(s)	5.3	6.3	3.6	4.3	31.2	6.8	4.9	-	11.8	6.9	3.5	-	-	-	4.2	14.8
L. To decrease (offset) the effects of some other drug(s)	.4	-	1.1	-	-	1.6	-	-	-	1.3	-	-	-	-	-	3.5
M. To get to sleep	14.8	8.3	25.8	15.4	-	10.0	13.8	19.0	21.3	11.7	20.0	-	-	13.4	15.2	12.4
N. As a substitute for heroin	.9	.3	1.1	.2	-	1.6	-	-	3.7	1.3	.9	-	-	-	-	7.2
O. Because I am "hooked"--I have to have it	1.3	1.0	1.1	.7	-	3.8	-	-	2.3	3.0	.6	-	-	-	-	10.4
Item 5230-5370 N(Wtd) ★	124	71	48	107	3	33	51	25	15	41	61	-	-	7	102	15

B099: When you take narcotics other than heroin how high do you usually get?

	TOTAL	M	F	White	Black	NE	NC	S	W	Yes	No	None	Mari- juana Only	Few Pills	More Pills	Any Her- oin
1. Not at all high	6.1	5.6	6.6	5.8	12.2	12.6	4.3	-	7.3	4.3	8.6	-	-	15.1	6.0	-
2. A little high	18.3	18.1	19.0	19.8	23.6	25.5	19.4	12.1	8.8	20.7	16.0	-	-	51.9	18.5	-
3. Moderately high	40.4	38.9	40.9	43.1	-	28.1	38.7	49.2	59.4	39.9	46.0	-	-	13.1	39.4	58.6
4. Very high	27.5	35.8	15.9	23.3	39.6	28.8	30.5	26.1	17.4	24.8	22.0	-	-	9.0	27.4	41.4
5. I don't take it to get high	7.6	1.5	17.6	8.0	24.6	5.0	7.2	12.6	7.1	10.3	7.4	-	-	10.9	8.6	-
Item 5380 N(Wtd) ★	130	75	49	111	4	36	52	25	17	43	63	-	-	6	107	14

B100: When you take narcotics other than heroin how long do you usually stay high?

	TOTAL	M	F	White	Black	NE	NC	S	W	Yes	No	None	Mari- juana Only	Few Pills	More Pills	Any Her- oin
1. Usually don't get high	15.4	7.8	24.7	15.7	36.8	20.4	11.3	13.0	20.6	15.3	18.2	-	-	34.2	14.1	-
2. One to two hours	16.7	20.0	12.6	18.1	23.6	17.2	17.7	18.9	10.2	17.7	14.7	-	-	25.8	18.7	-
3. Three to six hours	44.1	41.4	46.9	46.5	-	42.0	44.9	42.6	47.7	42.6	42.8	-	-	32.0	44.3	57.0
4. Seven to 24 hours	20.5	26.2	14.8	17.2	39.6	14.8	23.5	25.4	16.5	19.7	20.9	-	-	8.0	21.1	26.8
5. More than 24 hours	3.2	4.5	1.0	2.4	-	5.5	2.6	-	5.0	4.8	3.5	-	-	-	1.8	16.2
Item 5390 N(Wtd) ★	130	73	51	110	4	35	52	24	18	41	65	-	-	7	106	14

B101: What narcotics other than heroin have you taken during the last year without a doctor's orders? (Mark all that apply.)

	TOTAL	M	F	White	Black	NE	NC	S	W	Yes	No	None	Mari- juana Only	Few Pills	More Pills	Any Her- oin
A. Methadone	13.3	16.0	6.9	9.0	24.8	11.1	16.3	11.4	11.7	13.2	9.9	-	-	8.6	11.7	27.5
B. Opium	58.0	62.5	50.2	60.1	49.4	50.3	64.3	64.4	46.8	49.7	55.5	-	-	54.9	56.3	74.5
C. Morphine	14.7	13.5	15.0	14.7	-	7.9	15.7	15.6	24.4	18.3	14.0	-	-	-	11.0	48.1
D. Codeine	54.0	50.6	59.1	54.6	25.8	46.3	54.2	57.1	65.0	54.9	56.2	-	-	21.7	56.9	49.4
E. Demerol	14.4	14.7	14.5	14.1	-	13.0	12.4	19.0	16.7	10.1	18.1	-	-	8.6	14.5	16.5
F. Paregoric	8.1	3.9	14.3	8.6	-	10.0	4.7	14.8	4.8	10.2	8.3	-	-	-	7.6	15.6
G. Talwin	3.4	1.9	5.1	2.2	-	1.5	3.9	2.9	6.5	1.3	4.2	-	-	-	1.9	15.7
H. Laudanum	3.6	3.8	2.9	3.4	-	5.4	1.1	5.8	4.1	6.1	2.0	-	-	-	2.8	10.9
I. Other	12.0	14.5	7.4	13.2	-	10.9	14.5	15.5	2.0	17.0	9.6	-	-	-	10.8	21.2
J. Don't know the names of some I have used	25.4	21.9	30.0	25.7	-	22.3	29.8	22.9	22.4	24.3	28.8	-	-	14.8	22.1	54.9
Item 5400-5490 N(Wtd) ★	129	74	50	110	4	36	51	24	18	41	64	-	-	6	107	15

★=excludes respondents for whom question was inappropriate.

QUESTIONNAIRE FORM 1 1976	TOTAL	SEX		RACE		REGION				4YR COLLEGE PLANS		ILLICIT DRUG USE: LIFETIME				
		M	F	White	Black	NE	NC	S	W	Yes	No	None	Marijuana Only	Few Pills	More Pills	Any Heroin
Weighted No. of Cases:	3039	1426	1466	2356	338	715	950	919	454	1384	1321	1219	669	329	605	47
% of Weighted Total:	100.0	46.9	48.2	77.5	11.1	23.5	31.3	30.2	15.0	45.5	43.5	40.1	22.0	10.8	19.9	1.6

B102: Have you ever tried to stop using some narcotics other than heroin and found that you couldn't stop?

1. Yes	4.7	4.8	3.3	3.7	12.2	5.5	3.7	3.2	8.1	2.9	7.6	-	-	-	2.4	18.4
2. No	95.3	95.2	96.7	96.3	87.8	94.5	96.3	96.8	91.9	97.1	92.4	-	-	100.0	97.6	81.6
Item 5500 N(Wtd) ★	132	75	52	114	4	37	52	25	18	43	65	-	-	7	107	15

B103: What methods have you used for taking any of these narcotics other than heroin? (Mark all that apply.)

A. Sniffing or "snorting"	31.6	35.0	22.7	30.7	28.3	28.7	38.6	30.1	19.8	33.1	28.3	-	-	12.5	31.2	46.3
B. Smoking	59.1	64.5	49.9	57.9	63.2	50.2	75.8	54.2	36.9	56.0	56.0	-	-	40.5	57.9	70.5
C. Injection	6.7	8.7	3.8	5.0	-	5.5	6.6	4.7	12.6	4.8	9.5	-	-	-	2.0	43.6
D. By mouth	62.6	61.7	64.4	63.6	40.7	64.3	52.7	70.2	76.8	67.4	65.8	-	-	72.0	63.5	59.8
E. Other	6.1	7.4	4.1	5.7	-	5.2	7.2	8.0	2.0	4.5	5.5	-	-	-	4.9	18.0
Item 5510-5550 N(Wtd) ★	130	75	51	112	4	37	51	25	18	43	65	-	-	7	107	15

B104: Do you think you will be using any narcotics other than heroin without a doctor's orders five years from now?

1. I definitely will	.6	.5	.6	.5	.6	.9	.9	*	.3	.7	.5	.5	.4	-	.6	7.1
2. I probably will	3.1	3.6	2.6	3.3	2.2	3.9	3.0	2.7	2.7	2.3	3.7	.2	.5	1.5	12.8	14.9
3. I probably will not	17.3	19.5	14.9	17.6	12.4	16.5	17.1	17.2	19.4	16.3	17.9	8.3	14.8	31.7	31.7	46.2
4. I definitely will not	79.0	76.4	82.0	78.5	84.8	78.7	79.0	80.1	77.6	80.7	77.9	90.9	84.3	66.8	54.9	31.8
Item 5560 N(Wtd)	2802	1342	1402	2247	320	635	885	867	415	1323	1253	1179	622	307	536	42

B105: When (if ever) did you FIRST do each of the following things? Don't count anything you took because a doctor told you to.

B105A: Smoke cigarettes on a daily basis

8. Never	54.7	55.4	53.9	55.3	55.4	52.1	54.4	52.4	63.8	65.2	45.6	79.7	46.8	44.2	23.2	12.1
1. Grade 6 or below	4.6	5.7	3.5	4.6	3.8	4.1	5.4	4.0	4.9	3.9	5.1	3.1	5.4	4.0	6.4	14.8
2. Grade 7 or 8	9.9	10.7	9.1	10.2	6.2	12.9	9.8	7.8	9.7	7.7	12.0	4.1	10.4	9.9	20.3	24.2
3. Grade 9 (Freshman)	10.5	10.6	10.4	10.4	8.6	12.2	9.8	12.3	6.0	7.3	13.4	3.7	11.5	11.9	20.4	30.6
4. Grade 10 (Sophomore)	8.4	7.5	9.2	8.2	9.4	8.8	8.0	10.0	5.3	5.8	10.3	2.6	9.4	12.2	16.0	9.0
5. Grade 11 (Junior)	7.9	7.0	8.8	7.5	10.2	7.3	8.4	8.5	6.7	7.2	8.7	4.2	10.6	13.2	9.5	7.9
6. Grade 12 (Senior)	4.0	3.0	5.1	3.8	6.4	2.7	4.1	5.0	3.5	2.9	4.9	2.6	5.9	4.6	4.1	1.4
Item 5570 N(Wtd)	2667	1281	1343	2176	270	611	854	803	399	1267	1189	1105	586	293	543	45

B105B: Try an alcoholic beverages-- more than just a few sips

8. Never	9.2	7.4	10.8	8.5	16.5	5.2	7.2	13.7	11.2	10.0	8.6	21.3	1.2	2.1	.4	-
1. Grade 6 or below	7.4	9.6	5.3	7.3	4.8	8.8	7.0	5.0	10.8	6.1	8.4	4.1	6.4	11.2	12.5	16.2
2. Grade 7 or 8	21.3	26.4	15.9	21.8	11.9	26.2	22.8	16.2	20.3	20.3	21.9	10.5	21.9	23.3	37.3	46.7
3. Grade 9 (Freshman)	22.6	22.2	23.1	23.0	19.5	24.7	24.3	19.4	22.1	23.5	21.5	16.0	28.8	29.3	24.1	20.8
4. Grade 10 (Sophomore)	19.4	18.9	20.3	19.9	16.4	19.0	18.0	21.8	18.5	19.3	20.1	18.9	22.9	15.9	18.7	14.8
5. Grade 11 (Junior)	12.8	10.6	14.8	12.8	16.3	11.5	12.6	15.7	9.6	13.8	12.1	17.9	13.7	10.7	5.2	-
6. Grade 12 (Senior)	7.2	4.9	9.7	6.5	14.5	4.7	8.1	8.3	7.4	6.9	7.4	11.3	5.0	7.6	1.8	1.4
Item 5580 N(Wtd)	2538	1232	1262	2089	243	589	830	742	377	1188	1146	975	600	280	549	44

B105C: Try marijuana or hashish

8. Never	48.1	40.5	55.4	48.0	55.4	39.8	50.3	54.1	44.0	52.6	45.4	100.0	-	27.5	7.6	2.3
1. Grade 6 or below	.9	1.3	.6	.7	1.0	1.1	.7	.5	1.9	.7	1.1	-	.3	1.0	2.9	9.9
2. Grade 7 or 8	7.7	9.4	5.9	8.2	2.6	10.1	6.7	5.6	10.5	6.0	8.8	-	6.5	10.9	21.6	38.0
3. Grade 9 (Freshman)	13.9	16.5	11.5	13.9	9.1	16.3	12.7	11.7	17.2	11.8	15.4	-	19.5	21.3	31.7	37.1
4. Grade 10 (Sophomore)	13.7	15.9	11.7	14.0	12.2	15.3	14.5	12.2	12.8	12.5	14.1	-	29.3	17.1	23.7	7.7
5. Grade 11 (Junior)	10.1	11.4	8.7	9.9	12.0	13.0	10.1	8.3	9.2	10.7	9.5	-	27.6	14.3	9.9	3.6
6. Grade 12 (Senior)	5.6	5.0	6.2	5.4	7.6	4.4	5.0	7.6	4.4	5.6	5.8	-	16.9	7.8	2.5	1.4
Item 5590 N(Wtd)	2729	1305	1381	2225	283	619	871	832	407	1305	1215	1140	595	302	547	46

★=excludes respondents for whom question was inappropriate.　　*=less than .05 per cent.

QUESTIONNAIRE FORM 1 1976	TOTAL	SEX		RACE		REGION				4YR COLLEGE PLANS		ILLICIT DRUG USE: LIFETIME				
		M	F	White	Black	NE	NC	S	W	Yes	No	None	Mari- juana Only	Few Pills	More Pills	Any Her- oin
Weighted No. of Cases:	3039	1426	1466	2356	338	715	950	919	454	1384	1321	1219	669	329	605	47
% of Weighted Total:	100.0	46.9	48.2	77.5	11.1	23.5	31.3	30.2	15.0	45.5	43.5	40.1	22.0	10.8	19.9	1.6

B105D: Try LSD

	TOTAL	M	F	White	Black	NE	NC	S	W	Yes	No	None	Mari- juana Only	Few Pills	More Pills	Any Her- oin
8. Never	90.2	88.6	91.8	89.7	98.1	89.0	88.9	92.1	90.9	92.4	89.0	100.0	100.0	93.5	59.1	25.2
1. Grade 6 or below	*	*	-	*	-	-	-	-	.3	-	.1	-	-	-	.1	.8
2. Grade 7 or 8	.8	.6	1.0	.8	.6	1.1	.7	.6	1.1	.9	.6	-	-	.5	2.8	13.1
3. Grade 9 (Freshman)	2.4	2.4	2.4	2.6	.3	2.8	2.9	1.8	2.3	1.7	3.0	-	-	1.2	9.3	32.4
4. Grade 10 (Sophomore)	3.0	3.9	2.1	3.1	.4	2.9	2.7	3.4	2.9	2.2	3.7	-	-	.2	14.0	13.9
5. Grade 11 (Junior)	2.3	2.9	1.8	2.5	.4	3.2	2.8	1.5	1.6	1.8	2.1	-	-	2.4	9.7	11.9
6. Grade 12 (Senior)	1.2	1.6	.8	1.2	.2	1.0	2.1	.7	.9	1.0	1.6	-	-	2.1	4.9	2.8
Item 5600 N(Wtd)	2714	1291	1379	2205	289	617	864	830	403	1307	1201	1149	611	295	520	42

B105E: Try any psychedelic other than LSD

	TOTAL	M	F	White	Black	NE	NC	S	W	Yes	No	None	Mari- juana Only	Few Pills	More Pills	Any Her- oin
8. Never	89.9	87.6	92.0	89.3	97.7	88.6	89.2	91.0	91.0	93.0	87.3	100.0	100.0	94.2	53.0	23.9
1. Grade 6 or below	.1	.1	.1	.1	-	-	.1	-	.6	.2	.1	-	-	-	.5	2.5
2. Grade 7 or 8	.9	.9	.9	1.0	.6	1.3	.8	.7	1.0	1.0	.7	-	-	.5	4.0	11.6
3. Grade 9 (Freshman)	2.0	2.1	2.0	2.1	-	1.7	2.8	1.7	1.7	1.3	2.6	-	-	1.6	8.3	31.0
4. Grade 10 (Sophomore)	3.6	4.8	2.5	4.0	.6	3.6	2.9	4.5	3.2	1.9	5.1	-	-	1.2	17.5	23.6
5. Grade 11 (Junior)	2.6	3.4	2.0	2.7	.9	3.4	3.0	2.0	2.0	1.9	3.4	-	-	1.8	13.2	5.8
6. Grade 12 (Senior)	.8	1.1	.5	.8	.3	1.4	1.1	.1	.5	.7	.9	-	-	.8	3.8	1.6
Item 5610 N(Wtd)	2644	1259	1345	2150	288	601	836	814	392	1283	1163	1149	616	275	471	39

B105F: Try amphetamines

	TOTAL	M	F	White	Black	NE	NC	S	W	Yes	No	None	Mari- juana Only	Few Pills	More Pills	Any Her- oin
8. Never	82.3	82.3	82.4	80.9	95.4	83.1	80.9	83.8	80.9	87.2	78.1	100.0	100.0	75.6	23.4	13.9
1. Grade 6 or below	.2	.1	.3	.3	-	-	.3	.1	.8	.1	.4	-	-	.2	1.0	2.5
2. Grade 7 or 8	1.3	1.4	1.2	1.4	.6	1.4	1.1	1.2	1.9	.8	1.7	-	-	-	6.2	12.2
3. Grade 9 (Freshman)	3.4	3.0	3.6	3.6	.9	3.3	3.5	2.7	4.6	2.4	3.9	-	-	1.2	15.0	34.1
4. Grade 10 (Sophomore)	5.5	5.4	5.5	5.7	2.2	4.8	6.1	5.3	5.4	4.0	7.2	-	-	5.3	24.7	28.0
5. Grade 11 (Junior)	4.8	5.1	4.7	5.4	.5	4.7	4.5	5.2	5.1	3.7	5.6	-	-	8.7	21.1	6.2
6. Grade 12 (Senior)	2.5	2.8	2.2	2.8	.4	2.7	3.7	1.6	1.4	1.7	3.2	-	-	8.9	8.6	3.0
Item 5620 N(Wtd)	2629	1258	1331	2137	285	600	830	810	389	1281	1150	1148	612	252	484	39

B105G: Try quaaludes

	TOTAL	M	F	White	Black	NE	NC	S	W	Yes	No	None	Mari- juana Only	Few Pills	More Pills	Any Her- oin
8. Never	93.8	92.8	94.9	93.6	98.0	94.2	93.4	92.2	97.6	96.3	92.1	100.0	100.0	97.0	73.7	37.0
1. Grade 6 or below	.1	.1	.2	.1	-	.2	.2	-	.1	.1	.1	-	-	-	.6	1.0
2. Grade 7 or 8	.3	.5	.1	.3	-	.3	.2	.4	.3	.2	.4	-	-	-	1.1	6.6
3. Grade 9 (Freshman)	1.2	.8	1.5	1.3	-	1.3	1.4	1.3	.5	.8	1.6	-	-	-	5.1	21.1
4. Grade 10 (Sophomore)	1.9	2.4	1.4	2.0	1.2	2.0	2.0	2.4	.6	1.3	2.6	-	-	.7	8.3	20.2
5. Grade 11 (Junior)	1.9	2.7	1.1	1.9	.3	1.1	2.0	2.9	.5	1.0	2.2	-	-	1.7	7.8	14.1
6. Grade 12 (Senior)	.7	.7	.7	.8	.4	.7	.8	.8	.4	.4	1.0	-	-	.5	3.5	-
Item 5630 N(Wtd)	2703	1286	1378	2193	295	618	851	827	407	1300	1201	1151	616	295	510	37

B105H: Try barbiturates

	TOTAL	M	F	White	Black	NE	NC	S	W	Yes	No	None	Mari- juana Only	Few Pills	More Pills	Any Her- oin
8. Never	88.3	88.8	88.2	87.3	96.6	87.6	87.8	87.2	92.4	91.7	85.5	100.0	100.0	89.7	48.0	22.7
1. Grade 6 or below	.3	-	.5	.1	.6	.5	-	.4	.1	.2	.4	-	-	-	1.2	2.3
2. Grade 7 or 8	.6	.7	.5	.7	.6	.8	.4	.7	.8	.5	.6	-	-	.4	2.4	11.0
3. Grade 9 (Freshman)	2.5	2.3	2.7	2.7	.2	3.1	2.3	2.5	2.3	2.0	2.6	-	-	1.6	10.5	31.4
4. Grade 10 (Sophomore)	3.6	3.4	3.7	3.9	1.5	3.6	4.0	3.7	2.4	2.6	4.6	-	-	2.1	16.8	20.6
5. Grade 11 (Junior)	3.5	3.8	3.2	3.8	.5	3.6	4.3	3.5	1.8	1.8	5.2	-	-	3.0	16.9	9.1
6. Grade 12 (Senior)	1.2	.9	1.2	1.3	-	.7	1.2	1.8	.3	1.2	1.1	-	-	3.2	4.4	2.9
Item 5640 N(Wtd)	2648	1257	1349	2152	286	604	839	808	398	1273	1185	1148	615	265	485	39

B105I: Try tranquilizers

	TOTAL	M	F	White	Black	NE	NC	S	W	Yes	No	None	Mari- juana Only	Few Pills	More Pills	Any Her- oin
8. Never	88.6	90.1	87.3	87.6	95.9	90.5	89.5	85.6	89.5	90.4	87.3	100.0	100.0	79.3	54.2	33.3
1. Grade 6 or below	.4	.5	.2	.3	.3	.2	.3	.4	.8	.4	.4	-	-	1.7	.8	2.3
2. Grade 7 or 8	.6	.7	.6	.7	.6	.2	.4	1.3	.3	.3	.5	-	-	1.2	2.3	4.9
3. Grade 9 (Freshman)	2.2	2.0	2.3	2.4	.4	2.3	1.8	2.9	1.5	2.0	2.3	-	-	4.1	7.2	32.8
4. Grade 10 (Sophomore)	3.1	3.2	3.0	3.4	.6	3.2	3.1	3.3	3.0	2.6	3.4	-	-	3.9	13.5	19.5
5. Grade 11 (Junior)	3.8	3.0	4.6	4.4	.5	2.4	3.4	5.0	4.3	3.2	4.4	-	-	6.5	17.0	5.5
6. Grade 12 (Senior)	1.3	.5	2.0	1.3	1.8	1.2	1.5	1.5	.5	1.1	1.6	-	-	3.3	5.0	1.6
Item 5650 N(Wtd)	2603	1250	1314	2106	289	599	825	789	389	1252	1164	1148	606	231	483	39

* = less than .05 per cent.

QUESTIONNAIRE FORM 1 1976	TOTAL	SEX		RACE		REGION				4YR COLLEGE PLANS		ILLICIT DRUG USE: LIFETIME				
		M	F	White	Black	NE	NC	S	W	Yes	No	None	Marijuana Only	Few Pills	More Pills	Any Heroin
Weighted No. of Cases:	3039	1426	1466	2356	338	715	950	919	454	1384	1321	1219	669	329	605	47
% of Weighted Total:	100.0	46.9	48.2	77.5	11.1	23.5	31.3	30.2	15.0	45.5	43.5	40.1	22.0	10.8	19.9	1.6

B105J: Try cocaine

8. Never	91.1	88.4	93.7	91.4	92.9	90.7	91.7	92.4	88.1	94.1	89.5	100.0	100.0	88.9	66.2	24.1
1. Grade 6 or below	*	*	*	*	-	-	-	-	.2	*	*	-	-	-	-	2.2
2. Grade 7 or 8	.4	.6	.2	.4	-	.5	.2	.3	.7	.4	.4	-	-	-	1.3	9.4
3. Grade 9 (Freshman)	1.1	1.3	.7	.9	1.3	1.1	1.0	1.2	.8	.7	1.1	-	-	2.0	3.3	13.4
4. Grade 10 (Sophomore)	2.6	3.1	2.2	2.6	1.3	2.1	3.3	2.9	1.5	1.7	3.6	-	-	1.8	10.3	29.2
5. Grade 11 (Junior)	2.9	4.4	1.5	3.0	1.5	3.2	2.2	1.9	5.7	1.6	3.5	-	-	2.0	12.4	18.6
6. Grade 12 (Senior)	1.9	2.2	1.6	1.7	3.0	2.4	1.5	1.3	3.0	1.3	1.8	-	-	5.3	6.6	3.1
Item 5660 N(Wtd)	2709	1297	1371	2200	294	615	859	827	409	1306	1199	1150	616	292	513	44

B105K: Try heroin

8. Never	98.6	98.3	99.1	98.6	100.0	98.9	98.6	99.0	97.7	99.1	98.3	100.0	100.0	100.0	100.0	-
1. Grade 6 or below	.1	.1	-	.1	-	-	.1	.1	.3	.1	.2	-	-	-	-	6.5
2. Grade 7 or 8	.1	.1	.1	.2	-	.4	.1	-	.2	.1	.2	-	-	-	-	10.9
3. Grade 9 (Freshman)	.2	.3	.1	.2	-	.1	.2	.3	.2	.2	.2	-	-	-	-	16.2
4. Grade 10 (Sophomore)	.3	.3	.4	.3	-	.2	.3	.4	.5	.2	.4	-	-	-	-	26.2
5. Grade 11 (Junior)	.4	.5	.2	.3	-	.2	.4	.1	.9	.2	.4	-	-	-	-	26.8
6. Grade 12 (Senior)	.2	.3	.1	.2	-	.1	.3	.1	.3	.1	.2	-	-	-	-	13.3
Item 5670 N(Wtd)	2717	1300	1377	2205	295	613	857	836	411	1306	1207	1149	615	299	522	36

B105L: Try any narcotic other than heroin

8. Never	92.4	90.8	94.1	91.8	98.3	89.9	92.1	94.3	93.1	94.5	91.1	100.0	100.0	93.1	68.3	33.0
1. Grade 6 or below	.3	.2	.4	.3	-	.1	.2	.7	.1	.3	.4	-	-	.3	1.0	5.7
2. Grade 7 or 8	.4	.5	.4	.4	-	.3	.3	.3	.9	.2	.5	-	-	-	1.9	5.2
3. Grade 9 (Freshman)	1.3	1.9	.8	1.4	.3	1.9	1.5	.9	.7	1.0	1.5	-	-	.1	5.7	17.6
4. Grade 10 (sophomore)	2.0	2.1	1.8	2.2	.7	3.2	1.6	1.4	2.1	1.7	2.6	-	-	.8	8.8	13.6
5. Grade 11 (junior)	2.2	3.4	1.1	2.2	.3	3.0	2.1	1.6	2.1	1.5	2.3	-	-	1.9	9.5	18.1
6. Grade 12 (senior)	1.4	1.2	1.6	1.5	.4	1.5	2.1	.7	.9	.8	1.7	-	-	3.7	4.9	6.9
Item 5680 N(Wtd)	2628	1251	1337	2135	286	598	828	808	394	1265	1165	1148	610	259	477	37

These next questions are about your experiences in school.

D001: Some people like school very much. Others don't. How do you feel about going to school?

5. I like school very much	14.9	13.3	16.8	13.0	26.6	15.4	12.1	16.8	16.4	20.0	9.8	18.6	15.1	10.0	9.6	8.7
4. I like school quite a lot	31.7	29.5	33.6	32.3	30.5	28.2	31.6	33.9	32.6	38.6	25.5	37.3	30.0	35.1	21.8	13.6
3. I like school some	38.6	41.8	35.2	39.7	31.5	38.0	41.1	37.4	36.6	32.7	44.3	34.5	40.8	40.9	41.9	51.0
2. I don't like school very much	10.9	10.8	11.2	10.8	9.5	12.2	11.3	9.2	11.9	7.0	14.5	7.1	11.0	10.0	19.7	14.8
1. I don't like school at all	3.9	4.6	3.2	4.1	1.9	6.2	3.9	2.8	2.5	1.7	6.0	2.5	3.1	4.1	7.0	12.0
Item 7630 N(Wtd)	2775	1320	1398	2244	292	624	883	857	411	1365	1277	1168	614	305	522	40

D002: How often do you feel that the school work you are assigned is meaningful and important?

5. Almost always	10.8	8.9	12.8	9.1	22.8	10.2	8.5	14.1	10.0	12.1	9.5	13.4	9.7	8.8	7.8	1.3
4. Often	24.5	24.8	24.2	23.7	30.1	23.6	22.5	26.1	27.0	27.7	21.0	26.9	24.0	26.6	18.3	22.5
3. Sometimes	42.7	40.1	45.4	43.7	35.8	43.5	43.0	42.2	41.7	42.2	43.6	43.9	43.6	41.7	40.2	47.4
2. Seldom	18.9	22.5	15.5	20.2	9.7	19.2	22.4	15.2	18.6	16.3	21.1	14.3	19.2	19.2	29.1	22.2
1. Never	3.0	3.7	2.4	3.3	1.5	3.5	3.6	2.3	2.7	1.6	4.8	1.5	3.5	3.7	4.6	6.6
Item 5700 N(Wtd)	2768	1314	1396	2238	291	622	882	855	410	1363	1273	1166	612	304	521	40

D003: How interesting are most of your courses to you?

5. Very exciting and stimulating	4.7	4.0	5.4	3.0	18.1	4.0	2.8	7.0	5.1	5.1	3.9	5.8	5.5	1.1	3.1	1.4
4. Quite interesting	30.1	28.4	31.7	29.0	37.5	29.5	27.1	33.4	30.5	33.9	26.6	33.7	31.4	32.3	19.6	15.3
3. Fairly interesting	44.0	43.1	44.5	45.5	33.0	41.1	49.3	40.9	43.3	43.1	44.7	44.8	41.4	40.9	46.3	52.6
2. Slightly dull	16.1	17.9	14.7	17.1	7.6	18.0	16.3	14.2	17.2	14.0	18.4	12.3	16.8	19.7	22.9	17.3
1. Very dull	5.1	6.6	3.7	5.4	3.8	7.4	4.5	4.6	3.9	3.9	6.4	3.4	4.9	5.9	8.1	13.4
Item 5710 N(Wtd)	2761	1308	1396	2234	289	622	879	855	404	1358	1269	1166	609	305	516	39

* = less than .05 per cent.

QUESTIONNAIRE FORM 1 1976	TOTAL	SEX		RACE		REGION				4YR COLLEGE PLANS		ILLICIT DRUG USE: LIFETIME				
		M	F	White	Black	NE	NC	S	W	Yes	No	None	Mari-juana Only	Few Pills	More Pills	Any Her-oin
Weighted No. of Cases:	3039	1426	1466	2356	338	715	950	919	454	1384	1321	1219	669	329	605	47
% of Weighted Total:	100.0	46.9	48.2	77.5	11.1	23.5	31.3	30.2	15.0	45.5	43.5	40.1	22.0	10.8	19.9	1.6
D004: How important do you think the things you are learning in school are going to be for your later life?																
5. Very important	19.7	17.8	21.4	15.9	47.3	17.0	15.0	28.0	16.3	19.4	19.3	21.6	21.4	15.4	14.1	12.5
4. Quite important	26.7	25.9	27.9	27.1	27.9	22.9	26.5	29.5	27.2	31.2	22.9	31.1	24.6	26.3	20.7	27.0
3. Fairly important	32.4	33.6	30.8	33.6	18.1	33.9	34.1	27.3	37.0	32.2	32.5	30.9	33.6	35.3	34.3	26.9
2. Slightly important	18.2	19.3	17.3	20.2	5.5	22.3	20.7	13.5	16.2	15.6	21.1	14.6	17.7	18.6	27.0	21.4
1. Not at all important	3.0	3.5	2.5	3.1	1.1	3.9	3.6	1.7	3.4	1.6	4.2	1.8	2.7	4.4	4.0	12.1
Item 5720 N(Wtd)	2758	1303	1396	2230	288	618	878	856	406	1359	1264	1167	606	305	515	40
D005: How much competition for grades is there among students at your school?																
1. None	6.1	6.6	5.7	5.7	8.0	7.9	6.6	3.7	7.4	3.7	8.2	5.5	6.0	6.8	6.6	8.3
2. A little	21.6	20.9	21.9	22.6	15.8	18.9	20.8	23.3	23.6	19.9	23.9	20.8	21.1	21.4	23.6	26.4
3. Some	37.0	37.6	36.3	37.4	33.1	32.1	39.9	37.5	36.8	34.4	39.6	35.7	38.8	34.8	38.6	32.8
4. Quite a bit	25.6	25.1	26.0	25.2	26.5	27.7	24.8	24.6	26.2	29.4	22.0	27.9	23.5	26.0	23.6	21.5
5. A great deal	9.7	9.7	10.1	9.1	16.6	13.4	7.9	10.8	5.9	12.7	6.2	10.2	10.6	11.0	7.6	11.0
Item 5730 N(Wtd)	2775	1315	1393	2247	286	623	886	854	411	1352	1259	1165	617	302	520	41
D006: How do you think most of the students in your classes would feel if you cheated on a test?																
1. They would like it very much	1.5	1.6	1.4	1.1	3.5	2.2	.9	1.6	1.2	1.4	1.6	1.3	1.9	1.7	1.1	4.2
2. They would like it	2.9	3.5	2.3	2.3	8.5	2.0	1.8	4.7	3.1	2.2	3.4	2.8	3.3	2.5	2.5	.9
3. They would not care	74.6	77.1	72.4	76.0	65.6	77.7	74.1	75.5	69.2	71.2	78.3	70.0	76.8	76.3	83.1	83.8
4. They would dislike it	17.3	15.3	19.2	17.2	16.2	15.3	19.6	13.9	22.6	21.4	13.3	20.4	16.2	18.5	11.5	11.1
5. They would dislike it very much	3.7	2.5	4.8	3.4	6.2	2.8	3.6	4.4	3.8	3.8	3.3	5.5	1.8	1.0	1.9	-
Item 5740 N(Wtd)	2771	1312	1395	2246	285	622	883	856	410	1347	1263	1165	614	301	521	42
D007: How do you think most of the students in your classes would feel if you intentionally did things to make your teachers angry?																
1. They would like it very much	3.7	4.7	2.5	2.9	8.8	5.0	3.0	4.2	2.2	3.1	3.9	3.0	3.0	3.1	4.2	12.1
2. They would like it	10.6	13.2	8.4	10.9	10.4	10.5	11.6	10.2	9.2	10.6	10.8	9.6	9.5	12.4	13.3	10.6
3. They would not care	45.0	47.2	42.7	43.6	52.2	44.9	45.1	45.5	44.1	41.0	48.4	42.3	45.9	43.7	51.3	55.4
4. They would dislike it	34.9	30.1	39.6	36.9	22.2	34.2	36.0	33.4	36.6	39.1	31.7	38.2	35.9	35.2	28.8	20.5
5. They would dislike it very much	5.8	4.8	6.7	5.7	6.4	5.3	4.2	6.7	7.9	6.3	5.1	6.9	5.7	5.6	2.4	1.3
Item 5750 N(Wtd)	2759	1309	1386	2238	283	621	876	854	408	1341	1256	1160	614	300	517	41
D008: How often do you find that your friends encourage you to do things which your teachers wouldn't like?																
1. Never	32.0	20.6	42.7	29.2	47.9	34.2	26.3	35.7	33.3	31.5	33.4	35.1	29.5	23.6	29.9	33.1
2. Seldom	37.5	39.1	36.5	39.8	27.4	35.4	41.0	35.4	37.8	40.2	33.8	40.0	38.0	40.3	32.7	31.9
3. Sometimes	24.2	31.9	16.9	24.6	18.4	25.5	25.9	22.7	21.9	23.4	25.8	19.4	27.0	30.0	29.0	26.9
4. Often	5.2	6.8	3.5	5.4	4.9	4.0	5.9	5.2	5.8	3.9	6.2	4.6	5.0	4.7	7.2	5.3
5. Almost always	1.0	1.5	.4	.9	1.3	.9	.9	1.0	1.2	.9	.8	.9	.5	1.4	1.3	2.8
Item 5760 N(Wtd)	2761	1307	1390	2239	283	620	879	853	409	1339	1261	1160	611	302	519	42
D009: Have you ever been in a work-study program--that is, a program where you work on a job as part of your schooling?																
1. No, not ever	74.2	76.4	72.6	75.9	66.9	84.4	72.2	72.7	65.9	82.5	66.5	77.4	74.6	71.4	72.1	52.1
2. Yes, for a half year or less	9.2	8.5	9.8	8.3	14.7	7.1	7.8	8.3	16.7	6.8	11.6	7.7	8.6	12.0	10.1	13.7
3. Yes, for about a year	11.6	8.9	13.6	11.1	12.8	5.8	15.2	12.2	11.1	7.4	15.3	10.4	12.0	11.3	13.0	17.8
4. Yes, for about two years	3.9	4.5	3.5	4.0	3.6	2.4	3.8	5.2	4.0	2.3	5.6	3.2	4.7	3.3	4.3	7.6
5. Yes, for more than two years	1.2	1.7	.5	.8	2.1	.3	.9	1.5	2.3	1.0	1.0	1.4	.1	1.9	.5	8.9
Item 5770 N(Wtd)	2754	1301	1389	2236	281	616	875	853	410	1340	1255	1160	611	301	515	41

QUESTIONNAIRE FORM 1 1976	TOTAL	SEX		RACE		REGION				4YR COLLEGE PLANS		ILLICIT DRUG USE: LIFETIME				
		M	F	White	Black	NE	NC	S	W	Yes	No	None	Mari-juana Only	Few Pills	More Pills	Any Her-oin
Weighted No. of Cases:	3039	1426	1466	2356	338	715	950	919	454	1384	1321	1219	669	329	605	47
% of Weighted Total:	100.0	46.9	48.2	77.5	11.1	23.5	31.3	30.2	15.0	45.5	43.5	40.1	22.0	10.8	19.9	1.6

These last questions are about you and the counselors in your school.

D010: How many times this school year have you seen a counselor individually?

1. No times	11.5	12.1	10.5	11.0	13.9	6.8	11.5	17.2	6.7	7.7	15.0	12.2	7.9	10.5	12.0	8.7
2. 1 time	14.0	14.7	13.6	14.7	10.0	12.9	15.3	14.2	12.7	10.0	18.0	14.9	15.6	13.5	11.7	6.3
3. 2 times	20.8	19.8	21.6	21.8	14.9	21.7	19.8	20.6	21.9	19.3	22.7	19.8	22.3	22.4	20.5	27.0
4. 3 or 4 times	30.1	29.0	31.5	30.3	29.8	29.9	30.9	28.8	31.1	32.0	28.0	31.0	29.3	31.2	29.1	36.1
5. 5 - 7 times	13.1	14.1	12.0	13.2	12.3	14.3	15.0	10.0	13.6	16.6	9.9	13.4	12.6	12.2	14.3	9.9
6. 8 - 10 times	4.8	5.3	4.4	4.4	7.0	5.5	3.8	4.6	6.7	6.7	2.8	4.0	5.7	5.6	5.5	2.6
7. 11 or more times	5.7	4.9	6.4	4.5	12.0	9.0	3.7	4.6	7.4	7.7	3.7	4.8	6.6	4.6	6.7	9.5
Item 5780 N(Wtd)	2757	1304	1390	2238	280	620	878	849	410	1341	1256	1161	614	303	517	40

D011: How many times this school year have you seen a counselor as a part of a group of other students?

1. No times	53.0	52.4	53.5	54.1	43.1	54.3	54.4	50.5	52.8	48.1	58.8	50.9	55.8	49.8	56.3	52.0
2. 1 time	15.4	14.9	16.1	15.7	14.7	15.2	13.6	16.3	17.9	16.4	14.5	16.9	13.0	18.0	14.0	15.7
3. 2 times	15.4	16.1	14.5	15.2	17.0	14.2	16.4	16.9	11.7	15.4	15.1	15.3	15.0	16.9	13.9	12.4
4. 3 or 4 times	9.9	9.9	10.0	9.3	14.6	8.2	9.7	10.2	12.2	11.7	7.7	11.0	9.9	9.2	9.1	11.2
5. 5 - 7 times	2.9	2.7	3.0	2.8	5.1	3.1	3.0	3.0	2.4	3.9	1.9	3.2	3.2	1.4	2.8	2.2
6. 8 - 10 times	1.3	1.9	.7	1.3	1.9	1.6	1.0	1.5	1.2	1.8	.7	1.1	1.1	2.4	1.1	3.7
7. 11 or more times	2.1	2.1	2.2	1.8	3.6	3.3	1.9	1.6	1.7	2.7	1.3	1.6	1.9	2.3	2.8	2.9
Item 5790 N(Wtd)	2749	1299	1389	2232	281	615	878	848	408	1339	1255	1159	613	299	515	40

D012: Would you have preferred to see a counselor more or less often than you have during the past year?

5. Much more often	9.7	9.9	9.4	7.7	21.8	12.9	6.8	10.9	8.7	10.0	8.5	9.6	11.5	7.8	8.7	10.7
4. A little more often	23.6	22.9	23.9	23.2	24.5	21.3	25.6	23.5	22.4	24.7	22.6	25.2	24.4	22.9	19.5	27.2
3. About as often	52.9	52.8	53.6	55.6	38.7	52.5	52.3	52.4	56.1	55.4	50.8	53.7	51.3	53.6	53.7	52.6
2. A little less often	4.6	4.1	4.9	4.4	5.4	3.9	5.7	4.4	3.4	3.7	5.6	4.4	4.0	3.7	6.6	2.8
1. Much less often	9.2	10.2	8.2	9.2	9.6	9.3	9.5	8.8	9.3	6.2	12.5	7.1	8.9	11.9	11.6	6.7
Item 5800 N(Wtd)	2727	1296	1372	2214	280	605	874	846	402	1327	1244	1149	608	295	512	40

D013: How helpful have your sessions with a counselor been to you?

5. Extremely helpful	10.7	9.4	11.7	8.6	22.6	9.2	8.6	14.1	10.3	11.1	9.6	10.8	9.7	9.7	9.5	18.3
4. Quite helpful	26.0	28.3	23.4	25.4	28.7	20.4	25.5	28.3	30.4	28.4	23.7	28.3	26.5	24.6	22.3	20.5
3. Somewhat helpful	27.1	26.9	27.6	28.1	22.3	28.3	30.8	23.0	25.9	25.9	28.0	28.4	27.1	26.1	25.1	22.4
2. A little helpful	20.1	18.9	21.5	21.2	13.6	22.8	21.4	17.7	18.3	21.3	19.2	18.6	22.2	18.2	22.3	25.9
1. Not at all helpful	16.1	16.5	15.7	16.8	12.7	19.2	13.7	16.8	15.1	13.2	19.5	13.9	14.5	21.3	20.8	12.9
Item 5810 N(Wtd)	2699	1277	1362	2188	277	605	863	826	405	1319	1226	1138	604	296	504	39

	TOTAL	SEX		RACE		REGION				4YR COLLEGE PLANS		ILLICIT DRUG USE: LIFETIME				
QUESTIONNAIRE FORM 2 1976		M	F	White	Black	NE	NC	S	W	Yes	No	None	Mari-juana Only	Few Pills	More Pills	Any Her-oin
Weighted No. of Cases:	3036	1453	1445	2358	343	723	919	934	460	1450	1342	1223	687	343	597	69
% of Weighted Total:	100.0	47.9	47.6	77.7	11.3	23.8	30.3	30.8	15.2	47.8	44.2	40.3	22.6	11.3	19.7	2.3
A01: Taking all things together, how would you say things are these days--would you say you're very happy, pretty happy, or not too happy these days?																
3. Very happy	21.3	19.0	23.8	23.0	13.9	16.5	22.2	22.9	23.8	22.6	20.3	22.1	23.1	20.7	17.0	25.4
2. Pretty happy	66.8	71.3	63.3	67.4	67.7	68.8	68.4	65.0	64.3	67.0	67.5	67.8	66.8	68.6	68.7	50.7
1. Not too happy	11.9	9.7	13.0	9.6	18.7	14.7	9.6	12.1	12.0	10.4	12.1	10.2	10.1	10.4	14.3	23.9
Item 1190 N(Wtd)	2928	1383	1418	2282	331	696	879	911	442	1410	1293	1192	666	328	566	67
A02: The next questions ask about the kinds of things you do in your spare time, that is, time not spent in school, on homework, or on a paid job. How often do you do each of the following?																
A02A: Watch TV																
5. Almost everyday	70.6	70.7	70.5	69.1	82.1	69.7	67.7	76.7	65.7	67.2	74.3	74.1	68.9	70.4	67.2	60.9
4. At least once a week	23.2	23.8	22.8	24.7	15.0	23.6	26.6	18.8	24.9	25.6	20.8	20.4	24.8	23.8	26.8	23.2
3. Once or twice a month	4.1	3.2	5.1	4.3	1.2	4.2	4.0	2.9	6.3	4.8	3.4	3.4	4.4	4.7	4.7	8.7
2. A few times a year	1.3	1.5	1.1	1.4	.9	1.7	1.0	1.1	2.2	1.7	.9	1.4	1.6	.3	1.0	2.9
1. Never	.7	.8	.5	.6	.9	1.0	.8	.5	.9	.6	.6	.7	.3	.6	.3	4.3
Item 5820 N(Wtd)	3015	1441	1441	2348	340	717	915	926	458	1444	1333	1218	682	341	594	69
A02B: Go to movies																
5. Almost everyday	.1	.1	-	*	-	-	.2	-	.2	.1	.1	-	.1	.3	-	-
4. At least once a week	9.9	10.1	9.5	9.2	12.9	8.5	8.3	13.6	7.6	7.0	12.8	8.5	9.7	13.8	9.6	14.5
3. Once or twice a month	50.6	50.8	50.8	52.1	46.0	47.8	51.4	51.6	51.7	52.5	49.0	47.8	55.5	50.1	51.8	49.3
2. A few times a year	36.5	36.1	36.7	36.2	37.8	41.4	37.0	32.5	35.6	37.8	35.0	39.5	32.8	34.0	37.1	36.2
1. Never	2.9	2.9	2.9	2.5	2.9	2.2	3.1	2.2	4.8	2.6	3.1	4.2	2.0	2.1	1.3	1.4
Item 5830 N(Wtd)	3013	1442	1441	2349	341	718	913	925	458	1442	1336	1217	683	341	593	69
A02C: Attend art shows, musical performances, or theater plays																
5. Almost everyday	.1	.1	-	*	.3	.1	-	-	.7	.1	.1	.2	.1	-	.2	-
4. At least once a week	1.5	1.9	1.0	1.4	2.4	1.5	1.3	1.7	1.3	1.5	1.0	1.4	.9	2.3	1.0	7.2
3. Once or twice a month	10.4	10.1	10.8	10.4	11.9	10.8	11.1	8.7	11.6	12.3	7.9	9.5	9.0	9.9	13.3	15.9
2. A few times a year	54.2	49.6	59.8	56.5	48.4	56.5	55.6	51.3	53.9	64.5	44.4	56.0	53.8	58.9	54.1	39.1
1. Never	33.7	38.3	28.4	31.7	36.8	31.0	32.1	38.2	32.3	21.5	46.6	32.9	36.3	28.9	31.6	39.1
Item 5840 N(Wtd)	3018	1447	1438	2352	337	720	914	927	458	1444	1336	1215	686	343	595	69
A02D: Go to church or church-related events																
5. Almost everyday	3.3	2.1	4.5	2.9	5.4	1.3	3.1	3.9	5.5	4.0	2.6	5.0	1.3	2.1	2.5	2.9
4. At least once a week	40.9	36.3	46.5	41.6	41.1	40.1	42.8	43.0	33.9	45.2	37.5	54.0	37.4	40.5	23.1	15.9
3. Once or twice a month	16.0	16.3	15.7	14.9	26.2	13.0	15.0	21.2	12.3	16.6	15.5	15.3	15.6	16.1	16.8	23.2
2. A few times a year	22.6	25.2	19.6	22.4	20.8	25.3	22.2	20.6	23.2	19.1	25.7	16.9	26.2	23.2	28.1	29.0
1. Never	17.2	20.0	13.6	18.2	6.8	20.4	16.9	11.2	25.2	15.1	18.8	8.7	19.4	18.2	29.5	30.4
Item 5980 N(Wtd)	3003	1444	1429	2340	336	716	913	917	457	1436	1332	1212	679	336	594	69
A02E: Participate in community affairs or volunteer work																
5. Almost everyday	2.1	2.4	1.9	1.6	5.3	1.7	2.2	2.4	2.2	1.9	2.1	2.2	2.0	2.9	1.7	2.9
4. At least once a week	5.8	5.0	6.7	5.5	8.2	5.3	5.8	5.5	7.5	8.0	3.7	7.6	5.1	5.6	3.4	4.3
3. Once or twice a month	12.5	11.4	13.9	12.6	14.7	9.9	13.0	14.4	12.1	15.3	10.0	15.3	10.8	12.4	9.4	8.7
2. A few times a year	44.6	44.2	46.0	47.0	36.5	45.9	43.5	47.0	39.3	48.0	42.2	47.7	45.4	44.0	41.4	27.5
1. Never	34.9	36.9	31.6	33.2	35.6	37.2	35.5	30.6	39.1	26.7	42.0	27.3	36.6	35.1	44.1	58.0
Item 5860 N(Wtd)	3012	1446	1436	2350	340	715	913	929	455	1442	1337	1213	685	339	594	69

*=less than .05 per cent.

QUESTIONNAIRE FORM 2 1976	TOTAL	SEX		RACE		REGION				4YR COLLEGE PLANS		ILLICIT DRUG USE: LIFETIME				
		M	F	White	Black	NE	NC	S	W	Yes	No	None	Mari-juana Only	Few Pills	More Pills	Any Her-oin
Weighted No. of Cases:	3036	1453	1445	2358	343	723	919	934	460	1450	1342	1223	687	343	597	69
% of Weighted Total:	100.0	47.9	47.6	77.7	11.3	23.8	30.3	30.8	15.2	47.8	44.2	40.3	22.6	11.3	19.7	2.3
A02F: Play a musical instrument or sing																
5. Almost everyday	28.4	22.4	35.2	28.3	34.8	26.6	30.7	29.2	25.1	32.9	24.6	32.0	26.0	28.7	24.1	30.4
4. At least once a week	9.8	8.0	12.0	10.0	12.1	10.3	8.8	10.3	9.9	11.4	8.4	11.5	7.9	10.3	8.6	7.2
3. Once or twice a month	5.4	4.9	5.9	4.9	8.3	5.7	4.8	5.6	5.7	6.4	4.4	6.0	5.0	6.2	4.2	5.8
2. A few times a year	11.2	11.4	11.1	11.6	8.3	12.0	10.3	10.0	14.1	12.1	10.8	9.4	11.7	11.7	14.3	4.3
1. Never	45.1	53.3	35.7	45.2	36.6	45.5	45.4	44.8	44.9	37.2	51.8	41.1	49.6	42.8	48.6	53.6
Item 5870 N(Wtd)	3010	1444	1433	2347	339	717	911	928	454	1440	1334	1213	682	341	593	69
A02G: Do creative writing																
5. Almost everyday	5.5	4.4	6.4	4.7	8.8	6.7	4.4	5.5	5.7	5.8	4.4	4.6	4.9	5.0	7.4	11.6
4. At least once a week	8.9	6.8	11.2	8.9	9.7	10.6	8.4	8.0	9.0	12.4	6.0	10.3	7.8	8.5	8.2	8.7
3. Once or twice a month	15.8	13.4	18.7	16.3	16.8	17.9	14.8	15.6	14.9	20.6	11.1	16.9	12.1	18.2	16.3	15.9
2. A few times a year	25.3	23.9	26.8	25.6	28.0	24.0	24.9	25.5	27.7	29.3	21.0	25.3	26.7	29.0	23.5	17.4
1. Never	44.5	51.5	36.8	44.5	36.6	41.0	47.5	45.2	42.9	31.8	57.5	42.9	48.7	39.0	44.5	47.8
Item 5880 N(Wtd)	3008	1445	1432	2343	339	717	914	922	455	1438	1334	1213	678	341	595	69
A02H: Actively participate in sports, athletics or exercising																
5. Almost everyday	43.7	51.7	35.5	43.1	48.8	42.1	43.6	40.8	52.0	50.2	36.5	43.0	49.3	46.1	39.2	30.4
4. At least once a week	24.0	22.1	26.0	24.8	19.1	28.3	21.9	23.9	21.9	24.7	23.0	23.4	22.8	23.3	26.4	29.0
3. Once or twice a month	13.6	10.3	17.0	14.2	11.5	10.6	14.6	14.4	14.5	12.3	15.5	12.1	13.2	15.7	15.4	23.2
2. A few times a year	11.9	10.1	13.8	11.4	15.0	12.8	11.5	13.9	7.0	8.8	15.2	14.2	9.4	10.8	11.0	8.7
1. Never	6.8	5.7	7.7	6.5	5.9	6.3	8.3	6.9	4.6	4.0	9.8	7.4	5.6	3.8	8.3	10.1
Item 5890 N(Wtd)	3016	1450	1432	2349	340	717	915	928	456	1439	1338	1215	684	343	592	69
A02I: Do art or craft work																
5. Almost everyday	11.5	10.2	12.7	11.8	9.2	11.9	11.0	10.0	14.9	10.6	11.9	9.7	9.1	16.2	14.8	14.5
4. At least once a week	12.8	10.1	15.5	13.1	10.7	14.8	11.8	11.2	14.7	14.2	10.6	12.6	12.2	12.4	13.6	21.7
3. Once or twice a month	18.5	15.5	21.5	19.5	11.6	15.1	20.1	17.8	21.8	19.6	17.8	19.3	18.1	20.0	17.0	18.8
2. A few times a year	30.2	32.2	28.8	31.1	29.4	30.1	33.3	29.3	26.4	33.0	28.2	30.1	31.9	29.4	30.4	26.1
1. Never	27.0	31.9	21.6	24.5	39.2	28.0	23.8	31.8	22.2	22.6	31.6	28.4	28.9	22.1	24.2	20.3
Item 5900 N(Wtd)	3006	1444	1429	2343	337	714	909	928	455	1435	1335	1211	681	340	595	69
A02J: Work around the house, yard, garden, car, etc.																
5. Almost everyday	40.6	32.5	48.9	39.0	51.3	37.2	44.8	41.5	35.8	36.5	44.5	41.3	40.2	44.0	37.4	29.0
4. At least once a week	37.4	44.2	31.0	38.7	30.2	37.5	35.7	37.3	41.3	39.5	36.0	38.4	39.1	39.1	34.2	43.5
3. Once or twice a month	15.3	16.5	13.7	16.1	11.4	15.8	14.5	14.5	17.5	17.3	13.4	14.6	14.3	12.5	19.3	18.8
2. A few times a year	5.5	5.4	5.5	5.4	6.5	7.5	3.7	6.2	4.6	5.8	4.9	4.8	5.7	3.8	7.4	4.3
1. Never	1.2	1.4	.8	.8	.9	1.9	1.3	.5	.9	.8	1.3	.8	.6	.9	1.8	5.8
Item 5910 N(Wtd)	3028	1451	1443	2355	341	720	916	934	458	1449	1340	1220	686	343	597	69
A02K: Get together with friends, informally																
5. Almost everyday	51.5	55.2	47.9	51.9	51.2	55.1	50.6	49.6	52.1	50.2	52.4	40.5	54.8	54.4	65.6	67.6
4. At least once a week	35.7	34.0	38.0	36.4	35.3	32.4	36.4	36.7	37.5	37.8	34.5	40.8	38.0	35.7	25.8	26.5
3. Once or twice a month	9.6	7.5	11.6	9.4	8.5	9.8	10.4	9.2	8.5	9.2	10.2	14.5	5.8	7.3	6.0	1.5
2. A few times a year	2.4	2.3	2.2	1.7	4.4	2.2	1.9	3.5	1.7	2.4	2.3	3.4	1.2	1.8	1.8	4.4
1. Never	.7	.8	.4	.5	.6	.7	.8	.9	.4	.5	.6	.8	.3	.9	.5	1.5
Item 5920 N(Wtd)	3021	1448	1441	2354	340	717	915	930	459	1446	1340	1218	686	342	596	68
A02L: Go shopping or window-shopping																
5. Almost everyday	3.1	1.5	4.4	2.0	7.4	4.4	2.7	2.8	2.4	2.0	3.6	2.5	3.2	2.6	3.7	5.8
4. At least once a week	35.8	23.9	47.9	35.0	43.4	35.8	35.9	38.9	29.5	34.0	38.3	38.2	33.1	37.4	31.7	43.5
3. Once or twice a month	44.6	46.8	42.8	46.4	36.6	41.0	47.3	41.9	50.1	49.2	40.6	44.2	45.4	42.4	48.8	36.2
2. A few times a year	12.8	21.2	4.2	13.2	9.7	14.6	11.5	12.3	13.8	12.1	13.2	12.4	14.9	12.6	11.6	5.8
1. Never	3.6	6.4	.7	3.3	2.9	3.9	2.5	4.2	4.2	2.6	4.3	2.6	3.6	4.7	4.2	7.2
Item 5930 N(Wtd)	3017	1446	1442	2351	339	720	912	928	457	1445	1337	1218	685	342	596	69

QUESTIONNAIRE FORM 2 1976	TOTAL	SEX		RACE		REGION				4YR COLLEGE PLANS		ILLICIT DRUG USE: LIFETIME				
		M	F	White	Black	NE	NC	S	W	Yes	No	None	Mari- juana Only	Few Pills	More Pills	Any Her- oin
Weighted No. of Cases:	3036	1453	1445	2358	343	723	919	934	460	1450	1342	1223	687	343	597	69
% of Weighted Total:	100.0	47.9	47.6	77.7	11.3	23.8	30.3	30.8	15.2	47.8	44.2	40.3	22.6	11.3	19.7	2.3

A02M: Relax alone

	TOTAL	M	F	White	Black	NE	NC	S	W	Yes	No	None	Mar.	Few	More	Her.
5. Almost everyday	39.9	38.6	41.3	40.2	38.0	40.8	39.0	39.4	41.1	44.4	34.9	40.3	38.7	37.5	40.0	50.7
4. At least once a week	38.7	38.0	39.5	38.4	39.8	39.4	38.2	38.0	39.6	38.5	38.8	39.3	36.8	42.8	39.5	27.5
3. Once or twice a month	12.4	12.8	11.7	12.7	12.2	11.5	13.1	12.9	11.2	10.7	14.2	11.9	14.2	11.7	11.6	11.6
2. A few times a year	5.7	6.8	4.7	5.6	5.3	5.0	6.6	5.4	5.7	4.2	7.3	4.5	7.7	5.3	5.9	5.8
1. Never	3.4	3.7	2.9	3.1	4.7	3.1	3.1	4.2	2.4	2.2	4.7	4.0	2.3	2.6	2.9	5.8
Item 5940 N(Wtd)	3011	1446	1433	2347	337	715	911	929	455	1438	1335	1212	684	341	595	69

A02N: Read books, magazines, or newspapers

	TOTAL	M	F	White	Black	NE	NC	S	W	Yes	No	None	Mar.	Few	More	Her.
5. Almost everyday	59.3	58.4	61.5	60.2	58.8	63.0	61.4	55.8	56.1	67.3	53.2	60.5	59.6	61.8	59.0	50.7
4. At least once a week	25.6	25.0	25.7	25.3	25.3	24.6	24.4	26.0	28.6	23.5	26.5	26.1	25.7	25.1	24.3	29.0
3. Once or twice a month	9.6	10.1	9.1	9.8	9.1	7.9	8.6	12.1	9.0	6.4	12.9	9.3	8.2	9.0	12.1	7.2
2. A few times a year	3.7	3.8	2.9	3.0	5.0	2.9	3.7	4.1	4.1	2.3	4.8	3.5	3.9	3.2	2.7	5.8
1. Never	1.9	2.6	.8	1.7	1.8	1.7	1.7	2.0	2.0	.6	2.6	.7	2.8	.9	2.0	7.2
Item 5950 N(Wtd)	3026	1450	1442	2357	340	719	917	932	458	1448	1340	1220	686	343	597	69

A02O: Go to taverns, bars or nightclubs

	TOTAL	M	F	White	Black	NE	NC	S	W	Yes	No	None	Mar.	Few	More	Her.
5. Almost everyday	3.2	4.7	1.5	2.9	2.3	3.8	4.7	2.2	1.5	1.5	5.0	.7	2.6	1.8	7.1	18.8
4. At least once a week	18.1	22.6	13.8	19.0	17.3	20.3	22.4	17.5	7.0	14.4	21.5	10.0	21.7	19.1	26.0	37.7
3. Once or twice a month	18.9	20.2	16.9	18.8	20.2	22.3	20.5	18.2	11.7	19.9	17.1	12.1	23.6	24.3	24.3	17.4
2. A few times a year	18.2	18.7	17.7	17.5	23.4	20.3	16.5	18.3	17.8	20.7	15.3	17.5	20.8	20.8	16.7	13.0
1. Never	41.7	33.9	50.1	41.9	36.8	33.1	35.9	43.9	61.9	43.6	41.1	59.7	31.1	34.0	26.1	13.0
Item 5960 N(Wtd)	3013	1447	1434	2346	342	718	911	930	454	1442	1337	1212	687	341	593	69

A02P: Go to parties or other social affairs

	TOTAL	M	F	White	Black	NE	NC	S	W	Yes	No	None	Mar.	Few	More	Her.
5. Almost everyday	4.3	6.3	2.3	4.4	2.3	5.8	5.4	2.5	3.5	2.6	5.8	.8	3.2	2.9	10.6	24.6
4. At least once a week	26.5	27.7	24.9	25.2	31.9	28.2	29.7	20.8	29.0	27.1	25.4	13.9	31.6	30.9	39.9	42.0
3. Once or twice a month	39.0	37.1	41.4	40.4	38.0	38.3	35.8	41.4	41.2	41.8	36.6	41.7	42.4	39.9	33.5	24.6
2. A few times a year	26.0	24.1	28.1	26.3	24.3	24.6	24.6	31.4	20.0	25.1	27.4	37.2	20.4	23.3	13.9	8.7
1. Never	4.2	4.8	3.3	3.8	3.8	3.1	4.5	3.9	6.1	3.4	4.9	6.4	2.5	2.9	2.2	-
Item 5970 N(Wtd)	3026	1451	1441	2354	342	720	915	932	459	1449	1340	1218	687	343	597	69

A03: How much do you agree or disagree with each of the following statements?

A03A: In the United States, we put too much emphasis on making profits and not enough on human well-being

	TOTAL	M	F	White	Black	NE	NC	S	W	Yes	No	None	Mar.	Few	More	Her.
1. Disagree	3.2	4.7	1.5	2.4	3.6	3.5	2.4	3.7	3.3	2.9	2.9	2.4	4.0	4.7	1.5	9.1
2. Mostly disagree	8.7	11.3	6.0	9.0	8.1	8.5	8.1	9.1	9.3	9.5	7.9	9.1	10.0	9.2	6.5	6.1
3. Neither	12.9	16.1	9.8	13.3	7.2	12.7	14.9	9.8	15.6	11.6	13.5	13.0	13.0	9.2	14.0	16.7
4. Mostly agree	47.4	42.8	53.0	50.6	36.3	44.5	51.5	46.2	45.8	49.1	47.9	47.4	48.2	49.6	48.6	36.4
5. Agree	27.8	25.2	29.5	24.6	44.7	30.7	23.0	31.1	26.0	27.0	27.8	28.1	24.8	27.3	29.5	33.3
Item 5990 N(Wtd)	2980	1431	1422	2328	333	706	905	920	450	1428	1322	1204	678	337	587	66

A03B: People are too much concerned with material things these days

	TOTAL	M	F	White	Black	NE	NC	S	W	Yes	No	None	Mar.	Few	More	Her.
1. Disagree	4.4	5.3	3.2	3.2	9.4	4.4	3.6	5.5	3.5	3.1	5.3	4.3	3.1	3.8	4.2	5.8
2. Mostly disagree	6.2	8.1	3.9	5.5	8.2	7.4	4.6	6.4	6.8	5.8	6.1	4.9	8.5	5.9	5.9	5.8
3. Neither	8.9	11.2	6.5	9.0	7.6	9.4	9.0	6.9	12.5	8.9	8.6	8.3	9.6	9.4	9.8	8.7
4. Mostly agree	37.6	38.1	37.8	40.8	24.6	38.2	44.9	30.1	37.9	41.0	35.7	37.9	39.1	35.5	38.7	29.0
5. Agree	42.9	37.4	48.6	41.5	49.9	40.6	38.0	51.1	39.6	41.3	44.4	44.5	39.7	45.5	41.4	52.2
Item 6000 N(Wtd)	3009	1443	1435	2347	341	712	909	931	457	1442	1332	1215	680	341	594	69

QUESTIONNAIRE FORM 2 1976	TOTAL	SEX		RACE		REGION				4YR COLLEGE PLANS		ILLICIT DRUG USE: LIFETIME				
		M	F	White	Black	NE	NC	S	W	Yes	No	None	Mari-juana Only	Few Pills	More Pills	Any Her-oin
Weighted No. of Cases:	3036	1453	1445	2358	343	723	919	934	460	1450	1342	1223	687	343	597	69
% of Weighted Total:	100.0	47.9	47.6	77.7	11.3	23.8	30.3	30.8	15.2	47.8	44.2	40.3	22.6	11.3	19.7	2.3

A03C: Since it helps the economy to grow, people should be encouraged to buy more

	TOTAL	M	F	White	Black	NE	NC	S	W	Yes	No	None	Mari-juana Only	Few Pills	More Pills	Any Her-oin
1. Disagree	22.1	18.1	25.4	19.7	31.5	21.2	15.0	29.7	22.2	18.6	24.5	21.8	22.4	22.0	21.1	20.3
2. Mostly disagree	22.7	20.2	25.2	23.8	14.8	23.5	22.9	19.3	28.0	25.5	20.2	23.8	21.4	21.7	24.2	17.4
3. Neither	27.5	26.4	29.4	29.6	19.6	27.4	31.0	23.7	27.8	30.2	25.8	27.4	26.5	33.1	27.7	21.7
4. Mostly agree	18.0	21.3	14.4	18.0	19.6	18.1	20.9	17.0	14.2	17.4	18.8	17.2	19.9	16.4	18.2	21.7
5. Agree	9.6	14.1	5.5	8.9	14.5	9.7	10.1	10.0	7.8	8.4	10.6	9.9	9.8	6.7	8.6	18.8
Item 6010 N(Wtd)	2996	1440	1427	2339	337	711	909	927	450	1429	1332	1204	683	341	592	69

A03D: There is nothing wrong with advertising that gets people to buy things they don't really need

	TOTAL	M	F	White	Black	NE	NC	S	W	Yes	No	None	Mari-juana Only	Few Pills	More Pills	Any Her-oin
1. Disagree	43.6	39.6	48.4	44.2	40.9	49.9	37.7	46.5	40.0	45.7	42.5	44.6	42.0	43.3	44.9	40.6
2. Mostly disagree	22.9	21.6	24.1	24.4	17.8	21.6	25.3	20.6	24.8	23.7	22.1	23.2	22.8	22.2	23.4	18.8
3. Neither	11.3	11.9	10.6	11.8	10.4	9.1	14.6	9.3	11.9	11.0	11.7	10.1	11.0	12.9	13.5	8.7
4. Mostly agree	11.8	13.9	9.0	11.2	12.8	11.5	12.7	11.0	11.9	11.0	12.1	11.7	12.6	12.9	9.6	17.4
5. Agree	10.4	13.0	7.8	8.3	18.1	8.0	9.6	12.5	11.4	8.6	11.8	10.3	11.7	8.8	8.6	15.9
Item 6020 N(Wtd)	3009	1445	1431	2344	337	714	909	931	455	1437	1336	1210	684	342	594	69

A03E: There will probably be more shortages in the future, so Americans will have to learn how to be happy with fewer "things"

	TOTAL	M	F	White	Black	NE	NC	S	W	Yes	No	None	Mari-juana Only	Few Pills	More Pills	Any Her-oin
1. Disagree	6.5	6.9	5.6	5.7	7.3	8.4	5.6	5.4	7.6	6.5	5.8	5.5	5.5	9.9	6.6	10.1
2. Mostly disagree	6.9	7.3	6.6	7.1	5.9	10.0	6.6	5.9	4.8	7.1	6.4	6.7	7.6	6.4	6.2	7.2
3. Neither	9.6	9.7	9.0	9.7	8.5	10.2	10.4	7.6	10.9	9.5	9.3	8.5	10.9	9.0	9.8	11.6
4. Mostly agree	27.3	27.8	27.2	29.7	17.3	28.4	31.6	22.7	26.2	28.0	27.7	27.9	28.3	25.7	30.0	14.5
5. Agree	49.8	48.3	51.5	47.7	61.3	43.2	45.8	58.4	50.7	49.0	50.8	51.4	47.7	49.0	47.2	58.0
Item 6030 N(Wtd)	3017	1448	1438	2350	341	718	912	930	458	1444	1335	1216	685	343	593	69

A04: Below are several ways that people have used to protest about serious social issues. How much do you approve or disapprove of these actions?

A04A: Signing petitions

	TOTAL	M	F	White	Black	NE	NC	S	W	Yes	No	None	Mari-juana Only	Few Pills	More Pills	Any Her-oin
4. Strongly approve	24.5	26.6	22.8	26.8	15.1	29.5	22.0	20.9	29.3	30.6	18.5	23.7	25.9	23.1	26.4	24.6
3. Approve	44.2	44.3	44.9	46.8	30.9	43.6	48.9	40.2	43.8	46.9	43.8	43.5	46.2	44.7	47.0	31.9
2. Disapprove	4.2	4.3	4.0	3.7	5.6	3.7	3.5	5.6	3.7	2.6	5.6	5.1	2.7	4.1	3.2	4.3
1. Strongly disapprove	1.1	1.1	1.0	.6	3.6	.6	.8	1.6	1.5	.9	1.2	1.0	.9	.3	1.2	5.8
8. Don't know, or it depends	25.9	23.6	27.3	22.1	44.8	22.6	24.8	31.6	21.8	19.1	30.9	26.7	24.3	27.5	22.3	33.3
Item 6040 N(Wtd)	3000	1437	1433	2342	337	711	910	924	454	1436	1332	1210	679	342	591	69

A04B: Boycotting certain products or stores

	TOTAL	M	F	White	Black	NE	NC	S	W	Yes	No	None	Mari-juana Only	Few Pills	More Pills	Any Her-oin
4. Strongly approve	16.7	18.7	14.3	16.4	16.1	25.5	12.3	14.2	17.1	21.0	11.5	13.7	19.6	15.8	19.8	20.3
3. Approve	36.8	39.3	34.6	37.4	36.7	39.8	38.3	32.6	37.5	40.8	33.0	35.0	38.4	42.4	35.5	34.8
2. Disapprove	14.9	12.5	17.4	14.9	16.4	9.5	16.2	17.1	16.2	11.9	18.9	17.5	14.6	13.7	11.5	11.6
1. Strongly disapprove	4.1	4.8	3.2	3.7	5.3	2.5	3.6	5.5	4.4	2.9	5.2	4.5	2.2	3.2	5.1	4.3
8. Don't know, or it depends	27.5	24.7	30.5	27.7	25.8	22.6	29.6	30.6	24.8	23.4	31.4	29.4	25.1	24.9	28.2	27.5
Item 6050 N(Wtd)	2992	1443	1423	2335	341	713	906	922	451	1434	1326	1201	680	342	592	69

A04C: Lawful demonstrations

	TOTAL	M	F	White	Black	NE	NC	S	W	Yes	No	None	Mari-juana Only	Few Pills	More Pills	Any Her-oin
4. Strongly approve	17.1	20.2	14.1	17.2	16.5	22.8	14.6	14.2	19.0	21.0	13.0	13.4	18.5	17.6	23.0	23.1
3. Approve	47.3	48.3	47.1	49.3	41.4	50.4	47.7	45.8	44.6	49.7	46.2	45.1	49.3	47.6	51.2	50.8
2. Disapprove	11.1	9.8	12.0	10.2	14.4	8.8	11.1	13.4	9.9	8.5	13.2	13.1	10.0	12.4	7.1	4.6
1. Strongly disapprove	3.7	3.8	3.4	3.7	3.3	1.8	4.8	3.9	4.2	2.9	4.7	4.0	3.5	5.0	2.0	4.6
8. Don't know, or it depends	20.8	17.8	23.5	19.6	24.3	16.0	21.6	22.8	22.1	18.0	23.0	24.5	18.6	17.4	16.7	18.5
Item 6060 N(Wtd)	2992	1435	1428	2340	333	712	911	917	453	1435	1328	1205	681	340	592	65

QUESTIONNAIRE FORM 2 1976	TOTAL	SEX		RACE		REGION				4YR COLLEGE PLANS		ILLICIT DRUG USE: LIFETIME				
		M	F	White	Black	NE	NC	S	W	Yes	No	None	Mari- juana Only	Few Pills	More Pills	Any Her- oin
Weighted No. of Cases:	3036	1453	1445	2358	343	723	919	934	460	1450	1342	1223	687	343	597	69
% of Weighted Total:	100.0	47.9	47.6	77.7	11.3	23.8	30.3	30.8	15.2	47.8	44.2	40.3	22.6	11.3	19.7	2.3
A04D: Occupying buildings or factories																
4. Strongly approve	3.0	4.1	1.8	2.5	4.5	2.6	2.3	3.9	3.3	2.4	3.1	1.3	2.8	5.3	4.4	4.5
3. Approve	17.6	18.6	16.1	14.8	30.2	16.4	17.0	19.7	16.3	13.8	21.0	14.9	16.1	22.3	19.5	17.9
2. Disapprove	31.5	31.5	32.1	33.2	23.9	33.9	33.6	28.8	29.4	35.6	28.7	33.9	32.4	27.9	30.6	23.9
1. Strongly disapprove	15.2	19.1	11.7	17.0	5.4	12.7	16.9	14.1	18.1	18.2	12.7	19.6	14.9	17.2	6.7	7.5
8. Don't know, or it depends	32.6	26.9	38.3	32.6	36.0	34.4	30.1	33.6	33.1	30.0	34.6	30.3	33.9	27.0	38.8	47.8
Item 6070 N(Wtd)	2973	1427	1422	2328	331	700	901	918	453	1425	1325	1202	678	337	585	67
A04E: Wildcat strikes																
4. Strongly approve	3.1	4.3	1.5	2.8	2.2	3.6	2.5	2.8	4.2	2.6	2.9	1.8	2.7	3.3	5.6	5.8
3. Approve	9.2	12.8	4.9	8.9	11.7	7.8	10.4	9.3	8.5	8.5	9.3	6.1	9.2	9.7	11.8	21.7
2. Disapprove	32.4	31.4	34.1	33.3	28.3	32.1	31.6	32.6	34.5	33.5	32.5	32.5	32.7	33.7	33.1	33.3
1. Strongly disapprove	21.0	20.3	21.9	21.4	14.2	20.5	21.7	20.9	20.3	22.7	19.0	26.9	17.8	21.6	13.0	10.1
8. Don't know, or it depends	34.3	31.2	37.7	33.6	43.7	35.9	33.7	34.7	32.5	32.7	36.3	32.8	37.6	31.9	36.3	27.5
Item 6080 N(Wtd)	2959	1422	1412	2319	325	701	902	906	449	1412	1320	1199	673	329	586	69
A04F: Blocking traffic																
4. Strongly approve	2.0	2.4	1.2	1.6	2.1	2.7	1.3	1.6	2.6	1.8	1.8	.6	2.2	2.3	3.4	2.9
3. Approve	3.4	4.2	2.7	2.8	6.5	5.0	3.5	2.6	2.4	2.8	3.8	2.3	3.2	4.4	4.9	1.4
2. Disapprove	42.6	41.9	43.2	43.4	39.5	39.7	41.0	46.4	42.5	40.1	45.3	40.8	43.0	39.2	48.1	46.4
1. Strongly disapprove	42.1	41.2	43.6	43.4	36.0	41.5	44.3	39.8	43.0	46.5	38.7	48.2	40.2	44.4	32.9	33.3
8. Don't know, or it depends	10.0	10.3	9.3	8.8	15.6	11.1	10.0	9.4	9.4	8.7	10.4	8.0	11.5	9.4	10.8	15.9
Item 6090 N(Wtd)	3003	1444	1432	2345	339	713	908	926	456	1441	1332	1207	684	342	593	69
A04G: Damaging things																
4. Strongly approve	2.4	2.7	1.9	1.9	3.8	2.1	1.4	2.9	3.5	2.2	2.2	1.1	2.8	2.1	3.2	7.2
3. Approve	1.8	2.1	1.1	.9	5.3	1.4	1.9	2.4	1.1	1.3	1.9	1.9	1.0	1.0	2.9	2.9
2. Disapprove	21.0	22.9	19.0	18.8	30.8	21.0	18.8	23.9	19.3	16.6	25.2	18.1	21.0	20.9	25.1	29.0
1. Strongly disapprove	69.3	64.1	75.3	73.6	49.7	70.1	71.9	66.1	69.3	75.7	64.4	75.7	69.1	73.2	60.7	49.3
8. Don't know, or it depends	5.5	8.1	2.8	4.7	10.4	5.2	6.2	4.5	6.6	4.3	6.2	3.2	6.3	2.9	9.1	13.0
Item 6100 N(Wtd)	3006	1442	1435	2345	338	713	910	927	456	1439	1335	1209	685	340	593	69
A04H: Personal violence																
4. Strongly approve	2.2	2.2	1.9	1.7	4.1	2.1	1.5	2.6	2.6	1.7	2.2	1.3	1.9	2.6	2.9	5.8
3. Approve	3.2	4.5	1.9	2.5	8.0	2.0	3.5	4.3	2.4	2.2	4.1	2.6	2.3	2.6	5.2	4.3
2. Disapprove	19.9	21.7	17.3	18.1	24.6	20.5	16.1	22.3	21.3	17.6	21.2	17.3	20.8	20.2	21.2	21.7
1. Strongly disapprove	66.5	60.6	74.0	70.7	50.6	67.9	70.6	61.4	67.1	73.2	62.0	73.0	65.6	67.3	60.1	47.8
8. Don't know, or it depends	8.2	10.9	5.0	7.1	13.0	7.4	8.3	9.4	6.6	5.3	10.4	5.8	9.3	7.3	10.8	20.3
Item 6110 N(Wtd)	3007	1445	1434	2348	338	713	911	927	456	1441	1335	1209	686	342	594	69
A05: Do you think that you would prefer having a mate for most of your life, or would you prefer not having a mate?																
5. Definitely prefer to have a mate	58.6	52.8	65.1	61.7	45.6	57.6	58.2	61.2	55.8	57.3	61.6	61.6	60.7	57.2	53.6	53.6
4. Probably prefer to have a mate	26.5	29.0	23.9	26.1	25.6	30.1	27.0	21.9	29.2	28.7	24.6	25.5	26.4	25.8	29.6	27.5
3. Not sure	11.4	13.4	8.8	9.1	21.8	9.8	11.3	12.9	11.3	10.3	10.7	10.6	8.4	12.6	12.9	14.5
2. Probably prefer not to have a mate	2.6	3.6	1.6	2.3	6.2	1.8	2.7	3.3	2.7	3.0	2.1	2.0	3.6	3.2	2.5	5.8
1. Definitely prefer not to have a mate	.9	1.2	.5	.7	1.2	.8	.9	.9	.9	.8	1.0	.4	1.0	1.2	1.4	-
Item 6120 N(Wtd)	2989	1429	1433	2329	340	715	904	918	452	1437	1321	1206	675	341	591	69
A06: Which do you think you are most likely to choose in the long run?																
3. Getting married	74.2	69.4	80.0	78.3	59.6	76.7	73.8	73.3	73.1	78.1	72.6	79.0	74.0	73.7	69.3	57.4
2. I have no idea	18.6	23.8	12.6	16.4	24.7	18.5	18.8	18.1	19.8	17.0	18.4	15.7	18.5	18.7	22.5	25.0
1. Not getting married	5.9	6.4	5.2	4.0	14.5	4.4	5.6	6.7	6.9	4.9	6.4	4.4	6.1	6.0	6.6	16.2
8. Am already married	1.3	.4	2.2	1.3	1.2	.4	1.8	1.9	.5	.1	2.6	1.0	1.4	1.5	1.9	1.5
Item 6130 N(Wtd)	2911	1382	1403	2265	324	699	877	900	435	1398	1286	1175	654	331	579	68

QUESTIONNAIRE FORM 2 1976	TOTAL	SEX		RACE		REGION				4YR COLLEGE PLANS		ILLICIT DRUG USE: LIFETIME				
		M	F	White	Black	NE	NC	S	W	Yes	No	None	Mari- juana Only	Few Pills	More Pills	Any Her- oin
Weighted No. of Cases:	3036	1453	1445	2358	343	723	919	934	460	1450	1342	1223	687	343	597	69
% of Weighted Total:	100.0	47.9	47.6	77.7	11.3	23.8	30.3	30.8	15.2	47.8	44.2	40.3	22.6	11.3	19.7	2.3

A07: If you did get married (or are married)...

A07A: How likely do you think it is that you would stay married to the same person for life?

5. Very likely	61.9	57.7	66.5	63.2	52.7	57.0	64.3	64.8	58.9	61.0	63.2	70.1	56.1	61.7	53.3	50.7
4. Fairly likely	21.4	24.1	19.5	22.9	15.6	24.2	22.4	18.0	22.0	23.7	20.1	18.7	26.2	19.9	23.1	26.9
3. Uncertain	13.5	14.4	11.9	11.2	26.9	15.9	10.6	13.6	15.5	11.8	14.1	9.9	13.4	14.5	18.6	17.9
2. Fairly unlikely	2.0	2.5	1.4	1.7	2.7	2.0	1.5	2.3	2.3	2.4	1.5	.9	3.0	2.1	3.0	3.0
1. Very unlikely	1.2	1.3	.9	1.0	2.4	.9	1.3	1.2	1.4	1.1	1.2	.5	1.4	1.8	1.9	1.5
Item 6140 N(Wtd)	2924	1400	1396	2282	334	693	876	916	440	1394	1300	1174	665	337	576	67

A07B: How likely is it that you would want to have children?

5. Very likely	59.1	59.1	60.1	60.4	53.7	63.4	58.5	58.5	54.8	61.5	58.2	64.0	58.0	63.7	51.1	51.5
4. Fairly likely	18.7	21.4	15.9	18.9	17.2	16.6	20.0	17.1	23.0	18.4	18.2	17.4	20.4	15.9	21.7	13.6
3. Uncertain	13.1	12.7	13.2	12.8	13.6	12.2	12.6	14.6	12.5	12.2	13.6	11.6	12.4	11.1	16.1	18.2
2. Fairly unlikely	3.1	2.1	4.1	3.2	2.7	3.3	2.9	2.7	3.6	3.3	3.3	2.5	2.8	3.6	3.8	6.1
1. Very unlikely	4.2	3.6	4.3	3.8	5.0	3.6	4.4	4.2	4.3	3.7	4.5	3.2	4.5	3.9	5.0	7.6
8. Already have child(ren)	1.9	1.1	2.5	1.0	7.4	1.0	1.6	2.9	1.6	.9	2.6	1.4	1.6	1.8	2.3	3.0
Item 6150 N(Wtd)	2932	1401	1406	2285	337	691	882	919	440	1392	1310	1181	667	333	577	66

The questions in the next column ask you to imagine different kinds of married life that you might have. We want you to think about different ways you might share responsibilities for working, taking care of the home, and taking care of children. Please indicate how acceptable for you each of the different arrangements would be.

A08: Imagine you are married and have no children. How would you feel about each of the following working arrangements?

A08A: Husband works full-time, wife doesn't work

1. Not at all acceptable	25.4	14.0	36.8	23.5	38.0	33.2	21.9	24.0	22.7	28.8	21.0	22.6	27.0	25.3	26.9	26.5
2. Somewhat acceptable	32.1	30.3	34.2	32.3	28.4	29.9	34.5	31.9	31.8	32.1	33.0	32.7	29.6	35.3	33.4	29.4
3. Acceptable	33.0	42.6	23.5	34.6	25.1	29.7	33.6	33.3	36.6	30.9	35.4	34.3	33.6	31.2	32.0	32.4
4. Desirable	9.5	13.0	5.7	9.7	8.4	7.2	10.0	10.9	9.1	8.2	10.6	10.4	9.7	8.5	7.5	10.3
Item 6160 N(Wtd)	2993	1434	1431	2339	334	710	904	926	453	1434	1329	1215	678	340	587	68

A08B: Husband works full-time, wife works about half-time

1. Not at all acceptable	4.5	5.0	3.6	3.1	10.0	5.7	2.7	6.0	2.9	3.3	4.8	3.7	4.2	5.0	4.1	7.2
2. Somewhat acceptable	19.7	17.0	22.6	17.7	30.9	23.2	15.9	22.1	17.0	19.6	19.4	19.5	20.5	20.5	19.1	15.9
3. Acceptable	56.8	58.4	55.0	57.8	52.1	54.8	57.9	57.0	57.7	57.3	56.9	56.3	58.3	57.3	56.4	55.1
4. Desirable	18.9	19.6	18.8	21.2	7.0	16.3	23.5	15.0	22.4	19.9	18.9	20.4	17.0	17.2	20.2	21.7
Item 6170 N(Wtd)	2966	1422	1420	2322	330	706	897	915	447	1416	1322	1201	672	337	580	69

A08C: Both work full-time

1. Not at all acceptable	19.9	25.3	14.2	19.0	23.4	18.1	19.4	22.6	18.1	15.0	24.3	19.5	21.6	22.1	17.3	18.8
2. Somewhat acceptable	22.9	26.2	19.7	23.7	18.9	21.5	23.5	21.2	27.2	22.6	22.3	22.7	23.4	20.6	24.0	17.4
3. Acceptable	37.5	32.1	42.8	37.1	41.6	38.2	36.7	37.5	37.7	39.8	35.7	39.7	34.8	35.2	37.3	39.1
4. Desirable	19.7	16.3	23.4	20.3	16.5	22.1	20.4	18.7	17.0	22.6	17.6	18.1	20.3	22.1	21.6	23.2
Item 6180 N(Wtd)	2973	1422	1429	2322	334	706	898	920	448	1423	1321	1210	676	330	584	69

QUESTIONNAIRE FORM 2 1976	TOTAL	SEX		RACE		REGION				4YR COLLEGE PLANS		ILLICIT DRUG USE: LIFETIME				
		M	F	White	Black	NE	NC	S	W	Yes	No	None	Mari-juana Only	Few Pills	More Pills	Any Her-oin
Weighted No. of Cases: % of Weighted Total:	3036 100.0	1453 47.9	1445 47.6	2358 77.7	343 11.3	723 23.8	919 30.3	934 30.8	460 15.2	1450 47.8	1342 44.2	1223 40.3	687 22.6	343 11.3	597 19.7	69 2.3

A08D: Both work about half-time

1. Not at all acceptable	46.5	49.2	43.7	44.3	57.7	44.4	45.1	52.8	39.5	41.8	50.3	47.7	46.6	49.9	41.5	46.4
2. Somewhat acceptable	28.8	26.6	31.7	31.1	19.9	30.1	29.9	25.2	32.2	30.4	28.4	30.8	29.2	28.3	28.2	18.8
3. Acceptable	16.9	16.9	16.5	17.5	11.8	16.9	18.2	14.1	19.7	19.7	14.2	15.5	17.8	15.0	18.7	15.9
4. Desirable	7.8	7.4	8.1	7.1	10.6	8.6	6.7	7.8	8.9	8.0	7.1	6.1	6.5	6.8	11.7	17.4
Item 6190 N(Wtd)	2979	1425	1426	2329	331	710	896	922	451	1434	1317	1206	678	339	579	69

A08E: Husband works about half-time, wife works full-time

1. Not at all acceptable	66.0	69.8	62.1	65.1	71.1	61.5	65.0	71.6	64.0	59.6	71.9	68.0	69.6	64.0	59.8	59.4
2. Somewhat acceptable	21.1	17.6	25.3	22.2	19.3	24.2	20.5	19.4	20.8	25.0	18.0	20.8	19.3	24.5	23.7	18.2
3. Acceptable	9.8	8.1	11.0	10.5	4.5	10.3	11.6	6.4	12.4	12.7	6.9	9.0	8.8	10.0	12.4	10.1
4. Desirable	3.1	4.4	1.5	2.3	5.1	4.1	2.9	2.7	2.6	2.6	3.1	2.2	2.4	1.8	3.9	13.0
Item 6200 N(Wtd)	2983	1425	1431	2333	332	711	897	922	453	1429	1326	1204	678	339	587	69

A08F: Husband doesn't work, wife works full-time

1. Not at all acceptable	84.0	84.9	83.6	84.6	82.9	80.7	83.2	89.1	80.6	82.0	86.5	85.2	85.5	88.9	79.5	75.4
2. Somewhat acceptable	8.7	7.0	10.5	8.9	8.1	10.7	10.0	5.3	10.1	10.1	7.9	8.8	8.7	7.0	9.9	8.7
3. Acceptable	4.7	4.3	4.8	4.7	3.3	4.9	5.1	3.4	6.6	5.9	3.3	4.6	3.4	2.6	6.8	7.2
4. Desirable	2.5	3.8	1.0	1.8	5.7	3.5	1.8	2.4	2.9	2.0	2.3	1.3	2.4	1.5	3.8	8.7
Item 6210 N(Wtd)	2989	1431	1431	2336	334	709	903	923	454	1432	1327	1213	676	341	585	69

A09: Imagine you are married and have one or more pre-school children. How would you feel about each of the following working arrangements?

A09A: Husband works full-time, wife doesn't work

1. Not at all acceptable	6.1	4.5	7.5	4.3	16.7	6.6	5.2	7.3	4.9	6.1	5.7	5.9	5.4	5.0	7.1	7.2
2. Somewhat acceptable	12.4	9.2	15.4	9.9	26.3	13.8	8.8	14.1	14.3	11.8	12.6	11.8	13.4	12.1	12.5	7.2
3. Acceptable	35.3	36.0	34.3	33.9	38.8	37.9	33.7	35.5	34.0	32.3	37.5	32.3	34.5	40.9	35.9	44.9
4. Desirable	46.1	50.3	42.7	51.9	18.5	41.9	52.3	43.1	46.8	49.7	44.1	50.0	46.7	42.4	44.4	40.6
Item 6220 N(Wtd)	2999	1438	1433	2342	335	712	908	926	453	1436	1332	1213	679	340	590	69

A09B: Husband works full-time, wife works about half-time

1. Not at all acceptable	18.3	22.9	13.1	19.1	9.7	22.0	18.1	16.6	16.7	15.9	20.3	19.5	15.5	18.3	20.1	14.5
2. Somewhat acceptable	29.9	30.8	29.1	29.6	33.6	30.0	31.4	28.6	29.7	31.6	29.2	28.6	33.0	29.6	29.1	34.8
3. Acceptable	41.9	37.6	46.6	41.4	47.2	38.0	39.9	46.2	42.6	42.1	41.5	43.4	40.3	42.6	39.4	39.1
4. Desirable	9.9	8.6	11.3	9.9	9.4	10.0	10.6	8.6	11.0	10.4	9.1	8.6	11.1	9.5	11.5	11.6
Item 6230 N(Wtd)	3003	1436	1439	2341	339	713	907	928	455	1438	1333	1215	682	338	591	69

A09C: Both work full-time

1. Not at all acceptable	73.2	75.7	71.4	76.8	54.5	77.6	75.9	66.2	75.2	75.8	71.7	73.4	76.1	72.4	72.2	72.5
2. Somewhat acceptable	13.9	12.0	15.9	13.3	18.9	12.5	13.3	15.9	13.1	13.6	14.2	14.9	13.1	15.2	12.1	8.7
3. Acceptable	8.6	7.1	9.6	6.5	19.5	6.5	6.3	13.1	7.5	7.3	9.2	8.7	7.2	7.9	9.7	8.7
4. Desirable	4.3	5.2	3.1	3.5	7.2	3.4	4.6	4.8	4.2	3.4	4.9	3.0	3.5	4.4	5.8	11.6
Item 6240 N(Wtd)	2987	1431	1431	2337	334	706	904	924	452	1431	1327	1207	678	341	587	69

A09D: Both work about half-time

1. Not at all acceptable	51.6	55.0	47.8	50.7	54.5	50.7	51.2	55.2	46.1	45.4	57.3	52.6	53.4	52.4	46.9	50.0
2. Somewhat acceptable	29.3	26.5	32.7	30.7	24.4	27.3	31.1	27.1	33.3	32.4	27.8	30.4	28.2	28.4	30.7	27.9
3. Acceptable	14.1	13.4	14.8	14.2	13.6	16.4	13.3	12.5	15.5	16.6	11.3	13.2	13.8	13.3	16.8	11.8
4. Desirable	5.0	5.0	4.6	4.4	7.2	5.6	4.3	5.2	5.1	5.6	3.6	3.6	4.6	5.6	5.7	11.8
Item 6250 N(Wtd)	2977	1428	1424	2327	332	708	898	919	453	1427	1324	1208	674	338	584	68

QUESTIONNAIRE FORM 2 1976	TOTAL	SEX		RACE		REGION				4YR COLLEGE PLANS		ILLICIT DRUG USE: LIFETIME				
		M	F	White	Black	NE	NC	S	W	Yes	No	None	Mari-juana Only	Few Pills	More Pills	Any Her-oin
Weighted No. of Cases:	3036	1453	1445	2358	343	723	919	934	460	1450	1342	1223	687	343	597	69
% of Weighted Total:	100.0	47.9	47.6	77.7	11.3	23.8	30.3	30.8	15.2	47.8	44.2	40.3	22.6	11.3	19.7	2.3

A09E: Husband works about half-time, wife works full-time

1. Not at all acceptable	78.5	79.1	78.0	79.4	73.3	76.1	79.2	80.9	75.7	75.8	81.6	79.2	81.3	79.6	75.3	73.5
2. Somewhat acceptable	13.7	12.7	14.6	13.5	15.3	14.1	13.5	12.7	15.2	15.5	12.1	13.9	11.7	14.7	14.3	13.2
3. Acceptable	5.6	5.4	5.7	5.5	5.7	7.5	5.3	3.6	7.1	7.1	3.8	5.1	5.5	3.8	7.5	5.9
4. Desirable	2.3	2.8	1.7	1.6	5.4	2.1	2.0	2.9	1.8	1.6	2.5	1.8	1.3	1.8	2.9	5.9
Item 6260 N(Wtd)	2984	1430	1429	2334	333	708	902	922	453	1432	1325	1211	675	339	586	68

A09F: Husband doesn't work, wife works full-time

1. Not at all acceptable	83.6	84.4	83.4	83.4	85.2	81.0	82.6	88.3	80.6	80.0	87.9	83.7	85.7	85.0	82.6	73.1
2. Somewhat acceptable	7.5	6.5	8.2	8.0	4.2	7.5	9.7	4.4	9.7	8.7	6.0	7.5	6.3	6.8	8.7	11.9
3. Acceptable	5.9	5.4	6.3	6.3	3.3	8.2	5.4	4.1	6.8	8.3	3.7	5.9	5.9	6.2	6.0	4.5
4. Desirable	2.9	3.8	2.1	2.4	7.2	3.4	2.4	3.1	2.9	3.0	2.4	2.7	2.1	2.1	2.7	11.9
Item 6270 N(Wtd)	2988	1431	1431	2339	332	711	901	923	453	1433	1328	1212	679	340	587	67

A10: Imagine you are married and have one or more pre-school children. Imagine also that the husband is working full-time and the wife does not have a job outside the home. How would you feel about each of these arrangements for the day-to-day care of the child(ren)?

A10A: Wife does all child care

1. Not at all acceptable	28.9	26.2	32.2	29.9	24.6	32.1	28.3	27.4	28.6	34.0	23.7	30.1	28.0	27.1	30.5	26.1
2. Somewhat acceptable	29.6	29.0	30.5	30.2	28.5	26.3	31.1	31.3	28.4	27.2	32.3	30.7	29.5	27.7	29.5	21.7
3. Acceptable	29.1	28.1	29.3	27.1	35.7	28.5	26.6	31.2	30.8	27.1	30.7	29.2	28.2	30.7	27.6	30.4
4. Desirable	12.4	16.7	8.1	12.9	11.1	13.1	14.1	10.1	12.3	11.7	13.2	10.1	14.3	14.6	12.3	21.7
Item 6280 N(Wtd)	2983	1429	1427	2331	333	708	901	919	455	1431	1323	1210	678	336	586	69

A10B: Wife does most of it

1. Not at all acceptable	8.2	8.0	8.1	6.4	15.1	8.1	7.4	9.2	7.7	7.9	7.9	8.2	7.8	8.5	7.8	10.1
2. Somewhat acceptable	26.6	26.8	26.5	26.1	28.5	29.2	25.4	25.5	27.3	25.2	27.6	25.9	28.7	25.9	27.6	29.0
3. Acceptable	45.7	44.2	47.0	45.7	47.5	45.1	44.3	49.2	42.0	46.2	45.9	46.7	44.3	46.8	43.9	43.5
4. Desirable	19.5	20.9	18.4	21.9	8.9	17.6	22.8	15.9	23.1	20.8	18.7	19.2	19.3	18.8	20.6	18.8
Item 6290 N(Wtd)	2996	1434	1437	2337	337	712	906	924	455	1435	1332	1213	680	340	588	69

A10C: Both do it equally

1. Not at all acceptable	8.1	8.7	7.0	7.2	14.1	7.4	7.0	9.9	7.7	7.2	8.2	7.5	7.1	10.8	7.8	10.1
2. Somewhat acceptable	22.2	25.0	19.7	21.7	23.4	20.6	23.8	21.4	23.3	21.6	23.5	21.0	23.6	21.3	22.6	30.4
3. Acceptable	36.7	37.8	35.3	35.8	41.0	38.3	34.4	37.4	37.0	36.4	36.4	36.8	39.9	35.9	33.2	31.9
4. Desirable	32.9	28.4	38.0	35.3	21.3	33.6	34.7	31.3	31.7	34.9	31.9	34.8	29.3	32.1	36.6	27.5
Item 6300 N(Wtd)	2994	1435	1434	2342	334	712	906	922	454	1436	1329	1213	679	343	588	69

A10D: Husband does most of it

1. Not at all acceptable	62.1	58.1	66.7	62.0	62.7	63.2	59.3	64.5	60.9	61.7	62.6	63.8	60.9	66.8	58.0	56.5
2. Somewhat acceptable	29.4	31.8	26.8	30.2	25.0	28.5	31.6	27.2	30.8	30.7	28.7	27.6	32.2	23.8	34.0	34.8
3. Acceptable	6.1	7.1	4.9	6.0	6.6	5.4	6.6	6.0	6.4	5.7	6.3	6.4	4.6	6.5	5.8	7.2
4. Desirable	2.4	3.0	1.6	1.8	5.7	3.0	2.4	2.4	2.0	1.8	2.5	2.1	2.2	2.9	2.2	1.4
Item 6310 N(Wtd)	2984	1430	1431	2337	332	709	900	920	455	1432	1325	1211	677	340	586	69

A10E: Husband does all of it

1. Not at all acceptable	90.4	88.7	93.0	91.8	84.3	89.9	90.4	90.7	91.2	91.7	90.1	90.2	90.4	91.2	92.5	89.9
2. Somewhat acceptable	5.6	6.6	3.9	5.5	5.1	5.8	6.9	4.5	5.1	5.4	5.6	5.8	5.9	5.6	5.0	5.8
3. Acceptable	1.8	2.1	1.3	1.4	4.8	1.4	1.4	2.4	1.8	1.3	2.0	2.2	1.8	.9	1.0	1.4
4. Desirable	2.2	2.6	1.7	1.3	5.7	2.8	1.4	2.6	2.2	1.6	2.3	1.9	1.9	2.6	1.7	2.9
Item 6320 N(Wtd)	2989	1430	1433	2339	332	712	902	920	454	1433	1328	1212	680	340	585	69

QUESTIONNAIRE FORM 2 1976	TOTAL	SEX		RACE		REGION				4YR COLLEGE PLANS		ILLICIT DRUG USE: LIFETIME				
		M	F	White	Black	NE	NC	S	W	Yes	No	None	Mari-juana Only	Few Pills	More Pills	Any Heroin
Weighted No. of Cases:	3036	1453	1445	2358	343	723	919	934	460	1450	1342	1223	687	343	597	69
% of Weighted Total:	100.0	47.9	47.6	77.7	11.3	23.8	30.3	30.8	15.2	47.8	44.2	40.3	22.6	11.3	19.7	2.3

The next section of this questionnaire is about government and public affairs.

A11: Some people think about what's going on in government very often, and others are not that interested. How much of an interest do you take in government and current events?

	TOTAL	M	F	White	Black	NE	NC	S	W	Yes	No	None	Mari-juana Only	Few Pills	More Pills	Any Heroin
1. No interest at all	4.1	3.7	4.6	3.5	5.8	4.5	4.3	3.4	4.6	2.5	5.6	3.9	3.4	3.5	5.4	7.2
2. Very little interest	17.4	13.2	21.5	16.6	19.9	19.7	17.3	16.5	15.8	12.0	22.3	14.8	15.2	17.5	23.4	20.3
3. Some interest	48.5	47.2	49.2	49.0	44.7	46.9	49.3	49.2	48.1	45.6	52.0	49.5	50.7	47.7	43.9	43.5
4. A lot of interest	22.4	25.2	20.6	23.2	21.1	21.3	22.0	23.2	23.5	28.7	16.2	23.4	21.9	25.1	20.7	24.6
5. A very great interest	7.5	10.7	4.2	7.6	8.8	7.8	7.2	7.7	7.9	11.2	3.8	8.3	8.6	6.1	6.6	4.3
Item 6330 N(Wtd)	3007	1442	1440	2344	342	715	909	928	455	1447	1329	1218	684	342	590	69

A12: Do you think some of the people running the government are crooked or dishonest?

	TOTAL	M	F	White	Black	NE	NC	S	W	Yes	No	None	Mari-juana Only	Few Pills	More Pills	Any Heroin
1. Most of them are crooked or dishonest	14.8	15.0	14.5	13.8	17.9	17.1	14.3	15.2	11.7	10.7	18.2	12.6	16.3	10.0	19.6	18.8
2. Quite a few are	37.3	36.5	38.2	37.8	37.5	38.4	34.7	38.9	37.5	39.9	35.3	35.2	36.6	39.7	42.4	36.2
3. Some are	45.0	45.4	44.8	46.1	40.2	42.2	48.7	42.8	46.8	46.3	44.2	49.5	44.0	49.4	35.0	42.0
4. Hardly any are	2.5	2.6	2.4	2.1	4.1	1.8	2.2	3.0	2.9	2.6	2.3	2.6	2.8	.6	2.4	2.9
5. None at all are crooked or dishonest	.4	.5	.1	.2	.3	.4	.1	.1	1.3	.6	-	.2	.3	.3	.5	1.4
Item 6340 N(Wtd)	3004	1443	1437	2345	341	713	910	927	453	1443	1332	1217	680	340	592	69

A13: Do you think the government wastes much of the money we pay in taxes?

	TOTAL	M	F	White	Black	NE	NC	S	W	Yes	No	None	Mari-juana Only	Few Pills	More Pills	Any Heroin
1. Nearly all tax money is wasted	7.4	8.2	6.2	6.4	11.8	8.0	6.2	8.3	7.3	5.1	9.1	6.3	7.6	6.4	8.6	8.7
2. A lot of tax money is wasted	50.4	50.4	50.6	51.6	43.8	52.9	51.4	47.9	49.6	51.2	50.3	48.1	51.5	52.9	55.6	49.3
3. Some tax money is wasted	36.4	35.5	37.8	37.7	32.4	34.3	36.6	37.2	37.4	38.3	34.4	39.3	36.1	35.4	31.4	37.7
4. A little tax money wasted	5.3	5.4	5.0	4.2	10.3	4.8	5.6	5.7	4.6	5.1	5.8	5.9	4.6	5.0	4.1	2.9
5. No tax money is wasted	.5	.3	.4	*	2.1	.1	.1	.9	.9	.3	.4	.5	.1	.6	.2	1.4
Item 6350 N(Wtd)	3002	1445	1434	2345	340	711	910	927	454	1442	1333	1217	681	342	592	69

A14: How much of the time do you think you can trust the government in Washington to do what is right?

	TOTAL	M	F	White	Black	NE	NC	S	W	Yes	No	None	Mari-juana Only	Few Pills	More Pills	Any Heroin
1. Almost always	7.6	9.8	5.5	8.1	5.0	6.5	8.5	7.9	7.2	7.5	7.5	8.4	5.3	8.8	7.5	5.8
2. Often	36.8	38.6	35.5	40.3	19.2	36.7	39.2	34.4	37.1	41.4	32.8	38.5	40.7	37.5	31.2	36.2
3. Sometimes	41.8	38.4	45.1	41.2	45.7	40.8	40.9	42.9	43.0	39.6	44.4	41.0	41.5	41.3	44.2	46.4
4. Seldom	11.4	10.3	12.4	8.8	26.5	14.2	9.0	12.7	9.0	9.7	12.8	10.5	10.4	11.1	13.7	5.8
5. Never	2.4	2.8	1.5	1.6	3.8	2.0	2.4	1.9	3.7	1.7	2.6	1.6	2.1	.9	3.4	5.8
Item 6360 N(Wtd)	3000	1442	1434	2344	339	709	909	927	456	1443	1331	1217	680	341	590	69

A15: Do you feel that the people running the government are smart people who usually know what they are doing?

	TOTAL	M	F	White	Black	NE	NC	S	W	Yes	No	None	Mari-juana Only	Few Pills	More Pills	Any Heroin
1. They almost always know what they are doing	13.2	15.0	11.4	13.2	11.1	13.6	13.7	12.1	13.7	14.8	10.4	13.0	14.0	14.6	11.4	14.5
2. They usually know what they are doing	51.1	51.7	50.5	54.4	35.2	49.5	52.1	49.7	54.5	52.6	51.0	51.4	52.9	55.0	49.7	49.3
3. They sometimes know what they are doing	28.9	25.4	33.1	27.2	43.1	29.9	27.4	32.5	23.4	27.8	30.7	30.3	27.0	26.0	30.2	27.5
4. They seldom know what they are doing	5.3	6.0	4.3	4.1	9.4	5.5	5.3	4.7	6.4	4.0	6.3	4.6	5.3	4.1	6.3	5.8
5. They never know what they are doing	1.4	1.8	.8	1.2	1.2	1.5	1.5	.9	2.0	1.0	1.5	.7	1.0	-	2.7	4.3
Item 6370 N(Wtd)	3003	1443	1436	2345	341	713	910	927	453	1443	1331	1217	681	342	590	69

* = less than .05 per cent.

QUESTIONNAIRE FORM 2 1976	TOTAL	SEX		RACE		REGION				4YR COLLEGE PLANS		ILLICIT DRUG USE: LIFETIME				
		M	F	White	Black	NE	NC	S	W	Yes	No	None	Mari-juana Only	Few Pills	More Pills	Any Her-oin
Weighted No. of Cases:	3036	1453	1445	2358	343	723	919	934	460	1450	1342	1223	687	343	597	69
% of Weighted Total:	100.0	47.9	47.6	77.7	11.3	23.8	30.3	30.8	15.2	47.8	44.2	40.3	22.6	11.3	19.7	2.3

A16: Would you say the government is pretty much run for a few big interests looking out for themselves, or is it run for the benefit of all the people?

	TOTAL	M	F	White	Black	NE	NC	S	W	Yes	No	None	Mari-juana Only	Few Pills	More Pills	Any Her-oin
1. Nearly always run for a few big interests	9.8	10.0	9.0	9.0	11.8	11.8	8.3	9.4	10.5	9.0	9.9	8.6	11.1	7.7	11.7	10.3
2. Usually run for a few big interests	23.4	23.2	24.2	23.2	23.7	24.0	23.7	21.6	25.1	24.4	23.0	24.3	24.3	18.6	23.4	27.9
3. Run some for the big interests, some for the people	48.9	46.4	51.5	49.4	50.6	49.5	48.2	50.1	46.5	48.4	49.4	49.6	45.6	55.0	49.1	36.8
4. Usually run for the benefit of all the people	15.0	17.3	12.9	15.8	10.9	12.9	15.9	15.3	16.1	16.0	14.5	14.7	15.3	16.9	13.6	22.1
5. Nearly always run for the benefit of all the people	3.0	3.1	2.5	2.5	3.3	1.8	3.9	3.6	1.8	2.3	3.2	2.9	3.9	1.5	2.2	4.4
Item 6380 N(Wtd)	2979	1433	1423	2327	338	703	907	922	447	1433	1321	1216	675	338	582	68

A17: Have you ever done, or do you plan to do, the following things?

A17A: Vote in a public election

	TOTAL	M	F	White	Black	NE	NC	S	W	Yes	No	None	Mari-juana Only	Few Pills	More Pills	Any Her-oin
1. I probably won't do this	4.2	4.3	4.0	3.2	7.4	4.4	3.9	3.6	5.8	2.4	5.8	3.7	4.1	2.4	4.6	7.4
2. Don't know	7.7	6.5	8.8	5.5	15.4	8.6	5.6	9.0	8.1	4.1	10.6	8.4	5.3	8.0	6.8	11.8
3. I probably will do this	82.7	81.7	83.9	85.6	75.1	83.6	82.6	82.8	81.2	87.4	78.6	82.7	85.1	85.8	82.4	72.1
4. I have already done this	5.4	7.5	3.3	5.7	2.1	3.4	8.0	4.6	4.9	6.0	5.1	5.2	5.6	3.5	6.2	8.8
Item 6390 N(Wtd)	2970	1422	1426	2317	337	708	895	920	447	1429	1315	1201	676	339	585	68

A17B: Write to public officials

	TOTAL	M	F	White	Black	NE	NC	S	W	Yes	No	None	Mari-juana Only	Few Pills	More Pills	Any Her-oin
1. I probably won't do this	19.8	17.4	21.6	17.7	26.9	21.3	17.8	20.0	20.5	12.0	27.3	18.6	19.1	20.6	21.1	19.1
2. Don't know	44.4	44.4	44.6	44.8	43.8	41.5	45.5	46.9	42.1	41.4	47.5	44.3	44.5	43.3	44.7	50.0
3. I probably will do this	24.7	27.1	22.6	24.9	26.2	25.1	22.6	25.4	27.1	32.3	17.4	26.5	23.7	24.8	23.4	17.6
4. I have already done this	11.1	11.1	11.1	12.6	3.7	12.1	14.1	7.6	10.3	14.3	7.8	10.7	12.6	11.3	10.6	13.2
Item 6400 N(Wtd)	2870	1364	1392	2238	324	694	863	878	435	1385	1274	1159	649	335	564	68

A17C: Give money to a political candidate or cause

	TOTAL	M	F	White	Black	NE	NC	S	W	Yes	No	None	Mari-juana Only	Few Pills	More Pills	Any Her-oin
1. I probably won't do this	39.5	41.0	37.6	38.2	42.5	41.3	38.9	40.0	36.6	31.3	47.9	34.4	41.1	36.7	47.8	40.6
2. Don't know	37.3	35.9	39.0	38.1	35.1	36.9	37.9	36.0	39.3	40.3	35.3	41.8	38.0	34.6	29.7	31.9
3. I probably will do this	17.6	16.9	18.5	17.9	18.3	16.6	16.1	18.7	19.9	21.8	12.4	19.8	15.3	20.7	15.6	15.9
4. I have already done this	5.7	6.3	4.9	5.8	4.1	5.2	7.1	5.3	4.2	6.6	4.4	4.0	5.6	8.0	6.8	11.6
Item 6410 N(Wtd)	2990	1439	1430	2335	339	710	905	923	453	1439	1326	1215	679	338	590	69

A17D: Work in a political campaign

	TOTAL	M	F	White	Black	NE	NC	S	W	Yes	No	None	Mari-juana Only	Few Pills	More Pills	Any Her-oin
1. I probably won't do this	47.1	51.2	42.7	47.5	43.2	46.5	48.6	44.6	50.1	36.5	57.9	45.3	51.3	44.3	48.2	36.2
2. Don't know	35.3	32.9	37.9	34.7	38.7	36.1	34.3	36.6	33.3	39.9	30.7	37.5	32.9	34.6	33.7	39.1
3. I probably will do this	10.2	8.9	11.2	9.7	12.8	9.8	10.4	11.2	8.4	14.0	5.9	10.1	8.9	14.7	8.6	13.0
4. I have already done this	7.4	7.1	8.1	8.1	5.4	7.6	6.6	7.8	8.2	9.6	5.6	7.1	6.9	6.5	9.5	11.6
Item 6420 N(Wtd)	3000	1442	1437	2347	336	712	910	927	451	1445	1331	1217	684	341	591	69

A17E: Participate in a lawful demonstration

	TOTAL	M	F	White	Black	NE	NC	S	W	Yes	No	None	Mari-juana Only	Few Pills	More Pills	Any Her-oin
1. I probably won't do this	35.5	31.9	39.0	35.4	30.0	28.5	36.6	37.2	40.8	29.1	42.0	41.7	33.0	32.4	27.9	26.1
2. Don't know	44.1	44.2	43.6	44.4	44.8	45.8	45.5	43.1	40.6	45.5	42.2	44.5	45.7	39.4	44.8	36.2
3. I probably will do this	16.3	18.8	14.3	16.1	21.1	20.1	14.3	16.3	14.5	20.1	12.7	12.2	17.7	21.8	20.3	17.4
4. I have already done this	4.1	5.1	3.1	4.1	4.2	5.6	3.5	3.4	4.0	5.2	3.1	1.7	3.7	6.5	6.8	20.3
Item 6430 N(Wtd)	2987	1435	1431	2333	337	710	906	923	448	1434	1329	1210	682	340	587	69

A17F: Boycott certain products or stores

	TOTAL	M	F	White	Black	NE	NC	S	W	Yes	No	None	Mari-juana Only	Few Pills	More Pills	Any Her-oin
1. I probably won't do this	34.9	32.6	37.4	33.6	39.0	22.4	35.1	42.3	38.9	28.0	42.0	39.8	33.0	32.6	28.5	33.3
2. Don't know	40.0	39.7	40.3	40.7	38.1	42.7	43.6	34.7	39.6	40.9	39.6	38.3	41.2	39.7	43.0	31.9
3. I probably will do this	17.8	19.3	16.4	18.2	17.3	25.0	15.4	16.1	14.9	21.5	13.4	17.2	19.2	18.5	17.8	15.9
4. I have already done this	7.2	8.4	5.9	7.5	6.0	9.9	5.8	6.9	6.4	9.6	4.9	4.7	6.6	8.8	10.7	17.4
Item 6440 N(Wtd)	2994	1437	1436	2342	336	709	910	925	450	1444	1327	1216	682	340	589	69

QUESTIONNAIRE FORM 2 1976	TOTAL	SEX		RACE		REGION				4YR COLLEGE PLANS		ILLICIT DRUG USE: LIFETIME				
		M	F	White	Black	NE	NC	S	W	Yes	No	None	Marijuana Only	Few Pills	More Pills	Any Heroin
Weighted No. of Cases:	3036	1453	1445	2358	343	723	919	934	460	1450	1342	1223	687	343	597	69
% of Weighted Total:	100.0	47.9	47.6	77.7	11.3	23.8	30.3	30.8	15.2	47.8	44.2	40.3	22.6	11.3	19.7	2.3

A18: How much do you agree or disagree with each of the following statements?

A18A: The U.S. should begin a gradual program of disarming whether other countries do or not

	TOTAL	M	F	White	Black	NE	NC	S	W	Yes	No	None	Mari. Only	Few Pills	More Pills	Any Heroin
1. Disagree	43.5	55.2	31.8	45.8	31.8	42.5	40.6	48.8	39.7	44.5	42.2	42.9	46.8	45.6	41.4	37.3
2. Mostly disagree	18.8	17.7	19.5	19.7	14.2	20.9	22.0	14.6	17.9	20.9	17.1	19.7	18.6	18.3	18.4	14.9
3. Neither	20.3	14.1	26.7	19.8	21.3	18.9	20.8	19.0	24.6	17.5	23.7	19.8	19.9	21.0	21.4	16.4
4. Mostly agree	11.4	7.9	15.3	10.6	17.6	11.3	12.2	10.3	12.5	11.7	11.0	12.0	10.4	8.3	11.5	19.4
5. Agree	6.0	5.1	6.8	4.0	15.1	6.6	4.5	7.3	5.1	5.3	6.0	5.7	4.2	6.8	7.3	11.9
Item 6450 N(Wtd)	2944	1436	1392	2317	324	684	891	920	448	1421	1309	1196	673	338	575	67

A18B: There may be times when the U.S. should go to war to protect the rights of other countries

	TOTAL	M	F	White	Black	NE	NC	S	W	Yes	No	None	Mari. Only	Few Pills	More Pills	Any Heroin
1. Disagree	21.1	20.2	21.8	19.3	30.4	24.9	16.5	23.0	20.8	16.9	25.4	19.3	20.8	18.0	26.2	29.0
2. Mostly disagree	24.5	23.1	25.9	25.4	18.5	23.6	27.0	22.6	24.6	26.0	23.4	22.7	25.2	29.9	25.5	23.2
3. Neither	16.3	14.8	17.5	16.6	14.0	16.5	18.9	13.3	17.4	16.5	16.4	16.2	15.8	13.3	19.0	18.8
4. Mostly agree	24.9	25.1	24.8	26.5	17.6	24.5	25.6	25.2	23.7	28.8	21.3	27.5	25.7	24.3	20.0	17.4
5. Agree	13.2	16.7	9.9	12.1	19.6	10.4	12.1	16.0	13.6	11.7	13.6	14.4	12.7	14.8	9.2	10.1
Item 5690 N(Wtd)	2975	1436	1422	2328	336	702	899	926	448	1433	1320	1205	678	338	585	69

A18C: The U.S. should be willing to go to war to protect its own economic interests

	TOTAL	M	F	White	Black	NE	NC	S	W	Yes	No	None	Mari. Only	Few Pills	More Pills	Any Heroin
1. Disagree	8.4	7.9	8.5	7.8	8.7	11.4	6.0	7.0	11.8	8.7	7.8	7.1	8.6	6.2	11.7	8.8
2. Mostly disagree	11.4	10.2	12.8	11.8	7.2	13.5	11.7	8.9	12.7	12.7	9.7	9.3	12.1	12.4	13.9	13.2
3. Neither	17.6	17.3	18.4	19.0	9.9	18.7	21.3	12.1	20.3	18.0	18.0	18.7	17.6	16.0	17.5	22.1
4. Mostly agree	31.6	30.0	32.2	31.8	30.7	31.8	32.3	31.8	29.4	32.4	30.6	32.0	30.7	32.5	30.4	23.5
5. Agree	30.9	34.7	28.1	29.6	43.6	24.5	28.8	40.2	25.8	28.1	34.0	32.8	30.9	32.8	26.2	32.4
Item 6460 N(Wtd)	2961	1437	1405	2321	335	695	897	920	449	1431	1312	1195	677	338	588	68

A18D: The only good reason for the U.S. to go to war is to defend against an attack on our own country

	TOTAL	M	F	White	Black	NE	NC	S	W	Yes	No	None	Mari. Only	Few Pills	More Pills	Any Heroin
1. Disagree	8.3	9.7	7.0	8.0	12.5	7.6	7.9	10.2	6.5	8.2	8.1	8.4	8.2	9.1	7.2	7.2
2. Mostly disagree	12.4	13.3	11.4	13.0	10.7	13.3	11.4	12.6	12.8	13.2	11.8	12.9	13.6	10.9	9.9	10.1
3. Neither	8.8	7.1	10.6	8.9	9.3	8.4	11.3	7.0	8.1	8.7	8.7	9.0	9.6	7.9	8.2	14.5
4. Mostly agree	32.3	31.2	33.6	33.2	28.4	31.4	33.5	32.4	31.0	35.4	29.9	32.6	31.5	33.4	32.4	34.8
5. Agree	38.1	38.7	37.5	36.9	39.4	39.3	35.8	37.8	41.3	34.4	41.6	37.1	37.2	38.7	42.3	31.9
Item 6470 N(Wtd)	2975	1433	1420	2329	335	700	901	929	445	1434	1318	1206	674	341	586	69

A18E: The U.S. does not need to have greater military power than the soviet union

	TOTAL	M	F	White	Black	NE	NC	S	W	Yes	No	None	Mari. Only	Few Pills	More Pills	Any Heroin
1. Disagree	36.7	41.1	32.5	36.4	43.8	34.0	29.5	48.9	30.1	32.8	41.1	38.9	34.0	41.9	33.2	36.2
2. Mostly disagree	22.2	21.7	22.5	22.6	18.4	22.8	22.3	21.2	23.2	24.5	20.0	22.5	21.7	21.8	21.5	27.5
3. Neither	18.9	15.5	22.7	19.0	17.8	19.0	24.2	13.2	20.3	18.4	19.8	18.9	22.0	14.7	18.6	14.5
4. Mostly agree	12.5	11.4	13.4	12.8	11.2	12.1	15.1	10.0	13.4	13.6	10.9	12.0	12.9	11.8	12.5	14.5
5. Agree	9.6	10.3	9.0	9.2	9.1	12.2	8.9	6.6	13.2	10.8	8.2	7.7	9.3	10.3	14.2	5.8
Item 6480 N(Wtd)	2963	1434	1412	2325	331	694	897	924	448	1432	1317	1198	676	339	585	69

A18F: The U.S. ought to have much more military power than any other nation in the world

	TOTAL	M	F	White	Black	NE	NC	S	W	Yes	No	None	Mari. Only	Few Pills	More Pills	Any Heroin
1. Disagree	14.2	13.0	15.1	13.7	10.8	19.0	13.3	9.6	18.0	15.7	11.9	11.6	14.2	14.7	19.0	16.2
2. Mostly disagree	17.7	17.5	18.1	18.9	12.3	18.0	21.5	13.7	18.0	22.2	13.7	18.3	18.1	15.3	17.9	16.2
3. Neither	26.7	23.4	30.6	27.7	21.6	27.2	29.1	23.6	27.3	26.2	28.0	28.4	26.4	23.3	27.7	26.5
4. Mostly agree	20.4	20.9	19.0	19.8	24.9	18.0	19.9	23.7	18.4	18.6	21.2	21.0	21.1	22.7	15.7	25.0
5. Agree	21.1	25.2	17.1	19.9	30.5	17.8	16.1	29.6	18.4	17.2	25.2	20.9	20.1	23.9	19.7	16.2
Item 6490 N(Wtd)	2968	1434	1413	2324	334	695	899	923	450	1433	1316	1199	678	339	585	68

QUESTIONNAIRE FORM 2 1976	TOTAL	SEX		RACE		REGION				4YR COLLEGE PLANS		ILLICIT DRUG USE: LIFETIME				
		M	F	White	Black	NE	NC	S	W	Yes	No	None	Marijuana Only	Few Pills	More Pills	Any Heroin
Weighted No. of Cases:	3036	1453	1445	2358	343	723	919	934	460	1450	1342	1223	687	343	597	69
% of Weighted Total:	100.0	47.9	47.6	77.7	11.3	23.8	30.3	30.8	15.2	47.8	44.2	40.3	22.6	11.3	19.7	2.3

A18G: Our present foreign policy is based on our own narrow economic and power interests

1. Disagree	5.8	6.0	5.7	5.5	7.4	7.2	4.1	7.3	4.3	6.5	4.9	6.4	6.3	4.5	4.6	8.8
2. Mostly disagree	11.4	13.1	9.8	11.2	12.3	12.0	11.5	11.8	9.4	14.4	8.5	12.4	12.5	11.3	8.3	14.7
3. Neither	41.1	36.1	46.6	44.1	28.0	39.0	44.6	37.4	44.6	37.1	45.3	40.2	39.6	44.5	44.1	38.2
4. Mostly agree	27.8	29.7	25.6	27.4	30.5	26.3	29.3	26.8	29.3	28.9	27.2	26.2	29.6	24.9	30.1	23.5
5. Agree	13.8	15.1	12.3	11.9	21.8	15.5	10.4	16.7	12.4	13.1	14.2	14.8	11.9	14.8	13.0	14.7
Item 6500 N(Wtd)	2910	1417	1377	2284	325	684	885	904	437	1410	1293	1178	666	337	569	68

A18H: Servicemen should obey orders without question

1. Disagree	20.0	17.6	22.3	18.3	30.1	25.4	15.8	19.5	20.8	21.0	18.7	17.1	19.4	21.8	25.1	19.4
2. Mostly disagree	22.1	18.9	25.2	22.2	17.5	23.4	23.0	19.8	22.6	24.0	20.1	22.9	22.0	22.6	21.1	16.4
3. Neither	18.7	16.8	21.0	19.2	15.4	16.9	22.4	15.4	20.4	18.0	19.4	18.9	19.1	15.9	18.8	25.4
4. Mostly agree	26.4	29.9	23.1	28.0	22.0	22.7	27.4	29.3	23.9	26.1	26.9	26.8	25.0	28.8	26.5	23.9
5. Agree	12.9	16.9	8.3	12.3	15.1	11.5	11.4	15.9	12.2	11.0	14.8	14.4	14.5	10.9	8.3	13.4
Item 6510 N(Wtd)	2972	1437	1415	2332	332	697	901	924	451	1431	1322	1200	677	340	589	67

A19: This section deals with activities which may be against the rules or against the law. We hope you will answer all of these questions. However, if you find a question which you cannot answer honestly, we would prefer that you leave it blank. Remember, your answers will never be connected with your name. During the LAST 12 MONTHS, how often have you...

A19A: Argued or had a fight with either of your parents

1. Not at all	13.1	16.5	9.2	9.4	33.3	8.9	12.7	17.2	12.9	12.0	13.0	16.9	10.9	7.1	9.7	13.4
2. Once	9.9	10.7	9.2	8.4	18.5	8.3	8.9	12.0	10.0	11.6	8.1	12.9	8.8	10.3	4.8	4.5
3. Twice	11.9	11.1	12.1	11.8	8.8	12.6	10.4	12.6	12.2	11.8	12.1	12.9	9.9	13.2	11.2	9.0
4. 3 or 4 times	25.7	26.2	25.5	27.5	17.9	27.3	26.1	23.4	27.3	26.5	25.6	24.8	30.0	29.7	21.7	19.4
5. 5 or more times	39.4	35.6	43.8	42.7	21.5	43.0	42.1	34.9	37.7	38.0	41.3	32.6	40.4	39.7	52.5	52.2
Item 6520 N(Wtd)	2974	1428	1430	2334	330	707	900	915	451	1428	1326	1210	680	340	589	67

A19B: Hit an instructor or supervisor

1. Not at all	96.7	95.2	98.7	96.8	97.6	96.6	96.3	97.6	96.3	98.0	96.2	98.5	97.2	97.1	94.6	85.1
2. Once	1.9	2.8	.8	2.0	1.2	2.1	1.9	1.4	2.4	1.4	2.3	1.2	1.5	1.8	3.0	6.0
3. Twice	.8	1.2	.4	.8	1.2	.7	1.0	1.0	.7	.3	1.1	.2	1.0	.9	1.4	4.5
4. 3 or 4 times	.1	.2	-	.1	-	.1	.2	.1	.2	-	.2	-	.3	.3	.2	-
5. 5 or more times	.4	.5	.1	.3	.3	.4	.7	.1	.7	.3	.2	-	.1	.3	.8	3.0
Item 6530 N(Wtd)	2992	1440	1435	2345	334	712	908	918	454	1441	1327	1219	684	342	591	67

A19C: Gotten into a serious fight in school or at work

1. Not at all	85.8	80.6	91.8	86.7	85.9	85.7	86.3	86.8	83.5	89.5	83.7	92.4	84.1	79.8	81.0	69.1
2. Once	8.2	10.9	5.3	7.8	8.1	8.6	7.7	7.8	9.5	6.9	8.9	4.9	10.1	11.4	11.2	5.9
3. Twice	3.0	4.1	1.9	3.0	2.7	3.2	3.3	2.2	4.0	2.6	3.5	1.0	3.7	5.6	4.7	8.8
4. 3 or 4 times	1.8	2.6	1.0	1.6	2.7	1.4	1.4	2.4	2.0	.8	2.6	1.2	1.6	2.3	2.2	7.4
5. 5 or more times	1.0	1.7	.1	.9	.9	1.1	1.3	.8	.9	.4	1.3	.6	.6	1.2	.8	8.8
Item 6540 N(Wtd)	2994	1439	1435	2345	334	713	907	918	455	1441	1328	1220	684	342	590	68

A19D: Taken part in a fight where a group of your friends were against another group

1. Not at all	85.0	81.0	89.5	85.4	84.7	86.1	85.7	84.6	82.8	88.7	81.5	91.4	83.4	82.7	78.4	58.2
2. Once	8.9	10.2	7.4	8.8	9.3	7.2	9.2	9.0	11.2	7.3	11.1	6.0	9.7	9.4	12.4	17.9
3. Twice	2.8	3.9	1.5	2.6	4.2	3.1	1.9	3.5	2.6	1.5	3.5	1.1	3.5	3.8	4.2	7.5
4. 3 or 4 times	2.1	2.8	1.5	2.2	.6	1.8	2.6	1.6	2.2	1.7	2.5	1.0	1.9	3.5	2.7	10.4
5. 5 or more times	1.2	2.1	.3	1.1	1.2	1.7	.7	1.3	1.3	.8	1.4	.5	1.5	.6	2.4	6.0
Item 6550 N(Wtd)	2989	1435	1435	2342	334	711	907	916	454	1437	1327	1220	682	342	589	67

QUESTIONNAIRE FORM 2 1976	TOTAL	SEX		RACE		REGION				4YR COLLEGE PLANS		ILLICIT DRUG USE: LIFETIME				
		M	F	White	Black	NE	NC	S	W	Yes	No	None	Marijuana Only	Few Pills	More Pills	Any Heroin
Weighted No. of Cases:	3036	1453	1445	2358	343	723	919	934	460	1450	1342	1223	687	343	597	69
% of Weighted Total:	100.0	47.9	47.6	77.7	11.3	23.8	30.3	30.8	15.2	47.8	44.2	40.3	22.6	11.3	19.7	2.3
A19E: Hurt someone badly enough to need bandages or a doctor																
1. Not at all	90.2	83.6	97.6	90.9	91.0	91.7	90.5	89.2	89.2	91.9	89.5	95.4	90.1	87.6	85.8	64.7
2. Once	6.5	10.6	1.8	6.4	6.0	5.4	6.3	7.1	7.5	6.0	6.9	3.3	6.1	8.0	10.3	16.2
3. Twice	1.5	2.5	.3	1.3	.3	1.1	1.4	1.7	1.8	1.0	1.7	.5	1.9	2.9	1.9	2.9
4. 3 or 4 times	.9	1.6	.1	.8	.9	1.0	1.0	.9	.9	.7	1.1	.6	1.6	.6	.8	4.4
5. 5 or more times	.9	1.6	.1	.5	1.8	1.0	.8	1.1	.7	.5	.9	.2	.3	.9	1.4	11.8
Item 6560 N(Wtd)	2988	1437	1433	2341	335	710	908	917	454	1441	1326	1219	684	339	590	68
A19F: Used a knife or gun or some other thing (like a club) to get something from a person																
1. Not at all	97.5	96.1	99.3	98.2	95.2	97.6	98.7	96.6	96.5	98.3	97.3	99.2	98.2	98.0	95.1	82.4
2. Once	1.2	1.7	.6	1.0	2.1	1.3	.4	1.7	1.3	.7	1.5	.4	1.2	1.2	2.4	5.9
3. Twice	.5	.7	.1	.2	.9	.4	.6	.7	.4	.4	.5	.2	.1	-	.8	5.9
4. 3 or 4 times	.4	.8	.1	.3	.9	.4	.1	.5	.7	.5	.2	-	.3	.9	.8	1.5
5. 5 or more times	.4	.8	-	.2	.6	.4	.2	.3	.9	.2	.5	.2	-	-	.8	4.4
Item 6570 N(Wtd)	2992	1438	1435	2345	334	712	908	919	454	1440	1329	1222	683	342	590	68
A19G: Taken something not belonging to you worth under $50																
1. Not at all	69.0	59.9	78.6	68.1	76.4	67.4	66.0	74.5	66.7	70.6	67.8	81.6	64.6	64.5	51.9	50.0
2. Once	13.5	16.0	10.8	13.7	11.8	13.1	14.3	12.8	14.2	13.1	13.9	9.5	16.0	16.4	17.5	16.2
3. Twice	6.5	8.2	4.6	6.9	4.2	8.4	7.0	5.2	5.3	5.5	7.0	4.1	6.9	6.7	11.4	2.9
4. 3 or 4 times	5.3	6.5	3.9	5.5	4.5	5.3	6.8	3.0	6.9	5.3	5.5	2.2	5.7	6.7	9.2	17.6
5. 5 or more times	5.7	9.4	2.0	5.9	3.6	6.0	6.0	4.6	6.9	5.4	5.8	2.6	6.6	5.6	10.2	13.2
Item 6580 N(Wtd)	2964	1423	1424	2321	330	703	902	909	451	1424	1320	1209	681	341	578	68
A19H: Taken something not belonging to you worth over $50																
1. Not at all	93.9	89.7	98.7	94.7	93.7	93.5	93.2	95.4	92.5	96.0	92.4	99.1	93.0	93.8	87.7	70.1
2. Once	3.0	5.2	.6	2.7	3.3	2.8	3.5	2.8	3.1	2.1	3.8	.5	4.7	4.4	4.8	10.4
3. Twice	.9	1.3	.2	.8	.3	1.7	.9	.3	1.1	.6	1.1	.3	.9	.3	2.0	6.0
4. 3 or 4 times	.9	1.7	.2	.9	.9	.8	1.3	.4	1.1	.4	1.5	-	.7	.9	2.6	6.0
5. 5 or more times	1.2	2.0	.2	.9	1.5	1.0	1.1	1.0	2.2	.9	1.3	.2	.7	.9	2.9	6.0
Item 6590 N(Wtd)	2984	1431	1435	2337	334	711	903	916	454	1438	1326	1219	682	340	587	67
A19I: Taken something from a store without paying for it																
1. Not at all	67.7	62.2	74.0	68.6	63.4	63.6	68.5	70.2	67.8	71.2	64.6	83.8	63.3	63.5	47.4	36.8
2. Once	13.5	13.1	13.3	13.0	15.9	13.1	12.6	15.3	12.3	11.6	15.3	8.6	13.0	18.8	18.7	16.2
3. Twice	7.2	9.0	5.2	6.9	9.8	10.3	7.1	5.6	5.5	6.8	7.5	3.4	10.1	7.4	10.9	13.2
4. 3 or 4 times	4.9	5.7	4.2	5.3	3.0	6.4	5.3	3.5	4.6	4.6	5.2	2.1	5.9	6.2	9.2	7.4
5. 5 or more times	6.7	9.9	3.3	6.2	7.9	6.6	6.6	5.4	9.7	5.8	7.4	2.1	7.8	4.1	13.9	26.5
Item 6600 N(Wtd)	2979	1430	1432	2339	328	708	907	910	454	1433	1327	1213	683	340	589	68
A19J: Taken a car that didn't belong to someone in your family without permission of the owner																
1. Not at all	95.8	93.9	97.7	96.1	94.3	96.9	94.6	96.4	95.4	96.8	95.1	98.5	97.7	95.3	90.5	82.4
2. Once	2.1	3.0	1.2	1.9	3.0	1.5	3.0	1.8	1.5	1.7	2.3	1.1	.9	1.5	4.9	5.9
3. Twice	1.1	1.7	.6	1.1	.6	.8	1.0	1.1	2.0	.8	1.5	.2	.7	2.9	2.4	2.9
4. 3 or 4 times	.3	.1	.4	.1	1.2	.1	.3	.2	.2	.3	.2	-	.3	-	.3	4.4
5. 5 or more times	.7	1.3	.1	.7	.9	.4	1.1	.4	.7	.3	1.0	.2	.6	-	2.0	2.9
Item 6610 N(Wtd)	2993	1439	1436	2345	335	712	908	919	454	1442	1329	1222	684	342	590	68

QUESTIONNAIRE FORM 2 1976	TOTAL	SEX		RACE		REGION				4YR COLLEGE PLANS		ILLICIT DRUG USE: LIFETIME				
		M	F	White	Black	NE	NC	S	W	Yes	No	None	Marijuana Only	Few Pills	More Pills	Any Heroin
Weighted No. of Cases:	3036	1453	1445	2358	343	723	919	934	460	1450	1342	1223	687	343	597	69
% of Weighted Total:	100.0	47.9	47.6	77.7	11.3	23.8	30.3	30.8	15.2	47.8	44.2	40.3	22.6	11.3	19.7	2.3
A19K: Taken part of a car without permission of the owner																
1. Not at all	94.1	89.4	98.7	93.9	97.3	92.4	93.3	96.9	92.5	95.8	92.7	98.8	93.3	92.9	88.3	79.4
2. Once	3.2	5.4	1.0	3.3	1.8	3.8	4.0	1.5	3.5	2.0	3.9	.7	3.7	4.1	5.4	13.2
3. Twice	1.2	2.4	.2	1.4	-	2.3	1.1	.9	.7	.9	1.4	.2	1.6	1.5	2.2	1.5
4. 3 or 4 times	.8	1.4	.1	.6	.3	.8	1.0	-	1.5	.6	1.0	.2	.7	.9	1.9	1.5
5. 5 or more times	.8	1.5	.1	.9	.3	.6	.7	.7	1.8	.6	1.0	.1	.6	.9	2.0	2.9
Item 6620 N(Wtd)	2977	1429	1434	2336	330	709	905	910	454	1437	1324	1215	682	339	588	68
A19L: Gone into some house or building when you weren't supposed to be there																
1. Not at all	76.7	69.8	83.6	76.5	78.1	73.0	75.8	80.9	75.6	77.5	75.2	83.7	77.9	71.0	66.9	49.3
2. Once	11.5	14.1	9.3	11.7	12.0	12.9	10.6	11.1	11.7	11.1	12.2	9.5	9.5	16.7	14.6	20.9
3. Twice	5.6	8.3	3.1	5.8	3.6	6.0	5.9	4.5	7.0	5.2	6.2	3.5	6.4	5.9	7.1	17.9
4. 3 or 4 times	3.3	4.0	2.4	3.3	4.2	3.4	4.4	2.3	2.6	3.6	3.0	2.1	3.5	2.9	6.3	1.5
5. 5 or more times	2.9	4.0	1.5	2.8	2.1	4.5	3.3	1.2	3.1	2.5	3.2	1.2	2.6	3.8	4.9	10.4
Item 6630 N(Wtd)	2980	1436	1429	2337	333	705	905	917	454	1433	1329	1214	683	341	590	67
A19M: Set fire to someone's property on purpose																
1. Not at all	98.3	97.1	99.5	98.7	98.5	98.5	99.0	98.2	96.9	98.8	98.0	99.7	98.2	99.4	95.4	91.2
2. Once	.8	1.5	.2	.6	.9	.8	.6	.7	2.0	.7	1.0	.2	1.5	-	2.0	1.5
3. Twice	.5	.9	.1	.5	.3	.4	.3	.9	.4	.3	.6	.1	.3	.6	1.2	5.9
4. 3 or 4 times	.1	.1	-	*	-	-	.1	.2	.2	.1	.1	-	-	-	.3	1.5
5. 5 or more times	.3	.4	.1	.2	.3	.3	-	.2	.9	.1	.3	.1	-	-	1.0	-
Item 6640 N(Wtd)	2990	1439	1436	2346	334	711	907	919	453	1442	1329	1221	684	342	591	68
A19N: Damaged school property on purpose																
1. Not at all	88.1	82.0	94.4	88.0	89.2	85.8	86.9	91.4	86.9	90.3	86.4	94.1	85.3	86.8	81.0	74.2
2. Once	6.7	10.1	3.2	6.8	6.6	8.1	7.0	5.4	6.4	5.5	8.0	3.6	8.5	7.1	10.2	10.6
3. Twice	2.7	3.9	1.4	2.8	1.8	3.3	3.1	1.5	3.3	2.7	2.3	1.1	4.0	1.5	4.6	10.6
4. 3 or 4 times	1.4	2.1	.6	1.4	1.5	1.8	1.7	1.0	1.1	.9	1.8	.7	1.5	3.8	1.7	-
5. 5 or more times	1.1	2.0	.3	1.1	.9	.8	1.3	.7	2.0	.6	1.5	.6	.9	.6	2.7	4.5
Item 6650 N(Wtd)	2976	1432	1431	2334	333	706	904	915	451	1437	1322	1218	681	340	588	66
A19O: Damaged property at work on purpose																
1. Not at all	94.2	90.1	98.6	94.1	96.1	94.2	93.3	95.5	93.4	95.5	93.5	97.3	94.0	93.3	90.5	88.2
2. Once	3.1	5.2	.9	3.3	1.8	3.1	3.0	2.9	3.5	2.9	3.1	1.4	4.0	4.1	4.1	7.4
3. Twice	1.3	2.0	.4	1.2	1.2	1.3	1.9	.9	1.3	.6	1.7	.8	.9	1.2	2.5	1.5
4. 3 or 4 times	.6	1.3	-	.7	-	.8	.7	.1	1.3	.6	.8	.2	.4	1.2	1.4	1.5
5. 5 or more times	.7	1.3	.1	.7	.6	.7	1.1	.4	.4	.5	.8	.3	.7	.3	1.7	2.9
Item 6660 N(Wtd)	2980	1435	1433	2339	334	708	902	916	454	1440	1323	1219	679	341	591	68
A19P: Gotten into trouble with police because of something you did																
1. Not at all	82.3	72.0	92.7	81.4	91.3	86.2	77.1	84.9	81.2	86.4	78.4	92.9	79.2	78.9	69.3	48.5
2. Once	9.7	14.4	4.8	10.2	5.4	6.5	13.2	8.7	9.5	8.6	11.1	5.0	11.3	11.1	15.3	25.0
3. Twice	4.6	7.6	1.5	4.9	2.4	3.4	6.0	3.7	5.3	3.3	5.2	1.2	7.0	5.0	7.6	13.2
4. 3 or 4 times	2.4	4.0	.8	2.5	.9	3.0	2.3	2.0	2.6	1.2	3.6	.6	1.9	3.5	5.8	5.9
5. 5 or more times	1.1	1.9	.1	1.0	.3	1.1	1.4	.7	1.1	.5	1.7	.3	.6	1.2	2.2	8.8
Item 6670 N(Wtd)	2982	1436	1433	2340	332	710	903	916	453	1438	1327	1218	682	342	589	68
A20: The next questions are about some things which may have happened TO YOU. During the LAST 12 MONTHS, how often...																

*=less than .05 per cent.

QUESTIONNAIRE FORM 2 1976	TOTAL	SEX		RACE		REGION				4YR COLLEGE PLANS		ILLICIT DRUG USE: LIFETIME				
		M	F	White	Black	NE	NC	S	W	Yes	No	None	Mari- juana Only	Few Pills	More Pills	Any Her- oin
Weighted No. of Cases:	3036	1453	1445	2358	343	723	919	934	460	1450	1342	1223	687	343	597	69
% of Weighted Total:	100.0	47.9	47.6	77.7	11.3	23.8	30.3	30.8	15.2	47.8	44.2	40.3	22.6	11.3	19.7	2.3
A20A: Has something of yours (worth under $50) been stolen?																
1. Not at all	55.4	49.5	61.0	55.2	52.9	59.3	54.3	56.4	49.3	51.5	58.9	61.4	53.0	49.9	49.2	44.1
2. Once	25.8	26.6	25.7	26.0	27.7	23.5	26.5	25.8	28.1	28.1	23.6	24.5	26.0	29.1	26.8	30.9
3. Twice	10.8	12.9	8.4	10.8	9.7	10.3	11.5	9.4	12.7	11.7	10.0	8.4	12.6	13.1	12.0	14.7
4. 3 or 4 times	6.3	8.6	3.9	6.5	6.7	5.5	5.9	6.5	8.0	6.8	5.8	4.6	6.5	6.2	9.3	7.4
5. 5 or more times	1.7	2.4	1.1	1.5	3.0	1.4	1.7	2.0	1.8	1.8	1.7	1.2	1.8	2.1	2.7	2.9
Item 6680 N(Wtd)	2958	1422	1423	2324	329	706	894	911	448	1423	1316	1210	677	337	583	68
A20B: Has something of yours (worth over $50) been stolen?																
1. Not at all	87.8	84.0	91.8	89.1	82.8	89.7	89.0	86.9	83.9	87.2	88.7	90.9	88.0	87.0	82.7	74.2
2. Once	9.3	12.0	6.7	8.3	15.0	8.3	8.5	9.7	11.6	9.9	8.7	7.5	9.4	9.7	12.0	16.7
3. Twice	2.2	3.2	1.1	2.1	1.9	1.4	1.6	2.9	3.4	2.4	2.0	1.5	1.9	2.7	3.5	3.0
4. 3 or 4 times	.4	.5	.2	.4	-	.4	.5	.3	.7	.3	.5	.1	.3	.6	1.1	3.0
5. 5 or more times	.2	.4	.1	.2	.3	.3	.3	.1	.2	.2	.1	.1	.1	-	.5	1.5
Item 6690 N(Wtd)	2907	1390	1408	2287	320	697	875	895	440	1401	1292	1194	669	330	567	66
A20C: Has someone deliberately damaged your property (your car, clothing, etc.)?																
1. Not at all	69.2	61.0	77.5	69.4	71.1	73.2	68.2	68.9	65.4	69.6	69.4	73.8	71.4	62.8	61.7	57.4
2. Once	19.0	24.0	14.0	19.2	16.7	16.1	19.2	20.2	20.8	18.7	18.6	16.6	16.3	22.4	25.4	20.6
3. Twice	7.6	9.5	5.6	7.2	7.9	6.7	8.0	7.7	7.8	7.9	7.1	5.9	8.4	9.4	8.1	11.8
4. 3 or 4 times	3.4	4.1	2.3	3.2	4.0	3.6	3.1	2.8	4.7	3.0	3.7	2.8	3.4	4.1	3.6	2.9
5. 5 or more times	.9	1.3	.6	.9	.6	.6	1.3	.5	1.3	.8	1.2	.7	.6	.9	1.0	5.9
Item 6700 N(Wtd)	2965	1422	1432	2332	329	704	897	913	451	1426	1324	1214	681	339	583	68
A20D: Has someone injured you with a weapon (like a knife, gun, or club)?																
1. Not at all	95.0	92.5	97.9	96.3	91.5	95.9	95.4	93.7	95.8	96.3	94.6	97.5	96.0	90.6	93.8	82.4
2. Once	3.4	5.5	1.3	2.7	6.6	2.3	2.9	4.8	3.3	2.4	3.9	2.1	2.9	7.0	3.6	7.4
3. Twice	.9	1.3	.4	.5	1.5	1.1	.8	1.0	.9	.8	1.1	.2	.9	1.8	1.4	5.9
4. 3 or 4 times	.2	.4	.1	.2	.3	.4	.1	.3	-	.2	.2	.2	.1	.6	.2	1.5
5. 5 or more times	.4	.3	.3	.3	-	.3	.9	.2	.2	.3	.3	-	-	.3	1.0	2.9
Item 6710 N(Wtd)	2970	1426	1433	2335	331	706	899	914	450	1429	1324	1216	680	342	584	68
A20E: Has someone threatened you with a weapon, but not actually injured you?																
1. Not at all	84.0	78.3	90.2	85.6	77.6	84.8	84.8	83.0	83.1	85.3	83.4	90.9	84.3	77.2	76.0	64.2
2. Once	9.9	12.3	7.1	8.8	13.9	10.2	9.2	10.5	9.8	10.0	10.0	6.0	10.1	16.3	14.1	13.4
3. Twice	3.2	4.9	1.5	3.1	4.2	3.1	3.1	2.9	4.0	2.5	3.6	1.5	3.5	3.3	5.0	14.9
4. 3 or 4 times	1.6	2.3	.8	1.3	2.7	1.1	1.6	2.3	1.1	.9	1.6	.7	2.0	1.8	2.2	1.5
5. 5 or more times	1.2	2.1	.4	1.2	1.5	.6	1.3	1.3	2.0	1.3	1.3	.8	.1	1.5	2.7	6.0
Item 6720 N(Wtd)	2962	1427	1427	2329	330	706	895	912	450	1424	1322	1211	683	338	583	67
A20F: Has someone injured you on purpose without using a weapon?																
1. Not at all	85.2	83.1	87.7	85.5	84.8	83.7	84.3	88.1	83.9	85.5	85.4	90.0	86.5	80.1	78.5	77.9
2. Once	8.7	10.1	6.9	8.7	9.1	10.1	8.6	7.0	10.3	9.0	8.1	6.2	8.3	13.5	11.0	8.8
3. Twice	3.2	3.7	2.8	3.2	3.0	3.4	3.9	2.9	2.5	3.0	3.3	1.8	2.4	4.1	5.7	5.9
4. 3 or 4 times	1.7	1.9	1.3	1.4	1.8	2.0	1.8	1.5	1.3	1.2	2.0	1.4	2.1	1.5	1.7	2.9
5. 5 or more times	1.2	1.3	1.1	1.2	1.2	.9	1.4	.7	2.2	1.2	1.2	.5	.7	.9	3.1	2.9
Item 6730 N(Wtd)	2956	1419	1428	2323	329	705	897	906	447	1423	1318	1210	676	342	582	68
A20G: Has an unarmed person threatened you with injury, but not actually injured you?																
1. Not at all	72.9	64.6	81.3	72.2	74.9	73.1	72.0	73.3	73.2	73.0	72.2	80.2	72.0	66.3	63.7	61.8
2. Once	14.3	17.2	11.3	14.2	14.1	14.1	14.4	15.9	11.6	14.1	14.7	10.8	15.0	18.8	18.6	13.2
3. Twice	4.7	6.7	2.7	4.9	4.9	5.0	5.2	4.1	4.5	4.4	5.2	3.6	5.1	5.3	5.3	7.4
4. 3 or 4 times	3.9	5.8	1.9	4.2	3.1	4.0	3.7	4.0	3.8	4.4	3.3	2.6	4.7	5.6	4.6	4.4
5. 5 or more times	4.3	5.7	2.9	4.5	3.4	4.0	4.7	2.8	6.7	4.2	4.7	2.8	3.2	4.4	7.4	13.2
Item 6740 N(Wtd)	2958	1423	1425	2328	327	703	898	908	448	1420	1323	1208	682	341	581	68

QUESTIONNAIRE FORM 2 1976	TOTAL	SEX		RACE		REGION				4YR COLLEGE PLANS		ILLICIT DRUG USE: LIFETIME				
		M	F	White	Black	NE	NC	S	W	Yes	No	None	Marijuana Only	Few Pills	More Pills	Any Heroin
Weighted No. of Cases:	3036	1453	1445	2358	343	723	919	934	460	1450	1342	1223	687	343	597	69
% of Weighted Total:	100.0	47.9	47.6	77.7	11.3	23.8	30.3	30.8	15.2	47.8	44.2	40.3	22.6	11.3	19.7	2.3

A21: The following questions concern cigarettes, alcohol, and a number of other drugs. How difficult do you think it would be for you to get each of the following types of drugs, if you wanted some?

A21A: Marijuana (pot, grass)

	TOTAL	M	F	White	Black	NE	NC	S	W	Yes	No	None	Mar-juana Only	Few Pills	More Pills	Any Her-oin
1. Probably impossible	5.3	4.6	5.8	3.0	15.6	3.8	3.6	8.5	4.5	3.5	6.8	10.7	.4	2.1	.8	1.4
2. Very difficult	2.7	2.3	3.0	1.7	8.6	2.0	1.8	4.0	2.7	2.0	3.1	4.9	.9	1.5	.8	-
3. Fairly difficult	4.6	3.7	5.6	4.1	6.7	3.7	4.0	5.9	4.5	5.2	4.3	8.8	1.6	3.8	1.4	-
4. Fairly easy	28.3	25.8	31.3	29.8	20.8	23.8	30.4	29.2	29.1	29.1	28.7	35.4	28.3	29.0	15.4	21.7
5. Very easy	59.1	63.7	54.3	61.4	48.3	66.4	60.2	52.5	58.9	60.2	57.2	40.3	68.7	63.9	81.3	75.4
Item 6750 N(Wtd)	2941	1417	1414	2314	327	702	892	904	443	1413	1317	1185	681	341	589	69

A21B: LSD

	TOTAL	M	F	White	Black	NE	NC	S	W	Yes	No	None	Mar-juana Only	Few Pills	More Pills	Any Her-oin
1. Probably impossible	17.2	15.9	17.8	12.3	40.4	15.9	13.0	22.4	17.4	14.1	18.4	21.8	16.1	14.7	9.5	2.9
2. Very difficult	17.0	19.1	14.8	17.1	17.6	16.4	18.6	15.9	16.9	17.9	16.4	18.8	18.1	19.5	12.4	8.8
3. Fairly difficult	28.4	28.9	28.7	30.7	18.8	26.1	30.2	29.4	26.7	29.3	29.3	26.7	30.6	31.6	29.0	17.6
4. Fairly easy	28.9	26.8	31.0	32.2	14.2	31.7	31.2	24.1	29.9	30.7	27.6	26.8	29.1	25.7	36.1	36.8
5. Very easy	8.5	9.3	7.6	7.7	9.0	10.0	7.2	8.2	9.1	8.1	8.2	6.0	6.0	8.6	12.9	33.8
Item 6760 N(Wtd)	2890	1402	1382	2271	324	687	872	892	438	1389	1296	1158	663	339	587	68

A21C: Some other psychedelic (mescaline, peyote, psilocybin, PCP, etc.)

	TOTAL	M	F	White	Black	NE	NC	S	W	Yes	No	None	Mar-juana Only	Few Pills	More Pills	Any Her-oin
1. Probably impossible	18.6	17.3	19.6	13.5	45.8	18.0	13.1	25.1	17.5	15.2	20.8	25.2	17.9	16.1	5.9	8.7
2. Very difficult	18.6	18.5	18.9	18.7	19.0	17.4	19.2	19.0	18.4	20.7	16.9	22.1	19.4	20.3	11.0	7.2
3. Fairly difficult	27.1	27.5	27.1	29.3	17.4	27.4	29.6	24.1	27.8	28.4	26.7	26.7	27.1	28.1	30.3	14.5
4. Fairly easy	27.8	27.7	27.9	31.0	11.5	29.1	29.9	25.1	27.4	28.7	27.5	21.4	29.3	26.3	40.2	37.7
5. Very easy	7.9	8.9	6.7	7.6	6.5	8.1	8.2	6.8	9.0	7.0	8.0	4.5	6.2	9.6	12.6	29.0
Item 6770 N(Wtd)	2865	1395	1364	2252	321	678	869	882	435	1378	1282	1143	665	335	580	69

A21D: Amphetamines (uppers, pep pills, bennies, speed)

	TOTAL	M	F	White	Black	NE	NC	S	W	Yes	No	None	Mar-juana Only	Few Pills	More Pills	Any Her-oin
1. Probably impossible	12.0	11.2	12.5	7.9	33.0	11.4	8.0	16.4	12.3	9.6	13.5	18.4	9.3	7.4	3.2	4.3
2. Very difficult	9.2	9.1	9.5	8.7	13.0	9.3	8.2	10.4	8.7	10.6	7.8	12.9	10.8	7.1	2.2	1.4
3. Fairly difficult	17.0	18.6	15.7	17.6	14.2	16.6	17.5	17.5	15.5	18.5	16.3	18.0	20.2	20.1	11.8	8.7
4. Fairly easy	40.3	39.7	40.6	43.3	27.2	41.5	43.6	36.9	38.7	40.5	40.0	38.1	42.3	39.2	44.0	37.7
5. Very easy	21.5	21.4	21.7	22.5	13.0	21.3	22.6	18.8	24.8	20.9	22.2	12.7	17.6	26.0	38.7	47.8
Item 6780 N(Wtd)	2899	1408	1383	2277	324	685	880	895	439	1391	1300	1164	669	339	586	69

A21E: Barbiturates (downers, goofballs, reds, yellows, etc.)

	TOTAL	M	F	White	Black	NE	NC	S	W	Yes	No	None	Mar-juana Only	Few Pills	More Pills	Any Her-oin
1. Probably impossible	13.8	12.5	14.8	9.5	35.7	13.0	9.0	18.5	14.8	10.9	15.5	19.7	12.9	8.6	3.9	7.2
2. Very difficult	11.1	11.5	10.8	11.1	12.6	11.0	11.3	10.7	12.1	12.3	10.2	13.5	13.3	11.2	5.3	-
3. Fairly difficult	20.6	22.1	19.1	21.5	16.0	19.6	23.0	19.2	20.3	21.3	20.7	20.5	21.3	25.4	19.5	10.1
4. Fairly easy	35.5	34.9	36.3	38.4	23.7	37.8	36.0	33.4	34.9	36.8	34.6	34.1	37.1	32.8	39.0	42.0
5. Very easy	18.9	18.9	18.9	19.6	12.0	18.6	20.6	18.1	17.8	18.7	18.9	12.1	15.4	21.9	32.2	39.1
Item 6790 N(Wtd)	2885	1403	1374	2263	325	683	873	891	438	1382	1294	1154	668	338	584	69

A21F: Tranquilizers

	TOTAL	M	F	White	Black	NE	NC	S	W	Yes	No	None	Mar-juana Only	Few Pills	More Pills	Any Her-oin
1. Probably impossible	10.0	9.8	9.6	5.8	30.4	9.7	6.7	13.9	9.1	7.4	10.7	13.6	8.3	7.1	3.4	5.9
2. Very difficult	7.3	7.7	6.8	6.4	12.4	5.9	7.1	7.7	8.9	6.2	8.1	8.2	8.0	5.0	6.0	2.9
3. Fairly difficult	17.1	18.8	15.8	17.7	14.6	14.3	20.8	15.1	18.5	17.8	17.4	16.7	20.9	15.9	15.1	20.6
4. Fairly easy	36.2	36.3	35.8	38.7	23.9	41.4	35.3	34.7	33.3	38.2	35.4	36.9	37.9	36.5	35.3	26.5
5. Very easy	29.3	27.4	32.0	31.4	18.6	28.5	30.3	28.5	30.1	30.4	28.4	24.7	24.9	35.6	40.0	41.2
Item 6800 N(Wtd)	2899	1408	1385	2282	322	691	876	894	438	1391	1301	1165	671	340	583	68

QUESTIONNAIRE FORM 2 1976	TOTAL	SEX		RACE		REGION				4YR COLLEGE PLANS		ILLICIT DRUG USE: LIFETIME				
		M	F	White	Black	NE	NC	S	W	Yes	No	None	Marijuana Only	Few Pills	More Pills	Any Heroin
Weighted No. of Cases:	3036	1453	1445	2358	343	723	919	934	460	1450	1342	1223	687	343	597	69
% of Weighted Total:	100.0	47.9	47.6	77.7	11.3	23.8	30.3	30.8	15.2	47.8	44.2	40.3	22.6	11.3	19.7	2.3

A21G: Cocaine

1. Probably impossible	18.8	16.6	21.1	15.0	35.5	18.6	15.0	23.6	17.1	16.6	20.0	25.1	16.9	17.6	8.2	2.9
2. Very difficult	19.5	21.1	18.1	20.7	14.3	17.6	20.4	19.5	20.3	20.4	18.6	21.2	22.8	19.7	15.3	1.4
3. Fairly difficult	27.7	28.2	27.6	30.4	17.8	24.5	31.5	28.3	24.0	28.4	28.8	27.0	29.8	26.8	29.6	21.7
4. Fairly easy	24.9	23.5	26.0	26.1	20.2	28.7	25.5	20.8	25.9	26.3	23.4	20.8	23.4	26.5	33.2	39.1
5. Very easy	9.1	10.5	7.3	7.9	12.1	10.5	7.6	7.8	12.5	8.5	9.2	5.9	7.3	9.1	13.9	33.3
Item 6810 N(Wtd)	2868	1394	1368	2257	321	683	869	884	433	1375	1288	1143	662	340	582	69

A21H: Heroin (smack, horse)

1. Probably impossible	30.1	29.6	30.6	26.6	46.7	30.9	25.3	34.0	30.7	26.7	32.0	31.1	31.5	32.6	24.1	7.2
2. Very difficult	27.0	29.2	25.3	29.2	19.2	25.4	29.4	25.6	27.9	29.6	25.0	25.1	28.1	27.6	32.2	18.8
3. Fairly difficult	24.5	23.9	24.8	26.5	14.6	22.8	26.9	23.8	23.6	25.1	25.2	26.7	20.5	25.0	26.5	18.8
4. Fairly easy	13.3	11.8	14.7	13.5	11.8	16.6	13.3	11.7	11.2	13.9	12.6	12.2	15.8	10.0	12.5	33.3
5. Very easy	5.1	5.5	4.6	4.1	8.0	4.3	5.2	4.8	6.9	4.7	5.3	4.8	3.9	4.7	4.6	21.7
Item 6820 N(Wtd)	2871	1400	1365	2254	323	680	865	889	437	1377	1290	1144	663	340	584	69

A21I: Some other narcotic (methadone, opium, codeine, paregoric, etc.)

1. Probably impossible	23.6	21.6	25.2	18.6	46.5	21.9	19.8	29.7	21.0	20.0	25.9	29.1	23.3	22.3	12.2	4.3
2. Very difficult	23.3	25.1	21.2	25.1	16.6	23.1	24.8	21.3	24.7	26.0	21.2	22.8	24.9	28.4	21.5	13.0
3. Fairly difficult	26.3	27.2	25.7	28.4	15.4	26.6	28.3	25.0	24.7	26.7	26.4	25.2	27.5	22.0	32.9	17.4
4. Fairly easy	18.2	17.2	19.1	19.5	12.9	20.1	18.5	15.5	20.1	19.3	17.3	16.9	18.1	17.9	19.3	36.2
5. Very easy	8.8	8.9	8.7	8.4	8.6	8.4	8.8	8.6	9.8	7.9	9.1	6.0	6.2	9.4	14.1	27.5
Item 6830 N(Wtd)	2874	1400	1371	2256	325	681	867	888	438	1382	1286	1151	662	341	581	69

This section asks for your views and feelings about a number of different things.

D01: How satisfied are you with your life as a whole these days?

1. Completely dissatisfied	2.6	2.5	2.7	2.1	5.7	2.5	2.5	3.0	2.1	2.7	2.3	2.8	1.4	3.7	2.0	4.8
2. Quite dissatisfied	9.1	9.2	9.1	9.4	8.4	11.0	8.8	7.6	10.1	9.4	9.0	8.8	9.0	9.8	8.5	15.9
3. Somewhat dissatisfied	12.2	11.5	12.9	12.2	13.4	11.5	12.6	13.5	9.9	12.2	12.1	10.9	11.3	13.8	15.5	9.5
4. Neither, or mixed feelings	14.5	14.2	14.9	13.5	21.1	14.3	15.7	14.5	12.9	13.9	15.1	13.7	14.1	13.8	16.9	14.3
5. Somewhat satisfied	22.6	25.0	20.2	22.2	21.8	25.6	19.8	23.2	22.8	22.6	22.2	22.7	23.7	19.7	24.5	19.0
6. Quite satisfied	32.6	31.8	33.5	34.8	20.1	29.3	34.7	30.8	36.6	33.8	31.9	34.7	33.9	33.5	26.8	28.6
7. Completely satisfied	6.4	5.9	6.7	5.8	8.7	5.6	6.1	7.4	5.9	5.3	7.3	6.5	6.7	5.5	5.9	6.3
Item 6840 N(Wtd)	2814	1366	1389	2285	298	644	875	868	426	1421	1288	1163	654	325	555	63

D02: These next questions ask you to guess how well you might do in several different situations. How good do you think you would be...

D02A: As a husband or wife?

1. Poor	1.1	1.5	.7	.8	3.1	.3	1.3	1.6	1.2	.7	1.6	.7	1.7	1.5	.7	-
2. Not so good	2.0	2.3	1.8	1.9	4.1	1.2	2.1	2.6	1.9	2.4	1.8	1.8	1.5	1.5	3.1	3.1
3. Fairly good	11.9	13.6	10.4	11.5	13.9	9.1	11.9	14.3	11.0	10.4	12.9	11.3	11.1	10.5	14.0	21.9
4. Good	38.4	38.9	37.8	39.8	28.5	37.1	40.0	37.9	37.6	39.7	37.3	39.9	36.7	36.1	39.6	31.3
5. Very good	39.8	35.2	44.0	39.0	44.1	44.7	38.0	37.1	41.5	41.4	38.3	39.7	42.5	43.8	34.5	37.5
8. Don't know	6.8	8.4	5.2	7.0	6.4	7.4	6.7	6.4	6.6	5.4	8.2	6.4	6.5	6.5	8.1	6.3
Item 6850 N(Wtd)	2810	1361	1391	2282	295	645	871	870	426	1418	1290	1163	649	324	556	64

D02B: As a parent?

1. Poor	1.4	1.8	1.2	1.5	2.0	.9	1.3	2.3	.9	1.5	1.3	1.3	1.7	1.5	.9	6.3
2. Not so good	3.6	3.1	4.2	4.0	2.7	3.7	2.9	4.2	4.2	3.9	3.2	2.6	3.4	4.3	6.3	1.6
3. Fairly good	12.2	12.4	12.0	12.1	10.9	9.0	13.6	13.4	11.3	9.9	14.9	12.1	12.7	11.5	12.5	12.7
4. Good	38.1	38.7	37.7	39.9	27.3	36.0	40.2	36.6	40.0	38.6	37.9	39.8	36.1	36.2	37.9	31.7
5. Very good	36.8	35.3	38.1	34.7	50.2	41.8	33.7	35.9	37.2	40.1	32.9	36.5	38.1	38.4	34.1	42.9
8. Don't know	7.8	8.7	6.8	7.9	6.5	8.3	8.4	7.5	6.6	6.0	9.8	7.8	7.8	8.4	8.3	6.3
Item 6860 N(Wtd)	2795	1349	1389	2273	293	641	866	863	425	1419	1275	1159	645	323	554	63

QUESTIONNAIRE FORM 2 1976	TOTAL	SEX		RACE		REGION				4YR COLLEGE PLANS		ILLICIT DRUG USE: LIFETIME				
		M	F	White	Black	NE	NC	S	W	Yes	No	None	Marijuana Only	Few Pills	More Pills	Any Heroin
Weighted No. of Cases:	3036	1453	1445	2358	343	723	919	934	460	1450	1342	1223	687	343	597	69
% of Weighted Total:	100.0	47.9	47.6	77.7	11.3	23.8	30.3	30.8	15.2	47.8	44.2	40.3	22.6	11.3	19.7	2.3

D02C: As a worker on a job?

1. Poor	.4	.5	.1	.3	.7	.3	.1	.7	.2	.1	.6	.3	.2	.3	.9	-
2. Not so good	.5	.5	.5	.4	.7	.9	.3	.1	1.2	.4	.8	.3	.2	.9	1.3	-
3. Fairly good	5.8	5.2	6.4	5.9	6.3	4.9	6.3	6.5	5.2	5.2	6.3	5.9	5.3	5.4	7.1	1.6
4. Good	37.0	32.3	42.0	38.3	27.1	39.0	39.0	35.7	32.9	34.8	40.8	37.5	38.1	32.2	39.0	31.3
5. Very good	54.8	59.7	49.7	53.7	62.8	53.4	52.7	55.6	59.5	58.3	50.1	54.6	55.6	61.2	49.4	62.5
8. Don't know	1.4	1.7	1.2	1.3	2.4	1.3	1.6	1.5	1.2	1.3	1.4	1.3	.5	.3	2.4	6.3
Item 6870 N(Wtd)	2771	1338	1377	2255	288	638	861	851	420	1413	1260	1148	638	317	551	64

D03: Some people think a lot about the social problems of the nation and the world, and about how they might be solved. Others spend little time thinking about these issues. How much do you think about such things?

1. Never	3.8	4.3	3.3	3.3	5.1	3.8	3.9	3.0	5.2	2.1	5.4	3.7	4.0	2.2	4.2	8.1
2. Seldom	19.3	19.1	19.8	19.2	21.4	21.8	19.0	19.1	16.8	14.2	25.3	18.8	18.0	16.4	22.1	17.7
3. Sometimes	49.1	48.3	50.1	49.5	49.7	45.7	50.4	51.8	46.2	49.4	49.7	51.0	49.9	46.6	46.8	43.5
4. Quite often	22.5	22.9	21.9	22.8	19.0	22.7	22.3	21.0	26.1	27.7	16.4	22.0	24.8	27.8	18.7	21.0
5. A great deal	5.3	5.5	4.8	5.2	4.8	6.2	4.6	5.1	5.7	6.6	3.3	4.5	3.1	7.1	8.0	9.7
Item 6880 N(Wtd)	2796	1351	1385	2271	294	634	869	870	422	1421	1274	1159	645	324	551	62

D04: Now we'd like you to make some ratings of how honest and moral the people are who run the following organizations. To what extent are there problems of dishonesty and immorality in the leadership of...

D04A: Large corporations

1. Not at all	3.5	3.9	2.9	1.9	11.1	3.1	2.7	4.4	3.7	2.2	4.7	4.1	2.7	3.1	2.1	6.9
2. Slight	13.5	14.7	12.3	12.7	19.2	13.7	14.2	12.8	13.2	11.9	15.2	13.8	13.9	13.6	11.3	15.5
3. Moderate	31.1	32.7	29.3	33.0	20.9	31.6	32.9	29.9	28.5	33.0	29.5	33.7	30.4	31.5	27.3	25.9
4. Considerable	28.1	27.4	29.3	29.4	20.2	29.2	25.1	29.7	29.8	31.1	25.5	27.7	28.9	31.2	28.4	20.7
5. Great	9.2	10.5	7.4	9.2	7.7	10.6	8.7	7.7	11.0	10.8	6.7	7.8	9.9	8.3	12.2	10.3
8. No opinion	14.7	10.8	18.7	13.7	20.6	11.9	16.5	15.3	13.7	11.0	18.3	13.0	14.1	12.3	18.8	20.7
Item 6890 N(Wtd)	2718	1319	1340	2211	287	613	853	842	410	1375	1245	1134	619	324	532	58

D04B: Major labor unions

1. Not at all	3.5	4.4	2.6	2.3	9.6	3.1	3.6	3.8	3.7	2.4	4.2	4.9	3.0	2.8	1.7	5.1
2. Slight	13.1	14.2	12.0	12.4	19.2	12.4	12.2	14.7	12.7	12.1	14.3	12.0	14.0	15.7	12.3	5.1
3. Moderate	29.5	29.7	29.2	31.5	18.9	31.6	29.3	27.5	30.9	30.9	28.6	29.6	31.1	27.5	30.4	27.1
4. Considerable	25.8	25.7	26.3	26.3	21.0	24.7	25.5	26.3	23.3	29.6	22.1	26.2	24.1	31.5	24.3	25.4
5. Great	11.1	13.4	8.6	11.7	7.1	11.2	11.3	9.9	13.2	12.5	9.5	11.3	11.1	7.4	13.4	15.3
8. No opinion	16.9	12.5	21.3	15.8	24.6	14.3	18.1	17.8	16.2	12.6	21.1	16.0	16.9	15.1	17.9	22.0
Item 6900 N(Wtd)	2712	1325	1329	2212	281	614	851	839	408	1367	1248	1128	623	324	530	59

D04C: The nation's colleges and universities

1. Not at all	6.2	7.1	5.1	5.2	11.3	5.7	6.5	5.9	6.7	4.6	7.2	6.9	4.5	8.1	4.7	10.3
2. Slight	33.1	34.8	31.3	35.8	15.5	36.7	32.5	32.3	29.9	37.4	28.7	35.4	36.1	30.4	29.2	24.1
3. Moderate	26.6	25.8	27.3	26.9	28.2	27.2	27.0	25.7	26.9	28.3	25.2	24.8	26.8	29.5	28.9	25.9
4. Considerable	14.2	14.6	13.8	13.6	16.9	12.0	14.0	16.2	14.1	13.3	15.2	14.3	13.8	11.5	14.9	17.2
5. Great	4.9	4.8	5.1	4.1	9.9	4.1	3.8	6.4	5.2	5.3	4.3	5.3	3.0	8.4	4.2	5.2
8. No opinion	15.0	12.8	17.3	14.4	18.3	14.1	16.2	13.3	17.3	11.0	19.2	13.3	15.9	12.1	18.1	19.0
Item 6910 N(Wtd)	2707	1320	1329	2209	284	610	851	841	405	1369	1242	1123	623	322	530	58

D04D: The nation's public schools

1. Not at all	7.0	7.7	5.9	6.4	9.6	7.0	6.1	7.7	7.6	6.6	6.9	7.2	6.8	8.6	5.1	13.6
2. Slight	32.5	35.7	29.5	34.6	19.2	33.6	34.6	30.2	31.2	34.1	30.8	34.0	37.3	30.6	27.2	16.9
3. Moderate	26.7	25.1	28.2	27.9	22.8	27.6	25.4	26.1	29.7	28.9	25.4	27.4	23.1	31.8	27.0	33.9
4. Considerable	15.8	15.0	17.0	14.8	20.3	14.4	16.8	17.3	13.0	15.4	16.6	15.0	14.9	15.1	19.7	11.9
5. Great	7.5	6.6	8.5	6.2	16.0	7.2	5.4	10.1	7.4	7.9	6.7	7.2	5.0	5.6	11.0	11.9
8. No opinion	10.5	9.8	11.0	10.0	12.1	10.4	11.9	8.6	11.3	7.1	13.5	9.2	12.8	8.3	10.0	13.6
Item 6920 N(Wtd)	2707	1317	1331	2209	281	613	852	834	407	1371	1239	1128	616	324	529	59

QUESTIONNAIRE FORM 2 1976	TOTAL	SEX		RACE		REGION				4YR COLLEGE PLANS		ILLICIT DRUG USE: LIFETIME				
		M	F	White	Black	NE	NC	S	W	Yes	No	None	Mari- juana Only	Few Pills	More Pills	Any Her- oin
Weighted No. of Cases:	3036	1453	1445	2358	343	723	919	934	460	1450	1342	1223	687	343	597	69
% of Weighted Total:	100.0	47.9	47.6	77.7	11.3	23.8	30.3	30.8	15.2	47.8	44.2	40.3	22.6	11.3	19.7	2.3

D04E: Churches and religious organizations

	TOTAL	M	F	White	Black	NE	NC	S	W	Yes	No	None	Mari- juana Only	Few Pills	More Pills	Any Her- oin
1. Not at all	20.7	21.5	19.8	21.9	11.9	19.0	21.7	21.4	20.1	20.0	21.1	21.3	22.4	23.5	17.3	15.3
2. Slight	35.0	35.4	34.6	36.6	27.7	36.8	36.0	33.5	33.7	39.9	29.8	38.8	35.9	33.3	28.8	28.8
3. Moderate	13.6	12.4	15.1	13.9	12.3	15.7	12.3	13.0	14.7	13.7	13.7	12.8	10.9	16.0	17.5	13.6
4. Considerable	8.8	9.2	8.3	7.5	16.1	9.3	7.3	10.0	8.4	9.2	8.6	7.9	8.3	6.8	11.2	8.5
5. Great	8.5	9.3	7.8	7.6	16.1	6.9	8.5	9.7	9.1	7.4	9.8	8.5	7.5	10.2	8.4	8.5
8. No opinion	13.4	12.1	14.4	12.4	15.8	12.4	14.4	12.5	14.0	9.7	16.9	10.6	15.3	9.9	16.8	25.4
Item 6930 N(Wtd)	2704	1318	1327	2202	285	612	848	837	407	1368	1239	1129	616	324	525	59

D04F: The national news media (TV, magazines, news services)

	TOTAL	M	F	White	Black	NE	NC	S	W	Yes	No	None	Mari- juana Only	Few Pills	More Pills	Any Her- oin
1. Not at all	4.2	5.2	3.0	3.3	8.1	3.9	3.9	4.9	4.0	2.9	6.0	4.4	4.9	2.5	3.6	5.1
2. Slight	19.9	21.9	18.2	20.1	20.4	21.6	18.9	20.0	19.0	20.7	19.2	20.6	21.4	20.4	16.1	25.4
3. Moderate	32.2	34.1	29.9	33.6	22.5	33.3	32.8	28.9	35.6	36.7	27.3	32.9	30.3	35.5	32.4	20.3
4. Considerable	21.6	19.3	23.9	22.1	17.6	19.6	22.1	22.8	21.2	21.9	21.2	21.7	20.3	23.5	22.4	22.0
5. Great	11.1	9.9	12.5	10.9	13.7	11.4	10.3	13.1	8.4	11.0	11.5	10.7	11.8	9.6	12.5	11.9
8. No opinion	10.9	9.6	12.4	9.8	17.3	10.1	11.9	10.3	11.6	6.9	14.8	9.7	11.2	8.3	12.9	15.3
Item 6940 N(Wtd)	2700	1318	1323	2201	284	612	851	833	405	1366	1238	1123	617	324	527	59

D04G: The Presidency and the administration

	TOTAL	M	F	White	Black	NE	NC	S	W	Yes	No	None	Mari- juana Only	Few Pills	More Pills	Any Her- oin
1. Not at all	3.5	4.5	2.3	2.6	9.3	3.3	2.9	4.3	3.2	1.8	5.2	3.8	1.9	2.8	4.0	5.1
2. Slight	17.2	21.4	13.1	17.7	16.8	16.9	16.7	17.6	18.3	18.6	16.0	18.2	18.9	18.6	11.8	16.9
3. Moderate	28.4	29.2	27.6	30.5	16.1	27.7	30.9	25.7	29.6	31.3	25.5	31.1	26.7	31.0	25.6	16.9
4. Considerable	24.9	22.7	27.2	25.1	22.5	28.3	25.1	23.5	22.0	27.0	23.0	24.0	25.9	25.4	25.7	28.8
5. Great	15.0	13.9	16.2	14.6	18.9	14.9	13.3	17.8	12.8	15.0	15.0	13.1	15.0	13.9	20.2	13.6
8. No opinion	11.0	8.3	13.6	9.5	16.4	9.0	10.8	10.9	14.3	6.2	15.5	9.7	11.3	8.0	12.9	18.6
Item 6950 N(Wtd)	2698	1315	1324	2203	280	611	848	835	405	1365	1237	1124	618	323	526	59

D04H: Congress-that is, the U.S. Senate and House of Representatives

	TOTAL	M	F	White	Black	NE	NC	S	W	Yes	No	None	Mari- juana Only	Few Pills	More Pills	Any Her- oin
1. Not at all	3.9	4.9	2.7	2.6	12.0	3.5	2.7	5.6	3.4	2.0	5.9	4.4	3.1	2.2	3.8	8.6
2. Slight	16.5	19.5	13.3	16.7	17.6	16.7	16.3	16.4	17.5	18.1	15.0	16.4	19.0	16.7	13.7	20.7
3. Moderate	29.2	29.6	28.9	31.0	20.8	26.6	31.4	28.1	30.5	33.9	24.6	31.9	27.9	31.6	25.6	19.0
4. Considerable	24.5	23.9	25.2	25.3	16.5	29.3	23.1	23.6	22.2	26.3	22.7	23.5	25.3	28.5	24.0	24.1
5. Great	11.2	11.6	11.0	11.0	13.0	11.4	11.4	12.1	8.6	10.8	11.2	10.1	10.7	8.7	15.8	12.1
8. No opinion	14.7	10.6	18.9	13.5	19.7	12.7	15.1	14.3	17.7	9.0	20.6	13.7	14.1	12.4	17.0	17.2
Item 6960 N(Wtd)	2695	1316	1319	2196	284	605	849	834	406	1362	1236	1123	617	323	524	58

D04I: The U.S. Supreme Court

	TOTAL	M	F	White	Black	NE	NC	S	W	Yes	No	None	Mari- juana Only	Few Pills	More Pills	Any Her- oin
1. Not at all	9.5	12.4	6.4	8.8	11.6	9.9	8.7	9.4	11.1	9.8	9.1	11.8	9.3	7.1	5.7	12.3
2. Slight	27.5	30.8	23.8	28.6	21.1	29.1	27.9	26.0	27.1	31.8	22.9	26.7	33.0	29.2	24.3	15.8
3. Moderate	23.8	22.3	25.7	25.3	20.1	26.0	24.6	21.5	23.9	25.8	22.6	25.1	21.6	25.8	23.8	17.5
4. Considerable	13.7	12.6	14.9	13.4	13.4	13.4	11.4	16.8	12.1	13.6	13.5	13.4	12.7	15.8	14.4	15.8
5. Great	7.8	8.5	7.1	7.2	9.9	6.9	8.7	8.4	5.9	6.6	9.0	6.7	5.8	8.1	10.7	15.8
8. No opinion	17.8	13.4	22.1	16.7	23.9	14.7	18.6	17.9	20.0	12.5	22.9	16.4	17.7	14.3	20.7	24.6
Item 6970 N(Wtd)	2687	1310	1318	2188	284	605	842	834	406	1357	1234	1120	616	322	522	57

D04J: All the courts and the justice system in general

	TOTAL	M	F	White	Black	NE	NC	S	W	Yes	No	None	Mari- juana Only	Few Pills	More Pills	Any Her- oin
1. Not at all	5.9	6.4	5.0	4.8	11.0	3.8	5.7	7.0	7.4	4.6	7.0	6.6	4.9	6.3	4.6	10.3
2. Slight	25.0	27.8	22.2	26.0	19.8	26.0	23.6	24.1	28.5	27.8	22.4	26.7	28.7	22.6	20.3	15.5
3. Moderate	29.4	29.9	29.3	31.6	21.2	29.4	31.1	29.9	24.8	30.9	28.7	29.7	28.0	32.0	31.4	17.2
4. Considerable	17.7	17.4	18.2	17.2	17.0	18.9	17.5	17.4	17.1	19.7	15.4	17.4	16.4	20.4	18.9	13.8
5. Great	7.1	7.1	7.1	6.7	9.5	8.1	6.5	8.0	5.0	6.5	7.3	5.4	6.2	8.5	9.4	19.0
8. No opinion	14.9	11.5	18.1	13.7	20.8	13.8	15.6	13.8	17.6	10.5	19.3	14.2	15.9	10.3	15.5	22.4
Item 6980 N(Wtd)	2687	1312	1316	2189	283	603	845	834	404	1358	1233	1120	617	319	523	58

QUESTIONNAIRE FORM 2 1976	TOTAL	SEX		RACE		REGION				4YR COLLEGE PLANS		ILLICIT DRUG USE: LIFETIME				
		M	F	White	Black	NE	NC	S	W	Yes	No	None	Mari-juana Only	Few Pills	More Pills	Any Her-oin
Weighted No. of Cases:	3036	1453	1445	2358	343	723	919	934	460	1450	1342	1223	687	343	597	69
% of Weighted Total:	100.0	47.9	47.6	77.7	11.3	23.8	30.3	30.8	15.2	47.8	44.2	40.3	22.6	11.3	19.7	2.3

D04K: The police and other law enforcement agencies

	TOTAL	M	F	White	Black	NE	NC	S	W	Yes	No	None	Mari-juana Only	Few Pills	More Pills	Any Her-oin
1. Not at all	4.3	5.1	3.5	3.5	7.8	2.5	4.4	5.3	5.2	2.3	6.3	4.7	4.5	3.4	3.3	6.9
2. Slight	23.4	24.9	22.3	24.2	21.2	21.9	24.3	24.6	21.4	23.5	23.6	27.0	24.8	20.5	17.2	12.1
3. Moderate	29.7	30.2	29.0	31.8	19.8	30.3	30.1	27.4	32.8	33.7	26.2	31.0	31.6	31.1	27.2	13.8
4. Considerable	21.8	21.3	22.3	22.1	17.3	23.2	22.2	20.8	20.9	23.4	20.0	20.9	20.1	24.2	24.3	27.6
5. Great	11.3	11.4	11.2	9.9	19.4	13.7	9.1	12.6	9.6	11.2	10.9	7.1	10.0	13.0	18.9	25.9
8. No opinion	9.4	7.0	11.6	8.5	14.5	8.2	9.9	9.2	10.3	5.8	13.1	9.3	8.9	7.8	9.2	15.5
Item 6990 N(Wtd)	2693	1312	1322	2195	283	607	846	835	406	1364	1233	1123	617	322	523	58

D04L: The U.S. military

	TOTAL	M	F	White	Black	NE	NC	S	W	Yes	No	None	Mari-juana Only	Few Pills	More Pills	Any Her-oin
1. Not at all	6.7	7.4	5.8	6.3	8.9	6.4	5.2	8.6	6.7	4.8	8.7	7.9	6.3	6.6	5.5	1.8
2. Slight	29.1	31.2	27.2	30.5	22.8	29.6	29.6	30.6	24.4	31.6	26.1	28.8	34.4	31.3	24.5	22.8
3. Moderate	24.5	25.9	23.2	26.2	14.9	26.8	23.8	23.0	25.9	28.4	21.0	24.6	26.3	25.9	23.1	17.5
4. Considerable	13.4	14.4	12.6	13.1	14.6	12.7	14.8	11.8	14.8	13.6	13.1	14.1	10.7	13.1	15.3	15.8
5. Great	6.8	7.8	5.8	6.2	10.3	6.8	5.9	7.0	8.6	6.9	6.7	5.6	5.3	7.5	9.6	14.0
8. No opinion	19.4	13.4	25.4	17.7	28.1	17.7	20.7	19.0	19.7	14.5	24.5	19.0	17.0	15.6	22.2	26.3
Item 7000 N(Wtd)	2687	1307	1321	2191	281	605	846	830	406	1362	1231	1120	617	320	523	57

D05: How much do you agree or disagree with each of the following statements?

D05A: There is too much competition in this society

	TOTAL	M	F	White	Black	NE	NC	S	W	Yes	No	None	Mari-juana Only	Few Pills	More Pills	Any Her-oin
1. Disagree	9.5	13.4	5.8	9.3	13.1	8.1	8.3	12.4	7.8	10.5	8.3	10.5	8.9	9.5	7.6	8.6
2. Mostly disagree	13.3	16.5	9.9	14.1	11.0	11.6	13.2	14.1	14.2	16.0	10.9	13.5	13.5	15.5	11.8	12.1
3. Neither	22.3	26.4	18.2	22.3	22.7	16.8	24.0	23.3	24.6	19.2	25.5	20.7	25.5	23.0	21.3	19.0
4. Mostly agree	35.2	28.8	41.5	36.7	27.3	39.2	37.5	30.1	35.4	36.0	34.9	36.0	36.2	36.0	34.2	32.8
5. Agree	19.7	14.7	24.7	17.7	25.9	24.4	16.8	20.1	17.7	18.3	20.4	19.3	15.9	16.4	25.2	27.6
Item 7010 N(Wtd)	2678	1297	1321	2180	282	602	840	841	395	1342	1236	1112	616	317	527	58

D05B: Too many young people are sloppy about their grooming and clothing, and just don't care how they look

	TOTAL	M	F	White	Black	NE	NC	S	W	Yes	No	None	Mari-juana Only	Few Pills	More Pills	Any Her-oin
1. Disagree	14.6	15.6	13.4	14.6	14.0	17.4	13.9	13.7	13.2	12.8	16.2	11.0	18.1	13.5	18.9	18.3
2. Mostly disagree	26.4	26.1	26.7	27.8	20.3	27.7	26.4	24.8	27.6	30.8	21.8	23.3	28.4	31.7	27.3	35.0
3. Neither	19.9	22.1	17.7	21.3	11.2	22.5	24.1	13.1	21.1	18.8	21.1	17.4	22.3	15.4	25.6	16.7
4. Mostly agree	22.5	21.3	23.8	22.6	22.0	18.1	22.5	25.5	23.1	21.9	23.6	28.6	17.6	23.5	14.6	20.0
5. Agree	16.7	15.0	18.3	13.8	32.2	14.3	13.2	22.8	14.9	15.6	17.3	19.8	13.6	16.0	13.8	10.0
Item 7020 N(Wtd)	2713	1308	1344	2205	286	614	850	846	402	1366	1248	1131	619	319	535	60

D05C: There is too much hard rock music on the radio these days

	TOTAL	M	F	White	Black	NE	NC	S	W	Yes	No	None	Mari-juana Only	Few Pills	More Pills	Any Her-oin
1. Disagree	46.0	49.0	42.8	46.9	45.4	49.8	44.0	46.7	43.1	43.2	49.3	33.0	54.3	45.0	61.6	65.5
2. Mostly disagree	24.4	23.7	25.1	25.3	20.8	25.0	26.5	22.1	24.0	25.8	22.7	25.7	25.9	24.8	21.4	17.2
3. Neither	16.1	15.0	17.2	15.6	17.3	14.0	17.7	15.2	17.6	16.7	15.6	20.9	12.9	16.1	10.0	10.3
4. Mostly agree	7.8	5.6	10.1	7.1	10.2	7.2	6.4	9.1	8.9	8.0	7.5	11.6	4.4	7.8	4.0	6.9
5. Agree	5.8	6.8	4.7	5.1	6.7	4.1	5.4	7.0	6.4	6.3	4.9	9.0	2.5	6.5	3.0	-
Item 7030 N(Wtd)	2694	1297	1336	2183	284	613	853	825	404	1355	1239	1122	611	322	529	58

D05D: People should do their own thing, even if other people think it's strange

	TOTAL	M	F	White	Black	NE	NC	S	W	Yes	No	None	Mari-juana Only	Few Pills	More Pills	Any Her-oin
1. Disagree	3.3	3.0	3.0	2.8	4.5	2.0	2.0	5.4	3.1	2.9	3.6	4.4	1.3	2.8	1.7	6.7
2. Mostly disagree	5.8	4.6	4.6	5.9	5.9	4.2	4.8	7.2	7.0	6.0	5.6	7.5	4.8	6.8	3.3	3.3
3. Neither	13.3	12.9	13.8	14.2	9.0	10.6	14.7	13.4	14.0	14.2	12.5	16.5	14.3	9.0	9.1	10.0
4. Mostly agree	37.0	36.9	37.5	38.6	26.4	37.9	40.9	32.4	37.5	38.5	35.8	39.4	36.2	35.5	35.1	40.0
5. Agree	40.6	40.3	41.0	38.6	53.8	45.4	37.5	41.7	38.0	38.5	42.4	32.3	43.4	46.0	50.6	40.0
Item 7040 N(Wtd)	2732	1321	1351	2216	288	615	851	853	413	1378	1253	1136	622	324	538	60

MONITORING THE FUTURE

QUESTIONNAIRE FORM 2 1976	TOTAL	SEX		RACE		REGION				4YR COLLEGE PLANS		ILLICIT DRUG USE: LIFETIME				
		M	F	White	Black	NE	NC	S	W	Yes	No	None	Marijuana Only	Few Pills	More Pills	Any Heroin
Weighted No. of Cases:	3036	1453	1445	2358	343	723	919	934	460	1450	1342	1223	687	343	597	69
% of Weighted Total:	100.0	47.9	47.6	77.7	11.3	23.8	30.3	30.8	15.2	47.8	44.2	40.3	22.6	11.3	19.7	2.3

D05E: I get a real kick out of doing things that are a little dangerous

1. Disagree	24.2	14.2	34.3	20.6	46.0	21.3	19.9	31.8	21.3	24.7	23.5	29.4	18.7	19.9	19.9	23.3
2. Mostly disagree	21.2	17.0	24.9	22.3	18.1	20.3	22.7	21.1	19.6	23.3	19.6	25.2	19.4	22.4	15.0	23.3
3. Neither	24.8	27.0	22.9	26.1	17.1	25.4	27.9	20.1	27.4	24.7	24.9	22.8	26.8	25.8	27.3	15.0
4. Mostly agree	20.5	27.9	13.2	21.4	12.9	21.6	20.7	19.1	21.0	20.4	20.5	15.0	25.6	21.4	26.3	20.0
5. Agree	9.3	13.8	4.6	9.6	5.9	11.5	8.8	7.7	10.8	6.9	11.5	7.6	9.5	10.2	11.5	18.3
Item 7050 N(Wtd)	2721	1316	1345	2211	287	610	850	852	409	1372	1251	1136	620	322	532	60

D05F: I like to test myself every now and then by doing something a little risky

1. Disagree	23.8	14.9	32.7	21.8	36.9	20.1	19.7	30.4	23.8	23.8	23.8	29.9	18.9	21.0	17.1	20.0
2. Mostly disagree	17.2	15.3	18.8	17.8	14.6	16.4	19.8	16.0	15.5	18.1	16.4	19.4	16.8	17.6	12.0	20.0
3. Neither	21.1	20.4	21.5	21.7	16.0	20.9	20.6	19.0	26.5	21.1	21.0	19.8	24.0	20.4	23.3	15.0
4. Mostly agree	25.4	32.9	18.9	26.9	18.1	27.5	27.7	23.3	21.8	26.9	24.1	21.3	27.3	27.8	31.1	25.0
5. Agree	12.6	16.5	8.1	11.8	14.3	15.1	12.0	11.4	12.4	10.1	14.7	9.6	13.2	13.3	16.3	21.7
Item 7060 N(Wtd)	2720	1314	1347	2208	287	611	848	849	412	1372	1250	1133	620	324	533	60

D06: How many of your friends would you estimate...

D06A: Smoke cigarettes

1. None	6.3	5.6	6.7	5.4	10.0	4.4	5.7	6.0	10.8	7.5	4.6	10.5	2.9	4.3	2.6	-
2. A few	26.1	24.6	27.8	26.1	29.1	20.8	24.1	26.9	36.4	29.5	23.1	37.5	23.6	21.1	10.1	9.8
3. Some	30.9	33.8	28.5	33.2	16.6	30.2	32.4	29.8	31.3	33.7	28.3	30.0	36.0	32.7	28.5	13.1
4. Most	33.5	33.4	33.4	32.7	39.1	39.7	33.8	35.3	20.0	27.0	39.9	20.8	35.2	37.9	52.1	57.4
5. All	3.2	2.6	3.7	2.7	5.2	5.0	3.8	2.0	1.7	2.3	4.1	1.1	2.2	3.7	6.5	19.7
Item 7070 N(Wtd)	2745	1328	1356	2223	289	620	860	850	415	1381	1257	1138	627	327	537	61

D06B: Smoke marijuana (pot, grass) or hashish

1. None	17.1	12.1	22.3	16.6	20.8	10.7	17.7	20.6	18.3	16.9	17.7	33.2	6.2	10.1	2.0	3.3
2. A few	26.8	26.8	27.4	29.2	16.9	23.5	28.8	27.9	25.3	30.2	24.0	38.8	26.0	25.1	8.9	6.6
3. Some	25.4	27.8	22.6	24.5	27.5	24.3	26.8	25.4	24.3	26.6	24.1	20.7	38.1	28.7	21.2	8.2
4. Most	23.7	25.3	21.8	23.4	25.7	30.9	20.0	21.5	25.3	21.2	25.7	6.5	26.6	30.6	46.8	55.7
5. All	6.9	7.9	6.0	6.3	9.2	10.7	6.7	4.6	6.5	5.1	8.5	.7	4.0	5.5	21.0	27.9
Item 7080 N(Wtd)	2738	1322	1356	2220	284	618	857	848	415	1382	1251	1131	627	327	538	61

D06C: Take LSD

1. None	69.4	66.7	72.4	69.1	75.7	65.7	69.5	72.1	69.2	72.5	66.4	84.5	77.4	63.6	37.6	24.6
2. A few	20.2	22.1	18.2	20.7	15.0	20.6	20.5	18.8	22.0	19.8	20.8	10.9	20.2	28.3	34.6	27.9
3. Some	7.5	7.4	7.7	7.6	5.4	10.6	6.4	6.7	6.8	5.9	8.8	4.0	2.2	8.1	19.0	23.0
4. Most	1.9	2.7	1.1	1.9	1.1	1.8	2.6	1.3	1.7	1.0	2.9	.1	.2	-	6.9	16.4
5. All	.9	1.1	.6	.7	2.9	1.1	1.1	1.0	.2	.7	1.1	.5	.2	-	1.9	8.2
Item 7090 N(Wtd)	2718	1317	1342	2208	280	613	853	839	413	1369	1248	1119	625	321	537	61

D06D: Take other psychedelics (mescaline, peyote, PCP, etc.)

1. None	69.7	65.9	73.8	69.2	79.1	69.1	69.0	71.6	68.1	73.2	66.4	86.5	78.9	64.8	32.7	24.6
2. A few	20.4	22.7	17.9	20.8	14.0	19.7	19.8	20.6	22.5	18.7	21.9	11.3	18.7	27.8	36.2	27.9
3. Some	6.9	7.4	6.6	7.1	4.3	8.5	7.3	5.4	7.0	6.2	7.5	1.8	1.9	7.3	20.9	23.0
4. Most	2.1	2.8	1.3	2.3	.7	1.6	3.0	1.7	1.9	1.1	3.3	.2	.5	-	7.9	16.4
5. All	.9	1.4	.4	.7	2.2	1.1	.8	.8	.7	.9	.9	.3	.2	-	2.2	6.6
Item 7100 N(Wtd)	2724	1319	1345	2215	278	614	855	841	414	1376	1245	1122	621	327	541	61

QUESTIONNAIRE FORM 2 1976	TOTAL	SEX		RACE		REGION				4YR COLLEGE PLANS		ILLICIT DRUG USE: LIFETIME				
		M	F	White	Black	NE	NC	S	W	Yes	No	None	Marijuana Only	Few Pills	More Pills	Any Heroin
Weighted No. of Cases:	3036	1453	1445	2358	343	723	919	934	460	1450	1342	1223	687	343	597	69
% of Weighted Total:	100.0	47.9	47.6	77.7	11.3	23.8	30.3	30.8	15.2	47.8	44.2	40.3	22.6	11.3	19.7	2.3

D06E: Take amphetamines (uppers, pep pills, bennies, speed)

	TOTAL	M	F	White	Black	NE	NC	S	W	Yes	No	None	Marijuana Only	Few Pills	More Pills	Any Heroin
1. None	57.8	56.1	59.7	56.8	68.1	59.1	55.5	60.4	55.3	61.4	54.3	79.1	64.5	47.2	17.3	14.8
2. A few	27.2	28.5	26.0	28.1	20.3	26.6	26.9	27.0	29.0	26.6	27.5	17.3	29.2	39.6	37.4	27.9
3. Some	9.4	8.8	9.9	9.7	5.1	9.3	10.8	7.4	11.1	7.8	11.4	2.7	5.3	12.0	25.8	18.0
4. Most	4.3	5.0	3.4	4.6	2.2	3.6	5.4	3.7	4.1	3.3	5.2	.5	.8	1.2	16.0	26.2
5. All	1.3	1.6	.9	.9	4.0	1.3	1.5	1.4	.5	.9	1.7	.4	.2	-	3.3	13.1
Item 7110 N(Wtd)	2716	1316	1340	2210	276	613	854	836	414	1370	1242	1117	623	326	538	61

D06F: Take quaaludes (quads, methaqualone)

	TOTAL	M	F	White	Black	NE	NC	S	W	Yes	No	None	Marijuana Only	Few Pills	More Pills	Any Heroin
1. None	73.0	68.9	77.2	72.2	82.6	72.8	73.8	71.7	74.5	76.0	69.6	88.9	82.4	64.8	39.0	31.7
2. A few	17.5	20.6	14.5	18.4	9.4	17.4	15.9	18.9	18.2	16.3	19.0	9.0	15.2	27.8	31.6	20.0
3. Some	6.6	7.1	6.2	6.7	3.6	7.0	7.3	5.9	6.1	5.2	8.2	1.5	2.1	6.5	20.9	26.7
4. Most	2.0	2.4	1.5	2.0	1.8	1.6	2.0	2.6	.7	1.8	2.3	.4	.2	.9	6.4	16.7
5. All	.9	1.1	.6	.6	2.2	.8	1.1	.8	.5	.7	1.1	.4	.2	-	2.1	6.7
Item 7120 N(Wtd)	2700	1307	1335	2196	276	610	845	834	411	1361	1236	1113	619	324	531	60

D06G: Take barbiturates (downers, goofballs, reds, yellows, etc.)

	TOTAL	M	F	White	Black	NE	NC	S	W	Yes	No	None	Marijuana Only	Few Pills	More Pills	Any Heroin
1. None	63.7	61.2	66.4	63.1	73.1	62.9	61.9	65.5	65.0	67.9	59.1	82.1	71.4	54.0	27.7	16.7
2. A few	24.7	26.4	23.1	25.6	16.5	24.8	24.8	23.7	26.8	23.3	26.4	14.5	24.3	36.4	38.5	35.0
3. Some	8.1	7.8	8.2	8.1	5.0	8.5	9.2	7.6	5.8	6.2	10.2	2.7	3.7	8.6	22.3	21.7
4. Most	2.7	3.6	1.6	2.6	3.2	2.9	2.9	2.5	1.9	1.9	3.1	.3	.5	1.2	9.3	18.3
5. All	.9	1.1	.6	.6	2.2	.8	1.2	.7	.5	.7	1.1	.4	-	-	2.0	8.3
Item 7130 N(Wtd)	2715	1318	1338	2207	279	614	852	837	411	1370	1241	1119	622	324	538	60

D06H: Take tranquilizers

	TOTAL	M	F	White	Black	NE	NC	S	W	Yes	No	None	Marijuana Only	Few Pills	More Pills	Any Heroin
1. None	63.7	63.8	64.2	62.6	74.7	65.1	62.7	62.8	65.9	67.3	59.5	77.9	74.6	54.8	31.5	26.7
2. A few	26.3	25.9	26.6	27.9	15.9	25.6	26.4	27.2	25.5	25.0	28.1	18.4	22.5	37.7	39.9	31.7
3. Some	6.9	6.3	7.3	6.9	4.7	6.4	7.6	7.1	6.1	5.3	8.8	2.6	2.4	6.2	19.9	20.0
4. Most	2.3	3.0	1.5	2.2	2.5	2.3	2.4	2.0	2.4	1.9	2.3	.5	.5	.9	7.1	16.7
5. All	.8	1.0	.4	.5	2.5	.7	1.1	1.0	.2	.6	1.1	.5	-	.3	1.7	5.0
Item 7140 N(Wtd)	2707	1311	1337	2201	277	610	850	836	411	1365	1237	1115	621	321	537	60

D06I: Take cocaine

	TOTAL	M	F	White	Black	NE	NC	S	W	Yes	No	None	Marijuana Only	Few Pills	More Pills	Any Heroin
1. None	71.2	68.2	74.6	71.8	70.5	67.7	74.9	73.2	65.0	72.7	70.1	87.7	78.2	65.2	38.6	23.3
2. A few	19.0	20.7	17.0	19.0	17.6	20.5	17.1	17.9	22.4	19.0	18.9	9.8	18.5	26.1	33.6	25.0
3. Some	6.5	7.1	6.1	6.3	7.2	8.2	5.1	6.1	7.8	6.0	7.1	1.6	2.9	7.5	18.3	25.0
4. Most	2.4	2.8	1.8	2.3	2.2	2.6	1.8	2.0	3.9	1.8	2.8	.4	.3	.9	7.5	21.7
5. All	.9	1.1	.5	.5	2.2	1.0	.9	.7	1.0	.5	1.2	.4	-	.3	2.1	6.7
Item 7150 N(Wtd)	2700	1308	1334	2193	278	609	846	833	411	1360	1236	1114	616	322	536	60

D06J: Take heroin (smack, horse)

	TOTAL	M	F	White	Black	NE	NC	S	W	Yes	No	None	Marijuana Only	Few Pills	More Pills	Any Heroin
1. None	86.4	85.5	87.3	87.2	83.0	89.5	85.1	84.0	89.5	88.5	83.5	91.5	91.0	84.8	78.0	37.3
2. A few	10.8	11.5	10.2	10.7	9.7	7.7	12.0	12.5	9.3	9.6	12.5	6.9	7.9	14.3	17.3	35.6
3. Some	2.1	1.9	2.2	1.7	4.7	1.8	2.5	2.6	1.0	1.2	3.2	.9	.8	1.2	3.5	22.0
4. Most	.2	.3	.1	.2	.7	.3	.1	.5	-	.2	.2	.3	.2	-	.4	1.7
5. All	.5	.7	.2	.3	1.8	.7	.5	.6	.2	.4	.6	.4	.2	-	.6	5.1
Item 7160 N(Wtd)	2706	1312	1336	2200	277	611	850	835	410	1367	1237	1115	621	322	537	59

D06K: Take other narcotics (methadone, opium, codeine, paregoric, etc.)

	TOTAL	M	F	White	Black	NE	NC	S	W	Yes	No	None	Marijuana Only	Few Pills	More Pills	Any Heroin
1. None	75.9	73.1	79.0	76.3	75.5	75.4	75.9	77.2	73.8	78.4	73.0	88.3	84.8	70.6	49.7	25.0
2. A few	18.2	19.6	16.4	18.6	14.8	18.9	18.0	16.7	20.3	17.0	19.6	10.1	14.3	24.8	34.0	33.3
3. Some	3.8	4.6	3.1	3.3	6.5	3.6	3.1	4.3	4.7	3.2	4.5	1.0	.8	4.3	10.1	21.7
4. Most	1.4	1.6	1.1	1.5	1.1	1.5	2.1	1.2	.2	.8	1.9	.2	.2	.3	4.7	13.3
5. All	.7	1.1	.4	.4	1.8	.7	.9	.6	1.0	.5	1.1	.4	.2	-	1.5	6.7
Item 7170 N(Wtd)	2702	1314	1331	2198	277	610	849	836	408	1365	1235	1115	617	323	535	60

QUESTIONNAIRE FORM 2 1976	TOTAL	SEX		RACE		REGION				4YR COLLEGE PLANS		ILLICIT DRUG USE: LIFETIME				
		M	F	White	Black	NE	NC	S	W	Yes	No	None	Mari-juana Only	Few Pills	More Pills	Any Her-oin
Weighted No. of Cases: % of Weighted Total:	3036 100.0	1453 47.9	1445 47.6	2358 77.7	343 11.3	723 23.8	919 30.3	934 30.8	460 15.2	1450 47.8	1342 44.2	1223 40.3	687 22.6	343 11.3	597 19.7	69 2.3
D06L: Use inhalants (sniffing glue, aerosols, laughing gas, etc.)																
1. None	81.5	79.1	84.2	82.2	78.2	82.8	81.9	78.9	83.8	83.6	79.4	85.9	87.4	75.0	70.8	76.3
2. A few	14.3	15.9	12.3	14.0	13.8	13.0	14.7	15.5	13.0	13.1	15.6	11.1	11.0	20.4	21.8	13.6
3. Some	3.1	3.5	2.7	3.0	3.6	3.4	2.4	3.7	2.9	2.3	3.9	2.0	1.1	4.0	5.8	5.1
4. Most	.7	.9	.4	.4	2.5	.2	.7	1.2	.2	.5	.7	.6	.2	.9	.9	1.7
5. All	.5	.5	.4	.3	1.8	.8	.4	.6	-	.6	.4	.4	.2	-	.6	3.4
Item 7180 N(Wtd)	2697	1312	1328	2197	275	609	850	831	407	1362	1229	1108	618	324	537	59
D06M: Drink alcoholic beverages (liquor, beer, wine)																
1. None	5.0	4.5	5.3	3.6	11.4	2.5	4.2	6.5	7.1	3.9	5.7	8.6	2.6	2.5	1.7	1.7
2. A few	11.9	7.8	16.1	11.2	15.4	7.5	10.6	15.1	14.7	11.8	12.2	20.2	5.9	10.8	2.4	8.3
3. Some	18.5	17.2	19.9	18.4	22.1	15.9	15.6	22.7	19.8	19.9	17.4	25.6	15.0	17.0	9.7	8.3
4. Most	39.4	42.2	36.6	40.2	37.1	39.9	42.7	39.0	33.3	40.5	38.4	34.4	46.4	41.8	41.2	38.3
5. All	25.2	28.3	22.1	26.5	13.9	34.4	27.1	16.7	25.2	23.7	26.2	11.2	30.2	28.2	44.9	45.0
Item 7190 N(Wtd)	2723	1320	1345	2217	280	611	860	842	409	1369	1250	1125	625	323	537	60
D06N: Get drunk at least once a week																
1. None	19.3	14.5	24.2	17.5	30.5	16.4	17.4	22.0	22.1	20.8	17.8	30.1	12.0	17.5	7.1	5.0
2. A few	27.6	26.7	28.4	27.7	30.9	24.9	26.2	31.4	26.7	29.8	26.0	32.9	27.6	26.2	18.9	21.7
3. Some	26.5	28.3	24.5	27.2	20.0	25.7	27.9	24.9	27.9	26.8	25.9	23.6	30.5	26.2	28.6	21.7
4. Most	18.8	20.8	16.6	20.2	9.1	21.1	20.6	16.6	15.8	16.7	20.8	10.5	22.5	21.2	28.6	30.0
5. All	7.8	9.6	6.2	7.4	9.1	11.9	7.9	5.0	7.5	6.0	9.4	2.8	7.2	8.6	17.1	23.3
Item 7200 N(Wtd)	2732	1324	1350	2218	285	615	858	847	412	1375	1252	1129	626	325	539	60
E01: How much do you think people risk harming OTHERS or society in general, if they...																
E01A: Smoke one or more packs of cigarettes per day																
1. No risk	22.8	25.4	20.0	22.7	26.0	24.3	20.5	26.8	16.8	20.6	24.7	17.3	26.4	21.5	29.8	26.3
2. Slight risk	29.4	30.5	28.7	30.5	22.4	31.0	29.8	28.1	29.1	30.6	28.5	27.7	30.3	31.5	31.1	28.1
3. Moderate risk	28.6	26.8	30.3	29.3	24.2	26.2	32.6	24.8	32.1	30.0	27.5	30.7	27.4	30.2	25.5	31.6
4. Great risk	17.1	14.8	19.2	16.4	21.7	17.4	15.8	17.0	19.8	17.4	16.5	21.6	14.2	16.2	12.0	7.0
5. Can't say, drug unfamiliar	2.1	2.5	1.8	1.0	6.1	1.3	1.3	3.5	2.2	1.4	2.8	2.6	1.6	.6	1.7	7.0
Item 7320 N(Wtd)	2698	1300	1343	2198	277	610	843	839	405	1371	1223	1124	613	321	534	57
E01B: Try marijuana (pot, grass) once or twice																
1. No risk	38.5	42.2	34.7	39.9	31.9	48.6	37.9	30.9	40.2	37.1	39.6	16.8	47.9	47.3	64.3	71.4
2. Slight risk	30.0	29.4	30.7	31.1	23.2	25.9	29.7	34.1	28.3	32.1	28.1	34.0	33.2	27.6	22.5	12.5
3. Moderate risk	16.6	15.5	18.1	16.4	20.3	15.1	17.9	15.8	18.4	17.0	16.5	23.8	13.2	14.4	8.7	3.6
4. Great risk	11.2	9.5	12.7	9.9	18.1	7.5	11.0	14.3	10.7	10.5	12.0	19.9	3.9	10.0	2.6	5.4
5. Can't say, drug unfamiliar	3.7	3.4	3.8	2.7	6.2	3.0	3.5	5.0	2.5	3.3	3.9	5.7	2.0	.6	2.1	7.1
Item 7330 N(Wtd)	2674	1294	1327	2178	276	603	831	837	403	1357	1213	1113	608	319	529	56
E01C: Smoke marijuana occasionally																
1. No risk	30.4	33.3	27.2	30.7	29.2	38.5	27.9	26.4	31.8	28.3	32.6	10.8	36.7	38.2	55.9	65.5
2. Slight risk	30.0	31.1	29.1	31.3	22.5	30.8	32.6	26.8	29.8	30.9	28.7	27.0	37.5	34.4	27.8	17.2
3. Moderate risk	24.0	21.3	26.8	24.5	22.9	19.2	24.9	26.4	23.8	26.1	22.3	35.0	19.0	18.9	11.6	6.9
4. Great risk	11.9	10.9	13.0	10.9	17.3	8.5	11.2	14.8	12.5	11.5	12.4	21.2	4.6	7.9	3.4	3.4
5. Can't say, drug unfamiliar	3.7	3.4	4.0	2.6	8.5	3.0	3.2	5.5	2.0	3.3	4.0	5.9	2.0	.6	1.5	5.2
Item 7340 N(Wtd)	2674	1287	1332	2179	271	603	838	833	399	1360	1210	1113	605	317	533	58

QUESTIONNAIRE FORM 2 1976	TOTAL	SEX		RACE		REGION				4YR COLLEGE PLANS		ILLICIT DRUG USE: LIFETIME				
		M	F	White	Black	NE	NC	S	W	Yes	No	None	Mari-juana Only	Few Pills	More Pills	Any Her-oin
Weighted No. of Cases:	3036	1453	1445	2358	343	723	919	934	460	1450	1342	1223	687	343	597	69
% of Weighted Total:	100.0	47.9	47.6	77.7	11.3	23.8	30.3	30.8	15.2	47.8	44.2	40.3	22.6	11.3	19.7	2.3
E01D: Smoke marijuana regularly																
1. No risk	20.3	24.1	16.0	19.9	23.6	27.2	18.4	17.8	19.0	17.6	22.9	6.4	20.8	23.0	43.7	45.8
2. Slight risk	24.0	24.1	24.1	24.7	17.8	25.4	23.8	20.9	28.9	23.6	24.2	14.4	33.4	29.3	29.9	32.2
3. Moderate risk	24.8	24.4	25.1	26.0	17.8	24.3	28.4	22.2	23.7	27.9	21.9	28.2	27.2	26.2	16.6	11.9
4. Great risk	27.1	23.2	31.0	26.8	32.4	19.8	25.7	33.8	26.4	27.5	26.8	45.1	16.4	21.1	7.6	3.4
5. Can't say, drug unfamiliar	3.9	4.0	3.8	2.7	8.4	3.3	3.6	5.4	2.2	3.4	4.3	5.9	2.3	.6	2.3	5.1
Item 7350 N(Wtd)	2680	1297	1328	2183	275	602	839	838	401	1359	1218	1115	611	317	529	59
E01E: Try LSD once or twice																
1. No risk	10.4	11.9	9.0	9.9	15.1	13.9	10.5	8.6	9.3	9.5	11.2	5.6	10.0	9.5	19.4	28.8
2. Slight risk	20.1	18.1	22.1	21.1	15.8	22.2	21.5	17.8	18.8	21.0	19.6	17.8	19.7	18.4	26.4	25.4
3. Moderate risk	24.2	24.9	23.5	26.1	14.3	24.0	24.7	22.7	26.8	27.2	21.1	23.9	24.5	26.3	25.6	20.3
4. Great risk	32.9	34.2	31.7	31.9	38.6	28.3	31.0	37.0	35.3	31.9	34.0	39.4	31.9	36.7	18.6	16.9
5. Can't say, drug unfamiliar	12.3	10.8	13.6	10.9	16.2	11.4	12.5	14.0	10.0	10.2	14.2	13.3	13.7	8.9	9.8	6.8
Item 7360 N(Wtd)	2673	1291	1327	2180	272	604	842	827	399	1359	1210	1113	608	316	531	59
E01F: Take LSD regularly																
1. No risk	4.9	5.8	3.9	4.1	11.4	5.5	4.9	4.9	4.1	3.6	6.5	3.4	4.8	5.4	7.0	12.5
2. Slight risk	7.0	7.4	6.5	7.2	5.9	7.2	7.3	6.6	6.6	5.4	8.3	4.0	6.5	6.7	12.1	19.6
3. Moderate risk	18.1	19.0	17.4	19.6	9.9	21.6	19.6	13.2	20.2	19.6	16.5	14.1	20.1	18.4	25.5	17.9
4. Great risk	57.7	57.1	58.8	58.2	57.4	53.9	55.6	61.6	59.2	61.1	54.8	65.4	54.4	61.0	45.9	41.1
5. Can't say, drug unfamiliar	12.3	10.8	13.4	10.9	15.8	11.8	12.5	13.5	9.9	10.4	13.9	13.0	14.3	8.6	9.6	7.1
Item 7370 N(Wtd)	2656	1282	1324	2165	272	601	832	831	392	1350	1205	1105	603	315	529	56
E01G: Try heroin (smack, horse) once or twice																
1. No risk	6.8	7.4	6.1	6.2	11.0	9.9	6.2	5.4	6.3	5.7	8.0	4.9	6.1	7.6	9.5	20.7
2. Slight risk	13.8	13.1	14.8	14.9	8.4	13.7	15.6	12.3	13.8	15.1	12.6	13.9	14.7	11.0	14.1	20.7
3. Moderate risk	21.4	20.4	22.4	22.6	19.0	21.7	22.9	19.1	22.8	23.9	18.6	22.8	20.5	18.3	21.9	24.1
4. Great risk	42.9	45.6	40.4	42.3	45.4	40.1	38.7	48.0	45.3	43.1	43.0	43.0	41.1	51.7	40.6	29.3
5. Can't say, drug unfamiliar	15.1	13.6	16.4	14.1	16.5	14.5	16.7	15.3	12.0	12.2	17.8	15.3	17.5	11.7	13.7	5.2
Item 7380 N(Wtd)	2664	1281	1328	2172	273	598	834	831	400	1358	1205	1113	604	317	525	58
E01H: Take heroin occasionally																
1. No risk	4.5	5.3	3.5	3.7	10.8	5.3	4.1	4.8	3.5	3.3	5.8	3.4	4.8	5.0	4.7	12.3
2. Slight risk	7.8	6.9	8.8	7.5	10.4	8.5	7.8	7.3	7.7	6.7	8.8	7.6	5.9	8.5	8.7	22.8
3. Moderate risk	19.5	19.3	20.0	21.1	10.8	19.5	21.4	17.3	20.1	22.1	16.8	19.8	19.3	17.6	20.4	24.6
4. Great risk	53.5	55.3	51.7	54.1	52.0	51.9	50.5	55.9	57.0	56.2	51.0	54.7	52.3	58.0	52.2	35.1
5. Can't say, drug unfamiliar	14.8	13.4	16.0	13.7	16.0	14.7	16.3	14.8	11.7	11.7	17.7	14.3	17.7	11.0	14.0	7.0
Item 7390 N(Wtd)	2667	1288	1324	2177	269	599	833	833	402	1353	1210	1109	606	319	529	57
E01I: Take heroin regularly																
1. No risk	4.1	4.9	3.1	3.1	11.5	3.2	4.2	4.8	3.3	2.7	5.6	3.3	4.7	4.7	3.2	10.3
2. Slight risk	3.6	3.7	3.4	3.4	4.8	4.2	3.1	4.1	2.8	2.7	4.4	3.3	2.5	3.8	4.5	10.3
3. Moderate risk	10.7	10.9	10.7	11.0	10.0	12.0	11.2	9.2	11.2	10.3	11.2	9.4	11.2	9.8	12.5	19.0
4. Great risk	66.6	67.0	66.4	68.7	56.5	66.0	65.3	66.5	70.1	72.2	60.9	68.8	63.8	70.3	65.5	55.2
5. Can't say, drug unfamiliar	15.0	13.7	16.3	13.9	17.1	14.7	16.1	15.4	12.4	12.1	17.8	15.0	17.7	11.4	14.2	5.2
Item 7400 N(Wtd)	2654	1278	1323	2166	269	592	834	835	394	1351	1201	1105	599	317	528	58
E01J: Try barbiturates (downers, goofballs, reds, yellows, etc.) once or twice																
1. No risk	11.4	12.2	10.8	11.2	12.1	15.3	10.9	9.4	11.3	11.1	11.8	6.1	11.4	11.0	21.2	27.6
2. Slight risk	22.3	21.7	22.8	23.5	18.4	20.5	25.8	20.2	21.9	23.2	22.0	20.5	18.2	24.2	30.1	29.3
3. Moderate risk	24.0	24.3	23.4	25.3	16.5	23.8	22.8	23.2	28.6	25.9	22.2	22.3	23.3	30.2	25.9	20.7
4. Great risk	26.2	27.7	25.0	24.9	33.8	24.2	24.3	29.7	26.1	26.2	25.8	32.7	26.8	24.5	13.8	12.1
5. Can't say, drug unfamiliar	16.0	14.1	18.0	15.2	18.8	16.4	16.1	17.6	12.1	13.8	18.2	18.5	20.3	10.4	9.1	12.1
Item 7410 N(Wtd)	2668	1286	1327	2176	272	596	837	837	398	1356	1209	1113	605	318	528	58

QUESTIONNAIRE FORM 2 1976	TOTAL	SEX		RACE		REGION				4YR COLLEGE PLANS		ILLICIT DRUG USE: LIFETIME				
		M	F	White	Black	NE	NC	S	W	Yes	No	None	Mari-juana Only	Few Pills	More Pills	Any Her-oin
Weighted No. of Cases:	3036	1453	1445	2358	343	723	919	934	460	1450	1342	1223	687	343	597	69
% of Weighted Total:	100.0	47.9	47.6	77.7	11.3	23.8	30.3	30.8	15.2	47.8	44.2	40.3	22.6	11.3	19.7	2.3
E01K: Take barbiturates regularly																
1. No risk	5.5	6.3	4.6	4.6	11.9	5.4	5.2	6.0	5.0	4.0	7.1	3.2	5.8	4.1	8.6	22.4
2. Slight risk	10.6	10.2	11.0	11.1	7.4	9.8	13.4	8.5	10.3	9.6	11.8	6.6	8.6	13.7	19.3	19.0
3. Moderate risk	24.1	24.8	23.4	25.3	15.6	27.1	24.5	21.3	24.6	25.6	22.8	20.5	23.3	25.5	33.1	24.1
4. Great risk	43.3	44.0	42.7	43.5	45.0	40.8	40.1	46.3	47.6	46.7	39.6	51.7	41.4	44.6	29.1	24.1
5. Can't say, drug unfamiliar	16.4	14.7	18.1	15.4	19.7	16.8	16.9	17.7	12.5	14.2	18.8	18.2	20.8	12.1	9.8	10.3
Item 7420 N(Wtd)	2651	1279	1318	2162	269	591	830	831	399	1352	1198	1107	602	314	523	58
E01L: Try amphetamines (uppers, pep pills, bennies, speed) once or twice																
1. No risk	12.8	12.9	12.6	12.9	11.5	15.9	13.5	9.2	13.9	11.8	14.0	6.0	11.5	10.8	28.2	29.3
2. Slight risk	21.8	22.5	21.4	23.0	16.7	20.3	23.9	20.6	22.0	23.1	20.6	18.7	18.2	23.7	31.8	27.6
3. Moderate risk	24.5	23.6	25.0	25.4	18.9	23.1	25.1	23.8	26.8	26.3	22.9	24.1	23.7	33.5	21.7	22.4
4. Great risk	25.8	27.2	24.4	24.6	34.1	24.8	23.3	28.9	26.3	26.1	25.1	32.8	27.3	22.8	11.6	8.6
5. Can't say, drug unfamiliar	15.1	13.7	16.6	14.1	18.9	15.9	14.3	17.4	11.1	12.8	17.3	18.3	19.5	9.2	6.9	10.3
Item 7430 N(Wtd)	2654	1282	1318	2166	270	592	834	833	395	1351	1203	1109	600	316	525	58
E01M: Take amphetamines regularly																
1. No risk	6.6	7.4	5.7	5.9	13.8	6.4	7.0	7.0	5.3	4.9	8.4	3.5	5.8	6.6	12.8	19.0
2. Slight risk	11.3	11.5	11.1	11.7	9.2	12.0	12.4	9.5	11.1	8.2	14.8	5.6	8.2	10.3	25.1	24.1
3. Moderate risk	22.7	24.2	21.2	23.8	13.5	23.6	24.4	19.9	23.9	25.3	19.5	18.3	23.0	29.1	29.3	17.2
4. Great risk	43.2	42.5	43.9	43.8	41.5	40.4	41.1	44.9	48.8	48.0	38.3	53.6	42.1	43.7	25.0	25.9
5. Can't say, drug unfamiliar	16.2	14.3	18.0	14.8	21.9	17.6	15.1	18.8	10.9	13.6	19.0	19.0	20.8	10.6	7.9	13.8
Item 7440 N(Wtd)	2558	1235	1271	2097	260	581	799	800	377	1301	1160	1061	582	302	509	58
E01N: Try cocaine once or twice																
1. No risk	13.0	14.5	11.4	12.7	14.3	17.1	12.2	10.0	14.3	12.0	13.8	5.5	10.4	13.9	28.0	43.1
2. Slight risk	19.4	19.7	19.3	20.3	16.2	19.5	20.4	16.9	22.8	20.2	18.6	15.5	18.1	22.0	28.2	17.2
3. Moderate risk	22.3	21.2	23.3	23.5	17.0	21.5	23.0	22.2	22.0	23.9	21.1	23.1	23.6	25.6	19.2	12.1
4. Great risk	27.8	29.1	26.7	27.0	31.3	25.5	25.9	31.2	28.6	28.7	27.2	35.1	27.5	28.2	14.0	15.5
5. Can't say, drug unfamiliar	17.4	15.4	19.4	16.5	21.2	16.4	18.5	19.6	12.3	15.2	19.3	20.8	20.4	10.4	10.5	12.1
Item 7450 N(Wtd)	2620	1266	1301	2147	259	591	820	818	391	1334	1185	1089	597	309	522	58
E01O: Take cocaine regularly																
1. No risk	6.5	7.6	5.2	5.8	11.1	7.2	5.4	6.4	8.1	5.2	7.9	3.0	5.7	6.4	12.0	29.6
2. Slight risk	8.7	10.0	7.7	9.0	7.8	9.8	8.9	6.5	11.0	8.1	9.2	4.3	5.6	10.5	19.5	14.8
3. Moderate risk	18.9	19.1	18.8	19.4	15.2	20.8	20.0	15.7	20.4	19.1	18.7	13.4	20.8	20.7	26.3	27.8
4. Great risk	48.7	48.7	48.9	49.6	46.1	46.3	47.2	52.4	48.4	52.3	45.3	58.3	48.4	52.9	30.7	14.8
5. Can't say, drug unfamiliar	17.1	14.5	19.5	16.2	20.2	15.9	18.5	19.0	12.1	15.3	18.8	20.9	19.4	9.5	11.4	13.0
Item 7460 N(Wtd)	2470	1194	1226	2026	243	559	774	764	372	1259	1118	1021	558	295	498	54
E01P: Try one or two drinks of an alcoholic beverage (beer, wine, liquor)																
1. No risk	38.9	41.1	36.6	40.5	25.4	47.2	40.2	31.7	38.9	39.1	38.4	26.8	47.4	38.7	54.4	50.9
2. Slight risk	36.1	35.9	36.1	37.0	33.8	32.9	36.5	39.6	32.4	36.9	35.5	40.9	34.9	36.5	29.1	26.3
3. Moderate risk	15.7	14.1	17.5	15.0	19.5	13.0	14.3	17.2	19.8	15.5	16.5	20.9	11.5	16.0	10.1	8.8
4. Great risk	7.2	6.8	7.8	5.9	15.4	5.2	7.1	8.7	7.0	6.4	7.4	8.6	4.9	8.5	4.4	10.5
5. Can't say, drug unfamiliar	2.1	2.1	2.1	1.5	5.5	1.8	2.0	2.6	1.8	1.9	2.2	2.8	1.3	.6	1.9	3.5
Item 7470 N(Wtd)	2668	1288	1326	2178	272	598	835	836	398	1359	1208	1114	607	318	526	57
E01Q: Take one or two drinks nearly every day																
1. No risk	14.1	17.4	10.9	13.7	15.4	17.4	14.7	11.9	12.3	10.9	17.4	7.5	17.3	15.0	21.9	27.6
2. Slight risk	27.5	28.8	26.1	28.7	23.1	30.4	30.0	24.5	24.6	25.1	30.1	24.0	31.6	24.8	32.1	27.6
3. Moderate risk	35.1	34.0	36.5	36.1	27.5	33.6	32.9	36.9	38.6	40.2	30.3	39.4	33.6	36.1	29.3	27.6
4. Great risk	21.3	18.0	24.6	20.2	27.1	17.5	20.3	24.1	22.8	21.7	20.2	26.4	16.0	23.8	14.8	13.8
5. Can't say, drug unfamiliar	2.0	2.0	2.0	1.2	6.6	1.2	2.2	2.6	1.8	1.9	2.0	2.6	1.5	.3	1.9	3.4
Item 7480 N(Wtd)	2666	1285	1327	2175	273	593	836	838	399	1358	1210	1111	607	319	526	58

QUESTIONNAIRE FORM 2 1976	TOTAL	SEX M	SEX F	RACE White	RACE Black	REGION NE	REGION NC	REGION S	REGION W	4YR COLLEGE PLANS Yes	4YR COLLEGE PLANS No	ILLICIT DRUG USE: LIFETIME None	Marijuana Only	Few Pills	More Pills	Any Heroin
Weighted No. of Cases:	3036	1453	1445	2358	343	723	919	934	460	1450	1342	1223	687	343	597	69
% of Weighted Total:	100.0	47.9	47.6	77.7	11.3	23.8	30.3	30.8	15.2	47.8	44.2	40.3	22.6	11.3	19.7	2.3
E01R: Take four or five drinks nearly every day																
1. No risk	5.6	7.8	3.3	4.6	13.6	4.4	6.0	6.9	3.7	3.0	8.5	3.2	5.9	6.3	7.8	20.7
2. Slight risk	11.5	13.6	9.6	11.6	10.3	14.1	13.0	9.4	8.5	9.9	13.2	7.7	13.2	12.8	16.2	17.2
3. Moderate risk	27.0	29.1	25.2	28.2	19.4	32.1	27.1	23.3	26.9	25.2	29.1	24.1	32.0	22.5	32.1	17.2
4. Great risk	53.5	47.1	59.6	54.1	49.5	47.4	51.7	57.3	58.1	59.9	46.4	62.1	47.3	58.1	41.8	39.7
5. Can't say, drug unfamiliar	2.4	2.5	2.3	1.5	7.3	1.8	2.2	3.0	2.5	1.9	2.7	2.9	1.6	.3	2.1	3.4
Item 7490 N(Wtd)	2671	1290	1327	2180	273	595	837	838	401	1357	1212	1111	607	320	526	58
E01S: Have five or more drinks once or twice each weekend																
1. No risk	10.5	13.6	7.2	9.8	14.3	13.5	10.3	9.9	7.5	6.7	14.0	5.0	11.4	10.1	19.2	29.3
2. Slight risk	16.9	19.8	13.9	17.4	12.9	20.4	19.0	12.2	16.8	16.0	17.7	9.5	22.0	21.4	22.9	25.9
3. Moderate risk	30.3	28.8	31.3	31.5	22.1	30.5	32.9	29.2	26.6	31.6	28.8	26.1	36.7	30.5	33.0	25.9
4. Great risk	40.1	35.6	45.1	39.8	43.4	34.0	35.7	45.6	46.9	43.6	37.1	56.2	28.1	37.7	22.9	15.5
5. Can't say, drug unfamiliar	2.3	2.2	2.4	1.5	7.0	1.7	2.2	3.0	2.3	2.1	2.3	3.2	1.8	.3	1.9	3.4
Item 7500 N(Wtd)	2663	1286	1323	2174	272	594	835	835	399	1353	1210	1110	605	318	525	58
E02: Some people like school very much. Others don't. How do you feel about going to school?																
5. I like school very much	12.6	12.1	13.1	10.9	23.6	10.5	9.9	15.3	16.0	16.1	8.4	16.7	8.5	12.7	8.3	7.1
4. I like school quite a lot	28.7	26.8	30.8	29.5	25.5	26.8	29.0	30.0	27.9	36.0	21.3	34.1	28.3	29.7	18.3	16.1
3. I like school some	38.8	41.8	35.9	38.3	41.1	37.8	40.6	37.5	39.3	35.2	42.4	35.3	41.4	43.4	40.0	48.2
2. I don't like school very much	13.9	13.6	14.1	14.8	8.0	16.8	15.0	12.1	11.2	10.1	18.1	10.0	16.1	10.1	22.1	16.1
1. I don't like school at all	5.9	5.7	6.1	6.5	1.8	7.8	5.6	5.0	5.6	2.4	9.8	3.9	5.7	4.4	11.2	12.5
Item 7630 N(Wtd)	2670	1288	1329	2177	275	600	839	837	394	1351	1218	1118	614	316	520	56
E03: About how many hours do you spend in an average week on all your homework including both in school and out of school?																
1. 0 hours	9.9	13.3	6.3	9.6	8.8	10.0	10.9	9.0	9.5	4.5	15.6	6.8	11.6	9.2	13.7	15.3
2. 1-4 hours	44.9	45.9	44.1	45.0	48.5	43.8	42.6	48.7	43.3	37.2	53.5	42.1	46.6	43.5	50.2	47.5
3. 5-9 hours	22.5	21.6	23.2	22.3	25.7	21.2	22.3	23.4	22.8	27.5	16.7	24.8	21.2	23.5	18.9	20.3
4. 10-14 hours	11.1	10.3	12.0	11.6	8.1	13.7	10.3	9.4	12.6	15.4	6.5	12.1	11.1	12.7	8.4	10.2
5. 15-19 hours	5.0	4.0	6.1	5.1	3.7	4.5	6.3	3.9	5.1	7.0	3.1	5.9	5.8	3.8	3.4	1.7
6. 20-24 hours	3.0	2.6	3.4	3.2	.7	3.5	2.8	2.5	3.3	4.1	1.8	3.6	2.3	3.2	2.3	5.1
7. 25 or more hours	3.6	2.3	4.9	3.2	4.0	3.2	4.6	2.9	3.6	4.4	2.6	4.7	1.7	4.1	3.1	-
Item 7640 N(Wtd)	2667	1279	1334	2176	272	598	843	836	390	1356	1209	1117	605	315	524	59
E04: In general, how much say or influence do you feel each of the following has on HOW YOUR SCHOOL IS RUN?																
E04A: The principal																
1. Little or no influence	10.4	12.2	8.2	8.7	16.9	10.1	10.3	9.4	13.4	7.5	13.4	8.2	10.3	9.8	12.0	29.8
2. Some influence	13.8	13.8	13.5	12.2	22.8	14.7	14.5	13.1	11.9	13.8	13.7	12.5	13.0	14.3	16.3	17.5
3. Moderate influence	13.8	13.7	13.9	13.9	11.8	11.8	15.6	13.7	12.9	12.4	15.4	13.3	14.0	16.2	13.3	12.3
4. Considerable influence	27.4	27.2	27.9	29.6	14.0	29.0	27.2	26.0	28.2	27.5	27.0	28.4	27.2	27.3	28.0	12.3
5. A great deal of influence	34.8	33.1	36.5	35.6	34.2	34.8	32.3	37.7	33.6	38.8	30.5	37.6	35.5	32.4	30.2	26.3
Item 7650 N(Wtd)	2638	1261	1323	2152	272	587	834	830	387	1346	1193	1108	602	315	510	57
E04B: The teachers																
1. Little or no influence	8.2	9.0	7.2	6.8	12.7	7.8	9.5	7.2	8.0	5.9	10.7	6.3	6.5	9.9	11.6	19.6
2. Some influence	20.9	21.2	20.8	20.2	27.6	19.8	22.9	22.5	15.2	17.4	24.6	18.8	21.9	25.2	22.3	19.6
3. Moderate influence	31.3	32.8	29.8	33.3	22.4	32.0	32.9	27.9	33.7	33.5	29.2	31.8	32.5	29.6	30.8	25.0
4. Considerable influence	29.7	27.9	31.4	30.6	25.0	29.7	27.1	31.2	32.1	34.2	24.7	32.6	31.1	26.1	25.4	23.2
5. A great deal of influence	9.9	9.1	10.7	9.1	12.3	10.5	7.5	11.3	11.1	8.9	10.6	10.4	8.1	9.2	10.1	14.3
Item 7660 N(Wtd)	2640	1267	1320	2160	268	590	838	824	389	1348	1193	1105	604	314	516	56

QUESTIONNAIRE FORM 2 1976	TOTAL	SEX		RACE		REGION				4YR COLLEGE PLANS		ILLICIT DRUG USE: LIFETIME				
		M	F	White	Black	NE	NC	S	W	Yes	No	None	Mari-juana Only	Few Pills	More Pills	Any Her-oin
Weighted No. of Cases:	3036	1453	1445	2358	343	723	919	934	460	1450	1342	1223	687	343	597	69
% of Weighted Total:	100.0	47.9	47.6	77.7	11.3	23.8	30.3	30.8	15.2	47.8	44.2	40.3	22.6	11.3	19.7	2.3

E04C: The students

1. Little or no influence	31.2	32.7	30.3	32.4	26.8	29.5	34.0	31.1	27.9	28.3	34.2	29.6	31.3	28.2	38.0	26.8
2. Some influence	26.3	26.8	25.7	26.7	24.2	24.8	26.6	28.1	24.1	29.0	23.4	25.7	26.1	31.4	26.8	16.1
3. Moderate influence	18.4	19.1	17.8	19.1	12.8	19.4	18.1	17.5	19.5	19.8	17.1	21.0	18.4	14.4	14.6	21.4
4. Considerable influence	13.7	12.1	14.9	13.0	18.5	15.6	12.4	12.0	16.9	14.2	13.2	12.9	14.6	16.0	11.2	23.2
5. A great deal of influence	10.3	9.3	11.5	8.9	18.1	10.5	8.8	11.2	11.3	8.7	12.0	10.8	9.5	9.9	9.4	10.7
Item 7670 N(Wtd)	2635	1264	1318	2156	265	589	838	819	390	1346	1190	1106	597	312	519	56

E04D: Parents of students

1. Little or no influence	21.6	23.2	20.2	21.7	19.9	25.6	22.2	21.6	14.9	16.7	26.3	18.6	23.2	19.0	26.0	34.5
2. Some influence	32.5	32.9	32.7	34.2	23.8	29.8	32.6	34.4	32.4	33.3	32.1	33.2	33.8	32.2	32.4	20.0
3. Moderate influence	21.6	21.1	21.8	22.0	18.4	21.8	22.4	19.0	25.4	23.6	19.8	22.5	21.9	22.8	19.0	25.5
4. Considerable influence	14.5	13.7	15.1	14.4	16.1	13.8	14.2	14.2	17.5	16.8	12.3	15.4	12.0	16.7	14.5	10.9
5. A great deal of influence	9.6	9.0	10.2	7.8	21.8	9.0	8.6	10.7	10.0	9.7	9.6	10.2	9.0	9.3	8.3	10.9
Item 7680 N(Wtd)	2633	1262	1317	2158	261	587	838	819	389	1345	1188	1107	598	311	516	55

E05: Have you had any drug education courses or lectures in school?

1. No--GO TO Q.E09	15.7	16.8	14.4	15.1	18.1	15.6	13.6	17.7	16.2	14.1	17.6	18.8	15.0	12.5	11.1	22.0
2. No, and I wish I had-- GO TO Q.E09	5.1	5.2	5.1	4.6	8.8	4.3	5.3	5.9	4.0	4.5	5.9	5.0	6.5	6.6	3.1	-
3. Yes	79.2	78.1	80.5	80.3	73.1	80.1	81.2	76.3	79.8	81.5	76.6	76.1	78.5	81.0	85.8	78.0
Item 7690 N(Wtd)	2494	1182	1264	2073	227	559	788	776	371	1295	1110	1047	572	305	486	50

E06: Would you say that the information about drugs that you received in school classes or programs has...

1. Made you less interested in trying drugs	50.5	45.9	55.3	48.3	71.2	44.2	48.7	59.5	45.8	50.3	51.5	69.5	47.3	47.4	22.2	22.5
2. Not changed your interest in trying drugs	45.6	48.2	42.8	48.3	23.5	53.6	45.7	36.4	51.9	46.4	43.9	29.4	48.7	49.4	69.7	60.0
3. Made you more interested in trying drugs	4.0	6.0	2.0	3.4	5.3	2.2	5.8	4.0	2.4	3.3	4.6	1.1	4.0	3.2	8.1	20.0
Item 7840 N(Wtd) ★	1973	922	1017	1658	170	446	637	593	297	1056	849	796	446	247	419	40

E07: How many of the following drug education experiences have you had in high school? (Mark all that apply.)

A. A special course about drugs	22.7	23.7	21.7	22.2	26.6	26.9	22.9	18.8	24.1	26.1	18.8	23.8	20.6	25.5	20.6	18.4
B. Films, lectures, or discussions in one of my regular courses	75.7	75.7	75.5	77.4	64.7	76.9	77.9	70.8	78.9	79.0	72.8	78.1	75.9	72.5	74.6	63.2
C. Films or lectures, outside of my regular courses	28.8	28.6	28.9	28.1	33.5	23.1	26.5	37.4	24.8	29.8	27.7	30.7	25.2	30.0	26.9	23.7
D. Special discussions ("rap" groups) about drugs	24.7	24.0	25.7	23.6	28.9	26.9	24.0	25.4	21.1	24.4	24.9	19.7	23.2	30.4	30.8	36.8
Item 7850-7880 N(Wtd) ★	1979	926	1014	1662	173	446	637	602	294	1057	849	798	456	247	413	38

E08: Overall, how valuable were the experiences to you?

1. Little or no value	18.1	21.0	15.3	19.2	10.5	21.9	18.6	13.4	21.2	17.2	19.2	13.1	16.7	15.3	30.8	26.3
2. Some value	45.7	45.8	45.7	47.6	33.1	47.8	49.7	41.6	43.1	47.1	43.6	42.3	52.6	43.1	46.7	50.0
3. Considerable value	24.7	22.5	26.9	24.1	30.2	21.7	22.5	29.7	23.9	25.9	23.8	31.2	20.4	27.0	17.6	10.5
4. Great value	11.4	10.6	12.1	9.1	26.2	8.9	9.4	15.4	11.8	9.7	13.4	13.5	10.3	14.5	5.1	13.2
Item 7890 N(Wtd) ★	1985	932	1015	1665	172	448	640	599	297	1063	849	799	456	248	415	38

★ = excludes respondents for whom question was inappropriate.

QUESTIONNAIRE FORM 2 1976	TOTAL	SEX		RACE		REGION				4YR COLLEGE PLANS		ILLICIT DRUG USE: LIFETIME				
		M	F	White	Black	NE	NC	S	W	Yes	No	None	Marijuana Only	Few Pills	More Pills	Any Heroin
Weighted No. of Cases:	3036	1453	1445	2358	343	723	919	934	460	1450	1342	1223	687	343	597	69
% of Weighted Total:	100.0	47.9	47.6	77.7	11.3	23.8	30.3	30.8	15.2	47.8	44.2	40.3	22.6	11.3	19.7	2.3

E09: The next questions are about things you might own. First, which of the following products do you yourself PRESENTLY OWN? Count things that were given to you as well as things you bought, but only count those that are in good working order. (Mark ALL that you own.)

	TOTAL	M	F	White	Black	NE	NC	S	W	Yes	No	None	Marijuana Only	Few Pills	More Pills	Any Heroin
A. A hair dryer	66.6	55.4	77.7	70.6	35.0	67.9	68.7	67.2	59.0	67.7	65.9	65.2	64.5	70.7	71.6	64.8
B. Water or snow skis	15.6	18.5	12.7	17.8	.8	20.4	13.1	9.6	26.2	18.0	12.3	12.6	21.1	11.8	17.9	16.7
C. A camera	65.4	58.2	72.7	65.6	62.2	69.0	64.5	63.2	66.2	67.6	63.6	64.9	64.3	67.5	66.9	63.0
D. A watch	81.0	77.1	85.1	81.2	79.5	81.3	82.3	82.0	75.6	82.2	80.2	83.1	77.6	83.1	79.4	81.5
E. Hiking back pack	22.1	32.6	11.3	23.7	6.7	24.0	21.8	16.3	31.3	24.5	19.4	16.9	25.7	21.7	28.0	35.2
F. A clock radio	56.7	58.7	54.4	58.3	42.5	59.5	57.9	53.5	56.2	58.9	52.9	54.0	59.0	58.6	58.8	64.8
G. An electric shaver	33.6	34.9	32.5	37.4	7.5	36.4	36.5	29.1	32.1	33.2	33.8	31.5	34.2	34.4	38.1	37.0
H. A tennis racquet	50.3	50.4	50.0	54.7	22.0	54.6	52.5	43.5	53.7	59.8	39.3	51.3	51.1	52.9	48.8	38.9
I. A TV set	42.4	46.5	38.8	40.0	57.1	46.4	36.0	48.0	38.9	40.8	43.6	39.6	42.0	44.3	47.1	44.4
J. A bicycle	61.3	60.7	61.6	64.5	42.9	68.2	62.5	54.0	63.1	66.6	55.2	62.0	62.9	62.4	58.2	55.6
K. A car	43.7	55.6	31.7	46.6	23.6	31.3	44.0	50.0	48.3	37.9	50.2	37.5	48.1	46.8	48.1	64.8
L. A tape recorder	55.0	60.2	50.1	54.8	55.1	61.6	50.1	56.4	52.9	55.1	54.0	53.4	56.7	53.8	57.2	66.7
M. An electronic calculator	31.3	37.9	25.2	32.3	22.0	34.5	33.7	27.2	29.8	39.3	22.4	33.6	32.0	30.3	28.0	29.6
N. A boat or snowmobile	6.8	10.9	3.0	7.6	.8	8.2	7.1	5.9	6.1	5.9	7.7	5.4	7.5	4.5	9.9	13.0
Item 7700-7830 N(Wtd)	2630	1260	1315	2161	254	588	840	810	393	1345	1188	1099	603	314	514	54

E10: When, if ever, do you expect to buy each of these things? (If you already own one: When, if ever, do you expect to buy a better model?)

E10A: A hair dryer

	TOTAL	M	F	White	Black	NE	NC	S	W	Yes	No	None	Marijuana Only	Few Pills	More Pills	Any Heroin
0. Only if my present one wears out	52.9	44.9	60.2	55.5	36.3	53.6	54.3	54.8	44.5	52.5	54.5	53.4	51.1	57.9	52.0	50.0
4. Within the next year	14.1	12.0	16.6	13.2	18.5	13.8	14.3	13.1	16.1	15.7	12.1	13.5	12.4	17.2	16.1	8.0
3. Within 2 to 5 years	10.1	10.1	10.2	10.3	10.1	8.8	9.4	11.6	11.0	10.3	10.2	10.4	10.1	10.8	8.5	14.0
2. Later than 5 years	4.3	4.6	3.8	4.4	2.4	4.5	4.8	2.8	6.2	3.8	4.3	4.1	3.9	3.0	6.0	2.0
1. Probably not ever	18.6	28.4	9.3	16.6	33.1	19.4	17.3	17.7	22.4	17.6	18.8	18.5	22.6	11.4	17.5	26.0
Item 13700 N(Wtd)	2484	1154	1280	2043	248	558	788	785	353	1277	1121	1044	566	297	485	50

E10B: Water or snow skis

	TOTAL	M	F	White	Black	NE	NC	S	W	Yes	No	None	Marijuana Only	Few Pills	More Pills	Any Heroin
0. Only if my present one wears out	8.0	10.1	5.9	7.5	9.7	8.8	6.3	7.9	10.9	7.6	8.4	7.7	9.4	7.9	6.7	8.3
4. Within the next year	8.8	12.1	5.7	9.5	3.4	9.4	6.9	7.2	15.9	9.8	6.5	4.7	10.6	11.3	13.8	12.5
3. Within 2 to 5 years	16.0	17.2	15.0	17.8	2.5	19.5	13.7	14.2	19.5	19.3	12.6	13.7	16.4	20.5	18.2	14.6
2. Later than 5 years	11.1	12.4	9.9	11.5	6.8	8.6	12.4	9.7	15.0	14.1	7.8	10.9	9.9	14.4	12.3	10.4
1. Probably not ever	56.1	48.3	63.6	53.6	77.6	53.7	60.8	61.1	38.7	49.2	64.6	63.0	53.9	45.9	49.4	52.1
Item 13710 N(Wtd)	2459	1153	1256	2035	237	555	783	763	359	1272	1101	1035	566	292	478	48

E10C: A camera

	TOTAL	M	F	White	Black	NE	NC	S	W	Yes	No	None	Marijuana Only	Few Pills	More Pills	Any Heroin
0. Only if my present one wears out	42.4	34.0	50.6	42.6	42.0	40.3	42.4	43.7	42.7	42.3	43.3	42.2	41.9	44.7	42.1	40.8
4. Within the next year	19.5	18.6	20.1	19.3	33.6	17.8	16.8	23.1	20.1	18.8	20.1	19.9	17.2	22.3	17.4	24.5
3. Within 2 to 5 years	23.4	27.9	18.9	24.9	13.4	24.4	25.6	20.4	23.7	23.5	22.7	22.4	25.8	20.3	26.0	16.3
2. Later than 5 years	9.3	12.2	6.6	9.8	6.7	11.3	8.7	8.3	9.9	11.1	7.0	9.8	9.6	7.7	8.6	14.3
1. Probably not ever	5.4	7.3	3.7	5.4	4.2	6.4	6.5	4.5	3.6	4.4	6.8	5.7	4.8	5.0	5.7	6.1
Item 13720 N(Wtd)	2497	1178	1272	2063	238	566	797	771	363	1285	1123	1048	582	300	477	49

E10D: A watch

	TOTAL	M	F	White	Black	NE	NC	S	W	Yes	No	None	Marijuana Only	Few Pills	More Pills	Any Heroin
0. Only if my present one wears out	52.9	49.4	56.6	53.2	50.0	53.4	53.8	54.4	46.7	51.9	55.2	53.7	53.8	52.7	49.7	60.0
4. Within the next year	27.1	24.7	28.9	26.0	37.1	25.5	24.7	28.9	30.8	26.4	27.5	27.1	25.5	28.0	28.0	20.0
3. Within 2 to 5 years	11.9	14.6	9.2	12.3	8.1	11.9	13.3	10.0	13.2	13.9	9.3	12.0	13.3	9.5	12.5	6.0
2. Later than 5 years	4.8	6.6	3.1	5.1	2.4	5.3	5.6	3.7	4.4	5.0	4.2	4.1	5.8	5.4	4.5	10.0
1. Probably not ever	3.3	4.6	2.2	3.4	2.4	3.7	2.7	3.0	4.7	2.8	3.7	3.0	1.7	4.4	5.3	4.0
Item 13730 N(Wtd)	2519	1192	1277	2078	248	564	803	788	364	1294	1135	1071	573	296	489	50

QUESTIONNAIRE FORM 2 1976	TOTAL	SEX		RACE		REGION				4YR COLLEGE PLANS		ILLICIT DRUG USE: LIFETIME				
		M	F	White	Black	NE	NC	S	W	Yes	No	None	Marijuana Only	Few Pills	More Pills	Any Heroin
Weighted No. of Cases:	3036	1453	1445	2358	343	723	919	934	460	1450	1342	1223	687	343	597	69
% of Weighted Total:	100.0	47.9	47.6	77.7	11.3	23.8	30.3	30.8	15.2	47.8	44.2	40.3	22.6	11.3	19.7	2.3

E10E: Hiking back pack

0. Only if my present one wears out	14.8	21.3	8.3	15.2	7.3	14.9	15.6	11.0	20.8	15.1	14.3	11.9	19.0	13.2	16.4	22.4
4. Within the next year	12.6	12.5	12.9	12.7	12.0	12.7	13.6	11.3	13.1	13.6	11.4	9.8	11.7	15.7	16.4	22.4
3. Within 2 to 5 years	11.9	11.7	12.3	12.7	6.4	13.6	10.3	10.9	14.5	13.2	10.6	11.3	9.9	13.9	15.1	6.1
2. Later than 5 years	8.1	9.6	6.5	8.5	5.1	7.8	7.6	7.8	10.0	8.7	7.1	8.0	7.1	9.3	8.7	8.2
1. Probably not ever	52.7	45.0	60.0	51.0	69.2	50.7	52.9	59.0	41.9	49.4	56.6	59.1	52.2	48.2	43.2	38.8
Item 13740 N(Wtd)	2430	1131	1251	2013	234	550	777	753	351	1258	1092	1028	563	280	470	49

E10F: A clock radio

0. Only if my present one wears out	44.3	45.7	42.7	45.1	36.2	47.4	45.3	41.3	43.6	46.6	41.2	41.5	47.4	47.9	44.8	47.1
4. Within the next year	20.9	17.8	23.6	19.3	30.9	19.5	19.8	23.7	19.4	21.2	21.0	22.7	20.8	17.5	20.2	11.8
3. Within 2 to 5 years	15.7	15.3	16.5	16.4	14.4	14.6	16.4	16.3	14.7	14.4	17.4	16.2	14.1	17.8	15.3	9.8
2. Later than 5 years	8.0	8.8	7.2	8.5	4.1	8.1	8.0	7.2	9.7	8.4	7.3	9.5	6.7	6.8	6.8	5.9
1. Probably not ever	11.1	12.3	10.0	10.9	14.0	10.3	10.7	11.5	12.5	9.4	13.0	10.2	10.9	9.6	12.8	25.5
Item 13750 N(Wtd)	2485	1166	1270	2046	243	553	792	780	360	1276	1123	1054	567	292	484	51

E10G: An electric shaver

0. Only if my present one wears out	26.9	30.2	24.1	28.8	12.0	29.7	29.3	23.0	25.1	25.3	28.2	26.1	26.0	30.2	27.4	30.6
4. Within the next year	16.3	23.5	9.5	16.1	15.4	13.9	16.9	16.1	19.1	17.1	15.9	15.5	20.2	12.8	15.5	14.3
3. Within 2 to 5 years	11.2	14.8	7.8	11.3	12.0	10.6	10.6	12.4	10.9	10.8	11.5	11.2	10.1	13.9	10.4	10.2
2. Later than 5 years	5.9	7.3	4.4	6.0	5.1	6.0	5.7	5.6	6.6	6.6	4.9	6.8	5.3	2.8	6.2	6.1
1. Probably not ever	39.7	24.3	54.1	37.7	55.6	39.8	37.5	42.9	38.3	40.2	39.5	40.5	38.6	40.6	40.6	36.7
Item 13760 N(Wtd)	2448	1150	1249	2031	234	548	785	765	350	1255	1110	1035	565	288	471	49

E10H: A tennis racquet

0. Only if my present one wears out	36.6	37.4	36.1	38.8	21.2	41.8	39.5	30.7	34.8	42.4	29.7	38.1	37.6	36.6	34.0	25.6
4. Within the next year	17.4	16.8	17.6	16.1	26.0	16.5	13.1	22.5	17.1	19.3	15.6	16.6	17.1	18.1	18.4	21.3
3. Within 2 to 5 years	12.6	12.0	13.4	12.5	10.4	12.4	12.7	11.3	16.0	12.8	12.7	12.3	12.8	14.3	12.7	8.5
2. Later than 5 years	6.5	7.1	5.5	6.4	6.1	5.7	6.1	7.1	6.7	6.8	5.8	6.1	6.8	6.6	6.1	10.6
1. Probably not ever	26.9	26.7	27.4	26.2	36.4	23.8	28.6	28.3	25.3	18.7	36.2	26.9	25.7	24.0	28.6	34.0
Item 13770 N(Wtd)	2461	1155	1256	2041	231	558	787	760	356	1270	1106	1037	572	287	479	47

E10I: A TV set

0. Only if my present one wears out	30.5	32.8	28.3	28.4	42.1	33.3	25.9	35.7	25.1	29.1	31.5	29.3	31.9	30.7	29.8	34.7
4. Within the next year	15.8	14.9	16.4	14.5	24.0	10.4	16.6	19.1	15.0	12.4	20.0	13.8	14.6	17.9	18.6	20.4
3. Within 2 to 5 years	28.3	29.6	29.0	29.7	21.5	27.2	31.0	26.3	28.4	28.7	27.7	27.5	28.6	28.7	30.2	30.6
2. Later than 5 years	19.5	19.0	20.1	21.3	8.3	24.0	19.8	14.6	22.1	24.1	14.3	23.4	18.8	17.2	15.5	6.1
1. Probably not ever	5.9	5.7	6.2	6.0	3.7	5.0	6.5	4.2	9.3	5.7	6.3	6.0	5.9	5.4	5.8	8.2
Item 13780 N(Wtd)	2499	1183	1267	2059	242	558	796	779	366	1277	1136	1055	576	296	484	49

E10J: A bicycle

0. Only if my present one wears out	39.4	37.6	40.5	40.7	30.7	42.3	42.2	33.0	42.1	44.2	34.0	39.6	40.8	42.3	36.9	32.0
4. Within the next year	15.1	12.4	18.0	13.4	25.7	12.3	14.4	18.3	14.3	14.1	16.7	15.1	12.3	17.4	15.4	16.0
3. Within 2 to 5 years	13.4	12.5	14.2	13.1	12.9	13.7	14.2	13.2	11.5	14.1	12.7	13.9	14.2	10.6	14.4	8.0
2. Later than 5 years	8.5	10.2	7.1	9.0	7.5	7.2	8.7	8.4	10.4	8.8	8.0	9.4	8.4	7.8	7.1	12.0
1. Probably not ever	23.6	27.3	20.1	23.8	23.7	24.5	20.6	27.0	21.3	18.8	28.7	22.0	24.3	21.8	26.3	34.0
Item 13790 N(Wtd)	2473	1154	1271	2044	241	555	793	770	356	1268	1119	1044	569	293	480	50

E10K: A car

0. Only if my present one wears out	21.2	24.9	17.7	22.3	16.0	17.6	20.8	23.6	22.6	18.1	25.0	19.1	22.0	24.3	22.2	28.6
4. Within the next year	30.8	32.9	28.4	30.1	34.0	27.7	30.8	33.4	30.1	25.9	36.2	27.1	33.0	32.9	34.3	26.5
3. Within 2 to 5 years	30.6	28.5	32.8	30.9	29.6	33.3	31.7	27.1	31.7	35.5	25.3	32.4	30.9	29.6	28.6	26.5
2. Later than 5 years	15.1	11.3	18.9	15.1	17.2	19.6	13.6	14.4	12.9	19.3	10.3	18.8	12.6	12.2	12.5	14.3
1. Probably not ever	2.2	2.2	2.2	1.7	3.2	1.8	2.9	1.5	2.4	1.2	3.2	2.6	1.6	1.0	2.4	6.1
Item 13800 N(Wtd)	2532	1208	1273	2085	250	567	801	793	372	1301	1139	1068	573	304	496	49

QUESTIONNAIRE FORM 2 1976	TOTAL	SEX		RACE		REGION				4YR COLLEGE PLANS		ILLICIT DRUG USE: LIFETIME				
		M	F	White	Black	NE	NC	S	W	Yes	No	None	Mari- juana Only	Few Pills	More Pills	Any Her- oin
Weighted No. of Cases:	3036	1453	1445	2358	343	723	919	934	460	1450	1342	1223	687	343	597	69
% of Weighted Total:	100.0	47.9	47.6	77.7	11.3	23.8	30.3	30.8	15.2	47.8	44.2	40.3	22.6	11.3	19.7	2.3

E10L: A tape recorder

0. Only if my present one wears out	37.8	39.2	36.4	37.9	38.8	43.3	34.7	38.9	33.6	37.9	37.5	37.5	40.8	38.1	35.0	34.0
4. Within the next year	13.5	15.5	11.9	10.6	31.8	10.5	12.5	16.5	13.9	15.3	11.7	13.1	12.6	16.2	13.0	18.0
3. Within 2 to 5 years	16.1	18.1	14.2	16.2	16.3	12.3	16.3	16.5	21.1	16.8	14.8	17.8	11.5	16.5	18.4	6.0
2. Later than 5 years	10.7	10.4	11.1	11.6	5.3	9.7	11.4	9.4	13.6	11.6	9.8	11.7	9.2	10.3	10.4	8.0
1. Probably not ever	21.9	16.8	26.4	23.8	7.8	24.4	25.2	18.9	17.8	18.4	26.3	19.8	25.7	18.6	23.0	34.0
Item 13810 N(Wtd)	2485	1168	1267	2045	245	554	787	784	360	1271	1126	1049	573	291	483	50

E10M: An electric calculator

0. Only if my present one wears out	24.2	27.5	21.3	24.3	22.9	24.4	26.1	22.5	23.1	28.2	20.1	25.6	23.5	27.6	20.0	22.9
4. Within the next year	21.0	23.1	19.3	13.7	22.9	21.1	20.6	21.9	19.7	27.3	13.1	21.2	25.8	19.6	16.6	16.7
3. Within 2 to 5 years	13.3	14.6	12.2	13.7	11.7	12.7	11.5	13.8	17.1	15.4	10.4	13.9	11.3	12.6	14.4	10.4
2. Later than 5 years	9.8	9.6	10.0	10.2	7.9	8.8	9.7	8.6	14.2	8.2	11.6	10.1	8.5	10.1	9.8	12.5
1. Probably not ever	31.7	25.1	37.2	31.7	29.6	32.9	32.2	33.1	25.4	20.9	44.8	29.0	30.6	30.1	39.3	39.6
Item 13820 N(Wtd)	2457	1154	1255	2027	240	544	785	777	351	1270	1102	1050	565	286	471	48

E10N: A boat or snowmobile

0. Only if my present one wears out	4.7	6.4	3.0	3.8	10.2	6.4	4.2	4.6	3.1	3.5	5.6	4.9	4.3	4.5	5.0	8.3
4. Within the next year	3.7	5.8	1.5	3.4	6.0	2.0	4.8	4.2	2.8	1.8	5.5	2.4	4.1	4.9	3.8	6.3
3. Within 2 to 5 years	8.1	13.1	3.7	8.7	4.7	5.7	9.6	8.8	6.8	6.3	10.0	5.6	8.9	8.7	11.6	6.3
2. Later than 5 years	24.8	28.8	20.8	26.9	8.9	24.5	25.3	20.9	32.2	28.3	20.3	22.5	26.4	26.9	27.5	29.2
1. Probably not ever	58.8	46.0	71.0	57.2	70.6	61.4	56.0	61.4	55.0	60.0	58.7	64.7	56.1	54.9	52.1	47.9
Item 13830 N(Wtd)	2437	1137	1250	2019	235	547	778	761	351	1256	1098	1030	560	286	476	48

QUESTIONNAIRE FORM 3 1976	TOTAL	SEX		RACE		REGION				4YR COLLEGE PLANS		ILLICIT DRUG USE: LIFETIME				
		M	F	White	Black	NE	NC	S	W	Yes	No	None	Mari- juana Only	Few Pills	More Pills	Any Her- oin
Weighted No. of Cases:	3034	1471	1443	2378	332	709	945	925	455	1408	1399	1209	721	364	612	49
% of Weighted Total:	100.0	48.5	47.6	78.4	10.9	23.4	31.1	30.5	15.0	46.4	46.1	39.8	23.8	12.0	20.2	1.6

A01: Taking all things together, how would you say things are these days-would you say you're very happy, pretty happy, or not too happy these days?

3. Very happy	19.3	16.3	22.0	20.7	12.3	16.9	20.0	20.8	18.6	22.0	17.6	21.2	17.9	17.4	18.9	20.4
2. Pretty happy	67.1	70.6	65.1	68.6	65.7	65.9	69.9	64.9	68.0	66.3	68.5	65.8	69.2	71.6	65.3	59.2
1. Not too happy	13.6	13.2	12.8	10.7	22.0	17.3	10.1	14.3	13.4	11.8	13.9	13.0	12.9	11.0	15.8	20.4
Item 1190 N(Wtd)	3018	1464	1440	2368	332	706	940	924	447	1403	1396	1202	720	363	608	49

A02: Some people think a lot about the social problems of the nation and the world, and about how they might be solved. Others spend little time thinking about these issues. How much do you think about such things?

1. Never	1.8	2.5	1.0	1.5	3.0	3.0	.7	1.7	2.0	.6	2.9	1.5	2.4	1.1	2.0	4.1
2. Seldom	13.2	14.6	12.2	13.5	13.7	15.7	10.9	13.2	14.0	10.7	16.4	11.6	13.1	14.8	15.5	10.2
3. Sometimes	51.4	49.4	53.0	53.3	41.6	49.6	58.8	48.3	45.2	48.9	54.0	51.2	54.1	49.5	49.6	46.9
4. Quite often	28.2	27.9	28.7	27.1	31.0	26.7	26.2	30.0	31.3	32.4	23.3	29.0	26.4	28.6	28.8	34.7
5. A great deal	5.4	5.7	5.1	4.6	10.6	5.1	3.4	6.8	7.5	7.5	3.3	6.8	4.0	6.0	4.1	4.1
Item 6880 N(Wtd)	3018	1468	1437	2373	329	708	940	920	451	1402	1399	1205	719	364	607	49

A03: The next questions ask your opinions about a number of different topics. How much do you agree or disagree with each statement below?

A03A: Men and women should be paid the same money if they do the same work

1. Disagree	1.7	2.8	.5	1.1	3.3	3.0	1.1	1.5	1.3	1.6	1.6	1.7	1.5	1.4	1.8	4.1
2. Mostly disagree	2.0	3.5	.6	1.7	3.6	1.0	1.8	3.1	2.0	1.4	2.6	1.7	2.5	1.6	2.5	4.1
3. Neither	1.8	3.1	.2	1.6	1.5	2.3	1.5	1.7	1.5	1.7	1.6	1.7	1.4	1.1	2.1	4.1
4. Mostly agree	12.5	17.8	7.1	13.4	5.8	11.9	13.0	11.9	13.2	10.4	13.8	12.9	12.2	13.5	12.1	8.2
5. Agree	82.1	72.9	91.7	82.1	85.8	81.9	82.6	81.7	81.9	84.9	80.3	82.1	82.4	82.1	81.5	77.6
Item 7930 N(Wtd)	3027	1471	1440	2377	330	708	944	922	453	1407	1397	1206	721	364	611	49

A03B: Women should be considered as seriously as men for jobs as executives or politicians

1. Disagree	6.2	10.1	2.2	5.1	10.6	5.9	4.5	8.5	5.3	4.3	7.0	6.2	6.7	4.7	5.3	12.2
2. Mostly disagree	6.7	10.3	2.9	7.0	4.5	6.5	6.8	6.5	7.1	6.3	6.8	7.3	5.8	8.3	6.6	2.0
3. Neither	5.8	9.2	2.6	6.2	1.8	5.7	6.1	5.3	6.4	4.6	7.1	5.2	7.1	6.6	5.3	6.1
4. Mostly agree	26.4	30.1	22.4	27.8	19.1	22.8	30.1	25.3	26.5	26.3	27.5	26.8	26.5	25.9	25.8	24.5
5. Agree	54.9	40.4	70.1	53.9	64.2	59.1	52.5	54.2	54.4	58.4	51.6	54.4	53.9	54.5	57.1	55.1
Item 7940 N(Wtd)	3022	1469	1436	2371	330	706	942	922	452	1405	1395	1203	720	363	609	49

A03C: A woman should have exactly the same job opportunities as a man

1. Disagree	10.8	16.2	4.8	9.4	17.4	9.8	9.4	13.6	9.1	8.5	12.1	11.0	11.9	8.9	9.9	8.3
2. Mostly disagree	8.4	11.2	5.2	8.4	8.4	7.7	8.4	8.4	9.1	6.6	10.0	9.4	8.0	7.8	7.2	8.3
3. Neither	6.0	8.5	3.6	6.6	2.5	5.1	7.9	4.7	6.4	5.9	6.1	5.9	5.6	9.2	4.6	10.4
4. Mostly agree	28.5	28.5	28.6	30.0	20.6	23.7	31.4	27.2	32.1	29.9	27.8	29.3	27.9	25.0	29.9	29.2
5. Agree	46.4	35.5	57.8	45.7	51.4	53.6	42.8	46.1	43.1	49.1	44.0	44.3	46.7	48.9	48.3	41.7
Item 7950 N(Wtd)	3003	1454	1432	2366	321	705	938	909	452	1399	1383	1196	713	360	609	48

A03D: A woman should have exactly the same educational opportunities as a man

1. Disagree	1.0	1.4	.6	.5	3.1	.9	1.4	1.1	.4	.6	1.4	1.3	.7	1.1	.7	2.1
2. Mostly disagree	1.0	1.3	.6	.8	2.5	.9	.9	1.1	1.1	.2	1.3	.9	.7	1.4	.5	4.2
3. Neither	1.4	2.3	.3	1.3	-	1.3	1.6	1.2	1.3	1.0	1.7	1.3	1.1	1.4	1.8	-
4. Mostly agree	9.7	12.1	7.1	9.4	10.1	9.0	9.6	8.7	13.0	8.1	10.5	10.4	8.5	9.9	9.2	12.5
5. Agree	86.9	83.1	91.4	88.0	84.4	88.0	86.6	87.9	84.1	90.2	85.1	86.0	88.7	86.8	87.7	81.3
Item 7960 N(Wtd)	3011	1465	1429	2365	326	700	941	916	453	1395	1394	1197	715	363	611	48

QUESTIONNAIRE FORM 3 1976	TOTAL	SEX		RACE		REGION				4YR COLLEGE PLANS		ILLICIT DRUG USE: LIFETIME				
		M	F	White	Black	NE	NC	S	W	Yes	No	None	Mari- juana Only	Few Pills	More Pills	Any Her- oin
Weighted No. of Cases:	3034	1471	1443	2378	332	709	945	925	455	1408	1399	1209	721	364	612	49
% of Weighted Total:	100.0	48.5	47.6	78.4	10.9	23.4	31.1	30.5	15.0	46.4	46.1	39.8	23.8	12.0	20.2	1.6

A03E: It is usually better for everyone involved if the man is the achiever outside the home and the woman takes care of the home and family

1. Disagree	15.6	7.1	23.9	14.8	19.1	21.0	14.2	13.6	14.2	17.7	12.7	14.9	13.6	16.0	18.5	20.4
2. Mostly disagree	12.2	8.5	16.2	12.4	12.5	14.9	11.9	10.7	11.5	14.7	9.7	11.9	12.5	11.3	13.9	4.1
3. Neither	13.4	14.9	12.1	13.9	10.3	14.9	14.7	15.2	11.5	15.2	11.5	11.7	12.8	15.7	16.2	16.3
4. Mostly agree	29.2	31.1	26.9	30.1	24.3	24.7	32.8	28.5	30.1	28.5	30.9	29.5	32.5	29.5	25.4	30.6
5. Agree	29.6	38.4	20.9	28.8	33.4	24.3	26.4	36.8	29.9	23.8	35.3	31.9	28.5	27.5	26.2	26.5
Item 7970 N(Wtd)	3020	1469	1435	2372	329	704	943	922	452	1404	1396	1202	719	363	611	49

A03F: A preschool child is likely to suffer if the mother works

1. Disagree	12.3	7.5	16.5	9.2	30.2	14.3	9.6	14.7	9.4	11.4	12.1	10.8	12.3	16.7	11.4	21.7
2. Mostly disagree	12.9	8.0	18.3	12.7	17.1	15.2	12.1	12.1	12.9	14.1	12.0	11.6	12.2	15.0	15.8	10.9
3. Neither	12.3	11.8	12.6	13.4	8.7	14.3	12.3	10.1	13.8	12.5	11.8	13.0	11.0	12.5	12.4	15.2
4. Mostly agree	24.4	25.5	23.9	25.1	17.4	24.2	23.5	25.9	23.7	26.2	23.1	23.7	23.7	22.8	27.5	19.6
5. Agree	38.0	47.2	28.7	39.6	26.5	32.2	42.5	37.2	40.0	35.7	41.1	40.9	40.8	33.3	32.9	34.8
Item 7980 N(Wtd)	3000	1457	1428	2363	321	706	937	909	448	1400	1386	1197	716	360	607	46

A03G: A working mother can establish just as warm and secure a relationship with her children as a mother who does not work

1. Disagree	21.7	28.2	14.7	21.6	18.9	20.1	21.3	24.1	19.9	18.6	24.0	22.4	24.7	18.7	18.0	20.8
2. Mostly disagree	21.0	24.9	17.0	22.9	8.8	19.0	23.8	18.4	23.7	22.6	20.3	22.9	19.9	20.7	20.9	12.5
3. Neither	8.1	10.0	6.3	9.0	2.7	8.1	8.3	7.0	9.7	8.5	8.0	6.3	10.0	7.4	10.8	8.3
4. Mostly agree	23.0	18.6	27.4	23.6	21.6	21.0	22.1	24.7	24.6	23.5	22.8	21.6	22.7	22.9	24.7	22.9
5. Agree	26.2	18.2	34.5	23.0	47.9	31.6	24.4	25.6	22.3	26.8	24.8	27.0	22.7	30.3	25.5	35.4
Item 7990 N(Wtd)	3016	1464	1437	2368	328	705	937	922	452	1403	1393	1198	717	363	612	48

A04: The next questions are about pollution and the environment. How much do you agree or disagree with each statement below?

A04A: Pollution of most types has increased in the U.S. in the last ten years

1. Disagree	2.0	2.2	1.5	1.7	2.4	3.0	1.4	2.2	1.1	2.1	1.5	1.6	2.6	1.4	1.8	4.1
2. Mostly disagree	3.5	4.6	2.4	3.6	4.6	4.0	2.9	3.4	4.5	4.0	2.9	3.1	4.5	3.9	2.8	6.1
3. Neither	4.7	4.9	3.8	4.0	7.3	3.7	5.5	4.0	5.8	5.2	3.9	4.5	4.3	3.6	4.9	10.2
4. Mostly agree	22.2	21.6	23.3	22.8	18.9	22.3	23.9	21.1	20.9	22.6	22.7	23.8	21.0	24.5	21.4	14.3
5. Agree	67.6	66.6	69.0	67.9	67.1	66.9	66.3	69.5	67.7	66.1	69.1	67.1	67.5	66.7	69.1	65.3
Item 8000 N(Wtd)	3017	1468	1434	2370	328	708	940	920	449	1405	1393	1199	719	363	611	49

A04B: Government should take steps to deal with our environmental problems, even if it means that most of us pay higher prices or taxes

1. Disagree	9.6	11.2	7.8	7.5	20.2	11.3	5.0	14.1	7.8	6.8	11.7	9.1	10.4	8.0	9.7	14.3
2. Mostly disagree	9.2	9.4	8.8	9.1	9.5	8.6	9.4	8.9	10.7	8.9	9.6	9.3	8.9	11.6	8.5	4.1
3. Neither	14.1	12.4	16.4	14.6	10.7	13.3	15.1	12.7	16.0	12.5	15.6	11.7	13.1	18.3	18.0	16.3
4. Mostly agree	37.8	35.1	40.1	39.4	29.1	34.3	40.9	34.9	42.7	40.6	36.6	38.8	38.9	35.5	36.8	28.6
5. Agree	29.2	31.8	26.9	29.3	30.6	32.4	29.5	29.5	22.9	31.2	26.4	31.1	28.6	26.6	27.0	36.7
Item 8010 N(Wtd)	3017	1464	1437	2371	327	706	941	921	450	1405	1392	1201	718	361	611	49

A04C: I would prefer to pay more money for things that will last a long time, rather than have them cost less and break sooner

1. Disagree	.9	.8	1.0	.7	2.7	1.4	.6	1.2	.2	.4	1.4	.2	1.5	1.7	.7	2.0
2. Mostly disagree	1.1	1.6	.5	.8	2.4	1.1	1.4	.9	.7	.9	1.2	1.1	.4	.8	1.3	4.1
3. Neither	2.9	3.1	2.3	2.4	2.7	4.0	2.1	2.5	3.5	2.9	2.7	2.7	3.4	2.5	2.8	2.0
4. Mostly agree	20.8	21.0	20.4	21.8	13.1	18.2	22.0	19.5	25.1	21.8	19.0	20.7	18.9	25.6	21.3	16.3
5. Agree	74.3	73.5	75.8	74.3	79.0	75.3	73.8	76.0	70.5	74.1	75.7	75.3	75.9	69.1	74.1	73.5
Item 8020 N(Wtd)	3015	1464	1435	2368	328	705	939	919	451	1403	1394	1200	715	363	611	49

QUESTIONNAIRE FORM 3 1976	TOTAL	SEX		RACE		REGION				4YR COLLEGE PLANS		ILLICIT DRUG USE: LIFETIME				
		M	F	White	Black	NE	NC	S	W	Yes	No	None	Mari- juana Only	Few Pills	More Pills	Any Her- oin
Weighted No. of Cases:	3034	1471	1443	2378	332	709	945	925	455	1408	1399	1209	721	364	612	49
% of Weighted Total:	100.0	48.5	47.6	78.4	10.9	23.4	31.1	30.5	15.0	46.4	46.1	39.8	23.8	12.0	20.2	1.6

A04D: I would probably be willing to use a bicycle or mass transit (if available) rather than a car to get to work

	TOTAL	M	F	White	Black	NE	NC	S	W	Yes	No	None	Mari- juana Only	Few Pills	More Pills	Any Her- oin
1. Disagree	23.1	26.1	19.3	19.0	45.0	24.5	18.9	30.5	14.3	17.5	27.5	21.3	25.1	19.3	23.8	29.2
2. Mostly disagree	16.2	15.9	16.4	16.9	12.8	15.9	16.7	15.8	16.7	14.8	17.7	14.4	16.9	20.2	16.7	18.8
3. Neither	11.1	12.6	8.9	11.6	6.1	11.0	13.0	9.9	9.8	11.0	11.7	11.2	8.5	10.5	14.1	12.5
4. Mostly agree	25.5	24.2	27.8	27.0	20.8	25.3	25.6	23.5	29.4	28.6	22.4	28.4	26.4	22.7	21.6	22.9
5. Agree	24.2	21.2	27.7	25.4	15.0	23.5	25.7	20.3	29.8	28.1	20.7	24.7	23.2	27.3	23.8	16.7
Item 8030 N(Wtd)	3014	1463	1435	2368	327	703	940	922	449	1402	1394	1200	717	362	610	48

A04E: I would be willing to eat less meat and more grains and vegetables, if it would help provide food for starving people

	TOTAL	M	F	White	Black	NE	NC	S	W	Yes	No	None	Mari- juana Only	Few Pills	More Pills	Any Her- oin
1. Disagree	8.7	12.9	4.3	8.3	8.0	8.9	8.2	8.2	10.5	8.3	8.6	7.3	9.6	7.8	10.2	12.2
2. Mostly disagree	8.9	13.1	4.8	10.0	3.4	9.5	10.4	6.0	10.5	9.5	8.5	9.3	8.5	7.5	10.0	14.3
3. Neither	12.0	15.3	8.0	12.4	7.1	12.3	14.2	9.4	12.5	11.6	12.1	12.7	9.9	10.8	13.1	12.2
4. Mostly agree	31.8	31.8	31.5	32.9	27.3	30.5	31.4	33.8	30.1	31.3	33.2	32.6	32.8	32.2	29.5	24.5
5. Agree	38.7	26.8	51.4	36.4	54.3	38.9	35.8	42.6	36.6	39.5	37.7	38.2	39.2	41.9	37.4	36.7
Item 8040 N(Wtd)	3010	1461	1433	2367	326	705	939	917	448	1401	1391	1199	716	360	610	49

A05: In the following list you will find some statements about leisure time and work. Please show whether you agree or disagree with each statement.

A05A: I like the kind of work you can forget about after the work day is over

	TOTAL	M	F	White	Black	NE	NC	S	W	Yes	No	None	Mari- juana Only	Few Pills	More Pills	Any Her- oin
1. Disagree	17.1	18.8	15.8	15.2	28.7	20.0	12.6	20.0	16.0	19.2	14.4	19.5	16.6	18.0	12.5	19.1
2. Mostly disagree	15.9	15.5	15.6	16.1	13.4	17.7	17.5	13.5	14.3	19.5	12.5	15.8	17.4	14.9	15.3	12.8
3. Neither	12.4	14.4	10.4	13.3	5.8	10.5	12.3	12.3	15.8	14.7	10.5	13.1	11.3	10.8	13.0	14.9
4. Mostly agree	22.3	20.5	24.2	23.3	18.6	19.3	25.3	19.5	26.1	21.8	23.3	24.3	18.9	22.1	23.2	10.6
5. Agree	32.3	30.8	34.0	32.1	33.5	32.6	32.2	34.5	27.8	24.8	39.2	27.3	35.7	34.3	36.1	42.6
Item 8050 N(Wtd)	3007	1463	1433	2364	328	706	936	916	449	1402	1389	1196	718	362	609	47

A05B: To me, work is nothing more than making a living

	TOTAL	M	F	White	Black	NE	NC	S	W	Yes	No	None	Mari- juana Only	Few Pills	More Pills	Any Her- oin
1. Disagree	44.3	39.6	50.3	45.5	39.1	43.6	42.4	47.5	43.0	50.3	38.9	48.8	45.7	41.9	38.1	26.5
2. Mostly disagree	26.2	27.0	25.5	28.9	15.0	26.2	29.2	22.2	28.0	28.3	24.6	25.6	26.3	26.9	27.8	26.5
3. Neither	6.8	7.0	6.2	7.1	3.7	5.5	9.2	5.1	6.9	5.4	7.8	5.9	5.3	7.8	9.3	4.1
4. Mostly agree	11.6	12.7	9.5	10.7	14.4	13.7	11.0	11.0	10.7	9.2	13.5	10.0	12.2	14.7	12.1	10.2
5. Agree	11.1	13.7	8.4	7.8	28.1	10.9	8.2	14.2	11.6	6.7	15.1	9.8	10.6	8.6	12.6	32.7
Item 8060 N(Wtd)	3007	1463	1430	2363	327	706	936	918	447	1399	1390	1195	715	360	611	49

A05C: I expect my work to be a very central part of my life

	TOTAL	M	F	White	Black	NE	NC	S	W	Yes	No	None	Mari- juana Only	Few Pills	More Pills	Any Her- oin
1. Disagree	5.7	4.5	6.6	5.2	6.4	8.1	4.7	5.7	4.2	4.1	6.8	5.0	5.4	6.9	5.7	14.3
2. Mostly disagree	8.0	7.7	8.0	8.5	4.0	6.0	9.2	6.6	11.6	6.8	9.4	7.0	7.5	8.0	9.5	12.2
3. Neither	11.9	11.8	12.0	13.2	4.3	10.9	15.7	8.7	12.2	10.3	13.8	11.0	11.6	12.5	14.7	12.2
4. Mostly agree	34.4	35.0	34.2	35.8	30.3	34.4	36.8	30.8	36.5	37.6	31.6	35.9	33.5	34.6	33.6	22.4
5. Agree	40.0	40.9	39.0	37.3	55.0	40.6	33.7	48.3	35.2	41.2	38.4	41.0	41.7	37.4	36.7	36.7
Item 8070 N(Wtd)	3011	1468	1429	2366	327	704	938	920	449	1402	1389	1197	717	361	611	49

A05D: I want to do my best in my job, even if this sometimes means working overtime

	TOTAL	M	F	White	Black	NE	NC	S	W	Yes	No	None	Mari- juana Only	Few Pills	More Pills	Any Her- oin
1. Disagree	2.0	2.2	1.6	1.6	3.6	3.1	1.5	1.7	1.8	1.3	2.4	1.7	1.9	1.4	2.6	6.3
2. Mostly disagree	2.7	2.3	2.7	2.8	2.1	4.4	3.0	1.5	2.2	2.2	3.0	1.7	3.2	3.9	3.4	2.1
3. Neither	5.0	5.5	4.0	5.1	3.6	6.7	4.5	4.0	5.3	4.1	5.6	4.2	5.1	4.4	5.9	10.4
4. Mostly agree	33.0	33.3	32.8	35.4	22.9	31.6	36.4	27.8	38.8	37.4	29.7	29.8	34.4	34.0	37.6	22.9
5. Agree	57.3	56.6	58.9	55.1	67.2	54.4	54.8	65.0	51.9	55.1	59.4	62.7	55.4	56.6	50.2	56.3
Item 8080 N(Wtd)	3022	1467	1439	2370	332	706	942	922	451	1405	1395	1205	719	362	611	48

	TOTAL	SEX		RACE		REGION				4YR COLLEGE PLANS		ILLICIT DRUG USE: LIFETIME				
QUESTIONNAIRE FORM 3 **1976**		M	F	White	Black	NE	NC	S	W	Yes	No	None	Mari- juana Only	Few Pills	More Pills	Any Her- oin
Weighted No. of Cases:	3034	1471	1443	2378	332	709	945	925	455	1408	1399	1209	721	364	612	49
% of Weighted Total:	100.0	48.5	47.6	78.4	10.9	23.4	31.1	30.5	15.0	46.4	46.1	39.8	23.8	12.0	20.2	1.6

A05E: I would like to stay in the same job for most of my adult life

1. Disagree	15.1	13.2	16.3	13.8	21.2	16.4	13.7	16.2	13.4	12.4	16.9	11.8	15.5	15.2	18.9	28.6
2. Mostly disagree	11.2	9.8	12.3	11.3	10.6	13.2	10.2	9.3	13.8	11.8	10.7	10.3	13.5	10.7	10.7	12.2
3. Neither	16.3	16.0	17.2	16.4	12.4	17.0	17.1	14.8	16.7	17.6	15.3	16.7	15.7	15.4	17.8	12.2
4. Mostly agree	26.6	27.8	24.9	27.9	19.1	26.6	29.4	25.0	24.1	26.4	27.5	28.1	24.2	25.9	27.8	22.4
5. Agree	30.8	33.1	29.3	30.6	36.4	26.9	29.5	34.7	31.8	31.8	29.6	33.3	30.9	32.8	24.8	24.5
Item 8090 N(Wtd)	3015	1466	1433	2365	330	706	939	921	449	1400	1394	1200	718	363	608	49

A06: If you were to get enough money to live as comfortably as you'd like for the rest of your life, would you want to work?

1. I would want to work	78.1	77.0	79.7	77.5	79.5	75.3	81.1	77.9	76.7	80.6	76.1	81.7	76.8	78.8	73.1	60.0
2. I would not want to work	21.9	23.0	20.3	22.5	20.5	24.7	18.9	22.0	23.3	19.4	23.9	18.3	23.2	21.2	26.8	40.0
Item 8100 N(Wtd)	2940	1422	1412	2328	312	688	915	903	434	1379	1355	1172	702	353	598	45

The next questions are about living or working with people of different races. Please rate each of the statements below using the following terms:

Not at all acceptable: I'd avoid this if I possibly could.

Somewhat acceptable: I could live with this, but not be happy about it.

Acceptable: This would be O.K., or I'd be neutral about this.

Desirable: I'd really like this.

A07: How would you feel about...

A07A: Having close personal friends of another race?

1. Not at all acceptable	2.7	3.1	2.3	2.7	1.8	2.5	2.1	4.2	.9	1.4	4.0	2.2	2.2	3.6	2.5	10.2
2. Somewhat acceptable	6.9	8.7	4.8	7.1	5.2	5.7	6.4	9.4	4.9	5.9	7.7	6.6	6.5	8.9	7.1	6.1
3. Acceptable	56.3	61.1	51.6	58.4	51.2	54.0	57.2	59.0	52.0	53.5	59.6	54.6	57.0	56.4	58.6	53.1
4. Desirable	34.2	27.1	41.4	31.7	42.1	37.8	34.4	27.3	42.3	39.2	28.6	36.7	34.3	31.0	31.9	30.6
Item 8110 N(Wtd)	3014	1465	1434	2367	328	707	937	918	452	1401	1395	1206	718	358	608	49

A07B: Having a job with a supervisor of a different race?

1. Not at all acceptable	3.4	5.1	2.0	3.6	1.5	4.0	3.3	4.1	1.8	1.6	5.7	3.2	2.2	5.0	3.8	12.2
2. Somewhat acceptable	9.4	12.3	5.9	9.8	6.4	9.7	8.4	11.8	6.0	7.9	10.3	7.4	9.3	10.3	11.8	10.2
3. Acceptable	69.4	70.7	68.1	70.1	71.9	66.9	71.0	70.2	68.4	71.4	68.2	70.3	71.7	68.8	66.6	59.2
4. Desirable	17.8	11.9	24.1	16.5	20.5	19.4	17.3	14.0	23.9	19.1	15.9	19.2	16.7	15.6	17.8	16.3
Item 8120 N(Wtd)	3015	1466	1434	2368	327	708	938	917	452	1400	1395	1204	720	359	608	49

A07C: Having a family of a different race (but same level of education and income) move next door to you?

1. Not at all acceptable	5.6	6.9	4.1	5.3	4.6	4.4	4.7	9.0	2.4	4.0	7.2	5.1	4.2	7.8	5.1	12.2
2. Somewhat acceptable	11.2	13.5	8.7	12.3	8.2	9.6	10.9	14.9	6.7	8.8	13.6	10.5	11.6	10.4	13.2	16.3
3. Acceptable	56.7	59.9	53.4	57.6	53.2	57.8	56.6	56.8	55.1	56.2	57.4	55.8	60.0	58.3	54.6	46.9
4. Desirable	26.4	19.7	33.8	24.8	34.3	28.0	27.8	19.2	35.6	31.1	21.8	28.7	24.2	23.5	27.1	24.5
Item 8130 N(Wtd)	3010	1462	1433	2362	329	706	936	918	450	1400	1392	1204	718	357	606	49

QUESTIONNAIRE FORM 3 1976	TOTAL	SEX		RACE		REGION				4YR COLLEGE PLANS		ILLICIT DRUG USE: LIFETIME				
		M	F	White	Black	NE	NC	S	W	Yes	No	None	Mari-juana Only	Few Pills	More Pills	Any Her-oin
Weighted No. of Cases:	3034	1471	1443	2378	332	709	945	925	455	1408	1399	1209	721	364	612	49
% of Weighted Total:	100.0	48.5	47.6	78.4	10.9	23.4	31.1	30.5	15.0	46.4	46.1	39.8	23.8	12.0	20.2	1.6
A07D: Having your (future) children's friends be all of your race?																
1. Not at all acceptable	20.1	16.7	23.2	18.8	22.7	21.2	18.0	20.0	23.1	22.6	16.7	20.1	19.8	17.5	21.6	26.5
2. Somewhat acceptable	21.3	21.3	21.3	21.6	22.4	20.2	21.8	20.0	24.7	24.4	18.4	21.2	21.3	21.5	21.4	20.4
3. Acceptable	40.2	42.7	38.5	41.3	35.7	40.0	43.0	36.6	41.9	38.1	43.0	38.9	42.4	40.1	41.0	38.8
4. Desirable	18.4	19.2	17.1	18.2	18.9	18.6	17.1	23.3	10.5	14.8	21.9	19.8	16.4	21.2	16.1	14.3
Item 8140 N(Wtd)	2978	1451	1416	2341	322	698	928	906	446	1388	1378	1191	713	349	603	49
A07E: Having some of your (future) children's friends be of other races?																
1. Not at all acceptable	3.5	4.5	2.4	2.8	4.3	3.0	3.3	4.7	2.0	2.1	4.6	3.5	2.1	4.5	3.1	12.2
2. Somewhat acceptable	8.5	10.6	6.1	9.1	6.5	8.7	7.7	11.0	5.1	6.7	9.9	7.5	8.0	11.5	8.9	2.0
3. Acceptable	49.3	53.8	44.5	50.5	46.6	49.3	49.9	49.5	47.5	45.5	53.8	48.0	53.4	49.7	47.9	40.8
4. Desirable	38.7	31.0	46.9	37.6	42.3	38.9	39.1	34.9	45.3	45.7	31.7	41.0	36.6	34.6	40.0	42.9
Item 8150 N(Wtd)	2998	1456	1431	2361	324	704	934	912	448	1397	1389	1199	716	356	607	49
A08: How would you feel about having a job where...																
A08A: ...all the employees are of your race?																
1. Not at all acceptable	7.0	5.6	8.0	4.6	17.4	7.4	5.1	8.7	6.7	7.8	5.5	7.9	5.9	4.7	6.0	10.2
2. Somewhat acceptable	13.5	12.2	14.8	12.0	18.0	15.8	11.1	11.6	18.4	16.2	10.6	12.9	13.8	16.4	12.9	16.3
3. Acceptable	53.5	53.2	53.9	56.2	44.2	51.9	56.5	50.3	56.0	54.4	53.4	52.4	56.1	52.1	54.8	42.9
4. Desirable	26.1	29.0	23.3	27.1	20.4	24.9	27.3	29.4	18.9	21.7	30.6	26.7	24.3	26.7	26.2	30.6
Item 8160 N(Wtd)	3006	1461	1430	2361	328	707	937	913	450	1397	1390	1204	715	359	604	49
A08B: ...some employees are of a different race?																
1. Not at all acceptable	.8	1.1	.4	.7	.6	1.3	.5	.9	.2	.7	.9	.5	.8	.6	.8	6.1
2. Somewhat acceptable	5.4	6.8	3.7	5.3	4.0	4.0	6.3	6.2	4.0	3.4	6.9	4.4	5.7	5.6	5.6	12.2
3. Acceptable	65.1	69.1	60.8	67.5	53.1	63.9	66.5	65.4	63.6	63.5	67.1	63.1	65.6	67.9	66.7	61.2
4. Desirable	28.8	22.9	35.1	26.5	42.0	30.8	26.7	27.5	32.2	32.3	25.1	31.9	27.8	26.0	26.9	20.4
Item 8170 N(Wtd)	3008	1461	1434	2366	326	704	939	915	450	1401	1392	1204	719	358	606	49
A08C: ...most employees are of a different race?																
1. Not at all acceptable	14.1	16.4	12.0	15.7	7.3	12.1	14.7	19.3	6.0	11.5	16.6	12.7	15.0	14.7	15.3	20.4
2. Somewhat acceptable	32.0	34.4	29.7	35.3	21.1	28.9	35.8	34.6	23.9	33.9	31.3	29.9	34.3	32.2	33.7	36.7
3. Acceptable	45.0	41.7	48.4	43.4	50.2	48.1	42.5	38.1	60.0	46.3	43.8	48.5	43.1	43.9	42.1	26.5
4. Desirable	8.7	7.5	9.9	5.5	21.4	10.8	7.1	8.1	10.1	8.4	8.4	8.8	7.4	9.2	8.8	14.3
Item 8180 N(Wtd)	2999	1457	1429	2358	327	703	935	914	447	1396	1387	1201	714	360	603	49
A09: How would you feel about living in an area where...																
A09A: ...all the neighbors are of your race?																
1. Not at all acceptable	4.3	3.5	5.0	2.5	11.2	5.7	3.3	4.3	4.5	4.9	3.7	4.2	3.6	5.0	4.6	4.1
2. Somewhat acceptable	9.6	8.5	10.5	7.6	16.1	12.5	7.6	7.4	13.6	10.6	8.0	8.5	10.6	12.6	7.9	14.3
3. Acceptable	49.4	49.2	49.7	51.0	41.6	49.6	49.9	44.0	58.8	52.4	46.3	49.0	49.6	47.5	52.5	44.9
4. Desirable	36.7	38.7	34.8	38.9	31.0	32.0	39.2	44.3	23.4	32.0	42.2	38.2	36.2	35.2	35.1	36.7
Item 8190 N(Wtd)	3002	1454	1434	2357	329	703	934	916	449	1396	1392	1201	716	358	604	49
A09B: ...some of the neighbors are of other races?																
1. Not at all acceptable	2.4	2.8	1.9	2.3	2.1	1.8	1.9	3.9	1.1	1.8	3.0	2.5	1.5	4.4	1.6	8.2
2. Somewhat acceptable	9.3	10.7	7.6	9.2	8.5	7.7	8.4	14.1	4.0	7.3	10.8	8.5	9.3	9.2	10.0	14.3
3. Acceptable	64.7	68.0	61.3	66.6	57.6	62.6	67.4	63.1	65.9	64.0	65.6	63.3	67.1	64.2	65.9	55.1
4. Desirable	23.6	18.4	29.2	21.9	31.7	28.1	22.4	19.0	28.7	27.0	20.5	25.7	22.1	22.2	22.6	22.4
Item 8200 N(Wtd)	3010	1464	1432	2364	328	705	938	918	449	1401	1393	1201	718	360	607	49

QUESTIONNAIRE FORM 3 1976	TOTAL	SEX		RACE		REGION				4YR COLLEGE PLANS		ILLICIT DRUG USE: LIFETIME				
		M	F	White	Black	NE	NC	S	W	Yes	No	None	Mari-juana Only	Few Pills	More Pills	Any Her-oin
Weighted No. of Cases:	3034	1471	1443	2378	332	709	945	925	455	1408	1399	1209	721	364	612	49
% of Weighted Total:	100.0	48.5	47.6	78.4	10.9	23.4	31.1	30.5	15.0	46.4	46.1	39.8	23.8	12.0	20.2	1.6
A09C: ...most of the neighbors are of other races?																
1. Not at all acceptable	23.3	27.1	19.7	26.2	10.5	19.1	23.8	31.5	12.1	21.8	25.1	22.5	23.2	24.0	24.2	25.0
2. Somewhat acceptable	33.2	32.9	33.6	35.5	26.5	30.6	35.9	34.0	30.1	33.4	33.9	31.5	34.1	32.4	36.8	31.3
3. Acceptable	37.4	34.4	39.9	34.2	50.5	40.9	35.5	30.2	50.4	38.9	35.5	39.8	37.4	38.0	32.8	27.1
4. Desirable	6.2	5.6	6.7	4.1	12.6	9.6	4.9	4.3	7.4	5.9	5.6	6.1	5.3	5.6	6.1	16.7
Item 8210 N(Wtd)	2996	1453	1430	2354	325	700	936	911	448	1395	1385	1198	716	358	603	48
A10: How would you feel about having your (future) children go to schools where...																
A10A: ...all the children are of your race?																
1. Not at all acceptable	9.9	7.1	12.7	7.9	18.2	11.5	7.0	10.9	11.4	12.3	6.9	10.8	8.5	10.8	9.4	8.2
2. Somewhat acceptable	11.8	10.6	12.9	10.2	19.1	13.2	9.1	10.8	17.1	14.5	9.1	10.7	14.2	12.5	10.9	12.2
3. Acceptable	46.6	48.9	44.5	47.8	40.3	46.4	48.3	43.5	49.4	46.9	46.4	45.8	47.1	46.1	47.0	55.1
4. Desirable	31.8	33.4	30.0	34.1	22.2	28.9	35.5	34.9	21.8	26.3	37.6	32.7	30.2	30.6	32.8	24.5
Item 8220 N(Wtd)	3003	1459	1429	2362	325	703	940	911	449	1396	1390	1200	716	360	604	49
A10B: ...some of the children are of other races?																
1. Not at all acceptable	1.4	1.4	1.2	1.3	1.5	1.4	1.1	1.9	1.1	.9	1.7	1.3	1.0	1.7	1.5	6.1
2. Somewhat acceptable	6.5	8.3	4.2	5.8	8.0	7.3	6.1	7.0	5.6	4.9	7.5	5.6	6.0	7.2	6.9	18.4
3. Acceptable	61.8	65.6	58.1	63.5	53.4	58.5	65.1	63.4	57.0	57.6	66.5	61.4	62.2	63.3	62.1	49.0
4. Desirable	30.2	24.6	36.5	29.5	37.4	32.6	27.8	27.7	36.5	36.5	24.3	31.7	30.9	27.8	29.5	26.5
Item 8230 N(Wtd)	3006	1463	1429	2365	326	702	938	916	449	1396	1393	1198	719	360	607	49
A10C: ...most of the children are of other races?																
1. Not at all acceptable	25.6	29.4	21.8	28.7	11.8	21.3	26.1	33.3	15.5	24.5	26.7	24.8	26.1	24.2	27.4	22.4
2. Somewhat acceptable	32.9	33.7	32.3	35.8	21.7	32.0	35.9	30.6	32.8	33.5	32.9	32.0	32.7	32.5	36.0	36.7
3. Acceptable	34.9	31.1	38.5	31.5	50.9	38.5	32.8	29.8	44.0	35.9	33.8	36.4	34.8	35.8	31.6	30.6
4. Desirable	6.5	5.8	7.3	4.1	15.5	8.2	5.2	6.2	7.4	6.1	6.6	6.7	6.5	7.2	5.0	10.2
Item 8240 N(Wtd)	2993	1456	1422	2355	322	704	936	909	445	1384	1392	1196	713	360	602	49
A11: What race are your close friends?																
1. All my race	41.1	39.9	42.4	44.3	34.9	42.1	51.5	37.9	23.6	38.5	44.5	42.7	41.7	38.4	40.9	22.4
2. Almost all my race	29.8	29.9	29.9	31.8	23.1	26.4	29.3	31.5	32.9	30.2	29.8	28.9	29.5	35.6	29.3	18.4
3. Mostly my race	18.3	19.4	17.2	18.2	21.2	19.1	14.0	21.2	20.4	19.5	16.4	17.2	19.5	16.0	19.8	32.7
4. About half my race	6.7	6.2	7.1	4.7	12.8	7.1	3.4	7.0	12.7	7.0	6.2	6.5	5.9	7.8	6.7	14.3
5. Mostly other race(s)	2.4	2.6	2.3	.8	4.7	3.0	1.4	1.5	5.4	2.9	1.7	2.8	2.0	1.4	2.2	4.1
6. Almost all other race(s)	1.6	2.0	1.1	.2	3.7	2.1	.4	.9	4.8	1.9	1.3	1.8	1.4	.8	1.2	6.1
Item 8250 N(Wtd)	2989	1447	1430	2356	321	700	937	910	441	1392	1384	1199	713	357	597	49
A12: What race are the people in your neighborhood?																
1. All my race	59.6	58.0	61.4	65.2	46.2	49.6	72.8	65.1	36.3	56.0	64.9	60.9	61.3	54.5	60.1	44.9
2. Almost all my race	20.5	22.4	18.6	20.9	19.0	21.4	16.2	19.8	29.3	24.2	16.6	19.3	19.9	23.7	21.0	24.5
3. Mostly my race	9.5	9.4	9.7	8.7	15.3	11.7	6.8	8.5	13.7	9.4	9.7	9.5	8.8	9.2	9.7	22.4
4. About half my race	4.8	5.0	4.6	3.5	8.6	7.1	2.0	4.6	7.0	4.0	5.1	4.4	5.5	5.0	5.2	2.0
5. Mostly other race(s)	3.2	3.0	3.4	1.0	8.3	6.3	.9	1.4	7.2	3.8	2.2	3.5	2.8	4.7	2.2	4.1
6. Almost all other race(s)	2.4	2.3	2.2	.7	3.1	3.7	1.3	.5	6.5	2.5	1.6	2.4	1.8	2.8	2.0	4.1
Item 8260 N(Wtd)	2994	1454	1427	2354	327	701	936	914	444	1393	1386	1199	715	358	599	49
A13: What race were the students in the elementary school where you spent the most time?																
1. All my race	51.9	50.8	53.7	55.1	50.3	48.4	68.0	47.5	32.4	50.6	54.8	54.8	52.3	47.9	49.7	42.9
2. Almost all my race	22.3	23.5	20.8	24.5	10.7	19.7	19.9	25.1	26.1	23.0	21.2	19.6	22.9	25.8	25.8	10.2
3. Mostly my race	11.7	11.8	11.5	12.0	8.6	11.3	6.0	14.6	18.7	12.1	11.3	11.7	11.7	10.1	13.0	2.0
4. About half my race	8.8	8.1	9.0	6.7	16.0	13.3	3.6	9.6	11.0	8.1	9.0	8.7	8.4	9.2	7.5	30.6
5. Mostly other race(s)	2.9	3.0	2.8	1.1	8.6	4.3	1.3	2.0	5.9	3.2	2.2	3.1	2.8	2.8	2.0	2.0
6. Almost all other race(s)	2.4	2.8	2.2	.6	5.8	3.4	1.2	1.3	5.9	3.0	1.4	2.2	2.0	4.5	1.8	10.2
Item 8270 N(Wtd)	2993	1453	1431	2354	326	701	935	913	444	1393	1386	1201	717	357	600	49

QUESTIONNAIRE FORM 3 1976	TOTAL	SEX		RACE		REGION				4YR COLLEGE PLANS		ILLICIT DRUG USE: LIFETIME				
		M	F	White	Black	NE	NC	S	W	Yes	No	None	Mari-juana Only	Few Pills	More Pills	Any Her-oin
Weighted No. of Cases:	3034	1471	1443	2378	332	709	945	925	455	1408	1399	1209	721	364	612	49
% of Weighted Total:	100.0	48.5	47.6	78.4	10.9	23.4	31.1	30.5	15.0	46.4	46.1	39.8	23.8	12.0	20.2	1.6
A14: What race are the students in your present school (if you are in school)?																
1. All my race	19.3	20.8	18.2	22.1	6.7	16.5	35.5	8.7	11.7	16.1	22.6	21.4	18.6	17.1	18.8	12.2
2. Almost all my race	29.7	31.6	27.7	34.0	11.3	31.5	39.2	17.5	31.5	30.6	29.8	27.1	29.3	34.5	32.3	26.5
3. Mostly my race	21.2	21.8	21.2	23.5	11.7	18.8	15.0	27.4	25.5	24.0	19.3	21.8	23.0	20.2	20.1	14.3
4. About half my race	20.1	16.7	23.0	16.4	43.3	18.8	7.0	36.3	16.2	19.4	20.5	19.7	19.6	20.4	19.8	28.6
5. Mostly other race(s)	6.1	5.3	6.7	3.0	19.0	8.8	1.8	7.6	8.1	6.1	4.9	6.2	6.4	4.2	6.0	6.1
6. Almost all other race(s)	3.6	3.9	3.1	1.0	8.3	5.6	1.4	2.6	7.0	3.8	3.0	3.7	3.2	3.1	3.0	10.2
Item 8280 N(Wtd)	2997	1452	1432	2357	326	701	939	913	444	1394	1388	1201	716	357	601	49
A15: What race are the people that you work with on your job (if you have a job)?																
1. All my race	49.8	51.9	48.5	56.4	18.5	49.7	65.2	37.7	41.4	46.4	54.5	49.4	52.9	44.9	53.0	30.8
2. Almost all my race	20.9	20.4	21.4	22.7	12.5	17.8	17.6	26.1	22.4	21.5	21.0	21.9	19.1	21.6	22.3	12.8
3. Mostly my race	12.2	11.5	13.0	12.7	6.5	12.8	9.5	15.4	10.6	12.9	11.7	11.6	12.7	15.2	11.5	20.5
4. About half my race	7.3	6.8	7.6	5.5	19.4	7.5	3.7	10.1	8.9	8.2	6.1	7.5	5.8	7.4	7.2	17.9
5. mostly other race(s)	5.8	5.4	5.9	1.7	26.4	6.7	2.1	7.5	8.9	6.1	4.3	5.7	6.0	7.1	2.9	7.7
6. Almost all other race(s)	4.0	4.0	3.5	1.0	16.7	5.5	2.0	3.3	7.5	4.9	2.3	4.0	3.3	4.2	3.3	12.8
Item 8290 N(Wtd)	2331	1222	1023	1871	216	523	755	706	348	1059	1112	872	582	283	489	39
A16: How often do you do things (like having a conversation, eating together, playing sports) with people of other races?																
1. Not at all	12.9	11.7	14.2	14.4	5.8	12.4	19.3	9.1	8.1	9.2	16.3	14.5	11.3	11.5	12.3	12.2
2. A little	32.8	34.9	30.7	35.8	22.3	32.8	38.8	30.9	24.0	30.2	36.2	33.1	31.8	34.4	32.9	34.7
3. Some	35.2	34.8	35.8	34.8	35.7	34.1	30.1	39.6	39.1	36.3	33.5	33.1	36.6	35.5	36.9	34.7
4. A lot	19.1	18.6	19.3	15.0	36.3	20.7	11.8	20.6	28.5	24.4	13.9	19.3	20.3	18.7	17.8	18.4
Item 8300 N(Wtd)	2996	1454	1432	2355	328	701	934	917	445	1395	1386	1201	716	358	601	49
A17: Generally, how do you feel about the experiences you have had with people of other races?																
5. Very good	21.1	15.9	25.7	19.3	27.6	23.9	22.0	15.5	26.7	24.5	17.6	22.4	20.9	20.6	19.0	20.4
4. Mostly good	41.0	40.1	42.8	41.1	43.9	38.0	42.9	39.3	45.2	42.3	40.0	44.2	40.1	36.7	38.1	34.7
3. Mixed	33.4	38.2	28.3	35.1	24.8	34.1	31.4	38.4	26.0	30.2	37.0	30.1	34.9	37.3	37.2	30.6
2. Mostly bad	3.4	4.5	2.4	3.7	2.5	3.2	2.4	5.6	1.6	2.5	4.5	2.1	3.6	4.8	4.7	10.2
1. Very bad	1.0	1.2	.7	.9	1.2	.9	1.3	1.1	.5	.6	1.1	1.2	.6	.6	1.0	4.1
Item 8310 N(Wtd)	2965	1444	1412	2326	326	694	918	910	442	1385	1369	1189	703	354	599	49
A18: The next questions are about some of your own plans. Are you married or engaged?																
1. Married--SKIP TO Q.A20	1.4	1.0	1.7	1.2	1.5	.2	1.6	2.4	1.0	.5	2.4	1.0	1.3	1.8	1.4	5.0
2. Engaged	9.9	6.6	13.2	9.6	11.2	5.3	10.1	14.4	7.7	4.5	15.2	9.2	8.1	9.9	12.7	7.5
3. Neither	88.7	92.5	85.1	89.2	87.3	94.6	88.3	83.2	91.1	95.0	82.3	89.8	90.6	88.3	85.9	85.0
Item 8320 N(Wtd)	2788	1326	1375	2259	260	646	899	827	417	1321	1286	1116	668	333	566	40
A19: If it were just up to you, what would be the ideal time for you to get married?																
1. Within the next year or so	9.7	5.0	14.4	9.8	9.8	6.5	9.4	13.7	7.0	2.8	16.7	9.3	6.7	13.1	11.0	17.1
2. Two or three years from now	24.9	20.6	28.9	26.1	19.9	19.0	30.2	24.4	24.2	16.5	34.1	24.4	25.0	26.2	25.8	17.1
3. Four or five years from now	34.9	36.2	33.9	35.2	31.2	35.7	34.9	33.5	36.7	42.2	27.5	36.8	35.2	34.8	31.4	29.3
4. Over five years from now	25.8	32.4	19.5	25.6	27.9	34.2	21.5	23.0	27.8	35.1	16.6	24.8	28.9	21.7	26.9	24.4
5. I don't want to marry	4.7	5.9	3.3	3.4	11.2	4.8	4.0	5.4	4.1	3.4	5.2	4.6	3.9	4.5	4.7	9.8
Item 8330 N(Wtd) ★	2805	1348	1362	2248	276	664	897	831	414	1338	1279	1122	667	336	573	41

★=excludes respondents for whom question was inappropriate.

QUESTIONNAIRE FORM 3 1976	TOTAL	SEX		RACE		REGION				4YR COLLEGE PLANS		ILLICIT DRUG USE: LIFETIME				
		M	F	White	Black	NE	NC	S	W	Yes	No	None	Mari-juana Only	Few Pills	More Pills	Any Her-oin
Weighted No. of Cases:	3034	1471	1443	2378	332	709	945	925	455	1408	1399	1209	721	364	612	49
% of Weighted Total:	100.0	48.5	47.6	78.4	10.9	23.4	31.1	30.5	15.0	46.4	46.1	39.8	23.8	12.0	20.2	1.6

A20: Have you thought at all about whether you'd like to have children or how many you'd like to have?

3. I've thought about it a lot	41.7	29.5	54.4	40.7	51.1	40.2	42.4	43.6	39.0	40.2	43.0	42.6	41.9	38.1	42.5	41.7
2. I've thought about it a little	48.2	55.0	41.3	49.7	40.9	47.3	49.6	47.0	48.9	51.6	44.7	48.4	47.6	54.2	46.0	41.7
1. I haven't thought about it at all	10.1	15.6	4.4	9.6	8.0	12.5	8.0	9.4	12.2	8.3	12.3	9.0	10.5	7.6	11.5	16.7
Item 8340 N(Wtd)	2931	1419	1400	2307	313	679	911	897	444	1368	1359	1169	697	354	591	48

A21: All things considered, if you could have exactly the number of children you want, what number would you choose to have?

1. None	3.3	3.2	3.4	3.3	3.1	2.1	3.6	3.4	4.1	2.8	3.8	3.7	1.6	2.5	5.3	2.1
2. One	3.2	3.3	3.2	3.0	3.4	2.6	2.6	3.9	3.6	3.1	3.2	2.7	2.5	3.4	3.8	10.4
3. Two	44.9	45.3	44.3	46.0	40.1	38.2	43.9	51.1	45.1	43.0	46.7	41.2	48.5	43.1	49.9	31.3
4. Three	20.4	21.2	19.9	20.2	22.2	22.4	22.1	18.2	18.5	22.2	19.4	21.2	22.6	20.8	17.5	16.7
5. Four	12.5	10.2	14.7	12.5	14.2	16.0	12.3	10.4	12.1	12.7	12.0	15.7	9.4	13.8	9.3	8.3
6. Five	2.6	2.4	2.6	2.4	3.7	3.4	2.5	2.0	3.2	3.2	1.9	2.9	2.8	3.1	1.5	4.2
7. Six or more	3.4	3.0	3.8	2.9	6.2	3.9	3.1	2.6	5.0	3.3	3.6	3.5	2.8	4.2	2.7	10.4
8. Don't know	9.7	11.3	8.1	9.8	6.8	11.6	9.9	8.4	8.7	9.7	9.4	9.0	9.9	9.6	10.0	16.7
Item 8350 N(Wtd)	2974	1445	1418	2338	324	701	921	912	439	1386	1378	1188	709	355	601	48

A22: If the "population explosion" were NOT a problem, would you choose to have a larger number of children?

4. Yes, I'm sure I would want more	7.3	6.0	8.2	7.0	7.3	7.3	7.6	7.0	7.2	6.7	7.7	5.5	8.2	8.1	8.1	18.4
3. I probably would want more	13.1	12.3	14.3	13.3	11.0	11.9	12.8	12.6	16.3	14.2	12.4	13.1	12.7	13.5	13.6	20.4
2. I probably would not want more	35.5	36.8	34.1	36.7	32.6	35.6	37.6	36.2	29.5	37.5	33.6	37.4	35.6	36.2	32.9	20.4
1. I'm sure I would not want more	28.2	26.6	30.1	27.9	34.1	26.0	26.8	30.0	31.3	27.1	28.9	27.6	27.9	27.2	30.6	26.5
8. Don't know, no idea	16.0	18.3	13.3	15.1	14.9	19.3	15.1	14.3	15.7	14.5	17.3	16.5	15.8	15.2	14.9	16.3
Item 8360 N(Wtd)	3002	1456	1431	2357	328	703	934	918	447	1397	1393	1201	717	356	605	49

A23: If it were just up to you, how soon after getting married would you want to have your first child?

1. I don't want to have children (or get married)	4.3	4.4	4.1	3.7	6.5	3.2	4.3	4.6	5.5	3.4	5.0	4.7	2.0	3.4	6.0	8.5
2. I wouldn't wait at all	3.8	5.2	2.1	3.2	4.9	3.7	2.9	3.9	5.3	3.3	4.1	3.6	3.7	3.7	3.8	10.6
3. I would wait one year	25.0	29.5	20.7	24.2	29.0	29.3	23.6	23.0	25.6	22.7	27.9	25.9	28.0	26.2	20.5	21.3
4. I would wait two years	32.2	28.0	36.8	34.0	24.4	29.8	36.0	30.3	32.0	32.9	31.6	34.2	29.1	36.6	30.7	31.9
5. I would wait three years	14.0	11.0	17.1	14.6	10.5	13.2	14.7	14.8	11.9	16.5	11.2	14.4	14.7	11.3	14.7	6.4
6. I would wait four or five years	8.9	7.1	10.9	9.4	8.6	7.3	8.7	10.1	9.4	9.5	8.9	8.3	7.3	11.0	10.5	6.4
7. I would wait more than five years	2.2	2.1	2.3	2.3	2.2	1.0	1.7	3.8	1.1	2.3	2.3	1.8	2.3	1.4	3.5	2.1
8. Don't know, or already have a child	9.6	12.6	6.1	8.6	14.2	12.5	7.8	9.5	8.9	9.5	8.9	7.2	12.9	6.5	10.3	12.8
Item 8370 N(Wtd)	2972	1446	1417	2335	324	697	923	914	438	1384	1379	1191	708	355	600	47

A24: Now we'd like you to make some ratings of how good or bad a job you feel each of the following organizations is doing for the country as a whole. For each one, mark the circle that best describes how you feel. How good or bad a job is being done for the country as a whole by...

A24A: Large corporations?

1. Very poor	5.0	6.1	3.9	4.8	6.5	8.6	3.9	3.3	5.4	5.9	4.1	3.5	4.9	6.5	6.7	12.5
2. Poor	14.3	16.6	12.3	14.9	13.3	15.6	15.0	13.1	13.6	15.9	13.0	15.1	11.5	15.3	15.5	27.1
3. Fair	35.0	36.1	34.0	35.5	30.3	33.6	35.6	33.7	39.0	35.7	34.5	35.8	36.3	34.8	32.6	27.1
4. Good	25.5	25.9	25.2	26.5	23.5	23.7	24.3	29.8	22.0	25.1	26.8	26.1	28.5	23.2	24.0	20.8
5. Very good	5.8	5.0	6.5	5.2	8.7	4.9	6.8	6.5	3.6	5.3	6.1	6.0	4.8	7.1	5.5	6.3
8. No opinion	14.2	10.3	18.0	13.1	17.6	13.4	14.4	13.8	16.1	12.1	15.5	13.6	14.3	13.0	15.5	6.3
Item 8380 N(Wtd)	2971	1450	1413	2342	323	699	922	909	441	1384	1381	1188	713	353	599	48

QUESTIONNAIRE FORM 3 1976	TOTAL	SEX		RACE		REGION				4YR COLLEGE PLANS		ILLICIT DRUG USE: LIFETIME				
		M	F	White	Black	NE	NC	S	W	Yes	No	None	Mari- juana Only	Few Pills	More Pills	Any Her- oin
Weighted No. of Cases:	3034	1471	1443	2378	332	709	945	925	455	1408	1399	1209	721	364	612	49
% of Weighted Total:	100.0	48.5	47.6	78.4	10.9	23.4	31.1	30.5	15.0	46.4	46.1	39.8	23.8	12.0	20.2	1.6

A24B: Major labor unions?

1. Very poor	6.1	7.7	4.2	6.4	4.7	6.9	6.4	3.8	8.8	7.9	4.6	6.8	6.6	5.6	3.7	6.3
2. Poor	15.6	18.8	13.0	16.5	9.8	17.0	16.6	13.5	15.6	17.4	13.8	17.4	11.4	13.0	18.3	20.8
3. Fair	31.9	31.2	32.6	31.7	36.1	34.7	29.9	34.9	25.3	31.5	32.2	31.2	34.4	34.5	29.8	29.2
4. Good	26.0	26.4	25.8	26.2	25.3	23.9	25.5	27.0	28.3	26.3	26.1	25.1	26.2	29.1	27.0	22.9
5. Very good	6.8	6.3	7.1	6.6	6.0	6.3	7.7	6.5	6.3	5.6	7.9	6.0	6.8	7.3	7.5	10.4
8. No opinion	13.6	9.7	17.3	12.6	17.7	11.4	13.7	14.5	15.4	11.3	15.3	13.5	14.5	11.0	13.6	10.4
Item 8390 N(Wtd)	2962	1440	1413	2337	316	695	925	899	442	1384	1373	1186	709	354	597	48

A24C: The nation's colleges and universities?

1. Very poor	1.0	.8	.9	.6	2.2	1.7	.9	1.0	.2	.5	1.5	.8	.6	.6	.8	8.3
2. Poor	3.4	3.8	3.1	3.1	5.2	3.7	2.9	3.5	3.8	2.6	4.0	2.8	1.7	4.5	5.5	12.5
3. Fair	16.8	17.3	16.3	16.2	19.1	19.7	16.0	16.3	14.9	14.6	19.0	17.0	17.3	18.8	14.8	18.8
4. Good	42.9	42.7	42.8	44.7	37.3	41.5	43.9	41.9	44.7	44.7	41.2	46.0	43.2	38.4	40.6	29.2
5. Very good	30.7	31.1	30.9	31.0	29.6	27.8	30.7	33.4	29.8	34.9	27.0	28.9	32.3	32.4	32.4	18.8
8. No opinion	5.3	4.3	5.9	4.5	6.5	5.7	5.7	3.9	6.5	2.6	7.4	4.6	5.0	5.4	5.7	10.4
Item 8400 N(Wtd)	2980	1450	1426	2351	324	702	929	906	443	1388	1383	1193	716	352	601	48

A24D: The nation's public schools?

1. Very poor	5.0	5.0	5.0	4.7	5.2	5.6	4.1	5.7	4.5	4.8	5.1	4.2	3.4	5.6	7.5	14.6
2. Poor	14.1	15.6	12.8	13.7	16.0	16.7	13.4	13.4	12.6	15.5	11.7	12.4	13.7	17.7	15.6	22.9
3. Fair	32.2	31.8	32.4	32.7	26.9	35.5	30.8	29.2	36.3	33.1	31.8	31.3	32.0	33.8	32.3	39.6
4. Good	32.8	33.9	32.5	34.6	27.8	30.3	35.1	34.4	28.4	34.1	32.5	35.7	34.8	33.2	28.5	8.3
5. Very good	12.4	11.6	13.0	11.5	18.5	8.0	12.9	14.6	13.5	11.1	13.7	13.4	12.4	7.6	12.3	8.3
8. No opinion	3.5	2.3	4.3	2.8	5.6	3.8	3.6	2.6	4.5	1.4	5.1	3.0	3.6	2.0	3.8	8.3
Item 8410 N(Wtd)	2986	1451	1426	2351	324	702	932	909	444	1393	1384	1197	715	355	601	48

A24E: Churches and religious organizations?

1. Very poor	2.8	3.2	2.3	2.6	4.0	3.6	3.1	1.0	4.5	3.0	2.5	2.0	2.9	2.0	4.0	8.3
2. Poor	7.2	8.4	6.3	7.2	2.8	9.8	6.9	5.7	6.8	7.6	6.9	5.7	7.0	10.7	18.8
3. Fair	24.8	23.9	25.7	25.0	23.2	27.7	26.1	21.0	25.4	24.6	24.4	25.4	22.5	28.2	24.8	20.8
4. Good	34.8	34.6	35.1	35.8	32.8	33.8	35.4	36.7	31.1	36.7	33.9	34.5	39.4	34.6	31.5	29.2
5. Very good	20.5	20.0	21.1	20.2	25.7	13.4	19.4	27.3	20.2	18.7	22.4	24.4	17.2	20.6	16.9	12.5
8. No opinion	9.9	9.9	9.7	9.2	11.8	11.8	9.1	8.1	12.0	9.4	9.9	8.0	12.2	7.6	11.9	10.4
Item 8420 N(Wtd)	2979	1448	1423	2346	323	701	927	910	441	1387	1384	1194	716	355	597	48

A24F: The national news media (TV, magazines, news services)?

1. Very poor	3.4	3.9	3.2	3.5	3.4	3.8	2.5	3.4	4.7	3.4	3.6	3.4	2.1	2.5	4.3	16.7
2. Poor	7.7	8.9	6.4	8.3	3.1	7.1	9.5	5.5	9.6	8.5	6.6	6.7	7.2	8.2	9.8	10.4
3. Fair	24.5	24.6	24.5	25.7	15.2	24.0	27.1	22.9	22.6	25.3	23.9	26.1	24.9	23.9	22.8	14.6
4. Good	34.7	33.5	35.8	35.3	34.2	32.9	34.6	36.1	34.5	36.4	33.9	35.4	35.5	31.8	33.4	41.7
5. Very good	25.5	26.1	25.0	24.0	37.3	28.0	22.2	27.8	23.5	23.7	26.4	23.9	25.7	30.7	26.0	14.6
8. No opinion	4.3	3.0	5.0	3.1	6.8	4.0	4.1	4.2	5.2	2.7	5.5	4.5	4.6	2.5	3.7	4.2
Item 8430 N(Wtd)	2988	1454	1426	2356	322	703	929	911	446	1394	1385	1201	712	355	601	48

A24G: The President and his administration?

1. Very poor	11.0	10.6	11.3	10.1	15.3	15.8	9.2	9.4	10.6	10.8	11.3	8.2	11.2	13.2	14.0	22.9
2. Poor	16.6	17.4	16.1	15.8	22.2	17.1	16.4	16.7	16.0	14.7	17.8	14.7	16.6	16.9	20.9	20.8
3. Fair	38.7	39.2	38.6	40.6	30.3	37.5	39.6	37.7	41.2	40.8	37.7	41.0	37.2	40.2	35.8	29.2
4. Good	19.7	20.9	18.4	21.8	9.7	16.0	22.1	20.1	19.8	23.1	17.2	21.5	20.4	17.4	17.4	20.8
5. Very good	4.1	4.9	3.2	3.5	6.6	2.9	4.4	5.3	2.7	4.2	3.9	5.0	3.7	4.2	2.7	-
8. No opinion	9.9	6.9	12.4	8.2	15.9	10.7	8.2	10.8	9.9	6.4	12.0	9.6	10.8	8.1	9.2	8.3
Item 8440 N(Wtd)	2973	1442	1422	2344	320	701	922	906	444	1386	1379	1188	712	356	598	48

QUESTIONNAIRE FORM 3 1976	TOTAL	SEX		RACE		REGION				4YR COLLEGE PLANS		ILLICIT DRUG USE: LIFETIME				
		M	F	White	Black	NE	NC	S	W	Yes	No	None	Marijuana Only	Few Pills	More Pills	Any Heroin
Weighted No. of Cases:	3034	1471	1443	2378	332	709	945	925	455	1408	1399	1209	721	364	612	49
% of Weighted Total:	100.0	48.5	47.6	78.4	10.9	23.4	31.1	30.5	15.0	46.4	46.1	39.8	23.8	12.0	20.2	1.6

A24H: Congress--that is, the U.S. Senate and House of Representatives?

1. Very poor	7.4	7.7	6.9	6.9	8.0	9.6	5.9	7.0	8.1	7.6	7.4	6.4	6.7	8.5	9.0	14.6
2. Poor	16.6	20.0	13.7	17.6	10.5	17.3	17.3	15.3	16.9	16.7	16.2	14.6	16.5	17.2	20.0	27.1
3. Fair	37.9	37.5	38.4	38.9	33.7	36.4	39.0	38.3	36.9	38.3	38.3	38.3	37.9	36.6	38.9	27.1
4. Good	20.1	21.8	18.3	20.6	20.1	17.5	21.2	21.2	19.4	22.4	18.2	22.4	22.1	20.8	14.0	14.6
5. Very good	3.0	3.2	2.6	2.3	6.8	2.4	3.1	3.3	2.7	2.7	3.0	4.4	1.3	2.5	2.3	2.1
8. No opinion	15.0	9.7	20.0	13.5	20.4	16.8	13.3	14.9	15.8	12.3	16.9	13.9	15.4	14.4	15.5	16.7
Item 8450 N(Wtd)	2978	1448	1423	2346	323	701	925	909	444	1387	1383	1191	715	355	599	48

A24I: The U.S. Supreme Court?

1. Very poor	4.7	5.2	4.2	4.3	5.3	5.4	3.9	5.1	4.3	4.3	5.1	3.9	4.3	4.8	5.8	12.8
2. Poor	9.0	10.9	7.1	9.1	7.8	8.4	9.1	9.4	8.8	7.7	9.9	9.2	7.6	7.9	10.5	8.5
3. Fair	32.5	31.4	33.5	33.2	27.0	34.5	32.0	32.4	30.4	32.1	33.3	31.6	31.5	36.7	33.9	27.7
4. Good	27.9	31.2	25.1	29.2	24.5	27.4	28.0	26.4	31.7	31.1	25.1	30.7	27.3	28.8	23.9	25.5
5. Very good	7.5	8.3	6.6	7.1	11.8	6.8	8.2	7.3	7.5	9.0	6.1	8.3	8.7	5.1	5.8	4.3
8. No opinion	18.4	13.0	23.5	17.2	23.9	17.1	18.8	19.5	17.2	15.7	20.4	16.4	20.4	16.4	19.9	21.3
Item 8460 N(Wtd)	2972	1449	1416	2342	322	701	922	908	441	1385	1380	1189	714	354	599	47

A24J: All the courts and the justice system in general?

1. Very poor	8.3	9.4	7.2	8.0	7.5	10.1	7.4	8.1	7.7	8.7	7.9	6.8	7.4	8.5	10.9	15.2
2. Poor	17.0	19.5	14.3	18.5	9.7	17.7	19.0	14.0	17.4	18.0	15.9	18.2	13.9	17.5	18.5	21.7
3. Fair	36.1	34.4	38.4	38.1	26.5	36.5	36.7	36.9	32.4	34.7	38.4	34.9	37.9	38.4	37.1	26.1
4. Good	21.5	22.2	20.2	20.5	31.5	19.7	19.1	23.0	26.0	24.3	18.8	24.3	21.9	18.4	18.5	15.2
5. Very good	3.7	3.9	3.3	3.2	6.9	3.1	3.8	3.6	4.5	3.6	3.5	4.2	4.1	2.3	2.3	-
8. No opinion	13.5	10.4	16.5	11.8	18.1	12.7	14.0	14.3	12.2	10.8	15.7	11.8	14.9	15.3	12.8	21.7
Item 8470 N(Wtd)	2961	1444	1408	2331	321	701	922	897	442	1385	1369	1190	704	354	596	46

A24K: The police and other law enforcement agencies?

1. Very poor	6.8	7.9	5.6	5.6	13.4	8.5	4.8	7.5	6.7	5.9	7.4	4.3	5.9	4.8	11.2	29.2
2. Poor	15.2	14.7	15.5	15.0	15.0	15.3	17.8	14.2	11.7	14.6	15.3	12.6	15.3	16.3	19.1	22.9
3. Fair	33.5	32.9	34.5	33.9	30.2	37.0	33.8	30.7	32.6	34.8	32.5	33.6	31.7	35.2	36.7	20.8
4. Good	30.3	30.7	30.3	32.1	23.1	27.1	31.3	31.1	31.7	32.8	28.6	34.3	33.6	30.1	20.3	16.7
5. Very good	9.3	9.7	8.8	9.3	10.0	7.8	7.5	10.7	12.4	8.7	10.1	11.2	8.1	9.3	7.6	4.2
8. No opinion	5.0	4.2	5.5	4.3	8.1	4.3	4.6	5.8	4.9	3.1	6.2	4.1	5.3	4.2	5.2	8.3
Item 8480 N(Wtd)	2984	1452	1423	2352	321	705	928	906	445	1395	1382	1201	717	355	596	48

A24L: The U.S. military?

1. Very poor	3.5	4.0	2.9	3.2	3.1	5.4	2.7	1.9	5.9	4.5	2.5	2.1	3.2	2.0	6.2	18.8
2. Poor	5.5	5.3	5.9	5.8	3.7	4.0	7.4	4.2	7.0	5.9	5.0	5.3	4.3	5.6	6.9	14.6
3. Fair	24.3	25.5	23.6	25.0	18.5	23.2	24.4	23.9	26.8	26.8	22.1	24.1	22.3	24.2	27.9	20.8
4. Good	34.8	35.7	34.1	36.7	25.9	33.2	36.1	36.3	31.5	33.5	36.4	36.6	36.5	33.0	31.1	22.9
5. Very good	19.6	22.7	16.2	17.9	32.7	19.5	16.6	24.6	15.5	17.1	21.9	19.6	21.2	21.1	17.2	14.6
8. No opinion	12.3	6.8	17.4	11.4	16.0	14.9	12.8	9.2	13.1	12.3	12.1	12.2	12.6	13.8	10.6	8.3
Item 8490 N(Wtd)	2978	1448	1421	2343	324	699	922	913	444	1387	1382	1193	716	355	594	48

A25: All things considered, do you think the armed services presently have too much or too little influence on the way this country is run?

1. Far too little	4.0	4.6	3.6	3.6	6.6	4.2	2.1	6.0	3.5	3.8	4.4	3.8	3.7	3.4	4.6	12.8
2. Too little	18.1	18.7	17.5	18.5	16.3	16.4	18.7	20.6	14.2	16.0	19.4	19.0	18.1	17.8	16.3	14.9
3. About right	63.9	62.1	65.3	63.8	64.6	64.6	63.2	63.2	65.7	63.6	64.5	65.2	63.0	66.5	61.5	53.2
4. Too much	11.5	12.1	11.2	11.9	8.8	11.9	14.1	7.7	13.5	13.7	9.7	10.2	12.9	9.2	14.1	14.9
5. Far too much	2.5	2.5	2.5	2.1	4.4	2.9	1.9	2.6	3.0	2.9	2.1	1.8	2.3	3.2	3.4	6.4
Item 8500 N(Wtd)	2921	1437	1379	2303	319	683	910	899	429	1363	1357	1171	700	349	589	47

QUESTIONNAIRE FORM 3 1976	TOTAL	SEX		RACE		REGION				4YR COLLEGE PLANS		ILLICIT DRUG USE: LIFETIME				
		M	F	White	Black	NE	NC	S	W	Yes	No	None	Mari- juana Only	Few Pills	More Pills	Any Her- oin
Weighted No. of Cases:	3034	1471	1443	2378	332	709	945	925	455	1408	1399	1209	721	364	612	49
% of Weighted Total:	100.0	48.5	47.6	78.4	10.9	23.4	31.1	30.5	15.0	46.4	46.1	39.8	23.8	12.0	20.2	1.6

A26: Do you think the U.S. spends too much or too little on the armed services?

	TOTAL	M	F	White	Black	NE	NC	S	W	Yes	No	None	Mari- juana Only	Few Pills	More Pills	Any Her- oin
1. Far too little	4.7	6.4	2.8	4.4	3.5	4.5	3.9	5.0	5.8	5.4	3.7	4.7	4.7	3.1	4.3	14.6
2. Too little	22.5	28.1	17.0	23.5	23.0	17.9	21.3	28.4	20.3	22.2	22.3	23.5	20.9	21.4	24.0	12.5
3. About right	46.2	40.2	52.1	46.4	44.3	46.5	45.8	45.6	47.8	42.2	49.9	47.5	44.6	51.1	42.7	39.6
4. Too much	20.3	19.3	21.6	20.0	21.1	22.5	22.3	16.6	20.0	22.7	18.5	18.7	23.0	19.4	21.3	25.0
5. Far too much	6.3	5.9	6.5	5.7	8.2	8.4	6.7	4.2	6.1	7.3	5.7	5.6	6.7	4.9	7.8	8.3
Item 8510 N(Wtd)	*2917*	*1438*	*1375*	*2298*	*318*	*688*	*907*	*895*	*429*	*1364*	*1353*	*1168*	*697*	*350*	*588*	*48*

A27: Next are some questions which ask about your experiences and attitudes concerning particular drugs. First we want your answers about some drugs that can be bought at a drugstore without a doctor's prescription--sometimes called over-the-counter or non-prescription drugs. DURING THE LAST 12 MONTHS, on how many occasions have you...

A27A: ...used non-prescription drugs which are supposed to relieve pain (such as aspirin, Anacin, Bufferin, or Excedrin)?

	TOTAL	M	F	White	Black	NE	NC	S	W	Yes	No	None	Mari- juana Only	Few Pills	More Pills	Any Her- oin
1. 0 occasions	9.3	11.6	6.1	6.5	19.5	10.3	8.0	9.3	10.1	8.7	9.1	11.5	8.8	5.3	5.7	14.6
2. 1-2 occasions	18.6	21.0	16.2	17.3	25.9	17.6	17.1	20.0	20.6	17.7	19.0	22.3	17.1	19.0	12.5	16.7
3. 3-5 occasions	18.2	17.7	18.5	17.7	19.5	16.9	19.9	17.0	19.1	16.7	19.2	19.8	20.6	16.8	13.3	14.6
4. 6-9 occasions	15.7	17.2	14.2	16.8	11.0	15.6	15.2	15.6	16.6	16.2	15.4	15.4	16.1	18.7	15.3	8.3
5. 10-19 occasions	17.1	15.9	18.6	18.5	12.2	18.9	17.1	16.0	16.6	19.2	15.9	15.3	20.2	15.4	19.2	12.5
6. 20-39 occasions	10.5	8.6	12.8	11.5	7.0	10.1	10.6	12.0	7.6	10.9	10.6	8.1	9.0	13.4	15.3	10.4
7. 40 or more	10.7	8.0	13.6	11.6	5.5	10.7	12.0	10.1	9.4	10.5	10.9	7.8	8.1	11.5	18.7	22.9
Item 8520 N(Wtd)	*2996*	*1459*	*1433*	*2359*	*328*	*700*	*934*	*915*	*446*	*1399*	*1387*	*1204*	*719*	*358*	*609*	*48*

A27B: ...used non-prescription drugs that are supposed to help people get to sleep (such as Sleep-Eze, Sominex, or Nytol)?

	TOTAL	M	F	White	Black	NE	NC	S	W	Yes	No	None	Mari- juana Only	Few Pills	More Pills	Any Her- oin
1. 0 occasions	88.3	87.7	89.2	88.5	89.6	88.5	88.4	87.3	89.9	89.3	87.6	94.5	91.5	86.4	76.6	52.1
2. 1-2 occasions	6.7	6.5	7.0	7.0	5.2	6.7	6.5	8.1	4.3	6.5	7.1	3.2	5.9	9.2	12.5	10.4
3. 3-5 occasions	2.2	3.0	1.4	2.0	2.1	2.7	1.7	2.1	2.9	1.6	2.8	1.4	1.5	1.4	4.3	14.6
4. 6-9 occasions	1.0	1.0	.9	.9	1.5	.7	1.2	.9	1.3	1.4	.5	.5	.7	1.4	1.8	6.3
5. 10-19 occasions	.9	1.1	.8	1.0	.6	.9	1.3	.8	.7	.8	.9	.1	.4	1.4	2.8	6.3
6. 20-39 occasions	.3	.1	.3	.2	.6	.1	.1	.7	.2	.1	.3	-	.1	-	1.3	-
7. 40 or more	.5	.6	.3	.3	.6	.4	.9	.1	.7	.2	.7	.2	-	-	.7	10.4
Item 8530 N(Wtd)	*2993*	*1457*	*1432*	*2358*	*328*	*698*	*933*	*915*	*446*	*1396*	*1386*	*1204*	*717*	*359*	*606*	*48*

A27C: ...used non-prescription drugs that are supposed to help people stay awake (such as No-Doz, Wake, or Vivarin)?

	TOTAL	M	F	White	Black	NE	NC	S	W	Yes	No	None	Mari- juana Only	Few Pills	More Pills	Any Her- oin
1. 0 occasions	88.8	88.1	90.1	89.3	88.3	91.5	87.9	88.0	87.5	90.5	87.3	96.8	93.9	86.9	71.0	50.0
2. 1-2 occasions	5.3	5.8	4.3	5.3	4.6	3.4	4.9	6.8	5.8	4.9	6.0	1.8	4.0	7.3	12.4	6.3
3. 3-5 occasions	2.0	2.3	1.8	2.0	2.1	2.4	2.0	1.5	2.7	1.6	2.5	.4	1.3	3.1	4.4	12.5
4. 6-9 occasions	1.6	1.6	1.5	1.5	1.5	1.0	1.7	1.8	1.6	1.1	1.9	.2	.7	.6	5.3	8.3
5. 10-19 occasions	.6	.6	.6	.6	.3	.3	1.1	.2	.7	.6	.4	.1	.3	.6	1.6	2.1
6. 20-39 occasions	.9	.7	.9	.8	1.2	.1	1.2	1.1	1.1	.8	.9	.1	-	1.4	3.5	-
7. 40 or more	.9	1.0	.8	.6	1.8	1.0	1.3	.5	.9	.5	1.0	.4	-	.3	1.8	20.8
Item 8540 N(Wtd)	*2987*	*1454*	*1430*	*2356*	*326*	*696*	*933*	*911*	*447*	*1394*	*1385*	*1202*	*717*	*358*	*607*	*48*

A27D: ...used non-prescription drugs that are supposed to calm people down--keep them from being nervous or in a bad mood (such as Cope, Compoz, Devarex, or Miles Nervine)?

	TOTAL	M	F	White	Black	NE	NC	S	W	Yes	No	None	Mari- juana Only	Few Pills	More Pills	Any Her- oin
1. 0 occasions	90.8	92.3	89.9	91.7	88.7	91.5	91.9	88.6	92.2	94.1	88.6	96.8	96.0	84.9	79.3	56.3
2. 1-2 occasions	4.4	3.0	5.4	4.3	4.3	3.7	4.3	5.5	3.1	2.8	5.6	1.6	2.1	9.5	8.9	6.3
3. 3-5 occasions	1.7	1.8	1.7	1.7	2.1	1.0	1.2	2.7	2.0	1.1	2.3	.7	.8	1.7	4.8	4.2
4. 6-9 occasions	1.3	1.4	1.0	1.0	1.8	1.9	1.2	1.2	.7	.7	1.4	.2	1.0	2.0	2.3	12.5
5. 10-19 occasions	.6	.5	.6	.3	1.5	.9	.3	.5	.7	.6	.6	.3	-	.6	1.6	-
6. 20-39 occasions	.6	.3	.8	.6	.6	.4	.4	1.1	.2	.4	.8	-	.1	.8	1.5	10.4
7. 40 or more	.6	.5	.6	.4	.9	.4	.9	.4	1.1	.4	.7	.3	-	.6	1.3	10.4
Item 8550 N(Wtd)	*2992*	*1456*	*1432*	*2360*	*327*	*696*	*934*	*914*	*447*	*1398*	*1386*	*1204*	*717*	*358*	*608*	*48*

QUESTIONNAIRE FORM 3 1976	TOTAL	SEX		RACE		REGION				4YR COLLEGE PLANS		ILLICIT DRUG USE: LIFETIME				
		M	F	White	Black	NE	NC	S	W	Yes	No	None	Mari-juana Only	Few Pills	More Pills	Any Her-oin
Weighted No. of Cases:	3034	1471	1443	2378	332	709	945	925	455	1408	1399	1209	721	364	612	49
% of Weighted Total:	100.0	48.5	47.6	78.4	10.9	23.4	31.1	30.5	15.0	46.4	46.1	39.8	23.8	12.0	20.2	1.6

A28: Individuals differ in whether or not they disapprove of people doing certain things. Do YOU disapprove of people (who are 18 or older) doing each of the following?

A28A: Smoking one or more packs of cigarettes per day †

	TOTAL	M	F	White	Black	NE	NC	S	W	Yes	No	None	Mari-juana Only	Few Pills	More Pills	Any Heroin
1. Don't disapprove	34.1	34.9	32.7	34.1	29.3	36.9	32.6	32.6	35.8	28.0	39.8	21.7	37.2	35.5	51.9	45.8
2. Disapprove	35.8	36.8	35.5	36.0	39.9	33.1	37.3	39.1	29.9	37.3	35.1	38.7	38.7	34.6	29.2	27.1
3. Strongly disapprove	30.1	28.3	31.8	29.9	30.5	30.0	30.1	28.3	34.5	34.8	25.2	39.7	24.1	29.9	18.9	27.1
Item 8560 N(Wtd)	2987	1456	1427	2352	328	697	933	916	441	1395	1383	1200	715	358	607	48

A28B: Trying marijuana (pot, grass) once or twice

	TOTAL	M	F	White	Black	NE	NC	S	W	Yes	No	None	Mari-juana Only	Few Pills	More Pills	Any Heroin
1. Don't disapprove	61.6	65.3	57.4	63.7	50.9	70.7	60.3	54.4	64.8	60.0	63.0	27.6	84.7	76.1	89.8	85.4
2. Disapprove	20.0	19.1	21.2	20.1	20.1	16.7	22.2	21.2	18.1	20.4	19.7	35.8	11.4	11.8	5.2	8.3
3. Strongly disapprove	18.4	15.6	21.4	16.2	29.0	12.4	17.5	24.3	17.4	19.6	17.4	36.7	3.8	12.1	5.1	6.3
Item 8570 N(Wtd)	2988	1454	1432	2356	328	699	932	914	443	1396	1382	1200	718	356	610	48

A28C: Smoking marijuana occasionally

	TOTAL	M	F	White	Black	NE	NC	S	W	Yes	No	None	Mari-juana Only	Few Pills	More Pills	Any Heroin
1. Don't disapprove	52.2	57.7	46.2	53.9	44.7	60.8	49.9	46.7	55.0	49.6	54.1	17.7	71.9	66.6	85.7	81.3
2. Disapprove	21.7	19.5	24.1	22.1	19.5	21.9	23.7	21.1	18.7	21.9	22.4	32.0	18.9	18.1	8.1	8.3
3. Strongly disapprove	26.1	22.7	29.8	24.0	35.9	17.3	26.5	32.3	26.4	28.5	23.5	50.3	9.2	15.3	6.3	8.3
Item 8580 N(Wtd)	2985	1453	1429	2349	329	699	930	911	444	1390	1384	1194	718	359	608	48

A28D: Smoking marijuana regularly

	TOTAL	M	F	White	Black	NE	NC	S	W	Yes	No	None	Mari-juana Only	Few Pills	More Pills	Any Heroin
1. Don't disapprove	30.5	36.1	23.9	30.7	25.0	35.5	28.3	27.5	33.9	26.6	33.6	7.4	31.3	37.7	66.4	80.4
2. Disapprove	28.0	29.6	26.5	28.4	29.6	31.3	27.3	27.3	25.5	28.1	28.0	21.3	44.4	32.1	20.0	10.9
3. Strongly disapprove	41.5	34.3	49.5	40.8	45.4	33.2	44.6	45.3	40.5	45.3	38.4	71.2	24.2	30.1	13.6	8.7
Item 8590 N(Wtd)	2973	1452	1421	2345	324	696	927	910	440	1389	1374	1195	716	355	605	46

A28E: Trying LSD once or twice

	TOTAL	M	F	White	Black	NE	NC	S	W	Yes	No	None	Mari-juana Only	Few Pills	More Pills	Any Heroin
1. Don't disapprove	15.4	18.1	12.2	15.4	11.3	19.2	13.4	13.2	17.8	12.5	17.6	4.4	10.6	13.4	39.5	75.0
2. Disapprove	20.6	19.8	21.4	20.7	20.4	24.4	19.1	19.5	20.3	21.3	19.9	15.9	23.0	27.9	24.1	4.2
3. Strongly disapprove	64.0	62.2	66.3	63.8	68.3	56.4	67.5	67.2	61.9	66.2	62.5	79.7	66.4	58.8	36.4	20.8
Item 8600 N(Wtd)	2991	1456	1432	2357	328	698	934	916	443	1397	1384	1202	717	359	610	48

A28F: Taking LSD regularly

	TOTAL	M	F	White	Black	NE	NC	S	W	Yes	No	None	Mari-juana Only	Few Pills	More Pills	Any Heroin
1. Don't disapprove	4.7	6.1	2.8	3.9	6.1	4.7	3.2	5.2	6.6	3.3	5.4	2.8	2.4	3.1	9.0	31.9
2. Disapprove	15.5	17.2	13.6	14.8	19.0	20.1	13.6	14.7	13.9	12.2	18.5	9.2	16.0	19.1	23.6	34.0
3. Strongly disapprove	79.8	76.7	83.6	81.3	74.9	75.1	83.2	80.2	79.5	84.6	76.2	88.0	81.6	78.1	67.2	34.0
Item 8610 N(Wtd)	2980	1453	1424	2346	327	698	932	912	439	1395	1376	1199	713	356	609	47

A28G: Trying heroin (smack, horse) once or twice

	TOTAL	M	F	White	Black	NE	NC	S	W	Yes	No	None	Mari-juana Only	Few Pills	More Pills	Any Heroin
1. Don't disapprove	7.4	8.5	5.9	7.1	7.0	8.3	6.3	6.9	9.0	5.2	9.0	3.8	5.8	5.3	13.6	45.8
2. Disapprove	15.3	14.8	15.8	14.9	17.4	20.1	12.6	15.3	13.1	14.4	15.5	12.7	14.6	17.8	19.5	14.6
3. Strongly disapprove	77.3	76.7	78.4	78.0	75.6	71.4	81.1	77.8	77.9	80.3	75.5	83.4	79.5	76.9	66.8	37.5
Item 8620 N(Wtd)	2993	1458	1431	2357	328	700	935	915	443	1399	1384	1202	718	359	609	48

A28H: Taking heroin occasionally

	TOTAL	M	F	White	Black	NE	NC	S	W	Yes	No	None	Mari-juana Only	Few Pills	More Pills	Any Heroin
1. Don't disapprove	4.0	4.9	2.6	3.2	5.8	4.1	2.7	4.6	5.0	2.7	4.4	2.7	1.8	3.1	6.2	37.5
2. Disapprove	12.8	13.5	12.2	12.3	16.2	16.1	10.5	13.4	11.0	10.2	15.2	10.1	13.4	12.0	17.0	20.8
3. Strongly disapprove	83.2	81.6	85.2	84.5	78.3	79.6	86.8	81.9	84.0	87.0	80.4	87.2	84.8	85.0	76.9	41.7
Item 8630 N(Wtd)	2991	1456	1431	2355	327	700	931	916	444	1397	1384	1198	718	359	611	48

† = Wording changed from previous year.

QUESTIONNAIRE FORM 3 1976	TOTAL	SEX		RACE		REGION				4YR COLLEGE PLANS		ILLICIT DRUG USE: LIFETIME				
		M	F	White	Black	NE	NC	S	W	Yes	No	None	Mari-juana Only	Few Pills	More Pills	Any Her-oin
Weighted No. of Cases:	3034	1471	1443	2378	332	709	945	925	455	1408	1399	1209	721	364	612	49
% of Weighted Total:	100.0	48.5	47.6	78.4	10.9	23.4	31.1	30.5	15.0	46.4	46.1	39.8	23.8	12.0	20.2	1.6
A28I: Taking heroin regularly																
1. Don't disapprove	2.6	3.4	1.3	1.8	3.4	2.6	1.8	2.3	4.3	1.6	2.8	2.4	1.8	1.7	2.5	12.5
2. Disapprove	9.6	10.5	8.6	8.6	16.0	11.8	7.2	11.6	7.0	7.2	11.4	8.1	9.6	9.0	10.4	31.3
3. Strongly disapprove	87.9	86.2	90.1	89.5	80.9	85.6	91.0	86.1	88.6	91.3	85.7	89.4	88.5	89.3	87.0	58.3
Item 8640 N(Wtd)	2977	1453	1421	2350	324	696	935	906	440	1388	1380	1194	716	355	608	48
A28J: Trying a barbiturate (downer, goofball, red, yellow, etc.) once or twice																
1. Don't disapprove	18.6	19.9	17.0	19.5	10.8	22.9	16.2	17.5	19.2	15.0	21.6	5.0	12.1	17.2	49.3	70.8
2. Disapprove	22.6	22.4	22.9	23.0	20.6	24.8	22.4	20.4	24.4	22.1	23.1	19.3	23.7	31.1	23.4	16.7
3. Strongly disapprove	58.7	57.7	60.1	57.5	68.9	52.3	61.4	62.1	56.4	62.9	55.3	75.7	64.0	51.7	27.1	12.5
Item 8650 N(Wtd)	2972	1444	1425	2341	325	690	932	912	438	1389	1375	1197	712	354	606	48
A28K: Taking barbiturates regularly																
1. Don't disapprove	6.4	7.9	4.3	5.8	5.8	8.3	5.7	5.3	7.4	3.4	8.7	3.1	3.8	3.1	15.2	31.3
2. Disapprove	27.1	27.4	26.8	26.3	32.5	29.2	22.5	30.2	27.5	22.0	32.4	17.1	26.1	34.4	42.3	43.8
3. Strongly disapprove	66.5	64.7	68.9	67.9	62.0	62.5	71.8	64.7	65.0	74.6	59.0	79.8	70.2	62.6	42.5	25.0
Item 8660 N(Wtd)	2988	1454	1432	2356	326	699	934	912	443	1399	1382	1200	717	358	610	48
A28L: Trying an amphetamine (upper, pep pill, bennie, speed) once or twice																
1. Don't disapprove	24.9	25.9	23.1	26.1	15.0	26.8	25.0	21.7	28.4	20.8	28.1	6.2	17.7	28.8	63.9	75.0
2. Disapprove	23.5	23.6	23.7	23.5	22.4	26.9	21.5	21.9	25.2	23.4	23.9	23.6	26.6	29.6	17.4	6.3
3. Strongly disapprove	51.6	50.4	53.2	50.4	62.6	46.3	53.5	56.4	46.4	55.8	48.0	70.3	55.6	41.6	18.7	18.8
Item 8670 N(Wtd)	2988	1455	1431	2357	326	698	933	913	444	1399	1382	1200	717	358	610	48
A28M: Taking amphetamines regularly																
1. Don't disapprove	7.2	8.6	5.4	6.8	5.5	7.9	7.0	5.9	9.5	4.4	9.5	3.0	3.2	3.1	20.0	37.0
2. Disapprove	23.8	25.2	21.9	23.6	26.1	26.4	19.8	25.1	25.1	19.9	26.9	14.3	22.7	30.3	38.0	41.3
3. Strongly disapprove	69.0	66.2	72.7	69.6	68.4	65.7	73.3	69.1	65.2	75.7	63.6	82.7	74.1	66.9	42.1	21.7
Item 8680 N(Wtd)	2981	1450	1431	2352	326	696	933	909	442	1399	1375	1200	718	357	606	46
A28N: Trying cocaine once or twice																
1. Don't disapprove	17.6	20.6	13.9	17.3	14.4	20.5	13.9	16.4	23.3	14.1	19.8	4.4	10.8	19.4	45.9	74.5
2. Disapprove	20.5	20.5	20.9	20.3	23.3	24.4	19.4	18.7	20.5	20.5	20.4	16.5	24.1	26.8	20.9	8.5
3. Strongly disapprove	61.9	58.9	65.2	62.4	62.3	55.2	66.6	64.8	56.2	65.4	59.8	79.0	65.1	53.5	33.2	17.0
Item 8690 N(Wtd)	2982	1452	1430	2352	326	698	932	909	443	1396	1379	1198	719	355	608	47
A28O: Taking cocaine regularly																
1. Don't disapprove	6.1	7.7	3.8	5.3	6.0	7.9	3.7	6.1	7.9	3.8	7.5	2.8	2.8	4.0	13.1	50.0
2. Disapprove	18.5	21.3	15.5	17.8	21.5	20.5	15.6	18.0	22.2	15.5	20.8	10.9	17.3	21.4	32.1	29.2
3. Strongly disapprove	75.4	71.0	80.6	76.8	72.5	71.6	80.7	75.9	69.7	80.6	71.6	86.4	79.8	74.6	54.7	22.9
Item 8700 N(Wtd)	2957	1442	1416	2339	316	693	927	895	442	1390	1368	1188	713	351	605	48
A28P: Trying one or two drinks of an alcoholic beverage (beer, wine, liquor)																
1. Don't disapprove	81.7	83.3	80.2	84.5	68.1	89.3	86.4	73.6	76.9	79.1	84.7	66.6	93.3	88.5	93.4	89.6
2. Disapprove	11.7	10.8	12.6	10.1	17.5	8.9	9.4	16.0	12.4	13.2	10.0	21.0	4.7	9.0	3.6	8.3
3. Strongly disapprove	6.5	5.9	7.3	5.4	14.7	1.9	4.3	10.4	10.6	7.7	5.3	12.4	1.9	2.8	3.1	2.1
Item 8710 N(Wtd)	2988	1454	1433	2355	326	699	934	912	442	1397	1384	1200	718	357	610	48

QUESTIONNAIRE FORM 3 1976	TOTAL	SEX		RACE		REGION				4YR COLLEGE PLANS		ILLICIT DRUG USE: LIFETIME				
		M	F	White	Black	NE	NC	S	W	Yes	No	None	Mari-juana Only	Few Pills	More Pills	Any Her-oin
Weighted No. of Cases:	3034	1471	1443	2378	332	709	945	925	455	1408	1399	1209	721	364	612	49
% of Weighted Total:	100.0	48.5	47.6	78.4	10.9	23.4	31.1	30.5	15.0	46.4	46.1	39.8	23.8	12.0	20.2	1.6

A28Q: Taking one or two drinks nearly every day

1. Don't disapprove	31.1	37.3	24.2	31.7	22.6	35.5	30.9	26.9	33.0	26.0	35.6	17.9	35.3	37.3	46.7	56.5
2. Disapprove	42.1	41.5	43.1	42.8	41.8	43.4	42.3	42.7	38.2	41.5	42.7	42.3	45.2	42.9	37.2	32.6
3. Strongly disapprove	26.8	21.3	32.7	25.5	35.6	21.1	26.9	30.4	28.5	32.4	21.6	39.8	19.5	19.9	16.1	13.0
Item 8720 N(Wtd)	2976	1449	1428	2348	323	696	931	907	442	1394	1378	1197	714	357	608	46

A28R: Taking four or five drinks nearly every day

1. Don't disapprove	9.3	13.0	5.0	8.9	7.7	8.5	9.1	10.4	8.8	5.8	12.5	5.3	7.5	10.4	16.1	35.4
2. Disapprove	29.2	31.3	26.6	29.4	27.1	32.8	29.1	26.0	30.2	24.5	33.1	21.1	34.5	30.9	36.0	39.6
3. Strongly disapprove	61.5	55.7	68.4	61.7	65.5	58.7	61.8	63.6	60.9	69.7	54.3	73.5	57.8	58.7	47.9	25.0
Item 8730 N(Wtd)	2981	1449	1431	2349	325	698	929	911	443	1397	1379	1198	716	356	609	48

A28S: Having five or more drinks once or twice each weekend

1. Don't disapprove	41.4	47.8	34.0	43.5	26.0	44.4	46.0	36.5	37.6	35.3	46.9	22.0	49.5	43.9	65.5	72.9
2. Disapprove	26.6	26.6	27.1	26.3	26.6	30.1	25.6	24.8	26.7	27.0	26.5	29.8	27.8	29.6	17.5	22.9
3. Strongly disapprove	32.0	25.6	38.9	30.3	47.4	25.4	28.4	38.8	35.7	37.8	26.6	48.2	22.7	26.5	17.0	2.1
Item 8740 N(Wtd)	2978	1449	1428	2347	327	694	929	913	442	1390	1381	1195	715	355	611	48

A29: During the LAST 12 MONTHS, how often have you been around people who were taking each of the following to get high or for "kicks"?

A29A: Marijuana (pot, grass) or hashish

1. Not at all	20.5	16.7	24.6	19.7	24.6	15.2	21.1	24.9	18.9	20.5	20.8	41.2	4.7	13.7	3.9	-
2. Once or twice	21.8	21.2	22.5	21.0	27.7	20.1	23.1	22.9	19.8	22.2	21.1	32.3	20.9	15.7	6.4	14.6
3. Occasionally	25.1	27.4	23.0	25.9	23.4	25.7	24.3	24.8	26.5	26.7	24.5	17.8	39.6	28.0	20.8	10.4
4. Often	32.5	34.8	30.0	33.5	24.3	39.1	31.5	27.5	34.7	30.7	33.7	8.7	34.7	42.6	68.9	75.0
Item 20590 N(Wtd)	2980	1450	1429	2351	325	693	925	913	449	1392	1381	1197	718	357	610	48

A29B: LSD

1. Not at all	78.8	77.9	79.5	77.3	93.1	73.8	80.3	82.2	76.5	78.9	79.0	92.8	84.8	72.1	51.2	31.3
2. Once or twice	13.0	13.6	12.7	14.4	4.1	14.7	12.7	11.2	14.9	14.0	12.2	4.8	11.5	19.4	27.7	12.5
3. Occasionally	6.0	6.2	5.9	6.3	1.3	8.0	5.4	5.2	5.9	5.4	6.7	1.9	2.7	7.3	15.5	33.3
4. Often	2.2	2.4	1.9	1.9	1.6	3.5	1.6	1.3	2.7	1.8	2.2	.5	1.0	1.1	5.6	22.9
Item 20600 N(Wtd)	2959	1446	1413	2341	320	688	921	907	443	1383	1370	1188	710	355	607	48

A29C: Other psychedelics (mescaline, peyote, PCP, etc.)

1. Not at all	76.5	74.4	78.4	74.2	93.2	71.7	77.4	80.8	73.6	77.9	75.5	93.4	81.3	68.8	45.6	22.9
2. Once or twice	13.5	15.1	12.2	15.4	3.4	14.4	13.0	11.5	17.4	13.4	13.4	4.9	13.8	21.3	25.6	14.6
3. Occasionally	6.9	7.4	6.5	7.6	1.9	9.1	7.0	5.3	6.3	6.6	7.3	1.0	3.9	8.1	19.2	33.3
4. Often	3.1	3.0	3.0	2.8	1.9	4.8	2.6	2.4	2.7	2.2	3.8	.7	.8	1.7	9.4	27.1
Item 20610 N(Wtd)	2967	1446	1420	2340	323	693	923	908	443	1387	1376	1190	715	356	605	48

A29D: Amphetamines (uppers, pep pills, bennies, speed)

1. Not at all	59.6	58.9	60.3	56.4	80.7	60.5	55.6	64.5	56.4	63.1	55.8	81.3	64.9	47.6	20.2	12.5
2. Once or twice	20.3	21.4	19.1	22.1	11.3	18.7	21.5	19.4	22.1	18.9	21.7	13.6	22.2	29.2	26.3	20.8
3. Occasionally	13.2	13.5	13.0	14.6	4.0	13.3	15.0	10.9	14.1	13.2	13.8	3.8	10.6	17.8	32.5	16.7
4. Often	6.8	6.1	7.5	6.9	4.0	7.3	7.9	5.0	7.4	4.9	8.7	1.2	2.4	5.3	21.0	50.0
Item 20620 N(Wtd)	2979	1451	1427	2350	327	694	927	911	447	1393	1381	1195	717	359	609	48

QUESTIONNAIRE FORM 3 1976	TOTAL	SEX		RACE		REGION				4YR COLLEGE PLANS		ILLICIT DRUG USE: LIFETIME				
		M	F	White	Black	NE	NC	S	W	Yes	No	None	Mari-juana Only	Few Pills	More Pills	Any Her-oin
Weighted No. of Cases:	3034	1471	1443	2378	332	709	945	925	455	1408	1399	1209	721	364	612	49
% of Weighted Total:	100.0	48.5	47.6	78.4	10.9	23.4	31.1	30.5	15.0	46.4	46.1	39.8	23.8	12.0	20.2	1.6
A29E: Barbiturates (downers, goofballs, reds, yellows, etc.)																
1. Not at all	69.0	68.0	69.8	66.4	86.2	65.3	69.5	70.6	70.2	71.3	66.4	86.3	74.9	63.0	34.3	14.6
2. Once or twice	17.7	18.4	17.1	19.6	7.6	18.8	17.2	16.9	18.3	17.4	17.7	10.3	17.4	21.4	31.4	16.7
3. Occasionally	8.9	9.7	8.2	9.5	3.7	11.7	8.2	8.0	7.8	8.2	10.1	2.7	5.6	12.5	21.8	25.0
4. Often	4.5	3.9	4.9	4.5	2.1	4.2	5.1	4.5	3.6	3.2	5.6	.8	2.1	3.1	12.5	43.8
Item 20630 N(Wtd)	2981	1453	1426	2350	327	695	927	912	447	1393	1382	1195	718	359	609	48
A29F: Tranquilizers (Librium, Valium, Miltown)																
1. Not at all	67.7	71.8	63.3	64.9	88.8	65.9	68.1	68.2	68.8	68.2	67.3	80.7	76.6	57.1	40.5	23.4
2. Once or twice	17.7	16.2	19.5	19.3	8.1	16.7	16.9	18.3	19.6	17.5	18.0	12.9	14.3	24.6	27.0	25.5
3. Occasionally	9.1	8.1	10.2	9.8	1.6	11.9	8.8	8.5	6.5	10.1	8.1	4.1	6.6	14.3	18.9	10.6
4. Often	5.5	3.9	7.0	5.9	1.6	5.5	6.3	5.1	5.0	4.2	6.6	2.3	2.7	3.9	13.7	40.4
Item 20640 N(Wtd)	2973	1451	1424	2350	322	696	925	909	443	1393	1376	1194	715	357	608	47
A29G: Cocaine ("coke")																
1. Not at all	77.0	74.9	79.3	76.8	83.4	73.2	79.2	81.3	69.7	78.0	76.8	93.0	82.2	68.0	49.3	22.9
2. Once or twice	13.9	15.5	12.2	14.3	10.1	14.4	13.4	11.7	19.1	14.5	13.4	5.4	12.2	21.6	27.8	10.4
3. Occasionally	6.1	7.0	5.3	6.3	4.0	8.8	5.5	4.0	7.6	5.5	6.2	.7	4.6	8.7	16.0	22.9
4. Often	3.0	2.6	3.2	2.6	2.1	3.6	2.1	3.1	3.6	2.2	3.6	.9	1.0	2.0	6.9	43.8
Item 20650 N(Wtd)	2973	1449	1425	2346	326	694	926	907	446	1393	1377	1196	715	356	608	48
A29H: Heroin (smack, horse)																
1. Not at all	91.4	91.7	91.1	91.7	92.6	87.9	91.9	92.9	92.4	92.5	90.3	95.4	93.6	89.6	86.0	36.2
2. Once or twice	6.2	6.3	5.8	6.1	5.2	9.1	5.7	4.7	5.6	5.3	6.9	3.4	5.3	7.0	10.5	31.9
3. Occasionally	1.6	1.2	2.0	1.5	.9	2.3	1.5	1.5	.7	1.6	1.6	.7	.7	3.4	2.3	17.0
4. Often	.8	.7	1.1	.7	1.2	.9	.8	.7	1.3	.5	1.2	.5	.3	-	1.2	17.0
Item 20660 N(Wtd)	2974	1452	1423	2347	325	695	926	907	446	1395	1375	1194	717	356	608	47
A29I: Other narcotics (methadone, opium, codeine, paregoric, etc.)																
1. Not at all	81.9	81.2	82.3	81.2	89.2	77.3	83.4	85.2	78.9	84.0	80.2	93.1	88.8	78.6	58.7	25.0
2. Once or twice	12.4	13.2	11.9	13.1	8.6	14.9	11.1	10.6	14.8	11.9	12.5	5.4	9.2	16.4	25.4	31.3
3. Occasionally	3.9	4.3	3.4	4.1	1.2	5.8	3.6	2.9	3.6	2.9	4.7	.7	1.8	4.2	10.9	22.9
4. Often	1.8	1.3	2.4	1.6	.9	2.0	1.8	1.2	2.7	1.2	2.5	.8	.1	.8	5.0	20.8
Item 20670 N(Wtd)	2973	1451	1423	2346	325	692	924	911	446	1390	1381	1195	714	359	606	48
A29J: Alcoholic beverages (beer, wine, liquor)																
1. Not at all	6.0	5.6	5.8	4.8	10.9	4.2	4.0	8.5	7.9	5.4	6.0	11.7	1.5	2.8	2.0	4.2
2. Once or twice	10.7	8.9	12.7	9.5	18.3	10.6	10.4	11.1	10.4	10.6	10.5	19.1	6.2	5.9	2.8	2.1
3. Occasionally	26.2	26.1	26.4	25.2	36.0	23.6	25.0	29.7	26.0	28.7	23.7	34.5	25.6	24.4	12.7	14.6
4. Often	57.1	59.3	55.1	60.5	35.1	61.6	60.6	50.7	56.0	55.3	59.7	34.5	66.7	66.9	82.7	77.1
Item 20680 N(Wtd)	2950	1435	1416	2333	322	691	916	899	443	1380	1367	1181	712	353	607	48
This section asks for your views and feelings about a number of different things.																
D01: How satisfied are you with your life as a whole these days?																
1. Completely dissatisfied	2.6	2.2	3.0	2.3	5.3	2.9	1.9	3.3	2.4	2.2	3.2	2.7	2.3	.9	3.5	6.8
2. Quite dissatisfied	9.1	10.1	8.5	9.5	7.0	11.1	9.5	7.1	10.0	8.9	9.3	9.4	9.2	7.7	9.5	2.3
3. Somewhat dissatisfied	12.1	12.4	11.6	11.0	18.9	13.1	12.3	11.0	12.4	11.3	12.5	10.4	12.2	15.9	11.8	22.7
4. Neither, or mixed feelings	13.3	12.8	13.7	13.5	10.9	14.4	12.9	13.9	11.4	11.8	15.0	11.0	13.0	15.3	17.1	20.5
5. Somewhat satisfied	25.2	26.7	23.8	25.8	23.9	26.3	23.2	27.8	22.8	26.9	23.8	25.6	22.9	23.9	27.2	29.5
6. Quite satisfied	31.8	30.7	32.8	32.8	26.7	27.5	34.7	30.6	34.9	34.4	29.3	34.9	33.5	30.7	27.5	11.4
7. Completely satisfied	5.7	5.1	6.5	5.1	7.0	4.8	5.6	6.3	6.4	4.5	6.8	6.0	6.8	5.6	3.5	6.8
Item 6840 N(Wtd)	2854	1391	1393	2317	285	647	910	875	421	1386	1356	1159	687	339	578	44

QUESTIONNAIRE FORM 3 1976	TOTAL	SEX		RACE		REGION				4YR COLLEGE PLANS		ILLICIT DRUG USE: LIFETIME				
		M	F	White	Black	NE	NC	S	W	Yes	No	None	Mari- juana Only	Few Pills	More Pills	Any Her- oin
Weighted No. of Cases:	3034	1471	1443	2378	332	709	945	925	455	1408	1399	1209	721	364	612	49
% of Weighted Total:	100.0	48.5	47.6	78.4	10.9	23.4	31.1	30.5	15.0	46.4	46.1	39.8	23.8	12.0	20.2	1.6

D02: These questions are about your health at the present time.

D02A: Have you ever been bothered by shortness of breath when you were not exercising or working hard?

1. Never	68.8	72.9	64.2	68.5	73.5	70.9	68.6	66.7	70.5	73.2	65.2	77.2	72.3	58.6	54.5	52.3
2. Seldom	18.1	17.8	18.8	18.6	13.6	16.7	19.5	17.4	18.3	17.2	18.3	14.2	17.2	23.7	23.0	25.0
3. Sometimes	11.3	7.8	14.6	11.4	10.8	10.1	10.3	13.9	9.8	8.2	14.1	7.8	9.5	15.7	18.2	15.9
4. Often	1.9	1.4	2.3	1.6	2.4	2.5	1.6	1.9	1.7	1.4	2.4	.9	1.2	1.8	4.3	9.1
Item 8850 N(Wtd)	2855	1390	1395	2317	287	646	911	877	420	1384	1357	1160	686	338	578	44

D02B: Have you ever been bothered by your heart beating hard?

1. Never	63.4	67.5	58.9	61.9	70.4	62.7	63.2	62.4	66.7	65.4	61.4	69.0	65.2	58.8	53.2	45.5
2. Seldom	23.3	22.2	24.7	24.7	17.1	24.5	24.3	21.9	22.1	24.0	22.5	20.8	23.3	26.1	26.7	29.5
3. Sometimes	11.9	9.2	14.5	12.0	11.8	12.0	10.7	14.2	9.3	9.1	14.8	9.0	10.1	14.5	17.5	18.2
4. Often	1.4	1.1	1.9	1.3	1.0	.8	1.8	1.5	1.7	1.4	1.4	1.2	1.2	.6	2.6	6.8
Item 8860 N(Wtd)	2842	1381	1390	2307	287	640	905	878	420	1383	1348	1153	682	337	577	44

D02C: Have you ever had spells of dizziness?

1. Never	41.8	50.5	32.6	39.3	54.0	44.8	37.2	43.3	44.2	44.3	40.1	47.1	43.3	38.0	31.7	31.8
2. Seldom	35.4	33.8	37.1	37.5	22.8	30.5	40.4	32.8	37.3	35.0	35.6	35.0	35.8	36.2	36.4	34.1
3. Sometimes	19.8	13.9	26.1	20.4	18.2	21.3	19.4	21.0	15.9	18.3	21.1	16.4	17.1	24.0	26.9	20.5
4. Often	3.0	1.7	4.3	2.9	4.6	3.3	3.1	2.9	2.6	2.4	3.2	1.6	3.8	1.8	5.0	11.4
Item 8870 N(Wtd)	2839	1380	1388	2309	285	640	908	875	416	1378	1348	1151	684	334	577	44

D02D: Do your hands ever tremble enough to bother you?

1. Never	73.4	80.8	65.6	72.3	76.8	77.1	72.1	72.2	73.2	76.8	69.9	78.6	74.5	74.2	62.5	54.5
2. Seldom	16.0	12.4	19.9	17.2	10.9	14.3	16.4	15.5	18.7	14.4	18.2	14.4	17.0	13.4	20.8	9.1
3. Sometimes	8.2	5.4	11.0	8.2	8.4	6.8	9.5	9.2	5.7	6.9	9.2	5.5	6.7	9.8	13.0	25.0
4. Often	2.4	1.4	3.4	2.3	3.9	1.7	2.0	3.3	2.6	1.8	2.7	1.6	1.8	2.4	4.0	13.6
Item 8880 N(Wtd)	2842	1383	1390	2311	285	643	908	873	418	1382	1347	1154	682	337	578	44

D02E: Are you troubled by your hands sweating so that they feel damp and clammy?

1. Never	58.2	62.8	53.3	56.2	71.2	62.0	54.4	58.8	59.7	60.5	56.0	62.7	57.3	58.8	49.4	61.4
2. Seldom	24.9	23.0	26.9	26.2	15.8	23.8	26.0	23.4	27.0	24.1	26.4	22.6	25.4	23.1	30.7	18.2
3. Sometimes	12.1	10.6	13.8	12.7	9.8	9.7	14.9	12.7	8.8	11.1	12.3	11.1	12.8	11.3	13.5	11.4
4. Often	4.8	3.5	6.0	4.9	3.5	4.5	4.7	5.3	4.5	4.3	5.3	3.5	4.4	6.8	6.4	9.1
Item 8890 N(Wtd)	2845	1383	1390	2311	285	642	908	876	419	1381	1351	1157	682	337	577	44

D02F: Have there ever been times when you couldn't take care of things because you just couldn't get going?

1. Never	48.2	52.0	43.8	47.7	50.9	48.6	48.0	48.3	47.4	48.8	47.8	55.3	50.1	42.4	36.5	31.8
2. Seldom	31.4	31.3	31.5	31.8	29.3	31.4	30.7	31.4	32.8	32.1	30.6	28.5	31.7	37.7	33.0	31.8
3. Sometimes	17.4	14.5	20.6	17.6	16.4	17.5	17.9	17.1	17.0	16.2	18.5	14.4	15.5	16.3	25.2	27.3
4. Often	3.1	2.1	4.1	2.8	3.8	2.5	3.5	3.2	2.9	3.0	3.0	1.8	2.6	3.6	5.4	11.4
Item 8900 N(Wtd)	2841	1382	1387	2306	287	640	905	878	418	1379	1348	1151	684	337	576	44

D03: At any time during the LAST 12 MONTHS, have you felt in your own mind that you should REDUCE or STOP your use of...

QUESTIONNAIRE FORM 3 1976	TOTAL	SEX		RACE		REGION				4YR COLLEGE PLANS		ILLICIT DRUG USE: LIFETIME				
		M	F	White	Black	NE	NC	S	W	Yes	No	None	Mari-juana Only	Few Pills	More Pills	Any Her-oin
Weighted No. of Cases:	3034	1471	1443	2378	332	709	945	925	455	1408	1399	1209	721	364	612	49
% of Weighted Total:	100.0	48.5	47.6	78.4	10.9	23.4	31.1	30.5	15.0	46.4	46.1	39.8	23.8	12.0	20.2	1.6
D03A: Alcohol?																
1. Yes	32.9	37.5	28.0	32.3	34.3	29.6	34.0	36.9	28.2	32.1	34.2	22.8	38.2	35.8	40.9	39.0
2. No	54.1	51.9	56.3	55.9	41.4	63.3	55.6	46.6	51.2	52.7	55.1	48.6	58.8	57.0	56.3	56.1
8. Haven't used in last 12 months	13.0	10.7	15.7	11.8	24.2	7.3	10.4	16.5	20.5	15.3	10.6	28.6	3.0	7.3	2.8	4.9
Item 8910 N(Wtd)	2438	1238	1144	2048	198	558	807	708	365	1185	1157	877	638	302	538	41
D03B: Cigarettes?																
1. Yes	33.2	33.3	32.8	33.2	36.1	34.9	33.6	35.2	25.5	26.7	40.0	13.9	39.6	42.0	54.5	55.6
2. No	14.7	14.1	15.2	13.8	18.0	15.2	14.4	16.0	11.8	11.3	17.9	10.5	17.0	16.0	18.3	24.4
8. Haven't used in last 12 months	52.1	52.6	52.1	53.0	46.2	49.9	52.0	48.8	62.5	62.0	42.1	75.5	43.2	42.0	27.2	20.0
Item 8920 N(Wtd)	2721	1330	1327	2232	266	619	879	824	400	1332	1283	1078	664	326	563	45
D03C: Marijuana?																
1. Yes	18.1	22.7	13.2	18.3	16.1	19.6	18.0	17.6	17.2	18.4	17.9	-	35.9	23.7	30.0	21.4
2. No	27.8	30.0	25.6	28.1	22.7	34.9	26.1	24.5	27.6	23.3	32.1	-	41.4	39.5	54.4	73.8
8. Haven't used in last 12 months	54.1	47.3	61.2	53.7	60.7	45.6	55.9	57.9	55.2	58.3	50.0	100.0	22.7	37.1	15.6	2.4
Item 8930 N(Wtd)	2497	1221	1219	2082	211	562	823	739	373	1261	1144	1007	577	299	540	42
D03D: Psychedelics (LSD, etc.)?																
1. Yes	3.1	4.6	1.7	2.9	2.5	5.0	2.4	2.4	2.7	2.8	3.5	-	-	3.2	11.4	30.6
2. No	3.1	3.6	2.6	3.2	2.5	3.5	2.0	3.2	4.3	2.1	3.7	-	-	1.1	12.8	33.3
8. Haven't used in last 12 months	93.8	91.8	95.8	94.0	95.0	91.3	95.6	94.4	92.7	95.0	92.7	100.0	100.0	95.4	75.6	36.1
Item 8940 N(Wtd)	2415	1160	1202	2026	202	539	799	708	369	1231	1101	1007	609	280	446	36
D03E: Amphetamines (uppers)?																
1. Yes	4.5	5.6	3.4	4.4	3.9	5.1	4.4	4.0	4.4	3.5	5.5	-	-	3.1	19.9	27.5
2. No	7.5	8.4	6.9	7.9	3.4	7.5	6.9	7.0	9.9	5.4	9.4	-	-	5.4	33.9	50.0
8. Haven't used in last 12 months	88.1	86.1	89.7	87.7	92.7	87.4	88.7	89.0	85.6	91.2	85.0	100.0	100.0	91.5	46.3	25.0
Item 8950 N(Wtd)	2379	1162	1163	1994	205	546	770	701	362	1214	1083	1004	613	258	428	40
D03F: Quaaludes?																
1. Yes	1.7	2.3	1.2	1.7	1.4	2.9	1.5	1.9	.3	1.1	2.5	-	-	-	6.7	18.9
2. No	2.6	3.1	2.0	2.6	3.4	2.5	1.7	3.9	1.9	1.8	3.0	-	-	.4	9.6	45.9
8. Haven't used in last 12 months	95.7	94.6	96.8	95.8	95.2	94.7	96.8	94.2	97.8	97.0	94.5	100.0	100.0	99.6	83.9	35.1
Item 8960 N(Wtd)	2463	1184	1220	2076	207	550	809	737	366	1244	1133	1007	616	285	479	37
D03G: Barbiturates (downers)?																
1. Yes	3.3	3.7	2.9	3.0	2.5	4.4	2.6	3.7	2.2	2.3	4.3	-	-	2.2	14.1	20.0
2. No	4.3	5.2	3.7	4.5	2.0	3.7	3.7	6.4	2.5	2.7	5.9	-	-	1.1	17.9	52.5
8. Haven't used in last 12 months	92.4	91.2	93.4	92.5	95.0	91.9	93.9	89.9	95.1	95.0	89.8	100.0	100.0	97.0	67.9	27.5
Item 8970 N(Wtd)	2411	1168	1188	2021	201	541	782	723	365	1228	1104	1006	614	267	448	40
D03H: Cocaine?																
1. Yes	1.6	1.8	1.4	1.3	3.0	2.4	.9	2.1	1.4	1.2	2.0	-	-	1.4	5.0	29.4
2. No	3.3	4.1	2.6	3.3	3.0	3.3	1.6	4.2	5.4	2.3	4.1	-	-	.7	13.6	38.2
8. Haven't used in last 12 months	95.1	94.2	96.0	95.4	94.5	94.3	97.5	93.7	93.0	96.5	93.9	100.0	100.0	97.9	81.4	32.4
Item 8980 N(Wtd)	2451	1180	1216	2068	199	548	804	731	369	1232	1134	1007	614	280	479	34
D03I: Heroin?																
1. Yes	.5	.8	.2	.4	1.0	1.3	.2	.4	.3	.2	.7	-	-	.3	.4	19.4
2. No	.5	.7	.4	.3	2.5	.2	.4	.8	.5	.4	.6	-	-	-	.2	30.6
8. Haven't used in last 12 months	98.9	98.6	99.4	99.2	96.6	98.5	99.3	98.6	99.2	99.4	98.8	100.0	100.0	100.0	99.2	52.8
Item 8990 N(Wtd)	2475	1192	1226	2087	204	551	815	739	371	1245	1145	1006	614	289	491	36

QUESTIONNAIRE FORM 3 1976	TOTAL	SEX		RACE		REGION				4YR COLLEGE PLANS		ILLICIT DRUG USE: LIFETIME				
		M	F	White	Black	NE	NC	S	W	Yes	No	None	Marijuana Only	Few Pills	More Pills	Any Heroin
Weighted No. of Cases:	3034	1471	1443	2378	332	709	945	925	455	1408	1399	1209	721	364	612	49
% of Weighted Total:	100.0	48.5	47.6	78.4	10.9	23.4	31.1	30.5	15.0	46.4	46.1	39.8	23.8	12.0	20.2	1.6

D03J: Other narcotics?

1. Yes	1.8	2.4	1.1	1.8	1.0	3.1	1.6	1.6	.9	1.1	2.6	-	-	1.8	6.7	20.6
2. No	2.4	2.7	2.2	2.4	1.5	2.5	2.8	2.2	1.7	1.7	3.1	-	-	1.8	9.0	41.2
8. Haven't used in last 12 months	95.8	94.9	96.7	95.8	97.9	94.7	95.7	96.2	97.1	97.2	94.3	100.0	100.0	96.4	84.3	35.3
Item 9000 N(Wtd)	2361	1142	1164	1983	195	524	796	693	347	1195	1085	1001	609	277	402	34

IF YOU ARE CURRENTLY USING MARIJUANA, GO TO Q.D05

D04: Here are some reasons people give for not using marijuana, or for stopping use. If you have NEVER used marijuana, or if you have STOPPED using it, please tell us which reasons are true for you. (Mark all that apply.)

A. Concerned about possible psychological damage	55.2	50.1	59.6	57.1	44.8	50.7	59.3	53.1	56.1	60.3	49.0	67.2	40.2	44.1	35.8	9.1
B. Concerned about possible physical damage	53.6	49.0	57.8	55.8	43.8	46.5	58.4	51.4	56.9	58.3	47.9	64.6	38.3	44.7	37.4	9.1
C. Concerned about getting arrested	45.5	51.1	41.2	48.6	32.5	41.6	47.2	45.5	47.3	45.9	44.8	47.4	47.8	37.1	41.6	18.2
D. Concerned about becoming addicted to marijuana	34.7	32.8	36.5	35.4	33.5	32.1	35.7	35.9	33.2	35.0	35.0	42.3	26.5	22.9	21.6	9.1
E. It's against my beliefs	47.8	44.0	51.6	49.2	42.3	39.3	47.8	49.5	55.0	52.0	42.1	62.1	23.1	38.8	29.5	27.3
F. Concerned about loss of energy or ambition	28.7	30.7	27.2	30.2	22.7	26.0	28.1	29.4	32.4	33.1	23.9	31.5	23.6	25.3	26.8	27.3
G. Concerned about possible loss of control of myself	40.7	36.4	44.8	42.7	33.5	36.0	43.2	40.4	41.6	44.0	36.8	50.5	28.3	28.2	25.8	9.1
H. It might lead to stronger drugs	45.1	41.4	48.6	46.5	42.8	39.1	47.5	48.6	39.3	43.6	46.9	53.1	33.6	38.8	34.2	9.1
I. Not enjoyable, I didn't like it	23.9	24.4	23.6	24.7	20.6	24.1	24.9	21.8	26.3	23.2	25.4	13.4	49.6	30.6	23.7	27.3
J. My parents would disapprove	54.7	52.7	57.2	56.1	47.9	52.9	57.1	53.1	54.6	57.3	51.9	60.0	50.1	50.6	42.1	18.2
K. My husband/wife (or boyfriend/ girlfriend) would disapprove	28.1	27.0	29.3	29.5	19.1	21.6	29.5	30.7	27.9	24.5	32.6	28.1	27.0	34.7	25.8	-
L. I don't like being with the people who use it	33.8	33.2	35.2	34.3	29.4	28.3	33.0	36.4	37.8	33.5	34.6	42.4	20.2	24.1	23.7	36.4
M. My friends don't use it	29.7	26.2	33.1	32.5	16.0	20.8	34.3	30.7	29.0	30.2	29.1	38.4	17.1	18.8	21.1	-
N. I might have a bad trip	19.7	18.3	21.2	20.4	18.0	15.2	22.2	21.1	17.2	18.6	20.5	23.7	12.3	14.7	16.3	9.1
Item 9020-9150 N(Wtd) ★	1824	814	969	1491	194	361	627	574	262	960	800	1047	381	170	190	11

If you have never used alcohol, marijuana, or other drugs, GO TO Q.E01

D05A: Has your use of alcohol ever caused any of the following problems for you? (Mark all that apply.)

Responses to this set of questions are not included because of complexities in the presentation and interpretation of the data.

Item 9190-9330

D05M: Has your use of marijuana ever caused any of the following problems for you? (Mark all that apply.)

Responses to this set of questions are not included because of complexities in the presentation and interpretation of the data.

Item 9360-9500

★=excludes respondents for whom question was inappropriate.

QUESTIONNAIRE FORM 3 1976	TOTAL	SEX		RACE		REGION				4YR COLLEGE PLANS		ILLICIT DRUG USE: LIFETIME				
		M	F	White	Black	NE	NC	S	W	Yes	No	None	Mari- juana Only	Few Pills	More Pills	Any Her- oin
Weighted No. of Cases:	3034	1471	1443	2378	332	709	945	925	455	1408	1399	1209	721	364	612	49
% of Weighted Total:	100.0	48.5	47.6	78.4	10.9	23.4	31.1	30.5	15.0	46.4	46.1	39.8	23.8	12.0	20.2	1.6

D05O: Has your use of other drugs ever caused any of the following problems for you? (Mark all that apply.)

Responses to this set of questions are not included because of complexities in the presentation and interpretation of the data.

Item 9530-9670

E01: Some people think about what's going on in government very often, and others are not that interested. How much of an interest do you take in government and current events?

	TOTAL	M	F	White	Black	NE	NC	S	W	Yes	No	None	Mari.	Few	More	Heroin
5. A very great interest	6.9	9.1	4.9	5.9	10.6	7.9	4.9	6.8	9.8	10.7	2.5	8.2	6.1	5.6	4.8	11.6
4. A lot of interest	18.1	22.2	13.8	18.6	14.3	16.5	16.6	19.8	20.5	24.0	11.1	20.2	15.1	18.5	18.2	16.3
3. Some interest	48.1	49.1	46.8	49.0	43.8	44.4	51.1	48.4	46.0	46.5	50.8	49.0	49.1	45.5	47.1	41.9
2. Very little interest	20.8	14.6	27.2	20.7	21.5	22.7	22.2	20.4	15.7	16.3	25.9	17.8	23.8	24.1	22.0	20.9
1. No interest at all	6.2	5.0	7.3	5.8	9.8	8.4	5.2	4.7	8.3	2.5	9.7	4.9	6.1	6.0	7.8	11.6
Item 6330 N(Wtd)	2694	1297	1335	2208	265	595	869	835	396	1329	1265	1108	644	319	537	43

E02: Do you agree or disagree that most efforts to prevent (or clean up) pollution...

E02A: ...are just too expensive

	TOTAL	M	F	White	Black	NE	NC	S	W	Yes	No	None	Mari.	Few	More	Heroin
1. Disagree	24.0	25.5	22.3	23.5	25.2	28.4	22.1	23.4	22.3	25.2	22.2	23.4	24.5	25.2	23.5	25.6
2. Mostly disagree	24.6	25.0	24.6	26.0	19.3	23.7	24.9	24.0	26.9	29.6	19.3	25.9	24.1	23.6	24.7	16.3
3. Neither	28.4	26.8	29.6	28.5	24.0	26.0	30.9	28.1	27.4	25.4	32.0	26.1	29.3	28.9	32.4	23.3
4. Mostly agree	16.6	15.8	17.6	17.1	15.4	16.4	16.6	15.7	18.8	15.5	18.0	18.0	16.5	17.9	12.8	16.3
5. Agree	6.4	6.9	5.8	4.9	16.1	5.7	5.4	8.8	4.6	4.2	8.6	6.6	5.6	4.4	6.6	18.6
Item 9700 N(Wtd)	2683	1297	1320	2205	254	596	867	826	394	1323	1258	1103	642	318	531	43

E02B: ...cost more jobs than it's worth

	TOTAL	M	F	White	Black	NE	NC	S	W	Yes	No	None	Mari.	Few	More	Heroin
1. Disagree	29.4	29.1	29.5	29.7	26.7	34.6	27.0	29.0	27.0	32.0	25.8	29.4	29.6	28.9	28.7	28.6
2. Mostly disagree	26.4	27.1	25.8	27.7	21.9	24.2	28.0	25.9	27.5	29.5	23.3	27.6	27.2	24.4	25.9	23.8
3. Neither	29.2	28.1	30.3	29.6	24.7	25.8	31.9	27.7	31.4	26.1	33.1	28.8	28.0	28.6	30.6	31.0
4. Mostly agree	10.4	10.2	10.7	9.7	15.5	10.5	9.6	11.3	10.0	8.6	12.2	9.1	10.4	13.7	11.6	4.8
5. Agree	4.6	5.5	3.7	3.3	11.2	4.7	3.5	6.0	3.9	3.7	5.4	5.1	4.7	4.8	3.2	9.5
Item 9710 N(Wtd)	2664	1285	1315	2192	251	590	862	823	389	1311	1249	1093	635	315	533	42

E02C: ...are proposed by people who usually don't know what they are talking about

	TOTAL	M	F	White	Black	NE	NC	S	W	Yes	No	None	Mari.	Few	More	Heroin
1. Disagree	19.8	19.7	19.6	20.1	20.2	24.7	19.1	17.9	18.5	23.4	15.8	19.9	21.4	19.7	18.0	27.5
2. Mostly disagree	25.2	24.2	26.3	25.9	20.7	24.9	27.8	22.3	25.7	28.4	22.1	26.8	25.0	21.7	24.9	17.5
3. Neither	29.5	28.1	30.8	29.7	30.6	29.4	29.4	29.3	30.8	27.7	31.5	29.3	29.7	30.9	29.4	20.0
4. Mostly agree	15.3	16.1	14.9	15.4	12.8	12.4	15.6	16.3	16.7	13.6	17.0	13.5	14.0	17.8	18.9	15.0
5. Agree	10.1	11.9	8.4	8.9	16.1	8.8	8.1	14.1	8.2	6.9	13.5	10.5	10.2	9.9	8.8	20.0
Item 9720 N(Wtd)	2640	1276	1299	2180	242	582	853	815	389	1301	1239	1081	637	314	523	40

E02D: ...will not be enough anyhow

	TOTAL	M	F	White	Black	NE	NC	S	W	Yes	No	None	Mari.	Few	More	Heroin
1. Disagree	21.1	22.2	19.9	21.1	22.5	25.6	17.2	22.8	19.4	23.7	18.3	22.1	22.1	19.9	18.5	25.6
2. Mostly disagree	24.5	25.0	24.0	25.7	19.0	24.2	27.0	23.0	22.7	28.8	19.7	26.5	24.8	21.8	23.2	7.7
3. Neither	27.8	26.0	29.3	27.9	27.7	24.7	28.3	27.7	31.5	24.3	32.2	26.4	28.6	29.8	29.0	15.4
4. Mostly agree	18.7	18.7	19.5	18.5	18.6	16.7	21.0	16.8	20.7	17.4	20.3	16.5	18.4	22.1	20.0	30.8
5. Agree	7.8	8.2	7.2	6.7	12.6	8.6	6.6	9.7	5.7	5.9	9.4	8.3	6.0	6.4	9.5	17.9
Item 9730 N(Wtd)	2602	1254	1285	2158	231	570	849	797	387	1292	1214	1067	630	312	514	39

QUESTIONNAIRE FORM 3 1976	TOTAL	SEX		RACE		REGION				4YR COLLEGE PLANS		ILLICIT DRUG USE: LIFETIME				
		M	F	White	Black	NE	NC	S	W	Yes	No	None	Mari-juana Only	Few Pills	More Pills	Any Her-oin
Weighted No. of Cases:	3034	1471	1443	2378	332	709	945	925	455	1408	1399	1209	721	364	612	49
% of Weighted Total:	100.0	48.5	47.6	78.4	10.9	23.4	31.1	30.5	15.0	46.4	46.1	39.8	23.8	12.0	20.2	1.6

E02E: ...are useless because this society won't last long enough for such efforts to do any good

1. Disagree	40.1	39.7	40.4	41.5	31.0	42.0	39.6	39.1	40.6	46.8	33.0	42.9	42.0	36.1	36.7	25.0
2. Mostly disagree	23.3	25.4	21.6	24.1	20.5	22.5	24.8	22.2	23.7	24.1	22.2	24.2	21.8	26.2	21.2	35.0
3. Neither	22.4	20.1	24.4	22.1	23.0	21.4	23.2	22.2	22.7	18.5	26.9	19.5	25.0	23.6	24.1	17.5
4. Mostly agree	7.2	6.8	7.8	6.7	10.9	6.4	7.2	7.9	7.0	5.5	9.1	6.4	5.5	9.5	9.7	10.0
5. Agree	7.0	8.2	5.9	5.6	14.6	7.7	5.2	8.7	6.3	5.1	8.9	7.0	5.5	4.6	8.3	15.0
Item 9740 N(Wtd)	2614	1261	1289	2163	239	574	850	806	384	1296	1219	1076	633	305	518	40

E03: There has been talk about shortages of energy, food, and raw materials in this country. Do you think that in the coming years we will have plenty to meet our needs, a sufficient amount, or will we have to consume less?

1. Plenty to meet our needs	10.4	13.8	7.0	9.6	11.9	10.6	10.7	10.9	8.7	8.7	11.8	10.8	10.2	7.9	10.5	9.8
2. A sufficient amount	46.5	50.1	43.0	45.0	57.0	46.7	45.2	50.3	40.7	44.3	49.2	45.1	50.2	47.5	44.4	36.6
3. Will have to consume less	43.1	36.1	50.0	45.3	30.6	42.6	44.2	38.9	50.5	47.1	39.1	44.1	39.6	44.9	45.1	53.7
Item 9750 N(Wtd)	2572	1236	1280	2131	235	559	830	805	378	1281	1193	1077	608	303	505	41

E04: The questions in this section deal with population problems. How much do you agree or disagree with each statement?

E04A: Our government should help other countries to control their population

1. Disagree	22.8	25.0	20.6	22.1	27.0	24.2	20.4	23.7	23.8	20.5	25.0	21.8	21.5	23.4	24.3	27.9
2. Mostly disagree	16.3	15.8	16.5	16.1	17.5	19.2	17.4	14.9	12.3	17.6	15.4	17.6	18.5	12.0	13.3	23.3
3. Neither	20.9	21.1	20.9	21.3	16.7	17.5	21.2	21.4	23.8	19.0	22.7	19.8	20.4	19.9	25.7	14.0
4. Mostly agree	24.6	22.3	27.1	25.8	18.3	23.1	26.8	21.9	27.9	27.7	21.8	25.1	25.2	27.5	21.9	18.6
5. Agree	15.4	15.9	14.9	14.7	20.2	15.9	14.0	18.1	11.8	15.2	15.1	15.7	14.6	17.1	14.8	16.3
Item 9760 N(Wtd)	2669	1287	1313	2194	252	590	862	827	390	1315	1250	1108	632	316	526	43

E04B: Governments should avoid making policy about population and let the individual decide

1. Disagree	15.4	16.1	14.6	14.3	22.8	16.1	13.4	17.5	14.5	16.9	13.6	13.2	15.6	18.8	17.5	19.0
2. Mostly disagree	24.2	25.9	22.8	25.3	18.8	24.3	25.4	22.2	25.3	26.5	21.8	25.4	25.4	22.3	23.8	9.5
3. Neither	23.4	24.0	22.3	23.4	18.0	22.4	25.2	22.0	23.5	21.2	24.8	21.6	24.6	23.9	24.6	23.8
4. Mostly agree	21.0	19.0	23.0	21.7	18.4	19.0	24.2	20.1	19.1	21.3	21.2	21.5	21.5	20.1	20.2	19.0
5. Agree	16.0	15.0	17.3	15.3	21.6	18.3	11.8	18.2	17.3	14.2	18.5	18.4	12.9	15.0	13.9	28.6
Item 9770 N(Wtd)	2657	1281	1310	2189	250	585	861	824	387	1310	1246	1104	629	314	525	42

E04C: I feel strongly enough about preventing overpopulation that I'd be willing to limit my family to two children

1. Disagree	12.9	12.9	12.3	12.0	20.2	15.8	9.9	12.3	16.3	12.5	13.1	14.7	11.1	13.4	9.0	26.2
2. Mostly disagree	11.7	11.5	11.9	11.2	13.1	16.4	11.8	9.8	8.0	10.7	13.0	12.6	11.6	11.1	10.1	11.9
3. Neither	18.7	19.5	17.7	17.7	20.2	18.2	22.2	15.7	17.8	17.6	19.3	19.5	19.7	16.6	17.8	11.9
4. Mostly agree	22.7	23.5	22.3	23.6	17.9	20.4	24.0	22.9	23.0	23.4	22.3	21.2	24.3	26.1	21.6	19.0
5. Agree	34.1	32.5	35.8	35.5	28.6	29.3	31.9	39.2	35.1	35.9	32.3	31.9	33.2	32.8	41.5	33.3
Item 9780 N(Wtd)	2653	1274	1312	2182	252	584	855	827	387	1313	1240	1100	630	314	523	42

E04D: To help prevent overpopulation, I might decide not to have any children of my own

1. Disagree	50.1	48.2	51.5	50.2	48.8	55.1	47.7	50.3	47.4	49.4	50.9	52.1	51.0	48.4	45.1	58.5
2. Mostly disagree	18.2	20.6	15.9	17.9	20.4	18.7	19.5	16.4	18.0	19.6	16.7	17.6	19.1	20.9	16.4	17.1
3. Neither	15.6	17.0	14.4	15.6	14.4	13.9	18.1	14.1	16.1	14.5	16.6	14.8	18.0	16.1	14.6	7.3
4. Mostly agree	5.9	5.7	6.2	5.8	6.4	5.0	5.0	6.7	7.3	6.2	5.5	6.1	5.1	5.1	6.6	9.8
5. Agree	10.2	8.5	12.0	10.6	10.0	7.4	9.6	12.5	10.9	10.3	10.4	9.4	6.8	9.8	17.1	7.3
Item 9790 N(Wtd)	2648	1273	1309	2179	250	584	855	825	384	1309	1240	1100	629	316	519	41

QUESTIONNAIRE FORM 3 1976	TOTAL	SEX		RACE		REGION				4YR COLLEGE PLANS		ILLICIT DRUG USE: LIFETIME				
		M	F	White	Black	NE	NC	S	W	Yes	No	None	Marijuana Only	Few Pills	More Pills	Any Heroin
Weighted No. of Cases:	3034	1471	1443	2378	332	709	945	925	455	1408	1399	1209	721	364	612	49
% of Weighted Total:	100.0	48.5	47.6	78.4	10.9	23.4	31.1	30.5	15.0	46.4	46.1	39.8	23.8	12.0	20.2	1.6
E04E: High schools should offer instruction in birth control methods																
1. Disagree	7.7	7.8	7.7	7.5	10.6	7.1	7.2	9.1	7.0	5.5	10.2	10.8	6.2	3.8	5.3	17.1
2. Mostly disagree	5.2	6.2	4.1	5.0	4.3	4.8	6.2	4.0	6.2	5.0	6.5	6.5	5.3	3.5	2.9	9.8
3. Neither	12.8	14.8	10.9	12.8	11.8	9.8	14.2	13.3	13.2	10.9	14.5	13.5	14.5	9.8	11.6	2.4
4. Mostly agree	26.5	28.4	24.3	27.4	19.7	26.6	25.9	26.4	28.0	29.2	23.9	26.3	24.0	30.4	28.2	19.5
5. Agree	47.7	42.7	53.0	47.2	53.9	51.7	46.5	47.4	45.6	49.3	46.0	42.9	50.0	52.5	52.0	51.2
Item 9800 N(Wtd)	2652	1273	1313	2180	254	580	861	825	386	1307	1245	1096	628	316	525	41
E04F: I personally consider most methods of birth control to be immoral																
1. Disagree	45.3	39.4	51.6	47.8	32.2	46.2	46.3	43.3	45.3	48.9	41.4	40.6	47.4	45.0	52.6	50.0
2. Mostly disagree	19.1	22.4	16.1	20.5	10.6	20.0	19.8	18.2	18.3	19.9	18.4	18.6	19.6	22.3	19.4	9.5
3. Neither	21.0	23.7	17.9	20.5	21.2	19.4	21.7	20.2	23.3	18.3	23.6	22.0	20.9	21.4	17.3	28.6
4. Mostly agree	7.8	7.3	8.3	6.7	15.5	6.9	7.3	9.5	6.3	7.3	8.7	10.0	6.9	5.8	5.6	7.1
5. Agree	6.8	7.2	6.2	4.5	20.4	7.3	4.7	8.8	6.5	5.6	8.0	8.7	5.3	5.8	5.4	4.8
Item 9810 N(Wtd)	2613	1250	1297	2155	245	576	848	808	382	1294	1222	1073	623	309	521	42
E04G: The government should make birth control information and services available without cost to anyone who wants them																
1. Disagree	5.4	6.3	4.6	4.8	9.1	5.4	5.7	5.7	4.2	4.4	6.6	7.2	3.4	2.9	4.8	14.3
2. Mostly disagree	5.3	5.0	5.1	5.5	3.5	4.3	5.9	5.1	6.0	5.5	5.4	6.3	4.0	7.1	3.6	9.5
3. Neither	12.7	15.8	9.4	12.4	14.2	10.8	14.4	12.7	11.9	11.6	13.5	14.1	14.4	9.6	9.9	9.5
4. Mostly agree	24.0	27.9	20.7	24.9	16.5	24.0	26.6	20.1	26.5	26.0	22.0	25.1	22.6	25.6	23.1	11.9
5. Agree	52.5	45.1	60.2	52.3	57.1	55.6	47.4	56.3	51.4	52.5	52.4	47.3	55.8	54.8	58.3	57.1
Item 9820 N(Wtd)	2636	1263	1305	2162	254	576	853	821	385	1302	1235	1088	625	312	523	42
E05: How do you feel about giving food to foreign countries?																
1. I would share only or mostly with those countries that work on birth control	20.1	20.5	19.6	21.9	12.9	18.7	21.9	20.4	18.0	22.6	17.1	20.7	21.7	17.0	18.9	9.8
2. I would share with all needy countries	44.9	37.6	51.8	41.7	68.1	46.5	41.2	48.3	43.2	48.3	41.8	48.4	43.6	41.6	42.6	46.3
3. I feel we have no obligation to foreign countries	23.5	28.8	18.2	25.0	11.7	22.7	24.5	22.3	24.9	21.2	25.9	20.6	23.6	26.9	26.8	26.8
4. I don't care one way or the other	11.5	13.1	10.3	11.4	7.3	12.4	12.3	8.9	13.9	7.9	15.1	10.3	10.9	14.1	11.7	14.6
Item 9840 N(Wtd)	2592	1251	1278	2128	248	563	844	812	373	1272	1219	1085	605	305	514	41
E06: What do you think would be the ideal population size for the United States?																
1. Much smaller than it is now	12.3	11.2	12.9	11.8	15.7	12.4	9.6	12.5	17.9	10.8	12.7	10.4	10.9	12.4	16.3	19.5
2. Somewhat smaller than it is now	41.9	37.6	47.0	43.7	30.9	41.9	43.9	39.1	43.2	42.5	42.5	42.0	41.4	41.2	45.3	29.3
3. About the same as it is now	39.8	43.9	35.6	40.3	36.1	40.2	42.7	40.0	32.6	41.8	37.7	41.1	42.1	41.8	33.7	34.1
4. Somewhat larger than it is now	4.4	5.4	3.2	3.4	10.8	4.6	2.6	6.0	5.0	3.9	5.2	4.9	4.1	3.3	3.5	14.6
5. Much larger than it is now	1.6	1.7	1.3	.8	6.4	1.1	1.3	2.3	1.6	1.0	2.1	1.6	1.3	1.6	1.2	2.4
Item 9830 N(Wtd)	2610	1259	1284	2143	249	565	855	810	380	1293	1213	1092	613	306	514	41
E07: What do you think would be the ideal population size for the entire world?																
1. Much smaller than it is now	36.3	38.1	34.8	39.1	19.8	34.4	35.5	34.7	44.1	39.0	33.2	34.9	36.9	34.0	38.9	50.0
2. Somewhat smaller than it is now	39.1	38.1	40.0	40.6	29.3	42.2	42.7	35.7	33.8	39.7	38.8	39.6	39.4	41.7	39.5	12.5
3. About the same as it is now	19.7	19.1	20.3	17.6	33.1	19.3	18.1	22.7	17.6	17.1	22.6	20.4	19.2	20.0	16.9	30.0
4. Somewhat larger than it is now	3.1	3.4	2.9	2.0	11.6	2.1	2.6	4.4	2.9	2.9	3.3	3.2	2.8	3.0	2.8	5.0
5. Much larger than it is now	1.8	1.4	2.0	.8	6.6	2.0	1.1	2.5	1.9	1.3	2.2	1.8	1.5	1.3	2.0	2.5
Item 9850 N(Wtd)	2583	1249	1269	2129	242	561	845	801	376	1283	1199	1083	609	300	509	40

QUESTIONNAIRE FORM 3 1976	TOTAL	SEX		RACE		REGION				4YR COLLEGE PLANS		ILLICIT DRUG USE: LIFETIME				
		M	F	White	Black	NE	NC	S	W	Yes	No	None	Marijuana Only	Few Pills	More Pills	Any Heroin
Weighted No. of Cases:	3034	1471	1443	2378	332	709	945	925	455	1408	1399	1209	721	364	612	49
% of Weighted Total:	100.0	48.5	47.6	78.4	10.9	23.4	31.1	30.5	15.0	46.4	46.1	39.8	23.8	12.0	20.2	1.6

E08: Some people like school very much. Others don't. How do you feel about going to school?

5. I like school very much	16.9	14.4	18.9	13.8	37.6	14.6	14.6	20.7	17.4	20.9	12.9	22.3	16.4	12.4	9.4	7.0
4. I like school quite a lot	28.7	29.2	28.7	29.1	24.3	25.7	30.4	29.6	27.7	36.2	21.4	36.1	27.0	25.5	19.2	16.3
3. I like school some	36.7	39.6	33.7	38.6	27.0	37.7	36.4	34.9	39.3	32.5	40.7	31.1	40.4	45.2	39.8	27.9
2. I don't like school very much	12.5	12.1	12.7	13.0	7.6	14.4	13.8	10.8	10.3	8.1	16.9	7.8	12.8	11.5	20.8	27.9
1. I don't like school at all	5.2	4.7	5.9	5.5	3.4	7.6	4.8	4.0	5.0	2.4	8.2	2.8	3.4	5.4	10.9	18.6
Item 7630 N(Wtd)	2709	1299	1336	2210	263	591	876	845	397	1315	1274	1120	641	314	543	43

E09: Did you have a unit on sex education when you were in high school?

1. No, and I'm glad I didn't	7.7	9.0	6.0	7.6	5.0	7.8	6.0	9.3	7.5	7.0	8.2	7.8	8.7	6.2	6.4	14.6
2. No, and I wish I had	31.7	32.5	31.0	31.0	45.4	22.5	27.9	45.8	23.8	29.5	33.1	33.0	32.7	28.3	31.6	14.6
3. Yes, and it was very worthwhile	20.9	17.3	24.5	19.5	28.8	21.3	19.6	20.0	25.1	19.5	22.3	22.0	18.1	25.1	19.0	22.0
4. Yes, and it was somewhat worthwhile	28.4	28.6	28.4	30.1	15.8	34.1	32.8	18.6	31.5	31.7	26.0	27.9	30.8	29.6	25.6	34.1
5. Yes, but it was not worthwhile at all	11.3	12.6	10.1	11.8	5.0	14.2	13.8	6.3	12.4	12.3	10.2	9.4	9.7	10.7	17.3	14.6
Item 9860 N(Wtd)	2651	1271	1306	2157	260	577	857	830	387	1285	1249	1092	630	307	532	41

E10: Did you ever study about birth control methods in high school?

1. No, and I'm glad I didn't	11.0	14.5	7.7	11.0	10.9	10.5	10.0	10.3	15.4	11.0	10.9	13.1	10.9	7.9	8.7	14.6
2. No, and I wish I had	44.0	45.8	42.4	45.3	41.8	38.2	48.2	48.4	34.0	43.6	44.3	42.6	47.4	44.6	44.2	31.7
3. Yes, and it was very worthwhile	21.6	16.3	26.6	19.8	32.4	21.0	17.2	26.3	22.3	19.0	24.8	20.9	20.2	23.0	22.5	31.7
4. Yes, and it was somewhat worthwhile	17.7	17.5	17.8	18.2	12.5	22.1	19.0	12.1	20.4	20.1	15.1	18.5	16.8	19.3	16.2	14.6
5. Yes, but it was not worthwhile at all	5.6	5.9	5.4	5.7	2.3	8.4	5.5	2.8	7.6	6.3	4.9	4.8	4.6	4.9	8.5	4.9
Item 9870 N(Wtd)	2619	1251	1296	2137	256	571	848	818	382	1276	1234	1082	624	305	520	41

E11: Do you expect to vote in the Presidential election in November of 1976?

5. I definitely will	40.8	44.6	37.0	43.2	32.2	35.5	43.6	41.1	42.1	50.4	30.6	44.7	38.5	46.1	35.1	25.6
4. I probably will	30.6	30.2	31.4	31.0	29.5	27.4	33.0	31.2	28.7	27.1	34.4	29.3	32.0	25.5	35.3	23.3
3. I probably will not	12.0	11.5	12.7	11.3	14.3	13.1	11.4	12.2	11.4	6.9	17.2	10.2	13.4	12.3	11.7	16.3
2. I definitely will not	5.9	5.7	5.6	4.3	14.3	8.3	3.9	6.3	6.5	3.4	8.6	5.1	5.2	5.8	7.1	23.3
1. I will not be eligible to register to vote next November	10.7	8.0	13.5	10.3	9.7	15.7	8.3	9.3	11.4	12.2	9.2	10.7	11.0	10.0	11.1	11.6
Item 9920 N(Wtd)	2674	1291	1312	2182	258	580	870	837	387	1297	1258	1108	629	310	539	43

E12: Looking toward the future, how important would it be for you to have each of the following things?

E12A: At least one car

1. Not important	4.0	3.8	4.2	3.3	6.3	4.2	3.7	3.8	4.9	3.6	4.1	3.5	3.8	6.3	3.4	9.3
2. Somewhat important	18.5	15.9	20.4	16.9	32.0	22.7	15.0	18.1	21.0	20.2	15.9	20.8	17.7	16.6	14.8	20.9
3. Quite important	34.6	35.0	34.5	35.5	29.6	31.4	36.4	34.3	35.8	36.2	34.0	36.9	34.4	32.8	31.8	27.9
4. Extremely important	42.9	45.3	40.8	44.3	32.4	41.7	44.8	43.9	38.1	40.0	46.1	38.8	44.1	44.0	50.0	41.9
Item 13835 N(Wtd)	2651	1267	1311	2168	253	573	868	825	386	1292	1242	1101	631	302	528	43

E12B: At least two cars

1. Not important	59.7	50.6	68.4	59.1	65.4	64.1	60.1	55.1	61.9	60.1	58.3	61.6	58.9	53.5	59.8	53.5
2. Somewhat important	26.6	32.1	21.8	27.7	18.3	22.4	28.3	28.1	25.8	26.3	27.9	27.2	25.5	29.7	27.0	20.9
3. Quite important	9.0	11.7	6.3	9.2	7.7	7.1	8.4	11.1	8.9	9.6	8.8	7.5	10.5	11.6	8.6	7.0
4. Extremely important	4.6	5.6	3.5	4.0	8.5	6.2	3.0	5.9	3.7	4.0	4.9	3.6	4.9	5.3	4.8	18.6
Item 13840 N(Wtd)	2632	1262	1299	2159	246	566	865	819	383	1284	1234	1091	627	303	522	43

QUESTIONNAIRE FORM 3 1976	TOTAL	SEX		RACE		REGION				4YR COLLEGE PLANS		ILLICIT DRUG USE: LIFETIME				
		M	F	White	Black	NE	NC	S	W	Yes	No	None	Mari-juana Only	Few Pills	More Pills	Any Her-oin
Weighted No. of Cases:	3034	1471	1443	2378	332	709	945	925	455	1408	1399	1209	721	364	612	49
% of Weighted Total:	100.0	48.5	47.6	78.4	10.9	23.4	31.1	30.5	15.0	46.4	46.1	39.8	23.8	12.0	20.2	1.6
E12C: A large (full-sized) car																
1. Not important	67.3	59.1	75.6	67.8	61.9	66.8	69.4	64.4	69.9	66.6	68.1	68.1	67.1	68.5	67.7	58.5
2. Somewhat important	19.4	22.7	16.3	19.6	16.8	18.4	19.3	20.6	18.6	19.4	19.4	20.5	18.9	16.9	18.8	17.1
3. Quite important	8.1	11.4	5.1	8.0	10.7	8.6	7.7	8.0	8.6	8.5	7.9	7.3	7.4	11.6	7.3	14.6
4. Extremely important	5.2	6.9	3.0	4.6	10.2	6.4	3.6	7.0	2.9	5.6	4.6	4.1	6.6	3.0	6.2	9.8
Item 13850　N(Wtd)	2608	1243	1293	2145	244	560	855	811	382	1279	1220	1079	620	302	520	41
E12D: A new car every two or three years																
1. Not important	71.6	63.9	79.0	72.4	67.2	71.4	69.7	70.5	78.4	71.4	72.0	76.0	68.9	68.0	70.6	54.8
2. Somewhat important	17.5	21.1	14.4	17.4	18.5	17.6	19.3	17.5	13.3	17.8	17.1	16.0	18.1	18.2	18.1	26.2
3. Quite important	6.9	9.6	4.1	6.5	8.8	5.9	7.2	8.0	5.2	6.9	6.8	5.1	8.5	10.6	6.5	4.8
4. Extremely important	4.0	5.4	2.5	3.6	5.9	5.2	3.8	3.9	2.9	3.8	4.1	2.8	4.6	4.0	4.8	14.3
Item 13860　N(Wtd)	2620	1255	1292	2155	238	563	861	811	384	1279	1229	1088	624	303	520	42
E12E: Clothes in the latest style																
1. Not important	15.9	18.3	13.3	15.9	11.7	17.8	12.8	13.6	25.0	15.7	15.7	17.7	13.5	14.8	14.6	16.3
2. Somewhat important	43.3	42.1	45.1	44.7	35.2	42.7	45.3	42.4	41.4	43.3	44.1	45.6	41.3	43.4	43.5	25.6
3. Quite important	27.6	28.4	26.6	28.2	24.3	25.5	30.6	26.9	25.3	29.4	25.6	25.2	30.4	29.9	28.4	25.6
4. Extremely important	13.2	11.0	15.1	11.2	28.7	14.1	11.2	17.0	8.3	11.7	14.5	11.7	14.6	11.8	13.6	30.2
Item 13870　N(Wtd)	2644	1267	1304	2170	247	569	864	828	384	1284	1244	1093	629	304	529	43
E12F: A house of my own (instead of an apartment or condominium)																
1. Not important	21.3	14.9	27.6	21.6	20.6	21.4	21.4	20.1	23.3	22.4	20.4	21.4	19.2	20.4	24.3	21.4
2. Somewhat important	25.9	25.9	25.7	26.3	21.1	26.7	27.4	25.4	22.2	25.7	25.8	27.1	28.1	23.0	23.1	23.8
3. Quite important	28.6	32.8	24.4	28.8	24.7	26.4	29.1	28.2	31.5	28.2	29.3	27.7	28.5	31.9	28.5	16.7
4. Extremely important	24.2	26.3	22.2	23.3	33.6	25.3	21.9	26.5	23.3	23.8	24.5	23.9	24.0	25.0	24.1	40.5
Item 13880　N(Wtd)	2648	1273	1305	2173	247	569	868	824	387	1289	1241	1099	629	304	527	42
E12G: Lots of space around my house, a big yard																
1. Not important	14.1	11.6	16.7	13.3	16.5	11.9	13.8	14.7	17.3	13.3	15.1	13.4	14.6	15.7	13.5	14.0
2. Somewhat important	27.2	24.2	30.3	27.0	27.6	28.7	26.7	26.3	28.2	26.3	27.9	28.0	24.4	25.8	30.3	25.6
3. Quite important	31.4	35.6	27.2	32.7	26.3	29.2	33.2	32.5	28.2	32.0	31.5	30.3	35.0	29.1	31.5	20.9
4. Extremely important	27.3	28.6	25.8	27.0	29.6	30.1	26.5	26.6	26.4	28.4	25.6	28.4	26.0	29.4	24.6	41.9
Item 13890　N(Wtd)	2643	1262	1309	2171	243	571	865	819	387	1287	1242	1093	631	306	524	43
E12H: A well-kept garden and lawn																
1. Not important	11.2	11.1	11.1	11.0	9.6	13.5	10.3	10.2	11.9	11.4	10.9	10.8	8.7	13.2	13.7	9.3
2. Somewhat important	29.4	29.7	29.2	29.3	29.3	31.9	29.7	28.6	26.8	28.5	30.9	29.2	31.3	25.4	30.8	30.2
3. Quite important	35.8	35.3	36.5	37.1	30.5	33.1	36.8	36.5	35.8	36.6	35.1	34.7	38.1	37.0	35.2	27.9
4. Extremely important	23.7	23.8	23.3	22.7	30.5	21.7	23.1	24.8	25.5	23.4	23.0	25.3	22.0	24.4	20.4	32.6
Item 13900　N(Wtd)	2632	1258	1303	2164	239	571	861	811	388	1282	1235	1099	624	303	520	43
E12I: Major labor-saving appliances (washer, drier, dishwasher, etc.)																
1. Not important	13.2	11.9	14.6	12.5	16.4	14.5	11.8	12.1	16.5	13.2	13.1	12.5	10.6	14.4	15.4	23.8
2. Somewhat important	35.9	36.8	35.1	36.9	25.8	39.3	37.3	30.1	39.8	36.0	35.9	39.2	34.8	34.0	32.6	26.2
3. Quite important	32.6	34.8	30.5	33.5	28.3	29.5	34.6	34.7	27.9	33.0	32.2	29.5	37.6	31.0	33.2	31.0
4. Extremely important	18.4	16.6	19.8	17.1	29.5	16.8	16.2	23.1	15.8	18.0	18.8	18.7	16.8	20.6	18.8	19.0
Item 13910　N(Wtd)	2645	1268	1305	2170	244	573	865	821	387	1285	1241	1101	630	306	521	42
E12J: A high-quality stereo																
1. Not important	22.5	15.0	29.0	22.6	22.7	20.8	24.6	22.5	20.0	23.2	21.3	31.0	14.6	22.6	13.7	9.3
2. Somewhat important	32.8	30.6	35.5	33.7	27.1	31.9	34.5	31.3	33.3	32.0	34.6	35.0	36.8	31.1	26.1	16.3
3. Quite important	23.5	27.3	19.7	23.5	21.9	24.3	20.8	25.0	25.1	24.9	21.9	19.3	27.3	23.3	27.9	25.6
4. Extremely important	21.3	27.1	15.8	20.1	28.3	23.0	20.1	21.2	21.5	19.9	22.0	14.7	21.1	23.0	32.3	51.2
Item 13920　N(Wtd)	2650	1269	1308	2171	247	573	866	821	390	1287	1244	1103	630	305	524	43

QUESTIONNAIRE FORM 3 1976	TOTAL	SEX		RACE		REGION				4YR COLLEGE PLANS		ILLICIT DRUG USE: LIFETIME				
		M	F	White	Black	NE	NC	S	W	Yes	No	None	Mari-juana Only	Few Pills	More Pills	Any Her-oin
Weighted No. of Cases:	3034	1471	1443	2378	332	709	945	925	455	1408	1399	1209	721	364	612	49
% of Weighted Total:	100.0	48.5	47.6	78.4	10.9	23.4	31.1	30.5	15.0	46.4	46.1	39.8	23.8	12.0	20.2	1.6
E12K: A vacation house																
1. Not important	70.4	64.0	77.3	72.7	62.3	66.3	72.3	69.5	73.8	69.9	72.4	74.2	69.9	71.3	65.8	44.2
2. Somewhat important	17.5	21.0	14.0	16.9	17.2	18.4	16.3	19.0	16.1	18.2	16.5	15.8	17.8	15.8	20.8	25.6
3. Quite important	6.7	8.1	5.2	6.1	8.8	9.3	6.9	5.8	4.4	7.1	6.1	5.6	7.5	7.6	7.0	11.6
4. Extremely important	5.4	6.9	3.6	4.3	10.9	6.1	4.5	5.6	5.7	4.8	5.1	4.4	4.8	5.3	6.6	20.9
Item 13930 N(Wtd)	2629	1260	1297	2163	239	572	865	807	386	1284	1230	1095	628	303	514	43
E12L: A motor-powered, recreational vehicle (powerboat, snowmobile)																
1. Not important	63.2	49.7	76.5	62.9	69.0	67.0	63.3	63.9	56.6	68.1	59.8	69.2	61.2	60.6	57.6	41.9
2. Somewhat important	20.7	26.2	15.6	21.5	14.3	16.8	20.5	21.2	26.0	17.4	24.3	18.4	20.9	22.5	23.6	32.6
3. Quite important	9.0	13.6	4.7	9.2	7.3	9.6	9.6	8.3	8.2	8.8	8.9	7.3	10.6	10.4	10.4	4.7
4. Extremely important	7.0	10.4	3.1	6.3	9.4	6.6	6.6	6.6	9.3	5.7	7.0	5.2	7.1	6.5	8.4	23.3
Item 13940 N(Wtd)	2646	1265	1308	2170	245	572	864	820	389	1285	1242	1100	632	307	521	43

QUESTIONNAIRE FORM 4 1976	TOTAL	SEX		RACE		REGION				4YR COLLEGE PLANS		ILLICIT DRUG USE: LIFETIME				
		M	F	White	Black	NE	NC	S	W	Yes	No	None	Mari- juana Only	Few Pills	More Pills	Any Her- oin
Weighted No. of Cases: % of Weighted Total:	3027 100.0	1420 46.9	1479 48.9	2352 77.7	347 11.5	711 23.5	946 31.3	915 30.2	456 15.1	1341 44.3	1420 46.9	1273 42.1	679 22.4	320 10.6	586 19.4	56 1.9
A01: Taking all things together, how would you say things are these days--would you say you're very happy, pretty happy, or not too happy these days?																
3. Very happy	17.3	14.1	20.7	18.4	12.1	15.0	17.0	19.8	16.3	20.0	15.2	19.4	15.3	16.7	16.5	10.7
2. Pretty happy	68.0	71.4	66.0	70.1	59.7	66.5	69.1	67.4	69.1	65.6	71.4	68.0	68.6	65.7	70.3	69.6
1. Not too happy	14.7	14.5	13.2	11.4	28.2	18.5	13.8	12.8	14.3	14.3	13.4	12.6	15.9	17.9	13.2	19.6
Item 1190 N(Wtd)	3015	1413	1476	2344	347	707	942	913	453	1338	1417	1271	679	318	582	56
A02: Looking ahead to the next five years, do you think that things in this country will get better or worse?																
1. Get much better	3.4	3.9	2.5	3.0	4.3	2.5	3.7	3.7	3.3	3.9	3.0	2.9	3.8	5.3	3.1	3.6
2. Get somewhat better	33.7	36.6	31.6	33.7	38.0	35.5	31.7	36.0	30.6	38.0	30.5	32.7	36.6	33.5	31.6	39.3
3. Stay about the same	25.2	26.8	24.5	27.3	17.3	25.5	28.9	23.1	21.8	24.4	26.0	25.8	23.7	26.6	25.9	23.2
4. Get somewhat worse	31.5	27.5	34.6	30.7	31.1	30.7	30.5	31.2	35.7	28.4	33.9	30.8	31.9	28.5	33.8	25.0
5. Get much worse	6.1	5.3	6.8	5.3	8.9	5.9	5.2	5.8	8.8	5.3	6.7	7.7	4.0	6.0	5.5	8.9
Item 9940 N(Wtd)	3011	1413	1470	2339	347	707	941	909	454	1335	1412	1265	678	319	582	56
A03: Looking ahead to the next five years, do you think that things in the rest of the world will get better or worse?																
1. Get much better	1.9	2.3	1.3	1.4	4.4	1.1	2.3	2.5	1.1	1.9	1.7	1.5	1.6	2.8	1.2	9.1
2. Get somewhat better	21.3	21.7	20.9	19.8	30.8	22.4	21.2	20.5	21.5	21.7	20.6	20.9	22.9	19.6	20.8	23.6
3. Stay about the same	29.0	28.2	29.7	30.0	24.4	31.5	30.7	26.2	27.1	29.1	29.1	28.1	33.0	28.1	27.6	21.8
4. Get somewhat worse	38.8	38.5	39.8	40.6	29.4	38.1	37.7	40.9	38.1	39.4	38.9	39.0	34.9	43.8	42.4	32.7
5. Get much worse	8.9	9.2	8.4	8.2	11.0	7.0	8.1	9.8	12.2	7.8	9.6	10.5	7.6	6.0	8.1	12.7
Item 9950 N(Wtd)	2999	1410	1463	2332	344	704	939	906	451	1334	1404	1263	673	317	583	55
A04: How do you think your own life will go in the next five years-- do you think it will get better or worse?																
1. Get much better	38.8	36.4	40.8	37.9	47.4	40.0	36.6	40.7	37.8	43.1	35.0	35.9	39.6	39.4	41.6	60.7
2. Get somewhat better	48.0	50.0	47.0	49.6	41.9	48.5	50.6	44.6	48.9	45.8	50.4	49.5	49.2	45.6	46.4	26.8
3. Stay about the same	10.8	11.3	10.3	10.5	8.1	10.1	9.9	12.0	11.9	9.8	11.5	12.8	9.0	12.2	9.1	5.4
4. Get somewhat worse	1.8	1.7	1.6	1.8	1.2	1.1	2.2	2.3	1.1	.9	2.4	1.3	2.1	2.5	2.1	-
5. Get much worse	.5	.5	.4	.2	1.4	.3	.7	.4	.4	.3	.6	.5	.1	-	.9	5.4
Item 9960 N(Wtd)	3007	1412	1469	2339	346	703	941	912	452	1332	1412	1265	677	320	580	56
A05: Some people think a lot about the social problems of the nation and the world, and about how they might be solved. Others spend little time thinking about these issues. How much do you think about such things?																
1. Never	2.1	2.9	1.2	1.7	1.7	3.2	2.1	1.2	2.2	1.3	2.8	1.5	1.9	3.1	2.6	5.4
2. Seldom	16.3	17.0	15.7	17.0	12.7	17.3	15.9	14.8	18.5	12.5	19.8	15.5	17.7	18.8	16.2	8.9
3. Sometimes	48.3	48.9	48.2	49.6	41.6	49.2	52.2	44.2	46.9	46.0	50.4	50.0	50.4	43.4	44.2	46.4
4. Quite often	27.0	24.7	29.0	26.8	29.8	24.3	25.2	30.9	26.9	31.3	23.1	27.2	23.9	27.8	30.1	30.4
5. A great deal	6.3	6.5	6.0	4.9	14.2	5.9	4.7	8.9	5.5	9.0	4.0	5.8	6.0	7.2	7.0	10.7
Item 6880 N(Wtd)	3018	1417	1476	2348	346	709	944	912	454	1339	1417	1272	678	320	582	56
A06: These questions are about pollution and the environment. Please mark the circle that shows how much you agree or disagree with each statement below.																
A06A: In general, pollution has increased in the U.S. in the last ten years																
1. Disagree	3.1	4.1	1.8	2.4	5.3	2.8	3.5	3.9	1.1	2.3	3.2	2.2	3.1	4.4	3.3	3.7
2. Mostly disagree	4.9	6.4	3.3	5.1	5.0	6.7	3.2	5.4	4.9	5.6	3.6	4.7	4.8	4.1	5.2	1.9
3. Neither	3.4	4.1	2.7	3.4	3.2	3.7	3.6	2.9	3.1	3.1	3.7	2.5	3.1	6.6	4.1	1.9
4. Mostly agree	27.0	24.4	29.9	28.0	22.3	24.6	30.7	26.0	24.6	26.8	28.1	27.6	25.6	28.8	25.8	24.1
5. Agree	61.7	61.0	62.2	61.2	64.2	62.0	58.9	61.9	66.3	62.2	61.4	63.0	63.4	56.1	61.6	68.5
Item 9970 N(Wtd)	2997	1404	1469	2334	341	702	939	905	451	1330	1408	1262	673	319	581	54

QUESTIONNAIRE FORM 4 1976	TOTAL	SEX		RACE		REGION				4YR COLLEGE PLANS		ILLICIT DRUG USE: LIFETIME				
		M	F	White	Black	NE	NC	S	W	Yes	No	None	Marijuana Only	Few Pills	More Pills	Any Heroin
Weighted No. of Cases:	3027	1420	1479	2352	347	711	946	915	456	1341	1420	1273	679	320	586	56
% of Weighted Total:	100.0	46.9	48.9	77.7	11.5	23.5	31.3	30.2	15.1	44.3	46.9	42.1	22.4	10.6	19.4	1.9
A06B: The dangers of pollution are not really as great as government, the media, and environmental groups would like us to believe																
1. Disagree	43.2	42.2	44.4	44.8	39.7	44.9	40.3	43.5	45.8	47.2	40.2	43.6	43.0	42.9	43.9	45.5
2. Mostly disagree	25.8	24.1	27.5	27.4	20.0	25.2	28.2	23.3	26.6	27.2	24.8	25.9	25.9	25.7	26.1	20.0
3. Neither	7.8	8.9	6.5	7.4	7.8	8.7	7.2	7.1	8.7	6.3	9.2	8.4	8.5	5.6	6.4	10.9
4. Mostly agree	15.7	15.7	15.7	14.5	19.4	11.7	17.6	18.1	12.9	14.3	16.5	14.6	14.6	17.9	17.8	10.9
5. Agree	7.6	9.0	6.0	5.9	13.1	9.3	6.7	8.1	6.0	5.1	9.4	7.4	7.9	7.5	5.7	12.7
Item 9980 N(Wtd)	2988	1409	1460	2338	335	699	940	901	448	1325	1409	1264	672	319	578	55
A06C: America needs growth to survive, and that is going to require some increase in pollution																
1. Disagree	35.5	34.6	36.4	35.1	40.8	36.2	32.2	35.9	40.2	38.2	32.5	36.7	34.7	35.5	34.6	32.1
2. Mostly disagree	22.5	22.3	23.0	24.7	14.1	23.3	25.8	19.9	19.3	25.4	20.8	20.9	23.3	19.8	27.5	30.4
3. Neither	9.1	7.7	9.9	9.4	5.6	8.7	9.7	7.5	11.8	8.6	9.5	8.8	8.3	11.3	10.2	5.4
4. Mostly agree	18.5	19.5	17.6	18.8	15.5	18.0	19.0	18.9	17.1	16.0	20.6	18.9	20.5	19.8	14.1	14.3
5. Agree	14.5	15.9	13.1	12.0	24.3	13.9	13.3	17.7	11.6	11.8	16.5	14.7	13.4	13.8	13.6	17.9
Item 9990 N(Wtd)	3001	1407	1468	2336	341	705	943	903	450	1332	1410	1265	674	318	581	56
A06D: People will have to change their buying habits and way of life to correct our environmental problems																
1. Disagree	9.4	9.7	8.5	7.2	21.0	10.6	7.5	12.0	6.2	8.7	9.8	9.8	8.5	8.9	8.3	7.3
2. Mostly disagree	10.4	10.8	9.8	10.6	11.4	11.4	10.3	9.9	9.8	9.7	10.7	9.1	12.2	11.7	10.4	7.3
3. Neither	10.1	9.6	10.6	10.0	9.6	8.0	10.8	10.4	11.3	8.0	11.0	10.2	10.3	9.5	9.8	9.1
4. Mostly agree	32.7	32.1	33.9	35.2	21.0	32.6	33.0	32.6	32.7	33.9	32.8	34.0	31.0	37.0	31.8	40.0
5. Agree	37.4	37.7	37.1	37.0	37.3	37.4	38.3	35.2	40.0	39.8	35.7	37.1	37.8	32.9	39.7	34.5
Item 10000 N(Wtd)	2984	1401	1459	2320	343	700	929	905	450	1325	1398	1257	670	316	579	55
A06E: Government should take action to solve our environmental problems even if it means that some of the products we now use would have to be changed or banned																
1. Disagree	4.6	5.2	3.5	3.8	7.6	3.7	4.4	6.0	3.5	3.5	5.3	4.7	4.6	4.7	2.6	5.4
2. Mostly disagree	6.4	8.1	4.6	5.6	9.7	4.0	6.7	7.7	6.9	5.1	7.5	6.6	6.5	6.3	5.7	10.7
3. Neither	7.6	8.2	6.3	7.3	6.5	5.8	6.9	8.3	10.0	6.4	8.1	8.1	7.2	9.4	5.9	8.9
4. Mostly agree	30.8	30.6	31.5	31.9	28.2	31.1	34.0	28.2	29.0	31.5	31.1	33.3	28.6	28.8	29.4	30.4
5. Agree	50.6	47.9	54.1	51.3	48.4	55.5	47.9	49.8	50.6	53.6	48.0	47.2	53.1	50.5	56.3	42.9
Item 10010 N(Wtd)	3005	1413	1467	2343	341	701	940	912	451	1333	1410	1264	676	319	581	56
A06F: Government should place higher taxes on products which cause pollution in their manufacture or disposal, so that companies will be encouraged to find better ways to produce them																
1. Disagree	17.1	17.8	16.3	16.2	23.2	17.7	15.3	19.4	15.0	12.6	20.4	18.1	14.6	15.2	15.1	17.0
2. Mostly disagree	13.1	12.9	13.3	12.6	15.5	11.2	13.5	13.9	13.9	12.3	13.9	11.6	12.6	19.6	13.2	22.6
3. Neither	11.9	11.2	12.4	12.6	6.7	11.8	14.3	9.9	11.0	12.4	10.9	11.7	12.3	11.1	12.7	9.4
4. Mostly agree	25.1	24.0	26.5	26.6	16.4	24.8	25.8	24.1	25.8	26.9	24.1	27.4	25.1	24.4	22.1	24.5
5. Agree	32.8	34.2	31.6	32.0	38.1	34.6	31.1	32.6	34.4	35.8	30.7	31.1	35.6	29.4	37.0	24.5
Item 10020 N(Wtd)	3008	1413	1470	2343	341	705	942	908	453	1334	1411	1269	677	316	584	53
A06G: I wish that government would ban throwaway bottles and beverage cans																
1. Disagree	16.2	16.8	15.4	15.2	24.5	14.7	14.9	20.2	13.4	13.5	18.2	16.7	16.2	15.7	13.9	17.0
2. Mostly disagree	9.5	9.7	9.7	9.6	8.6	8.2	10.2	9.1	10.7	9.6	9.6	10.8	8.0	9.4	9.5	11.3
3. Neither	17.0	16.1	18.2	17.5	12.7	18.0	17.2	16.0	17.6	17.7	16.9	17.9	16.5	18.2	16.7	13.2
4. Mostly agree	20.3	18.5	21.6	20.1	21.2	20.9	23.0	17.7	19.0	20.5	20.1	19.7	21.0	21.7	21.0	17.0
5. Agree	36.9	38.7	35.0	37.6	33.0	38.2	34.7	37.0	39.3	38.6	35.2	35.0	38.4	34.9	39.1	39.6
Item 10030 N(Wtd)	2975	1395	1458	2318	339	694	930	902	448	1317	1399	1253	666	318	576	53

QUESTIONNAIRE FORM 4 1976	TOTAL	SEX		RACE		REGION				4YR COLLEGE PLANS		ILLICIT DRUG USE: LIFETIME				
		M	F	White	Black	NE	NC	S	W	Yes	No	None	Mari- juana Only	Few Pills	More Pills	Any Her- oin
Weighted No. of Cases:	3027	1420	1479	2352	347	711	946	915	456	1341	1420	1273	679	320	586	56
% of Weighted Total:	100.0	46.9	48.9	77.7	11.5	23.5	31.3	30.2	15.1	44.3	46.9	42.1	22.4	10.6	19.4	1.9

A06H: T.V. commercials stimulate people to buy a lot of things they don't really need

1. Disagree	5.1	6.7	3.4	4.1	9.1	5.5	3.7	6.5	4.2	3.8	5.9	5.6	5.0	2.5	3.4	11.3
2. Mostly disagree	5.1	6.3	4.0	4.9	5.0	4.0	4.6	6.3	6.1	4.1	5.9	4.6	6.4	5.6	4.1	5.7
3. Neither	6.1	7.0	4.9	6.5	3.2	6.2	6.0	5.6	7.2	6.4	5.2	5.9	4.9	7.5	7.4	9.4
4. Mostly agree	25.0	26.8	23.7	25.6	21.6	24.5	27.4	24.6	21.7	24.4	26.0	24.2	24.6	28.1	26.7	20.8
5. Agree	58.6	53.2	63.9	58.9	60.8	59.8	58.3	57.1	60.7	61.2	57.0	59.7	59.1	56.6	58.4	52.8
Item 10040 N(Wtd)	3014	1412	1475	2347	342	707	940	911	456	1336	1415	1270	675	320	584	53

A06I: T.V. commercials do a lot of good by showing new products that we might not know about otherwise

1. Disagree	9.8	10.2	9.5	9.9	8.5	12.2	7.5	9.7	11.2	11.2	8.5	9.3	10.6	9.8	10.6	9.4
2. Mostly disagree	13.1	11.9	14.5	14.9	5.6	16.3	11.5	10.2	17.2	15.3	11.8	14.7	12.7	10.4	13.4	11.3
3. Neither	13.5	14.1	12.9	14.7	5.6	16.3	13.2	10.2	16.1	15.3	11.9	14.1	13.9	14.2	12.3	18.9
4. Mostly agree	34.2	33.6	34.9	35.4	28.9	32.6	39.2	31.6	31.3	34.0	35.3	32.6	33.0	39.4	37.6	35.8
5. Agree	29.4	30.3	28.3	25.1	51.5	22.5	28.6	38.2	24.0	24.2	32.6	29.4	29.8	26.2	26.2	26.4
Item 10050 N(Wtd)	3006	1408	1472	2339	342	706	939	908	454	1334	1408	1264	678	317	583	53

A06J: My family and I often buy things we don't really need; we could get along with much less

1. Disagree	13.1	12.6	13.1	10.1	29.9	15.5	10.2	14.2	12.9	11.0	14.3	13.6	14.1	11.6	9.8	20.8
2. Mostly disagree	13.2	14.8	11.5	13.2	11.1	14.2	12.0	13.0	14.4	13.5	12.1	13.7	11.5	14.2	13.6	17.0
3. Neither	9.3	11.3	7.2	9.2	7.3	10.0	9.4	7.8	10.6	9.5	9.1	9.5	10.4	9.7	7.1	11.3
4. Mostly agree	30.3	30.7	29.8	32.5	22.6	30.8	35.0	25.1	29.7	32.2	29.7	28.7	32.3	30.2	34.5	18.9
5. Agree	34.2	30.8	38.4	35.0	29.3	29.2	33.4	39.8	32.2	33.8	34.7	34.6	31.8	34.0	35.0	34.0
Item 10060 N(Wtd)	2991	1400	1468	2330	341	698	935	908	451	1333	1402	1260	672	318	580	53

A06K: By the year 2000, engineers and scientists will probably have invented devices that will solve our pollution problems

1. Disagree	11.3	12.2	10.1	11.0	10.9	10.9	11.4	11.1	12.4	10.5	11.5	11.6	12.0	11.3	9.5	13.2
2. Mostly disagree	17.1	16.6	17.7	19.0	10.0	16.8	18.3	16.0	17.7	18.7	15.6	17.9	16.2	17.8	17.1	11.3
3. Neither	23.1	21.7	24.2	24.8	13.2	22.6	23.6	20.7	27.8	21.9	24.2	22.2	20.7	22.2	28.6	24.5
4. Mostly agree	31.0	31.3	31.2	31.2	29.9	32.5	31.1	31.2	28.0	33.4	29.6	30.8	32.6	33.8	29.7	28.3
5. Agree	17.4	18.3	16.8	14.0	36.1	17.2	15.6	21.1	14.1	15.6	19.1	17.4	18.5	15.0	15.3	24.5
Item 10070 N(Wtd)	3007	1408	1473	2342	341	704	940	909	453	1334	1412	1268	677	320	580	53

A07: In your own actions--the things you buy and the things you do-- how much of an effort do you make to conserve energy and protect the environment?

1. None	5.2	5.5	4.9	4.5	8.4	7.4	5.1	4.7	3.0	4.3	5.8	4.9	4.9	5.6	5.4	4.3
2. A little	25.1	26.4	23.2	25.0	24.8	26.4	24.7	23.6	27.1	24.3	24.6	23.5	27.7	29.7	23.2	14.9
3. Some	56.2	54.3	58.9	57.5	54.5	53.5	58.2	57.8	53.2	55.7	58.7	57.8	56.3	51.3	57.7	51.1
4. Quite a bit	13.4	13.9	13.0	13.0	12.1	12.8	11.9	13.9	16.9	15.7	10.9	13.8	11.1	13.4	13.8	29.8
Item 10080 N(Wtd)	2858	1321	1419	2240	323	664	897	865	432	1290	1335	1207	639	306	560	47

The next questions are about work.

A08: Different people may look for different things in their work. Below is a list of some of these things. Please read each one, then indicate how important this thing is for you.

QUESTIONNAIRE FORM 4 1976	TOTAL	SEX		RACE		REGION				4YR COLLEGE PLANS		ILLICIT DRUG USE: LIFETIME				
		M	F	White	Black	NE	NC	S	W	Yes	No	None	Mari- juana Only	Few Pills	More Pills	Any Her- oin
Weighted No. of Cases:	3027	1420	1479	2352	347	711	946	915	456	1341	1420	1273	679	320	586	56
% of Weighted Total:	100.0	46.9	48.9	77.7	11.5	23.5	31.3	30.2	15.1	44.3	46.9	42.1	22.4	10.6	19.4	1.9

A08A: A job where you can see the results of what you do

	TOTAL	M	F	White	Black	NE	NC	S	W	Yes	No	None	Mari- juana Only	Few Pills	More Pills	Any Her- oin
1. Not important	1.5	1.6	1.3	1.3	2.3	1.8	1.4	1.6	.9	1.6	1.5	1.7	1.2	1.9	.7	1.8
2. A little important	7.4	8.5	6.2	7.4	6.1	9.0	7.2	6.1	7.5	6.3	7.6	6.6	9.0	7.5	7.3	7.1
3. Pretty important	32.9	34.7	31.8	34.6	22.7	33.3	35.5	27.9	37.0	32.7	33.9	34.2	35.2	29.1	31.0	28.6
4. Very important	58.2	55.3	60.7	56.7	68.8	55.8	55.9	64.4	54.8	59.5	57.0	57.5	54.8	61.3	61.2	64.3
Item 10090 N(Wtd)	3012	1417	1474	2344	343	708	938	915	451	1337	1415	1271	677	320	578	56

A08B: A job that has high status and prestige

	TOTAL	M	F	White	Black	NE	NC	S	W	Yes	No	None	Mari- juana Only	Few Pills	More Pills	Any Her- oin
1. Not important	14.0	12.4	15.5	15.1	8.8	14.0	12.9	14.4	15.4	15.1	13.2	13.6	11.9	13.2	18.9	8.9
2. A little important	29.6	27.4	32.2	32.6	17.4	27.0	36.4	24.2	30.4	30.0	29.4	30.8	29.8	32.9	27.6	14.3
3. Pretty important	36.4	38.6	34.2	36.8	32.1	36.9	36.1	36.4	36.2	35.1	38.2	36.1	38.5	35.4	36.4	30.4
4. Very important	20.0	21.6	18.1	15.5	41.8	22.0	14.7	25.0	17.9	19.7	19.3	19.3	20.0	18.5	17.1	46.4
Item 10100 N(Wtd)	2983	1406	1461	2327	340	699	933	904	447	1328	1402	1262	671	319	572	56

A08C: A job which is interesting to do

	TOTAL	M	F	White	Black	NE	NC	S	W	Yes	No	None	Mari- juana Only	Few Pills	More Pills	Any Her- oin
1. Not important	.6	.8	.2	.3	.9	.7	.5	.5	.4	.3	.9	.6	-	.3	.7	3.6
2. A little important	1.8	2.6	1.0	1.3	5.0	1.1	1.5	3.1	1.3	1.2	2.2	1.6	2.2	1.6	.9	9.1
3. Pretty important	9.6	12.6	6.3	8.7	11.5	10.1	9.6	9.3	9.1	8.2	10.9	8.7	9.7	12.5	9.0	12.7
4. Very important	88.0	84.0	92.4	89.7	82.9	87.9	88.4	87.1	89.4	90.4	86.0	89.0	88.3	85.3	89.4	72.7
Item 10110 N(Wtd)	2999	1409	1470	2336	339	702	936	910	451	1332	1409	1268	673	319	577	55

A08D: A job where the chances for advancement and promotion are good

	TOTAL	M	F	White	Black	NE	NC	S	W	Yes	No	None	Mari- juana Only	Few Pills	More Pills	Any Her- oin
1. Not important	2.1	1.9	2.2	1.9	1.8	2.7	2.2	1.3	2.4	2.6	1.6	2.5	1.2	1.9	1.9	3.6
2. A little important	9.1	8.2	9.7	9.4	5.8	7.9	9.5	7.9	12.9	10.0	8.6	8.3	10.4	8.5	10.7	5.5
3. Pretty important	31.8	30.9	33.7	34.8	20.2	30.1	36.0	27.7	34.2	33.3	31.2	33.3	28.8	35.1	30.5	29.1
4. Very important	56.9	58.9	54.4	53.8	72.2	59.1	52.2	63.0	50.7	54.1	58.6	55.9	59.8	54.9	56.8	61.8
Item 10120 N(Wtd)	3007	1417	1470	2342	342	705	939	914	450	1334	1413	1270	676	319	577	55

A08E: A job that gives you an opportunity to be directly helpful to others

	TOTAL	M	F	White	Black	NE	NC	S	W	Yes	No	None	Mari- juana Only	Few Pills	More Pills	Any Her- oin
1. Not important	2.8	4.2	1.3	2.9	1.5	3.4	2.2	2.2	4.2	3.1	2.3	2.4	3.8	.9	3.8	1.9
2. A little important	12.4	18.2	6.4	13.4	7.3	11.4	14.0	10.5	14.8	12.1	12.5	10.2	12.0	14.7	16.5	18.5
3. Pretty important	33.8	37.8	31.0	35.2	29.7	33.9	34.3	33.6	33.2	32.0	36.2	31.5	37.0	33.8	35.7	31.5
4. Very important	51.0	39.7	61.3	48.6	61.5	51.4	49.5	53.7	47.8	52.7	49.0	55.9	47.0	50.9	44.0	48.1
Item 10130 N(Wtd)	3008	1414	1473	2341	343	704	939	913	452	1336	1413	1271	676	320	577	54

A08F: A job which provides you with a chance to earn a good deal of money

	TOTAL	M	F	White	Black	NE	NC	S	W	Yes	No	None	Mari- juana Only	Few Pills	More Pills	Any Her- oin
1. Not important	2.0	1.6	2.3	2.1	1.2	2.5	1.6	1.8	2.4	3.2	1.1	2.6	1.2	1.3	2.1	3.6
2. A little important	12.0	10.2	14.1	13.4	4.4	11.3	13.0	10.7	13.3	16.4	8.1	14.2	10.2	11.1	10.0	16.4
3. Pretty important	39.1	34.4	44.0	43.7	17.4	39.0	43.9	34.6	38.5	39.6	39.4	40.4	39.6	39.4	39.8	27.3
4. Very important	47.0	53.8	39.5	40.9	77.0	47.2	41.5	52.9	45.8	40.8	51.3	42.9	49.1	48.3	48.1	54.5
Item 10140 N(Wtd)	3002	1413	1471	2339	339	706	937	908	452	1333	1412	1271	674	315	578	55

A08G: A job where you have the chance to be creative

	TOTAL	M	F	White	Black	NE	NC	S	W	Yes	No	None	Mari- juana Only	Few Pills	More Pills	Any Her- oin
1. Not important	6.8	7.9	5.8	7.0	6.1	7.7	7.7	5.7	5.5	5.8	7.8	7.1	7.0	8.1	5.7	9.1
2. A little important	23.1	24.4	22.5	24.0	19.9	18.9	26.7	22.5	23.7	20.1	25.8	23.0	22.6	27.2	22.6	23.6
3. Pretty important	34.3	34.3	33.5	34.3	36.5	33.8	33.2	35.1	35.8	34.2	34.8	34.1	37.4	30.9	32.6	34.5
4. Very important	35.8	33.3	38.1	34.6	37.7	39.7	32.4	36.6	34.7	40.0	31.6	35.7	33.1	33.8	39.0	34.5
Item 10150 N(Wtd)	3006	1416	1471	2341	342	705	937	912	452	1336	1414	1268	676	320	579	55

QUESTIONNAIRE FORM 4 1976	TOTAL	SEX		RACE		REGION				4YR COLLEGE PLANS		ILLICIT DRUG USE: LIFETIME				
		M	F	White	Black	NE	NC	S	W	Yes	No	None	Mari- juana Only	Few Pills	More Pills	Any Her- oin
Weighted No. of Cases:	3027	1420	1479	2352	347	711	946	915	456	1341	1420	1273	679	320	586	56
% of Weighted Total:	100.0	46.9	48.9	77.7	11.5	23.5	31.3	30.2	15.1	44.3	46.9	42.1	22.4	10.6	19.4	1.9

A08H: A job where the skills you learn will not go out of date

1. Not important	4.5	4.0	4.7	4.3	3.8	6.0	4.1	4.3	3.3	4.9	4.1	4.2	4.1	6.9	4.0	3.6
2. A little important	10.2	9.9	10.5	10.3	7.9	10.4	11.0	9.0	10.6	10.0	10.4	10.1	10.1	10.0	10.2	8.9
3. Pretty important	31.0	29.4	33.4	32.9	24.0	31.5	32.1	28.7	32.2	32.2	30.6	33.1	30.0	34.4	28.9	23.2
4. Very important	54.4	56.6	51.4	52.5	64.3	52.0	52.7	57.9	54.1	52.9	54.9	52.6	55.8	48.8	57.0	64.3
Item 10160 N(Wtd)	3000	1411	1470	2336	342	702	934	913	451	1332	1411	1263	676	320	577	56

A08I: A job that gives you a chance to make friends

1. Not important	2.9	3.8	1.9	2.4	5.2	3.8	2.8	2.5	2.2	2.7	2.7	2.7	2.5	4.1	2.3	10.9
2. A little important	10.5	13.2	7.6	9.8	14.0	10.5	8.7	11.9	11.1	10.1	10.5	9.5	10.8	10.3	11.8	12.7
3. Pretty important	32.6	36.5	29.2	32.7	33.2	32.7	33.2	30.3	36.1	32.2	33.2	30.4	36.3	35.9	33.8	27.3
4. Very important	54.0	46.5	61.2	55.1	47.2	53.0	55.4	55.1	50.9	55.1	53.6	57.4	50.3	50.0	52.2	50.9
Item 10170 N(Wtd)	3003	1414	1469	2337	343	704	935	913	452	1331	1414	1265	678	320	577	55

A08J: A job which uses your skills and abilities--lets you do the things you can do best

1. Not important	.6	.6	.4	.3	1.2	.7	.5	.2	1.1	.4	.4	.6	-	-	.5	3.6
2. A little important	3.2	4.5	1.9	3.2	2.9	3.1	3.7	2.6	3.5	2.7	3.3	3.0	3.2	4.4	2.8	3.6
3. Pretty important	25.6	30.0	21.8	26.8	19.0	25.9	26.7	23.6	27.0	23.1	28.1	23.7	28.7	25.6	26.5	23.2
4. Very important	70.6	64.9	76.0	69.7	77.0	70.3	69.1	73.6	68.4	73.7	68.0	72.7	67.9	69.7	70.2	69.6
Item 10180 N(Wtd)	3008	1414	1474	2341	343	703	938	915	452	1335	1414	1270	677	320	578	56

A08K: A job that is worthwhile to society

1. Not important	3.8	5.4	2.1	3.6	3.6	5.4	3.5	2.8	4.0	3.4	3.9	2.6	4.9	3.5	4.2	7.5
2. A little important	14.7	17.6	11.6	14.4	15.0	14.1	15.0	13.1	18.5	12.7	16.2	12.8	14.8	17.4	15.5	22.6
3. Pretty important	37.0	38.4	35.9	39.2	29.1	36.6	39.9	35.5	34.7	35.2	38.8	35.9	38.5	34.1	41.0	39.6
4. Very important	44.5	38.6	50.3	42.8	52.3	43.9	41.7	48.6	42.8	48.6	41.2	48.5	41.9	45.1	39.3	32.1
Item 10190 N(Wtd)	2981	1401	1464	2329	333	702	927	902	449	1328	1398	1255	676	317	573	53

A08L: A job where you have more than two weeks vacation

1. Not important	23.3	19.0	27.3	24.7	19.0	22.3	25.4	23.4	20.0	23.2	23.9	24.3	24.1	22.3	21.8	23.2
2. A little important	36.1	33.5	39.1	38.1	28.4	33.1	40.0	34.6	35.4	35.6	37.4	36.7	35.9	40.3	35.3	28.6
3. Pretty important	23.5	25.0	22.2	22.0	30.1	24.0	21.9	25.3	22.5	22.0	24.4	21.7	23.6	24.8	24.9	30.4
4. Very important	17.1	22.6	11.4	15.2	22.5	20.6	12.6	16.8	22.0	19.3	14.4	17.4	16.4	12.6	18.2	17.9
Item 10200 N(Wtd)	3004	1414	1471	2340	342	704	937	913	449	1334	1412	1269	675	318	578	56

A08M: A job where you get a chance to participate in decision making

1. Not important	6.2	6.4	6.0	6.5	2.9	6.5	6.0	6.6	5.1	5.3	7.1	5.8	5.9	6.3	7.3	3.6
2. A little important	25.1	23.6	26.7	26.6	19.8	23.9	27.3	23.3	26.4	21.0	28.9	24.9	25.6	26.6	24.0	25.5
3. Pretty important	42.1	41.7	42.8	42.6	37.0	39.7	43.3	42.2	43.6	43.0	41.7	42.3	41.6	43.8	43.8	29.1
4. Very important	26.5	28.2	24.4	24.2	39.9	29.9	23.6	28.0	24.9	30.8	22.3	27.1	26.9	23.8	24.8	41.8
Item 10210 N(Wtd)	3002	1414	1472	2338	343	703	934	914	450	1336	1410	1268	676	320	576	55

A08N: A job which leaves a lot of time for other things in your life

1. Not important	3.0	2.9	3.1	2.4	5.3	4.0	2.8	3.2	1.3	2.3	3.5	3.2	3.1	2.8	2.1	3.6
2. A little important	18.5	15.6	21.8	19.4	15.8	17.5	21.2	16.7	17.9	21.3	16.9	18.9	17.7	21.6	19.3	16.1
3. Pretty important	40.4	38.6	42.0	41.0	37.0	38.3	43.3	37.4	43.4	38.7	42.4	40.1	41.8	38.6	41.1	41.1
4. Very important	38.2	43.0	33.2	37.2	41.6	40.0	32.8	42.7	37.6	37.8	37.1	37.9	37.5	37.0	37.5	37.5
Item 10220 N(Wtd)	2998	1408	1471	2335	341	702	934	910	452	1331	1409	1265	674	319	576	56

QUESTIONNAIRE FORM 4 1976	TOTAL	SEX		RACE		REGION				4YR COLLEGE PLANS		ILLICIT DRUG USE: LIFETIME				
		M	F	White	Black	NE	NC	S	W	Yes	No	None	Marijuana Only	Few Pills	More Pills	Any Heroin
Weighted No. of Cases:	3027	1420	1479	2352	347	711	946	915	456	1341	1420	1273	679	320	586	56
% of Weighted Total:	100.0	46.9	48.9	77.7	11.5	23.5	31.3	30.2	15.1	44.3	46.9	42.1	22.4	10.6	19.4	1.9

A08O: A job which allows you to establish roots in a community and not have to move from place to place

1. Not important	11.6	11.6	11.1	11.3	10.2	13.6	10.4	11.0	12.3	14.6	8.3	10.3	10.9	12.9	12.8	25.0
2. A little important	16.6	17.0	16.4	17.3	12.0	18.9	16.0	15.1	17.2	19.2	14.0	15.0	17.6	15.4	19.8	19.6
3. Pretty important	30.1	29.5	30.9	31.0	26.9	31.6	33.2	26.0	29.9	30.1	30.8	30.1	29.2	32.4	32.3	25.0
4. Very important	41.7	41.9	41.7	40.3	50.6	36.0	40.4	48.0	40.6	36.1	46.9	44.6	42.6	39.3	35.1	30.4
Item 10230 N(Wtd)	2996	1409	1466	2331	342	700	936	912	448	1330	1408	1267	672	318	576	56

A08P: A job which leaves you mostly free of supervision by others

1. Not important	10.8	10.2	11.4	11.2	9.9	8.7	11.1	12.8	9.5	11.6	10.5	12.4	9.6	9.7	9.7	8.9
2. A little important	28.8	25.2	32.1	29.9	23.7	28.8	30.8	26.6	28.8	27.8	29.2	30.1	29.4	27.9	26.6	17.9
3. Pretty important	37.4	36.5	39.0	37.5	38.3	37.8	37.6	36.3	38.6	37.2	38.4	37.3	37.3	40.4	38.2	26.8
4. Very important	23.0	28.0	17.6	21.3	28.4	24.6	20.4	24.3	23.1	23.4	21.9	20.2	23.8	21.9	25.4	44.6
Item 10240 N(Wtd)	3000	1413	1468	2336	342	704	934	911	451	1333	1409	1264	676	319	578	56

A08Q: A job that offers a reasonably predictable, secure future

1. Not important	1.5	1.3	1.4	1.3	2.0	2.6	1.4	1.1	.9	1.5	1.3	1.1	.9	1.9	1.7	7.3
2. A little important	5.6	5.9	5.4	5.6	5.0	5.2	5.7	5.6	6.0	6.8	4.5	4.4	7.2	5.3	6.4	7.3
3. Pretty important	31.3	31.1	31.6	33.7	17.5	33.9	33.9	26.1	32.2	32.0	31.4	31.2	30.3	35.0	31.6	29.1
4. Very important	61.7	61.6	61.5	59.4	75.1	58.5	59.0	67.2	60.9	59.7	62.9	63.2	61.5	57.5	60.4	58.2
Item 10250 N(Wtd)	2998	1409	1472	2337	342	699	935	914	450	1333	1411	1265	676	320	576	55

A08R: A job where you can learn new things, learn new skills

1. Not important	1.5	2.1	.8	1.5	.6	2.0	1.7	1.0	1.3	2.1	1.0	1.7	1.0	1.3	1.4	1.8
2. A little important	11.4	14.0	9.2	13.0	5.2	9.5	12.9	11.0	12.0	13.8	9.7	11.1	11.7	13.4	11.1	10.7
3. Pretty important	40.3	41.7	39.2	42.1	31.4	39.1	45.0	36.2	40.8	40.6	40.6	38.9	41.8	44.4	41.8	37.5
4. Very important	46.9	42.1	50.8	43.5	62.8	49.4	40.6	51.8	45.9	43.4	48.7	48.3	45.6	41.3	45.7	50.0
Item 10260 N(Wtd)	3004	1411	1474	2338	344	706	932	915	451	1336	1408	1270	673	320	576	56

A08S: A job where you do not have to pretend to be a type of person that you are not

1. Not important	4.4	6.1	2.6	3.8	8.8	4.4	3.9	5.2	4.2	3.6	5.0	3.2	4.8	6.0	4.7	14.3
2. A little important	4.8	6.7	2.5	4.6	3.5	5.1	5.3	4.0	5.1	3.9	5.5	5.0	3.9	5.7	4.0	5.4
3. Pretty important	17.7	21.9	14.0	17.8	13.6	17.6	17.6	17.0	18.9	16.9	18.3	17.0	17.2	18.2	19.8	17.9
4. Very important	73.1	65.3	80.9	73.8	74.3	72.8	73.3	73.9	71.5	75.6	71.3	74.9	74.1	69.8	71.6	62.5
Item 10270 N(Wtd)	2997	1409	1468	2336	339	705	933	911	449	1332	1409	1266	673	318	577	56

A08T: A job that most people look up to and respect

1. Not important	7.2	8.3	6.0	7.2	5.8	7.5	6.0	7.3	9.2	7.6	6.7	5.8	8.2	7.2	9.4	8.9
2. A little important	20.0	22.0	18.9	22.5	8.8	21.1	22.3	14.8	24.3	20.3	20.1	19.1	20.5	21.6	22.4	26.8
3. Pretty important	38.6	37.8	39.6	40.3	31.6	37.7	42.6	36.6	35.5	38.0	39.8	38.8	39.6	36.9	39.5	30.4
4. Very important	34.2	31.9	35.6	30.1	53.8	33.7	29.2	41.2	31.3	34.1	33.4	36.1	31.8	34.4	28.8	32.1
Item 10280 N(Wtd)	3000	1414	1468	2337	342	703	934	915	448	1332	1410	1267	674	320	577	56

A08U: A job that permits contact with a lot of people

1. Not important	8.5	11.6	5.6	8.7	8.2	8.4	8.3	8.0	10.5	7.1	9.4	7.8	10.9	8.1	7.8	12.7
2. A little important	20.5	25.5	16.0	20.8	19.9	17.8	20.8	20.5	24.1	19.7	21.6	20.2	21.7	18.4	22.1	20.0
3. Pretty important	37.3	38.1	36.2	37.9	36.0	38.2	37.1	37.4	35.9	37.2	37.5	35.9	36.8	36.9	41.5	36.4
4. Very important	33.7	24.6	42.2	32.6	36.0	35.6	34.0	34.1	29.2	36.1	31.5	36.2	30.7	36.9	28.5	32.7
Item 10290 N(Wtd)	2998	1408	1472	2336	342	706	933	912	448	1333	1407	1264	672	320	578	55

QUESTIONNAIRE FORM 4 1976	TOTAL	SEX		RACE		REGION				4YR COLLEGE PLANS		ILLICIT DRUG USE: LIFETIME				
		M	F	White	Black	NE	NC	S	W	Yes	No	None	Mari-juana Only	Few Pills	More Pills	Any Her-oin
Weighted No. of Cases:	3027	1420	1479	2352	347	711	946	915	456	1341	1420	1273	679	320	586	56
% of Weighted Total:	100.0	46.9	48.9	77.7	11.5	23.5	31.3	30.2	15.1	44.3	46.9	42.1	22.4	10.6	19.4	1.9

A08V: A job with an easy pace that lets you work slowly

	TOTAL	M	F	White	Black	NE	NC	S	W	Yes	No	None	Mj Only	Few Pills	More Pills	Heroin
1. Not important	28.5	30.3	27.5	30.4	22.8	26.5	30.2	25.7	33.8	32.7	25.2	27.8	31.4	25.6	31.3	21.8
2. A little important	38.8	36.5	40.9	40.0	36.1	39.3	40.2	37.3	38.3	38.0	40.2	38.4	37.6	45.6	37.9	43.6
3. Pretty important	23.7	22.6	24.2	22.1	27.2	24.2	22.1	27.2	18.6	21.7	25.3	24.9	22.3	18.8	23.8	18.2
4. Very important	9.0	10.4	7.4	7.5	13.9	10.0	7.4	9.7	9.2	7.8	9.2	8.9	8.6	10.0	7.1	16.4
Item 10300 N(Wtd)	2991	1407	1467	2333	338	698	932	914	447	1328	1409	1264	672	320	575	55

A08W: A job where most problems are quite difficult and challenging

	TOTAL	M	F	White	Black	NE	NC	S	W	Yes	No	None	Mj Only	Few Pills	More Pills	Heroin
1. Not important	19.2	17.9	20.2	18.8	21.3	18.5	20.3	20.2	16.3	14.1	23.8	16.9	19.9	21.0	21.4	25.5
2. A little important	36.5	34.5	38.9	38.5	30.0	34.5	37.9	35.9	38.2	33.9	39.1	36.8	35.1	39.5	36.8	25.5
3. Pretty important	31.1	32.3	30.4	31.0	32.4	33.0	28.5	30.7	34.2	36.1	26.3	32.1	31.5	28.2	31.4	25.5
4. Very important	13.1	15.4	10.5	11.6	16.3	14.0	13.3	13.1	11.2	15.8	10.7	14.2	13.5	11.0	10.4	21.8
Item 10310 N(Wtd)	2993	1407	1472	2335	343	702	932	911	448	1332	1408	1266	673	319	576	55

A09: What kind of work do you think you will be doing when you are 30 years old? Mark the one that comes closest to what you expect to be doing.

	TOTAL	M	F	White	Black	NE	NC	S	W	Yes	No	None	Mj Only	Few Pills	More Pills	Heroin
01. Laborer (car washer, sanitary worker, farm laborer)	.4	.6	-	.4	-	.2	1.1	-	.2	.1	.7	.3	.6	.7	.2	-
02. Service worker (cook, waiter, barber, janitor, gas station attendant, practical nurse, beautician)	2.5	.5	4.2	2.5	2.2	2.4	3.4	1.9	1.6	.8	4.0	2.1	2.0	3.7	2.8	-
03. Operative or semi-skilled worker (garage worker, taxicab, bus or truck driver, assembly line worker, welder)	3.7	7.1	.3	4.1	1.1	2.6	4.7	2.7	5.2	.3	7.1	2.6	4.4	2.7	3.9	16.3
04. Sales clerk in a retail store (shoe salesperson, department store clerk, drug store clerk)	1.7	.5	3.0	1.4	1.8	1.1	2.2	1.2	3.1	.4	2.9	1.5	2.0	2.4	1.5	-
05. Clerical or office worker (bank teller, bookkeeper, secretary, typist, postal clerk or carrier, ticket agent)	11.8	1.7	21.7	11.2	17.6	11.8	12.5	13.0	8.0	5.1	18.9	14.0	8.1	13.6	11.3	7.0
06. Protective service (police officer, fireman, detective)	3.8	6.8	1.0	4.0	2.2	4.2	4.0	3.4	3.5	3.5	4.2	3.5	5.3	2.4	3.2	4.7
07. Military service	2.7	4.5	.9	2.4	5.4	2.1	2.3	3.2	3.3	1.4	3.7	2.9	2.0	1.7	3.3	7.0
08. Craftsman or skilled worker (carpenter, electrician, brick layer, mechanic, machinist, tool and die maker, telephone installer)	10.5	20.6	.5	10.6	6.5	8.3	12.1	9.6	12.5	3.0	17.0	7.8	11.7	12.9	12.8	14.0
09. Farm owner, farm manager	2.4	3.5	1.5	2.8	.4	2.4	1.8	2.6	3.3	2.1	2.3	2.4	2.7	3.4	1.7	-
10. Owner of small business (restaurant owner, shop owner)	3.7	5.9	1.4	3.7	3.2	5.0	3.0	3.3	4.0	3.1	3.8	2.4	5.3	2.0	5.0	9.3
11. Sales representative (insurance agent, real estate broker, bond salesman)	.9	1.5	.2	.9	.7	.8	.7	1.2	.7	.9	.8	.8	1.3	1.4	.4	-
12. Manager or administrator (office manager, sales manager, school administrator, government official)	4.2	5.0	3.5	4.4	4.3	5.0	3.5	4.4	4.0	6.6	1.8	4.0	5.5	2.0	5.0	-
13. Professional without doctoral degree (registered nurse, librarian, engineer, architect, social worker, technician, accountant, actor, artist, musician)	27.3	21.9	32.6	27.3	29.0	30.8	24.5	27.9	26.4	42.0	13.5	28.9	27.7	27.2	24.7	25.6
14. Professional with doctoral degree or equivalent (lawyer, physician, dentist, scientist, college professor)	11.4	13.4	10.0	11.1	14.7	15.9	8.1	11.1	12.0	21.6	1.9	12.6	10.6	10.9	11.1	11.6
15. Full-time homemaker or housewife	6.3	.1	12.3	7.0	2.2	2.4	8.9	6.8	5.9	2.4	10.9	9.0	2.7	5.4	5.6	-
16. Don't know-GO TO Q.A13	6.8	6.6	7.0	6.3	8.6	5.0	7.4	7.8	6.6	6.8	6.6	5.1	8.1	7.8	7.6	7.0
Item 10320 N(Wtd)	2787	1303	1381	2232	279	660	881	821	425	1274	1298	1186	640	294	539	43

QUESTIONNAIRE FORM 4 1976	TOTAL	SEX		RACE		REGION				4YR COLLEGE PLANS		ILLICIT DRUG USE: LIFETIME				
		M	F	White	Black	NE	NC	S	W	Yes	No	None	Mari- juana Only	Few Pills	More Pills	Any Her- oin
Weighted No. of Cases:	3027	1420	1479	2352	347	711	946	915	456	1341	1420	1273	679	320	586	56
% of Weighted Total:	100.0	46.9	48.9	77.7	11.5	23.5	31.3	30.2	15.1	44.3	46.9	42.1	22.4	10.6	19.4	1.9

A10: How likely do you think it is that you will actually get to do this kind of work?

1. Not very likely	1.4	1.6	.7	.9	3.8	.8	1.5	2.0	1.5	.8	2.2	1.0	2.0	1.4	1.6	4.2
2. Somewhat likely	8.0	8.3	7.3	7.3	9.9	9.1	8.7	6.5	8.0	7.7	7.4	7.5	7.0	10.6	8.4	10.4
3. Fairly likely	24.7	27.5	22.2	24.0	24.9	28.6	21.9	23.6	26.3	25.1	23.9	23.9	29.6	22.5	21.5	14.6
4. Very likely	43.1	41.8	44.7	44.2	42.7	41.3	42.7	44.4	43.9	48.1	39.0	45.2	40.4	44.7	41.7	37.5
5. Certain	15.4	12.5	18.4	15.6	16.0	14.7	16.3	15.9	13.8	14.9	16.3	14.2	14.5	15.5	19.0	22.9
6. I already do this kind of work	7.4	8.2	6.7	8.0	3.1	5.6	9.1	7.6	6.0	3.4	11.1	8.2	6.5	5.3	8.0	8.3
Item 10330 N(Wtd) ★	2664	1252	1306	2106	293	640	827	798	399	1201	1250	1153	587	284	511	48

A11: How certain are you that this kind of work is a good choice for you?

1. Not at all certain	3.7	4.0	2.8	3.4	4.7	4.2	4.1	3.5	2.5	3.1	4.2	2.6	4.2	4.9	4.3	6.3
2. Somewhat certain	9.5	9.7	9.2	8.7	13.6	10.4	8.5	9.7	9.5	7.6	10.5	8.8	10.1	11.9	8.9	10.4
3. Fairly certain	29.5	31.4	27.7	30.1	25.8	29.2	29.7	28.2	32.3	31.2	28.1	28.6	31.0	29.7	28.2	31.3
4. Very certain	38.1	36.1	40.9	39.0	37.3	36.4	39.4	38.3	38.1	38.1	38.9	38.8	37.4	37.4	39.8	25.0
5. Completely certain	19.2	18.8	19.4	18.8	18.6	19.9	18.3	20.2	17.7	19.9	18.2	21.1	17.3	15.7	18.6	31.3
Item 10340 N(Wtd) ★	2682	1264	1312	2119	295	643	835	802	402	1209	1256	1156	596	286	515	48

A12: How satisfying do you think this kind of work will be for you?

1. Not very satisfying	.7	.8	.6	.6	1.4	.5	.8	.9	.5	.3	1.0	.4	.7	.7	.8	6.3
2. Somewhat satisfying	6.8	5.9	7.2	5.9	10.2	6.8	6.6	8.5	4.2	4.1	9.4	7.1	7.6	7.0	6.6	2.1
3. Quite satisfying	24.6	28.3	21.3	25.0	22.8	25.8	22.8	25.1	24.8	20.4	27.5	23.1	25.3	23.1	25.8	31.3
4. Very satisfying	39.4	39.0	40.0	39.4	39.1	39.0	40.5	37.4	41.9	41.3	38.3	40.0	39.8	40.9	38.6	35.4
5. Extremely satisfying	28.5	26.0	31.0	29.1	26.5	28.0	29.2	28.1	28.8	33.9	23.7	29.4	26.7	28.3	28.3	25.0
Item 10350 N(Wtd) ★	2683	1263	1316	2123	294	644	837	800	403	1208	1260	1160	596	286	515	48

A13: To what extent do you think the things listed below will prevent you from getting the kind of work you would like to have?

A13A: Your religion

1. Not at all	89.2	87.4	91.3	90.9	83.8	89.3	90.0	87.8	90.1	91.1	88.5	88.7	90.0	91.0	91.3	79.2
2. Somewhat	4.8	5.1	4.2	4.3	6.1	4.7	4.7	4.6	5.4	5.1	4.3	5.2	4.4	4.8	4.0	1.9
3. A lot	1.4	2.1	.8	1.3	1.2	1.5	1.3	1.7	.7	.9	1.6	1.7	1.2	1.0	.5	1.9
8. Don't know	4.7	5.4	3.7	3.6	8.9	4.4	3.9	6.1	4.0	3.0	5.6	4.4	4.4	3.2	4.0	15.1
Item 10360 N(Wtd)	2869	1344	1415	2239	327	680	892	874	424	1287	1352	1217	642	311	551	53

A13B: Your sex

1. Not at all	77.1	86.6	68.3	78.4	74.5	77.7	76.0	75.9	81.6	75.7	78.3	78.0	81.5	72.7	74.7	62.3
2. Somewhat	15.4	6.7	23.9	15.6	15.0	15.1	17.6	14.8	12.7	18.6	13.1	15.2	12.3	17.9	18.2	20.8
3. A lot	4.9	5.0	4.7	4.4	5.5	3.7	5.0	6.3	3.5	3.7	5.7	4.0	3.7	7.5	4.9	15.1
8. Don't know	2.6	1.8	3.2	1.6	4.9	3.7	1.5	3.0	2.4	2.0	2.9	2.8	2.6	1.9	2.3	1.9
Item 10370 N(Wtd)	2874	1348	1416	2244	326	682	894	872	425	1290	1355	1220	643	308	554	53

A13C: Your race

1. Not at all	82.2	82.3	83.7	91.3	39.0	80.9	85.3	79.4	83.7	81.6	84.7	83.1	83.3	81.4	86.2	66.0
2. Somewhat	10.3	10.2	9.6	5.3	34.4	10.6	8.0	12.1	11.1	11.6	8.1	9.8	10.2	9.6	8.2	22.6
3. A lot	4.0	3.7	3.9	1.7	14.5	4.0	3.7	5.0	2.4	3.9	3.7	3.6	3.9	4.5	2.9	7.5
8. Don't know	3.4	3.9	2.9	1.7	12.1	4.4	3.0	3.4	2.8	3.0	3.6	3.4	2.6	4.2	2.9	1.9
Item 10380 N(Wtd)	2872	1348	1414	2238	331	681	893	875	423	1287	1356	1218	645	311	551	53

A13D: Your family background

1. Not at all	84.8	83.7	86.4	87.9	73.8	85.3	83.6	83.6	88.9	86.4	83.2	85.9	87.1	82.0	84.0	77.4
2. Somewhat	8.3	8.3	8.2	7.2	12.3	7.7	9.2	9.0	6.4	7.8	8.9	8.2	6.4	10.3	9.8	5.7
3. A lot	2.7	3.5	1.8	1.9	5.2	1.9	2.8	3.3	2.4	1.9	3.4	2.5	2.3	2.9	2.2	13.2
8. Don't know	4.2	4.5	3.6	3.0	8.3	5.2	4.4	4.1	2.4	3.8	4.6	3.5	4.2	4.5	4.2	3.8
Item 10390 N(Wtd)	2868	1347	1414	2242	324	679	891	873	425	1287	1354	1217	642	311	550	53

★ = excludes respondents for whom question was inappropriate.

QUESTIONNAIRE FORM 4 1976	TOTAL	SEX		RACE		REGION				4YR COLLEGE PLANS		ILLICIT DRUG USE: LIFETIME				
		M	F	White	Black	NE	NC	S	W	Yes	No	None	Mari-juana Only	Few Pills	More Pills	Any Her-oin
Weighted No. of Cases:	3027	1420	1479	2352	347	711	946	915	456	1341	1420	1273	679	320	586	56
% of Weighted Total:	100.0	46.9	48.9	77.7	11.5	23.5	31.3	30.2	15.1	44.3	46.9	42.1	22.4	10.6	19.4	1.9
A13E: Your political views																
1. Not at all	80.2	80.0	81.1	83.0	66.7	76.6	81.7	79.4	84.8	82.1	79.0	82.1	82.1	77.7	80.9	66.0
2. Somewhat	9.3	9.9	8.1	8.5	13.0	10.0	9.5	9.2	7.7	9.6	8.6	7.7	9.7	11.3	10.3	15.1
3. A lot	2.5	3.1	1.8	1.9	4.6	2.7	1.9	2.9	2.6	2.1	2.9	2.4	2.0	2.3	2.0	3.8
8. Don't know	8.0	7.0	8.9	6.6	16.0	10.9	6.8	8.5	4.9	6.2	9.5	7.7	6.2	9.0	6.9	13.2
Item 10400 N(Wtd)	2870	1346	1413	2240	324	679	891	872	427	1287	1354	1215	641	310	554	53
A13F: Your education																
1. Not at all	49.7	48.8	51.3	49.7	57.6	53.2	45.2	52.1	48.8	55.7	44.8	52.2	52.0	48.4	45.1	26.4
2. Somewhat	24.8	25.0	24.5	25.4	20.0	23.5	26.3	23.1	27.3	19.4	29.6	22.3	24.7	27.9	27.9	41.5
3. A lot	22.0	22.4	21.2	21.9	18.8	18.7	25.8	21.3	20.8	21.7	22.3	22.6	19.7	20.2	23.3	28.3
8. Don't know	3.4	3.8	2.8	3.0	3.9	4.7	2.8	3.3	3.0	3.1	3.3	2.8	3.8	3.2	3.8	3.8
Item 10410 N(Wtd)	2880	1360	1412	2249	330	678	892	877	432	1288	1363	1222	639	312	559	53
A13G: Lack of vocational training																
1. Not at all	50.8	50.1	51.9	52.4	48.3	53.4	49.0	51.5	49.1	58.0	44.6	53.4	49.1	52.6	49.0	32.1
2. Somewhat	26.9	27.6	25.8	26.9	23.5	25.1	28.6	26.0	28.5	22.0	31.4	25.2	29.2	25.3	27.0	50.9
3. A lot	13.3	14.1	12.9	12.9	15.2	9.5	15.3	12.8	16.3	10.1	16.4	12.3	12.7	12.3	16.3	11.3
8. Don't know	8.9	8.1	9.5	7.8	13.0	11.9	7.1	9.6	6.1	9.9	7.7	9.2	9.0	9.7	7.4	5.7
Item 10420 N(Wtd)	2855	1348	1398	2227	323	672	886	873	424	1273	1358	1213	636	308	551	53
A13H: Lack of ability																
1. Not at all	57.7	58.0	57.4	58.2	59.9	59.7	54.0	58.5	60.5	60.3	55.0	55.5	60.0	60.1	59.1	49.1
2. Somewhat	16.9	16.9	16.8	16.8	17.0	17.0	16.2	16.8	18.7	13.8	20.0	17.5	17.1	17.2	15.6	15.1
3. A lot	20.4	20.4	20.5	20.5	16.4	17.9	25.0	19.8	16.4	21.3	19.6	22.6	18.3	16.6	19.2	30.2
8. Don't know	5.0	4.6	5.3	4.4	6.8	5.5	4.9	5.1	4.4	4.7	5.3	4.4	4.5	6.2	6.2	3.8
Item 10430 N(Wtd)	2860	1346	1407	2234	324	677	884	870	428	1284	1347	1215	638	308	552	53
A13I: Not knowing the right people																
1. Not at all	45.6	41.2	49.8	46.1	41.0	40.3	45.7	47.8	49.5	41.0	49.5	48.5	43.5	45.0	44.1	39.6
2. Somewhat	36.6	39.3	34.3	37.2	34.6	38.3	36.8	35.7	34.8	41.0	33.4	35.5	36.9	36.8	38.6	26.4
3. A lot	10.5	12.8	7.9	10.0	12.7	12.5	10.5	8.5	11.0	10.6	10.0	9.0	12.5	12.4	8.3	24.5
8. Don't know	7.4	6.8	8.0	6.7	11.7	8.7	7.0	7.9	4.7	7.4	7.1	7.0	7.0	6.2	8.8	7.5
Item 10440 N(Wtd)	2870	1352	1412	2245	324	678	895	870	428	1289	1357	1223	639	307	555	53
A13J: Not wanting to work hard																
1. Not at all	62.9	61.4	64.3	63.1	64.2	64.8	59.4	63.8	65.1	62.2	63.6	61.4	65.3	64.1	64.6	50.9
2. Somewhat	10.4	12.6	8.3	10.0	10.4	10.6	10.6	9.8	10.6	10.6	10.1	8.5	11.0	13.3	11.6	15.1
3. A lot	23.7	23.0	24.5	24.7	20.2	21.3	26.8	23.5	21.7	24.9	23.0	27.1	21.4	19.7	21.2	28.3
8. Don't know	2.9	2.9	3.0	2.3	5.2	3.2	3.2	2.7	2.6	2.3	3.2	3.0	2.5	2.9	2.7	5.7
Item 10450 N(Wtd)	2860	1346	1406	2231	327	677	884	875	424	1283	1355	1214	639	309	553	53
A13K: Not wanting to conform																
1. Not at all	52.1	50.5	53.7	52.7	51.6	51.9	50.6	52.1	55.5	48.7	55.7	53.0	51.8	56.9	49.7	46.2
2. Somewhat	22.4	24.9	20.2	22.8	19.5	24.8	23.9	20.6	18.9	28.0	17.4	21.0	21.9	22.0	24.9	28.8
3. A lot	14.0	13.9	14.1	14.5	9.7	13.0	14.8	13.3	15.3	13.8	14.8	15.5	12.1	10.9	15.2	11.5
8. Don't know	11.5	10.6	12.1	10.0	19.2	10.3	10.7	13.9	10.0	9.6	12.1	10.6	14.1	10.2	10.2	13.5
Item 10460 N(Wtd)	2832	1335	1394	2219	318	669	887	858	418	1274	1341	1209	626	304	551	52
A14: If you were to get enough money to live as comfortably as you'd like for the rest of your life, would you want to work?																
1. I would want to work	80.5	80.0	80.8	80.2	82.3	79.3	79.1	82.4	81.4	83.1	78.0	83.5	78.6	81.8	76.6	76.9
2. I would not want to work	19.5	20.0	19.2	19.7	17.7	20.7	20.9	17.6	18.6	16.9	22.0	16.5	21.4	18.2	23.4	25.0
Item 8100 N(Wtd)	2987	1407	1465	2335	339	702	934	905	446	1328	1410	1263	674	319	580	52

QUESTIONNAIRE FORM 4 1976	TOTAL	SEX		RACE		REGION				4YR COLLEGE PLANS		ILLICIT DRUG USE: LIFETIME				
		M	F	White	Black	NE	NC	S	W	Yes	No	None	Marijuana Only	Few Pills	More Pills	Any Heroin
Weighted No. of Cases:	3027	1420	1479	2352	347	711	946	915	456	1341	1420	1273	679	320	586	56
% of Weighted Total:	100.0	46.9	48.9	77.7	11.5	23.5	31.3	30.2	15.1	44.3	46.9	42.1	22.4	10.6	19.4	1.9

A15: How much do you agree or disagree with each statement below?

A15A: One sees so few good or happy marriages that one questions it as a way of life

	TOTAL	M	F	White	Black	NE	NC	S	W	Yes	No	None	Mari-juana Only	Few Pills	More Pills	Any Heroin
1. Disagree	29.3	27.4	30.8	31.0	21.9	29.6	31.7	26.9	28.4	31.2	28.7	35.6	26.6	25.5	24.4	14.8
2. Mostly disagree	22.9	22.6	23.7	25.4	13.8	21.5	25.3	21.5	23.0	27.4	20.0	23.0	25.7	22.0	22.1	14.8
3. Neither	16.5	18.3	14.4	16.1	12.3	17.2	16.1	15.0	19.2	15.4	16.0	14.4	16.9	18.9	18.7	18.5
4. Mostly agree	17.3	17.0	17.6	16.0	23.1	18.2	16.4	18.9	14.5	15.9	18.5	14.0	16.6	20.4	21.3	27.8
5. Agree	14.1	14.8	13.5	11.5	29.1	13.6	10.7	17.8	14.5	10.2	16.7	13.0	14.3	13.2	13.7	24.1
Item 10470 N(Wtd)	2980	1403	1462	2336	333	693	934	907	447	1328	1404	1261	670	318	578	54

A15B: It is usually a good idea for a couple to live together before getting married in order to find out whether they really get along

	TOTAL	M	F	White	Black	NE	NC	S	W	Yes	No	None	Mari-juana Only	Few Pills	More Pills	Any Heroin
1. Disagree	29.1	21.6	36.9	29.2	33.6	19.2	29.0	37.9	27.1	28.8	29.5	44.1	22.2	19.1	13.1	3.7
2. Mostly disagree	14.9	14.1	15.9	16.1	10.2	11.5	16.7	16.0	14.0	15.7	15.1	17.1	13.0	15.9	13.9	1.9
3. Neither	15.5	16.4	14.5	16.1	11.4	17.6	14.8	13.4	17.6	16.7	14.5	14.7	17.3	12.8	15.8	22.2
4. Mostly agree	19.0	21.8	16.6	19.5	15.5	22.4	19.6	14.8	20.7	20.5	17.8	12.1	22.7	28.1	23.4	29.6
5. Agree	21.5	26.2	16.2	19.0	29.2	29.4	19.7	17.8	20.9	18.4	23.2	11.8	24.9	24.1	33.7	42.6
Item 10480 N(Wtd)	2996	1414	1470	2342	342	697	938	911	450	1334	1415	1268	675	320	581	54

A15C: Having a close intimate relationship with only one partner is too restrictive for the average person

	TOTAL	M	F	White	Black	NE	NC	S	W	Yes	No	None	Mari-juana Only	Few Pills	More Pills	Any Heroin
1. Disagree	36.1	27.9	44.9	37.6	34.0	32.0	37.3	37.1	37.7	37.0	36.9	42.3	32.6	31.4	32.0	20.8
2. Mostly disagree	22.2	22.8	22.0	24.0	13.7	24.5	22.6	20.3	21.9	23.6	20.9	21.6	20.5	23.3	26.8	26.4
3. Neither	14.0	15.7	12.2	14.0	11.6	15.7	13.2	13.6	13.6	13.2	13.5	12.9	15.7	16.4	12.6	15.1
4. Mostly agree	16.2	19.5	12.9	15.1	20.6	16.0	16.5	17.1	14.5	15.4	17.5	14.5	17.5	18.6	16.8	18.9
5. Agree	11.4	14.2	8.0	9.3	20.3	11.5	10.4	12.0	12.3	10.7	11.3	8.8	13.5	10.7	11.9	18.9
Item 10490 N(Wtd)	2980	1406	1462	2335	335	693	936	903	448	1327	1410	1261	674	318	578	53

A15D: Having a job takes away from a woman's relationship with her husband

	TOTAL	M	F	White	Black	NE	NC	S	W	Yes	No	None	Mari-juana Only	Few Pills	More Pills	Any Heroin
1. Disagree	48.4	36.0	61.2	47.3	60.4	52.5	45.2	52.3	41.2	50.7	46.0	48.9	49.3	50.2	46.0	40.7
2. Mostly disagree	24.8	27.0	22.6	26.3	15.7	22.4	27.4	21.8	29.3	26.5	23.8	24.5	26.2	23.5	26.3	27.8
3. Neither	11.5	16.2	7.2	11.4	12.7	11.7	11.0	11.2	13.0	10.1	12.6	11.8	9.4	11.9	13.0	11.1
4. Mostly agree	10.3	13.9	6.4	10.8	6.8	9.9	11.0	9.1	12.8	9.2	11.2	10.1	10.2	10.7	10.0	13.0
5. Agree	4.9	6.8	2.6	4.2	4.1	3.7	5.5	5.8	4.0	3.5	6.4	4.8	4.9	3.4	4.7	9.3
Item 10500 N(Wtd)	2976	1402	1462	2327	338	695	930	903	447	1326	1405	1261	669	319	578	54

A15E: Having a job gives a wife more of a chance to develop herself as a person

	TOTAL	M	F	White	Black	NE	NC	S	W	Yes	No	None	Mari-juana Only	Few Pills	More Pills	Any Heroin
1. Disagree	4.5	4.7	4.0	3.7	7.8	4.3	3.8	5.2	5.1	3.7	5.2	5.3	3.4	2.2	4.2	7.7
2. Mostly disagree	5.4	7.6	3.1	5.4	4.2	5.2	6.1	5.0	4.9	5.0	5.4	5.0	5.0	5.9	6.4	3.8
3. Neither	11.8	17.2	6.1	12.4	8.1	11.5	12.3	9.1	16.9	10.8	12.2	10.9	13.1	12.2	12.6	15.4
4. Mostly agree	29.4	33.8	25.3	30.2	26.6	26.5	31.9	28.5	30.3	27.3	32.2	29.2	30.6	29.1	28.4	32.7
5. Agree	48.9	36.7	61.4	48.4	53.7	52.7	46.0	52.3	42.8	53.2	45.0	49.5	47.9	50.6	48.4	40.4
Item 10510 N(Wtd)	2984	1404	1468	2338	335	695	933	906	449	1331	1408	1262	674	320	578	52

A15F: Being a father and raising children is one of the most fulfilling experiences a man can have

	TOTAL	M	F	White	Black	NE	NC	S	W	Yes	No	None	Mari-juana Only	Few Pills	More Pills	Any Heroin
1. Disagree	5.5	6.1	5.0	5.0	7.8	4.4	5.3	6.4	6.1	5.2	6.2	6.2	4.4	2.5	5.6	16.7
2. Mostly disagree	5.4	5.5	5.1	5.6	2.7	5.9	6.5	4.3	5.0	5.2	5.4	5.0	5.3	6.3	6.2	11.1
3. Neither	20.1	18.6	22.2	21.8	10.5	21.8	20.5	16.9	23.3	20.3	19.7	19.3	19.4	21.1	24.2	13.0
4. Mostly agree	31.8	31.3	32.3	32.5	30.5	32.6	33.8	29.6	30.7	33.7	31.1	29.7	31.1	42.3	32.6	35.2
5. Agree	37.1	38.4	35.4	35.0	48.5	35.3	34.1	42.8	35.0	35.6	37.6	39.9	39.9	27.8	31.2	22.2
Item 10520 N(Wtd)	2950	1409	1430	2309	334	680	922	904	443	1315	1395	1251	666	317	567	54

QUESTIONNAIRE FORM 4 1976	TOTAL	SEX		RACE		REGION				4YR COLLEGE PLANS		ILLICIT DRUG USE: LIFETIME				
		M	F	White	Black	NE	NC	S	W	Yes	No	None	Marijuana Only	Few Pills	More Pills	Any Heroin
Weighted No. of Cases:	3027	1420	1479	2352	347	711	946	915	456	1341	1420	1273	679	320	586	56
% of Weighted Total:	100.0	46.9	48.9	77.7	11.5	23.5	31.3	30.2	15.1	44.3	46.9	42.1	22.4	10.6	19.4	1.9

A15G: Most mothers should spend more time with their children than they do now

	TOTAL	M	F	White	Black	NE	NC	S	W	Yes	No	None	Mari.	Few	More	Any
1. Disagree	5.7	6.2	5.2	6.0	4.1	8.0	4.8	4.7	5.8	6.0	5.7	5.0	5.8	6.3	7.1	7.4
2. Mostly disagree	8.9	9.2	9.1	9.5	6.2	11.5	10.4	7.1	5.6	10.2	7.7	8.2	9.4	9.7	9.5	14.8
3. Neither	21.5	25.2	17.6	23.0	12.6	25.5	22.2	15.5	25.4	25.5	17.1	19.5	24.3	19.5	24.0	27.8
4. Mostly agree	30.1	29.4	30.6	31.4	21.5	29.5	31.6	30.0	28.1	28.6	32.2	29.9	28.8	34.6	29.9	25.9
5. Agree	33.8	29.9	37.6	30.1	55.3	25.4	30.9	42.6	35.0	29.8	37.4	37.5	31.6	30.2	29.6	24.1
Item 10530 N(Wtd)	2983	1406	1467	2336	340	689	936	911	448	1331	1410	1269	670	318	578	54

A15H: If a wife works, her husband should take a greater part in housework and child-care

	TOTAL	M	F	White	Black	NE	NC	S	W	Yes	No	None	Mari.	Few	More	Any
1. Disagree	10.2	11.8	8.2	9.6	9.6	11.1	10.7	8.6	10.4	8.1	11.5	10.8	8.8	8.8	11.8	7.4
2. Mostly disagree	9.4	8.0	10.4	9.4	7.6	7.8	9.7	10.6	9.3	7.4	11.3	10.4	8.3	10.0	9.2	5.6
3. Neither	12.5	13.3	11.6	12.1	12.9	13.1	13.3	11.3	12.7	12.0	12.6	11.9	13.9	13.2	11.6	14.8
4. Mostly agree	33.4	36.3	30.8	35.4	24.9	31.7	33.5	32.7	37.3	34.4	33.9	33.5	33.8	34.5	35.3	20.4
5. Agree	34.4	30.7	39.0	33.4	44.7	36.3	32.8	36.9	30.0	38.0	30.8	33.4	35.2	33.9	32.2	51.9
Item 10540 N(Wtd)	2987	1409	1466	2336	342	694	934	909	450	1330	1410	1265	674	319	578	54

A16: How much TV do you estimate you watch on an average weekday?

	TOTAL	M	F	White	Black	NE	NC	S	W	Yes	No	None	Mari.	Few	More	Any
1. None	4.9	4.6	5.2	5.4	1.2	5.0	5.5	3.2	6.7	6.1	3.5	5.2	3.6	5.0	5.5	11.3
2. Half-hour or less	10.1	10.7	9.6	11.1	5.9	10.3	9.6	9.5	12.3	12.1	8.4	8.2	11.4	10.0	13.3	15.1
3. About one hour	17.0	20.0	14.3	18.6	7.3	18.5	19.3	12.4	19.2	19.8	14.5	17.1	15.0	15.7	20.7	20.8
4. About two hours	20.8	20.5	21.2	22.2	11.7	21.8	22.1	19.7	18.3	21.9	20.1	20.2	23.2	23.2	18.2	15.1
5. About three hours	19.7	20.0	19.1	19.5	24.0	17.7	19.6	22.7	16.6	17.3	22.2	19.6	19.8	19.1	20.7	15.1
6. About four hours	12.1	11.2	12.9	11.2	17.3	11.6	11.7	12.2	13.4	10.7	13.2	12.2	11.9	13.2	10.5	15.1
7. Five hours or more	15.5	12.9	17.8	12.1	32.3	15.1	12.4	20.2	13.2	12.2	18.0	17.5	15.3	13.8	11.2	11.3
Item 10550 N(Wtd)	2987	1407	1470	2338	341	696	935	910	447	1331	1412	1266	673	319	581	53

A17: In the past year, how many books have you read just because you wanted to--that is, without their being assigned?

	TOTAL	M	F	White	Black	NE	NC	S	W	Yes	No	None	Mari.	Few	More	Any
1. None	11.2	15.1	7.4	11.1	6.5	12.1	13.1	9.3	10.0	6.7	14.6	9.8	13.5	8.9	12.7	13.0
2. One	10.6	12.3	9.0	10.4	10.3	10.8	10.0	10.6	11.7	8.4	12.6	10.1	11.0	11.2	10.3	13.0
3. Two to five	38.6	41.2	35.7	38.1	43.7	38.7	36.1	38.7	43.4	37.7	39.0	40.2	39.4	33.9	37.2	33.3
4. Six to ten	15.1	14.1	16.3	15.2	17.3	17.8	14.2	14.9	13.1	16.8	13.9	14.3	15.6	16.9	15.2	18.5
5. Ten or more	24.4	17.3	31.8	25.2	22.0	20.4	26.6	26.4	22.1	30.4	19.9	25.6	20.7	28.8	24.7	20.4
Item 10560 N(Wtd)	2981	1403	1467	2334	341	695	930	904	452	1333	1405	1270	673	313	584	54

A18: Some people think about what's going on in government very often, and others are not that interested. How much of an interest do you take in government and current events?

	TOTAL	M	F	White	Black	NE	NC	S	W	Yes	No	None	Mari.	Few	More	Any
1. No interest at all	4.7	4.3	4.9	3.3	8.2	5.8	4.3	4.5	4.0	3.0	5.8	3.8	3.9	7.3	5.0	7.4
2. Very little interest	19.6	15.3	23.3	19.2	20.8	19.2	20.5	18.5	20.2	12.5	25.9	18.4	22.1	16.4	21.1	16.7
3. Some interest	47.6	46.2	49.2	49.1	40.5	48.0	49.1	44.1	50.8	45.1	49.9	50.0	45.4	45.1	46.6	40.7
4. A lot of interest	20.2	23.2	17.4	20.6	21.7	18.6	18.8	24.3	17.3	27.4	13.7	20.0	19.0	23.3	20.1	27.8
5. A very great interest	8.0	11.0	5.1	7.9	8.8	8.4	7.3	8.6	7.8	11.8	4.8	7.8	9.5	8.2	7.4	7.4
Item 6330 N(Wtd)	2982	1404	1470	2334	341	692	932	907	451	1334	1408	1269	674	317	582	54

A19: Some people think that there ought to be changes in the amount of influence and power that certain organizations have in our society. Do you think the following organizations should have more influence, less influence, or about the same amount of influence as they have now?

QUESTIONNAIRE FORM 4 1976	TOTAL	SEX		RACE		REGION				4YR COLLEGE PLANS		ILLICIT DRUG USE: LIFETIME				
		M	F	White	Black	NE	NC	S	W	Yes	No	None	Marijuana Only	Few Pills	More Pills	Any Heroin
Weighted No. of Cases:	3027	1420	1479	2352	347	711	946	915	456	1341	1420	1273	679	320	586	56
% of Weighted Total:	100.0	46.9	48.9	77.7	11.5	23.5	31.3	30.2	15.1	44.3	46.9	42.1	22.4	10.6	19.4	1.9
A19A: Large corporations?																
1. Much less	12.5	15.0	10.3	14.1	5.4	16.0	9.8	11.2	15.5	17.5	8.9	11.8	12.8	11.8	15.0	18.2
2. Less	39.0	40.8	37.9	43.7	20.2	39.9	43.4	33.3	40.1	46.1	33.5	39.8	40.5	39.8	39.3	21.8
3. Same as now	25.0	24.7	25.2	24.7	24.1	21.7	26.3	26.8	24.1	18.2	31.3	24.4	24.6	28.3	25.4	27.3
4. More	7.6	8.0	7.0	5.8	17.0	6.0	5.8	11.7	5.7	5.7	9.1	7.5	6.9	7.0	6.3	18.2
5. Much more	3.2	2.5	3.2	1.3	9.2	2.8	2.6	4.7	1.8	1.6	3.7	3.5	2.7	1.6	1.9	7.3
8. No opinion	12.7	9.0	16.5	10.3	24.1	13.5	12.1	12.5	12.8	11.0	13.4	12.9	12.5	11.1	12.1	9.1
Item 10570 N(Wtd)	2947	1392	1451	2310	336	687	925	896	439	1322	1392	1260	666	314	568	55
A19B: Major labor unions?																
1. Much less	11.8	15.6	8.1	13.7	2.4	11.1	13.0	8.9	16.3	15.1	9.8	13.6	10.5	11.2	10.2	18.2
2. Less	26.8	30.0	23.8	26.6	7.6	26.8	28.1	24.8	27.6	32.8	22.3	28.9	26.8	26.5	25.1	18.2
3. Same as now	26.2	24.6	28.1	26.6	26.3	24.7	26.9	25.4	28.3	23.7	28.8	25.7	25.8	25.2	30.0	18.2
4. More	16.1	16.3	15.5	13.7	27.5	15.7	15.3	18.5	13.3	13.4	18.2	12.6	18.4	18.5	16.1	30.9
5. Much more	6.4	5.2	7.4	4.0	15.8	6.6	5.1	8.7	4.1	4.5	7.4	6.0	6.6	6.7	6.3	7.3
8. No opinion	12.8	8.4	17.1	11.2	19.4	15.0	11.5	13.6	10.4	10.6	13.5	13.2	12.0	11.8	12.3	9.1
Item 10580 N(Wtd)	2947	1393	1448	2312	335	687	924	895	442	1322	1391	1260	664	313	570	55
A19C: Churches and religious organizations?																
1. Much less	4.8	7.1	2.5	5.2	.3	6.7	4.9	2.5	5.9	5.5	4.2	4.2	4.5	4.8	6.5	3.6
2. Less	8.4	9.7	7.2	9.0	4.5	10.0	8.1	4.9	13.4	9.7	7.0	7.5	8.5	8.9	9.6	12.7
3. Same as now	34.1	37.0	32.0	37.0	18.3	39.5	36.6	25.4	38.0	36.8	32.8	30.4	36.6	38.3	38.6	29.1
4. More	24.4	23.3	25.7	25.0	21.6	20.1	26.3	28.2	19.5	24.2	24.6	26.4	25.5	22.0	19.8	18.2
5. Much more	19.8	14.3	24.1	16.2	44.6	12.8	15.8	32.1	14.1	17.4	21.7	24.9	16.5	17.3	14.2	14.5
8. No opinion	8.6	8.6	8.5	7.7	10.8	10.8	8.3	7.0	9.1	6.4	9.6	6.6	8.4	8.3	11.1	20.0
Item 10590 N(Wtd)	2946	1391	1449	2311	334	688	924	895	440	1324	1389	1258	667	313	570	55
A19D: The national news media (TV, magazines, news services)?																
1. Much less	7.3	9.3	5.1	8.1	2.1	6.9	6.7	7.2	9.3	8.9	6.0	7.3	6.7	6.7	8.7	12.7
2. Less	22.9	24.2	22.0	25.8	12.6	25.3	26.0	18.4	21.7	26.7	19.7	24.1	24.1	22.9	21.4	10.9
3. Same as now	41.1	40.4	42.2	42.8	32.1	37.2	43.4	39.6	45.0	40.4	42.9	42.0	44.5	39.8	38.8	30.9
4. More	14.5	13.6	15.1	12.3	26.4	15.0	12.4	17.3	12.4	12.7	15.6	13.1	12.6	15.9	16.5	27.3
5. Much more	7.0	6.0	7.8	4.9	17.1	7.2	5.5	9.3	5.4	5.6	8.1	7.1	5.6	8.0	7.3	9.1
8. No opinion	7.2	6.4	7.8	6.1	9.9	8.5	5.9	8.2	6.3	5.6	7.6	6.6	6.7	6.4	7.4	12.7
Item 10600 N(Wtd)	2938	1392	1442	2307	333	685	920	891	442	1320	1388	1261	659	314	565	55
A19E: The Presidency and the administration?																
1. Much less	5.1	5.5	4.5	4.9	4.8	5.4	5.1	5.0	5.0	4.3	6.0	4.8	5.3	4.8	4.9	10.9
2. Less	17.4	16.5	18.1	17.7	18.2	19.7	18.7	13.3	19.7	18.4	17.0	15.2	18.1	20.1	20.6	21.8
3. Same as now	38.2	39.9	36.9	40.5	28.9	37.6	40.4	35.5	39.9	41.6	36.0	41.2	36.7	33.4	39.3	18.2
4. More	16.5	17.6	15.9	17.5	11.3	14.3	17.0	18.4	14.3	18.0	15.5	16.5	18.3	18.8	14.1	18.2
5. Much more	9.9	10.7	9.0	8.1	17.9	8.9	7.7	13.4	9.3	8.3	11.1	10.2	9.2	12.1	7.7	14.5
8. No opinion	12.8	9.6	15.6	11.2	19.0	14.1	11.1	14.0	11.8	9.3	14.4	12.0	12.7	10.8	13.4	18.2
Item 10610 N(Wtd)	2946	1390	1451	2309	336	686	923	896	441	1323	1392	1262	663	314	568	55
A19F: The Congress--that is, the U.S. Senate and House of Representatives?																
1. Much less	4.0	4.5	3.5	3.8	3.0	3.8	4.2	3.8	4.1	3.5	4.9	3.6	3.9	5.7	3.5	9.1
2. Less	12.9	13.4	12.3	13.5	9.8	10.2	14.1	13.2	13.9	12.3	13.0	11.1	15.1	12.7	12.7	16.4
3. Same as now	37.7	37.9	37.3	39.9	28.6	36.3	39.3	36.9	37.6	40.5	36.0	39.3	34.0	37.6	41.8	23.6
4. More	22.6	24.3	21.6	22.9	22.6	23.9	21.9	22.1	22.8	26.5	19.2	23.5	24.9	20.4	20.5	16.4
5. Much more	9.0	10.6	7.1	7.5	14.0	10.6	7.0	10.2	8.2	7.1	10.2	8.0	8.5	11.1	9.3	10.9
8. No opinion	13.9	9.3	18.2	12.3	21.7	15.5	13.2	13.7	13.2	10.1	16.8	14.4	13.7	12.4	12.0	23.6
Item 10620 N(Wtd)	2944	1391	1449	2308	336	686	923	896	439	1320	1393	1262	662	314	567	55

QUESTIONNAIRE FORM 4 1976	TOTAL	SEX		RACE		REGION				4YR COLLEGE PLANS		ILLICIT DRUG USE: LIFETIME				
		M	F	White	Black	NE	NC	S	W	Yes	No	None	Mari-juana Only	Few Pills	More Pills	Any Her-oin
Weighted No. of Cases:	3027	1420	1479	2352	347	711	946	915	456	1341	1420	1273	679	320	586	56
% of Weighted Total:	100.0	46.9	48.9	77.7	11.5	23.5	31.3	30.2	15.1	44.3	46.9	42.1	22.4	10.6	19.4	1.9

A19G: The U.S. Supreme Court?

	TOTAL	M	F	White	Black	NE	NC	S	W	Yes	No	None	Mari-juana Only	Few Pills	More Pills	Any Heroin
1. Much less	2.9	3.6	2.0	2.8	1.8	2.7	3.0	2.8	3.4	2.7	3.3	2.6	1.8	3.8	3.0	11.1
2. Less	8.1	8.6	7.7	8.6	4.2	7.7	8.3	8.8	7.1	7.5	8.7	8.0	7.8	9.6	7.6	7.4
3. Same as now	41.3	40.3	42.5	43.9	31.1	41.2	43.2	37.9	44.9	44.1	39.8	42.0	43.0	36.3	45.4	25.9
4. More	23.6	26.8	20.7	24.2	22.5	23.4	24.1	24.6	20.7	25.4	21.9	23.0	26.6	26.1	21.7	14.8
5. Much more	10.2	11.0	9.3	8.6	19.5	10.0	8.7	12.0	10.3	9.9	10.2	10.8	8.1	11.8	8.8	16.7
8. No opinion	13.8	9.6	17.7	11.8	20.7	15.0	12.8	13.9	13.9	10.3	15.9	13.7	12.8	12.1	13.3	24.1
Item 10630 N(Wtd)	2929	1379	1447	2301	334	679	921	890	439	1314	1386	1255	658	314	566	54

A19H: All the courts and the justice system in general?

	TOTAL	M	F	White	Black	NE	NC	S	W	Yes	No	None	Mari-juana Only	Few Pills	More Pills	Any Heroin
1. Much less	2.6	3.5	1.7	2.5	1.5	1.9	3.6	2.1	2.7	2.3	3.1	2.7	2.1	2.2	2.3	9.1
2. Less	7.7	9.1	6.2	7.8	6.6	7.9	7.6	8.1	6.8	7.4	7.7	6.4	8.1	8.0	9.2	7.3
3. Same as now	39.3	39.1	39.5	41.0	33.1	39.2	41.2	37.4	39.0	41.2	38.3	39.7	39.1	34.9	43.3	36.4
4. More	25.7	27.7	24.9	27.2	22.0	25.0	25.7	24.7	29.3	30.1	22.9	25.4	28.7	31.4	23.0	14.5
5. Much more	11.0	11.0	10.4	10.0	14.2	10.4	9.9	13.4	9.3	8.9	12.0	12.1	9.0	10.9	9.7	16.4
8. No opinion	13.7	9.7	17.3	11.6	22.6	15.7	12.0	14.5	12.7	10.3	15.8	13.8	12.8	12.2	12.5	16.4
Item 10640 N(Wtd)	2936	1387	1444	2303	332	681	923	891	441	1317	1390	1257	663	312	566	55

A19I: The police and other law enforcement agencies?

	TOTAL	M	F	White	Black	NE	NC	S	W	Yes	No	None	Mari-juana Only	Few Pills	More Pills	Any Heroin
1. Much less	3.9	5.3	2.4	3.7	3.9	3.5	5.2	2.7	4.3	3.0	5.0	2.2	3.0	4.5	6.7	10.9
2. Less	9.3	10.5	7.6	8.9	11.4	12.6	10.2	6.0	9.0	9.7	8.7	5.8	8.4	10.9	15.8	23.6
3. Same as now	28.8	28.9	29.0	30.1	21.6	29.2	28.4	26.4	33.9	30.5	27.5	26.4	33.9	29.1	30.6	16.4
4. More	28.9	29.3	29.2	30.9	22.8	26.3	31.9	28.3	28.0	30.1	28.2	33.2	28.8	26.5	23.6	16.4
5. Much more	21.8	19.7	23.6	20.6	28.4	20.2	17.5	29.3	18.3	21.0	23.2	25.9	18.7	22.7	16.2	21.8
8. No opinion	7.2	6.3	8.1	5.8	12.3	8.2	6.8	7.2	6.5	5.8	7.5	6.4	7.4	6.4	7.2	10.9
Item 10650 N(Wtd)	2944	1388	1451	2308	334	684	924	893	443	1321	1393	1259	664	313	568	55

A19J: The U.S. military?

	TOTAL	M	F	White	Black	NE	NC	S	W	Yes	No	None	Mari-juana Only	Few Pills	More Pills	Any Heroin
1. Much less	4.8	5.8	3.6	4.8	2.7	6.0	5.5	2.0	7.0	6.2	3.5	3.4	5.0	5.4	6.2	9.1
2. Less	8.7	8.5	8.2	9.0	7.1	12.4	8.4	5.5	10.2	11.4	6.5	7.1	9.0	10.2	10.2	10.9
3. Same as now	39.7	39.6	40.9	42.9	29.8	39.7	43.9	33.8	42.3	41.0	38.7	41.6	41.4	38.5	39.9	18.2
4. More	21.1	22.4	19.9	22.0	15.2	18.5	20.5	25.3	17.6	20.0	22.8	21.2	21.8	21.3	18.9	25.5
5. Much more	13.4	15.6	11.0	10.6	26.2	9.9	9.7	21.8	9.5	10.9	15.6	13.9	12.5	14.6	11.5	23.6
8. No opinion	12.5	8.1	16.5	10.7	19.0	13.4	12.0	11.6	13.6	10.5	13.0	12.8	10.2	9.9	13.6	12.7
Item 10660 N(Wtd)	2945	1388	1452	2308	336	685	922	896	442	1323	1392	1261	664	314	567	55

The next questions ask your views about drugs.

A20: Do you think that people (who are 18 or older) should be prohibited by law from doing each of the following?

A20A: Smoking cigarettes

	TOTAL	M	F	White	Black	NE	NC	S	W	Yes	No	None	Mari-juana Only	Few Pills	More Pills	Any Heroin
1. No	78.4	77.5	79.2	79.9	71.1	82.2	80.3	75.8	73.5	77.0	80.5	70.3	83.3	84.1	87.1	80.0
2. Not sure	7.3	7.3	7.4	6.8	9.3	5.6	6.2	9.0	8.7	8.0	6.3	10.2	6.4	7.6	2.2	3.6
3. Yes	14.3	15.2	13.4	13.2	19.5	12.3	13.4	15.1	17.8	15.1	13.1	19.5	10.1	8.3	10.7	14.5
Item 10770 N(Wtd)	2963	1398	1458	2319	343	684	931	900	449	1328	1393	1259	671	314	582	55

A20B: Smoking marijuana (pot, grass) in private

	TOTAL	M	F	White	Black	NE	NC	S	W	Yes	No	None	Mari-juana Only	Few Pills	More Pills	Any Heroin
1. No	58.7	58.7	58.2	58.4	60.1	68.6	58.4	51.7	57.9	59.3	57.9	34.1	71.4	76.7	84.7	85.7
2. Not sure	13.8	14.6	13.1	13.5	14.8	11.9	14.9	14.5	12.9	14.5	13.2	18.8	13.7	9.5	5.5	3.6
3. Yes	27.5	26.8	28.7	28.0	25.4	19.3	26.7	33.7	29.0	26.2	28.9	47.1	14.9	13.9	9.8	10.7
Item 10780 N(Wtd)	2972	1401	1462	2332	338	688	933	901	451	1329	1404	1262	672	317	582	56

QUESTIONNAIRE FORM 4 1976	TOTAL	SEX		RACE		REGION				4YR COLLEGE PLANS		ILLICIT DRUG USE: LIFETIME				
		M	F	White	Black	NE	NC	S	W	Yes	No	None	Mari- juana Only	Few Pills	More Pills	Any Her- oin
Weighted No. of Cases:	3027	1420	1479	2352	347	711	946	915	456	1341	1420	1273	679	320	586	56
% of Weighted Total:	100.0	46.9	48.9	77.7	11.5	23.5	31.3	30.2	15.1	44.3	46.9	42.1	22.4	10.6	19.4	1.9

A20C: Smoking marijuana in public places

1. No	22.5	25.9	18.7	20.9	24.6	27.1	22.0	21.4	18.8	20.4	23.4	11.6	21.0	28.1	40.1	53.6
2. Not sure	18.4	18.7	18.0	19.1	12.3	23.1	18.1	14.7	19.0	17.4	19.1	9.5	22.8	24.9	28.0	23.2
3. Yes	59.1	55.5	63.3	59.9	63.0	49.9	59.9	63.7	62.2	62.2	57.5	79.0	56.3	46.7	31.9	23.2
Item 10790　N(Wtd)	2977	1399	1469	2332	341	694	935	902	447	1331	1404	1269	668	317	583	56

A20D: Taking LSD in private

1. No	22.4	23.7	20.9	20.3	28.1	25.3	21.0	21.4	22.8	19.5	23.8	16.4	17.8	21.3	37.1	50.0
2. Not sure	12.5	11.6	13.4	12.1	14.2	14.4	12.4	10.8	12.9	11.5	13.4	10.5	9.9	15.6	16.4	21.4
3. Yes	65.1	64.7	65.7	67.6	57.7	60.3	66.6	67.8	64.3	69.1	62.7	73.1	72.2	62.9	46.4	28.6
Item 10800　N(Wtd)	2961	1395	1462	2326	338	688	928	897	448	1325	1401	1261	669	315	580	56

A20E: Taking LSD in public places

1. No	10.9	12.9	8.2	8.2	17.9	12.2	10.2	11.2	9.3	7.8	12.0	9.5	9.8	11.8	11.0	17.0
2. Not sure	7.2	7.6	7.0	7.1	6.9	8.0	7.4	7.1	6.2	5.4	9.3	3.8	5.9	8.3	13.9	30.2
3. Yes	81.9	79.5	84.8	84.7	75.5	79.7	82.5	81.7	84.4	86.8	78.7	86.7	84.5	80.3	74.9	54.7
Item 10810　N(Wtd)	2974	1400	1464	2333	335	689	935	900	450	1327	1404	1265	676	314	582	53

A20F: Taking amphetamines (uppers) or barbiturates (downers) in private

1. No	28.6	28.8	28.3	27.9	28.2	31.2	30.5	24.0	29.8	25.5	31.0	19.4	21.4	27.7	53.2	55.4
2. Not sure	17.9	18.8	17.3	17.5	19.0	19.0	16.3	19.1	17.4	18.9	17.3	16.2	16.8	24.5	18.9	21.4
3. Yes	53.5	52.4	54.4	54.6	52.8	49.9	53.2	57.0	52.8	55.6	51.8	64.4	61.8	47.4	27.9	23.2
Item 10820　N(Wtd)	2959	1394	1457	2317	337	690	921	899	449	1325	1395	1260	672	310	581	56

A20G: Taking amphetamines or barbiturates in public places

1. No	12.9	15.1	10.4	10.7	16.5	15.2	12.8	11.9	11.3	9.6	14.7	9.4	9.5	10.8	20.8	30.4
2. Not sure	11.0	11.8	10.5	10.9	12.4	10.0	11.6	11.5	10.6	9.2	12.8	6.9	9.2	13.6	19.9	26.8
3. Yes	76.1	73.1	79.1	78.4	71.2	74.9	75.6	76.5	78.1	81.2	72.5	83.6	81.4	75.6	59.3	42.9
Item 10830　N(Wtd)	2985	1408	1468	2340	340	692	937	904	452	1334	1409	1270	677	316	583	56

A20H: Taking heroin (smack, horse) in private

1. No	17.2	18.5	15.7	14.8	26.5	17.8	17.5	16.3	17.5	14.4	18.6	15.2	16.0	15.5	20.3	36.4
2. Not sure	10.4	9.9	10.8	9.3	13.0	11.3	9.8	10.2	10.2	9.1	11.2	9.9	8.1	13.9	11.5	16.4
3. Yes	72.4	71.5	73.6	75.9	60.5	71.0	72.6	73.4	72.1	76.4	70.3	75.0	75.7	70.6	68.0	47.3
Item 10840　N(Wtd)	2978	1402	1469	2336	339	690	935	902	451	1332	1406	1267	675	316	582	55

A20I: Taking heroin in public places

1. No	9.8	12.1	7.1	7.2	18.5	10.6	9.2	10.8	8.2	7.5	10.5	9.3	8.6	9.8	8.8	19.6
2. Not sure	5.3	5.6	5.3	4.9	7.1	5.9	5.5	5.4	3.8	3.9	6.6	3.6	5.5	7.0	6.7	17.9
3. Yes	84.8	82.3	87.6	87.9	74.4	83.5	85.3	83.8	87.8	88.6	83.0	87.1	85.9	83.2	84.7	64.3
Item 10850　N(Wtd)	2970	1398	1462	2329	336	691	927	900	452	1328	1402	1265	672	316	580	56

A20J: Getting drunk in private

1. No	71.1	72.0	70.2	73.2	61.2	75.7	74.7	64.0	70.4	70.1	73.1	57.5	78.3	81.8	85.4	85.5
2. Not sure	13.4	12.8	13.9	12.3	20.0	12.2	11.3	16.9	12.2	14.4	11.6	19.5	11.5	7.5	5.9	7.3
3. Yes	15.6	15.2	15.9	14.4	18.8	12.2	13.9	19.0	17.4	15.6	15.3	22.9	10.2	10.7	8.8	9.1
Item 10860　N(Wtd)	2972	1401	1464	2328	340	691	935	898	449	1329	1403	1260	676	318	581	55

QUESTIONNAIRE FORM 4 1976	TOTAL	SEX		RACE		REGION				4YR COLLEGE PLANS		ILLICIT DRUG USE: LIFETIME				
		M	F	White	Black	NE	NC	S	W	Yes	No	None	Marijuana Only	Few Pills	More Pills	Any Heroin
Weighted No. of Cases:	3027	1420	1479	2352	347	711	946	915	456	1341	1420	1273	679	320	586	56
% of Weighted Total:	100.0	46.9	48.9	77.7	11.5	23.5	31.3	30.2	15.1	44.3	46.9	42.1	22.4	10.6	19.4	1.9

A20K: Getting drunk in public places

	TOTAL	M	F	White	Black	NE	NC	S	W	Yes	No	None	Mari. Only	Few Pills	More Pills	Any Her.
1. No	27.8	30.1	25.0	27.9	22.4	30.5	32.8	22.1	24.6	23.0	32.2	18.2	29.4	32.1	40.2	53.6
2. Not sure	21.6	20.8	22.5	22.6	16.2	24.1	24.0	16.8	22.1	20.9	22.8	16.7	26.7	21.1	25.4	25.0
3. Yes	50.7	49.1	52.4	49.5	61.8	45.4	43.1	61.1	53.5	56.1	45.0	65.1	43.9	46.9	34.4	21.4
Item 10870 N(Wtd)	2973	1401	1464	2328	340	689	933	899	452	1329	1404	1264	674	318	579	56

A21: In particular, there has been a great deal of public debate about whether marijuana use should be legal. Which of the following policies would you favor?

	TOTAL	M	F	White	Black	NE	NC	S	W	Yes	No	None	Mari. Only	Few Pills	More Pills	Any Her.
1. Using marijuana shoud be entirely legal	32.6	35.4	29.3	32.0	33.5	38.7	31.9	28.0	33.4	31.9	32.7	11.5	37.0	46.1	62.8	74.5
2. It shoud be a minor violation --like a parking ticket-- but not a crime	29.0	27.7	30.2	29.5	29.7	32.9	29.7	26.6	26.9	30.9	27.8	23.7	40.6	35.0	25.3	14.5
3. It should be a crime	25.4	24.6	26.5	26.4	20.2	16.2	23.9	32.2	29.0	25.5	26.0	47.1	11.8	10.1	5.9	5.5
4. Don't know	13.0	12.4	14.0	12.2	16.3	12.2	14.5	13.1	10.7	11.7	13.4	17.7	10.6	8.8	6.2	5.5
Item 10880 N(Wtd)	2964	1399	1462	2328	337	687	933	895	449	1331	1399	1264	670	317	581	55

A22: If it were legal for people to USE marijuana, should it also be legal to SELL marijuana?

	TOTAL	M	F	White	Black	NE	NC	S	W	Yes	No	None	Mari. Only	Few Pills	More Pills	Any Her.
1. No	23.0	21.8	24.0	22.4	23.0	17.4	23.8	24.8	26.4	21.6	24.8	37.3	14.4	15.1	7.5	14.5
2. Yes, but only to adults	49.8	52.8	47.2	50.8	49.9	54.1	47.3	49.7	48.8	54.3	45.9	38.7	59.7	60.1	59.0	49.1
3. Yes, to anyone	13.3	13.3	12.9	12.8	13.7	13.7	13.6	13.0	12.6	11.3	14.3	8.9	12.6	12.3	22.1	27.3
4. Don't know	13.9	12.2	15.9	13.9	13.1	14.8	15.2	12.5	12.2	12.7	14.9	15.2	13.2	12.6	11.5	9.1
Item 10890 N(Wtd)	2977	1403	1469	2335	343	688	938	901	451	1331	1409	1267	675	318	583	55

A23: If marijuana were legal to use and legally available, which of the following would you be most likely to do?

	TOTAL	M	F	White	Black	NE	NC	S	W	Yes	No	None	Mari. Only	Few Pills	More Pills	Any Her.
1. Not use it, even if it were legal and available	50.4	45.3	56.4	51.4	50.7	42.9	48.8	56.3	53.8	53.5	48.6	83.6	33.6	31.4	14.7	3.6
2. Try it	8.1	7.7	8.6	7.7	10.3	8.3	9.4	8.1	5.2	9.2	7.8	8.8	10.4	9.7	2.9	3.6
3. Use it about as often as I do now	24.7	28.0	21.4	25.5	17.4	30.4	25.2	19.8	25.1	23.3	24.9	1.0	33.0	38.1	55.1	62.5
4. Use it more often than I do now	7.1	8.3	5.5	7.4	5.6	7.4	6.8	7.1	7.6	6.4	7.8	.2	9.3	8.2	18.2	25.0
5. Use it less than I do now	1.5	1.6	1.5	1.2	3.5	1.9	1.5	1.2	1.8	1.4	1.5	.6	1.8	2.5	2.4	1.8
6. Don't know	8.1	9.1	6.7	6.8	12.7	9.3	8.3	7.6	7.0	6.2	9.5	5.9	11.6	10.1	6.7	3.6
Item 10900 N(Wtd)	2968	1402	1466	2331	339	685	938	899	446	1332	1405	1266	670	318	584	56

This section asks for your views and feelings about a number of different things.

D01: How satisfied are you with your life as a whole these days?

	TOTAL	M	F	White	Black	NE	NC	S	W	Yes	No	None	Mari. Only	Few Pills	More Pills	Any Her.
1. Completely dissatisfied	2.6	2.5	2.6	2.0	5.7	3.1	2.1	3.1	1.7	1.8	2.8	2.5	2.5	2.6	2.6	4.1
2. Quite dissatisfied	8.6	9.3	7.8	8.6	8.4	8.2	9.2	8.6	7.8	8.6	8.2	8.3	8.2	8.1	10.4	8.2
3. Somewhat dissatisfied	13.3	13.8	12.7	13.5	16.5	13.5	13.3	12.3	15.4	12.6	14.0	12.8	14.1	14.3	13.0	18.4
4. Neither, or mixed feelings	14.4	14.3	14.7	13.5	16.5	15.9	14.3	13.3	14.7	14.6	14.4	12.1	14.6	17.9	17.8	8.2
5. Somewhat satisfied	25.0	27.0	22.7	25.0	26.3	23.0	24.2	27.7	23.9	25.6	24.3	23.5	27.9	23.7	24.0	30.6
6. Quite satisfied	30.4	27.5	33.6	33.2	18.5	30.7	31.4	29.5	29.9	32.4	29.1	33.8	28.4	27.3	28.8	22.4
7. Completely satisfied	5.7	5.6	5.9	4.7	8.1	5.7	5.4	5.5	6.6	4.3	7.3	6.9	4.2	6.5	3.8	8.2
Item 6840 N(Wtd)	2820	1337	1414	2276	297	635	900	862	422	1319	1379	1216	637	308	546	49

D02: FOR THOSE WHO HAVE A JOB: All things considered, how satisfied are you with your present job?

	TOTAL	M	F	White	Black	NE	NC	S	W	Yes	No	None	Mari. Only	Few Pills	More Pills	Any Her.
1. Completely dissatisfied	5.3	5.3	4.9	4.5	13.1	6.6	5.3	4.8	4.9	5.2	5.4	5.6	2.8	5.2	7.1	10.0
2. Quite dissatisfied	10.6	11.6	9.7	10.5	9.8	10.5	9.3	11.9	11.3	9.6	11.3	10.6	10.5	11.4	11.9	3.3
3. Somewhat dissatisfied	15.6	16.0	15.2	15.5	21.3	15.0	16.1	15.9	14.7	14.8	16.2	14.1	16.6	16.1	15.7	26.7
4. Neither, or mixed feelings	13.5	14.3	12.4	12.9	14.8	15.6	12.0	13.3	14.3	16.7	10.6	11.5	14.6	16.6	14.2	23.3
5. Somewhat satisfied	24.8	26.1	22.7	25.7	21.3	22.8	26.9	24.0	23.8	24.9	25.3	24.9	26.1	20.2	25.8	16.7
6. Quite satisfied	22.2	19.1	26.5	23.5	11.5	22.2	23.3	20.6	23.0	20.8	23.3	25.4	19.9	23.3	19.0	6.7
7. Completely satisfied	8.0	7.7	8.5	7.4	8.2	7.2	7.1	9.5	7.5	8.0	7.9	7.9	9.5	6.7	6.2	10.0
Item 10910 N(Wtd)	1696	874	774	1434	122	333	602	496	265	771	846	710	391	193	337	30

QUESTIONNAIRE FORM 4 1976	TOTAL	SEX		RACE		REGION				4YR COLLEGE PLANS		ILLICIT DRUG USE: LIFETIME				
		M	F	White	Black	NE	NC	S	W	Yes	No	None	Mari-juana Only	Few Pills	More Pills	Any Her-oin
Weighted No. of Cases:	3027	1420	1479	2352	347	711	946	915	456	1341	1420	1273	679	320	586	56
% of Weighted Total:	100.0	46.9	48.9	77.7	11.5	23.5	31.3	30.2	15.1	44.3	46.9	42.1	22.4	10.6	19.4	1.9

D03: People have different opinions about world problems. How much do you agree or disagree with each of the following statements?

D03A: I feel that I can do very little to change the way the world is today

1. Disagree	10.3	11.3	9.3	9.3	15.6	11.4	9.0	12.0	8.4	12.1	8.5	11.0	9.5	10.2	9.2	10.4
2. Mostly disagree	21.4	19.1	23.5	21.6	19.0	22.6	20.2	21.3	21.9	27.4	16.2	22.8	17.4	21.5	24.2	22.9
3. Neither	23.4	23.4	23.7	23.4	22.8	21.9	24.6	23.2	23.9	19.4	27.3	24.0	21.3	26.7	21.6	31.3
4. Mostly agree	29.5	29.9	29.1	31.6	21.5	28.3	31.3	27.2	32.3	30.5	28.8	28.4	34.2	28.1	29.1	18.8
5. Agree	15.3	16.2	14.3	14.0	21.1	15.7	14.8	16.3	13.8	10.6	19.1	13.8	17.4	13.5	15.6	18.8
Item 10920 N(Wtd)	2769	1306	1394	2236	289	625	889	849	406	1296	1348	1204	619	303	532	48

D03B: It does little good to clean up air and water pollution because this society will not last long enough for it to matter

1. Disagree	44.9	45.3	44.9	46.6	37.5	48.4	42.1	44.2	47.5	52.7	37.9	45.3	46.8	39.9	45.4	46.9
2. Mostly disagree	29.1	28.1	29.8	31.2	21.2	27.3	33.4	25.9	28.9	30.7	28.5	27.7	29.6	34.0	31.1	12.2
3. Neither	13.1	13.0	13.1	12.3	13.4	13.6	11.8	14.2	12.5	9.0	16.2	13.6	12.5	13.5	12.8	8.2
4. Mostly agree	7.1	7.1	7.3	5.9	16.3	5.5	6.8	9.5	5.4	4.0	9.9	6.6	6.0	10.2	6.0	12.2
5. Agree	5.8	6.5	5.0	4.0	11.7	5.2	5.9	6.1	5.6	3.6	7.6	6.7	5.0	2.3	4.7	20.4
Item 10930 N(Wtd)	2765	1304	1393	2238	283	618	888	851	408	1291	1349	1204	615	303	531	49

D03C: When things get tough enough, we'll put our minds to it and find a technological solution

1. Disagree	7.4	7.2	7.4	7.0	7.8	9.9	5.5	7.4	7.4	6.4	8.3	8.3	4.6	7.6	7.8	6.1
2. Mostly disagree	10.9	11.4	10.4	10.8	7.8	9.8	11.6	10.7	11.4	11.6	10.2	10.0	10.9	17.2	8.9	16.3
3. Neither	18.7	17.2	20.3	19.7	12.8	19.9	18.4	17.1	21.3	16.2	20.8	19.2	18.2	19.5	18.8	10.2
4. Mostly agree	37.8	36.3	39.1	39.2	31.9	37.3	40.1	35.8	37.9	40.6	36.3	36.8	38.6	34.7	41.3	42.9
5. Agree	25.1	27.8	22.9	23.3	39.4	23.1	24.3	29.0	22.0	25.2	24.4	25.8	27.4	21.1	23.4	24.5
Item 10940 N(Wtd)	2753	1297	1390	2228	282	614	886	849	404	1288	1344	1200	614	303	526	49

D03D: When I think about all the terrible things that have been happening, it is hard for me to hold out much hope for the world

1. Disagree	18.8	20.7	17.2	19.4	16.4	18.2	17.8	20.2	19.0	21.8	15.1	19.7	20.6	14.3	17.0	18.4
2. Mostly disagree	28.6	28.7	28.4	30.4	20.7	28.0	29.1	26.5	32.8	33.8	24.5	28.8	29.5	31.7	27.7	16.3
3. Neither	21.3	20.7	21.7	21.6	17.9	22.0	23.9	18.7	19.8	19.5	23.1	21.1	21.4	19.7	24.1	14.3
4. Mostly agree	22.3	21.8	22.9	21.7	26.8	22.1	22.2	23.2	20.8	17.8	26.5	20.5	21.6	25.0	23.7	28.6
5. Agree	9.0	7.9	9.9	6.9	18.2	9.3	7.0	11.5	7.5	7.0	10.7	9.8	6.9	9.3	7.6	20.4
Item 10950 N(Wtd)	2737	1292	1378	2216	280	610	883	845	399	1277	1341	1198	607	300	523	49

D03E: I often wonder if there is any real purpose to my life in light of the world situation

1. Disagree	27.5	27.3	27.5	28.4	24.2	29.3	25.1	28.3	28.8	32.8	22.5	31.2	24.1	24.8	25.9	16.7
2. Mostly disagree	21.5	19.8	22.9	23.2	11.6	21.2	21.5	19.3	26.8	23.6	19.8	21.9	22.3	23.5	20.8	10.4
3. Neither	24.2	26.1	22.8	24.3	21.7	26.0	26.7	21.4	22.3	20.3	27.9	22.5	25.9	25.2	25.7	27.1
4. Mostly agree	18.5	19.2	18.1	18.0	24.2	16.1	20.8	19.9	14.1	16.2	20.9	17.3	20.0	19.5	18.0	27.1
5. Agree	8.2	7.5	8.7	6.2	18.4	7.6	6.0	11.1	8.2	7.2	9.0	7.0	7.6	7.0	9.7	18.8
Item 10960 N(Wtd)	2731	1285	1378	2210	277	608	881	838	403	1273	1339	1194	609	302	518	48

D03F: My guess is that this country will be caught up in a major world upheaval in the next 10 years

1. Disagree	13.1	15.5	11.2	12.7	16.2	12.0	12.6	14.7	12.3	14.0	11.8	13.0	14.5	12.3	11.7	13.3
2. Mostly disagree	17.5	18.8	16.0	18.3	13.3	18.4	19.2	15.8	15.8	19.2	15.8	17.2	16.8	21.9	16.7	15.6
3. Neither	33.1	28.7	37.6	34.5	25.9	33.0	33.9	30.3	37.4	31.5	34.8	33.6	32.3	30.9	34.8	31.1
4. Mostly agree	22.0	23.7	20.2	22.0	20.1	23.1	21.8	22.2	20.4	22.1	22.6	19.8	24.6	22.9	23.3	26.7
5. Agree	14.3	13.4	15.0	12.6	24.8	13.4	12.4	17.0	14.1	13.3	15.0	16.4	11.7	12.0	13.6	13.3
Item 10970 N(Wtd)	2721	1284	1370	2203	278	610	878	835	398	1274	1331	1187	613	301	515	45

QUESTIONNAIRE FORM 4 1976	TOTAL	SEX		RACE		REGION				4YR COLLEGE PLANS		ILLICIT DRUG USE: LIFETIME				
		M	F	White	Black	NE	NC	S	W	Yes	No	None	Marijuana Only	Few Pills	More Pills	Any Heroin
Weighted No. of Cases:	3027	1420	1479	2352	347	711	946	915	456	1341	1420	1273	679	320	586	56
% of Weighted Total:	100.0	46.9	48.9	77.7	11.5	23.5	31.3	30.2	15.1	44.3	46.9	42.1	22.4	10.6	19.4	1.9

D03G: Nuclear or biological annihilation will probably be the fate of all mankind, within my lifetime

1. Disagree	22.8	25.2	20.9	24.0	19.6	23.6	22.0	21.7	25.4	28.0	17.6	23.5	23.8	20.5	22.5	12.8
2. Mostly disagree	18.9	20.9	16.9	20.2	12.0	19.6	18.6	18.0	20.1	21.9	16.0	20.1	19.9	15.4	17.9	10.6
3. Neither	34.7	27.7	41.5	34.7	33.7	34.6	35.9	33.6	34.6	29.4	40.0	34.0	34.0	40.3	34.5	38.3
4. Mostly agree	14.0	14.9	13.2	13.1	18.8	14.1	14.5	15.7	9.4	12.7	15.6	12.7	13.6	15.8	14.8	29.8
5. Agree	9.6	11.3	7.5	8.1	16.3	8.0	9.0	11.2	10.4	8.1	10.8	9.8	8.7	8.4	10.3	10.6
Item 10980 N(Wtd)	2688	1272	1351	2176	276	601	869	824	393	1263	1310	1181	597	298	507	47

D03H: The human race has come through tough times before, and will do so again

1. Disagree	4.8	6.2	3.5	4.5	6.8	5.3	4.4	4.7	5.3	4.1	5.3	5.7	3.3	3.3	4.7	6.4
2. Mostly disagree	7.2	6.8	7.4	6.3	11.9	6.6	5.7	8.8	7.8	7.0	7.3	6.5	7.4	7.6	8.8	4.3
3. Neither	18.1	18.4	17.8	18.3	16.2	18.4	18.4	16.2	21.4	16.1	20.0	18.0	17.0	22.9	16.9	25.5
4. Mostly agree	37.3	36.4	38.2	38.8	29.9	38.2	39.8	35.8	33.7	38.0	37.5	38.4	36.4	35.2	37.0	34.0
5. Agree	32.6	32.2	33.1	32.0	34.5	31.5	31.8	34.6	31.9	34.8	29.9	31.3	35.9	31.2	32.5	27.7
Item 10990 N(Wtd)	2715	1272	1376	2198	278	604	880	833	398	1268	1333	1187	607	301	514	47

The next questions are about alcohol use-- this time asking separately about beer, wine, and hard liquor.

D04: On how many occasions (if any) have you had beer to drink...

D04A: ...in your lifetime?

1. 0 occasions	13.1	9.6	16.2	12.5	17.0	7.5	11.3	18.4	14.8	12.8	13.3	26.1	3.2	4.5	2.5	-
2. 1-2	11.8	9.7	13.9	10.8	19.0	10.0	11.5	13.1	12.5	12.7	10.9	18.7	7.9	10.0	3.6	4.3
3. 3-5	9.2	7.3	11.0	8.5	16.2	6.1	9.5	11.3	8.7	10.8	7.6	13.5	8.4	5.9	3.4	2.2
4. 6-9	8.4	7.2	9.3	8.1	10.1	9.7	6.3	8.4	10.9	8.5	8.2	10.6	6.5	9.7	5.0	2.2
5. 10-19	9.7	8.2	11.2	9.1	13.8	10.0	9.0	10.8	8.7	10.6	9.3	9.8	10.4	12.8	6.5	4.3
6. 20-39	11.4	10.1	12.6	11.9	8.1	12.9	13.0	9.8	9.2	10.9	12.3	8.3	16.2	16.2	11.1	4.3
7. 40 or more	36.4	47.8	25.7	39.0	15.8	43.8	39.3	28.3	35.4	33.7	38.4	13.1	47.4	41.0	67.7	82.6
Item 11000 N(Wtd)	2629	1225	1340	2164	247	589	852	795	393	1251	1272	1126	597	290	524	46

D04B: ...during the last 12 months?

1. 0 occasions	24.8	19.3	29.9	23.0	38.7	19.3	20.4	31.2	29.5	26.0	23.3	42.7	12.2	17.0	8.1	2.2
2. 1-2	13.2	10.3	16.0	12.1	21.0	11.5	12.8	15.1	12.9	14.8	11.9	18.2	11.8	12.4	5.2	4.3
3. 3-5	10.6	8.7	12.3	10.1	14.7	10.2	10.6	11.4	9.8	10.3	10.8	13.3	8.4	9.5	8.3	4.3
4. 6-9	9.7	9.4	10.1	9.6	8.4	10.3	10.1	8.9	9.6	9.7	10.1	8.9	11.8	10.6	8.1	2.2
5. 10-19	12.1	12.7	11.3	13.0	5.9	13.8	13.5	9.7	11.9	11.4	12.8	6.9	19.1	17.0	12.7	13.0
6. 20-39	10.9	11.3	10.7	11.5	7.6	12.4	12.6	8.1	10.3	9.9	12.2	5.3	15.2	14.5	15.2	17.4
7. 40 or more	18.7	28.3	9.8	20.6	3.8	22.7	20.1	15.5	16.3	17.9	18.9	4.6	21.6	19.1	42.6	56.5
Item 11010 N(Wtd)	2585	1209	1312	2133	238	581	842	775	387	1232	1254	1101	592	283	519	46

D04C: ...during the last 30 days?

1. 0 occasions	40.2	31.5	48.6	37.9	57.3	35.1	34.6	46.8	47.3	42.3	37.8	63.0	27.7	29.1	17.1	2.2
2. 1-2	18.2	17.4	19.5	18.0	23.4	15.8	18.4	20.4	16.9	18.6	18.2	18.5	20.3	18.7	14.6	10.9
3. 3-5	13.7	15.0	12.4	14.4	7.1	16.0	14.4	10.4	15.6	14.3	13.6	8.7	19.0	20.1	14.8	10.9
4. 6-9	12.2	14.1	10.2	13.0	5.0	16.2	15.4	8.5	6.2	12.0	12.4	6.1	17.0	11.8	19.4	17.4
5. 10-19	9.9	13.1	6.8	10.6	5.0	9.8	11.2	8.9	9.1	8.4	11.3	2.8	11.3	14.2	19.6	17.4
6. 20-39	3.7	5.7	1.7	3.9	1.7	3.4	3.9	4.1	3.1	3.0	4.0	.6	3.2	3.8	9.2	21.7
7. 40 or more	2.1	3.4	.8	2.3	.8	3.8	2.1	.8	1.8	1.3	2.8	.1	1.3	2.1	5.2	19.6
Item 11020 N(Wtd)	2595	1216	1316	2145	239	582	850	778	385	1235	1261	1100	595	289	521	46

D05: Think back over the LAST TWO WEEKS. How many times have you had five or more 12-ounce cans of beer (or the equivalent) in a row?

1. None	67.0	54.4	78.6	65.4	82.8	61.2	64.2	73.5	69.1	72.2	62.3	88.3	55.8	60.4	42.3	10.3
2. Once	9.0	9.7	8.4	9.7	3.9	10.2	10.2	7.2	7.6	9.0	8.2	5.2	14.2	9.1	10.3	7.7
3. Twice	7.9	12.0	4.4	8.1	5.2	9.4	6.9	7.0	9.7	6.8	9.1	2.9	11.2	14.7	11.5	10.3
4. Three to five times	10.8	15.4	6.0	11.1	6.0	12.5	12.3	8.5	9.9	9.2	12.8	2.2	14.7	11.2	23.8	28.2
5. Six to nine times	2.8	4.8	1.1	3.0	1.3	2.8	4.1	1.9	1.6	1.1	4.2	.5	2.4	3.9	6.9	7.7
6. Ten or more times	2.5	3.7	1.4	2.7	.9	4.0	2.4	1.9	1.8	1.6	3.4	1.0	1.7	1.1	5.0	33.3
Item 11030 N(Wtd)	2569	1178	1329	2132	233	577	837	773	382	1230	1225	1115	579	285	504	39

QUESTIONNAIRE FORM 4 1976	TOTAL	SEX		RACE		REGION				4YR COLLEGE PLANS		ILLICIT DRUG USE: LIFETIME				
		M	F	White	Black	NE	NC	S	W	Yes	No	None	Mari-juana Only	Few Pills	More Pills	Any Her-oin
Weighted No. of Cases:	3027	1420	1479	2352	347	711	946	915	456	1341	1420	1273	679	320	586	56
% of Weighted Total:	100.0	46.9	48.9	77.7	11.5	23.5	31.3	30.2	15.1	44.3	46.9	42.1	22.4	10.6	19.4	1.9

D06: On how many occasions (if any) have you had wine to drink...

D06A: ...in your lifetime?

1. 0 occasions	14.6	14.7	14.1	13.1	20.5	8.7	13.8	19.6	15.3	13.5	15.4	26.5	5.5	6.1	4.3	2.2
2. 1-2	16.2	15.5	17.1	16.0	19.7	11.3	15.2	20.2	17.9	14.1	17.8	22.4	15.2	10.7	7.2	11.1
3. 3-5	16.9	16.1	17.7	17.4	12.3	15.0	19.4	17.0	14.0	16.4	17.5	17.5	19.9	20.4	11.4	6.7
4. 6-9	16.1	15.1	17.2	16.4	15.2	16.0	15.7	16.2	16.8	16.8	15.6	14.9	17.4	21.4	14.3	8.9
5. 10-19	13.9	15.3	12.5	14.4	12.3	17.1	14.4	11.7	12.2	15.2	12.7	7.9	18.8	16.8	20.2	11.1
6. 20-39	10.1	8.7	11.6	10.5	9.0	14.3	9.8	7.0	10.6	11.6	9.0	5.5	12.9	11.4	16.3	15.6
7. 40 or more	12.3	14.7	9.8	12.1	10.7	17.6	11.7	8.4	13.2	12.4	11.9	5.3	10.2	13.2	26.4	44.4
Item 11040 N(Wtd)	2585	1214	1308	2130	244	586	847	766	386	1223	1250	1100	597	280	516	45

D06B: ...during the last 12 months?

1. 0 occasions	33.0	32.5	33.4	31.7	39.1	23.4	30.1	42.1	36.2	28.8	37.1	47.9	22.9	27.0	17.7	11.4
2. 1-2	24.3	23.9	24.9	24.7	22.7	22.7	26.5	24.7	21.3	23.0	26.0	26.1	27.8	23.4	18.3	15.9
3. 3-5	17.2	17.6	17.0	17.4	16.4	17.3	19.3	15.2	16.3	19.6	14.7	14.8	20.7	18.6	19.2	4.5
4. 6-9	11.0	11.2	10.8	11.2	9.2	15.6	10.6	7.8	11.3	12.1	9.6	5.5	13.7	13.5	16.7	29.5
5. 10-19	7.8	7.6	8.0	8.2	7.1	11.6	8.0	4.5	8.4	9.9	6.1	3.4	8.4	11.7	14.6	6.8
6. 20-39	4.1	4.1	4.2	4.3	3.8	6.1	3.1	4.1	3.1	4.3	3.8	1.5	4.6	3.6	8.2	13.6
7. 40 or more	2.5	3.2	1.7	2.5	1.7	3.5	2.3	1.6	3.1	2.3	2.6	.9	1.9	2.2	5.2	15.9
Item 11050 N(Wtd)	2553	1199	1292	2104	238	578	838	756	381	1213	1237	1084	593	274	515	44

D06C: ...during the last 30 days?

1. 0 occasions	65.5	66.0	65.4	65.6	62.1	54.7	66.2	72.6	66.1	62.0	68.5	79.5	59.4	57.1	50.8	31.0
2. 1-2	20.6	20.3	20.5	20.5	21.7	24.7	20.5	17.0	22.1	23.8	17.9	14.7	25.5	24.4	24.9	31.0
3. 3-5	8.2	8.0	8.1	8.5	7.2	12.8	7.8	5.0	8.2	8.0	8.3	3.1	9.6	13.1	14.1	11.9
4. 6-9	3.2	2.8	3.8	3.0	4.7	4.5	3.1	2.7	2.4	3.6	2.8	1.8	2.3	3.6	6.1	11.9
5. 10-19	1.5	1.6	1.5	1.6	1.3	1.9	1.4	1.9	.5	1.2	1.9	.6	2.0	1.1	2.9	7.1
6. 20-39	.8	.9	.5	.5	2.6	1.0	.7	.8	.5	1.1	.5	.2	1.2	.4	1.2	4.8
7. 40 or more	.2	.4	.2	.2	.4	.5	.1	-	.5	.2	.2	-	-	-	.2	4.8
Item 11060 N(Wtd)	2551	1197	1293	2101	235	576	841	753	380	1212	1236	1082	596	275	510	42

D07: Think back over the LAST TWO WEEKS. How many times have you had five or more 4-ounce glasses of wine in a row (or the equivalent, which is about three-fourths of a bottle)?

1. None	87.5	85.4	89.6	88.2	82.6	85.4	86.2	89.8	89.1	89.5	85.8	95.6	86.7	84.7	76.7	53.5
2. Once	5.6	5.6	5.5	5.5	6.4	6.8	5.5	5.3	4.4	5.4	5.3	2.5	5.3	6.5	10.9	9.3
3. Twice	4.6	6.6	2.5	4.3	6.4	4.9	5.8	3.0	4.4	3.1	6.0	1.2	5.6	6.2	8.5	23.3
4. Three to five times	1.6	1.5	1.6	1.3	3.0	2.1	1.3	1.5	1.3	1.0	2.1	.5	1.9	1.5	3.0	2.3
5. Six to nine times	.4	.5	.2	.3	-	.3	.6	.1	-	.2	.5	.1	.2	.4	.8	4.7
6. Ten or more times	.4	.3	.4	.3	1.3	.5	.6	.1	.5	.7	.2	.1	.5	.4	.4	7.0
Item 11070 N(Wtd)	2557	1195	1302	2110	236	574	840	756	387	1214	1232	1096	587	275	506	43

These next questions are about hard liquor. (Hard liquor includes whiskey, Scotch, bourbon, gin, vodka, rum, etc., or mixed drinks made with liquor.)

D08: On how many occasions (if any) have you had liquor to drink...

D08A: ...in your lifetime?

1. 0 occasions	20.2	18.3	22.0	17.0	43.8	11.8	17.4	30.1	19.6	19.8	19.9	36.6	9.0	9.1	3.9	6.7
2. 1-2	13.3	13.0	13.6	12.6	20.7	12.3	10.2	16.1	15.9	14.6	12.3	20.2	11.7	9.1	2.2	6.7
3. 3-5	12.9	13.1	12.9	13.1	12.0	12.5	15.1	9.6	15.7	14.1	12.3	16.0	14.2	13.0	6.7	2.2
4. 6-9	12.4	12.9	12.4	13.1	7.0	12.5	13.7	12.1	10.2	12.2	12.5	9.5	18.6	16.5	9.4	11.1
5. 10-19	14.6	14.9	14.2	16.1	5.8	17.0	15.3	12.3	13.8	15.6	14.0	8.3	21.4	21.8	17.5	6.7
6. 20-39	11.3	9.8	12.9	12.4	5.0	15.1	11.6	8.5	11.0	10.8	12.1	4.7	13.7	14.4	21.6	6.7
7. 40 or more	15.3	18.2	11.9	15.7	5.8	19.0	16.8	11.3	14.1	12.9	16.9	4.4	11.5	15.8	38.8	60.0
Item 11080 N(Wtd)	2587	1216	1306	2130	242	578	847	778	383	1234	1246	1103	598	285	510	45

QUESTIONNAIRE FORM 4 1976	TOTAL	SEX		RACE		REGION				4YR COLLEGE PLANS		ILLICIT DRUG USE: LIFETIME				
		M	F	White	Black	NE	NC	S	W	Yes	No	None	Mari-juana Only	Few Pills	More Pills	Any Her-oin
Weighted No. of Cases:	3027	1420	1479	2352	347	711	946	915	456	1341	1420	1273	679	320	586	56
% of Weighted Total:	100.0	46.9	48.9	77.7	11.5	23.5	31.3	30.2	15.1	44.3	46.9	42.1	22.4	10.6	19.4	1.9

D08B: ...during the last 12 months?

1. 0 occasions	30.8	28.8	32.7	27.2	59.9	22.2	25.1	42.8	32.8	30.8	30.4	52.4	17.6	16.5	9.3	6.5
2. 1-2	19.7	19.9	19.7	19.9	15.6	18.8	21.9	16.9	22.0	19.8	20.2	22.5	21.8	19.7	11.5	13.0
3. 3-5	15.2	16.9	13.8	15.9	10.5	16.5	15.5	14.2	14.7	16.2	14.6	10.9	20.9	20.1	15.5	19.6
4. 6-9	12.1	10.5	13.5	13.2	6.3	14.1	13.4	10.0	10.8	11.8	12.3	7.2	17.1	15.8	16.5	4.3
5. 10-19	11.4	11.9	11.1	12.8	5.1	14.8	11.6	9.6	9.7	11.5	11.3	4.8	13.4	16.2	20.2	15.2
6. 20-39	5.3	5.3	5.0	5.3	1.3	7.7	6.0	3.0	4.2	5.7	4.7	1.3	5.5	6.7	12.1	10.9
7. 40 or more	5.4	6.6	4.2	5.8	1.7	5.8	6.6	3.5	5.8	4.1	6.4	1.0	3.7	5.3	14.9	32.6
Item 11090 N(Wtd)	2563	1205	1292	2114	237	568	846	767	381	1218	1243	1090	597	284	504	46

D08C: ...during the last 30 days?

1. 0 occasions	55.8	55.6	56.1	52.8	76.5	47.3	53.0	62.5	61.7	56.2	55.4	75.1	49.5	45.7	29.4	20.0
2. 1-2	21.4	20.2	22.4	23.1	11.8	24.5	22.1	19.7	18.4	22.6	20.5	16.5	28.2	25.2	21.9	28.9
3. 3-5	12.2	13.2	11.1	12.8	8.0	15.0	11.7	10.2	13.4	12.1	12.4	5.6	12.8	17.0	24.1	8.9
4. 6-9	5.8	5.8	6.0	6.1	1.7	7.5	6.8	5.1	3.1	5.4	6.4	1.6	6.5	6.7	13.4	6.7
5. 10-19	3.0	3.6	2.6	3.3	1.3	3.7	4.0	1.7	2.6	2.4	3.2	.5	1.8	4.3	7.7	17.8
6. 20-39	1.0	.4	1.4	1.1	-	.9	1.7	.8	.3	.7	1.3	.5	.7	1.1	2.0	4.4
7. 40 or more	.7	1.2	.4	.7	.8	1.2	.8	.4	.5	.6	.8	-	.5	-	1.4	13.3
Item 11100 N(Wtd)	2570	1208	1297	2119	238	575	847	767	381	1227	1241	1094	596	282	507	45

D09: Think back over the LAST TWO WEEKS. How many times have you had five or more mixed drinks or shot-glasses of hard liquor in a row?

1. None	80.2	76.6	83.9	79.6	87.0	75.1	77.9	84.0	85.3	84.2	76.3	93.5	77.9	76.3	59.9	30.8
2. Once	8.7	9.4	7.9	9.2	5.2	10.1	9.5	6.8	8.6	7.8	9.9	3.3	11.9	10.0	16.0	15.4
3. Twice	5.2	6.2	3.9	5.3	4.3	7.3	4.7	5.2	2.9	4.1	6.4	1.6	4.7	7.2	12.1	10.3
4. Three to five times	3.8	5.3	2.6	3.9	2.6	4.1	5.5	3.0	1.6	3.0	4.7	1.3	4.0	3.9	9.0	10.3
5. Six to nine times	1.2	1.5	.9	1.2	.9	1.4	1.7	.7	.8	.6	1.8	.3	1.2	1.8	1.8	15.4
6. Ten or more times	.8	.9	.7	.9	.4	1.8	.7	.1	.8	.4	1.0	.1	.3	.7	1.2	20.5
Item 11110 N(Wtd)	2521	1169	1287	2089	231	562	823	763	373	1217	1200	1086	580	279	489	39

These next questions ask for your opinions about the military services in the United States.

E01: To what extent do you think the following opportunities are available to people who work in the military services?

E01A: A chance to get ahead

1. To a very little extent	5.9	8.0	3.8	5.4	8.0	5.0	7.5	3.3	9.1	5.8	6.2	5.7	6.9	5.5	4.7	17.8
2. To a little extent	11.8	13.9	10.1	11.7	10.9	11.9	10.2	12.3	14.1	9.9	12.9	11.4	9.2	13.1	14.5	15.6
3. To some extent	46.2	48.1	44.1	48.2	29.9	49.1	47.1	42.9	47.0	48.6	44.4	45.9	48.7	44.6	46.3	28.9
4. To a great extent	25.9	20.2	31.7	26.2	29.9	23.5	27.3	28.8	20.4	26.1	26.2	26.8	25.5	27.3	24.8	24.4
5. To a very great extent	10.1	9.9	10.4	8.6	21.2	10.5	7.9	12.7	8.9	9.7	10.3	10.2	9.7	9.7	9.6	13.3
Item 11120 N(Wtd)	2625	1238	1322	2130	274	579	851	813	383	1233	1281	1169	577	289	488	45

E01B: A chance to get more education

1. To a very little extent	3.5	4.8	2.2	3.1	4.4	2.9	4.5	1.7	6.0	2.5	4.4	3.7	4.2	2.1	2.5	10.9
2. To a little extent	6.3	8.5	4.2	6.0	5.1	8.7	4.7	5.5	7.9	6.5	5.9	5.4	6.7	6.9	6.8	13.0
3. To some extent	29.5	32.2	27.0	30.2	23.1	29.6	30.7	27.2	31.9	31.6	27.3	30.6	30.1	28.6	27.2	23.9
4. To a great extent	42.1	37.8	46.1	43.1	38.8	40.0	44.4	44.0	36.6	41.3	43.5	41.8	42.0	44.1	44.3	19.6
5. To a very great extent	18.6	16.8	20.5	17.6	28.6	18.9	15.9	21.6	17.8	18.1	18.8	18.4	17.0	18.6	19.2	32.6
Item 11130 N(Wtd)	2623	1241	1318	2129	273	578	850	812	382	1231	1280	1167	578	290	485	46

E01C: A chance to advance to a more responsible position

1. To a very little extent	3.4	4.8	2.1	3.1	5.1	4.2	4.2	2.2	3.1	3.2	3.4	3.3	3.8	1.0	3.5	15.6
2. To a little extent	7.2	9.7	4.8	7.1	4.4	7.1	5.9	5.5	13.6	7.4	6.9	6.2	8.8	8.0	6.8	8.9
3. To some extent	34.6	35.4	33.7	35.4	26.1	36.3	37.8	30.3	34.1	35.5	34.0	34.7	35.5	36.3	33.1	22.2
4. To a great extent	39.3	36.3	42.5	40.7	35.7	36.0	39.6	43.2	35.2	38.6	40.3	40.2	37.4	36.3	43.0	28.9
5. To a very great extent	15.5	13.8	17.0	13.7	28.7	16.2	12.6	18.7	13.9	15.3	15.5	15.7	14.6	18.0	13.6	22.2
Item 11140 N(Wtd)	2617	1236	1318	2127	272	575	851	811	381	1228	1279	1163	577	289	486	45

QUESTIONNAIRE FORM 4 1976	TOTAL	SEX		RACE		REGION				4YR COLLEGE PLANS		ILLICIT DRUG USE: LIFETIME				
		M	F	White	Black	NE	NC	S	W	Yes	No	None	Marijuana Only	Few Pills	More Pills	Any Heroin
Weighted No. of Cases:	3027	1420	1479	2352	347	711	946	915	456	1341	1420	1273	679	320	586	56
% of Weighted Total:	100.0	46.9	48.9	77.7	11.5	23.5	31.3	30.2	15.1	44.3	46.9	42.1	22.4	10.6	19.4	1.9

E01D: A chance to have a personally more fulfilling job

1. To a very little extent	5.8	7.9	3.7	5.8	5.6	6.3	5.5	4.7	7.9	7.5	4.2	5.3	6.6	3.4	7.0	20.5
2. To a little extent	12.4	16.0	8.9	13.0	6.7	12.0	12.4	10.5	17.4	14.4	10.6	11.6	12.8	13.8	13.6	13.6
3. To some extent	37.7	36.1	39.2	39.7	24.8	37.2	41.3	34.6	36.9	39.0	36.3	36.4	40.4	35.9	40.0	22.7
4. To a great extent	31.2	28.4	33.7	30.9	33.3	31.9	30.8	33.1	26.9	27.4	35.2	32.8	28.7	33.1	29.3	25.0
5. To a very great extent	12.8	11.4	14.4	10.6	29.3	12.6	10.0	17.0	10.8	11.7	13.6	14.1	11.5	13.4	10.1	20.5
Item 11150 N(Wtd)	2606	1234	1310	2118	270	573	848	806	379	1224	1277	1160	572	290	485	44

E01E: A chance to get their ideas heard

1. To a very little extent	15.6	20.4	11.0	16.2	10.3	17.3	14.3	12.8	22.0	21.6	10.1	14.2	15.8	16.5	18.0	22.2
2. To a little extent	22.1	23.5	20.9	23.4	14.5	21.7	23.2	20.4	23.9	24.5	20.0	21.2	22.9	24.2	23.2	15.6
3. To some extent	37.4	32.9	41.3	38.1	31.3	39.7	38.9	35.8	33.7	36.7	38.0	37.1	39.6	33.7	38.3	28.9
4. To a great extent	17.7	16.3	19.0	16.5	27.5	14.3	16.8	22.6	14.6	11.7	23.5	19.6	15.5	18.2	15.1	22.2
5. To a very great extent	7.3	6.9	7.8	5.7	16.4	7.1	6.9	8.5	5.8	5.6	8.3	7.9	6.2	7.0	5.4	11.1
Item 11160 N(Wtd)	2583	1223	1299	2106	262	567	841	798	377	1210	1267	1153	568	285	478	45

E02: To what extent is it likely that a person in the military can get things changed and set right if he is being treated unjustly by a superior?

1. To a very little extent	21.6	23.7	19.1	22.4	11.5	22.8	23.3	17.0	25.6	26.3	16.9	18.3	22.5	24.6	26.3	27.9
2. To a little extent	29.0	28.2	30.6	30.6	22.6	29.7	30.0	26.7	30.5	29.6	28.8	29.7	31.0	29.9	26.3	23.3
3. To some extent	34.4	31.2	37.3	34.1	36.8	33.6	33.9	36.7	31.5	32.5	36.3	36.0	32.4	32.4	34.0	25.6
4. To a great extent	11.6	12.6	11.1	10.2	22.2	10.3	10.0	15.5	8.6	9.1	13.9	12.5	10.9	9.5	10.8	14.0
5. To a very great extent	3.4	4.3	2.5	2.7	6.5	3.4	2.9	3.9	3.8	2.6	4.2	3.5	3.0	3.2	2.7	11.6
Item 11170 N(Wtd)	2561	1221	1275	2085	261	556	836	798	371	1210	1246	1138	561	284	482	43

E03: To what extent do you think there is any discrimination against women who are in the armed services?

1. To a very little extent	19.6	21.7	17.2	19.5	17.9	19.3	19.5	19.6	19.9	19.0	20.0	19.9	22.0	17.6	16.6	22.2
2. To a little extent	29.1	30.0	28.2	29.7	25.6	28.2	30.3	29.0	30.5	26.5	31.3	29.2	32.6	23.6	28.8	20.0
3. To some extent	36.8	34.5	39.6	37.1	35.9	38.0	35.9	36.3	38.0	39.2	35.0	37.7	32.1	36.3	41.0	28.9
4. To a great extent	10.2	10.0	10.3	9.8	14.5	9.9	9.6	10.9	10.0	11.1	9.2	9.6	9.4	15.1	9.5	13.3
5. To a very great extent	4.4	3.7	4.7	3.9	6.1	4.3	4.5	4.4	3.8	4.1	4.5	3.6	3.8	7.0	4.4	13.3
Item 11180 N(Wtd)	2562	1209	1289	2087	262	553	841	797	371	1206	1255	1146	555	284	476	45

E04: To what extent do you think there is any discrimination against black people who are in the armed services?

1. To a very little extent	35.3	38.9	31.8	37.3	21.8	30.2	36.1	38.9	33.5	32.3	37.6	37.2	34.6	33.3	32.6	35.6
2. To a little extent	27.2	26.7	27.7	28.3	22.9	29.3	25.8	25.3	31.3	28.4	26.4	26.8	28.5	24.6	30.4	13.3
3. To some extent	26.8	23.1	30.4	25.8	33.2	29.6	28.9	23.7	24.5	28.8	25.4	27.0	24.5	30.5	27.1	26.7
4. To a great extent	7.5	7.9	7.1	6.2	14.5	7.5	5.6	9.0	8.8	7.8	7.1	6.3	8.3	8.4	8.7	11.1
5. To a very great extent	3.2	3.4	2.8	2.5	7.6	3.4	3.6	3.2	1.9	2.8	3.6	2.7	4.1	2.8	1.5	13.3
Item 11190 N(Wtd)	2550	1209	1278	2073	262	557	840	790	364	1198	1250	1135	555	285	473	45

E05: Do you personally feel that you would receive more just and fair treatment as a civilian or as a member of the military service?

1. Much more fair in the military service	6.2	8.0	4.8	5.2	13.9	5.0	5.0	8.4	6.1	5.2	7.1	6.8	5.5	6.3	5.0	4.8
2. More fair in the military service	11.8	12.1	11.7	11.7	15.1	13.1	13.3	10.6	9.1	11.6	11.7	12.0	12.5	10.9	12.6	7.1
3. About the same	44.6	41.9	47.4	44.9	41.3	41.5	45.7	47.2	41.3	42.6	47.1	45.5	43.3	48.4	41.5	38.1
4. More fair as a civilian	14.1	17.7	10.7	15.1	8.1	14.4	14.9	12.6	14.9	16.7	11.0	13.0	14.8	14.0	16.4	14.3
5. Much more fair as a civilian	9.3	11.9	6.7	9.9	5.4	10.8	8.5	8.0	11.2	11.0	7.5	7.8	11.3	8.1	10.5	16.7
6. Question not appropriate for me	14.0	8.5	18.8	13.2	16.2	15.3	12.4	13.1	17.1	12.8	15.6	14.9	12.3	11.9	14.5	19.0
Item 11200 N(Wtd)	2563	1206	1294	2086	259	557	832	799	375	1203	1254	1143	559	285	477	42

QUESTIONNAIRE FORM 4 1976	TOTAL	SEX		RACE		REGION				4YR COLLEGE PLANS		ILLICIT DRUG USE: LIFETIME				
		M	F	White	Black	NE	NC	S	W	Yes	No	None	Mari-juana Only	Few Pills	More Pills	Any Her-oin
Weighted No. of Cases:	3027	1420	1479	2352	347	711	946	915	456	1341	1420	1273	679	320	586	56
% of Weighted Total:	100.0	46.9	48.9	77.7	11.5	23.5	31.3	30.2	15.1	44.3	46.9	42.1	22.4	10.6	19.4	1.9

E06: In some countries the military forces have taken over and thrown out the civilian government. Do you think there is any chance that this could happen in the United States?

5. It probably will happen in the U.S.	3.3	3.6	3.0	2.2	9.4	2.3	3.5	3.9	3.0	2.0	4.1	3.3	3.4	1.4	2.3	7.1
4. It may happen in the U.S.	10.5	9.9	10.9	8.9	20.3	9.5	8.5	13.6	10.0	8.8	12.0	10.8	11.3	7.4	9.5	16.7
3. It is certainly possible, but not very likely	44.4	41.6	47.1	45.3	39.1	41.2	45.9	43.6	47.7	44.6	44.4	44.0	41.9	50.2	46.4	38.1
2. It is nearly impossible	30.5	31.9	29.6	32.7	18.0	35.1	30.9	28.1	27.5	33.3	28.5	30.2	29.7	33.3	32.6	31.0
1. It could never happen in the U.S.	11.3	13.2	9.5	10.9	13.3	12.0	11.2	10.7	11.9	11.4	11.0	11.6	13.7	7.7	9.2	9.5
Item 11210 N(Wtd)	2550	1208	1280	2077	256	558	828	793	371	1206	1237	1135	556	285	476	42

E07: If YOU felt that it was necessary for the U.S. to fight in some future war, how likely is it that you would volunteer for military service in that war?

1. I'm sure that I would volunteer	9.5	14.2	5.0	9.6	8.2	7.3	9.0	11.6	9.2	8.2	10.9	9.0	10.4	7.4	10.8	7.0
2. I would very likely volunteer	6.6	10.5	2.9	6.5	7.8	5.0	5.9	7.7	8.4	6.6	6.7	6.3	8.8	6.3	4.0	18.6
3. I would probably volunteer	14.0	18.5	10.1	13.5	14.5	11.3	14.9	16.5	10.6	14.5	13.5	12.9	14.2	16.5	12.7	25.6
4. I would probably NOT volunteer	22.2	21.3	22.7	23.2	16.4	22.3	22.4	22.5	20.9	22.2	22.3	24.7	21.9	20.0	19.4	9.3
5. I would very likely NOT volunteer	8.8	6.7	11.0	9.4	5.1	10.4	8.9	7.8	8.1	8.9	8.9	8.9	8.6	9.1	9.0	2.3
6. I would definitely NOT volunteer	14.8	11.1	18.4	14.0	22.3	16.8	13.1	13.4	18.4	14.6	14.7	15.0	14.0	17.9	14.4	7.0
7. In my opinion, there is no such thing as a "necessary" war	24.2	17.6	29.8	23.8	25.8	26.8	25.8	20.6	24.7	24.8	23.0	23.2	22.1	22.8	29.8	30.2
Item 11220 N(Wtd)	2558	1205	1291	2089	256	560	833	796	369	1210	1242	1136	557	285	480	43

E08: How closely do your ideas agree with your PARENTS' ideas about (...)

Our ideas are...

E08A: What you should do with your life

1. Very similar	25.5	21.8	28.4	25.1	27.3	24.6	24.0	26.8	27.2	29.6	21.8	29.9	20.1	28.2	21.0	15.6
2. Mostly similar	44.2	45.6	43.2	46.9	29.2	45.8	47.7	38.1	46.1	47.7	41.3	45.4	47.5	43.3	41.8	22.2
3. Mostly different	13.2	14.8	11.8	13.4	12.9	13.3	12.4	14.4	12.7	10.1	15.7	9.8	14.8	14.8	17.0	24.4
4. Very different	10.2	9.0	11.5	8.6	20.8	9.9	9.2	13.1	7.1	7.5	12.8	9.1	9.8	9.3	12.3	22.2
8. Don't know	6.9	8.7	5.1	5.9	9.8	6.4	6.7	7.5	7.1	5.2	8.5	5.8	7.7	4.1	7.9	15.6
Item 11230 N(Wtd)	2643	1236	1343	2150	264	578	863	810	393	1240	1292	1162	581	291	505	45

E08B: What you do in your leisure time

1. Very similar	9.2	7.7	10.4	9.3	7.6	9.2	8.8	8.8	11.0	10.6	7.8	13.1	7.1	6.9	4.7	4.4
2. Mostly similar	32.6	28.7	36.3	34.2	26.0	30.5	33.9	32.3	33.7	34.8	31.6	39.0	32.4	27.9	24.3	11.1
3. Mostly different	28.5	31.8	26.0	29.1	26.3	28.2	29.2	28.7	27.6	29.3	27.2	26.8	29.6	33.1	28.3	24.4
4. Very different	25.4	26.6	23.8	24.1	30.9	28.4	24.2	25.6	23.0	21.6	28.9	18.0	25.5	29.0	38.7	42.2
8. Don't know	4.2	5.2	3.4	3.3	9.2	4.0	3.9	4.5	4.8	3.8	4.7	3.3	5.4	3.4	4.2	17.8
Item 11240 N(Wtd)	2638	1234	1341	2148	262	577	861	808	392	1241	1289	1162	577	290	506	45

E08C: How you dress--what clothes you wear

1. Very similar	21.2	16.7	25.5	21.6	23.5	20.5	20.1	22.7	22.0	23.9	18.6	23.2	20.2	20.3	19.0	11.1
2. Mostly similar	42.2	40.4	44.5	44.8	25.4	41.2	43.9	38.7	46.8	44.0	41.3	44.4	44.7	41.7	37.2	20.0
3. Mostly different	18.9	23.4	14.6	18.6	19.6	20.1	19.6	18.6	16.1	18.7	18.9	17.6	16.9	22.1	22.6	24.4
4. Very different	14.6	14.9	13.6	12.4	24.6	15.1	13.8	16.9	11.0	10.9	17.9	12.4	15.0	13.1	17.2	28.9
8. Don't know	3.1	4.6	1.8	2.6	6.5	2.9	2.6	3.2	4.1	2.5	3.3	2.3	3.3	2.8	4.0	13.3
Item 11250 N(Wtd)	2631	1229	1339	2141	260	577	856	807	391	1235	1288	1159	575	290	505	45

QUESTIONNAIRE FORM 4 1976	TOTAL	SEX		RACE		REGION				4YR COLLEGE PLANS		ILLICIT DRUG USE: LIFETIME				
		M	F	White	Black	NE	NC	S	W	Yes	No	None	Marijuana Only	Few Pills	More Pills	Any Heroin
Weighted No. of Cases:	3027	1420	1479	2352	347	711	946	915	456	1341	1420	1273	679	320	586	56
% of Weighted Total:	100.0	46.9	48.9	77.7	11.5	23.5	31.3	30.2	15.1	44.3	46.9	42.1	22.4	10.6	19.4	1.9
E08D: How you spend your money																
1. Very similar	12.3	10.0	14.3	11.9	16.0	11.1	12.6	11.9	14.1	14.5	10.4	16.1	9.6	10.1	8.3	2.2
2. Mostly similar	34.5	30.0	39.0	36.2	26.6	35.1	34.8	31.2	39.9	38.8	31.0	39.3	36.3	32.3	26.1	15.6
3. Mostly different	23.9	25.3	22.6	24.7	17.6	22.6	24.2	26.7	18.9	23.1	24.7	22.1	23.7	28.5	25.7	24.4
4. Very different	25.3	29.8	20.8	23.3	35.2	26.3	24.5	27.1	22.3	20.7	29.2	18.9	26.7	25.3	34.7	46.7
8. Don't know	4.0	5.0	3.2	3.7	4.7	5.0	3.9	3.0	4.9	3.0	4.6	3.5	3.7	4.2	5.3	11.1
Item 11260 N(Wtd)	2628	1225	1338	2143	256	579	854	804	391	1233	1286	1157	573	288	505	45
E08E: What things are O.K. to do when you are on a date																
1. Very similar	14.6	12.7	16.7	14.2	18.1	12.4	13.6	16.4	16.4	14.7	14.3	18.9	11.6	12.0	9.6	9.1
2. Mostly similar	31.4	29.4	33.3	33.0	23.2	30.4	32.5	30.7	32.1	35.0	28.9	35.1	31.7	28.5	25.5	36.4
3. Mostly different	19.6	19.8	19.3	19.9	18.1	17.1	20.7	21.3	17.7	20.4	18.8	16.4	21.7	24.1	23.7	11.4
4. Very different	21.8	21.9	21.3	20.8	25.2	25.4	20.4	21.3	20.5	17.9	25.8	16.5	21.0	25.8	31.3	27.3
8. Don't know	12.6	16.2	9.4	12.1	15.4	14.7	12.9	10.4	13.3	12.2	12.3	13.1	13.9	9.6	9.8	15.9
Item 11270 N(Wtd)	2611	1217	1330	2130	254	566	856	799	390	1224	1280	1152	567	291	502	44
E08F: Whether it is O.K. to drink																
1. Very similar	21.9	18.8	24.5	22.1	19.4	15.7	20.9	23.5	29.7	23.4	20.2	30.6	11.9	14.1	19.0	15.9
2. Mostly similar	30.1	31.6	29.0	31.6	22.9	34.4	29.8	26.2	32.8	33.5	27.4	31.8	32.6	31.6	24.0	20.5
3. Mostly different	20.5	20.5	20.6	20.3	22.5	21.2	22.9	19.4	16.5	19.8	21.4	16.7	24.2	25.1	22.2	31.8
4. Very different	22.5	23.3	21.8	22.0	25.7	22.6	21.4	26.5	16.3	18.7	25.6	16.0	24.9	25.4	31.1	22.7
8. Don't know	5.0	5.8	4.1	4.0	9.5	6.1	4.9	4.5	4.7	4.5	5.4	5.0	6.3	3.4	3.6	9.1
Item 11280 N(Wtd)	2611	1215	1332	2131	253	572	855	797	387	1229	1276	1150	570	291	501	44
E08G: Whether it is O.K. to use marijuana																
1. Very similar	36.4	31.5	41.0	38.0	28.2	27.1	36.3	42.1	38.6	37.7	35.6	61.9	18.5	21.1	11.0	4.5
2. Mostly similar	13.1	14.2	12.2	13.3	11.0	13.7	12.8	10.2	18.4	14.8	11.7	14.6	13.2	11.4	11.4	15.9
3. Mostly different	10.0	11.3	8.6	10.0	9.4	11.1	11.6	7.2	10.6	11.4	8.5	4.9	13.7	15.6	14.3	15.9
4. Very different	33.1	34.4	31.6	32.6	35.7	38.1	31.9	33.5	27.2	29.3	36.6	11.1	45.4	45.3	58.4	56.8
8. Don't know	7.5	8.6	6.5	6.1	15.3	10.0	7.5	7.0	5.2	6.9	7.7	7.5	9.3	6.6	5.0	6.8
Item 11290 N(Wtd)	2610	1214	1333	2130	255	569	854	801	386	1227	1277	1152	568	289	502	44
E08H: Whether it is O.K. to use other drugs																
1. Very similar	50.0	46.1	54.3	52.8	37.3	44.6	49.8	52.1	54.0	55.0	45.6	69.9	51.6	35.9	16.9	2.3
2. Mostly similar	13.9	14.3	13.0	14.2	11.1	16.5	14.3	11.2	14.7	15.5	12.5	13.3	15.5	17.1	12.7	9.1
3. Mostly different	5.0	5.4	4.7	4.7	7.5	3.4	6.0	5.3	4.4	4.7	5.0	2.3	3.2	10.1	9.1	15.9
4. Very different	24.0	26.1	21.6	23.0	27.4	27.5	23.1	23.6	21.7	18.9	28.7	8.4	22.4	28.6	54.0	61.4
8. Don't know	7.2	8.1	6.3	5.4	17.1	8.2	6.8	7.8	5.2	5.8	8.2	5.9	7.3	8.4	7.1	9.1
Item 11300 N(Wtd)	2599	1207	1329	2120	252	563	853	796	387	1225	1270	1148	562	287	504	44
E08I: What values are important in life																
1. Very similar	30.4	29.9	31.0	29.7	39.2	27.8	28.5	34.1	31.0	32.7	28.1	39.3	29.5	23.8	16.7	13.6
2. Mostly similar	40.2	40.0	41.2	42.6	27.8	39.4	41.7	38.8	41.5	42.3	39.2	38.5	42.2	42.3	43.4	38.6
3. Mostly different	14.2	13.9	14.1	14.0	14.1	17.6	13.9	13.3	11.5	12.2	15.6	9.5	13.9	19.9	21.7	15.9
4. Very different	10.2	10.8	9.1	8.9	12.9	9.8	10.3	10.3	10.5	8.9	11.1	7.7	8.6	9.8	14.7	27.3
8. Don't know	5.0	5.6	4.6	4.8	5.9	5.6	5.7	3.6	5.1	4.0	5.9	4.9	6.0	4.2	3.4	4.5
Item 11310 N(Wtd)	2605	1211	1331	2125	255	569	848	798	390	1224	1273	1153	567	286	502	44
E08J: The value of education																
1. Very similar	48.3	48.4	48.3	47.4	53.5	46.1	44.3	51.3	54.0	57.7	39.7	53.4	47.4	46.4	41.6	25.6
2. Mostly similar	35.8	33.6	38.1	38.7	20.7	34.4	40.9	32.5	33.4	33.1	38.8	34.3	38.1	35.3	38.0	34.9
3. Mostly different	8.0	9.0	7.0	7.5	10.9	11.0	6.9	8.4	5.4	5.0	10.9	6.1	7.5	10.7	10.4	16.3
4. Very different	6.2	6.4	5.6	5.0	11.7	6.3	5.8	7.0	5.4	3.2	8.7	4.5	5.8	6.2	8.2	18.6
8. Don't know	1.7	2.5	1.1	1.5	3.1	2.1	2.2	1.0	1.5	.9	2.0	1.7	1.1	1.0	1.6	7.0
Item 11320 N(Wtd)	2613	1216	1332	2128	256	575	849	800	389	1228	1276	1152	570	289	502	43

QUESTIONNAIRE FORM 4 1976	TOTAL	SEX		RACE		REGION				4YR COLLEGE PLANS		ILLICIT DRUG USE: LIFETIME				
		M	F	White	Black	NE	NC	S	W	Yes	No	None	Mari-juana Only	Few Pills	More Pills	Any Her-oin
Weighted No. of Cases: % of Weighted Total:	3027 100.0	1420 46.9	1479 48.9	2352 77.7	347 11.5	711 23.5	946 31.3	915 30.2	456 15.1	1341 44.3	1420 46.9	1273 42.1	679 22.4	320 10.6	586 19.4	56 1.9
E08K: What are appropriate roles for women																
1. Very similar	25.3	19.5	30.1	25.2	30.6	21.8	23.0	29.7	26.3	27.3	23.4	30.1	22.3	25.4	19.5	9.5
2. Mostly similar	40.7	41.2	40.8	43.2	24.2	39.8	43.9	36.9	42.7	40.9	41.2	40.8	41.3	42.9	39.8	40.5
3. Mostly different	14.1	15.2	12.9	14.1	13.1	15.4	14.5	13.5	12.8	13.3	14.6	11.8	14.8	16.0	16.7	21.4
4. Very different	8.3	7.4	9.1	6.8	15.1	8.3	7.9	9.6	6.5	7.2	9.3	6.6	7.3	5.9	11.7	21.4
8. Don't know	11.6	16.7	7.1	10.7	17.1	14.5	10.7	10.4	12.0	11.4	11.6	10.5	14.5	9.8	12.3	7.1
Item 11330 N(Wtd)	2589	1197	1329	2111	252	565	848	792	384	1221	1263	1149	560	287	497	42
E08L: Conservation and pollution issues																
1. Very similar	23.2	22.4	23.5	23.2	23.0	22.3	21.8	25.6	22.9	25.7	20.7	26.8	22.1	23.6	18.1	14.0
2. Mostly similar	37.3	37.0	37.9	39.7	24.6	36.9	39.1	35.3	37.9	41.8	34.5	36.9	39.5	40.3	35.9	23.3
3. Mostly different	9.9	12.6	7.4	9.5	11.1	10.5	9.7	10.5	8.3	8.9	10.5	8.6	9.4	11.8	11.2	20.9
4. Very different	6.1	7.2	4.9	5.3	11.1	4.8	5.7	6.4	8.1	4.6	7.4	5.2	4.8	4.5	8.7	20.9
8. Don't know	23.5	20.7	26.4	22.4	30.2	25.5	23.8	22.2	22.6	19.0	26.9	22.6	24.4	19.4	26.0	20.9
Item 11340 N(Wtd)	2586	1207	1318	2110	252	564	845	793	385	1220	1262	1143	565	288	493	43
E08M: Racial issues																
1. Very similar	24.7	23.7	25.4	23.6	36.3	23.0	23.2	28.5	22.6	27.3	22.2	28.5	23.1	22.8	20.6	14.0
2. Mostly similar	32.0	35.1	29.6	33.7	24.7	29.8	32.9	33.3	30.4	33.9	30.5	30.8	36.3	31.1	31.3	30.2
3. Mostly different	14.6	15.1	14.4	15.5	8.4	17.2	14.5	12.7	14.8	17.5	12.0	14.1	15.1	18.7	13.7	16.3
4. Very different	10.7	9.5	11.2	10.2	8.8	12.1	10.7	9.0	12.2	9.5	11.6	8.4	8.5	11.8	15.1	32.7
8. Don't know	18.1	16.5	19.4	17.1	22.3	17.9	18.7	16.6	19.7	11.7	23.7	18.2	17.1	15.6	19.2	9.3
Item 11350 N(Wtd)	2586	1205	1317	2111	251	564	844	793	385	1215	1264	1141	562	289	496	43
E08N: Religion																
1. Very similar	34.3	30.1	37.5	32.4	50.2	28.0	32.2	40.8	34.8	35.6	33.2	41.7	32.0	31.0	23.2	22.7
2. Mostly similar	32.6	33.7	31.8	35.0	21.1	33.1	34.1	32.6	29.1	33.9	31.9	31.2	37.6	32.8	31.3	27.3
3. Mostly different	14.0	15.0	13.3	14.6	10.4	17.7	13.2	12.8	13.0	14.5	13.4	11.3	13.6	16.7	19.2	20.5
4. Very different	11.1	12.4	10.1	10.6	11.2	12.6	11.7	8.9	11.9	10.0	12.0	8.7	9.9	10.5	16.5	18.2
8. Don't know	8.0	8.9	7.3	7.4	6.8	8.8	8.8	5.1	10.6	6.1	9.5	7.1	6.9	9.4	9.9	13.6
Item 11360 N(Wtd)	2587	1206	1319	2109	251	565	848	789	385	1223	1257	1138	566	287	496	44
E08O: Politics																
1. Very similar	16.3	16.7	15.7	16.0	17.8	16.2	15.5	18.8	13.0	17.1	15.8	19.1	15.2	15.9	11.2	15.9
2. Mostly similar	31.6	33.2	30.5	33.9	22.1	26.4	33.5	33.5	31.3	34.9	29.1	33.4	31.3	32.9	28.7	22.7
3. Mostly different	13.3	15.5	11.2	13.8	7.9	18.1	12.5	9.4	16.1	14.9	11.8	12.3	13.3	13.1	17.1	9.1
4. Very different	8.7	10.5	7.1	8.0	11.5	9.0	8.6	8.4	9.3	7.4	9.6	7.2	8.0	9.3	10.0	27.3
8. Don't know	30.0	24.1	35.5	28.4	40.7	30.3	30.0	29.8	30.3	25.7	33.8	27.9	32.3	29.1	32.7	25.0
Item 11370 N(Wtd)	2601	1214	1322	2119	253	568	851	796	386	1222	1270	1147	566	289	498	44

The next questions ask about how your parents and your friends feel about some of the things we have been asking you about.

E09: How do you think your PARENTS feel (or would feel) about YOU doing each of the following things?

E09A: Smoking one or more packs of cigarettes per day

	TOTAL	M	F	White	Black	NE	NC	S	W	Yes	No	None	Mari-juana Only	Few Pills	More Pills	Any Her-oin
1. Not disapprove	12.4	13.7	11.0	11.5	15.3	14.1	12.9	11.4	10.9	8.6	15.5	8.0	12.1	13.0	20.1	31.8
2. Disapprove	36.3	37.7	35.0	36.2	38.3	35.7	37.7	38.1	30.6	35.1	37.9	30.4	36.5	45.2	41.6	54.5
3. Strongly disapprove	51.3	48.7	54.1	52.3	46.4	50.3	49.5	50.6	58.3	56.4	46.5	61.6	51.6	41.8	38.2	13.6
Item 11380 N(Wtd)	2625	1224	1332	2131	261	575	855	809	386	1234	1274	1148	578	292	502	44

QUESTIONNAIRE FORM 4 1976	TOTAL	SEX		RACE		REGION				4YR COLLEGE PLANS		ILLICIT DRUG USE: LIFETIME				
		M	F	White	Black	NE	NC	S	W	Yes	No	None	Marijuana Only	Few Pills	More Pills	Any Heroin
Weighted No. of Cases:	3027	1420	1479	2352	347	711	946	915	456	1341	1420	1273	679	320	586	56
% of Weighted Total:	100.0	46.9	48.9	77.7	11.5	23.5	31.3	30.2	15.1	44.3	46.9	42.1	22.4	10.6	19.4	1.9
E09B: Trying marijuana (pot, grass) once or twice.																
1. Not disapprove	12.6	13.5	11.8	12.3	12.8	13.9	13.4	9.7	15.4	13.8	11.1	4.4	13.1	17.4	24.9	44.7
2. Disapprove	27.1	29.7	24.3	27.4	23.4	29.7	27.4	24.6	27.8	27.4	26.3	18.5	34.8	31.1	32.5	44.7
3. Strongly disapprove	60.3	56.9	64.0	60.3	63.8	56.5	59.3	65.8	56.6	58.8	62.6	77.1	52.2	51.5	42.6	10.6
Item 11390 N(Wtd)	2638	1234	1335	2142	265	575	860	813	389	1235	1284	1155	580	293	502	47
E09C: Smoking marijuana occasionally																
1. Not disapprove	7.0	8.6	5.4	6.1	10.0	8.0	6.8	5.7	8.5	6.7	6.8	2.9	5.5	8.2	13.5	40.4
2. Disapprove	23.3	24.7	21.7	23.3	24.3	25.6	21.9	22.9	23.7	22.6	23.8	12.8	28.8	27.6	35.7	38.3
3. Strongly disapprove	69.7	66.8	72.9	70.6	66.0	66.4	71.3	71.3	67.5	70.8	69.5	84.4	65.6	64.2	50.8	21.3
Item 11400 N(Wtd)	2629	1231	1329	2137	259	574	857	811	388	1233	1280	1152	579	293	498	47
E09D: Smoking marijuana regularly																
1. Not disapprove	3.7	5.2	2.3	2.7	7.7	3.0	3.8	3.8	4.6	2.8	4.4	2.2	2.2	4.4	5.8	23.4
2. Disapprove	17.3	20.2	14.4	16.3	21.1	18.8	16.2	17.1	18.0	14.9	19.0	8.9	18.8	23.2	28.0	38.3
3. Strongly disapprove	79.0	74.6	83.4	81.0	71.3	78.0	80.0	79.2	77.6	82.3	76.5	88.9	79.0	72.4	66.2	38.3
Item 11410 N(Wtd)	2635	1231	1334	2141	261	574	860	812	389	1235	1283	1151	581	293	503	47
E09E: Trying LSD once or twice																
1. Not disapprove	2.6	3.4	1.7	1.6	5.4	2.4	1.8	3.8	2.3	1.9	3.2	2.4	1.6	2.7	2.0	19.1
2. Disapprove	10.4	12.4	8.6	8.9	16.9	10.3	9.7	10.9	11.3	9.3	11.3	7.3	10.3	13.0	13.3	25.5
3. Strongly disapprove	87.0	84.2	89.6	89.4	77.8	87.3	88.6	85.3	86.6	88.8	85.5	90.3	88.3	84.2	84.7	53.2
Item 11420 N(Wtd)	2632	1229	1334	2138	261	573	856	815	388	1235	1280	1151	580	292	502	47
E09F: Trying an amphetamine (upper, pep pill, bennie, speed) once or twice																
1. Not disapprove	2.9	3.6	2.1	2.0	5.0	2.1	2.7	3.3	3.9	2.3	3.2	2.0	1.2	3.8	3.0	27.7
2. Disapprove	13.0	14.8	11.0	11.8	16.8	13.4	11.6	12.6	16.5	12.2	13.7	8.5	10.7	15.7	22.5	25.5
3. Strongly disapprove	84.1	81.5	86.9	86.1	78.6	84.5	85.7	83.9	79.6	85.6	83.2	89.5	88.1	80.5	74.5	46.8
Item 11430 N(Wtd)	2634	1233	1333	2140	262	575	856	816	388	1233	1282	1149	582	293	502	47
E09G: Taking one or two drinks nearly every day																
1. Not disapprove	10.0	14.2	6.0	9.1	12.3	9.3	11.0	9.3	10.1	6.5	12.7	6.4	9.0	10.6	15.0	47.8
2. Disapprove	25.0	29.2	21.0	24.7	23.8	26.4	26.6	21.5	26.9	24.0	25.9	20.2	28.9	25.7	29.6	26.1
3. Strongly disapprove	65.0	56.6	73.0	66.2	63.8	64.3	62.4	69.2	62.7	69.5	61.4	73.3	61.9	63.7	55.4	26.1
Item 11440 N(Wtd)	2628	1228	1331	2138	260	572	857	814	386	1230	1278	1151	578	292	500	46
E09H: Taking four or five drinks nearly every day																
1. Not disapprove	3.5	5.1	1.9	2.7	5.0	3.3	4.1	3.5	2.3	2.4	4.3	2.4	2.4	3.7	3.6	27.7
2. Disapprove	16.1	20.7	11.8	14.9	20.7	15.3	15.3	16.8	17.8	11.8	19.8	11.9	16.3	17.0	21.6	31.9
3. Strongly disapprove	80.5	74.1	86.3	82.4	74.3	81.4	80.7	79.8	79.8	85.8	75.9	85.6	81.5	78.9	74.8	38.3
Item 11450 N(Wtd)	2630	1226	1336	2139	261	574	859	810	387	1229	1283	1153	577	294	500	47
E09I: Having five or more drinks once or twice each weekend																
1. Not disapprove	14.1	19.1	9.5	13.9	11.9	15.1	17.0	9.8	15.2	9.9	17.5	6.8	16.0	13.7	24.6	56.5
2. Disapprove	26.6	28.3	24.5	26.4	24.9	28.9	28.1	22.7	27.8	26.0	27.5	21.3	27.1	34.2	32.3	23.9
3. Strongly disapprove	59.3	52.7	66.1	59.8	63.2	56.0	54.8	67.7	57.0	64.2	55.1	71.9	56.9	52.4	43.3	19.6
Item 11460 N(Wtd)	2627	1228	1329	2135	261	571	858	810	388	1228	1281	1148	582	292	499	46

QUESTIONNAIRE FORM 4
1976

	TOTAL	SEX		RACE		REGION				4YR COLLEGE PLANS		ILLICIT DRUG USE: LIFETIME				
		M	F	White	Black	NE	NC	S	W	Yes	No	None	Marijuana Only	Few Pills	More Pills	Any Heroin
Weighted No. of Cases:	3027	1420	1479	2352	347	711	946	915	456	1341	1420	1273	679	320	586	56
% of Weighted Total:	100.0	46.9	48.9	77.7	11.5	23.5	31.3	30.2	15.1	44.3	46.9	42.1	22.4	10.6	19.4	1.9

E10: Some people like school very much. Others don't. How do you feel about going to school?

	TOTAL	M	F	White	Black	NE	NC	S	W	Yes	No	None	Mari-juana Only	Few Pills	More Pills	Any Heroin
5. I like school very much	13.6	10.4	16.4	11.7	28.2	9.4	12.3	17.9	14.0	18.5	9.4	18.0	10.4	11.7	8.9	7.0
4. I like school quite a lot	29.2	28.0	30.7	29.6	29.0	29.4	29.5	28.3	30.1	35.0	23.6	32.3	29.8	27.8	24.1	16.3
3. I like school some	40.2	43.2	36.9	41.4	30.2	40.7	40.6	39.1	40.4	35.7	44.5	37.0	45.0	38.5	42.3	34.9
2. I don't like school very much	10.6	10.6	10.7	11.1	7.1	11.3	11.6	9.2	10.1	8.0	13.1	8.6	9.5	15.1	14.5	11.6
1. I don't like school at all	6.5	7.8	5.3	6.2	5.1	9.2	6.0	5.6	5.4	2.9	9.3	4.2	5.4	7.2	10.3	30.2
Item 7630 N(Wtd)	2619	1219	1333	2138	255	575	854	805	386	1230	1273	1153	578	291	497	43

E11: The next questions are about some things which may have happened TO YOU while you you were at school (inside or outside or in a schoolbus). During the LAST 12 MONTHS, how often...

E11A: Has something of yours (worth under $50) been stolen?

	TOTAL	M	F	White	Black	NE	NC	S	W	Yes	No	None	Mari-juana Only	Few Pills	More Pills	Any Heroin
1. Not at all	63.8	58.0	69.5	63.0	65.8	65.3	63.9	64.2	60.2	60.8	66.5	68.4	60.2	56.8	61.9	42.6
2. Once	23.3	26.3	20.4	23.9	20.4	21.7	23.7	21.8	27.6	25.5	21.4	22.3	25.8	28.4	21.3	14.9
3. Twice	7.9	8.6	6.8	7.8	11.2	8.6	8.2	7.9	6.0	8.6	7.0	5.2	9.5	8.9	10.1	23.4
4. 3 or 4 times	3.3	4.4	2.3	3.5	1.5	3.0	2.9	3.7	3.4	3.8	3.0	2.8	2.4	4.8	3.8	6.4
5. 5 or more times	1.8	2.8	1.1	1.7	1.2	1.4	1.3	2.4	2.6	1.3	2.1	1.3	1.9	1.0	2.8	12.8
Item 9871 N(Wtd)	2610	1216	1326	2119	260	568	856	802	384	1224	1269	1144	578	292	494	47

E11B: Has something of yours (worth over $50) been stolen?

	TOTAL	M	F	White	Black	NE	NC	S	W	Yes	No	None	Mari-juana Only	Few Pills	More Pills	Any Heroin
1. Not at all	92.2	90.2	94.4	92.6	91.2	93.4	91.4	91.8	93.0	91.8	93.0	95.0	91.2	89.3	90.8	62.2
2. Once	6.1	7.5	4.4	6.2	4.2	4.9	7.0	6.5	4.9	6.7	5.1	4.3	7.1	7.6	7.2	22.2
3. Twice	1.0	1.3	.8	.7	2.3	1.0	1.2	.7	1.0	1.0	1.0	.6	.7	2.1	1.0	4.4
4. 3 or 4 times	.4	.8	-	.4	1.1	.3	.4	.5	.5	.5	.4	.1	.9	.7	.4	2.2
5. 5 or more times	.3	.2	.5	.1	1.1	.2	.1	.5	.5	.2	.6	.1	.2	.3	.4	6.7
Item 9872 N(Wtd)	2616	1219	1329	2124	262	572	856	803	385	1231	1268	1149	579	289	498	45

E11C: Has someone deliberately damaged your property (your car, clothing, etc.)?

	TOTAL	M	F	White	Black	NE	NC	S	W	Yes	No	None	Mari-juana Only	Few Pills	More Pills	Any Heroin
1. Not at all	74.2	66.0	81.9	74.9	70.2	77.7	72.8	74.4	71.1	75.6	73.6	77.8	73.6	73.6	69.8	46.8
2. Once	16.9	20.7	13.4	16.0	24.4	14.6	17.9	17.2	18.1	16.7	16.8	14.9	17.9	16.2	19.6	27.7
3. Twice	5.5	8.5	2.6	5.9	2.7	4.7	6.2	5.3	6.0	4.9	5.9	5.0	4.9	7.7	5.8	6.4
4. 3 or 4 times	2.2	3.1	1.4	2.0	2.3	1.8	2.5	2.3	2.1	1.9	2.3	1.4	2.4	2.5	3.4	2.1
5. 5 or more times	1.2	1.7	.7	1.2	1.2	1.1	.8	1.0	2.6	.9	1.4	1.0	1.0	.4	1.2	14.9
Item 9873 N(Wtd)	2605	1216	1324	2118	258	570	857	798	381	1226	1263	1147	576	284	496	47

E11D: Has someone injured you with a weapon (like a knife, gun, or club)?

	TOTAL	M	F	White	Black	NE	NC	S	W	Yes	No	None	Mari-juana Only	Few Pills	More Pills	Any Heroin
1. Not at all	94.3	91.2	97.5	95.0	92.3	93.0	94.4	95.1	94.0	96.4	92.8	96.4	94.3	94.1	92.6	61.7
2. Once	3.4	5.4	1.4	3.3	4.6	3.9	3.4	3.1	3.6	2.4	4.4	2.4	3.6	3.4	4.6	14.9
3. Twice	1.2	1.9	.5	.8	1.9	1.6	1.5	1.0	.3	.6	1.4	.8	1.2	.7	2.0	8.5
4. 3 or 4 times	.5	.6	.2	.4	1.1	.9	.2	.7	.3	.4	.5	.3	-	1.4	.6	2.1
5. 5 or more times	.6	.9	.3	.5	.4	.5	.5	.2	1.8	.2	.9	.1	1.0	.3	.4	12.8
Item 9874 N(Wtd)	2616	1221	1328	2126	261	571	858	803	384	1229	1271	1150	578	290	497	47

E11E: Has someone threatened you with a weapon, but not actually injured you?

	TOTAL	M	F	White	Black	NE	NC	S	W	Yes	No	None	Mari-juana Only	Few Pills	More Pills	Any Heroin
1. Not at all	87.5	81.6	93.1	88.6	83.5	87.7	87.7	87.2	87.0	89.3	86.6	91.7	87.3	85.1	82.6	53.2
2. Once	7.5	10.2	5.0	7.0	9.2	7.6	7.0	7.6	8.3	7.2	7.7	5.0	7.8	10.4	10.5	14.9
3. Twice	2.4	3.7	1.1	2.1	3.1	1.6	2.6	3.1	2.1	1.9	2.6	1.3	2.8	2.1	3.8	10.6
4. 3 or 4 times	1.3	2.0	.4	1.2	1.1	2.1	1.6	.6	.5	.8	1.4	1.2	.3	1.7	1.6	4.3
5. 5 or more times	1.3	2.3	.5	1.1	2.7	1.1	1.1	1.5	2.3	.8	1.7	.7	1.7	.7	1.4	17.0
Item 9875 N(Wtd)	2609	1220	1324	2122	261	569	857	799	384	1228	1265	1146	577	289	495	47

QUESTIONNAIRE FORM 4 1976	TOTAL	SEX		RACE		REGION				4YR COLLEGE PLANS		ILLICIT DRUG USE: LIFETIME				
		M	F	White	Black	NE	NC	S	W	Yes	No	None	Mari-juana Only	Few Pills	More Pills	Any Her-oin
Weighted No. of Cases:	3027	1420	1479	2352	347	711	946	915	456	1341	1420	1273	679	320	586	56
% of Weighted Total:	100.0	46.9	48.9	77.7	11.5	23.5	31.3	30.2	15.1	44.3	46.9	42.1	22.4	10.6	19.4	1.9
E11F: Has someone injured you on purpose without using a weapon?																
1. Not at all	86.4	83.1	89.9	86.8	85.7	85.2	84.9	88.5	86.9	87.5	86.0	90.3	85.0	85.4	82.0	61.7
2. Once	7.7	9.1	5.8	7.5	7.3	8.1	8.4	6.6	7.3	6.5	8.8	5.9	7.5	9.0	10.7	14.9
3. Twice	3.1	3.9	2.3	2.6	5.4	2.6	3.6	3.1	2.6	3.3	2.3	1.7	4.3	2.8	4.2	8.5
4. 3 or 4 times	1.5	2.0	.9	1.6	.4	2.1	1.5	1.1	.8	1.2	1.7	1.2	1.6	2.1	1.6	2.1
5. 5 or more times	1.4	2.0	.9	1.4	1.5	1.9	1.4	.5	2.4	1.4	1.3	.9	1.6	.7	1.8	12.8
Item 9876 N(Wtd)	2609	1219	1323	2121	259	569	856	802	382	1224	1268	1149	575	288	495	47
E11G: Has an unarmed person threatened you with injury, but not actually injured you?																
1. Not at all	78.7	71.2	86.1	78.8	75.8	79.4	78.8	78.7	77.5	79.6	77.8	84.6	74.5	79.1	72.3	53.2
2. Once	10.1	11.6	8.6	9.6	14.6	10.0	9.4	11.6	8.9	10.5	10.1	7.0	13.0	10.5	12.5	21.3
3. Twice	3.9	6.0	1.8	3.9	3.8	3.3	4.0	3.4	5.7	4.2	3.7	2.3	4.9	5.2	5.5	8.5
4. 3 or 4 times	2.9	4.5	1.4	3.1	2.7	3.0	2.8	2.7	3.1	2.6	3.2	2.6	2.4	1.4	4.2	8.5
5. 5 or more times	4.3	6.7	2.1	4.6	3.5	4.2	4.9	3.6	5.0	3.2	5.1	3.6	5.2	3.8	5.3	10.6
Item 9877 N(Wtd)	2608	1217	1325	2120	260	569	854	802	383	1224	1268	1147	576	287	495	47

QUESTIONNAIRE FORM 5 1976	TOTAL	SEX		RACE		REGION				4YR COLLEGE PLANS		ILLICIT DRUG USE: LIFETIME				
		M	F	White	Black	NE	NC	S	W	Yes	No	None	Mari-juana Only	Few Pills	More Pills	Any Her-oin
Weighted No. of Cases:	3008	1473	1427	2356	356	713	930	906	460	1415	1398	1174	678	381	606	70
% of Weighted Total:	100.0	49.0	47.4	78.3	11.8	23.7	30.9	30.1	15.3	47.0	46.5	39.0	22.5	12.7	20.1	2.3

A01: Taking all things together, how would you say things are these days--would you say you're very happy, pretty happy, or not too happy these days?

3. Very happy	18.0	16.2	20.1	18.8	15.3	18.0	16.3	18.7	20.3	20.6	16.0	21.5	17.3	13.4	15.4	14.3
2. Pretty happy	68.8	70.8	67.1	70.5	61.0	66.3	72.8	68.0	66.4	67.8	70.1	67.7	70.3	73.9	69.2	61.4
1. Not too happy	13.1	13.0	12.8	10.6	23.4	15.7	11.0	13.4	13.1	11.5	13.9	10.8	12.4	12.6	15.4	25.7
Item 1190 N(Wtd)	2998	1468	1425	2351	354	706	929	905	459	1412	1397	1172	676	380	603	70

A02: Some people think a lot about the social problems of the nation and the world, and about how they might be solved. Others spend little time thinking about these issues. How much do you think about such things?

1. Never	1.3	1.8	.7	1.1	.9	1.6	1.7	.7	1.5	.9	1.6	1.0	1.3	1.8	1.0	2.9
2. Seldom	14.5	15.7	13.4	15.4	9.1	16.2	16.9	10.6	14.6	11.0	17.6	13.0	14.5	15.0	17.1	17.1
3. Sometimes	51.1	50.5	51.6	52.4	43.2	49.7	51.9	51.6	50.8	47.4	55.9	52.9	53.7	50.1	47.7	37.1
4. Quite often	27.3	26.2	28.7	26.4	34.7	27.4	24.4	30.4	27.2	32.6	21.6	26.9	25.1	28.6	29.0	37.1
5. A great deal	5.7	5.8	5.6	4.7	12.2	5.1	5.2	6.8	5.7	8.1	3.4	6.1	5.3	4.7	5.5	4.3
Item 6880 N(Wtd)	2996	1467	1423	2351	352	708	928	902	459	1411	1393	1171	676	381	604	70

A03: Of all the problems facing the nation today, how often do you worry about each of the following?

A03A: Chance of nuclear war

1. Never	20.8	16.2	25.3	19.9	24.9	23.3	22.4	17.4	20.0	18.0	23.7	20.5	21.6	18.8	21.8	15.7
2. Seldom	37.1	37.3	36.7	38.3	29.8	36.7	36.7	38.4	36.0	37.5	37.8	38.2	35.7	35.8	36.4	48.6
3. Sometimes	31.7	33.7	30.1	31.8	32.1	30.6	32.4	30.5	33.8	32.9	29.6	30.1	32.5	34.5	32.9	25.7
4. Often	10.5	12.8	7.9	10.0	13.2	9.3	8.4	13.5	10.5	11.6	8.8	11.1	10.2	10.9	8.9	10.0
Item 11660 N(Wtd)	2992	1465	1420	2350	349	708	928	901	456	1409	1390	1168	676	377	605	70

A03B: Population growth

1. Never	11.3	14.0	8.1	10.3	16.3	15.3	10.7	10.4	8.3	10.6	12.0	10.5	10.5	9.4	13.2	15.7
2. Seldom	32.2	37.5	27.2	34.1	24.8	31.6	34.8	31.8	28.4	31.1	33.5	32.3	34.6	30.4	31.7	30.0
3. Sometimes	37.7	34.5	40.9	38.3	32.9	34.6	38.6	37.1	42.0	37.8	37.2	38.7	36.8	41.2	34.4	40.0
4. Often	18.8	14.0	23.7	17.3	26.2	18.6	15.9	20.7	21.2	20.6	17.3	18.4	18.0	19.2	20.7	15.7
Item 11670 N(Wtd)	2988	1465	1416	2350	343	708	926	897	457	1409	1389	1164	673	381	605	70

A03C: Crime and violence

1. Never	1.2	1.7	.5	1.0	1.2	1.3	1.4	.7	1.5	.9	1.4	.5	1.3	1.9	1.3	4.3
2. Seldom	9.9	14.2	5.3	10.6	4.6	9.1	10.0	9.4	11.6	8.5	11.2	8.0	12.4	8.0	10.9	14.3
3. Sometimes	34.8	40.8	29.1	38.2	20.5	36.4	36.2	30.9	36.9	34.8	35.2	32.8	35.6	34.7	38.0	42.9
4. Often	54.2	43.2	65.0	50.2	73.8	53.4	52.4	59.1	49.8	55.9	52.1	58.7	50.8	55.7	49.8	38.6
Item 11680 N(Wtd)	2983	1464	1416	2343	347	706	926	893	458	1407	1391	1165	675	375	605	70

A03D: Pollution

1. Never	3.9	4.2	3.3	2.9	8.7	3.8	4.0	4.7	1.8	2.8	4.3	3.7	3.4	4.5	3.3	5.8
2. Seldom	17.7	19.1	16.2	17.3	21.3	15.7	17.8	19.5	17.3	16.1	19.8	17.4	16.2	15.5	21.1	14.5
3. Sometimes	42.4	42.2	43.1	43.4	41.7	39.4	45.5	43.8	37.9	40.4	44.9	43.4	45.8	39.6	38.8	37.7
4. Often	36.1	34.6	37.4	36.5	28.0	41.1	32.8	32.0	43.2	40.6	31.1	35.5	34.6	40.4	36.8	42.0
Item 11690 N(Wtd)	2983	1464	1411	2347	343	708	926	892	456	1407	1387	1160	674	381	603	69

A03E: Energy shortages

1. Never	5.1	5.0	5.0	4.2	9.2	6.5	5.0	4.8	3.9	4.4	5.6	4.5	4.4	5.0	6.4	5.7
2. Seldom	24.2	22.2	26.4	24.4	24.1	24.6	26.2	20.9	26.1	22.9	25.8	21.6	26.5	26.8	24.8	35.7
3. Sometimes	42.3	42.3	42.5	43.6	34.1	43.0	42.7	41.4	42.5	42.7	41.5	41.4	44.8	38.5	42.6	35.7
4. Often	28.4	30.5	26.2	27.8	32.4	25.9	26.2	33.0	27.6	30.0	27.1	32.3	24.1	29.7	26.1	21.4
Item 11700 N(Wtd)	2991	1467	1418	2350	349	707	928	900	456	1412	1390	1169	676	377	605	70

QUESTIONNAIRE FORM 5 1976	TOTAL	SEX		RACE		REGION				4YR COLLEGE PLANS		ILLICIT DRUG USE: LIFETIME				
		M	F	White	Black	NE	NC	S	W	Yes	No	None	Mari-juana Only	Few Pills	More Pills	Any Her-oin
Weighted No. of Cases:	3008	1473	1427	2356	356	713	930	906	460	1415	1398	1174	678	381	606	70
% of Weighted Total:	100.0	49.0	47.4	78.3	11.8	23.7	30.9	30.1	15.3	47.0	46.5	39.0	22.5	12.7	20.1	2.3
A03F: Race relations																
1. Never	12.4	15.3	9.6	12.7	8.9	13.2	13.4	10.0	14.2	9.6	15.2	11.2	13.5	11.0	13.5	17.1
2. Seldom	33.5	36.3	30.5	36.2	19.5	31.3	35.4	30.9	38.0	31.4	35.2	32.7	33.9	35.7	33.1	30.0
3. Sometimes	33.5	31.3	35.6	34.2	30.2	33.8	34.0	33.7	31.4	34.8	32.8	35.6	34.5	31.8	30.2	32.9
4. Often	20.6	17.0	24.3	16.9	41.4	21.8	17.4	25.4	16.4	24.1	16.7	20.5	18.3	21.5	23.3	20.0
Item 11710 N(Wtd)	2991	1467	1417	2348	348	707	927	899	458	1409	1393	1167	676	381	602	70
A03G: Hunger and poverty																
1. Never	7.1	11.2	2.5	6.5	6.4	6.8	7.5	7.5	6.3	5.4	8.3	5.5	8.1	8.5	6.6	14.3
2. Seldom	29.1	36.4	22.1	32.4	14.9	26.0	33.6	26.7	29.8	28.2	30.8	26.8	31.3	29.2	31.2	31.4
3. Sometimes	40.7	37.0	44.6	42.5	31.6	41.6	40.3	38.4	44.6	41.4	40.5	42.2	41.3	37.9	39.9	38.6
4. Often	23.0	15.5	30.8	18.6	47.1	25.7	18.7	27.3	19.3	24.9	20.4	25.5	19.3	24.1	22.3	15.7
Item 11720 N(Wtd)	2981	1460	1414	2346	342	709	922	893	457	1409	1382	1159	675	377	606	70
A03H: Using open land for housing or industry																
1. Never	26.1	25.6	26.9	25.3	31.5	28.5	26.0	25.4	24.1	25.4	26.6	26.3	24.2	26.5	27.0	27.1
2. Seldom	31.8	29.7	33.9	32.7	29.2	30.7	33.3	33.3	27.1	32.7	31.5	34.0	32.6	31.5	28.2	22.9
3. Sometimes	23.6	25.3	21.6	23.6	23.1	21.7	24.4	23.6	24.7	22.7	23.9	22.3	25.1	23.3	24.9	25.7
4. Often	18.6	19.6	17.5	18.4	16.2	19.3	16.3	17.5	24.1	19.2	17.9	17.5	18.2	18.8	20.1	24.3
Item 11730 N(Wtd)	2991	1467	1418	2351	346	706	927	901	457	1408	1393	1168	677	378	603	70
A03I: Urban decay																
1. Never	31.9	31.8	32.0	31.2	35.9	27.7	32.3	34.6	31.9	25.6	38.4	31.4	29.0	30.4	36.4	28.6
2. Seldom	40.5	40.9	40.6	42.9	31.0	34.4	42.9	42.6	40.7	42.5	39.2	44.6	41.9	37.3	35.1	38.6
3. Sometimes	21.8	21.8	21.4	21.4	21.4	29.3	21.3	16.9	21.2	24.4	18.7	18.3	23.8	24.8	23.2	27.1
4. Often	5.9	5.4	6.0	4.5	11.9	8.7	3.6	5.8	6.0	7.5	3.8	5.6	5.5	7.7	5.5	5.7
Item 11740 N(Wtd)	2974	1457	1412	2339	345	700	926	896	452	1405	1382	1158	673	375	604	70
A03J: Economic problems																
1. Never	6.0	5.9	5.9	5.6	5.5	6.8	5.3	5.5	7.2	4.0	7.3	3.9	5.9	6.6	8.1	14.3
2. Seldom	26.3	25.9	27.1	27.5	21.1	24.8	28.9	25.4	25.2	24.3	28.5	26.5	25.8	25.3	27.6	32.9
3. Sometimes	42.9	42.4	43.3	43.6	43.1	38.0	43.5	44.6	45.8	42.4	44.3	44.6	42.6	43.8	40.6	31.4
4. Often	24.8	25.7	23.8	23.3	30.3	30.5	22.1	24.4	21.7	29.3	20.1	25.1	25.7	24.3	23.8	22.9
Item 11750 N(Wtd)	2989	1466	1416	2348	346	706	926	901	456	1408	1391	1167	674	379	604	70
A03K: Drug abuse																
1. Never	8.9	12.2	5.4	8.8	8.0	8.5	8.1	9.8	9.8	7.1	10.1	7.1	7.9	7.4	11.9	28.6
2. Seldom	23.7	28.3	19.7	25.5	11.8	24.9	25.0	17.7	31.0	25.9	22.4	22.9	25.8	23.5	23.2	25.7
3. Sometimes	35.8	35.7	35.4	37.3	27.3	37.5	37.6	34.3	31.9	35.6	36.4	35.7	39.0	36.8	33.9	21.4
4. Often	31.6	23.7	39.5	28.4	52.9	29.0	29.3	38.2	27.3	31.3	31.1	34.3	27.4	32.3	31.0	25.7
Item 11760 N(Wtd)	2991	1466	1419	2349	348	706	927	900	458	1411	1391	1168	675	378	604	70
A04: How well do you think your experiences and training (at home, school, work, etc.) have prepared you to be a good...																
A04A: Husband or wife																
1. Poorly	2.5	3.1	1.8	2.5	.6	3.2	2.5	2.2	1.8	2.6	2.4	1.4	3.2	.8	3.7	7.6
2. Not so well	6.0	7.4	4.5	6.4	3.0	5.7	6.5	5.3	6.8	5.9	6.1	4.5	7.3	3.5	7.8	13.6
3. Fairly well	24.4	30.2	18.5	25.5	19.1	22.9	25.5	23.3	26.4	23.3	25.9	20.3	28.0	27.6	27.5	22.7
4. Well	38.8	37.3	40.0	38.7	37.4	39.4	39.2	39.7	35.6	38.5	39.4	41.9	36.0	39.7	35.3	39.4
5. Very well	28.4	21.9	35.3	26.9	39.5	28.9	26.4	29.5	29.3	29.7	26.1	31.7	25.3	28.6	25.8	18.2
Item 11770 N(Wtd)	2897	1409	1388	2294	329	686	895	872	444	1369	1354	1126	656	370	590	66

	TOTAL	SEX		RACE		REGION				4YR COLLEGE PLANS		ILLICIT DRUG USE: LIFETIME				
QUESTIONNAIRE FORM 5 **1976**		M	F	White	Black	NE	NC	S	W	Yes	No	None	Mari-juana Only	Few Pills	More Pills	Any Her-oin
Weighted No. of Cases:	3008	1473	1427	2356	356	713	930	906	460	1415	1398	1174	678	381	606	70
% of Weighted Total:	100.0	49.0	47.4	78.3	11.8	23.7	30.9	30.1	15.3	47.0	46.5	39.0	22.5	12.7	20.1	2.3
A04B: Parent																
1. Poorly	2.9	3.4	2.6	3.1	.3	2.5	3.2	2.7	3.6	3.1	2.9	1.9	3.8	.5	4.6	10.4
2. Not so well	7.5	9.7	5.1	8.2	4.1	9.6	8.5	5.1	7.6	7.4	7.5	5.7	8.5	8.0	9.3	13.4
3. Fairly well	24.2	27.9	20.4	26.0	15.0	19.9	26.8	24.1	25.7	21.5	27.4	23.7	24.2	24.8	25.7	26.9
4. Well	36.0	36.2	35.9	36.4	32.3	36.5	37.4	35.3	33.9	35.0	37.3	36.2	36.0	38.9	36.1	26.9
5. Very well	29.3	22.7	36.0	26.3	48.4	31.7	24.2	32.8	29.2	33.1	24.9	32.6	27.5	27.5	24.3	22.4
Item 11780 N(Wtd)	2934	1429	1404	2312	341	690	909	887	448	1386	1367	1150	661	375	592	67
A04C: Worker on a job																
1. Poorly	1.0	1.4	.6	1.1	-	1.3	.7	1.1	1.5	.9	1.1	.9	1.2	.5	1.2	2.9
2. Not so well	4.4	4.0	4.7	4.6	3.7	4.7	5.2	3.3	4.6	3.9	4.8	4.0	4.3	4.0	5.8	2.9
3. Fairly well	15.9	16.6	15.3	16.5	11.0	15.6	16.5	13.3	20.3	16.8	15.5	13.6	14.8	16.9	21.1	14.7
4. Well	39.9	40.1	40.1	41.5	32.3	40.4	43.5	38.4	34.9	39.0	41.8	42.0	40.6	37.0	39.0	33.8
5. Very well	38.7	37.9	39.3	36.3	53.3	38.0	34.2	43.8	38.9	39.5	36.8	39.4	39.1	41.5	33.1	45.6
Item 11790 N(Wtd)	2979	1460	1415	2344	347	706	920	900	453	1401	1386	1162	675	378	602	68
A05: Apart from the particular kind of work you want to do, how would you rate each of the following settings as a place to work?																
A05A: Working in a large corporation																
1. Not at all acceptable	9.4	9.1	9.6	9.9	3.4	11.2	8.4	7.5	11.9	9.3	9.5	7.7	10.2	5.8	12.1	20.3
2. Somewhat acceptable	32.0	30.6	33.5	34.0	24.3	33.6	34.1	28.2	33.3	30.9	33.5	32.2	32.2	32.5	32.2	21.7
3. Acceptable	44.6	45.7	43.5	42.8	52.3	40.1	42.4	50.3	44.5	45.4	43.6	44.2	44.7	47.8	44.2	40.6
4. Desirable	14.0	14.6	13.3	13.3	20.0	15.0	15.0	14.0	10.4	14.4	13.4	15.8	12.9	13.6	11.5	17.4
Item 11800 N(Wtd)	2988	1463	1420	2348	350	705	924	905	454	1411	1389	1169	676	381	602	69
A05B: Working in a small business																
1. Not at all acceptable	5.1	5.7	4.4	3.8	10.1	5.5	4.3	6.2	3.7	5.0	4.9	4.7	5.5	4.5	4.3	10.0
2. Somewhat acceptable	23.5	25.4	21.9	21.8	33.3	27.8	20.7	23.0	23.3	23.3	22.8	23.6	21.5	20.2	26.6	24.3
3. Acceptable	50.3	50.5	49.9	51.5	44.8	47.1	52.3	49.3	53.1	52.6	48.3	49.6	51.8	50.9	49.5	51.4
4. Desirable	21.1	18.4	23.8	23.0	11.8	19.6	22.6	21.4	20.0	19.2	24.1	22.1	21.1	24.4	19.6	15.7
Item 11810 N(Wtd)	2982	1458	1420	2344	348	705	923	899	454	1406	1388	1166	674	377	602	70
A05C: Working in a government agency																
1. Not at all acceptable	21.1	21.6	20.9	22.0	17.1	20.2	23.3	18.7	23.2	15.2	26.4	19.4	19.6	22.7	23.7	30.0
2. Somewhat acceptable	27.7	27.5	27.9	28.8	22.3	24.0	29.1	27.3	30.9	27.8	28.6	26.8	29.5	25.6	28.2	31.4
3. Acceptable	33.1	33.4	32.6	32.5	33.3	36.6	31.9	32.3	31.6	36.5	30.2	34.6	34.2	32.2	31.8	24.3
4. Desirable	18.1	17.6	18.6	16.8	27.2	19.2	15.5	21.7	14.6	20.5	14.9	19.3	16.7	19.5	16.3	14.3
Item 11820 N(Wtd)	2979	1459	1416	2346	345	704	924	898	453	1407	1384	1162	675	379	600	70
A05D: Working in the military service																
1. Not at all acceptable	39.2	36.6	41.9	40.3	30.9	39.7	40.3	34.6	45.1	41.5	36.9	37.9	38.6	37.7	44.0	45.7
2. Somewhat acceptable	29.1	30.0	28.5	29.8	26.0	30.1	29.2	26.8	31.6	30.1	28.7	28.9	30.3	32.9	26.8	18.6
3. Acceptable	20.6	20.5	20.7	20.0	24.3	20.5	21.4	22.4	15.3	18.9	22.2	21.7	19.4	19.9	19.6	18.6
4. Desirable	11.2	12.9	8.9	9.9	18.6	9.6	9.2	16.0	8.0	9.5	12.2	11.5	12.0	9.5	9.7	18.6
Item 11830 N(Wtd)	2983	1460	1418	2342	350	707	926	898	452	1410	1387	1166	677	377	598	70
A05E: Working in a school or university																
1. Not at all acceptable	23.7	29.9	17.1	24.4	16.7	22.3	25.8	23.6	21.6	13.6	33.5	19.5	26.7	24.9	25.6	35.7
2. Somewhat acceptable	28.0	31.2	25.3	28.9	23.6	28.6	26.7	27.0	31.6	24.3	31.5	26.5	26.5	28.4	32.6	15.7
3. Acceptable	30.0	25.9	33.8	30.1	30.7	30.0	30.4	31.4	26.7	34.1	26.3	32.1	29.5	29.4	27.7	38.6
4. Desirable	18.4	13.1	23.8	16.6	29.0	19.1	17.2	18.1	20.1	28.0	8.7	22.0	17.2	17.2	14.3	10.0
Item 11840 N(Wtd)	2983	1460	1417	2343	348	707	925	899	453	1409	1386	1166	675	377	602	70

QUESTIONNAIRE FORM 5 1976	TOTAL	SEX		RACE		REGION				4YR COLLEGE PLANS		ILLICIT DRUG USE: LIFETIME				
		M	F	White	Black	NE	NC	S	W	Yes	No	None	Marijuana Only	Few Pills	More Pills	Any Heroin
Weighted No. of Cases:	3008	1473	1427	2356	356	713	930	906	460	1415	1398	1174	678	381	606	70
% of Weighted Total:	100.0	49.0	47.4	78.3	11.8	23.7	30.9	30.1	15.3	47.0	46.5	39.0	22.5	12.7	20.1	2.3

A05F: Working in a police department or police agency

	TOTAL	M	F	White	Black	NE	NC	S	W	Yes	No	None	Mar. Only	Few Pills	More Pills	Any Her.
1. Not at all acceptable	27.4	29.5	24.1	25.3	34.4	28.7	24.9	28.9	27.5	24.3	29.3	20.9	25.6	26.8	38.0	42.9
2. Somewhat acceptable	28.9	29.5	28.8	30.5	25.7	29.5	32.2	27.5	24.2	31.4	26.9	31.9	30.8	27.6	22.6	24.3
3. Acceptable	29.5	27.5	32.4	30.0	28.0	28.8	28.8	28.9	33.3	30.7	29.2	33.6	28.3	32.1	24.8	17.1
4. Desirable	14.2	13.5	14.7	14.2	11.8	13.0	14.2	14.9	15.0	13.6	14.6	13.6	15.4	13.4	14.5	17.1
Item 11850 N(Wtd)	2985	1463	1417	2348	346	705	925	901	454	1409	1390	1166	676	380	602	70

A05G: Working in a social service organization

	TOTAL	M	F	White	Black	NE	NC	S	W	Yes	No	None	Mar. Only	Few Pills	More Pills	Any Her.
1. Not at all acceptable	17.8	27.0	8.0	19.2	10.2	17.6	19.1	17.7	15.6	13.9	21.4	17.1	19.6	18.7	17.1	18.8
2. Somewhat acceptable	30.0	37.4	22.4	30.7	21.5	30.2	28.7	30.3	32.2	28.3	31.7	29.2	30.2	31.1	29.7	33.3
3. Acceptable	32.7	27.2	38.2	30.9	44.2	31.9	32.2	34.1	32.2	34.9	30.3	34.5	33.3	30.9	29.6	31.9
4. Desirable	19.5	8.4	31.3	19.1	24.1	20.3	20.0	18.0	20.0	23.0	16.7	19.2	16.9	19.3	23.6	17.4
Item 11860 N(Wtd)	2981	1459	1417	2346	344	705	921	900	454	1406	1389	1165	675	379	602	69

A05H: Working with a small group of partners

	TOTAL	M	F	White	Black	NE	NC	S	W	Yes	No	None	Mar. Only	Few Pills	More Pills	Any Her.
1. Not at all acceptable	11.7	10.1	12.8	10.1	17.3	12.3	11.7	12.9	8.7	9.0	13.3	11.4	11.8	11.6	10.4	17.1
2. Somewhat acceptable	27.7	25.9	30.0	27.1	34.0	26.4	25.9	31.4	26.2	26.3	28.9	28.8	29.0	27.4	24.3	25.7
3. Acceptable	41.7	43.8	40.0	43.3	32.6	40.1	43.0	42.1	41.0	43.5	40.5	44.2	39.9	39.2	41.8	41.4
4. Desirable	18.9	20.3	17.2	19.4	16.1	21.1	19.6	13.7	24.0	21.1	17.3	15.6	19.2	21.8	23.5	15.7
Item 11870 N(Wtd)	2988	1466	1418	2350	347	705	924	901	458	1409	1392	1164	676	380	605	70

A05I: Working on your own (self-employed)

	TOTAL	M	F	White	Black	NE	NC	S	W	Yes	No	None	Mar. Only	Few Pills	More Pills	Any Her.
1. Not at all acceptable	12.3	6.4	18.5	11.6	15.5	11.0	11.9	14.0	12.3	9.4	15.1	15.4	10.8	9.7	10.5	5.7
2. Somewhat acceptable	18.0	14.5	21.7	18.4	17.5	19.2	18.3	16.6	18.5	17.8	18.2	19.4	17.6	16.6	17.1	12.9
3. Acceptable	26.5	28.3	24.5	26.7	25.9	25.1	28.5	25.5	26.7	28.4	25.1	26.9	27.9	26.1	26.2	11.4
4. Desirable	43.2	50.8	35.3	43.2	41.4	44.8	41.5	44.0	42.5	44.4	41.6	38.2	43.9	47.4	46.2	71.4
Item 11880 N(Wtd)	2989	1465	1418	2348	348	708	924	902	454	1412	1388	1169	675	380	602	70

A06: If you were to get enough money to live as comfortably as you'd like for the rest of your life, would you want to work?

	TOTAL	M	F	White	Black	NE	NC	S	W	Yes	No	None	Mar. Only	Few Pills	More Pills	Any Her.
1. I would want to work	81.9	82.1	82.1	82.2	80.8	79.3	82.6	83.0	82.6	85.2	79.3	85.5	81.4	85.9	75.0	67.6
2. I would not want to work	18.1	17.9	17.8	17.8	19.2	20.8	17.4	17.0	17.4	14.8	20.7	14.5	18.6	14.1	25.1	30.9
Item 8100 N(Wtd)	2954	1438	1412	2326	344	702	912	886	454	1395	1369	1161	668	375	589	68

A07: The next questions are about race relations. How much have you gotten to know people of other races...

A07A: In school?

	TOTAL	M	F	White	Black	NE	NC	S	W	Yes	No	None	Mar. Only	Few Pills	More Pills	Any Her.
1. Not at all	13.2	13.6	13.0	15.6	2.3	15.5	22.8	4.6	7.3	13.5	13.2	12.7	14.6	12.6	13.9	14.9
2. A little	22.5	23.6	21.4	25.1	11.4	23.3	26.9	14.8	27.7	22.9	22.9	23.8	22.0	19.9	24.0	20.9
3. Some	27.2	29.5	25.5	28.4	21.4	25.6	24.6	31.1	27.5	26.5	28.0	27.8	23.8	29.4	28.2	25.4
4. A lot	33.0	29.6	35.6	26.5	63.1	30.4	18.8	48.4	35.5	32.9	31.9	31.3	35.1	34.1	31.0	35.8
8. Does not apply to me	4.1	3.7	4.5	4.5	1.4	5.2	7.0	1.2	1.8	4.2	4.0	4.4	4.5	4.2	2.9	3.0
Item 11890 N(Wtd)	2981	1458	1417	2338	350	708	922	900	451	1403	1388	1168	673	381	596	67

A07B: In your neighborhood?

	TOTAL	M	F	White	Black	NE	NC	S	W	Yes	No	None	Mar. Only	Few Pills	More Pills	Any Her.
1. Not at all	39.7	38.0	41.8	44.9	19.5	37.5	49.6	34.1	34.1	39.7	40.7	41.4	41.3	39.1	37.9	36.8
2. A little	18.7	21.6	15.5	18.3	16.6	21.1	16.1	16.5	24.6	19.6	17.6	16.4	20.2	20.7	20.8	11.8
3. Some	14.9	15.2	14.1	13.2	16.9	17.4	10.4	15.5	19.0	14.9	14.1	14.1	13.4	15.0	15.9	20.6
4. A lot	12.3	12.2	12.4	7.3	40.1	12.3	6.4	17.9	12.8	10.3	13.6	11.9	11.6	10.2	11.7	23.5
8. Does not apply to me	14.4	13.0	16.3	16.3	6.9	11.6	17.4	16.0	9.7	15.5	14.0	16.2	13.4	15.0	13.6	8.8
Item 11900 N(Wtd)	2978	1456	1415	2337	349	707	920	899	452	1402	1389	1164	673	381	596	68

QUESTIONNAIRE FORM 5 1976	TOTAL	SEX		RACE		REGION				4YR COLLEGE PLANS		ILLICIT DRUG USE: LIFETIME				
		M	F	White	Black	NE	NC	S	W	Yes	No	None	Marijuana Only	Few Pills	More Pills	Any Heroin
Weighted No. of Cases:	3008	1473	1427	2356	356	713	930	906	460	1415	1398	1174	678	381	606	70
% of Weighted Total:	100.0	49.0	47.4	78.3	11.8	23.7	30.9	30.1	15.3	47.0	46.5	39.0	22.5	12.7	20.1	2.3

A07C: In church?

1. Not at all	43.7	45.6	42.0	47.3	28.5	45.3	47.7	39.7	41.2	42.0	46.2	40.1	47.7	41.5	48.7	43.9
2. A little	16.8	16.1	17.1	16.6	18.0	16.1	19.0	16.1	14.9	17.8	15.4	19.3	14.9	17.6	13.3	12.1
3. Some	12.2	11.2	12.9	10.3	17.4	11.4	10.4	13.2	14.9	12.1	12.7	12.6	10.6	13.9	10.5	13.6
4. A lot	6.9	6.8	7.1	4.0	22.4	5.0	3.9	10.8	8.2	6.2	6.4	9.8	4.0	6.8	4.7	1.5
8. Does not apply to me	20.4	20.3	20.8	21.8	13.7	22.1	19.0	20.3	20.7	22.0	19.3	18.1	22.7	20.2	22.9	27.3
Item 11910 N(Wtd)	2962	1449	1409	2325	344	702	916	895	449	1397	1380	1159	671	381	593	66

A07D: On sports teams?

1. Not at all	23.0	19.1	27.5	26.4	8.1	25.9	33.1	12.0	19.6	20.6	26.4	23.6	24.6	17.9	26.6	13.6
2. A little	14.8	15.0	14.3	14.9	14.2	15.5	14.1	15.1	14.5	14.2	15.1	14.9	13.5	18.7	12.4	19.7
3. Some	20.4	23.6	17.4	19.6	21.4	18.4	18.6	23.0	22.0	20.0	20.4	20.6	19.5	18.9	21.0	27.3
4. A lot	22.9	29.3	15.8	18.7	45.2	19.4	14.5	32.3	26.5	25.2	19.8	21.1	26.5	24.7	19.5	19.7
8. Does not apply to me	18.9	13.0	25.0	20.3	11.3	20.8	19.6	17.7	17.1	20.0	18.3	19.8	16.1	19.7	20.7	21.2
Item 11920 N(Wtd)	2962	1451	1406	2328	345	702	918	893	449	1396	1381	1158	672	380	590	66

A07E: In clubs?

1. Not at all	32.6	35.0	30.4	35.9	17.7	33.9	43.9	22.0	28.7	28.8	36.6	31.0	36.8	29.2	33.8	32.3
2. A little	17.9	19.2	16.5	18.1	16.9	16.6	17.5	18.5	19.2	20.0	16.0	17.2	17.9	18.9	18.2	13.8
3. Some	18.2	16.1	19.9	17.3	21.5	17.4	13.1	25.1	16.0	20.4	15.7	21.6	14.7	18.2	13.9	29.2
4. A lot	12.3	11.5	12.9	9.0	29.9	10.5	6.6	18.3	14.9	13.6	10.6	13.0	12.9	11.1	11.3	7.7
8. Does not apply to me	19.1	18.2	20.2	19.7	13.7	21.6	19.0	16.1	21.2	17.2	21.1	17.1	17.6	22.6	22.9	16.9
Item 11930 N(Wtd)	2963	1451	1409	2331	344	703	915	896	449	1399	1382	1162	672	380	595	65

A07F: On a job?

1. Not at all	21.2	22.2	20.4	24.1	7.5	27.1	26.6	12.1	19.4	21.1	22.0	24.1	20.8	17.9	18.9	22.7
2. A little	14.4	15.5	13.5	15.3	10.4	14.2	16.2	12.1	16.0	14.7	14.8	13.7	15.3	16.9	14.4	9.1
3. Some	20.8	21.9	18.9	20.6	21.2	20.1	19.9	22.2	20.7	20.2	21.5	19.7	21.0	19.3	22.1	30.3
4. A lot	28.2	29.6	26.8	24.0	46.7	23.7	21.8	37.5	29.8	27.1	27.4	24.8	28.7	30.9	30.5	31.8
8. Does not apply to me	15.3	10.7	20.4	16.1	14.2	15.2	15.3	16.1	13.8	17.0	14.3	17.5	14.3	15.3	13.9	6.1
Item 11940 N(Wtd)	2971	1458	1409	2335	345	706	920	895	449	1399	1384	1160	672	379	597	66

A08: Thinking about the country as a whole, would you say relations between white people and black people have been getting better, getting worse, or staying pretty much the same?

1. Better	21.9	22.5	21.3	22.1	24.6	20.6	19.4	23.6	25.7	25.0	18.7	21.5	21.9	21.3	22.4	23.5
2. A little better	46.6	45.0	48.8	46.0	50.4	45.8	49.7	44.0	46.8	48.2	45.1	48.5	46.6	45.3	46.4	36.8
3. Same	22.0	21.9	21.7	22.2	19.0	22.7	22.4	22.0	20.1	19.9	24.4	21.1	21.6	24.7	22.3	22.1
4. A little worse	6.2	6.7	5.7	6.7	3.1	6.3	5.9	7.2	4.9	4.4	7.8	5.9	7.0	5.8	5.5	11.8
5. Worse	3.2	4.0	2.3	3.0	2.5	4.4	2.7	3.2	2.5	2.6	4.0	2.9	2.8	3.2	3.4	8.8
Item 11950 N(Wtd)	2978	1459	1415	2335	353	709	921	901	447	1398	1391	1166	670	380	597	68

The next questions are about driving.

A09: Do you have a driver's license?

1. Yes	86.9	92.6	80.8	91.0	64.0	76.4	93.0	88.0	88.2	86.0	88.4	85.1	89.7	90.1	85.7	94.0
2. No, but I soon will-- GO TO Q.A13	10.3	5.8	15.1	7.5	26.0	19.9	5.5	8.4	8.8	10.7	9.2	10.8	8.6	7.3	12.7	4.5
3. No--GO TO Q.A13	2.8	1.5	4.1	1.5	9.9	3.7	1.4	3.5	2.9	3.3	2.4	4.2	1.8	2.7	1.6	1.5
Item 11960 N(Wtd)	2874	1423	1357	2314	292	673	902	859	441	1369	1333	1120	663	372	573	67

A10: Do you own a car?

1. Yes	45.6	55.5	33.7	47.1	24.6	34.2	43.8	54.2	47.8	41.1	50.0	40.3	47.1	51.3	48.7	58.7
2. No, but I expect to own one in another year or two	34.5	30.2	39.5	32.8	52.9	37.4	34.8	32.1	34.7	31.4	37.1	32.8	34.0	34.6	38.1	33.3
3. No	19.9	14.2	26.8	20.1	22.5	28.4	21.4	13.6	17.5	27.5	13.0	27.0	19.0	14.0	13.2	9.5
Item 11970 N(Wtd) ★	2498	1316	1099	2102	187	514	838	756	389	1178	1179	952	594	335	491	63

★ = excludes respondents for whom question was inappropriate.

QUESTIONNAIRE FORM 5 1976	TOTAL	SEX M	SEX F	RACE White	RACE Black	NE	NC	S	W	4YR COLLEGE PLANS Yes	No	None	Marijuana Only	Few Pills	More Pills	Any Heroin
Weighted No. of Cases:	3008	1473	1427	2356	356	713	930	906	460	1415	1398	1174	678	381	606	70
% of Weighted Total:	100.0	49.0	47.4	78.3	11.8	23.7	30.9	30.1	15.3	47.0	46.5	39.0	22.5	12.7	20.1	2.3

A11: Are you able to use someone else's car when you want to?

	TOTAL	M	F	White	Black	NE	NC	S	W	Yes	No	None	Marijuana Only	Few Pills	More Pills	Any Heroin
1. Yes, whenever I wish	31.3	29.0	34.7	32.3	24.7	28.7	31.0	34.0	30.4	31.6	32.0	33.5	31.9	30.2	27.5	39.7
2. Yes, most of the time	45.8	44.4	46.8	46.0	45.2	45.3	46.2	45.4	46.2	49.1	41.7	47.0	45.4	48.2	44.1	31.7
3. Sometimes	15.6	17.4	13.2	14.8	20.4	15.8	16.1	14.9	15.3	13.9	17.1	12.7	15.9	14.1	20.3	14.3
4. Rarely	4.9	6.0	3.8	4.7	5.4	5.1	5.3	4.1	5.5	3.4	6.4	4.3	4.2	5.7	5.5	9.5
5. Never	2.5	3.0	1.6	2.2	4.3	5.1	1.4	1.7	2.6	2.0	2.8	2.6	2.4	1.8	2.5	4.8
Item 11980 N(Wtd) ★	2483	1309	1092	2092	186	512	832	754	385	1172	1172	947	592	334	487	63

A12: Do you make an effort to cut down on driving, in order to save gasoline?

	TOTAL	M	F	White	Black	NE	NC	S	W	Yes	No	None	Marijuana Only	Few Pills	More Pills	Any Heroin
1. Not at all	14.6	16.3	12.2	13.9	12.4	20.8	14.7	10.9	13.1	12.2	16.0	12.1	15.5	14.1	17.6	23.8
2. Not very much	32.0	31.3	32.3	32.9	25.4	30.3	35.0	30.0	32.0	33.0	31.3	29.4	35.6	34.4	30.8	33.3
3. Yes, to some extent	41.9	41.6	43.2	42.1	46.5	37.7	40.0	47.7	39.9	43.8	40.6	46.0	38.1	41.3	39.6	34.9
4. Yes, quite a bit	7.7	7.7	7.9	7.7	6.5	6.3	6.8	7.6	11.6	7.9	7.8	8.5	6.9	6.0	8.8	6.3
8. Don't know	3.8	3.2	4.5	3.2	9.7	4.9	3.3	3.7	3.4	3.1	4.3	4.0	4.0	4.2	3.1	1.6
Item 11990 N(Wtd) ★	2487	1314	1091	2095	185	509	836	754	388	1173	1174	948	593	334	490	63

A13: Do you make an effort to cut down on the amount of electricity you use in order to save energy?

	TOTAL	M	F	White	Black	NE	NC	S	W	Yes	No	None	Marijuana Only	Few Pills	More Pills	Any Heroin
1. Not at all	8.2	10.6	5.7	8.2	6.3	9.9	10.2	6.3	5.7	7.5	8.4	6.0	11.7	9.4	7.4	11.6
2. Not very much	27.3	29.5	24.9	28.4	24.2	25.3	30.5	26.0	26.9	26.9	29.1	26.4	25.9	27.0	32.0	31.9
3. Yes, to some extent	46.1	43.0	49.7	46.8	43.3	45.9	43.2	47.4	49.7	47.4	45.2	49.0	44.9	43.0	44.4	46.4
4. Yes, quite a bit	15.9	14.2	17.4	14.4	23.6	16.1	14.2	18.0	14.8	16.7	14.2	16.8	14.8	17.8	13.4	10.1
8. Don't know	2.4	2.7	2.3	2.1	2.6	2.8	2.1	2.3	2.6	1.4	3.2	1.8	2.5	2.9	2.7	1.4
Item 12000 N(Wtd)	2982	1462	1417	2340	351	708	922	900	453	1405	1390	1167	675	381	597	69

A14: In the house or apartment where you live, is an effort made to reduce heat during the winter, in order to save energy?

	TOTAL	M	F	White	Black	NE	NC	S	W	Yes	No	None	Marijuana Only	Few Pills	More Pills	Any Heroin
1. Not at all	8.1	8.4	7.5	6.6	15.0	8.1	7.5	9.2	6.9	7.1	8.3	7.8	8.6	7.3	7.5	14.5
2. Not very much	18.6	20.1	17.1	18.3	20.1	15.1	19.7	18.6	22.0	16.9	20.5	18.2	19.6	18.1	17.8	24.6
3. Yes, to some extent	42.2	41.9	42.9	43.3	37.4	40.6	43.2	40.7	45.9	42.4	42.8	44.1	40.4	39.4	44.1	36.2
4. Yes, quite a bit	28.8	27.3	30.5	30.2	24.4	33.2	28.2	29.2	22.4	32.2	25.6	27.5	30.0	33.3	28.0	24.6
8. Don't know	2.3	2.4	2.0	1.6	2.8	2.8	1.6	2.2	2.9	1.4	2.8	2.3	1.2	1.8	2.7	1.4
Item 12010 N(Wtd)	2980	1459	1417	2338	353	707	920	902	451	1402	1391	1167	673	381	597	69

A15: How do you feel about each of the following?

A15A: How much do you enjoy shopping for things like clothes, records, sporting goods, and books?

	TOTAL	M	F	White	Black	NE	NC	S	W	Yes	No	None	Marijuana Only	Few Pills	More Pills	Any Heroin
1. Not at all	2.7	4.7	.5	2.7	.3	3.7	3.5	.6	4.0	2.2	3.1	2.3	3.3	1.0	3.5	2.9
2. Not very much	10.1	15.6	4.0	10.8	5.7	8.5	10.1	10.0	12.8	9.3	10.6	8.4	12.2	9.4	9.4	23.2
3. Pretty much	33.5	44.7	21.8	35.9	19.0	31.4	35.4	31.7	36.7	33.9	32.8	31.3	35.9	33.3	34.9	37.7
4. Very much	53.7	34.9	73.6	50.6	75.1	56.3	51.1	57.9	46.2	54.5	53.6	57.9	48.5	56.2	52.0	37.7
Item 12020 N(Wtd)	2986	1461	1419	2342	353	707	924	903	452	1407	1391	1171	672	381	598	69

A15B: How much do you care about having the latest fashion in your clothes, records, leisure activities, and so on?

	TOTAL	M	F	White	Black	NE	NC	S	W	Yes	No	None	Marijuana Only	Few Pills	More Pills	Any Heroin
1. Not at all	4.8	6.5	3.0	4.8	1.7	7.2	3.9	3.6	5.3	4.8	4.6	4.4	4.8	4.5	5.4	4.4
2. Not very much	24.6	28.5	20.1	25.9	15.7	24.3	22.5	23.1	32.0	27.1	21.4	25.2	26.7	21.0	23.6	29.4
3. Pretty much	40.1	39.1	41.1	42.0	28.0	37.9	44.5	36.9	41.1	37.5	43.4	39.9	40.6	39.1	42.3	30.9
4. Very much	30.5	25.9	35.8	27.3	54.3	30.6	28.9	36.5	21.4	30.4	30.7	30.6	28.1	35.4	28.6	35.3
Item 12030 N(Wtd)	2981	1462	1415	2342	350	708	923	898	453	1407	1391	1168	673	381	598	68

★ = excludes respondents for whom question was inappropriate.

QUESTIONNAIRE FORM 5 1976	TOTAL	SEX		RACE		REGION				4YR COLLEGE PLANS		ILLICIT DRUG USE: LIFETIME				
		M	F	White	Black	NE	NC	S	W	Yes	No	None	Mari-juana Only	Few Pills	More Pills	Any Her-oin
Weighted No. of Cases:	3008	1473	1427	2356	356	713	930	906	460	1415	1398	1174	678	381	606	70
% of Weighted Total:	100.0	49.0	47.4	78.3	11.8	23.7	30.9	30.1	15.3	47.0	46.5	39.0	22.5	12.7	20.1	2.3

A15C: How much do you care about whether your family has most of the things your friends and neighbors have?

1. Not at all	28.7	26.4	30.8	27.4	31.1	34.0	25.8	25.9	31.6	28.2	28.6	26.2	30.4	26.7	30.9	33.8
2. Not very much	47.6	49.0	46.4	49.6	37.2	46.0	50.2	45.4	49.6	48.7	47.5	48.9	49.5	45.8	46.4	41.2
3. Pretty much	16.9	17.8	16.4	17.6	14.5	14.8	18.0	18.1	15.9	17.5	16.3	17.8	15.2	18.3	16.5	14.7
4. Very much	6.8	6.9	6.4	5.4	17.2	5.5	6.0	10.8	2.9	5.8	7.6	7.1	4.9	9.0	6.2	8.8
Item 12040 N(Wtd)	2972	1458	1408	2336	344	705	921	893	452	1402	1385	1166	671	378	593	68

A16: When you are older, do you expect to own more possessions than your parents do now, or about the same, or less?

I expect to own...

1. Much less than my parents	1.9	1.5	2.3	1.6	2.3	1.0	1.7	2.2	2.9	1.9	1.9	1.6	1.3	1.3	3.2	4.5
2. Somewhat less than my parents	10.4	9.3	11.6	11.2	4.0	8.3	10.2	10.5	14.0	9.7	11.2	9.8	8.5	10.4	14.6	9.1
3. About as much as my parents	40.5	36.4	44.8	44.1	21.2	37.8	43.8	38.8	41.6	38.6	43.1	43.6	42.1	40.4	34.5	25.8
4. Somewhat more than my parents	34.5	37.0	32.1	32.9	45.3	37.8	34.6	34.0	29.8	35.3	33.7	32.9	36.3	37.2	33.4	30.3
5. Much more than my parents	12.7	16.0	9.2	10.1	26.9	15.0	9.7	14.5	11.8	14.5	9.9	12.0	11.5	10.4	14.3	30.3
Item 12050 N(Wtd)	2954	1442	1411	2316	353	698	908	898	450	1392	1379	1165	667	376	589	66

A17: Compared with your parents, what is the smallest amount that you could be content or satisfied to own?

The least I could be content to own is...

1. Much less than my parents	12.7	10.6	14.9	13.3	6.7	13.0	12.7	12.3	13.1	14.1	12.2	11.9	13.5	11.2	13.5	19.7
2. Somewhat less than my parents	33.6	31.0	36.7	37.4	15.2	30.7	36.9	30.2	38.1	36.2	31.5	35.0	33.0	32.5	35.9	24.2
3. About as much as my parents	37.2	39.5	34.3	36.9	39.1	38.7	37.1	37.2	34.9	34.6	39.7	37.7	37.1	39.2	36.1	27.3
4. Somewhat more than my parents	12.8	14.9	10.7	10.2	28.0	13.0	11.4	14.7	11.9	11.2	13.6	11.7	13.8	13.3	11.1	15.2
5. Much more than my parents	3.7	4.0	3.4	2.2	11.1	4.7	1.9	5.6	2.3	3.8	2.9	3.7	2.6	3.7	3.6	13.6
Item 12060 N(Wtd)	2938	1440	1399	2314	343	687	911	895	444	1380	1379	1155	666	375	585	66

A18: These next questions ask your opinions about a number of different topics. How much do you agree or disagree with each statement below?

A18A: We ought to worry about our own country and let the rest of the world take care of itself

1. Disagree	20.3	19.6	21.0	17.9	33.3	20.4	19.1	22.2	18.8	23.8	17.1	20.9	20.7	20.5	18.3	16.4
2. Mostly disagree	21.9	20.3	23.8	23.6	12.8	21.8	23.4	19.7	23.5	24.1	19.9	22.7	21.0	19.5	24.5	17.9
3. Neither	14.0	14.8	13.1	14.5	11.6	14.2	15.2	12.4	14.4	13.7	14.1	12.6	11.8	15.8	17.1	16.4
4. Mostly agree	28.8	28.8	29.2	29.7	24.9	28.5	28.2	28.4	31.2	28.4	29.1	30.6	31.0	28.4	25.7	19.4
5. Agree	15.0	16.5	12.9	14.2	17.7	15.0	14.2	17.3	11.9	10.1	19.7	13.0	15.7	15.5	14.6	29.9
Item 12070 N(Wtd)	2969	1456	1410	2337	345	705	915	898	452	1400	1389	1165	668	380	596	67

A18B: It would be better if we all felt more like citizens of the world than of any particular country

1. Disagree	12.1	14.9	8.4	12.4	8.1	11.5	11.1	13.4	12.7	11.5	12.5	10.9	13.7	6.8	15.6	13.2
2. Mostly disagree	14.7	17.6	12.0	15.4	11.6	14.1	16.7	13.1	15.0	16.1	13.8	16.1	14.2	16.1	12.9	13.2
3. Neither	17.7	17.8	17.5	18.4	11.9	19.7	18.4	15.3	17.9	17.4	17.3	17.4	17.9	17.6	18.0	13.2
4. Mostly agree	27.8	24.7	31.7	28.7	26.7	24.9	28.0	29.6	28.3	27.6	28.3	28.9	26.1	30.8	26.0	22.1
5. Agree	27.6	25.2	30.4	25.0	41.6	29.8	25.8	28.5	26.1	27.3	28.0	26.6	28.1	28.4	27.4	38.2
Item 12080 N(Wtd)	2954	1451	1398	2324	344	704	914	895	441	1394	1380	1161	663	380	588	68

QUESTIONNAIRE FORM 5 1976	TOTAL	SEX		RACE		REGION				4YR COLLEGE PLANS		ILLICIT DRUG USE: LIFETIME				
		M	F	White	Black	NE	NC	S	W	Yes	No	None	Mari- juana Only	Few Pills	More Pills	Any Her- oin
Weighted No. of Cases:	3008	1473	1427	2356	356	713	930	906	460	1415	1398	1174	678	381	606	70
% of Weighted Total:	100.0	49.0	47.4	78.3	11.8	23.7	30.9	30.1	15.3	47.0	46.5	39.0	22.5	12.7	20.1	2.3
A18C: I find it hard to be sympathetic toward starving people in foreign lands, when there is so much trouble in our own country																
1. Disagree	30.3	20.4	40.5	28.5	40.3	32.3	26.3	32.0	32.0	32.0	28.1	30.1	29.3	32.3	29.6	33.8
2. Mostly disagree	23.4	22.4	24.8	25.9	14.1	23.9	26.1	21.1	21.3	26.2	21.4	26.9	22.0	18.6	23.4	13.2
3. Neither	13.9	16.4	11.2	14.0	10.1	13.2	15.6	11.4	16.8	14.8	13.6	12.4	15.1	16.8	14.1	14.7
4. Mostly agree	18.9	22.8	14.9	19.6	17.3	18.6	18.9	19.1	19.2	16.8	20.7	18.2	20.4	21.0	19.2	13.2
5. Agree	13.5	18.1	8.6	12.1	18.2	12.0	13.1	16.3	10.7	10.2	16.3	12.3	13.3	11.5	13.8	25.0
Item 12090 N(Wtd)	2966	1457	1406	2331	347	706	919	894	447	1401	1383	1159	668	381	595	68
A18D: Maybe some minority groups do get unfair treatment, but that's no business of mine																
1. Disagree	41.4	32.4	51.1	38.1	60.0	45.5	38.1	40.2	44.1	48.6	34.7	42.9	40.5	39.3	42.2	38.8
2. Mostly disagree	30.2	32.3	28.1	33.0	16.2	30.3	32.4	27.5	30.6	31.1	29.8	30.6	29.2	31.4	30.5	29.9
3. Neither	17.0	20.8	13.1	18.2	8.7	12.9	20.0	18.4	14.1	13.4	20.0	16.4	17.7	15.8	16.9	14.9
4. Mostly agree	6.5	8.3	4.5	6.3	8.4	5.7	5.8	7.6	6.9	3.5	9.0	6.4	6.3	7.7	5.7	7.5
5. Agree	4.9	6.3	3.3	4.5	7.0	5.6	3.7	6.1	4.3	3.4	6.4	3.6	6.2	5.8	4.6	10.4
Item 12100 N(Wtd)	2959	1451	1406	2328	345	699	916	897	447	1399	1382	1163	665	379	593	67
A18E: I get very upset when I see other people treated unfairly																
1. Disagree	2.8	3.0	2.5	2.6	3.5	2.0	2.9	2.4	4.9	2.3	3.1	2.9	2.7	1.6	2.2	10.3
2. Mostly disagree	4.4	5.9	2.6	4.6	3.2	5.3	4.9	3.5	4.2	3.9	5.1	4.8	2.7	3.7	5.7	4.4
3. Neither	8.8	13.0	4.2	9.0	5.5	8.5	10.6	7.8	7.1	8.1	9.3	7.9	9.7	7.7	8.9	11.8
4. Mostly agree	31.4	37.5	25.9	33.8	21.4	28.7	34.3	31.1	30.4	29.6	33.2	30.9	33.4	33.8	29.7	26.5
5. Agree	52.5	40.6	65.0	50.0	66.5	55.5	47.3	55.1	53.3	56.2	49.4	53.4	51.6	53.3	53.7	45.6
Item 12110 N(Wtd)	2967	1457	1407	2334	346	703	918	898	448	1400	1386	1162	668	379	596	68
A18F: I would agree to a good plan to make a better life for the poor, even if it cost me money																
1. Disagree	7.2	9.3	4.7	7.4	4.6	7.0	7.6	6.5	7.9	5.8	8.8	5.9	6.8	5.8	10.2	13.8
2. Mostly disagree	10.6	13.3	7.7	11.4	7.5	11.5	9.2	10.7	11.7	9.3	11.9	9.6	12.2	12.1	9.5	15.4
3. Neither	24.3	26.8	22.2	26.7	12.4	22.8	28.9	20.1	25.8	23.2	25.5	24.5	23.7	23.4	26.1	21.5
4. Mostly agree	35.4	32.4	38.4	35.6	30.8	34.1	36.3	36.2	33.7	36.9	34.1	36.4	34.0	36.6	35.6	29.2
5. Agree	22.6	18.2	27.1	18.9	44.4	24.4	18.1	26.6	20.9	24.9	19.8	23.5	23.1	22.1	18.8	21.5
Item 12120 N(Wtd)	2944	1448	1395	2317	347	697	906	896	445	1392	1375	1158	658	380	590	65
A18G: It's not really my problem if others are in trouble and need help																
1. Disagree	40.6	31.1	50.5	38.1	52.9	46.2	36.1	41.4	40.0	45.3	35.9	41.8	39.0	38.5	41.7	33.8
2. Mostly disagree	35.0	37.7	32.9	38.4	19.4	34.0	37.9	34.4	32.0	35.9	35.2	36.3	35.1	35.6	34.4	30.9
3. Neither	12.8	16.5	9.2	13.4	8.1	10.0	15.4	11.8	14.1	10.4	15.4	11.2	14.3	15.3	12.4	16.2
4. Mostly agree	7.6	10.0	5.3	7.1	12.4	6.6	7.6	7.9	8.9	6.2	8.6	7.3	7.4	7.4	8.3	10.3
5. Agree	3.8	4.6	2.3	3.0	7.2	3.3	3.1	4.6	4.7	2.2	5.0	3.4	4.2	2.9	3.4	8.8
Item 12130 N(Wtd)	2959	1450	1406	2328	346	697	918	897	447	1399	1381	1164	666	379	590	68
A18H: Americans could change their eating habits to provide more food for the hungry people in other parts of the world, and at the same time be healthier themselves																
1. Disagree	9.8	12.6	6.6	9.5	12.9	8.3	9.2	11.7	9.7	8.5	11.3	8.0	10.3	9.2	10.8	23.9
2. Mostly disagree	10.4	13.0	7.9	10.3	12.6	10.5	9.2	11.9	10.1	10.5	10.6	8.8	10.5	11.8	11.4	17.9
3. Neither	14.5	16.2	12.4	13.9	13.7	16.7	14.3	12.8	15.1	13.7	14.8	12.5	18.4	13.2	14.6	14.9
4. Mostly agree	29.4	29.6	29.2	32.0	20.6	29.8	32.7	27.6	25.8	30.1	29.2	33.2	28.8	28.4	26.2	22.4
5. Agree	35.8	28.6	43.9	34.4	40.6	34.8	34.7	35.9	39.6	37.1	34.2	37.5	31.9	37.1	36.8	22.4
Item 12140 N(Wtd)	2967	1457	1409	2330	350	707	918	897	445	1401	1385	1164	667	380	595	67

QUESTIONNAIRE FORM 5 1976	TOTAL	SEX		RACE		REGION				4YR COLLEGE PLANS		ILLICIT DRUG USE: LIFETIME				
		M	F	White	Black	NE	NC	S	W	Yes	No	None	Mari- juana Only	Few Pills	More Pills	Any Her- oin
Weighted No. of Cases:	3008	1473	1427	2356	356	713	930	906	460	1415	1398	1174	678	381	606	70
% of Weighted Total:	100.0	49.0	47.4	78.3	11.8	23.7	30.9	30.1	15.3	47.0	46.5	39.0	22.5	12.7	20.1	2.3

A18I: My family and I often buy things we really don't need; we could get along with much less

1. Disagree	12.8	13.5	12.0	9.9	28.7	16.8	8.1	15.2	11.4	11.3	14.0	13.0	11.5	12.6	12.1	23.5
2. Mostly disagree	14.6	16.5	12.0	15.9	10.6	16.7	16.4	12.2	12.3	15.5	13.2	13.1	17.8	12.6	15.6	11.8
3. Neither	13.6	15.3	11.6	13.2	10.9	14.9	14.0	10.7	16.6	12.9	13.5	12.8	15.7	11.8	12.8	19.1
4. Mostly agree	30.2	31.4	29.4	32.2	20.1	28.6	31.4	28.4	33.6	30.8	30.7	30.7	28.7	37.3	28.4	17.6
5. Agree	28.8	23.3	35.1	28.9	29.3	23.2	29.9	33.6	26.0	29.6	28.6	30.5	26.2	25.7	31.0	27.9
Item 10060 N(Wtd)	2968	1457	1406	2332	348	707	919	895	446	1401	1386	1164	668	381	596	68

A18J: Most people will have fuller and happier lives if they choose legal marriage rather than staying single, or just living with someone

1. Disagree	23.9	19.6	28.8	23.7	27.7	30.7	20.8	22.1	23.1	23.3	24.3	14.9	24.5	25.1	37.3	56.7
2. Mostly disagree	14.2	15.5	13.0	14.7	11.3	16.8	16.3	10.5	13.3	14.2	14.5	12.0	17.7	16.9	13.9	6.0
3. Neither	23.7	27.4	19.6	23.8	20.2	22.4	25.9	20.8	26.7	24.7	22.3	23.2	25.3	22.8	24.4	14.9
4. Mostly agree	16.7	16.8	16.1	16.5	17.1	14.1	18.2	17.1	16.9	17.3	16.6	19.4	16.8	15.6	11.8	11.9
5. Agree	21.5	20.8	22.5	21.3	24.0	16.0	18.7	29.4	20.0	20.5	22.3	30.4	15.6	19.6	12.6	10.4
Item 12150 N(Wtd)	2959	1450	1406	2330	346	701	918	895	445	1391	1388	1163	665	378	595	67

A18K: Parents should encourage just as much independence in their daughters as in their sons

1. Disagree	6.1	9.4	2.7	5.3	8.9	6.1	4.0	7.8	7.4	5.2	6.9	5.8	6.8	5.5	5.7	7.5
2. Mostly disagree	7.9	11.4	4.3	7.8	7.7	7.1	8.4	7.5	8.9	8.0	7.4	9.1	8.1	6.1	7.2	7.5
3. Neither	8.7	13.5	3.3	8.8	6.6	8.0	9.9	7.6	9.8	8.0	8.5	8.2	9.8	8.2	7.6	14.9
4. Mostly agree	24.4	29.5	19.6	24.7	21.5	24.3	26.3	21.5	26.8	24.3	24.9	26.5	25.4	24.2	20.6	17.9
5. Agree	52.8	36.2	70.1	53.3	55.3	54.5	51.4	55.6	47.3	54.5	52.3	50.4	50.2	55.8	59.1	52.2
Item 12160 N(Wtd)	2964	1454	1410	2332	349	703	917	896	448	1399	1387	1164	666	380	596	67

A18L: Being a mother and raising children is one of the most fulfilling experiences a woman can have

1. Disagree	6.3	4.0	8.8	6.5	4.6	7.8	6.3	5.2	6.2	7.0	5.5	5.9	6.3	6.2	6.7	16.1
2. Mostly disagree	7.6	5.8	9.5	8.0	4.3	8.0	8.4	6.9	6.7	7.3	8.3	5.6	9.1	8.6	9.3	9.7
3. Neither	27.6	39.9	15.8	30.5	15.9	27.5	29.0	24.2	31.8	31.2	24.2	23.0	30.9	30.5	32.8	25.8
4. Mostly agree	25.6	23.4	28.0	26.3	19.7	23.9	28.2	24.3	25.6	26.6	25.2	27.6	25.3	25.7	22.8	22.6
5. Agree	32.8	27.0	37.9	28.8	55.7	32.6	28.1	39.4	29.7	27.9	36.9	37.9	28.4	29.2	28.4	25.8
Item 12170 N(Wtd)	2896	1387	1408	2271	345	690	893	879	434	1370	1356	1144	651	370	580	62

A18M: Most fathers should spend more time with their children than they do now

1. Disagree	1.8	1.8	1.9	1.6	1.4	1.9	1.4	2.5	1.3	1.4	2.3	1.6	1.8	1.3	1.9	9.0
2. Mostly disagree	2.6	3.3	1.6	2.5	2.0	2.9	3.1	1.9	2.9	2.5	2.7	2.2	2.7	3.7	3.1	1.5
3. Neither	12.9	14.1	11.7	13.6	6.9	15.6	13.7	8.8	14.8	12.5	13.1	10.5	12.7	13.5	16.5	17.9
4. Mostly agree	31.7	35.5	28.5	34.1	19.5	31.1	36.4	26.6	33.3	32.8	31.8	30.9	32.2	32.4	32.9	32.8
5. Agree	51.0	45.3	56.3	48.1	69.9	48.7	45.4	60.2	47.6	50.8	50.1	54.9	50.5	48.8	45.8	38.8
Item 12180 N(Wtd)	2954	1447	1405	2323	349	700	915	894	445	1397	1377	1161	667	377	589	67

A18N: The husband should make all the important decisions in the family

1. Disagree	36.7	22.5	51.7	36.5	38.1	41.6	35.4	36.5	31.8	39.5	34.4	35.7	34.1	37.4	42.5	41.2
2. Mostly disagree	20.8	22.1	19.7	22.1	15.2	20.8	22.9	17.2	23.7	22.1	19.6	21.3	21.2	20.5	21.5	11.8
3. Neither	16.2	22.5	9.8	16.9	12.3	15.0	17.2	15.6	17.2	16.4	16.1	15.4	18.9	14.7	14.7	17.6
4. Mostly agree	14.3	16.8	11.2	13.6	16.3	12.5	14.3	15.6	14.5	13.6	14.7	15.4	13.8	15.5	11.5	17.6
5. Agree	12.1	16.1	7.5	10.8	18.1	10.1	10.2	15.1	12.8	8.4	15.1	12.2	12.0	11.8	9.8	11.8
Item 12190 N(Wtd)	2963	1456	1407	2330	349	702	918	896	447	1401	1385	1166	666	380	591	68

QUESTIONNAIRE FORM 5 1976	TOTAL	SEX		RACE		REGION				4YR COLLEGE PLANS		ILLICIT DRUG USE: LIFETIME				
		M	F	White	Black	NE	NC	S	W	Yes	No	None	Mari- juana Only	Few Pills	More Pills	Any Her- oin
Weighted No. of Cases:	3008	1473	1427	2356	356	713	930	906	460	1415	1398	1174	678	381	606	70
% of Weighted Total:	100.0	49.0	47.4	78.3	11.8	23.7	30.9	30.1	15.3	47.0	46.5	39.0	22.5	12.7	20.1	2.3

A19: Some people think about what's going on in government very often, and others are not that interested. How much of an interest do you take in government and current events?

1. No interest at all	4.9	4.6	4.9	4.3	4.8	6.6	5.0	3.1	5.2	2.9	6.6	3.1	4.6	5.5	5.4	15.2
2. Very little interest	17.7	15.5	19.8	17.2	16.8	20.4	17.9	16.1	16.4	12.3	22.6	17.4	15.9	19.3	18.5	21.2
3. Some interest	48.7	45.2	52.7	48.8	49.7	46.5	50.3	48.7	49.1	46.5	51.3	49.0	49.4	45.4	50.0	39.4
4. A lot of interest	21.6	24.7	18.6	22.4	21.6	20.4	20.4	24.2	21.1	28.5	15.2	23.0	21.8	24.8	19.2	15.2
5. A very great interest	7.1	10.0	4.0	7.2	7.1	6.2	6.4	8.0	8.1	9.9	4.3	7.5	8.3	5.0	6.9	7.6
Item 6330 N(Wtd)	2967	1452	1416	2330	352	707	916	897	446	1401	1384	1169	674	379	590	66

A20: If you have at least an average income in the future, how likely is it that you will contribute money to the following organizations? If you have already contributed, mark the last circle only. Are you likely to contribute to...

A20A: The United Fund or other community charities?

1. Definitely not	4.1	5.4	2.4	3.5	5.5	3.7	4.9	3.1	4.7	3.1	4.9	2.9	5.6	3.2	4.5	8.8
2. Probably not	13.5	15.2	12.0	14.3	8.4	13.1	13.2	12.3	17.2	11.7	15.5	11.8	12.4	16.4	15.6	19.1
3. Don't know	37.1	36.5	37.4	36.8	38.0	34.7	34.9	37.4	44.7	34.1	40.1	35.5	39.1	34.7	39.7	39.7
4. Probably will	30.6	30.7	30.6	30.6	32.3	29.4	32.3	32.5	25.3	34.5	27.0	33.9	28.7	33.4	26.7	13.2
5. Definitely will	4.5	4.4	4.8	4.2	6.9	5.8	3.5	4.9	3.8	5.3	3.7	5.9	3.0	5.3	3.3	2.9
6. Already have	10.1	7.8	12.9	10.7	8.9	13.3	11.1	9.5	4.3	11.5	8.9	10.0	11.2	6.6	10.2	16.2
Item 12200 N(Wtd)	2931	1437	1397	2302	347	694	903	891	443	1388	1368	1156	663	377	577	68

A20B: International relief organizations (CARE, UNICEF, etc.)?

1. Definitely not	4.2	6.1	2.1	3.9	3.5	3.6	4.0	4.4	5.0	3.8	4.4	3.1	5.6	4.3	3.9	7.4
2. Probably not	12.2	15.8	8.4	13.4	7.2	11.0	12.5	11.7	14.7	10.9	13.8	11.7	12.9	12.0	12.2	22.1
3. Don't know	30.7	32.8	28.2	30.6	30.1	27.8	29.9	32.1	33.2	25.4	34.7	28.0	29.9	34.0	32.4	32.4
4. Probably will	34.1	32.4	35.9	33.2	38.6	34.1	33.1	34.8	34.3	36.8	32.0	37.9	31.4	30.5	33.8	16.2
5. Definitely will	8.1	5.5	10.7	6.9	13.9	10.2	7.0	8.7	6.1	10.7	5.4	8.5	9.3	9.6	6.0	2.9
6. Already have	10.8	7.5	14.8	12.0	6.7	13.1	13.6	8.2	6.8	12.4	9.8	10.8	10.8	9.6	11.3	17.6
Item 12210 N(Wtd)	2928	1433	1396	2301	345	693	905	887	443	1384	1373	1150	665	374	583	68

A20C: Minority group organizations (NAACP, SCLS, etc.)?

1. Definitely not	12.0	15.6	8.0	13.4	3.5	12.4	10.9	13.3	11.0	11.2	12.8	11.7	13.3	9.6	12.1	19.4
2. Probably not	24.8	25.8	23.9	28.3	8.1	23.7	26.3	24.3	24.5	24.1	26.1	25.3	25.2	22.9	26.7	23.9
3. Don't know	39.8	38.2	41.5	42.0	23.1	38.8	44.2	33.6	44.8	37.7	42.5	39.5	37.9	45.1	38.5	40.3
4. Probably will	17.0	14.3	19.9	14.1	36.3	18.1	14.1	20.7	14.0	18.7	14.9	18.4	16.3	16.5	15.0	11.9
5. Definitely will	4.8	4.2	5.4	1.8	21.6	5.3	3.3	6.2	4.7	6.0	3.2	4.2	5.8	3.7	5.3	1.5
6. Already have	1.5	1.8	1.3	.5	7.2	1.6	1.3	2.0	.9	2.1	.7	1.0	1.3	2.1	2.6	-
Item 12220 N(Wtd)	2942	1445	1396	2311	347	695	912	890	444	1389	1378	1156	670	375	585	67

A20D: Church or religious organizations?

1. Definitely not	5.5	6.2	4.6	5.5	2.0	7.2	4.7	2.7	10.2	5.8	5.2	4.1	5.7	4.5	7.9	14.7
2. Probably not	8.7	9.2	8.4	9.6	4.3	10.8	8.8	5.2	12.4	8.5	9.4	5.5	10.9	7.7	13.5	11.8
3. Don't know	14.2	16.3	11.6	14.0	11.0	16.2	12.8	12.3	17.9	11.4	16.2	10.3	16.9	13.0	17.8	25.0
4. Probably will	24.6	24.6	24.5	24.3	24.6	25.0	25.1	26.1	20.4	20.0	28.6	24.8	24.1	26.1	23.8	17.6
5. Definitely will	15.7	14.4	16.9	14.5	26.0	12.2	15.9	19.9	12.7	18.8	13.1	20.8	12.7	17.3	8.9	5.9
6. Already have	31.2	29.4	34.0	32.2	32.1	28.9	32.7	33.9	26.2	35.5	27.6	34.6	29.7	31.4	28.3	25.0
Item 12230 N(Wtd)	2938	1436	1401	2308	346	696	914	886	442	1392	1372	1158	663	376	584	68

QUESTIONNAIRE FORM 5 1976	TOTAL	SEX		RACE		REGION				4YR COLLEGE PLANS		ILLICIT DRUG USE: LIFETIME				
		M	F	White	Black	NE	NC	S	W	Yes	No	None	Marijuana Only	Few Pills	More Pills	Any Heroin
Weighted No. of Cases:	3008	1473	1427	2356	356	713	930	906	460	1415	1398	1174	678	381	606	70
% of Weighted Total:	100.0	49.0	47.4	78.3	11.8	23.7	30.9	30.1	15.3	47.0	46.5	39.0	22.5	12.7	20.1	2.3

A20E: Political parties or organizations?

	TOTAL	M	F	White	Black	NE	NC	S	W	Yes	No	None	Mari-juana Only	Few Pills	More Pills	Any Heroin
1. Definitely not	20.1	21.5	18.6	19.5	19.1	24.6	17.1	18.6	21.5	16.7	23.0	17.6	22.3	19.1	21.2	33.3
2. Probably not	28.1	25.8	30.6	28.7	26.5	27.0	29.1	27.3	29.3	26.4	30.2	28.5	28.7	23.9	31.0	24.2
3. Don't know	32.3	31.6	32.8	32.0	33.2	32.2	34.4	31.1	30.4	32.9	31.6	32.6	30.9	36.2	29.3	31.8
4. Probably will	13.2	13.0	13.3	13.1	15.9	10.5	10.9	17.7	12.7	15.9	10.4	14.4	12.2	12.8	12.2	9.1
5. Definitely will	3.2	4.0	2.3	3.4	2.9	3.2	4.0	2.5	2.9	4.0	2.3	3.8	1.7	5.6	2.8	1.5
6. Already have	3.2	4.1	2.4	3.4	2.4	2.5	4.4	2.7	3.2	4.1	2.3	3.0	4.3	2.4	3.3	1.5
Item 12240 N(Wtd)	2917	1426	1392	2296	340	692	899	885	441	1377	1371	1156	656	376	580	66

A20F: Citizen lobbies (Common Cause, Public Citizen, etc.)?

	TOTAL	M	F	White	Black	NE	NC	S	W	Yes	No	None	Mari-juana Only	Few Pills	More Pills	Any Heroin
1. Definitely not	10.0	10.7	9.2	9.4	10.5	10.9	7.8	10.4	11.9	8.3	11.6	9.7	10.1	7.4	11.7	12.5
2. Probably not	24.5	24.6	23.9	25.4	19.5	23.9	26.2	22.4	25.8	23.5	25.9	24.9	25.1	24.9	22.7	29.7
3. Don't know	45.1	43.6	46.7	45.8	41.7	45.0	46.6	45.6	41.6	44.6	45.5	44.6	45.5	46.2	45.9	31.3
4. Probably will	15.9	15.9	16.0	15.4	21.3	15.7	14.7	16.4	17.3	18.6	13.0	16.5	15.0	15.4	15.8	21.9
5. Definitely will	3.1	3.7	2.7	2.9	4.7	3.2	3.2	3.5	2.2	3.6	2.6	3.2	2.7	4.8	2.7	3.1
6. Already have	1.4	1.5	1.4	1.2	2.0	1.3	1.4	1.7	1.1	1.4	1.4	1.3	1.7	1.3	1.4	1.6
Item 12250 N(Wtd)	2936	1443	1393	2311	343	695	905	891	445	1392	1372	1158	666	377	582	64

A20G: Charities to help fight diseases (Cancer, Heart Disease, etc.)?

	TOTAL	M	F	White	Black	NE	NC	S	W	Yes	No	None	Mari-juana Only	Few Pills	More Pills	Any Heroin
1. Definitely not	1.3	1.9	.4	.7	2.0	1.4	.9	1.3	1.8	.9	1.5	.9	1.8	.8	.7	7.6
2. Probably not	2.7	4.0	1.3	2.8	2.0	2.9	2.5	2.1	3.8	1.7	3.5	2.0	3.5	4.2	2.1	4.5
3. Don't know	10.6	13.8	6.5	9.9	10.3	10.5	9.3	9.7	15.5	7.7	12.5	8.9	10.4	9.3	12.7	22.7
4. Probably will	36.3	40.5	32.1	37.2	35.5	33.5	39.3	35.8	35.4	36.8	36.0	36.5	36.3	36.0	38.9	18.2
5. Definitely will	27.7	23.6	32.1	26.7	34.7	28.1	27.8	27.2	28.4	30.3	25.5	30.7	26.8	27.0	24.7	24.2
6. Already have	21.4	16.0	27.4	22.7	15.5	23.6	20.1	23.9	15.3	22.7	21.1	21.0	21.3	22.8	21.1	21.2
Item 12260 N(Wtd)	2945	1438	1407	2314	349	698	906	897	444	1393	1376	1165	663	378	584	66

A20H: Organizations concerned with population problems (Planned Parenthood, ZPG, etc.)?

	TOTAL	M	F	White	Black	NE	NC	S	W	Yes	No	None	Mari-juana Only	Few Pills	More Pills	Any Heroin
1. Definitely not	7.6	9.5	5.1	7.1	6.6	6.8	7.1	7.4	9.9	7.2	7.7	8.0	8.6	5.3	5.6	7.5
2. Probably not	17.4	21.3	13.7	18.5	13.3	18.8	19.2	14.9	16.7	18.1	17.9	18.8	16.5	17.0	16.8	16.4
3. Don't know	38.4	39.6	.37.0	38.6	37.9	38.3	38.5	38.5	38.7	36.2	39.6	38.8	39.2	39.3	34.5	34.3
4. Probably will	26.6	22.6	31.0	26.9	28.3	24.6	26.4	28.9	25.2	27.5	25.7	26.2	26.2	27.3	29.2	29.9
5. Definitely will	8.1	5.7	10.3	7.0	11.8	9.6	6.7	8.8	7.0	9.3	7.0	6.9	8.1	8.5	10.6	7.5
6. Already have	1.9	1.2	2.7	1.8	2.3	1.9	2.0	1.6	2.7	1.8	2.2	1.1	1.5	2.7	3.4	4.5
Item 12270 N(Wtd)	2945	1444	1402	2317	346	695	912	894	444	1396	1379	1161	665	377	585	67

A20I: Organizations concerned with environmental problems (Sierra Club, Friends of Earth, etc.)?

	TOTAL	M	F	White	Black	NE	NC	S	W	Yes	No	None	Mari-juana Only	Few Pills	More Pills	Any Heroin
1. Definitely not	6.4	8.1	4.4	5.6	8.1	7.2	5.9	6.0	7.0	5.0	7.4	5.1	7.0	6.6	6.8	13.4
2. Probably not	15.3	14.5	16.1	14.9	17.9	15.4	15.6	16.1	13.3	12.8	17.8	16.8	13.2	16.3	13.2	20.9
3. Don't know	38.6	36.1	40.8	38.7	40.8	34.4	41.1	40.7	36.4	35.7	41.8	39.2	39.0	41.3	35.7	22.4
4. Probably will	24.4	25.7	23.7	25.1	22.5	25.1	23.0	23.9	27.2	27.6	21.6	24.7	24.8	21.3	26.5	26.9
5. Definitely will	12.1	12.1	12.1	12.3	8.4	14.1	11.8	10.3	13.0	15.0	9.0	11.4	12.9	11.3	13.5	14.9
6. Already have	3.2	3.5	2.9	3.4	2.0	3.9	2.7	3.0	3.6	3.9	2.4	2.8	3.0	3.2	4.3	3.0
Item 12280 N(Wtd)	2950	1444	1406	2321	346	697	913	895	445	1398	1380	1160	669	380	585	67

Now we have a different kind of question.

A21: How satisfied are you with your life as a whole these days?

	TOTAL	M	F	White	Black	NE	NC	S	W	Yes	No	None	Mari-juana Only	Few Pills	More Pills	Any Heroin
1. Completely dissatisfied	1.8	1.9	1.6	1.5	3.4	1.3	1.9	2.2	1.8	1.5	2.0	2.0	1.6	1.9	.8	7.2
2. Quite dissatisfied	5.5	5.4	5.4	5.6	5.2	7.0	5.2	4.8	5.3	5.2	6.3	3.9	7.0	5.3	6.7	10.1
3. Somewhat dissatisfied	11.1	11.6	10.4	10.5	14.1	12.0	11.0	9.9	12.4	10.7	11.1	8.6	9.5	13.3	14.3	21.7
4. Neither, or mixed feelings	14.5	14.3	14.4	13.8	13.5	13.4	16.2	12.8	15.7	13.8	14.8	11.7	15.8	14.9	17.4	18.8
5. Somewhat satisfied	25.9	26.9	25.1	26.3	26.4	23.8	26.2	28.9	22.8	24.9	27.0	24.1	25.5	28.2	29.4	20.3
6. Quite satisfied	35.2	34.6	36.2	36.5	29.6	37.4	34.5	34.4	34.7	38.0	32.8	42.1	35.0	31.6	27.7	17.4
7. Completely satisfied	6.0	5.2	6.9	5.9	8.0	5.3	4.9	6.9	7.3	5.9	6.0	7.8	5.4	5.1	3.7	5.8
Item 6840 N(Wtd)	2954	1451	1407	2322	348	701	912	890	452	1396	1374	1167	671	376	596	69

QUESTIONNAIRE FORM 5 1976	TOTAL	SEX		RACE		REGION				4YR COLLEGE PLANS		ILLICIT DRUG USE: LIFETIME				
		M	F	White	Black	NE	NC	S	W	Yes	No	None	Mari- juana Only	Few Pills	More Pills	Any Her- oin
Weighted No. of Cases:	3008	1473	1427	2356	356	713	930	906	460	1415	1398	1174	678	381	606	70
% of Weighted Total:	100.0	49.0	47.4	78.3	11.8	23.7	30.9	30.1	15.3	47.0	46.5	39.0	22.5	12.7	20.1	2.3

A22: These questions are about whether you think women are discriminated against in each of the following areas. To what extent are women discriminated against...

A22A: In getting a college education?

	TOTAL	M	F	White	Black	NE	NC	S	W	Yes	No	None	Mari- juana Only	Few Pills	More Pills	Any Her- oin
1. Not at all	42.7	46.5	38.9	41.7	47.0	38.9	41.6	48.4	39.5	40.4	44.9	44.3	43.7	41.2	40.8	36.2
2. Very little	30.3	29.4	31.7	33.8	17.7	32.1	33.2	25.6	31.0	35.1	26.7	31.6	29.7	33.0	29.4	24.6
3. Some	14.2	10.3	18.0	14.3	11.0	16.8	15.3	11.0	14.0	14.9	13.8	12.4	14.2	13.0	18.4	15.9
4. A good deal	2.9	2.3	3.3	2.1	4.6	2.9	1.9	3.5	3.8	2.5	2.8	2.6	3.9	2.1	1.8	4.3
5. A great deal	2.2	2.8	1.8	1.3	7.8	1.7	1.8	3.2	2.0	1.7	2.8	2.5	1.0	4.0	1.3	2.9
8. Don't know	7.7	8.9	6.2	6.8	11.9	7.5	6.2	8.3	10.0	5.4	9.0	6.7	7.7	6.9	8.2	17.4
Item 12290 N(Wtd)	2956	1450	1410	2328	345	697	914	893	451	1403	1373	1169	671	376	598	69

A22B: In gaining positions of leadership over men and women?

	TOTAL	M	F	White	Black	NE	NC	S	W	Yes	No	None	Mari- juana Only	Few Pills	More Pills	Any Her- oin
1. Not at all	5.5	7.3	3.5	4.8	9.0	6.0	4.8	5.4	6.0	4.4	6.1	4.9	7.0	4.0	5.1	11.6
2. Very little	12.0	14.2	9.5	12.0	10.2	11.3	11.2	12.8	12.9	11.7	11.8	11.9	14.7	9.8	10.1	13.0
3. Some	33.6	36.9	30.1	35.0	25.9	30.7	35.5	33.3	34.7	35.3	32.2	36.1	32.1	36.2	30.0	23.2
4. A good deal	26.9	24.0	30.3	28.2	19.8	29.8	27.3	23.5	28.5	28.5	26.1	27.0	24.7	26.3	30.8	21.7
5. A great deal	15.8	10.3	21.6	14.6	23.0	16.6	16.0	17.4	10.9	16.5	15.5	14.4	15.3	17.0	17.5	21.7
8. Don't know	6.3	7.4	5.0	5.4	12.0	5.2	5.3	7.7	7.3	3.6	8.3	5.7	6.0	6.9	6.6	8.7
Item 12300 N(Wtd)	2949	1448	1406	2323	343	697	912	891	449	1401	1370	1166	672	376	594	69

A22C: In obtaining executive positions in business?

	TOTAL	M	F	White	Black	NE	NC	S	W	Yes	No	None	Mari- juana Only	Few Pills	More Pills	Any Her- oin
1. Not at all	6.5	7.8	4.9	4.9	13.2	6.5	5.9	7.3	5.8	4.9	7.6	5.1	8.6	4.8	6.1	10.1
2. Very little	12.5	13.2	11.6	12.6	11.8	11.4	13.1	12.9	12.5	11.7	13.3	14.7	12.8	10.4	9.6	11.6
3. Some	28.1	29.8	26.6	29.0	22.9	25.5	29.4	28.4	28.5	27.1	29.0	27.7	28.2	29.8	27.9	23.2
4. A good deal	27.0	26.3	27.5	28.6	18.2	28.5	28.1	24.7	27.2	30.5	25.0	25.8	27.1	29.8	28.7	24.6
5. A great deal	16.5	12.5	21.0	15.7	22.6	20.0	15.2	16.6	13.8	18.6	14.8	17.7	13.6	16.2	17.8	18.8
8. Don't know	9.4	10.4	8.4	9.1	11.5	8.2	8.2	10.0	12.2	7.2	10.4	8.9	9.7	9.0	10.1	11.6
Item 12310 N(Wtd)	2944	1450	1402	2324	340	695	914	887	449	1399	1369	1164	671	376	595	69

A22D: In obtaining top jobs in the professions?

	TOTAL	M	F	White	Black	NE	NC	S	W	Yes	No	None	Mari- juana Only	Few Pills	More Pills	Any Her- oin
1. Not at all	9.3	11.3	7.3	8.0	15.5	9.5	7.0	12.0	8.0	8.2	9.9	7.9	11.3	8.6	9.2	15.9
2. Very little	16.6	18.5	14.9	16.7	16.7	14.5	15.2	18.5	19.3	16.5	16.8	17.3	17.8	16.6	14.3	15.9
3. Some	28.2	28.7	27.5	29.6	20.5	27.0	31.1	26.0	28.2	30.3	26.5	28.2	28.8	27.8	27.9	24.6
4. A good deal	23.0	20.9	25.1	23.7	18.5	25.0	24.6	20.9	21.1	24.0	22.3	23.3	19.9	23.3	26.7	18.8
5. A great deal	15.0	11.7	18.5	14.2	20.2	17.1	14.8	15.1	12.0	15.1	15.2	15.6	14.5	15.0	13.6	15.9
8. Don't know	7.9	9.0	6.7	7.8	8.6	6.9	7.3	7.6	11.3	5.9	9.3	7.7	7.8	8.6	8.1	8.7
Item 12320 N(Wtd)	2939	1446	1402	2323	336	692	910	887	450	1398	1368	1164	670	374	595	69

A22E: In getting skilled labor jobs?

	TOTAL	M	F	White	Black	NE	NC	S	W	Yes	No	None	Mari- juana Only	Few Pills	More Pills	Any Her- oin
1. Not at all	8.0	9.2	6.8	7.1	12.3	8.0	7.6	8.4	8.3	7.4	8.3	6.6	9.7	8.3	8.6	5.8
2. Very little	18.2	20.1	16.5	18.6	15.0	17.6	19.9	16.9	18.1	16.6	20.2	18.5	20.3	14.5	18.0	14.5
3. Some	29.5	29.8	29.1	30.4	25.2	30.0	30.1	27.0	32.4	31.3	28.2	29.0	31.0	29.0	29.9	30.4
4. A good deal	20.2	18.9	21.3	21.1	16.4	21.0	20.7	21.0	17.0	22.0	18.6	21.8	17.2	23.1	18.6	23.2
5. A great deal	12.6	10.7	14.6	11.8	20.2	12.5	11.9	15.6	8.5	13.1	12.3	13.4	10.9	12.9	12.6	11.6
8. Don't know	11.4	11.1	11.8	11.1	10.9	10.9	9.8	11.1	15.8	9.5	12.2	10.8	10.9	12.1	12.4	14.5
Item 12330 N(Wtd)	2935	1441	1404	2316	341	687	910	890	448	1393	1370	1162	670	373	596	69

A22F: In getting elected to political office?

	TOTAL	M	F	White	Black	NE	NC	S	W	Yes	No	None	Mari- juana Only	Few Pills	More Pills	Any Her- oin
1. Not at all	5.6	7.6	3.6	4.7	9.0	5.2	4.9	6.3	6.0	4.6	6.3	4.5	7.6	6.1	4.4	8.7
2. Very little	9.2	12.2	5.8	9.5	9.0	8.0	9.2	8.8	12.0	10.2	8.1	9.6	9.8	8.2	8.7	10.1
3. Some	22.8	25.2	20.6	23.4	20.4	22.4	21.1	25.2	22.3	22.1	23.8	24.0	21.8	21.0	23.3	17.4
4. A good deal	23.2	23.9	22.5	24.6	15.2	24.0	23.2	22.4	23.6	25.9	21.3	23.3	23.0	26.9	21.1	21.7
5. A great deal	31.5	22.5	40.9	31.0	36.2	33.2	33.6	29.9	27.6	32.2	31.2	31.8	30.8	30.1	34.2	26.1
8. Don't know	7.7	8.6	6.7	6.8	10.2	7.2	7.9	7.8	8.0	5.0	9.2	6.8	6.9	7.7	8.4	17.4
Item 12340 N(Wtd)	2949	1449	1408	2326	343	696	913	890	449	1402	1373	1168	671	376	596	69

QUESTIONNAIRE FORM 5 1976	TOTAL	SEX		RACE		REGION				4YR COLLEGE PLANS		ILLICIT DRUG USE: LIFETIME				
		M	F	White	Black	NE	NC	S	W	Yes	No	None	Mari- juana Only	Few Pills	More Pills	Any Her- oin
Weighted No. of Cases:	3008	1473	1427	2356	356	713	930	906	460	1415	1398	1174	678	381	606	70
% of Weighted Total:	100.0	49.0	47.4	78.3	11.8	23.7	30.9	30.1	15.3	47.0	46.5	39.0	22.5	12.7	20.1	2.3

A22G: In getting equal pay for equal work?

1. Not at all	13.6	18.3	9.1	12.9	16.7	15.8	10.6	14.8	13.8	12.7	14.6	12.8	16.6	11.7	12.8	15.9
2. Very little	20.5	24.5	16.6	21.8	16.1	18.6	21.9	21.0	19.3	20.3	20.9	21.2	19.8	23.7	18.5	26.1
3. Some	24.7	24.4	25.0	25.8	19.3	23.6	26.9	22.2	26.7	25.0	25.0	23.9	26.2	24.5	24.7	18.8
4. A good deal	18.5	16.2	20.9	19.2	14.0	19.1	17.9	17.3	21.1	21.1	16.1	19.7	15.8	20.5	18.8	17.4
5. A great deal	16.4	10.4	22.2	14.6	25.1	17.1	17.1	17.0	13.1	16.1	16.4	16.7	15.2	15.2	17.5	11.6
8. Don't know	6.3	6.3	6.0	5.7	8.8	5.9	5.5	7.8	6.0	4.8	7.0	5.7	6.5	4.5	7.6	11.6
Item 12350 N(Wtd)	*2945*	*1447*	*1407*	*2325*	*342*	*692*	*913*	*890*	*450*	*1398*	*1374*	*1165*	*673*	*376*	*595*	*69*

A23: The next questions ask for your opinions on the effects of using certain drugs and other substances. First, how much do you think people risk harming themselves (physically or in other ways), if they...

A23A: Smoke one or more packs of cigarettes per day

1. No risk	2.0	2.3	1.6	1.3	4.3	2.2	1.4	2.4	2.2	1.1	2.4	2.1	1.0	1.6	2.3	7.4
2. Slight risk	9.3	8.6	9.8	9.0	9.6	8.5	10.7	9.6	6.8	6.6	11.6	6.3	12.4	8.5	10.4	16.2
3. Moderate risk	30.6	31.8	29.6	32.0	26.4	29.6	33.3	30.0	27.5	27.0	34.8	28.9	29.1	32.0	34.7	32.4
4. Great risk	56.4	55.0	57.9	56.7	55.4	58.1	53.4	56.1	60.4	64.0	49.3	60.9	55.7	56.9	51.6	38.2
5. Can't say drug unfamiliar	1.8	2.4	1.0	1.1	4.3	1.6	1.1	1.9	3.1	1.4	1.7	1.9	1.9	1.3	1.0	4.4
Item 12360 N(Wtd)	*2950*	*1457*	*1403*	*2328*	*345*	*695*	*914*	*888*	*454*	*1401*	*1375*	*1165*	*671*	*378*	*599*	*68*

A23B: Try marijuana (pot, grass) once or twice

1. No risk	49.7	52.1	47.1	51.9	35.0	57.6	51.6	41.8	49.1	49.2	49.7	21.7	67.0	59.6	75.5	79.7
2. Slight risk	25.2	25.6	25.3	26.1	22.2	23.5	26.6	26.4	22.7	27.1	23.8	31.7	24.5	22.9	17.7	11.6
3. Moderate risk	10.4	8.1	12.5	9.9	12.8	8.7	9.9	10.9	12.8	11.3	9.9	17.8	5.9	6.4	4.5	1.4
4. Great risk	11.4	11.1	11.7	9.9	22.2	7.5	9.4	16.1	12.3	10.0	12.7	22.2	2.1	10.6	1.8	4.3
5. Can't say drug unfamiliar	3.3	3.2	3.5	2.3	8.2	2.6	2.5	4.7	3.3	2.4	3.8	6.5	.4	1.1	.8	2.9
Item 12370 N(Wtd)	*2951*	*1456*	*1405*	*2332*	*343*	*693*	*918*	*886*	*454*	*1399*	*1378*	*1163*	*673*	*376*	*600*	*69*

A23C: Smoke marijuana occasionally

1. No risk	30.0	32.4	27.7	31.0	23.0	37.3	29.1	26.9	26.5	27.4	31.6	6.9	36.7	35.3	60.0	63.8
2. Slight risk	28.5	28.9	27.5	29.8	21.6	29.5	30.3	25.3	29.9	30.1	27.6	22.7	40.1	32.4	26.0	17.4
3. Moderate risk	23.1	22.0	24.6	23.0	21.6	21.0	24.5	23.3	23.2	26.4	21.0	36.8	16.8	18.0	9.5	10.1
4. Great risk	15.0	13.4	16.7	13.7	22.4	10.0	13.1	19.6	17.5	13.5	15.9	27.2	5.5	13.3	3.2	7.2
5. Can't say drug unfamiliar	3.4	3.2	3.3	2.4	7.2	2.0	2.9	4.9	3.1	2.5	3.9	6.3	.9	1.1	1.2	1.4
Item 12380 N(Wtd)	*2950*	*1452*	*1409*	*2327*	*348*	*691*	*916*	*891*	*452*	*1400*	*1375*	*1166*	*671*	*377*	*600*	*69*

A23D: Smoke marijuana regularly

1. No risk	13.9	16.2	11.7	13.2	13.6	14.2	13.9	14.9	11.7	10.1	16.7	3.0	15.1	16.0	28.8	43.5
2. Slight risk	20.1	22.3	17.8	21.7	14.2	25.3	19.2	16.6	20.5	20.1	20.4	5.8	27.2	24.7	36.2	26.1
3. Moderate risk	23.8	24.2	23.3	24.8	16.5	27.2	26.6	18.5	23.6	28.0	20.2	21.9	31.5	24.5	20.0	15.9
4. Great risk	38.6	34.1	43.7	37.6	48.0	30.7	37.0	45.1	41.2	39.1	38.7	62.9	25.1	33.5	13.7	15.9
5. Can't say drug unfamiliar	3.5	3.3	3.6	2.6	7.5	2.7	3.1	5.0	3.1	2.8	4.2	6.5	1.2	1.3	1.5	-
Item 12390 N(Wtd)	*2944*	*1447*	*1406*	*2322*	*346*	*691*	*915*	*883*	*454*	*1400*	*1371*	*1161*	*669*	*376*	*600*	*69*

A23E: Try LSD once or twice

1. No risk	6.0	6.4	5.4	5.1	7.0	7.7	5.9	5.1	4.8	4.4	7.0	2.6	3.7	4.8	13.7	15.9
2. Slight risk	15.9	13.6	17.4	16.4	9.6	18.6	17.9	12.3	14.9	14.2	16.9	9.8	14.5	18.6	26.8	36.2
3. Moderate risk	23.5	21.7	25.9	25.7	14.8	24.7	24.5	22.1	22.4	25.1	23.3	21.3	24.3	28.9	21.7
4. Great risk	45.7	48.6	43.3	45.1	54.1	41.1	42.4	49.8	51.2	48.4	43.4	56.5	47.3	44.6	24.7	26.1
5. Can't say drug unfamiliar	8.9	9.8	8.0	7.6	14.5	7.7	9.2	10.8	6.4	7.9	9.4	9.8	10.1	9.8	6.0	1.4
Item 12400 N(Wtd)	*2941*	*1446*	*1405*	*2323*	*344*	*688*	*912*	*887*	*455*	*1397*	*1372*	*1162*	*670*	*377*	*598*	*69*

QUESTIONNAIRE FORM 5 1976	TOTAL	SEX		RACE		REGION				4YR COLLEGE PLANS		ILLICIT DRUG USE: LIFETIME				
		M	F	White	Black	NE	NC	S	W	Yes	No	None	Mari- juana Only	Few Pills	More Pills	Any Her- oin
Weighted No. of Cases:	3008	1473	1427	2356	356	713	930	906	460	1415	1398	1174	678	381	606	70
% of Weighted Total:	100.0	49.0	47.4	78.3	11.8	23.7	30.9	30.1	15.3	47.0	46.5	39.0	22.5	12.7	20.1	2.3
A23F: Take LSD regularly																
1. No risk	1.8	2.1	1.4	.9	5.6	1.6	1.2	2.9	1.5	1.0	2.3	1.9	1.0	1.1	1.7	8.7
2. Slight risk	1.6	1.5	1.6	1.3	1.2	1.7	2.1	1.5	.9	.8	2.0	.1	1.0	1.3	4.2	10.1
3. Moderate risk	7.4	7.5	7.1	7.7	4.7	9.1	8.8	5.9	4.9	6.1	8.5	3.5	6.8	7.4	14.3	20.3
4. Great risk	80.8	79.6	82.8	83.0	76.0	80.3	79.3	79.4	87.0	84.9	78.4	85.6	81.5	81.2	73.8	59.4
5. Can't say drug unfamiliar	8.4	9.3	7.2	7.1	12.6	7.4	8.6	10.3	5.7	7.2	8.7	9.0	9.4	9.0	5.9	2.9
Item 12410 N(Wtd)	2937	1446	1403	2321	342	691	908	885	453	1401	1366	1157	672	377	596	69
A23G: Try heroin (smack, horse) once or twice																
1. No risk	3.2	3.3	3.1	2.2	7.2	3.9	2.0	4.3	2.6	2.4	3.9	2.4	2.2	2.1	4.7	17.4
2. Slight risk	8.8	7.6	9.4	8.8	6.1	10.2	9.5	7.9	6.6	7.9	9.8	6.5	5.4	9.8	14.9	27.5
3. Moderate risk	20.3	17.9	22.8	21.2	12.2	19.1	21.9	18.2	22.9	20.4	19.9	19.9	19.4	21.2	22.6	17.4
4. Great risk	58.9	61.6	56.8	60.0	61.4	58.1	57.5	60.0	61.0	61.6	57.1	62.2	62.8	57.1	51.8	34.8
5. Can't say drug unfamiliar	8.8	9.6	7.9	7.8	13.0	8.7	9.2	9.6	6.8	7.8	9.4	9.0	10.1	9.8	6.2	2.9
Item 12420 N(Wtd)	2941	1450	1404	2325	345	687	913	887	454	1404	1366	1161	670	378	598	69
A23H: Take heroin occasionally																
1. No risk	1.8	2.0	1.5	.9	5.5	1.9	1.1	2.6	1.3	1.1	2.3	1.7	1.3	1.6	1.5	4.3
2. Slight risk	2.0	1.6	2.3	1.7	3.2	1.7	2.0	2.6	1.1	1.2	2.8	1.2	1.0	2.4	3.7	8.7
3. Moderate risk	12.4	8.8	15.2	11.9	8.7	15.0	12.1	11.0	11.5	12.0	12.9	10.9	9.1	12.7	17.0	27.5
4. Great risk	75.6	78.5	73.5	78.4	70.3	73.3	76.6	74.1	80.0	78.6	73.1	77.5	78.6	74.0	72.5	56.5
5. Can't say drug unfamiliar	8.3	9.0	7.3	7.1	12.2	8.1	8.3	9.6	5.9	7.1	9.0	8.6	10.0	9.3	5.2	2.9
Item 12430 N(Wtd)	2941	1448	1406	2325	343	688	915	885	454	1403	1368	1160	672	377	599	69
A23I: Take heroin regularly																
1. No risk	1.8	1.9	1.5	.8	5.9	1.6	1.1	2.9	1.8	1.0	2.2	1.8	1.3	1.6	1.2	7.2
2. Slight risk	.1	-	.2	.1	.3	.3	.1	-	-	.1	.1	-	.1	.5	.2	-
3. Moderate risk	1.2	1.4	1.1	.9	2.6	1.2	1.0	1.7	.9	.7	1.8	.6	.9	1.6	1.5	7.2
4. Great risk	88.6	87.4	90.2	91.3	78.9	88.9	89.4	85.9	91.6	91.4	86.8	88.9	88.1	87.2	91.6	82.6
5. Can't say drug unfamiliar	8.3	9.3	7.0	7.0	12.3	8.0	8.4	9.6	5.8	6.8	9.2	8.6	9.5	9.1	5.4	4.3
Item 12440 N(Wtd)	2938	1450	1401	2323	341	687	913	886	452	1400	1368	1162	672	375	596	69
A23J: Try barbiturates (downers, goofballs, reds, yellows, etc.) once or twice																
1. No risk	10.3	9.2	10.7	10.1	7.6	11.3	10.5	9.3	9.9	9.0	11.1	3.2	5.6	9.5	27.2	33.3
2. Slight risk	20.0	20.0	20.3	21.6	10.5	22.6	21.7	16.6	19.6	19.5	20.4	13.4	15.7	23.3	33.7	43.5
3. Moderate risk	27.8	26.7	29.6	29.3	22.1	28.1	30.2	24.1	30.1	30.6	26.1	29.1	30.3	33.7	22.3	13.0
4. Great risk	32.5	34.3	30.8	31.7	41.0	30.7	28.6	37.5	32.7	32.3	32.5	41.7	38.6	26.3	12.7	5.8
5. Can't say drug unfamiliar	9.4	9.9	8.7	7.3	19.2	7.4	8.9	12.5	7.5	8.4	9.9	12.5	9.8	7.4	4.2	4.3
Item 12450 N(Wtd)	2948	1453	1406	2328	344	691	915	888	455	1404	1374	1163	674	377	600	69
A23K: Take barbiturates regularly																
1. No risk	2.2	2.3	1.7	1.2	5.8	1.6	1.9	3.2	1.8	1.3	2.6	1.9	1.5	1.6	2.5	8.7
2. Slight risk	4.3	4.4	4.1	4.4	2.9	4.4	5.6	4.2	2.2	2.9	5.2	.6	2.5	3.7	11.9	23.2
3. Moderate risk	16.5	16.4	16.7	17.5	10.5	16.9	18.8	13.4	17.1	14.9	18.4	8.6	14.2	17.6	32.6	27.5
4. Great risk	67.7	66.9	68.8	69.7	61.8	69.7	65.1	66.7	72.1	73.1	63.7	76.7	71.8	69.1	49.2	36.2
5. Can't say drug unfamiliar	9.3	9.8	8.5	7.1	19.0	7.3	8.8	12.6	6.9	7.8	10.1	12.1	10.0	7.7	3.7	4.3
Item 12460 N(Wtd)	2939	1449	1405	2325	343	687	913	888	451	1397	1373	1161	671	376	598	69
A23L: Try amphetamines (uppers, pep pills, bennies, speed) once or twice																
1. No risk	12.6	12.2	12.5	12.5	8.5	13.5	13.8	10.9	12.6	10.8	13.8	3.1	6.9	13.5	33.4	46.4
2. Slight risk	19.2	19.5	19.2	20.5	12.8	20.2	21.0	17.2	17.9	18.6	20.0	12.7	16.2	25.5	31.2	29.0
3. Moderate risk	26.3	25.2	27.7	27.9	18.7	28.1	28.1	22.6	27.4	29.6	24.3	29.3	28.5	29.7	18.5	11.6
4. Great risk	33.4	34.2	32.8	32.2	43.4	30.6	29.4	38.4	36.0	33.4	33.2	43.6	38.6	25.5	14.5	7.2
5. Can't say drug unfamiliar	8.5	8.9	8.0	6.8	16.3	7.6	7.9	10.9	6.4	7.5	8.8	11.4	9.8	6.4	2.3	5.8
Item 12470 N(Wtd)	2942	1449	1404	2325	343	687	916	886	453	1401	1373	1162	671	377	599	69

QUESTIONNAIRE FORM 5 1976	TOTAL	SEX		RACE		REGION				4YR COLLEGE PLANS		ILLICIT DRUG USE: LIFETIME				
		M	F	White	Black	NE	NC	S	W	Yes	No	None	Marijuana Only	Few Pills	More Pills	Any Heroin
Weighted No. of Cases:	3008	1473	1427	2356	356	713	930	906	460	1415	1398	1174	678	381	606	70
% of Weighted Total:	100.0	49.0	47.4	78.3	11.8	23.7	30.9	30.1	15.3	47.0	46.5	39.0	22.5	12.7	20.1	2.3

A23M: Take amphetamines regularly

1. No risk	2.2	2.4	1.6	1.2	5.0	1.5	2.4	2.8	1.5	1.3	2.6	1.6	1.5	1.6	3.2	7.2
2. Slight risk	5.9	6.1	5.6	6.0	5.5	5.5	6.3	5.8	5.3	3.9	7.4	.7	2.7	6.1	16.6	29.0
3. Moderate risk	15.6	16.4	14.3	16.6	9.0	16.7	18.4	12.4	14.2	14.9	16.4	8.0	12.8	19.6	30.3	29.0
4. Great risk	67.3	65.7	69.8	69.0	64.4	67.8	63.9	68.1	72.3	72.2	63.9	78.3	72.6	65.3	46.4	31.9
5. Can't say drug unfamiliar	9.0	9.3	8.6	7.3	16.0	8.3	9.0	10.9	6.4	7.8	9.7	11.4	10.4	7.4	3.5	2.9
Item 12480 N(Wtd)	2940	1449	1404	2324	343	687	914	886	452	1398	1374	1163	671	377	595	69

A23N: Try cocaine once or twice

1. No risk	10.1	11.4	8.4	9.7	8.5	13.0	9.1	7.9	12.0	8.0	12.0	2.3	4.5	10.1	27.4	42.0
2. Slight risk	15.1	15.4	14.3	15.4	12.0	17.1	16.3	13.2	13.1	14.3	15.2	7.7	10.9	23.1	28.4	26.1
3. Moderate risk	25.1	23.6	27.3	26.1	22.7	24.4	26.3	24.9	24.5	27.3	24.1	26.6	29.0	24.7	19.7	14.5
4. Great risk	39.1	39.5	38.9	39.2	43.4	36.4	36.5	42.1	42.1	40.4	37.8	49.4	43.6	32.7	19.8	17.4
5. Can't say drug unfamiliar	10.6	10.1	11.0	9.6	13.1	9.1	11.8	11.7	8.2	9.8	10.9	13.8	12.1	9.3	4.5	-
Item 12490 N(Wtd)	2927	1443	1397	2314	343	684	909	884	449	1392	1365	1156	668	376	595	69

A23O: Take cocaine regularly

1. No risk	2.6	3.3	1.9	1.7	5.3	2.6	2.0	3.3	2.4	1.9	2.8	1.6	1.4	1.9	4.9	13.4
2. Slight risk	4.0	4.6	3.2	3.9	3.8	4.1	4.2	3.8	4.0	3.0	4.6	.4	2.0	5.6	10.6	17.9
3. Moderate risk	10.6	11.9	9.2	10.7	8.8	11.3	10.4	9.8	11.6	9.3	12.0	4.0	8.1	13.6	23.4	20.9
4. Great risk	72.3	69.8	75.6	74.4	68.1	72.5	72.1	71.4	74.2	76.1	69.8	80.7	76.2	70.4	56.2	46.3
5. Can't say drug unfamiliar	10.5	10.5	10.2	9.2	13.9	9.3	11.4	11.9	7.8	9.7	10.8	13.2	12.5	8.8	5.1	1.5
Item 12500 N(Wtd)	2918	1443	1391	2309	339	681	907	880	450	1392	1361	1155	665	375	594	67

A23P: Try one or two drinks of an alcoholic beverage (beer, wine, liquor)

1. No risk	57.7	58.7	56.7	61.2	38.8	66.9	60.2	50.1	53.6	57.7	58.1	40.6	69.4	61.0	76.6	69.6
2. Slight risk	27.8	27.5	28.2	27.2	31.9	23.4	28.7	30.7	27.2	28.3	27.8	35.5	22.9	26.8	19.0	20.3
3. Moderate risk	8.7	8.0	9.5	7.4	17.1	6.1	7.5	11.4	10.4	8.9	8.7	14.8	5.5	7.2	2.5	1.4
4. Great risk	4.8	5.0	4.8	4.0	9.0	2.6	2.8	6.9	8.2	4.7	4.4	7.6	1.9	5.0	1.7	8.7
5. Can't say drug unfamiliar	.8	.8	.7	.3	3.5	1.0	.8	.9	.7	.4	.9	1.5	.1	.3	-	-
Item 12510 N(Wtd)	2949	1453	1408	2331	345	691	916	889	453	1402	1376	1163	673	377	599	69

A23Q: Take one or two drinks nearly every day

1. No risk	12.4	16.0	8.5	12.0	11.4	13.3	13.2	13.0	8.2	9.1	15.2	6.7	14.5	10.3	21.1	17.4
2. Slight risk	29.5	31.1	27.3	30.5	26.1	28.4	30.3	28.3	31.6	26.9	32.3	23.5	33.2	31.2	33.9	39.1
3. Moderate risk	35.8	34.0	38.3	36.6	29.3	37.7	37.0	34.0	34.1	38.6	33.9	40.8	34.4	38.4	28.9	24.6
4. Great risk	21.2	17.7	25.0	20.4	29.6	19.4	18.4	23.6	25.4	24.9	17.4	27.3	17.1	19.6	15.7	18.8
5. Can't say drug unfamiliar	1.1	1.2	.9	.5	3.5	1.3	1.1	1.1	.9	.6	1.2	1.7	.7	.5	.3	-
Item 12520 N(Wtd)	2940	1445	1405	2322	341	690	915	883	452	1400	1370	1160	668	378	598	69

A23R: Take four or five drinks nearly every day

1. No risk	3.8	5.2	1.9	2.9	5.5	2.5	4.7	4.4	2.6	2.2	4.7	2.1	3.9	2.9	5.9	10.4
2. Slight risk	8.5	10.8	6.3	8.8	6.7	8.3	9.2	8.8	7.1	5.5	11.4	5.2	11.8	6.6	11.1	17.9
3. Moderate risk	25.1	26.2	23.5	26.4	18.6	24.1	28.5	22.7	24.7	22.3	28.1	19.3	27.1	25.7	33.7	23.9
4. Great risk	61.0	56.3	66.7	61.2	63.7	63.9	56.0	62.0	64.7	69.3	53.5	71.4	55.8	64.2	48.9	44.8
5. Can't say drug unfamiliar	1.6	1.6	1.5	.7	5.2	1.3	1.5	2.1	.9	.7	2.1	2.1	1.5	.8	.5	4.5
Item 12530 N(Wtd)	2939	1448	1404	2321	344	689	910	887	453	1401	1369	1163	668	377	597	67

A23S: Have five or more drinks once or twice each weekend

1. No risk	12.9	15.5	10.0	13.0	9.3	13.7	14.8	11.5	10.6	9.5	16.0	5.1	15.0	14.3	23.6	20.3
2. Slight risk	20.1	23.0	17.5	21.3	13.1	20.8	22.7	17.3	19.6	17.2	22.5	11.8	26.5	20.1	27.1	30.4
3. Moderate risk	28.8	29.7	28.0	29.5	24.4	32.4	27.7	27.1	28.4	31.9	26.4	29.6	32.7	27.0	25.1	23.2
4. Great risk	37.0	30.4	43.7	35.7	50.0	31.7	33.5	42.9	40.7	40.9	33.6	51.9	25.1	38.1	23.5	23.2
5. Can't say drug unfamiliar	1.2	1.3	.9	.6	3.2	1.2	1.3	1.2	.9	.6	1.5	1.6	.7	.5	.5	2.9
Item 12540 N(Wtd)	2951	1454	1408	2331	344	691	917	889	454	1404	1377	1163	672	378	601	69

QUESTIONNAIRE FORM 5 1976	TOTAL	SEX		RACE		REGION				4YR COLLEGE PLANS		ILLICIT DRUG USE: LIFETIME				
		M	F	White	Black	NE	NC	S	W	Yes	No	None	Marijuana Only	Few Pills	More Pills	Any Heroin
Weighted No. of Cases:	3008	1473	1427	2356	356	713	930	906	460	1415	1398	1174	678	381	606	70
% of Weighted Total:	100.0	49.0	47.4	78.3	11.8	23.7	30.9	30.1	15.3	47.0	46.5	39.0	22.5	12.7	20.1	2.3

This section asks for your views and feelings about a number of different things.

D01: Do you agree or disagree with each of the following?

D01A: I take a positive attitude toward myself

	TOTAL	M	F	White	Black	NE	NC	S	W	Yes	No	None	Mari-juana Only	Few Pills	More Pills	Any Heroin
1. Disagree	1.8	1.7	1.7	1.4	3.2	2.0	1.6	1.7	1.9	1.2	2.2	2.0	1.5	.8	1.8	3.1
2. Mostly disagree	7.1	6.1	8.2	7.6	2.9	8.0	6.7	5.7	9.3	5.3	9.2	5.7	6.8	7.9	9.3	1.6
3. Neither	9.4	9.0	9.7	9.6	6.1	9.5	10.9	7.8	9.3	7.1	11.9	8.6	9.0	9.8	12.1	7.8
4. Mostly agree	48.8	47.0	50.7	52.1	31.9	49.8	53.1	44.7	46.3	49.1	48.5	48.5	49.8	48.2	48.9	57.8
5. Agree	33.0	36.1	29.8	29.3	55.5	30.6	27.8	40.1	33.3	37.5	28.2	35.2	32.9	33.5	27.9	29.7
Item 12550 N(Wtd)	2841	1388	1384	2292	310	650	899	862	430	1390	1342	1131	647	367	569	64

D01B: Good luck is more important than hard work for success

	TOTAL	M	F	White	Black	NE	NC	S	W	Yes	No	None	Mari-juana Only	Few Pills	More Pills	Any Heroin
1. Disagree	38.9	36.8	41.2	38.1	47.7	38.0	34.9	45.1	36.5	39.3	38.3	39.5	37.9	40.9	37.1	39.7
2. Mostly disagree	38.1	39.5	37.0	41.1	19.6	36.3	44.2	32.8	38.6	40.3	36.0	39.9	38.0	37.3	37.8	33.3
3. Neither	13.7	14.6	12.6	13.7	10.8	15.5	13.8	11.4	15.6	13.6	14.0	12.2	14.4	13.6	16.0	11.1
4. Mostly agree	6.5	6.3	6.5	5.5	12.1	7.4	5.2	7.0	6.7	4.8	8.4	5.6	7.3	5.4	6.9	9.5
5. Agree	2.8	2.7	2.7	1.6	9.8	2.9	1.9	3.8	2.3	2.1	3.3	2.7	2.6	2.7	2.1	6.3
Item 12560 N(Wtd)	2831	1386	1377	2285	306	645	898	858	430	1386	1336	1129	647	367	563	63

D01C: I feel I am a person of worth, on an equal plane with others

	TOTAL	M	F	White	Black	NE	NC	S	W	Yes	No	None	Mari-juana Only	Few Pills	More Pills	Any Heroin
1. Disagree	1.8	1.9	1.8	1.4	3.6	1.7	1.8	2.2	1.4	.9	2.8	1.5	1.9	2.7	2.1	1.6
2. Mostly disagree	3.9	4.0	3.6	3.7	3.9	3.5	4.3	4.5	2.3	3.0	4.9	3.4	4.3	3.3	3.4	9.5
3. Neither	8.8	8.5	8.9	9.6	4.6	9.1	10.7	6.0	9.5	5.3	12.1	8.2	7.9	10.3	10.1	4.8
4. Mostly agree	40.6	38.8	42.2	42.4	27.8	41.6	42.8	37.7	40.7	38.3	42.8	42.9	38.2	37.0	41.7	36.5
5. Agree	44.9	46.8	43.4	42.8	60.1	44.1	40.4	49.6	46.0	52.4	37.3	44.1	47.7	46.5	42.7	46.0
Item 12570 N(Wtd)	2829	1383	1378	2284	306	649	898	852	430	1386	1334	1127	646	368	564	63

D01D: I am able to do things as well as most other people

	TOTAL	M	F	White	Black	NE	NC	S	W	Yes	No	None	Mari-juana Only	Few Pills	More Pills	Any Heroin
1. Disagree	1.1	1.0	1.3	1.0	2.3	1.2	.7	1.4	1.2	.9	1.3	1.3	1.1	.8	1.1	1.6
2. Mostly disagree	3.1	3.1	3.0	3.0	3.0	2.3	3.5	3.3	2.8	2.4	3.9	2.8	3.6	2.5	3.0	1.6
3. Neither	6.1	5.4	6.7	6.3	5.0	5.4	7.0	4.9	7.5	4.0	8.0	5.5	6.8	5.2	6.6	9.5
4. Mostly agree	45.1	42.4	47.8	46.9	35.0	45.9	49.0	40.9	43.9	41.6	48.7	45.8	42.8	48.1	44.7	36.5
5. Agree	44.6	48.2	41.2	42.8	54.5	45.0	39.8	49.3	44.6	51.0	38.2	44.7	45.9	43.2	44.7	52.4
Item 12580 N(Wtd)	2817	1374	1374	2277	303	647	892	850	428	1384	1323	1122	643	366	562	63

D01E: Every time I try to get ahead, something or somebody stops me

	TOTAL	M	F	White	Black	NE	NC	S	W	Yes	No	None	Mari-juana Only	Few Pills	More Pills	Any Heroin
1. Disagree	21.4	22.0	21.3	20.7	26.8	24.2	18.2	20.8	25.4	25.2	17.7	22.9	21.7	20.8	19.2	19.4
2. Mostly disagree	34.3	33.3	35.5	36.8	21.2	35.3	36.6	31.3	33.8	37.6	30.4	36.6	34.1	34.2	33.0	22.6
3. Neither	22.6	23.2	21.8	22.6	22.2	21.0	24.1	21.6	23.9	21.8	23.5	20.8	23.4	24.0	25.0	19.4
4. Mostly agree	15.8	15.4	16.1	15.4	18.0	15.4	15.5	18.3	11.7	11.8	20.3	14.0	16.3	15.0	16.3	30.6
5. Agree	5.8	6.1	5.4	4.6	11.4	4.0	5.6	7.9	4.9	3.5	8.2	5.6	4.6	6.0	6.4	9.7
Item 12590 N(Wtd)	2824	1379	1377	2280	306	649	898	852	426	1383	1331	1125	646	366	563	62

D01F: Planning only makes a person unhappy since plans hardly ever work out anyway

	TOTAL	M	F	White	Black	NE	NC	S	W	Yes	No	None	Mari-juana Only	Few Pills	More Pills	Any Heroin
1. Disagree	30.4	28.1	32.7	30.5	32.2	29.6	27.3	32.8	33.2	35.5	25.5	33.7	29.3	30.9	25.4	17.7
2. Mostly disagree	33.7	36.7	31.1	36.3	19.1	32.9	36.9	31.1	33.2	36.8	29.8	34.8	35.0	33.1	32.3	30.6
3. Neither	14.4	14.2	14.3	14.0	14.5	16.2	15.3	12.0	15.0	13.2	15.8	12.1	15.0	15.6	16.9	22.6
4. Mostly agree	13.7	13.7	13.5	12.7	18.8	14.7	13.6	13.5	12.9	9.9	18.0	12.3	13.2	12.6	17.8	4.8
5. Agree	7.8	7.3	8.4	6.4	15.1	6.6	6.9	10.8	5.8	4.7	10.9	7.1	7.3	7.9	7.8	22.6
Item 12600 N(Wtd)	2819	1377	1375	2279	304	641	897	853	428	1380	1330	1122	645	366	563	62

QUESTIONNAIRE FORM 5 1976	TOTAL	SEX		RACE		REGION				4YR COLLEGE PLANS		ILLICIT DRUG USE: LIFETIME				
		M	F	White	Black	NE	NC	S	W	Yes	No	None	Mari-juana Only	Few Pills	More Pills	Any Her-oin
Weighted No. of Cases:	3008	1473	1427	2356	356	713	930	906	460	1415	1398	1174	678	381	606	70
% of Weighted Total:	100.0	49.0	47.4	78.3	11.8	23.7	30.9	30.1	15.3	47.0	46.5	39.0	22.5	12.7	20.1	2.3

D01G: People who accept their condition in life are happier than those who try to change things

1. Disagree	19.5	18.8	20.4	19.6	19.5	22.0	17.2	19.2	21.5	23.0	16.5	18.9	20.2	19.6	20.4	18.3
2. Mostly disagree	26.0	26.4	25.6	27.7	18.5	26.3	28.2	24.3	24.8	32.8	20.0	28.1	27.2	26.7	21.1	21.7
3. Neither	18.4	19.9	17.1	19.0	11.4	20.3	20.3	14.1	20.8	17.9	18.5	19.0	17.0	17.4	20.0	26.7
4. Mostly agree	21.5	22.0	21.0	21.6	23.5	18.6	22.1	23.4	21.0	16.8	25.6	19.9	22.9	21.8	22.5	16.7
5. Agree	14.5	12.9	15.8	12.1	26.8	13.1	12.2	19.1	12.3	9.5	19.3	14.2	12.8	14.3	15.9	18.3
Item 12610　N(Wtd)	2799	1368	1365	2269	298	636	893	845	424	1369	1324	1113	643	363	560	60

D01H: On the whole, I'm satisfied with myself

1. Disagree	3.0	3.4	2.6	2.6	4.9	3.4	2.2	3.2	3.8	2.3	3.9	2.0	2.3	3.9	4.3	9.7
2. Mostly disagree	8.9	8.5	9.3	8.9	8.9	9.4	7.6	9.2	10.4	9.1	9.2	7.2	9.7	8.9	11.0	14.5
3. Neither	9.0	9.3	8.4	9.4	4.9	8.7	12.0	6.3	8.2	8.1	9.7	7.0	9.5	12.2	9.4	17.7
4. Mostly agree	41.2	40.7	42.3	42.9	30.9	41.8	42.2	39.8	41.2	40.4	42.0	41.0	41.6	43.9	40.9	33.9
5. Agree	37.8	38.1	37.3	36.2	50.3	36.5	36.0	41.5	36.5	39.9	35.2	42.7	36.9	31.1	34.3	24.2
Item 12620　N(Wtd)	2811	1370	1374	2270	304	641	894	851	425	1378	1324	1123	642	360	563	62

D01I: People like me don't have much of a chance to be successful in life

1. Disagree	55.2	52.6	57.8	55.1	58.4	59.1	50.8	56.1	56.5	63.9	45.9	56.3	57.7	54.0	52.7	46.8
2. Mostly disagree	27.3	28.4	26.5	29.0	16.7	26.7	28.8	26.7	26.4	25.6	29.3	28.3	26.5	24.2	27.2	27.4
3. Neither	9.8	9.7	9.6	10.1	7.2	7.8	12.5	7.8	11.3	6.5	13.2	9.5	7.8	13.2	10.0	12.9
4. Mostly agree	5.3	6.3	4.1	4.3	9.2	5.1	5.8	5.7	3.3	2.5	8.2	3.6	5.9	5.2	7.7	6.5
5. Agree	2.5	3.0	1.9	1.5	8.2	1.1	2.1	3.9	2.6	1.5	3.4	2.3	1.9	3.3	2.5	6.5
Item 12630　N(Wtd)	2804	1370	1368	2265	305	641	890	848	425	1373	1322	1121	641	363	558	62

Drug use has different meanings to different people. We want to know how you think most people your age view others who use various drugs. The first questions are about marijuana.

D02: Most people my age believe that those who use marijuana once or twice a week are:

D02A: Ambitious

1. Much less than average	22.2	21.8	22.6	21.1	28.9	19.7	20.7	25.0	23.1	23.2	20.6	29.2	19.0	19.0	15.0	12.5
2. Less than average	27.3	25.8	29.1	28.8	19.0	28.0	29.1	24.0	28.9	31.3	24.3	30.6	27.6	30.1	21.8	12.5
3. About average	41.3	43.5	38.3	42.3	33.1	43.3	42.1	40.7	37.5	38.1	44.2	31.9	45.0	41.4	52.7	58.9
4. More than average	7.6	7.4	8.0	6.6	14.8	6.9	6.3	8.8	8.7	6.6	8.4	6.7	7.2	7.4	8.6	8.9
5. Much more than average	1.8	1.6	1.9	1.3	4.2	2.1	1.8	1.4	1.8	.9	2.6	1.4	1.4	2.1	1.9	8.9
Item 12780　N(Wtd)	2554	1265	1231	2078	263	568	822	783	381	1264	1200	1009	584	326	533	56

D02B: Antisocial

1. Much less than average	23.0	21.9	24.4	22.1	29.1	27.3	19.4	25.0	20.3	21.7	23.9	21.8	22.3	21.4	26.3	30.2
2. Less than average	27.5	27.8	27.3	27.7	28.7	27.8	27.6	26.0	29.7	28.4	26.7	29.0	25.8	28.3	26.8	17.0
3. About average	36.8	37.1	36.2	38.0	25.5	36.3	39.9	35.4	33.5	37.2	36.6	34.5	41.0	36.3	37.3	35.8
4. More than average	10.6	10.9	9.9	10.6	10.4	6.9	10.9	10.7	15.1	10.8	10.5	12.0	8.4	11.8	9.5	9.4
5. Much more than average	2.2	2.3	2.1	1.6	6.0	1.8	2.3	2.9	1.4	1.9	2.3	2.7	2.3	2.5	.2	5.7
Item 12790　N(Wtd)	2487	1246	1184	2035	251	554	800	763	370	1244	1157	977	573	322	518	53

D02C: Conforming

1. Much less than average	18.1	16.2	20.3	17.2	24.2	17.6	16.2	21.2	16.8	17.4	18.6	20.8	15.0	17.5	17.1	17.0
2. Less than average	25.5	27.7	23.8	26.1	24.6	24.3	23.0	26.5	30.0	25.8	25.4	26.4	25.9	25.2	24.4	18.9
3. About average	41.5	41.6	40.7	41.8	35.7	43.3	47.4	36.7	36.1	39.8	43.3	35.4	45.5	41.7	47.3	49.1
4. More than average	10.9	11.1	10.6	11.2	9.5	11.5	9.2	11.4	12.7	12.6	9.2	12.8	10.0	11.5	8.1	7.5
5. Much more than average	4.0	3.4	4.5	3.7	6.0	3.5	4.0	4.0	4.4	4.4	3.5	4.5	3.5	4.1	3.1	7.5
Item 12800　N(Wtd)	2474	1241	1176	2018	252	547	795	769	363	1235	1157	984	572	314	509	53

QUESTIONNAIRE FORM 5 1976	TOTAL	SEX		RACE		REGION				4YR COLLEGE PLANS		ILLICIT DRUG USE: LIFETIME				
		M	F	White	Black	NE	NC	S	W	Yes	No	None	Marijuana Only	Few Pills	More Pills	Any Heroin
Weighted No. of Cases:	3008	1473	1427	2356	356	713	930	906	460	1415	1398	1174	678	381	606	70
% of Weighted Total:	100.0	49.0	47.4	78.3	11.8	23.7	30.9	30.1	15.3	47.0	46.5	39.0	22.5	12.7	20.1	2.3
D02D: Criminal																
1. Much less than average	24.2	23.8	24.6	23.4	28.2	28.7	22.6	24.6	19.6	23.6	24.3	17.4	27.5	26.4	30.9	32.7
2. Less than average	20.1	19.0	21.4	20.2	22.4	20.5	18.4	21.8	19.6	20.2	20.1	19.1	20.3	21.2	22.0	10.9
3. About average	30.0	29.5	30.1	31.0	22.4	28.7	34.1	28.9	25.5	30.4	29.5	30.0	31.1	28.2	29.7	34.5
4. More than average	19.5	21.0	18.1	20.1	15.4	17.1	19.3	17.1	28.7	20.6	18.8	24.8	16.7	18.1	14.2	16.4
5. Much more than average	6.2	6.8	5.7	5.4	11.6	5.0	5.6	7.5	6.7	5.2	7.3	8.6	4.5	5.8	3.2	5.5
Item 12810 N(Wtd)	2541	1260	1222	2072	259	561	824	783	373	1260	1194	1009	582	326	528	55
D02E: Emotionally unstable																
1. Much less than average	21.3	22.8	19.8	21.1	24.2	24.8	17.6	24.0	18.8	20.4	22.5	15.7	23.1	24.0	27.3	23.2
2. Less than average	21.3	21.6	21.0	21.4	23.4	21.9	19.9	21.6	23.1	21.1	21.3	20.0	22.7	22.8	22.5	17.9
3. About average	33.1	33.5	32.9	33.3	27.4	30.6	38.4	30.0	31.6	32.4	34.1	30.3	35.8	32.6	34.8	44.6
4. More than average	16.9	15.8	18.1	17.4	15.1	16.9	16.1	16.4	19.6	19.5	14.2	23.1	12.8	15.7	11.0	8.9
5. Much more than average	7.4	6.4	8.3	6.8	9.9	5.8	8.0	8.0	7.0	6.6	8.0	10.9	5.4	4.9	4.0	5.4
Item 12820 N(Wtd)	2534	1257	1220	2074	252	556	826	779	373	1256	1189	1006	576	325	528	56
D02F: Interesting																
1. Much less than average	16.6	13.9	19.2	16.3	19.6	15.0	15.8	17.8	17.8	16.4	16.4	26.2	10.2	13.9	7.7	7.4
2. Less than average	21.4	21.0	22.1	21.9	18.8	18.7	22.5	21.4	23.0	23.7	19.4	28.3	18.4	20.4	14.0	9.3
3. About average	40.9	42.1	39.8	42.0	33.3	41.6	43.3	37.3	42.2	40.4	41.9	31.5	48.8	41.4	49.6	48.1
4. More than average	14.8	17.0	12.3	14.4	15.7	16.9	13.4	15.4	13.5	14.9	14.3	9.9	17.0	18.2	19.0	20.4
5. Much more than average	6.3	6.2	6.5	5.5	12.5	7.6	4.9	8.0	3.5	4.7	7.8	4.2	5.6	6.2	9.6	16.7
Item 12830 N(Wtd)	2521	1248	1215	2062	255	555	822	775	370	1247	1188	1005	576	324	520	54
D02G: Rebellious																
1. Much less than average	14.6	14.1	15.3	13.5	21.3	13.3	12.9	17.8	13.4	12.9	16.5	11.5	17.1	14.1	16.5	20.0
2. Less than average	18.1	18.6	17.7	17.6	21.3	20.3	16.8	19.0	15.6	16.5	19.7	15.2	19.7	23.1	19.5	10.9
3. About average	32.1	31.8	32.2	32.1	30.8	31.9	34.2	30.9	30.4	29.8	34.7	28.9	33.1	30.0	38.3	40.0
4. More than average	25.8	26.9	24.5	27.8	15.0	26.3	26.3	21.8	32.3	30.4	21.1	31.1	24.2	24.4	19.7	18.2
5. Much more than average	9.5	8.7	10.4	9.1	11.1	8.2	9.8	10.4	8.3	10.4	8.1	13.4	6.1	8.4	5.9	10.9
Item 12840 N(Wtd)	2514	1247	1210	2057	253	548	816	779	372	1249	1179	1003	574	320	522	55
D02H: Sensible																
1. Much less than average	23.9	21.3	26.4	23.9	23.0	21.4	24.3	24.9	24.5	25.3	22.2	36.6	17.3	18.7	12.2	12.5
2. Less than average	27.3	25.5	29.9	28.0	23.8	27.0	28.2	25.5	30.0	30.0	25.7	31.1	27.6	26.2	22.6	12.5
3. About average	35.9	38.8	32.4	36.7	31.3	39.7	36.4	34.0	33.0	33.7	37.5	23.1	43.4	38.6	48.3	48.2
4. More than average	9.1	10.5	7.7	8.3	14.1	8.0	8.1	11.0	9.3	8.2	10.2	6.6	8.0	10.3	13.3	16.1
5. Much more than average	3.7	3.9	3.7	3.1	7.4	4.0	2.9	4.6	3.3	2.8	4.4	2.5	3.7	6.5	3.6	8.9
Item 12850 N(Wtd)	2516	1243	1212	2054	256	551	818	779	367	1243	1185	999	572	321	526	56
D02I: Sexually permissive																
1. Much less than average	12.3	10.8	13.7	11.6	16.6	11.9	10.9	14.3	12.2	10.3	14.3	14.9	10.6	12.3	8.8	17.9
2. Less than average	14.8	14.1	15.7	14.1	20.2	13.0	14.3	16.4	14.9	14.7	14.8	18.2	14.9	12.6	11.1	5.4
3. About average	38.3	38.3	38.5	39.5	28.9	43.4	40.1	34.4	35.0	39.0	38.5	31.6	45.0	36.5	44.8	41.1
4. More than average	23.3	25.8	20.6	24.8	15.4	21.9	24.3	22.4	25.2	25.7	20.6	24.5	18.3	26.1	25.4	21.4
5. Much more than average	11.3	11.1	11.4	9.9	19.0	9.9	10.5	12.4	12.7	10.5	11.8	11.0	11.1	12.6	10.1	14.3
Item 12860 N(Wtd)	2512	1244	1210	2053	253	548	818	776	369	1242	1183	995	578	318	524	56
D02J: Weak-willed																
1. Much less than average	17.2	15.9	18.7	15.5	28.1	17.9	13.7	20.9	15.9	14.8	19.0	16.6	17.3	18.0	16.0	32.7
2. Less than average	19.8	20.2	19.4	20.1	19.2	20.9	20.4	19.4	17.5	19.6	20.6	17.7	21.5	20.5	21.9	10.9
3. About average	35.5	37.9	33.0	36.6	25.4	38.3	37.0	31.9	35.6	35.1	36.1	26.6	43.2	36.0	42.9	43.6
4. More than average	17.3	17.8	16.7	18.3	13.1	13.7	18.3	17.1	21.0	20.9	13.5	23.0	10.7	18.0	15.1	7.3
5. Much more than average	10.3	8.2	12.2	9.5	14.2	9.2	10.6	10.8	10.0	9.6	10.8	16.1	7.3	7.5	4.0	7.3
Item 12870 N(Wtd)	2535	1257	1219	2066	260	554	819	790	371	1254	1190	1012	577	322	524	55

QUESTIONNAIRE FORM 5 1976	TOTAL	SEX		RACE		REGION				4YR COLLEGE PLANS		ILLICIT DRUG USE: LIFETIME				
		M	F	White	Black	NE	NC	S	W	Yes	No	None	Mari-juana Only	Few Pills	More Pills	Any Her-oin
Weighted No. of Cases:	3008	1473	1427	2356	356	713	930	906	460	1415	1398	1174	678	381	606	70
% of Weighted Total:	100.0	49.0	47.4	78.3	11.8	23.7	30.9	30.1	15.3	47.0	46.5	39.0	22.5	12.7	20.1	2.3

D03: Most people my age believe that those who use illicit drugs other than marijuana once or twice a week are:

D03A: Ambitious

1. Much less than average	36.7	34.9	38.7	36.5	45.2	35.2	33.4	39.4	40.1	39.5	33.4	41.7	38.2	31.9	28.3	33.3
2. Less than average	30.9	30.9	30.7	32.5	18.3	32.2	33.5	27.4	30.5	33.9	28.2	29.1	32.9	37.5	30.2	19.6
3. About average	21.9	22.9	20.7	22.1	16.2	23.1	22.6	21.1	20.6	19.3	24.2	19.6	19.6	18.9	30.6	27.5
4. More than average	7.0	7.7	6.3	5.9	12.9	5.5	7.2	7.8	6.8	5.5	8.6	6.1	6.0	7.6	7.9	9.8
5. Much more than average	3.6	3.6	3.7	3.0	7.5	4.2	3.4	4.4	1.7	1.7	5.6	3.6	3.1	4.0	3.0	9.8
Item 12890 N(Wtd)	2390	1194	1143	1952	241	506	776	753	354	1194	1122	960	547	301	494	51

D03B: Antisocial

1. Much less than average	22.1	20.2	24.5	21.1	34.5	18.8	20.7	26.1	21.7	20.4	23.9	25.6	21.4	18.1	19.1	17.0
2. Less than average	28.7	29.4	27.6	28.5	26.5	30.2	26.1	29.1	31.2	28.5	29.5	29.3	28.2	31.2	27.0	27.7
3. About average	27.7	26.9	28.7	28.8	18.1	30.2	29.9	24.5	26.3	27.0	27.9	23.7	27.1	30.9	33.1	36.2
4. More than average	14.9	16.4	13.4	15.3	12.6	14.3	16.5	13.7	14.7	17.4	12.5	14.8	15.3	11.4	17.7	6.4
5. Much more than average	6.6	7.1	5.8	6.4	8.4	6.3	6.9	6.5	6.6	6.8	6.2	6.6	8.1	8.7	3.1	10.6
Item 12900 N(Wtd)	2348	1180	1115	1920	238	504	759	739	346	1181	1096	944	543	298	481	47

D03C: Conforming

1. Much less than average	27.0	26.0	28.0	26.5	36.7	23.6	23.6	31.0	30.5	29.0	24.9	30.4	25.9	23.8	23.5	26.1
2. Less than average	28.7	30.9	26.7	29.6	20.0	29.0	29.9	28.1	27.6	29.5	28.4	27.0	29.6	33.0	30.4	19.6
3. About average	28.4	27.8	28.8	27.9	26.3	29.0	29.7	26.5	28.7	24.9	31.3	26.0	29.1	24.8	32.3	41.3
4. More than average	10.8	10.4	11.3	11.2	9.6	12.4	11.4	9.9	8.8	12.0	9.4	10.6	9.7	12.6	11.7	6.5
5. Much more than average	5.2	4.8	5.2	4.7	7.5	6.2	5.5	4.6	4.4	4.7	5.9	6.0	5.8	5.8	2.3	8.7
Item 12910 N(Wtd)	2333	1170	1111	1905	240	500	747	744	341	1173	1090	941	537	294	480	46

D03D: Criminal

1. Much less than average	16.5	16.4	16.8	15.1	25.6	16.8	16.3	18.8	11.8	14.1	19.0	15.4	18.2	15.1	17.7	20.4
2. Less than average	16.4	16.2	16.8	16.4	16.5	15.4	16.1	18.4	14.7	16.1	17.0	15.3	15.7	17.7	17.7	14.3
3. About average	22.4	20.8	24.6	23.0	15.7	24.7	22.7	21.5	20.5	21.0	23.4	20.9	19.9	22.1	27.9	28.6
4. More than average	27.6	29.8	24.8	28.5	22.3	27.0	29.6	23.4	33.1	31.1	24.1	28.5	27.4	28.1	26.7	14.3
5. Much more than average	17.0	16.9	17.0	17.1	19.4	16.2	15.3	18.1	19.9	17.9	16.4	19.8	18.8	16.7	9.8	22.4
Item 12920 N(Wtd)	2383	1186	1143	1944	242	507	771	757	347	1188	1119	961	548	299	491	49

D03E: Emotionally unstable

1. Much less than average	15.7	15.8	15.7	14.3	25.1	14.4	15.5	18.7	11.6	14.3	16.8	15.1	17.4	16.0	14.7	12.5
2. Less than average	17.6	18.2	17.2	17.3	21.0	16.6	16.9	19.6	16.3	16.7	18.8	17.4	15.4	18.0	19.3	25.0
3. About average	21.9	22.1	21.5	21.9	18.1	22.5	22.2	22.3	18.9	18.3	25.1	18.6	22.3	20.3	26.1	31.3
4. More than average	27.4	28.0	26.7	29.0	18.1	30.2	28.9	22.2	31.7	32.6	22.5	28.6	25.2	29.0	28.7	16.7
5. Much more than average	17.5	16.0	19.0	17.5	17.7	16.6	16.6	17.2	21.5	17.9	16.8	20.4	19.4	16.3	11.2	12.5
Item 12930 N(Wtd)	2393	1193	1150	1954	243	507	779	761	344	1193	1122	968	551	300	491	48

D03F: Interesting

1. Much less than average	30.1	27.8	31.9	30.4	30.3	27.2	28.9	31.3	33.9	31.2	28.6	35.9	27.6	34.1	20.9	12.5
2. Less than average	29.8	30.6	29.2	30.5	25.7	31.8	30.8	27.6	29.9	33.6	26.0	31.0	32.4	23.8	28.6	27.1
3. About average	26.8	27.3	26.8	27.6	17.4	27.0	28.6	24.9	26.4	24.0	30.0	22.2	28.0	27.8	33.3	37.5
4. More than average	9.2	10.2	7.8	8.3	16.2	10.1	8.1	11.0	6.6	8.2	10.1	7.6	7.1	10.6	13.5	8.3
5. Much more than average	4.1	4.0	4.3	3.1	10.4	3.9	3.6	5.2	3.2	2.9	5.1	3.3	4.9	4.0	3.7	14.6
Item 12940 N(Wtd)	2385	1189	1144	1945	241	507	776	754	348	1191	1121	961	550	302	489	48

D03G: Rebellious

1. Much less than average	14.7	14.7	14.7	13.1	25.6	13.5	12.7	18.6	12.4	12.2	17.5	14.1	16.2	13.9	14.0	20.0
2. Less than average	17.3	17.3	17.3	16.7	18.2	17.1	17.8	17.5	15.5	14.8	20.0	14.6	16.4	21.4	19.9	14.0
3. About average	22.6	22.2	23.0	22.5	20.7	23.3	21.6	23.0	22.7	19.5	25.7	20.5	22.1	21.4	27.5	28.0
4. More than average	26.9	28.5	25.3	28.6	19.4	28.7	28.8	22.4	29.9	32.0	21.7	28.6	26.8	25.4	26.3	20.0
5. Much more than average	18.5	17.4	19.6	19.3	16.1	17.1	18.9	18.3	19.5	21.6	14.9	22.1	18.6	18.0	12.3	18.0
Item 12950 N(Wtd)	2380	1185	1143	1942	242	502	777	753	348	1192	1113	964	548	295	487	50

QUESTIONNAIRE FORM 5 1976	TOTAL	SEX		RACE		REGION				4YR COLLEGE PLANS		ILLICIT DRUG USE: LIFETIME				
		M	F	White	Black	NE	NC	S	W	Yes	No	None	Marijuana Only	Few Pills	More Pills	Any Heroin
Weighted No. of Cases:	3008	1473	1427	2356	356	713	930	906	460	1415	1398	1174	678	381	606	70
% of Weighted Total:	100.0	49.0	47.4	78.3	11.8	23.7	30.9	30.1	15.3	47.0	46.5	39.0	22.5	12.7	20.1	2.3

D03H: Sensible

1. Much less than average	41.6	38.8	44.6	43.4	34.9	41.0	41.3	40.5	45.5	46.5	36.8	48.4	40.2	42.1	31.9	22.4
2. Less than average	29.3	30.4	28.0	30.1	23.7	31.2	30.6	26.9	28.8	32.2	26.5	27.2	34.2	28.5	30.0	22.4
3. About average	17.9	19.0	16.7	16.9	18.3	17.9	18.1	19.3	14.1	11.9	24.3	14.1	15.4	17.9	26.3	36.7
4. More than average	6.7	7.1	6.3	6.2	10.8	5.4	6.8	7.3	7.2	5.8	7.3	5.5	5.9	6.3	9.5	6.1
5. Much more than average	4.5	4.6	4.5	3.4	12.0	4.4	3.0	6.1	4.6	3.5	5.3	4.8	4.4	5.0	2.3	12.2
Item 12960 N(Wtd)	2378	1187	1139	1942	241	503	777	751	347	1190	1115	959	547	302	486	49

D03I: Sexually permissive

1. Much less than average	16.2	15.6	16.9	15.1	24.8	16.7	14.4	18.2	15.3	13.5	19.2	17.0	16.5	16.2	15.2	12.2
2. Less than average	16.0	16.1	15.8	15.4	17.8	15.1	16.7	17.4	12.7	14.1	17.9	16.8	16.5	16.5	13.7	14.3
3. About average	29.9	29.9	30.0	30.3	25.6	33.1	29.6	27.5	31.2	30.5	29.6	25.9	32.4	31.6	33.8	30.6
4. More than average	23.4	24.6	21.9	24.9	13.6	20.9	25.0	22.0	26.0	26.7	19.6	25.3	17.6	20.2	28.3	22.4
5. Much more than average	14.6	13.7	15.4	14.2	18.2	14.5	14.3	15.0	14.7	15.3	13.7	15.0	17.0	15.8	9.2	20.4
Item 12970 N(Wtd)	2368	1179	1137	1932	242	498	771	753	346	1182	1112	952	546	297	488	49

D03J: Weak-willed

1. Much less than average	20.7	21.1	20.3	18.7	34.8	20.8	18.5	25.7	14.3	18.2	22.9	20.8	21.2	20.1	19.6	30.6
2. Less than average	16.6	16.0	17.2	17.0	13.5	16.4	17.1	16.7	15.4	14.8	18.2	15.4	16.6	16.8	16.8	14.3
3. About average	22.0	22.8	21.2	22.2	16.0	20.8	23.3	21.3	22.3	18.5	26.1	18.2	21.4	22.8	27.8	30.6
4. More than average	20.4	20.1	21.0	22.2	12.3	24.4	21.3	16.4	21.1	25.6	15.1	20.5	20.1	18.8	22.9	14.3
5. Much more than average	20.4	20.1	20.3	19.8	23.0	17.6	20.0	19.7	26.9	22.9	17.7	25.3	18.8	21.5	13.1	8.2
Item 12980 N(Wtd)	2385	1187	1145	1943	244	500	774	760	350	1192	1116	963	548	298	489	49

D04: Which best describes the law IN YOUR STATE regarding marijuana? Possession in private of an ounce or less of marijuana (by an adult) is...

1. A criminal offense, carrying a possible jail sentence	37.5	41.3	33.6	37.8	38.0	43.2	34.8	43.2	23.1	39.2	35.9	36.8	36.1	38.2	39.7	50.0
2. A criminal offense, carrying a possible fine but not a jail sentence	16.7	17.7	15.6	16.9	16.6	19.9	17.0	15.0	14.7	16.3	16.5	14.3	18.1	17.2	20.0	18.3
3. A non-criminal offense - like a traffic ticket - carrying a small fine and no criminal record at all	9.8	11.6	7.7	9.6	7.0	5.6	10.2	3.7	28.2	10.2	9.1	6.3	11.4	10.2	14.4	10.0
4. I don't know if the offense is criminal, but I know it only carries a fine	8.5	7.5	9.5	8.1	12.2	6.8	9.0	8.2	10.4	8.3	8.7	7.6	8.2	11.4	8.1	5.0
5. Not a legal offense at all	2.1	2.5	1.8	1.6	3.7	1.4	1.7	3.2	2.0	1.7	2.6	1.9	2.1	2.3	1.5	10.0
6. I just don't know	25.4	19.4	31.8	26.0	22.5	23.5	27.2	26.8	21.6	24.1	27.2	33.1	24.2	20.7	16.5	5.0
Item 13050 N(Wtd)	2668	1304	1299	2176	271	592	863	818	394	1315	1248	1061	607	343	541	60

These next questions ask your views about different lifestyles that have been in the news lately.

D05: A man and a woman who live together without being married are...

1. Experimenting with a worth-while alternative lifestyle	19.1	20.2	17.5	19.1	18.6	24.8	17.7	16.0	20.1	20.2	18.2	14.5	21.1	18.6	24.8	39.0
2. Doing their own thing and not affecting anyone else	52.3	53.8	51.3	52.6	49.5	54.8	54.5	49.0	50.5	48.6	55.9	44.2	58.3	57.0	58.5	50.8
3. Living in a way that could be destructive to society	8.4	8.2	8.4	8.3	10.0	5.9	7.8	10.1	9.7	9.4	7.2	11.7	7.5	7.4	3.7	1.7
4. Violating a basic principle of human morality	13.8	11.7	16.0	13.9	15.1	9.0	13.3	18.8	12.2	15.5	12.2	23.2	8.1	10.9	5.3	3.4
8. None of the above	6.3	6.0	6.8	6.1	7.2	5.4	6.8	6.0	7.5	6.5	6.4	6.5	5.2	6.0	7.7	6.8
Item 12770 N(Wtd)	2712	1313	1333	2206	279	613	877	820	402	1333	1269	1086	617	349	544	59

QUESTIONNAIRE FORM 5 1976	TOTAL	SEX		RACE		REGION				4YR COLLEGE PLANS		ILLICIT DRUG USE: LIFETIME				
		M	F	White	Black	NE	NC	S	W	Yes	No	None	Mari-juana Only	Few Pills	More Pills	Any Her-oin
Weighted No. of Cases:	3008	1473	1427	2356	356	713	930	906	460	1415	1398	1174	678	381	606	70
% of Weighted Total:	100.0	49.0	47.4	78.3	11.8	23.7	30.9	30.1	15.3	47.0	46.5	39.0	22.5	12.7	20.1	2.3

D06: A man and a woman who decide to have and raise a child out of wedlock are...

1. Experimenting with a worth- while alternative lifestyle	8.5	9.7	7.3	7.3	14.0	11.6	7.5	7.9	7.3	8.6	8.5	8.4	8.9	7.2	8.5	13.8
2. Doing their own thing and not affecting anyone else	34.0	35.5	32.3	32.5	42.3	35.4	34.9	32.5	32.8	30.4	37.2	26.4	38.0	34.8	42.1	55.2
3. Living in a way that could be destructive to society	21.9	20.7	23.0	23.7	15.8	19.0	22.0	24.8	20.5	23.2	21.4	22.9	19.6	27.2	20.6	12.1
4. Violating a basic principle of human morality	21.9	22.0	22.1	22.9	15.1	17.5	24.1	22.9	22.0	22.9	20.6	29.6	20.0	18.0	13.6	6.9
8. None of the above	13.7	12.2	15.2	13.6	13.2	16.5	11.6	11.8	17.3	15.0	12.3	12.7	13.3	13.0	15.3	12.1
Item 12880 N(Wtd)	2694	1304	1325	2196	272	611	869	815	400	1320	1267	1076	616	345	544	58

The next questions give examples of different living arrangements for people with children.

E01: First example: Two children are living with their parents. What is unusual about this family is that a number of other relatives live on the same block, including grandparents, aunts and uncles, and cousins. They often do things together as a group, and all the adults take some part in caring for the children.

E01A: What effect do you think this living arrangement has on the children?

1. Very harmful	5.7	6.1	5.5	5.2	7.7	4.0	6.1	7.0	4.8	4.2	7.5	5.4	7.1	6.1	4.5	3.5
2. Mostly harmful	19.3	17.7	20.9	20.3	17.9	17.3	21.0	19.4	18.0	17.9	20.1	19.2	18.3	22.5	17.9	26.3
3. Don't know	36.7	40.7	32.8	36.7	31.1	36.0	40.6	32.7	37.6	33.6	39.6	34.3	37.1	38.3	40.2	33.3
4. Mostly beneficial	27.9	25.9	29.9	28.5	25.6	30.2	24.3	29.4	29.3	32.1	24.4	29.6	26.7	24.5	29.1	22.8
5. Very beneficial	10.3	9.6	11.0	9.3	17.6	12.6	7.8	11.6	10.3	12.2	8.5	11.4	11.0	8.4	8.2	14.0
Item 13150 N(Wtd)	2689	1308	1315	2189	273	597	879	813	399	1320	1264	1083	607	347	537	57

E01B: What effect do you think this living arrangement has on the parents?

1. Very harmful	5.0	4.3	5.7	4.9	5.9	3.2	5.6	6.0	4.0	4.4	5.7	4.6	4.9	7.2	4.5	3.5
2. Mostly harmful	21.7	19.0	24.5	22.7	16.5	19.7	24.7	19.6	22.3	20.0	23.2	21.4	23.3	20.5	22.5	14.0
3. Don't know	40.2	44.7	35.2	39.5	42.1	37.9	43.8	38.5	39.3	38.7	41.4	39.3	39.1	41.6	40.7	38.6
4. Mostly beneficial	25.4	24.7	26.5	26.3	22.0	29.7	21.0	27.0	25.3	27.5	24.0	26.2	25.0	23.7	24.9	31.6
5. Very beneficial	7.7	7.3	8.1	6.6	13.2	9.3	4.9	8.8	9.0	9.3	5.8	8.6	7.6	6.6	7.1	10.5
Item 13160 N(Wtd)	2689	1310	1315	2189	273	599	875	815	399	1319	1264	1085	609	346	538	57

E01C: What effect do you think this living arrangement has on the grandparents?

1. Very harmful	3.1	3.4	2.5	2.5	5.3	2.0	2.9	4.3	2.5	2.0	4.1	2.4	4.0	2.3	3.9	1.8
2. Mostly harmful	8.9	8.1	9.9	8.7	11.3	7.7	10.1	9.5	7.0	7.4	10.1	9.7	8.1	9.9	7.7	7.0
3. Don't know	34.8	37.5	31.8	34.3	34.0	32.0	38.2	33.5	34.3	30.3	39.4	31.6	35.4	41.3	36.1	28.1
4. Mostly beneficial	33.8	31.4	36.7	35.5	27.2	33.8	34.1	32.8	35.3	37.4	30.9	37.2	31.1	30.8	32.7	35.1
5. Very beneficial	19.4	19.6	19.1	19.0	22.3	24.6	14.7	19.9	20.8	22.9	15.6	19.2	21.5	15.7	19.6	28.1
Item 13170 N(Wtd)	2674	1304	1307	2185	265	594	871	810	399	1314	1259	1082	605	344	535	57

E01D: How would you feel about this living arrangement if you were one of the parents?

1. Unacceptable	45.2	42.1	48.1	46.9	35.4	37.4	53.0	42.6	45.2	44.5	45.5	44.7	44.3	48.1	44.6	50.0
2. Acceptable--it would be O.K.	35.1	36.5	33.8	35.2	37.3	39.0	31.1	37.7	32.8	35.6	35.2	37.7	32.9	33.2	34.9	32.1
3. Desirable--I'd really like it	7.5	8.0	7.0	7.1	8.4	8.7	4.8	8.7	9.3	8.5	6.5	7.1	9.4	7.7	5.7	10.7
8. Don't know	12.2	13.4	11.1	10.7	19.0	14.7	11.3	11.2	12.6	11.4	12.8	10.5	13.6	11.0	14.8	8.9
Item 13180 N(Wtd)	2631	1262	1307	2149	263	585	853	796	396	1310	1219	1066	596	337	522	56

QUESTIONNAIRE FORM 5 1976	TOTAL	SEX		RACE		REGION				4YR COLLEGE PLANS		ILLICIT DRUG USE: LIFETIME				
		M	F	White	Black	NE	NC	S	W	Yes	No	None	Mari-juana Only	Few Pills	More Pills	Any Her-oin
Weighted No. of Cases:	3008	1473	1427	2356	356	713	930	906	460	1415	1398	1174	678	381	606	70
% of Weighted Total:	100.0	49.0	47.4	78.3	11.8	23.7	30.9	30.1	15.3	47.0	46.5	39.0	22.5	12.7	20.1	2.3

E02: Second example: Several couples, some with children and some with no children, all live on the same block and are good friends. The families often do things together as a group, and all the adults take some part in caring for the children.

E02A: What effect do you think this living arrangement has on the children?

	TOTAL	M	F	White	Black	NE	NC	S	W	Yes	No	None	Mar.	Few	More	Heroin
1. Very harmful	3.5	4.1	2.9	3.2	5.4	2.9	3.2	4.5	3.1	3.4	3.7	4.2	3.5	2.3	2.8	3.6
2. Mostly harmful	13.6	13.5	13.5	14.2	10.0	12.7	17.5	11.8	10.5	14.8	12.5	15.8	12.6	13.7	11.7	5.5
3. Don't know	30.8	33.2	28.4	30.0	33.3	29.6	29.8	31.4	33.9	26.1	35.4	28.1	29.9	37.0	32.7	34.5
4. Mostly beneficial	41.1	38.9	44.0	42.0	37.9	41.1	40.5	41.0	42.9	44.0	38.5	41.0	41.0	37.9	43.8	41.8
5. Very beneficial	10.9	10.4	11.2	10.6	14.2	13.9	9.0	11.5	9.7	11.7	10.0	11.0	12.9	9.0	9.0	16.4
Item 13280 N(Wtd)	2653	1292	1298	2171	261	584	869	808	392	1303	1253	1077	595	343	532	55

E02B: What effect do you think this living arrangement has on the parents?

	TOTAL	M	F	White	Black	NE	NC	S	W	Yes	No	None	Mar.	Few	More	Heroin
1. Very harmful	2.4	3.0	1.8	2.1	4.6	2.1	2.2	3.2	1.5	1.7	3.2	2.6	2.4	2.1	1.3	5.5
2. Mostly harmful	9.8	9.4	10.1	9.7	9.2	7.9	11.7	9.7	8.7	9.7	9.4	10.9	7.8	11.8	9.3	5.5
3. Don't know	32.8	34.3	31.0	31.5	39.8	30.4	33.5	32.6	35.2	29.0	36.7	32.5	31.3	32.1	35.3	36.4
4. Mostly beneficial	43.2	42.1	44.7	45.0	32.6	45.6	42.9	42.4	41.6	46.3	40.9	42.2	46.0	42.6	43.3	32.7
5. Very beneficial	11.8	11.2	12.4	11.7	13.4	13.9	9.6	12.1	12.9	13.3	9.9	11.8	12.5	11.5	10.8	21.8
Item 13290 N(Wtd)	2640	1281	1294	2160	261	583	862	807	389	1294	1248	1074	591	340	529	55

E02C: What effect do you think this living arrangement has on the couples with no children?

	TOTAL	M	F	White	Black	NE	NC	S	W	Yes	No	None	Mar.	Few	More	Heroin
1. Very harmful	3.0	2.7	3.2	2.5	5.3	2.7	3.4	3.2	2.3	2.6	3.4	3.0	3.0	3.5	2.1	1.8
2. Mostly harmful	9.4	9.1	9.4	8.9	11.4	6.3	9.2	12.2	8.4	9.4	9.3	9.4	9.6	10.2	9.2	5.4
3. Don't know	40.3	43.4	37.4	39.3	47.0	39.8	40.7	39.5	42.1	38.2	42.6	40.8	38.0	39.4	42.5	39.3
4. Mostly beneficial	36.0	34.1	38.0	38.5	23.1	34.6	37.3	34.7	37.2	38.2	33.7	36.2	36.7	35.3	35.5	39.3
5. Very beneficial	11.3	10.8	12.0	10.8	12.9	16.5	9.4	10.4	9.9	11.6	11.0	10.6	12.7	11.4	10.9	14.3
Item 13300 N(Wtd)	2650	1289	1298	2166	264	583	865	810	392	1300	1250	1077	592	343	532	56

E02D: How would you feel about this living arrangement for yourself as a parent?

	TOTAL	M	F	White	Black	NE	NC	S	W	Yes	No	None	Mar.	Few	More	Heroin
1. Unacceptable	20.8	19.4	22.3	20.5	23.0	18.9	21.8	20.9	21.0	21.6	19.8	23.4	21.1	18.3	17.6	14.8
2. Acceptable--it would be O.K.	49.8	49.8	49.8	50.7	43.8	50.2	47.5	50.6	52.7	50.5	50.3	47.7	51.3	53.0	52.7	29.6
3. Desirable--I'd really like it	14.1	14.5	13.6	14.9	9.4	14.1	15.3	13.4	12.7	14.8	12.6	13.9	14.4	12.1	13.4	31.5
8. Don't know	15.3	16.3	14.3	13.9	23.8	16.7	15.3	15.1	13.5	13.0	17.4	14.9	13.2	16.9	16.4	22.2
Item 13310 N(Wtd)	2602	1258	1285	2131	256	576	847	793	385	1294	1210	1062	589	338	507	54

E02E: How would you feel about this living arrangement for yourself if you were married with no children?

	TOTAL	M	F	White	Black	NE	NC	S	W	Yes	No	None	Mar.	Few	More	Heroin
1. Unacceptable	20.5	19.1	21.9	20.7	21.5	19.1	21.6	20.7	20.0	21.2	19.7	21.0	21.0	18.9	21.4	17.9
2. Acceptable--it would be O.K.	50.1	49.3	50.7	51.0	44.5	50.9	50.1	49.3	50.8	51.1	50.0	50.4	50.8	52.7	49.3	35.7
3. Desirable--I'd really like it	11.0	10.5	11.6	11.3	8.7	11.9	11.2	11.2	9.0	11.5	10.0	10.8	11.8	10.4	9.6	23.2
8. Don't know	18.3	21.1	15.8	16.9	25.3	17.9	17.1	18.8	20.3	16.2	20.3	17.8	16.3	18.0	19.7	23.2
Item 13320 N(Wtd)	2644	1286	1295	2160	265	580	869	805	390	1299	1247	1072	595	338	529	56

E03: Third example: Two married couples with children, a divorced parent with children, and several unmarried adults all live on the same block and are good friends. They often do things together as a group, and all the adults take some part in caring for the children.

QUESTIONNAIRE FORM 5 1976	TOTAL	SEX		RACE		REGION				4YR COLLEGE PLANS		ILLICIT DRUG USE: LIFETIME				
		M	F	White	Black	NE	NC	S	W	Yes	No	None	Mari- juana Only	Few Pills	More Pills	Any Her- oin
Weighted No. of Cases:	3008	1473	1427	2356	356	713	930	906	460	1415	1398	1174	678	381	606	70
% of Weighted Total:	100.0	49.0	47.4	78.3	11.8	23.7	30.9	30.1	15.3	47.0	46.5	39.0	22.5	12.7	20.1	2.3

E03A: What effect do you think this living arrangement has on the children of the married couples?

1. Very harmful	6.1	7.7	4.8	5.8	9.5	5.6	6.0	7.4	4.4	5.1	7.4	6.5	4.9	6.9	5.6	10.7
2. Mostly harmful	18.6	18.2	19.0	19.4	14.1	19.8	20.6	16.5	16.5	19.9	17.0	19.7	18.0	20.0	17.7	8.9
3. Don't know	45.8	48.4	43.3	44.9	44.7	43.3	45.6	46.1	49.1	42.4	48.6	42.7	47.6	46.9	48.4	44.6
4. Mostly beneficial	24.7	22.3	26.9	26.0	20.6	25.4	24.3	24.1	26.4	27.3	22.7	25.7	25.3	22.1	24.2	25.0
5. Very beneficial	4.7	3.5	6.0	3.9	11.1	6.1	3.4	5.9	3.6	5.3	4.4	5.3	4.3	4.2	4.2	10.7
Item 13420 N(Wtd)	2615	1274	1278	2136	262	571	860	798	387	1290	1227	1065	588	335	521	56

E03B: What effect do you think this living arrangement has on the children of the divorced parent?

1. Very harmful	5.5	5.8	5.3	5.3	6.2	5.3	5.4	6.1	5.2	4.9	6.0	6.1	3.8	6.3	5.2	8.9
2. Mostly harmful	22.2	21.0	23.8	21.3	28.2	21.1	25.3	20.4	20.7	22.2	22.1	25.1	19.8	21.5	20.3	17.9
3. Don't know	39.9	43.7	35.6	38.7	42.5	35.1	39.4	45.3	36.8	34.5	44.8	36.5	41.0	39.4	44.1	41.1
4. Mostly beneficial	26.9	25.2	28.8	29.4	17.4	32.2	25.5	22.7	30.8	31.9	22.3	26.8	31.1	26.9	24.8	17.9
5. Very beneficial	5.5	4.3	6.5	5.4	6.2	6.3	4.4	5.5	6.5	6.4	4.7	5.7	4.4	5.4	5.6	14.3
Item 13430 N(Wtd)	2605	1269	1275	2131	259	569	858	793	386	1288	1224	1061	586	335	521	56

E03C: What effect do you think this living arrangement has on the married couples?

1. Very harmful	3.6	4.5	2.7	3.5	3.9	2.6	3.5	4.7	2.6	3.3	4.0	3.6	3.2	5.4	2.7	3.7
2. Mostly harmful	14.0	13.8	14.3	14.0	16.3	14.1	15.3	13.3	12.5	14.1	13.5	14.4	13.8	13.5	14.1	9.3
3. Don't know	51.2	53.0	49.3	50.6	52.9	47.7	51.8	53.0	52.2	49.4	52.7	50.4	50.3	48.9	54.5	55.6
4. Mostly beneficial	26.6	25.1	28.2	28.0	18.7	30.5	25.8	24.4	27.5	28.3	25.6	26.1	28.5	29.4	24.9	22.2
5. Very beneficial	4.5	3.6	5.4	3.9	8.2	5.1	3.6	4.7	4.9	4.9	4.2	5.6	3.9	2.7	3.7	7.4
Item 13440 N(Wtd)	2601	1263	1275	2129	257	568	856	791	385	1280	1225	1060	585	333	519	54

E03D: What effect do you think this living arrangement has on the divorced parent?

1. Very harmful	3.4	3.9	2.7	2.8	7.7	3.0	2.8	5.0	1.8	2.9	4.0	3.7	2.9	3.0	2.3	9.1
2. Mostly harmful	17.5	16.6	18.6	16.8	21.9	16.9	19.4	16.3	16.8	15.4	19.1	18.7	16.0	17.8	16.1	16.4
3. Don't know	49.7	50.2	49.3	49.1	53.5	43.7	50.5	54.0	47.6	47.5	51.8	47.5	51.1	51.8	52.1	47.3
4. Mostly beneficial	24.5	24.4	24.3	26.4	12.7	30.3	22.8	20.6	27.9	28.0	21.3	25.8	26.1	22.3	23.5	18.2
5. Very beneficial	5.0	4.8	5.0	4.9	4.2	6.2	4.4	4.2	5.8	6.2	3.7	4.4	4.1	5.4	6.0	10.9
Item 13450 N(Wtd)	2598	1264	1271	2124	260	568	857	793	380	1284	1222	1060	587	332	514	55

E03E: What effect do you think this living arrangement has on the unmarried adults?

1. Very harmful	4.3	5.1	3.5	4.0	7.0	4.2	3.9	5.4	2.9	3.2	5.6	5.3	3.1	4.5	3.1	1.9
2. Mostly harmful	11.4	10.2	12.4	10.7	14.3	9.2	12.5	11.0	12.6	10.6	11.9	12.3	10.1	10.7	10.5	13.2
3. Don't know	54.5	55.2	54.1	54.1	55.8	50.2	55.4	55.3	56.8	53.4	55.2	52.0	55.9	54.0	57.6	56.6
4. Mostly beneficial	25.1	24.7	25.4	26.5	18.2	29.7	23.9	24.2	23.3	27.9	23.1	26.7	25.6	24.8	24.0	15.1
5. Very beneficial	4.7	5.0	4.5	4.7	4.7	6.7	4.3	4.1	4.2	5.1	4.3	3.6	5.3	6.0	4.5	13.2
Item 13460 N(Wtd)	2593	1261	1270	2121	258	566	855	790	382	1279	1222	1058	587	335	512	53

E03F: How would you feel about this living arrangement for yourself as a married parent?

1. Unacceptable	28.6	29.0	28.1	29.5	23.1	29.4	30.8	25.8	28.5	29.4	27.3	30.2	29.5	31.6	23.3	25.9
2. Acceptable--it would be O.K.	43.3	41.4	44.9	44.5	36.9	41.4	43.3	44.9	42.6	43.4	44.2	43.5	43.3	41.6	45.3	37.0
3. Desirable--I'd really like it	4.7	4.5	5.2	4.6	6.2	5.5	4.2	4.7	5.2	5.1	4.5	4.0	5.0	5.4	6.0	5.6
8. Don't know	23.3	25.2	21.9	21.4	33.8	23.9	21.7	24.7	23.8	22.1	24.1	22.3	22.3	21.4	25.4	31.5
Item 13470 N(Wtd)	2596	1255	1278	2120	260	565	857	791	383	1282	1222	1058	584	332	519	54

QUESTIONNAIRE FORM 5 1976	TOTAL	SEX		RACE		REGION				4YR COLLEGE PLANS		ILLICIT DRUG USE: LIFETIME				
		M	F	White	Black	NE	NC	S	W	Yes	No	None	Mari-juana Only	Few Pills	More Pills	Any Her-oin
Weighted No. of Cases:	3008	1473	1427	2356	356	713	930	906	460	1415	1398	1174	678	381	606	70
% of Weighted Total:	100.0	49.0	47.4	78.3	11.8	23.7	30.9	30.1	15.3	47.0	46.5	39.0	22.5	12.7	20.1	2.3
E03G: How would you feel about this living arrangement for yourself as a divorced parent?																
1. Unacceptable	24.7	25.0	24.3	24.0	29.4	24.1	26.8	24.7	21.0	23.9	25.4	25.9	24.8	25.9	21.4	20.4
2. Acceptable--it would be O.K.	38.2	35.8	40.7	40.2	27.9	39.1	37.1	37.3	40.9	41.5	35.5	36.8	41.6	38.9	38.4	37.0
3. Desirable--I'd really like it	6.6	6.1	7.0	6.7	6.1	6.0	6.4	6.1	8.7	7.3	5.8	6.3	6.0	5.1	7.5	7.4
8. Don't know	30.5	33.2	28.0	29.1	36.3	30.8	29.6	31.9	29.4	27.3	33.2	30.9	27.7	29.5	32.4	37.0
Item 13480 N(Wtd)	2593	1254	1276	2115	262	565	854	793	381	1278	1221	1056	584	332	518	54
E04: Some people like school very much. Others don't. How do you feel about going to school?																
5. I like school very much	15.4	15.0	15.8	13.4	28.6	14.0	11.0	20.1	17.7	20.4	10.0	20.9	12.2	14.2	8.9	13.8
4. I like school quite a lot	28.0	24.6	31.4	28.5	28.3	24.5	29.9	27.9	29.1	36.1	19.9	35.9	26.8	23.7	18.7	8.6
3. I like school some	38.7	42.3	35.1	39.4	33.7	39.5	41.4	35.2	38.8	33.2	44.2	32.8	40.6	44.8	43.6	41.4
2. I don't like school very much	12.4	12.1	12.6	13.3	5.8	14.7	12.7	11.2	10.7	7.2	17.5	7.2	14.2	12.1	19.0	27.6
1. I don't like school at all	5.6	6.0	5.1	5.5	3.6	7.4	5.0	5.6	4.0	3.1	8.2	3.3	6.2	5.2	10.0	8.6
Item 7630 N(Wtd)	2697	1303	1327	2193	276	605	875	815	402	1321	1264	1079	613	346	541	58
E05: How important is each of the following for being looked up to or having high status in your school?																
E05A: Coming from the right family																
1. No importance	12.9	14.0	11.2	11.1	20.8	16.4	9.8	12.3	15.4	12.3	13.4	11.4	13.9	12.8	14.3	23.2
2. Little importance	23.5	24.1	23.2	24.7	16.7	27.4	23.6	19.9	25.0	24.9	22.8	22.4	27.5	19.7	23.2	28.6
3. Moderate importance	34.0	34.7	33.5	36.1	21.6	30.9	36.5	34.7	32.1	35.5	32.1	32.9	33.8	35.4	36.3	25.0
4. Great importance	18.0	16.0	20.1	17.9	18.6	15.0	20.9	17.3	17.7	17.6	18.7	21.2	14.8	20.0	16.4	5.4
5. Very great importance	11.5	11.2	12.0	10.2	22.3	10.5	9.2	15.7	9.6	9.7	13.0	12.1	10.0	11.9	9.8	19.6
Item 13580 N(Wtd)	2658	1290	1305	2168	269	592	860	810	396	1310	1243	1067	603	345	531	56
E05B: Being a leader in student activities																
1. No importance	7.6	7.6	7.3	6.9	10.8	8.8	6.2	7.8	8.4	4.7	10.7	6.1	8.1	7.6	8.8	19.6
2. Little importance	14.5	15.2	13.9	14.3	12.6	16.9	13.5	12.5	17.0	12.5	16.6	10.2	16.3	12.9	21.0	21.4
3. Moderate importance	33.0	35.0	31.1	33.9	27.1	35.5	31.7	32.1	33.7	34.3	31.3	29.8	35.0	38.1	34.0	26.8
4. Great importance	30.1	29.6	30.6	30.6	28.6	27.7	32.9	30.0	27.3	34.3	26.0	35.3	26.7	30.5	25.3	17.9
5. Very great importance	14.9	12.7	16.9	14.2	20.8	11.0	15.8	17.5	13.7	14.2	15.3	18.5	13.8	10.9	10.9	12.5
Item 13590 N(Wtd)	2655	1284	1307	2167	269	591	861	807	395	1309	1241	1066	602	341	533	56
E05C: Having a nice car																
1. No importance	15.1	12.6	17.5	12.4	31.1	17.8	13.1	16.7	12.4	14.3	16.5	15.5	17.2	10.6	14.9	10.7
2. Little importance	28.8	26.4	31.1	29.7	23.7	31.2	28.7	28.1	26.6	28.6	29.0	29.7	25.6	31.4	27.3	39.3
3. Moderate importance	31.9	33.4	30.6	33.4	20.0	31.9	34.2	28.4	33.9	34.2	29.3	30.4	35.2	32.3	33.1	23.2
4. Great importance	16.6	18.9	14.0	17.2	15.2	12.5	17.7	17.9	17.2	16.3	16.7	15.4	14.7	20.2	18.1	16.1
5. Very great importance	7.7	8.7	6.8	7.3	10.0	6.6	6.3	8.9	9.9	6.7	8.5	8.8	7.1	5.6	6.6	10.7
Item 13600 N(Wtd)	2652	1282	1306	2162	270	590	857	810	395	1304	1240	1063	605	341	531	56
E05D: Getting good grades																
1. No importance	5.1	5.3	5.0	5.0	4.1	6.1	4.7	4.2	6.6	3.6	7.0	2.9	7.0	4.7	7.5	11.1
2. Little importance	15.9	16.4	15.3	17.4	7.1	16.9	17.2	13.6	16.5	16.6	15.5	13.5	17.6	15.6	20.2	16.7
3. Moderate importance	35.7	36.8	35.0	38.3	20.5	35.2	37.1	34.5	36.4	37.1	34.6	34.2	34.6	37.9	37.5	44.4
4. Great importance	26.5	25.8	26.8	26.7	23.5	25.3	28.1	25.5	27.0	27.7	25.7	30.6	23.8	23.5	24.7	13.0
5. Very great importance	16.7	15.6	17.9	12.5	44.8	16.6	13.0	22.1	13.7	15.1	17.3	18.7	17.1	18.2	10.0	16.7
Item 13610 N(Wtd)	2638	1273	1301	2151	268	586	854	804	393	1298	1234	1058	601	340	530	54

	TOTAL	SEX		RACE		REGION				4YR COLLEGE PLANS		ILLICIT DRUG USE: LIFETIME				
QUESTIONNAIRE FORM 5 1976		M	F	White	Black	NE	NC	S	W	Yes	No	None	Mari- juana Only	Few Pills	More Pills	Any Her- oin
Weighted No. of Cases:	3008	1473	1427	2356	356	713	930	906	460	1415	1398	1174	678	381	606	70
% of Weighted Total:	100.0	49.0	47.4	78.3	11.8	23.7	30.9	30.1	15.3	47.0	46.5	39.0	22.5	12.7	20.1	2.3
E05E: Being a good athlete																
1. No importance	8.4	7.1	9.7	7.4	13.7	8.5	7.6	10.2	6.6	5.1	11.8	6.3	10.0	7.4	10.0	15.1
2. Little importance	11.2	10.3	12.3	10.2	15.6	10.4	12.6	10.9	9.9	8.6	14.3	10.3	10.0	11.6	13.0	15.1
3. Moderate importance	28.2	29.5	26.9	28.5	21.8	30.1	25.8	29.1	28.7	27.5	28.5	24.7	31.2	26.1	34.2	22.6
4. Great importance	31.1	33.3	28.2	32.0	28.6	31.4	30.3	30.6	33.2	35.4	26.6	34.5	29.5	33.8	25.7	20.8
5. Very great importance	21.1	19.9	22.9	21.7	20.2	19.7	23.7	19.3	21.3	23.4	18.8	24.2	19.3	20.8	17.0	26.4
Item 13620 N(Wtd)	2635	1273	1299	2151	262	589	854	797	394	1295	1235	1059	600	337	530	53
E05F: Knowing a lot about intellectual matters																
1. No importance	10.9	9.9	12.0	11.0	8.2	12.5	10.6	9.8	11.4	8.9	13.2	8.7	12.6	12.0	11.6	16.4
2. Little importance	27.7	26.3	29.5	30.2	15.3	27.1	30.3	24.8	28.6	28.7	27.3	27.6	26.9	26.7	30.3	30.9
3. Moderate importance	38.1	39.6	36.6	39.1	28.4	37.0	39.1	35.9	42.0	38.7	37.8	36.8	38.9	41.9	39.0	30.9
4. Great importance	17.1	18.1	15.6	15.2	29.1	17.1	16.8	19.1	13.4	17.5	15.9	19.2	15.1	14.4	15.2	16.4
5. Very great importance	6.3	6.1	6.4	4.5	18.7	6.3	3.3	10.5	4.6	6.1	5.8	7.7	6.6	4.7	4.0	5.5
Item 13630 N(Wtd)	2645	1278	1304	2157	268	586	859	806	395	1301	1236	1063	602	341	528	55
E05G: Planning to go to college																
1. No importance	14.7	14.1	15.3	14.5	13.5	15.1	14.8	15.2	12.9	8.2	21.4	11.5	14.9	16.7	18.4	25.9
2. Little importance	23.1	23.5	23.0	24.6	15.4	23.1	24.8	19.9	25.9	23.4	23.9	23.4	22.4	22.2	23.9	29.6
3. Moderate importance	32.5	33.0	32.2	35.0	19.9	31.5	34.7	30.4	33.8	33.2	31.8	32.7	31.8	32.7	35.6	18.5
4. Great importance	17.9	18.7	16.9	17.1	23.7	17.1	17.5	20.2	15.5	20.5	14.8	20.3	17.1	16.1	14.4	18.5
5. Very great importance	11.6	10.7	12.7	8.8	27.1	13.1	8.0	14.3	11.9	14.7	8.1	12.2	13.8	11.7	8.0	7.4
Item 13640 N(Wtd)	2649	1281	1304	2161	266	590	862	803	394	1306	1236	1065	603	342	528	54
E06: How about using drugs (other than marijuana or alcohol)--does that cause a student to be looked up to or looked down on?																
E06A: Among the majority of students in my school, such drug use is...																
1. Looked down on a lot	16.0	18.8	13.2	15.4	21.7	11.0	13.4	22.4	15.7	17.3	14.1	18.0	17.6	17.8	8.5	14.0
2. Looked down on some	22.0	20.9	23.2	22.8	18.0	20.2	25.4	20.0	21.6	24.7	20.0	28.0	20.0	18.3	17.6	5.3
3. Neither or mixed	52.9	51.2	54.6	53.9	41.9	57.4	52.9	49.2	54.3	51.3	54.2	46.3	54.1	55.0	62.4	66.7
4. Looked up to some	6.9	7.4	6.4	6.1	12.9	8.4	6.8	5.6	7.1	5.0	8.9	5.6	6.2	6.8	9.8	7.0
5. Looked up to a lot	2.2	1.8	2.5	1.7	5.5	2.9	1.5	2.7	1.3	1.6	2.9	2.1	2.3	2.1	1.9	8.8
Item 13650 N(Wtd)	2628	1266	1299	2140	272	580	851	803	394	1294	1228	1048	601	338	529	57
E06B: Among my own group of friends, such drug use is...																
1. Looked down on a lot	34.9	34.4	35.7	36.1	33.2	29.1	33.4	38.1	40.2	41.0	28.8	54.8	27.8	28.7	12.1	5.3
2. Looked down on some	18.0	16.5	19.5	18.2	16.0	17.8	17.4	17.8	19.9	19.7	16.6	20.3	19.7	18.6	11.5	7.0
3. Neither or mixed	36.8	37.4	36.1	36.2	36.2	40.2	40.1	33.4	31.3	32.4	40.8	21.2	43.7	42.6	53.9	54.4
4. Looked up to some	7.1	8.2	5.9	6.6	9.7	9.1	5.5	7.4	6.8	4.5	9.5	2.4	6.7	7.7	14.9	14.0
5. Looked up to a lot	3.2	3.4	2.9	2.9	4.9	3.6	3.5	3.4	1.8	2.6	4.2	1.1	2.2	2.4	7.6	19.3
Item 13660 N(Wtd)	2627	1269	1295	2143	268	580	851	800	396	1294	1228	1052	600	338	529	57
E07: How often have you been around people who were taking each of the following to get high or for "kicks"?																
E07A: Marijuana (pot, grass) or hashish																
1. Never	18.5	15.2	21.4	17.6	25.8	13.4	17.1	23.0	19.9	18.1	19.4	37.8	3.0	10.3	5.5	-
2. Once or twice	21.4	22.0	20.9	21.7	18.7	17.6	22.6	21.8	23.6	23.9	19.4	32.3	19.6	17.4	5.8	3.4
3. Occasionally	25.8	26.7	25.1	25.5	25.8	25.0	28.2	24.0	25.1	27.6	24.0	20.3	40.5	30.6	17.7	20.3
4. Often	34.3	35.9	32.5	35.2	29.2	43.9	32.1	31.1	31.3	30.3	37.1	9.5	37.0	41.8	71.1	76.3
Item 8750 N(Wtd)	2644	1286	1292	2155	267	581	861	801	402	1295	1241	1058	602	340	532	59

QUESTIONNAIRE FORM 5 1976	TOTAL	SEX M	F	RACE White	Black	REGION NE	NC	S	W	4YR COLLEGE PLANS Yes	No	ILLICIT DRUG USE: LIFETIME None	Marijuana Only	Few Pills	More Pills	Any Heroin
Weighted No. of Cases:	3008	1473	1427	2356	356	713	930	906	460	1415	1398	1174	678	381	606	70
% of Weighted Total:	100.0	49.0	47.4	78.3	11.8	23.7	30.9	30.1	15.3	47.0	46.5	39.0	22.5	12.7	20.1	2.3
E07B: LSD																
1. Never	70.7	71.5	69.6	68.8	87.5	66.6	70.0	73.9	71.9	72.9	68.7	88.2	74.7	68.9	37.8	13.6
2. Once or twice	16.4	15.1	18.0	17.7	7.8	17.1	17.0	15.8	15.7	17.2	15.6	8.7	16.9	21.9	28.1	18.6
3. Occasionally	9.8	9.4	10.4	10.7	3.5	12.5	10.0	7.6	9.6	7.7	11.9	3.0	6.9	8.3	25.2	35.6
4. Often	3.1	4.1	2.0	2.8	1.2	3.8	2.9	2.7	3.0	2.3	3.8	.3	1.3	.9	9.1	30.5
Item 8760 N(Wtd)	2608	1268	1275	2131	257	574	851	789	395	1280	1228	1040	593	338	527	59
E07C: Other psychedelics (mescaline, peyote, PCP, etc.)																
1. Never	72.9	72.5	73.2	71.5	87.0	68.8	72.4	75.6	74.7	76.1	70.1	91.8	79.0	69.2	36.4	13.6
2. Once or twice	15.1	14.7	15.6	16.1	6.9	17.5	14.4	13.2	16.7	14.3	15.9	5.8	13.9	20.4	32.2	10.2
3. Occasionally	8.6	9.0	8.3	9.2	3.8	9.8	9.5	8.2	5.8	7.1	10.1	1.6	5.5	9.6	22.1	42.4
4. Often	3.4	3.9	2.8	3.2	2.3	4.2	3.8	2.8	2.8	2.7	4.0	.9	1.3	.6	9.3	33.9
Item 8770 N(Wtd)	2607	1269	1273	2125	262	573	850	788	396	1275	1233	1043	595	334	525	59
E07D: Quaaludes (quads, methaqualone)																
1. Never	77.7	77.5	77.5	76.4	90.3	75.8	78.1	76.2	82.4	80.5	75.2	94.1	81.0	75.9	47.9	19.0
2. Once or twice	12.6	12.3	12.5	13.6	7.8	12.6	12.2	13.2	12.5	12.4	13.2	4.4	12.1	17.9	25.7	19.0
3. Occasionally	6.8	7.4	6.5	7.2	1.6	8.8	7.1	6.7	3.3	5.1	8.0	1.3	5.5	5.4	18.7	27.6
4. Often	2.9	2.9	2.8	2.8	.8	3.0	2.6	3.7	1.8	2.1	3.6	.3	1.4	1.2	7.7	36.2
Item 8780 N(Wtd)	2584	1260	1261	2110	258	565	842	786	391	1262	1224	1036	585	336	518	58
E07E: Barbiturates (downers, goofballs, reds, yellows, etc.)																
1. Never	63.3	63.8	62.5	61.2	80.5	59.3	62.1	65.6	66.8	67.3	59.9	85.5	68.2	52.5	25.8	8.5
2. Once or twice	20.8	20.3	21.3	22.1	11.9	22.3	20.8	18.5	22.8	20.2	21.1	11.4	21.6	33.8	31.3	13.6
3. Occasionally	12.2	11.9	12.9	13.0	6.1	14.0	13.9	11.3	8.0	9.7	14.8	2.5	8.9	11.3	33.2	40.7
4. Often	3.7	3.9	3.4	3.6	1.5	4.2	3.1	4.5	2.3	2.9	4.2	.6	1.3	2.1	9.7	39.0
Item 8790 N(Wtd)	2614	1273	1276	2131	261	570	850	794	400	1280	1234	1042	598	337	527	59
E07F: Tranquilizers (Librium, Valium, Miltown)																
1. Never	65.9	69.5	61.8	63.7	84.0	64.7	66.1	65.2	68.6	68.7	63.5	85.2	71.2	59.6	30.3	13.3
2. Once or twice	19.4	18.0	21.2	21.0	9.5	18.6	19.2	19.4	20.7	19.4	19.5	10.6	19.0	27.3	33.2	15.0
3. Occasionally	10.7	8.9	12.6	11.4	4.2	11.6	11.2	11.1	7.9	9.0	12.3	3.5	7.8	10.4	26.0	40.0
4. Often	4.0	3.6	4.2	3.9	1.9	4.9	3.6	4.3	2.8	2.8	4.7	.8	1.9	2.4	10.7	31.7
Item 8800 N(Wtd)	2605	1263	1276	2123	263	569	852	792	392	1276	1229	1040	591	337	524	60
E07G: Cocaine ("coke")																
1. Never	72.9	70.5	75.1	73.1	79.2	67.5	74.9	76.0	70.3	75.5	71.5	89.8	79.0	69.2	40.3	11.9
2. Once or twice	16.3	18.0	14.9	16.5	13.3	19.2	15.3	14.0	19.5	15.9	16.2	7.8	14.8	21.6	31.6	23.7
3. Occasionally	7.4	7.7	7.1	7.7	5.3	9.2	6.5	7.3	7.1	6.3	8.1	1.9	4.7	6.8	18.7	40.7
4. Often	3.3	3.8	2.8	2.7	1.9	3.9	3.4	2.8	3.0	2.2	4.1	.5	1.5	2.1	9.2	25.4
Item 8810 N(Wtd)	2606	1267	1275	2124	264	567	851	795	394	1277	1229	1043	595	338	519	59
E07H: Heroin (smack, horse)																
1. Never	86.5	86.9	85.9	86.8	89.7	85.1	88.1	84.6	88.8	89.3	84.3	92.7	90.3	86.6	76.4	20.3
2. Once or twice	9.0	8.3	9.9	9.0	6.9	8.8	8.2	11.0	7.4	7.5	10.5	5.7	7.2	9.2	15.6	32.2
3. Occasionally	3.4	3.2	3.4	3.3	2.7	4.7	2.7	3.4	2.5	2.5	4.0	1.5	2.2	3.0	5.9	32.2
4. Often	1.1	1.5	.7	.8	.8	1.6	.9	1.0	1.3	.9	1.3	.2	.3	1.5	2.3	16.9
Item 8820 N(Wtd)	2608	1271	1271	2126	262	571	851	792	393	1275	1232	1041	595	336	526	59
E07I: Other narcotics (methadone, opium, codeine, paregoric, etc.)																
1. Never	77.2	75.3	78.9	76.5	86.4	73.5	77.8	77.3	80.7	79.8	74.9	91.7	84.0	76.2	46.6	13.8
2. Once or twice	15.1	15.8	14.5	15.8	11.0	17.8	14.8	14.1	13.5	14.0	16.0	6.2	10.9	17.9	34.4	37.9
3. Occasionally	5.7	6.5	5.1	5.8	2.3	6.3	5.8	6.1	4.3	4.5	6.7	1.7	3.7	5.4	14.0	24.1
4. Often	2.0	2.4	1.5	1.9	.4	2.3	1.8	2.5	1.3	1.6	2.3	.3	1.2	.6	5.0	25.9
Item 8830 N(Wtd)	2606	1268	1272	2125	264	567	852	793	394	1275	1232	1045	595	336	521	58

	TOTAL	SEX		RACE		REGION				4YR COLLEGE PLANS		ILLICIT DRUG USE: LIFETIME				
QUESTIONNAIRE FORM 5 1976		M	F	White	Black	NE	NC	S	W	Yes	No	None	Mari- juana Only	Few Pills	More Pills	Any Her- oin
Weighted No. of Cases:	3008	1473	1427	2356	356	713	930	906	460	1415	1398	1174	678	381	606	70
% of Weighted Total:	100.0	49.0	47.4	78.3	11.8	23.7	30.9	30.1	15.3	47.0	46.5	39.0	22.5	12.7	20.1	2.3
E07J: Inhalants (glue, laughing gas, snappers, etc.)																
1. Never	78.7	76.8	80.2	78.2	89.3	76.4	79.3	78.5	80.9	79.7	77.8	87.3	81.8	76.3	63.9	44.8
2. Once or twice	15.5	16.7	14.8	16.4	6.1	16.9	14.1	16.2	15.5	15.1	15.9	9.8	13.5	17.1	26.2	36.2
3. Occasionally	4.1	4.3	3.9	3.9	3.4	3.9	4.6	4.3	2.8	3.5	4.6	2.2	3.7	5.4	6.7	5.2
4. Often	1.7	2.3	1.1	1.5	1.1	2.8	2.0	1.0	.8	1.6	1.5	.7	1.0	1.5	3.2	13.8
Item 8835 N(Wtd)	2603	1269	1271	2123	261	568	851	792	393	1274	1229	1040	593	334	526	58
E07K: Alcoholic beverages (beer, wine, liquor)																
1. Never	9.4	8.9	9.9	7.9	21.2	8.3	7.5	10.9	12.2	8.5	10.5	16.3	6.3	6.2	1.9	1.7
2. Once or twice	9.2	7.8	10.4	8.7	11.0	6.2	8.6	11.4	10.2	10.0	8.7	16.4	4.0	8.0	2.3	3.4
3. Occasionally	25.1	24.8	25.0	24.9	26.9	22.5	23.3	27.5	28.1	27.6	22.8	33.7	22.3	23.6	13.2	10.2
4. Often	56.2	58.4	54.7	58.6	40.5	62.7	60.7	50.2	49.5	53.8	58.0	33.6	67.4	62.5	82.5	86.4
Item 8840 N(Wtd)	2633	1281	1286	2147	264	577	857	797	402	1292	1240	1052	602	339	531	59

Cross-Time Index of Questionnaire Items, 1975-1978

Introduction to the Indexing Conventions

This cross-time index of question locations is organized in numerical sequence according to item reference number, which is the unique numerical identifier assigned to each question in the study.

The Content Index may be used in two major ways:

1. **Locating a Question Across Years.** Having located a question of interest in the Descriptive Results section, the reader may determine in what other years that same question has appeared simply by looking it up here under its unique item reference number. The Index will show all years in which that item has appeared and also show its location each year (by questionnaire form, section, and item number). All items will retain their unique reference numbers in future years as well, and thus may be located in exactly the same way in subsequent volumes in this series.

EXAMPLE: A reader interested in a particular item about enjoying the fast pace of today's life would find that it has been assigned item Reference Number 1210. The index entry for item 1210 shows that this item has appeared in Section A of questionnaire Form 1 in all annual surveys in the series. Its question number was 4B in 1975 and 2B thereafter. By looking up the same item reference number in the index of any other volume of interest, the reader can ascertain the page location in that volume for the descriptive results on the same question.

2. **Locating Questions by Subject Area.** Given an interest in some particular subject area, one can quickly scan the Index to locate all questions dealing with that area. Table 3 shows the 19 general subject areas into which all items are classified, along with the alphabetical code assigned each

area. (Category A, Drugs, is further subdivided into numerically identified subcategories.)

EXAMPLE: A reader interested in items dealing with religion should first locate the relevant code in Table 3: Code G, "Religion." The second step is to scan all pages of the item index looking for entries in Column G under the heading Subject Area, noting for every item showing a G, its item reference number and page location in this volume. The reader may or may not find the abbreviated description of the item (given in the third column of the index and further described below) helpful in deciding whether to look up a particular item in the Descriptive Results section. Some of these descriptions are rather clear as to their meaning, but others are less so.

Definitions of the Column Headings

The definitions of column headings, and the conventions used for the entries in each column, are given below under the numbers indicated in the following key.

① **Item Reference Number.** A unique identification number is assigned to each question for the duration of this research and reporting series. It appears below that question in the Descriptive Results section, as well as in this index and the indices of all other volumes in the series.

② **Page Location.** The second column of the Question Index gives the page number of the present volume on which a verbatim statement of the question may be found along with this year's descriptive results.

③ **Item Description (Abbreviated).** This is a brief mnemonic description — up to 16 characters in length — which attempts to characterize the content of the question. Originally developed for question identification on OSIRIS computer files, it may in many cases allow one to determine the relevance of the question to one's own interest and thus reduce the number of irrelevant questions which must be looked up in the Descriptive Results section.

④ **Questionnaire Location by Year.** An entry is provided for every year in which an item appeared in one of the study's questionnaire forms. The six (or fewer) characters comprising the entry indicate the form in which the question appeared, the section of that form, and the question number. Take as an example the questionnaire location 1A004A. This location code indicates that the question appeared in Form 1, Section A, and was labeled as Question 4a.

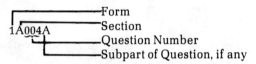

Occasionally an entry will be enclosed in parentheses. This indicates that there was a change (usually minor) in the wording of the question and/or the answer alternatives in subsequent years.

A form number (ranging from 1 to 5) is usually shown in the first character location. However, two substitute characters will replace the form number at times:

+ A plus sign indicates that the item appeared in all five forms that year and that it appeared in the same location on all forms.
* An asterisk indicates that the item appeared in four forms (Forms 2 through 5) and in the same location on all forms.

⑤ **Subject Area.** Table 3 shows the subject content areas which have been distinguished here and gives the alphabetical code assigned to each of them. Every question item in the index has been classified into one or more of the subject areas, and the alphabetical codes for those subject areas are printed in the appropriate column(s) next to each item under the general heading "Subject Area." A separate column has been assigned to each subject area code to facilitate rapid scanning. (Note that area A, dealing with drugs, has been given numerically identified subcategories because there were so many questions dealing with this general subject area.)

Figure 2

Guide to Cross-Time Index

① ITEM REFERENCE NUMBER	② PAGE LOCATION (IN THIS VOLUME)	③ ITEM DESCRIPTION (ABBREVIATED)	④ QUESTIONNAIRE LOCATION BY YEAR (FORM, SECTION, AND QUESTION NUMBER) 1975	1976	1977	1978	⑤ SUBJECT AREA A	B C D E F G H I	J K L M N O P Q R S
10	16	R'S BIRTH YEAR		+C001	+C001	+C001			R
20	16	R'S BIRTH MONTH		+C002	+C002	+C002			R
30	16	R'S SEX		+C003	+C003	+C003			R
40	16	R'S RACE		+C004	+C004	+C004			R
50	16	R SPD >TIM R-URB		+C005	+C005	+C005			R
60	17	R NOT MARRIED		+C006	+C006	+C006		D	R
80	17	R'S HSHLD ALONE		+C007A	+C007A	+C007A			M R
90	17	R'S HSHLD FATHER		+C007B	+C007B	+C007B			M R
100	17	R'S HSHLD MOTHER		+C007C	+C007C	+C007C			M R
110	17	R'S HSHLD BR/SR		+C007D	+C007D	+C007D			M R
120	17	R'S HSHLD GRPRNT		+C007E	+C007E	+C007E			M R
130	17	R'S HSHLD SPOUSE		+C007F	+C007F	+C007F			M R
140	17	R'S HSHLD CHLDRN		+C007G	+C007G	+C007G			M R
150	17	R'S HSHLD RELTVS		+C007H	+C007H	+C007H			M R
160	17	R'S HSHLD NONRLT		+C007I	+C007I	+C007I			M R
310	17	FATHR EDUC LEVEL		+C008	+C008	+C008		B	R
320	17	MOTHR EDUC LEVEL		+C009	+C009	+C009		B	R
330	17	MOTH PD JB R YNG		+C010	+C010	+C010		C	R
340	18	R'S POLTL PRFNC		+C011	+C011	+C011		H	R
350	18	R'POL BLF RADCL		+C012	+C012			H	R
360	18	R'S RELGS PRFNC		+C013A	+C013A	+C013A		G	R
370	18	R'ATTND REL SVC		+C013B	+C013B	+C013B		G	R
380	18	RLGN IMP R'S LF		+C013C	+C013C	+C013C		G	R
390	19	WHEN R XPCT GRAD		+C014	+C014	+C014		B	R
400	19	R'S HS PROGRAM		+C015	+C015	+C015		B	R
410	19	RT SF SCH AB>AVG		+C016	+C016	+C016			R
420	19	RT SF INTELL>AVG		+C017	+C017	+C017			R
430	19	#DA/4W SC MS ILL		+C018A	+C018A	+C018A		B	
440	19	#DA/4W SC MS CUT		+C018B	+C018B	+C018B		B	
450	20	#DA/4W SC MS OTH		+C018C	+C018C				
460	20	#DA/4W SKP CLASS		+C019					
470	20	R HS GRADE/D=1		+C0??					R
480	20	R WL DO VOC/TEC							R
490	20	R WL DO ARMD FC							
500	20	R WL DO 2YR CLG							
510	21	R WL DO 4YR CLG							
520	21	R WL DO GRD/...							
530	21	R WNT...							

Table 3

Subject Area Key
(Referenced by letter in the Question Index)

A. **Drugs.** Drug use and related attitudes and beliefs, drug availability and exposure, surrounding conditions and social meaning of drug use. Views of significant others regarding drugs.

A01   Use of Drugs
        A01A — . . . in lifetime
        A01B — . . . in the last 12 months
        A01C — . . . in the last 30 days
        A01D — Quantity used
        A01E — How high? (How often?)
        A01F — How long high?
        A01G — Incidence of first use
        A01H — Use with other drugs
        A01I — Try to stop?
        A01J — . . . on doctor's orders?
        A01K — Bad trip?
        A01L — Kinds of drugs

A02   Exposure to Drug Use
        A02A — Friends' use of drugs
        A02B — Exposure to users

A03   Availability of Drugs

A04   Expected Future Use

A05   Conditions of Use
        A05A — Alone
        A05B — With others
        A05C — Settings
        A05D — Mode of drug administration

A06   Reasons for Use, Abstention, and Stopping

A07   Problems with Drugs

A08   Sources of Help regarding Drugs

A09   Parental Awareness of Use

A10   Drug Education

A11   Own Attitudes regarding Drugs and Drug Users
        A11A — For adults
        A11C — For own children
        A11D — Perception of drug users

A12   Others' Attitudes regarding Drugs and Drug Users
        A12A — Parents
        A12B — Friends
        A12C — Students in school
        A12D — Perception of Drug Users

Table 3 (continued)

A13 Legal Issues regarding Drugs
    A13A — Preferred legality for adults
    A13C — Own response to legalization
    A13D — Knowledge of marijuana laws

A14 Risk of Drug Harm
    A14A — To self
    A14B — To others

B. **Education.** Educational lifestyle, values, experiences, and environments. Media usage.

C. **Work and Leisure.** Vocational values, meaning of work and leisure, work and leisure activities, preferences regarding occupational characteristics and type of work setting.

D. **Sex Roles and Family.** Values, attitudes, and expectations about marriage, family structure, sex roles, and sex discrimination.

E. **Family Plans and Population Concerns.** Values, attitudes, and expectations about personal family plans. Views on sexual mores and concerns about overpopulation.

F. **Conservation, Materialism, Equity, Etc.** Values, attitudes, and expectations related to conservation, pollution, materialism, equity, and the sharing of resources. Preferences regarding type of dwelling and urbanicity.

G. **Religion.** Religious affiliation, practices, and views.

H. **Politics.** Political affiliation, activities, and views.

I. **Social Change.** Values, attitudes, and expectations about social change.

J. **Social Problems.** Concern with various social problems facing the nation and the world.

K. **Major Social Institutions.** Confidence in and commitment to various major social institutions (business, unions, branches of government, press, organized religion, military, etc.).

L. **Military.** Views about the armed services and the use of military force. Personal plans for military service.

M. **Interpersonal Relationships.** Qualitative and quantitative characteristics of cross-age and peer relationships. Interpersonal conflict.

N. **Race Relations.** Attitudes toward and experiences with other racial groups.

O. **Concern for Others.** Radius of concern for others, voluntary and charitable activities.

P. **Happiness.** Happiness and life satisfaction, overall and in specific life domains.

Q. **Other Personality Variables.** Attitudes about self (including self-esteem), locus of control, loneliness, optimism, trust in others, somatic symptoms, importance placed on various life goals, counter-culture orientation.

R. **Background and School.** Demographic and family background characteristics, curriculum and grades in high school, victimization in school.

S. **Deviant Behavior and Victimization.** Delinquent behaviors, driving violations and accidents, violations and accidents under the influence of drugs, victimization experiences.

ITEM REFERENCE NUMBER	PAGE LOCATION (IN THIS VOLUME)	ITEM DESCRIPTION (ABBREVIATED)	1975	1976	1977	1978	A	B	C	D	E	F	G	H	I	J	K	L	M	N	O	P	Q	R	S
10	16	R'S BIRTH YEAR		+C001	+C001	+C001																		R	
20	16	R'S BIRTH MONTH		+C002	+C002	+C002																		R	
30	16	R'S SEX		+C003	+C003	+C003																		R	
40	16	R'S RACE		+C004	+C004	+C004																		R	
50	16	R SPD >TIM R-URB		+C005	+C005	+C005																		R	
60	17	R NOT MARRIED		+C006	+C006	+C006				D														R	
80	17	R'S HSHLD ALONE		+C007A	+C007A	+C007A														M					R	
90	17	R'S HSHLD FATHER		+C007B	+C007B	+C007B														M					R	
100	17	R'S HSHLD MOTHER		+C007C	+C007C	+C007C														M					R	
110	17	R'S HSHLD BR/SR		+C007D	+C007D	+C007D														M					R	
120	17	R'S HSHLD GRPRNT		+C007E	+C007E	+C007E														M					R	
130	17	R'S HSHLD SPOUSE		+C007F	+C007F	+C007F														M					R	
140	17	R'S HSHLD CHLDRN		+C007G	+C007G	+C007G														M					R	
150	17	R'S HSHLD RELTVS		+C007H	+C007H	+C007H														M					R	
160	17	R'S HSHLD NONRLT		+C007I	+C007I	+C007I														M					R	
310	17	FATHR EDUC LEVEL		+C008	+C008	+C008		B																	R	
320	17	MOTHR EDUC LEVEL		+C009	+C009	+C009		B																	R	
330	17	MOTH PD JB R YNG		+C010	+C010	+C010			C																R	
340	18	R'S POLTL PRFNC		+C011	+C011	+C011								H											R	
350	18	R'POL BLF RADCL		+C012	+C012	+C012								H											R	
360	18	R'S RELGS PRFNC		+C013A	+C013A	+C013A							G												R	
370	18	R'ATTND REL SVC		+C013B	+C013B	+C013B							G												R	
380	18	RLGN IMP R'S LF		+C013C	+C013C	+C013C							G												R	
390	19	WHEN R XPCT GRAD		+C014	+C014	+C014		B																	R	
400	19	R'S HS PROGRAM		+C015	+C015	+C015		B																	R	
410	19	RT SF SCH AB>AVG		+C016	+C016	+C016																			R	
420	19	RT SF INTELL>AVG		+C017	+C017	+C017																			R	
430	19	#DA/4W SC MS ILL		+C018A	+C018A	+C018A		B																		
440	19	#DA/4W SC MS CUT		+C018B	+C018B	+C018B		B																		
450	20	#DA/4W SC MS OTH		+C018C	+C018C	+C018C		B																		
460	20	#DA/4W SKP CLASS		+C019	+C019	+C019		B																		
470	20	R HS GRADE/D=1		+C020	+C020	+C020																			R	
480	20	R WL DO VOC/TEC		+C021A	+C021A	+C021A		B	C																R	
490	20	R WL DO ARMD FC		+C021B	+C021B	+C021B		B											L						R	
500	20	R WL DO 2YR CLG		+C021C	+C021C	+C021C		B																	R	
510	21	R WL DO 4YR CLG		+C021D	+C021D	+C021D		B																	R	
520	21	R WL DO GRD/PRF		+C021E	+C021E	+C021E		B																	R	
530	21	R WNTDO VOC/TEC		+C022A	+C022A	+C022A		B	C																R	
540	21	R WNTDO ARMD FC		+C022B	+C022B	+C022B		B											L						R	
550	21	R WNTDO 2YR CLG		+C022C	+C022C	+C022C		B																	R	
560	21	R WNTDO 4YR CLG		+C022D	+C022D	+C022D		B																	R	
570	21	R WNTDO GRD/PRF		+C022E	+C022E	+C022E		B																	R	
580	21	R WNTDO NONE		+C022F	+C022F	+C022F		B																	R	
590	21	HRS/W WRK SCHYR		+C023	+C023	+C023			C																	
600	21	R$/AVG WEEK JOB		+C024A	+C024A	+C024A																			R	
610	22	R$/AVG WEEK OTH		+C024B	+C024B	+C024B																			R	
620	22	#X/AV WK GO OUT		+C025	+C025	+C025			C											M						
630	22	#X DATE 3+/WK		+C026	+C026	+C026			C											M						
640	22	DRIVE>200 MI/WK		+C027	+C027	+C027						F														
650	22	#X/12MO R TCKTD		+C028	+C028	+C028	A07A																			S
660	23	#TCKTS AFT DRNK		+C029A	+C029A	+C029A	A07A																			S
670	23	#TCKTS AFT MARJ		+C029B	+C029B	+C029B	A07A																			S
680	23	#TCKTS AFT OTDG		+C029C	+C029C	+C029C	A07A																			S
690	23	#ACCIDNTS/12 MO		+C030	+C030	+C030	A07A																			S
700	23	#ACDTS AFT DRNK		+C031A	+C031A	+C031A	A07A																			S
710	23	#ACDTS AFT MARJ		+C031B	+C031B	+C031B	A07A																			S
720	24	#ACDTS AFT OTDG		+C031C	+C031C	+C031C	A07A																			S
730	24	R'S BRANCH SERV		+C032	+C032	+C032													L						R	
740	24	R XPCTS B OFFCR		+C033	+C033	+C033													L						R	
750	24	R XPCTS MLTR CR		+C034	+C034	+C034													L						R	
760	24	EVR SMK CIG,REGL	1A018	+B001	+B001	(+B001)	A01A																			
			*B01				A01A																			
780	41	#CIGS SMKD/30DAY	1A020	1B003	1B003	1B003	A01C																			
	24		*B02	*B02	*B02	*B02	A01C																			
790	25	EVER DRINK	1A026	*B03	*B03	*B03	A01A																			
			*B03				A01A																			

ITEM REFERENCE NUMBER	PAGE LOCATION (IN THIS VOLUME)	ITEM DESCRIPTION (ABBREVIATED)	QUESTIONNAIRE LOCATION BY YEAR (FORM, SECTION, AND QUESTION NUMBER)				SUBJECT AREA	
			1975	1976	1977	1978	A	B C D E F G H I J K L M N O P Q R S
810	42	#X DRNK/LIFETIME	1A028A	1B007A	1B007A	1B007A	A01A	
	25		*B04A	*B04A	*B04A	*B04A	A01A	
820	42	#X DRNK/LAST12MO	1A028B	1B007B	1B007B	1B007B	A01B	
	25		*B04B	*B04B	*B04B	*B04B	A01B	
830	42	#X DRNK/LAST30DA	1A028C	1B007C	1B007C	1B007C	A01C	
	25		*B04C	*B04C	*B04C	*B04C	A01C	
840	25	#X DRK ENF FL HI	*B05	*B05	*B05	*B05	A01E	
850	44	5+DRK ROW/LST 2W	1A035	1B012	1B012	1B012	A01D	
	25		*B06	*B06	*B06	*B06	A01D	
860		#XMJ+HS/LIFETIME	1A044A				A01A	
	26		*B07A	*B07A	*B07A	*B07A	A01A	
870		#XMJ+HS/LAST12MO	1A044B				A01B	
	26		*B07B	*B07B	*B07B	*B07B	A01B	
880		#XMJ+HS/LAST30DA	1A044C				A01C	
	26		*B07C	*B07C	*B07C	*B07C	A01C	
890	50	#X LSD/LIFETIME	1A057A	1B029A	1B029A	1B029A	A01A	
	26		*B08A	*B08A	*B08A	*B08A	A01A	
900	50	#X LSD/LAST 12MO	1A057B	1B029B	1B029B	1B029B	A01B	
	27		*B08B	*B08B	*B08B	*B08B	A01B	
910	50	#X LSD/LAST 30DA	1A057C	1B029C	1B029C	1B029C	A01C	
	27		*B08C	*B08C	*B08C	*B08C	A01C	
920	53	#X PSYD/LIFETIME	1A071A	1B038A	1B038A	1B038A	A01A	
	27		*B09A	*B09A	*B09A	*B09A	A01A	
930	53	#X PSYD/LAST12MO	1A071B	1B038B	1B038B	1B038B	A01B	
	27		*B09B	*B09B	*B09B	*B09B	A01B	
940	53	#X PSYD/LAST30DA	1A071C	1B038C	1B038C	1B038C	A01C	
	27		*B09C	*B09C	*B09C	*B09C	A01C	
950	69	#X COKE/LIFETIME	1A144A	1B076A	1B076A	1B076A	A01A	
	28		*B10A	*B10A	*B10A	*B10A	A01A	
960	69	#X COKE/LAST12MO	1A144B	1B076B	1B076B	1B076B	A01B	
	28		*B10B	*B10B	*B10B	*B10B	A01B	
970	69	#X COKE/LAST30DA	1A144C	1B076C	1B076C	1B076C	A01C	
	28		*B10C	*B10C	*B10C	*B10C	A01C	
980	55	#X AMPH/LIFETIME	1A087A	1B043A	1B043A	1B043A	A01A	
	28		*B11A	*B11A	*B11A	*B11A	A01A	
990	55	#X AMPH/LAST12MO	1A087B	1B043B	1B043B	1B043B	A01B	
	28		*B11B	*B11B	*B11B	*B11B	A01B	
1000	55	#X AMPH/LAST30DA	1A087C	1B043C	1B043C	1B043C	A01C	
	29		*B11C	*B11C	*B11C	*B11C	A01C	
1010	59	#X QUAD/LIFETIME	1A102A	1B053A	1B053A	1B053A	A01A	
	29		*B12A	*B12A	*B12A	*B12A	A01A	
1020	59	#X QUAD/LAST12MO	1A102B	1B053B	1B053B	1B053B	A01B	
	29		*B12B	*B12B	*B12B	*B12B	A01B	
1030	59	#X QUAD/LAST30DA	1A102C	1B053C	1B053C	1B053C	A01C	
	29		*B12C	*B12C	*B12C	*B12C	A01C	
1040	60	#X BRBT/LIFETIME	1A116A	1B057A	1B057A	1B057A	A01A	
	29		*B13A	*B13A	*B13A	*B13A	A01A	
1050	60	#X BRBT/LAST12MO	1A116B	1B057B	1B057B	1B057B	A01B	
	30		*B13B	*B13B	*B13B	*B13B	A01B	
1060	60	#X BRBT/LAST30DA	1A116C	1B057C	1B057C	1B057C	A01C	
	30		*B13C	*B13C	*B13C	*B13C	A01C	
1070	64	#X TRQL/LIFETIME	1A131A	1B067A	1B067A	1B067A	A01A	
	30		*B14A	*B14A	*B14A	*B14A	A01A	
1080	65	#X TRQL/LAST12MO	1A131B	1B067B	1B067B	1B067B	A01B	
	30		*B14B	*B14B	*B14B	*B14B	A01B	
1090	65	#X TRQL/LAST30DA	1A131C	1B067C	1B067C	1B067C	A01C	
	30		*B14C	*B14C	*B14C	*B14C	A01C	
1100	73	#X "H"/LIFETIME	1A158A	1B085A	1B085A	1B085A	A01A	
	31		*B15A	*B15A	*B15A	*B15A	A01A	
1110	73	#X "H"/LAST 12MO	1A158B	1B085B	1B085B	1B085B	A01B	
	31		*B15B	*B15B	*B15B	*B15B	A01B	
1120	74	#X "H"/LAST 30DA	1A158C	1B085C	1B085C	1B085C	A01C	
	31		*B15C	*B15C	*B15C	*B15C	A01C	
1130	78	#X NARC/LIFETIME	1A173A	1B095A	1B095A	1B095A	A01A	
	31		*B16A	*B16A	*B16A	*B16A	A01A	
1140	78	#X NARC/LAST12MO	1A173B	1B095B	1B095B	1B095B	A01B	

ITEM REFERENCE NUMBER	PAGE LOCATION (IN THIS VOLUME)	ITEM DESCRIPTION (ABBREVIATED)	1975	1976	1977	1978	A	B	C	D	E	F	G	H	I	J	K	L	M	N	O	P	Q	R	S
	31		*B16B	*B16B	*B16B	*B16B	A01B																		
1150	78	#X NARC/LAST30DA	1A173C	1B095C	1B095C	1B095C	A01C																		
	32		*B16C	*B16C	*B16C	*B16C	A01C																		
1160	32	#X INHL/LIFETIME		*B17A	*B17A	*B17A	A01A																		
1170	32	#X INHL/LAST12MO		*B17B	*B17B	*B17B	A01B																		
1180	32	#X INHL/LAST30DA		*B17C	*B17C	*B17C	A01C																		
1190	*	VRY HPY THS DAYS		+A001	+A001	+A001																P	Q	R	
1200	33	US NEEDS PLANNG	1A004A	1A002A	1A002A	1A002A									I										
1210	33	ENJOY FAST PACE	1A004B	1A002B	1A002B	1A002B									I								Q		
1220	33	THG CHG 2 QUICK	1A004D	1A002C	1A002C	1A002C									I								Q		
1230	33	X AHEAD TOUGHER	1A004G	1A002D	1A002D	1A002D									I								Q		
1240	33	TM SPT ADLT MST	1A006	1A003	1A003	1A003													M						
1250	34	LK MR TM ADLT	1A007	1A004	1A004	1A004													M						
1260	34	LK MR TM YG CHD	1A008	1A005	1A005	1A005													M						
1270	34	SAT PRESENT JOB	1A009A	1A006A	1A006A	1A006A			C													P			
1280	34	SAT NEIGHBORHOD	1A009B	1A006B	1A006B	1A006B																P			
1290	34	SAT PRSNL SAFTY	1A009C	1A006C	1A006C	1A006C																P			
1300	35	SAT OWN PROP SF	1A009D	1A006D	1A006D	1A006D																P			
1310	35	SAT EDUC EXPRNCS	1A009E	1A006E	1A006E	1A006E		B														P			
1320	35	SAT OWN FRIENDS	1A009F	1A006F	1A006F	1A006F													M			P			
1330	35	SAT GT ALNG PRNT	1A009G	1A006G	1A006G	1A006G													M			P			
1340	35	SAT YOURSELF	1A009H	1A006H	1A006H	1A006H																P	Q		
1350	35	SAT STD OF LVG	1A009I	1A006I	1A006I	1A006I						F										P			
1360	36	SAT TIME FR THGS	1A009J	1A006J	1A006J	1A006J																P			
1370	36	SAT SPD LEISR	1A009K	1A006K	1A006K	1A006K			C													P			
1380	36	SAT LIFE AS WHLE	1A009L	1A006L	1A006L	1A006L																P			
1390	36	SAT GOVT OPRTNG		1A006M	1A006M	1A006M								H			K								
1400	36	SAT AMT OF FUN		1A006N	1A006N	1A006N																P	Q	R	
1410	36	IMP B SUCCSS WK		1A007A	1A007A	1A007A			C														Q		
1420	37	IMP GD MRRG&FAM		1A007B	1A007B	1A007B				D													Q		
1430	37	IMP LOTS OF $		1A007C	1A007C	1A007C						F											Q		
1440	37	IMP TM RCRN&HBY		1A007D	1A007D	1A007D			C														Q		
1450	37	IMP STRG FRDSHP		1A007E	1A007E	1A007E													M				Q		
1460	37	IMP STEADY WORK		1A007F	1A007F	1A007F			C														Q		
1470	37	IMP CNTRBTN SOC		1A007G	1A007G	1A007G															O		Q		
1480	37	IMP LDR COMUNTY		1A007H	1A007H	1A007H													M				Q		
1490	37	IMP CHLD BTR OPP		1A007I	1A007I	1A007I																	Q		
1500	38	IMP LIV CLS PRNT		1A007J	1A007J	1A007J													M				Q		
1510	38	IMP GT AWY AREA		1A007K	1A007K	1A007K																	Q		
1520	38	IMP CRRCT INEQL		1A007L	1A007L	1A007L															O		Q		
1530	38	IMP NEW XPRNCE		1A007M	1A007M	1A007M																	Q		
1540	38	IMP FND PRPS LF		1A007N	1A007N	1A007N																	Q		
1550	38	PPL CAN B TRSTD	1A010	1A008	1A008	1A008																	Q		
1560	38	PPL TRY B HLPFL	1A011	1A009	1A009	1A009																	Q		
1570	39	PPL TRY BE FAIR	1A012	1A010	1A010	1A010																	Q		
1580	39	-OBY LW=-GD CTZN		1A011A	1A011A	1A011A								H											
1590	39	GD CTZN ALG GOVT		1A011B	1A011B	1A011B								H											
1600	39	GD CTZN CHG GOVT	1A013B	1A011C	1A011C	1A011C								H											
1610	39	VOTE->MAJ IMPCT		1A011D	1A011D	1A011D								H	I										
1620	39	CTZN GRP HV EFCT		1A011E	1A011E	1A011E								H	I										
1630	40	OUR SYST ST BS	1A013C	1A011F	1A011F	1A011F								H											
1640	40	US NEEDS GROWTH	1A013E	1A011G	1A011G	1A011G						F													
1650	40	LV THNGS TO GOD	1A004C	1A011H	1A011H	1A011H									I										
1660	40	GO SCH ENJY XPR	1A013I	1A011I	1A011I	1A011I		B																	
1670	40	DO WL SC IMP/JB	1A013H	1A011J	1A011J	1A011J		B	C																
1680	41	SMK CIG DLY/12G	1A019	1B002	1B002	(1B002)	A01G																		
1690	41	*TRY STP SMK&FL	1A021	1B004	1B004	1B004	A01I																		
1700	41	*WNT STP SMK NW	1A022	1B005	1B005	1B005	A01I																		
1710	41	NO SMK IN 5 YR	1A023	1B006	1B006	1B006	A04A																		
1720	42	#X/YR ALC ALONE		1B008A	1B008A	1B008A	A05A																		
1730	42	#X/YR ALC-2 PPL		1B008B	1B008B	1B008B	A05B																		
1740	43	#X/YR ALC@PARTY		1B008C	1B008C	1B008C	A05C																		
1750	43	#X/YR ALC-DT/SP		1B008D	1B008D	1B008D	A05B																		
1760	43	#X/YR ALC-ADLTS		1B008E	1B008E	1B008E	A05B																		
1770	43	#X/YR ALC-DATIM		1B008F	1B008F	1B008F	A05C																		
1780	43	#X/YR ALC@HOME		1B008G	1B008G	1B008G	A05C																		

* Descriptive results for Forms 1, 2, 3, 4, and 5, respectively, can be found on pages 33, 88, 118, 142, and 168.

ITEM REFERENCE NUMBER	PAGE LOCATION (IN THIS VOLUME)	ITEM DESCRIPTION (ABBREVIATED)	QUESTIONNAIRE LOCATION BY YEAR (FORM, SECTION, AND QUESTION NUMBER)				SUBJECT AREA	
			1975	1976	1977	1978	A	B C D E F G H I J K L M N O P Q R S
1790	43	#X/YR ALC@SCHL		1B008H	1B008H	1B008H	A05C	
1810	43	#X/YR ALCIN CAR		1B008I	1B008I	1B008I	A05C	
1820	44	ALC EXPERIMENT		1B009A	1B009A	1B009A	A06A	
1830	44	ALC RELAX	1A032A	1B009B	1B009B	1B009B	A06A	
1840	44	ALC GET HIGH	1A032B	1B009C	1B009C	1B009C	A06A	
1850	44	ALC SEEK INSGHT	1A032C	1B009D	1B009D	1B009D	A06A	
1860	44	ALC GD TM FRNDS	1A032D	1B009E	1B009E	1B009E	A06A	
1870	44	ALC FIT IN GRP	1A032E	1B009F	1B009F	1B009F	A06A	
1880	44	ALC GET AWY PRB	1A032F	1B009G	1B009G	1B009G	A06A	
1890	44	ALC BOREDOM	1A032G	1B009H	1B009H	1B009H	A06A	
1900	44	ALC ANGR&FRSTRN	1A032H	1B009I	1B009I	1B009I	A06A	
1910	44	ALC GT THRU DAY	1A032J	1B009J	1B009J	1B009J	A06A	
1920	44	ALC INCRS EF DR	1A032K	1B009K	1B009K	1B009K	A06A	
1930	44	ALC DECRS EF DR	1A032L	1B009L	1B009L	1B009L	A06A	
1940	44	ALC GET SLEEP		1B009M	1B009M	1B009M	A06A	
1950	44	ALC TASTES GOOD	1A032N	1B009N	1B009N	1B009N	A06A	
1960	44	ALC I AM HOOKED	1A032M	1B009O	1B009O	1B009O	A06A	
1970	44	#X DRK ENF FL 4	1A033	1B010	1B010	1B010	A01E	
1980	44	DRK AL,HI24+HR	1A034	1B011	1B011	1B011	A01F	
1990	45	#X/2W,3-4 DR RW	1A036	1B013	1B013	1B013	A01D	
2000	45	#X/2WK,2 DRK RW	1A037	1B014	1B014	1B014	A01D	
2010	45	#X/2WK,JST 1DRK	1A038	1B015	1B015	1B015	A01D	
2020	45	*TRY STP ALC&FL	1A039	1B016	1B016	1B016	A01D	
2030	45	NO ALC IN 5 YR	1A040	1B017	1B017	1B017	A04A	
2040	46	#X HASH/LIFETIM		1B018A	1B018A	1B018A	A01A	
2050	46	#X HASH/LAST12M		1B018B	1B018B	1B018B	A01B	
2060	46	#X HASH/LAST30D		1B018C	1B018C	1B018C	A01C	
2070	46	#X MARJ/LIFETIME		1B019A	1B019A	1B019A	A01A	
2080	46	#X MARJ/LAST12MO		1B019B	1B019B	1B019B	A01B	
2090	46	#X MARJ/LAST30DA		1B019C	1B019C	1B019C	A01C	
2100	47	#X/YR MJ ALONE	1A045	1B020A	1B020A	1B020A	A05A	
2110	47	#X/YR MJ-2 PPL		1B020B	1B020B	1B020B	A05B	
2120	47	#X/YR MJ@PARTY		1B020C	1B020C	1B020C	A05C	
2130	47	#X/YR MJ-DT/SP		1B020D	1B020D	1B020D	A05B	
2140	47	#X/YR MJ-ADLTS		1B020E	1B020E	1B020E	A05B	
2150	47	#X/YR MJ-DATIME		1B020F	1B020F	1B020F	A05C	
2160	48	#X/YR MJ@HOME		1B020G	1B020G	1B020G	A05C	
2170	48	#X/YR MJ@SCHL		1B020H	1B020H	1B020H	A05C	
2190	48	#X/YR MJIN CAR		1B020I	1B020I	1B020I	A05C	
2200	48	#X OVL MJ+ ALC		1B021	1B021	1B021	A06A	
2210	48	MJ EXPERIMENT	1A049A	1B022A	1B022A	1B022A	A06A	
2220	48	MJ RELAX	1A049B	1B022B	1B022B	1B022B	A06A	
2230	48	MJ GET HIGH	1A049C	1B022C	1B022C	1B022C	A06A	
2240	48	MJ SEEK INSIGHT	1A049D	1B022D	1B022D	1B022D	A06A	
2250	48	MJ GD TM FRNDS	1A049E	1B022E	1B022E	1B022E	A06A	
2260	48	MJ FIT IN GRP	1A049F	1B022F	1B022F	1B022F	A06A	
2270	48	MJ GET AWY PRB	1A049G	1B022G	1B022G	1B022G	A06A	
2280	48	MJ BOREDOM	1A049H	1B022H	1B022H	1B022H	A06A	
2290	48	MJ ANGR&FRUSTRN	1A049I	1B022I	1B022I	1B022I	A06A	
2300	48	MJ GET THRU DAY	1A049K	1B022J	1B022J	1B022J	A06A	
2310	48	MJ INCRS EF DRG	1A049L	1B022K	1B022K	1B022K	A06A	
2320	48	MJ DECRS EF DRG	1A049M	1B022L	1B022L	1B022L	A06A	
2330	48	MJ I AM HOOKED		1B022M	1B022M	1B022M	A06A	
2340	49	MJ/HSH,VRY HIGH	1A050	1B023	1B023	1B023	A01E	
2350	49	MJ/HSH,HI 24+HR	1A051	1B024	1B024	1B024	A01F	
2360	49	JOINT/DA LST MO		1B025	1B025	1B025	A01D	
2370	49	OZS.MJ LST MO/6		1B026	1B026	1B026	A01D	
2380	49	*TRY STP MJ &FL	1A052	1B027	1B027	1B027	A01I	
2390	49	NO MJ/HSH IN5YR	1A053	1B028	1B028	1B028	A04A	
2400	50	#X/YR LSD ALONE		1B030A	1B030A	1B030A	A05A	
2410	50	#X/YR LSD-2 PPL		1B030B	1B030B	1B030B	A05B	
2420	51	#X/YR LSD@PARTY		1B030C	1B030C	1B030C	A05C	
2430	51	#X/YR LSD-DT/SP		1B030D	1B030D	1B030D	A05B	
2440	51	#X/YR LSD-ADLTS		1B030E	1B030E	1B030E	A05B	
2450	51	#X/YR LSD-DATIM		1B030F	1B030F	1B030F	A05C	
2460	51	#X/YR LSD@HOME		1B030G	1B030G	1B030G	A05C	

ITEM REFERENCE NUMBER	PAGE LOCATION (IN THIS VOLUME)	ITEM DESCRIPTION (ABBREVIATED)	QUESTIONNAIRE LOCATION BY YEAR (FORM, SECTION, AND QUESTION NUMBER)				SUBJECT AREA	
			1975	1976	1977	1978	A	B C D E F G H I J K L M N O P Q R S
2470	51	#X/YR LSD@SCHL		1B030H	1B030H	1B030H	A05C	
2490	51	#X/YR LSDIN CAR		1B030I	1B030I	1B030I	A05C	
2500	52	#X OVL LSD+ ALC		1B031A	1B031A	1B031A	A01H	
2510	52	#X OVL LSD+ MJ		1B031B	1B031B	1B031B	A01H	
2520	52	LSD EXPERIMENT	1A062A	1B032A	1B032A	1B032A	A06A	
2530	52	LSD RELAX	1A062B	1B032B	1B032B	1B032B	A06A	
2540	52	LSD GET HIGH	1A062C	1B032C	1B032C	1B032C	A06A	
2550	52	LSD SEEK INSGHT	1A062D	1B032D	1B032D	1B032D	A06A	
2560	52	LSD GD TM FRNDS	1A062E	1B032E	1B032E	1B032E	A06A	
2570	52	LSD FIT IN GRP	1A062F	1B032F	1B032F	1B032F	A06A	
2580	52	LSD GT AWY PRB	1A062G	1B032G	1B032G	1B032G	A06A	
2590	52	LSD BOREDOM	1A062H	1B032H	1B032H	1B032H	A06A	
2600	52	LSD ANGR&FRSTRN	1A062I	1B032I	1B032I	1B032I	A06A	
2610	52	LSD GT THRU DAY	1A062K	1B032J	1B032J	1B032J	A06A	
2620	52	LSD INCRS EF DR	1A062L	1B032K	1B032K	1B032K	A06A	
2630	52	LSD DCRS EF DRG	1A062M	1B032L	1B032L	1B032L	A06A	
2640	52	LSD I AM HOOKED		1B032M	1B032M	1B032M	A06A	
2650	52	LSD,GET VERY HI	1A063	1B033	1B033	1B033	A01E	
2660	52	LSD,HIGH 24+ HR	1A064	1B034	1B034	1B034	A01F	
2670	53	1+ BAD TRIP LSD	1A065	1B035	1B035	1B035	A01K	
2680	53	*TRY STP LSD&FL	1A066	1B036	1B036	1B036	A01I	
2690	53	NO LSD IN 5 YRS	1A067	1B037	1B037	1B037	A04A	
2700	54	PSYD,GT VERY HI	1A077	1B039	1B039	1B039	A01E	
2710	54	PSYD,HI 24+ HRS	1A078	1B040	1B040	1B040	A01F	
2720	54	TKN YR,MESCALIN	1A079A	1B041A	1B041A	1B041A	A01L	
2730	54	TKN YR,PEYOTE	1A079B	1B041B	1B041B	1B041B	A01L	
2740	54	TKN YR,PSILOCYB	1A079C	1B041C	1B041C	1B041C	A01L	
2750	54	TKN YR,PCP		1B041D	1B041D	1B041D	A01L	
2760	54	TKN YR,CNCT THC	1A079D	1B041E	1B041E	1B041E	A01L	
2770	54	TKN YR,OTH PSYD	1A079E	1B041F	1B041F	1B041F	A01L	
2780	54	TKN YR,DK NAME	1A079F	1B041G	1B041G	1B041G	A01L	
2790	54	DR TOLD TK AMPH	1A085	1B042	1B042	1B042	A01J	
2800	55	#X/YR AMPH ALNE		1B044A	1B044A	1B044A	A05A	
2810	55	#X/YR AMPH-2PPL		1B044B	1B044B	1B044B	A05B	
2820	56	#X/YR AMPH@PRTY		1B044C	1B044C	1B044C	A05C	
2830	56	#X/YR AMPH-DT/S		1B044D	1B044D	1B044D	A05B	
2840	56	#X/YR AMPH-ADLT		1B044E	1B044E	1B044E	A05B	
2850	56	#X/YR AMPH-DATM		1B044F	1B044F	1B044F	A05C	
2860	56	#X/YR AMPH@HOME		1B044G	1B044G	1B044G	A05C	
2880	56	#X/YR AMPH@SCHL		1B044H	1B044H	1B044H	A05C	
2890	56	#X/YR AMPH@CAR		1B044I	1B044I	1B044I	A05C	
2900	57	#X OVL AMPH+ALC		1B045A	1B045A	1B045A	A01H	
2910	57	#X OVL AMPH+MJ		1B045B	1B045B	1B045B	A01H	
2920	57	#X OVL AMPH+LSD		1B045C	1B045C	1B045C	A01H	
2930	57	#X OVL AMPH+PSY		1B045D	1B045D	1B045D	A01H	
2940	57	AMPH EXPERIMENT	1A092A	1B046A	1B046A	1B046A	A06A	
2950	57	AMPH RELAX	1A092B	1B046B	1B046B	1B046B	A06A	
2960	57	AMPH GET HIGH	1A092C	1B046C	1B046C	1B046C	A06A	
2970	57	AMPH SK INSIGHT	1A092D	1B046D	1B046D	1B046D	A06A	
2980	57	AMPH GD TM FRND	1A092E	1B046E	1B046E	1B046E	A06A	
2990	57	AMPH FIT IN GRP	1A092F	1B046F	1B046F	1B046F	A06A	
3000	57	AMPH GT AWY PRB	1A092G	1B046G	1B046G	1B046G	A06A	
3010	57	AMPH BOREDOM	1A092H	1B046H	1B046H	1B046H	A06A	
3020	57	AMPH ANGR&FRSTN	1A092I	1B046I	1B046I	1B046I	A06A	
3030	57	AMPH GT THRU DA	1A092K	1B046J	1B046J	1B046J	A06A	
3040	57	AMPH INCR EF DR	1A092L	1B046K	1B046K	1B046K	A06A	
3050	57	AMPH DCRS EF DR	1A092M	1B046L	1B046L	1B046L	A06A	
3060	57	AMPH STAY AWAKE	1A092N	1B046M	1B046M	1B046M	A06A	
3070	57	AMPH GET>ENERGY	1A092O	1B046N	1B046N	1B046N	A06A	
3080	57	AMPH LOSE WGHT	1A092P	1B046O	1B046O	1B046O	A06A	
3090	57	AMPH I AM HOOKD	1A092Q	1B046P	1B046P	1B046P	A06A	
3100	58	AMPH,GT VERY HI	1A093	1B047	1B047	1B047	A01E	
3110	58	AMPH,HI 24+ HRS	1A094	1B048	1B048	1B048	A01F	
3120	58	TKN YR,BENZDRIN	1A095A	1B049A	1B049A	1B049A	A01L	
3130	58	TKN YR,DEXEDRIN	1A095B	1B049B	1B049B	1B049B	A01L	
3140	58	TKN YR,METHDRIN	1A095C	1B049C	1B049C	1B049C	A01L	

ITEM REFERENCE NUMBER	PAGE LOCATION (IN THIS VOLUME)	ITEM DESCRIPTION (ABBREVIATED)	QUESTIONNAIRE LOCATION BY YEAR (FORM, SECTION, AND QUESTION NUMBER)				SUBJECT AREA	
			1975	1976	1977	1978	A	B C D E F G H I J K L M N O P Q R S
3150	58	TKN YR,RITALIN	1A095D	1B049D	1B049D	1B049D	A01L	
3160	58	TKN YR,PRELUDIN	1A095E	1B049E	1B049E	1B049E	A01L	
3170	58	TKN YR,DEXAMYL	1A095F	1B049F	1B049F	1B049F	A01L	
3180	58	TKN YR,METHAMPH	1A095G	1B049G	1B049G	1B049G	A01L	
3190	58	TKN YR,OTH AMPH	1A095H	1B049H	1B049H	1B049H	A01L	
3200	58	TKN YR,DNT KN N	1A095I	1B049I	1B049I	1B049I	A01L	
3210	58	MTHD AMPH-MOUTH		1B050A	1B050A	1B050A	A05D	
3220	58	MTHD AMPH-INJCT		1B050B	1B050B	1B050B	A05D	
3230	58	MTHD AMPH-OTHER		1B050C	1B050C	1B050C	A05D	
3240	58	*TRY STP AMP&FL	1A096	1B051	1B051	1B051	A01I	
3250	58	NO AMPH IN 5YR	1A097	1B052	1B052	1B052	A04A	
3260	59	QUAD GT VERY HI	1A108	1B054	1B054	1B054	A01E	
3270	60	QUAD,HI 24+ HRS	1A109	1B055	1B055	1B055	A01F	
3280	60	DR TOLD TK BARB	1A114	1B056	1B056	1B056	A01J	
3290	61	#X/YR BRBT ALNE		1B058A	1B058A	1B058A	A05A	
3300	61	#X/YR BRBT-2PPL		1B058B	1B058B	1B058B	A05B	
3310	61	#X/YR BRBT@PRTY		1B058C	1B058C	1B058C	A05C	
3320	61	#X/YR BRBT-DT/S		1B058D	1B058D	1B058D	A05B	
3330	61	#X/YR BRBT-ADLT		1B058E	1B058E	1B058E	A05B	
3340	61	#X/YR BRBT-DATM		1B058F	1B058F	1B058F	A05C	
3350	62	#X/YR BRBT@HOME		1B058G	1B058G	1B058G	A05C	
3360	62	#X/YR BRBT@SCHL		1B058H	1B058H	1B058H	A05C	
3380	62	#X/YR BRBT@CAR		1B058I	1B058I	1B058I	A05C	
3390	62	#X OVL BARB+ALC		1B059A	1B059A	1B059A	A01H	
3400	62	#X OVL BARB+MJ		1B059B	1B059B	1B059B	A01H	
3410	62	#X OVL BARB+LSD		1B059C	1B059C	1B059C	A01H	
3420	62	#X OVL BARB+PSY		1B059D	1B059D	1B059D	A01H	
3430	63	#X OVL BARB+AMP		1B059E	1B059E	1B059E	A01H	
3440	63	#X OVL BARB+QUA		1B059F	1B059F	1B059F	A01H	
3450	63	BARB EXPERIMENT	1A121A	1B060A	1B060A	1B060A	A06A	
3460	63	BARB RELAX	1A121B	1B060B	1B060B	1B060B	A06A	
3470	63	BARB GET HIGH	1A121C	1B060C	1B060C	1B060C	A06A	
3480	63	BARB SK INSIGHT	1A121D	1B060D	1B060D	1B060D	A06A	
3490	63	BARB GD TM FRND	1A121E	1B060E	1B060E	1B060E	A06A	
3500	63	BARB FIT IN GRP	1A121F	1B060F	1B060F	1B060F	A06A	
3510	63	BARB GT AWY PRB	1A121G	1B060G	1B060G	1B060G	A06A	
3520	63	BARB BOREDOM	1A121H	1B060H	1B060H	1B060H	A06A	
3530	63	BARB ANGR&FRSTN	1A121I	1B060I	1B060I	1B060I	A06A	
3540	63	BARB GT THRU DA	1A121K	1B060J	1B060J	1B060J	A06A	
3550	63	BARB INCR EF DR	1A121L	1B060K	1B060K	1B060K	A06A	
3560	63	BARB DCRS EF DR	1A121M	1B060L	1B060L	1B060L	A06A	
3570	63	BARB GET SLEEP	1A121N	1B060M	1B060M	1B060M	A06A	
3575		BARB RLV PHYS PN				1B060N	A06A	
3580	63	BARB I AM HOOKD	1A121O	1B060N	1B060N	1B060O	A06A	
3590	63	BARB,GT VERY HI	1A122	1B061	1B061	1B061	A01E	
3600	63	BARB,HI 24+ HRS	1A123	1B062	1B062	1B062	A01F	
3610	64	TKN YR,PHNOBARB	1A124A	1B063A	1B063A	1B063A	A01L	
3620	64	TKN YR,SECONAL	1A124B	1B063B	1B063B	1B063B	A01L	
3630	64	TKN YR,TUINAL	1A124C	1B063C	1B063C	1B063C	A01L	
3640	64	TKN YR,NEMBUTAL	1A124D	1B063D	1B063D	1B063D	A01L	
3650	64	TKN YR,LUMINAL	1A124E	1B063E	1B063E	1B063E	A01L	
3660	64	TKN YR,DESBUTAL	1A124F	1B063F	1B063F	1B063F	A01L	
3670	64	TKN YR,AMYTAL	1A124G	1B063G	1B063G	1B063G	A01L	
3680	64	TKN YR,ADRNOCAL	1A124H	1B063H	1B063H	1B063H	A01L	
3690	64	TKN YR,OTH BRBT	1A124I	1B063I	1B063I	1B063I	A01L	
3700	64	TKN YR,DNT KNOW	1A124J	1B063J	1B063J	1B063J	A01L	
3710	64	TRY STP BARB&FL	1A125	1B064	1B064	1B064	A01I	
3720	64	NO BARB IN 5YR	1A126	1B065	1B065	1B065	A04A	
3730	64	DR TOLD TK TRNQ	1A129	1B066	1B066	1B066	A01J	
3740	65	#X/YR TRQL ALNE		1B068A	1B068A	1B068A	A05A	
3750	65	#X/YR TRQL-2PPL		1B068B	1B068B	1B068B	A05B	
3760	65	#X/YR TRQL@PRTY		1B068C	1B068C	1B068C	A05C	
3770	66	#X/YR TRQL-DT/S		1B068D	1B068D	1B068D	A05B	
3780	66	#X/YR TRQL-ADLT		1B068E	1B068E	1B068E	A05B	
3790	66	#X/YR TRQL-DATM		1B068F	1B068F	1B068F	A05C	
3800	66	#X/YR TRQL@HOME		1B068G	1B068G	1B068G	A05C	

ITEM REFERENCE NUMBER	PAGE LOCATION (IN THIS VOLUME)	ITEM DESCRIPTION (ABBREVIATED)	QUESTIONNAIRE LOCATION BY YEAR (FORM, SECTION, AND QUESTION NUMBER)				SUBJECT AREA	
			1975	1976	1977	1978	A	B C D E F G H I J K L M N O P Q R S
3810	66	#X/YR TRQL@SCHL		1B068H	1B068H	1B068H	A05C	
3830	66	#X/YR TRQL@CAR		1B068I	1B068I	1B068I	A05C	
3840	67	#X OVL TRQL+ALC		1B069A	1B069A	1B069A	A01H	
3850	67	#X OVL TRQL+MJ		1B069B	1B069B	1B069B	A01H	
3860	67	#X OVL TRQL+LSD		1B069C	1B069C	1B069C	A01H	
3870	67	#X OVL TRQL+PSY		1B069D	1B069D	1B069D	A01H	
3880	67	#X OVL TRQL+AMP		1B069E	1B069E	1B069E	A01H	
3890	67	#X OVL TRQL+QUA		1B069F	1B069F	1B069F	A01H	
3900	67	#X OVL TRQL+BRB		1B069G	1B069G	1B069G	A01H	
3910	68	TRNQ EXPERIMENT	1A136A	1B070A	1B070A	1B070A	A06A	
3920	68	TRNQ RELAX	1A136B	1B070B	1B070B	1B070B	A06A	
3930	68	TRNQ GET HIGH	1A136C	1B070C	1B070C	1B070C	A06A	
3940	68	TRNQ SK INSIGHT	1A136D	1B070D	1B070D	1B070D	A06A	
3950	68	TRNQ GD TM FRND	1A136E	1B070E	1B070E	1B070E	A06A	
3960	68	TRNQ FIT IN GRP	1A136F	1B070F	1B070F	1B070F	A06A	
3970	68	TRNQ GT AWY PRB	1A136G	1B070G	1B070G	1B070G	A06A	
3980	68	TRNQ BOREDOM	1A136H	1B070H	1B070H	1B070H	A06A	
3990	68	TRNQ ANGR&FRSTN	1A136I	1B070I	1B070I	1B070I	A06A	
4000	68	TRNQ GT THRU DA	1A136K	1B070J	1B070J	1B070J	A06A	
4010	68	TRNQ INCR EF DR	1A136L	1B070K	1B070K	1B070K	A06A	
4020	68	TRNQ DCRS EF DR	1A136M	1B070L	1B070L	1B070L	A06A	
4030	68	TRNQ GET SLEEP	1A136N	1B070M	1B070M	1B070M	A06A	
4035		TRNQ RLV PHYS PN				1B070N	A06A	
4040	68	TRNQ I AM HOOKD	1A136O	1B070N	1B070N	1B070O	A06A	
4050	68	TRNQ,GT VERY HI	1A137	1B071	1B071	1B071	A01E	
4060	68	TRNQ,HI 24+ HRS	1A138	1B072	1B072	1B072	A01F	
4070	68	TKN YR,LIBRIUM		1B073A	1B073A	1B073A	A01L	
4080	68	TKN YR,VALIUM		1B073B	1B073B	1B073B	A01L	
4090	68	TKN YR,MILTOWN		1B073C	1B073C	1B073C	A01L	
4100	68	TKN YR,EQUANIL		1B073D	1B073D	1B073D	A01L	
4110	68	TKN YR,MEPRBMTE		1B073E	1B073E	1B073E	A01L	
4120	68	TKN YR,SERAX		1B073F	1B073F	1B073F	A01L	
4130	68	TKN YR,ATARAX		1B073G	1B073G	1B073G	A01L	
4140	68	TKN YR,TRANXENE		1B073H	1B073H	1B073H	A01L	
4150	68	TKN YR,VISTARIL		1B073I	1B073I	1B073I	A01L	
4160	68	TKN YR,DNT KNW		1B073J	1B073J	1B073J	A01L	
4170	69	*TRY STP TRQ&FL	1A139	1B074	1B074	1B074	A01I	
4180	69	NO TRNQ IN 5YR	1A140	1B075	1B075	1B075	A04A	
4190	70	#X/YR COKE ALNE		1B077A	1B077A	1B077A	A05A	
4200	70	#X/YR COKE-2PPL		1B077B	1B077B	1B077B	A05B	
4210	70	#X/YR COKE@PRTY		1B077C	1B077C	1B077C	A05C	
4220	70	#X/YR COKE-DT/S		1B077D	1B077D	1B077D	A05B	
4230	70	#X/YR COKE-ADLT		1B077E	1B077E	1B077E	A05B	
4240	70	#X/YR COKE-DATM		1B077F	1B077F	1B077F	A05C	
4250	70	#X/YR COKE@HOME		1B077G	1B077G	1B077G	A05C	
4260	71	#X/YR COKE@SCHL		1B077H	1B077H	1B077H	A05C	
4280	71	#X/YR COKE@CAR		1B077I	1B077I	1B077I	A05C	
4290	71	#X OVL COKE+ALC		1B078A	1B078A	1B078A	A01H	
4300	71	#X OVL COKE+MJ		1B078B	1B078B	1B078B	A01H	
4310	71	#X OVL COKE+LSD		1B078C	1B078C	1B078C	A01H	
4320	71	#X OVL COKE+PSY		1B078D	1B078D	1B078D	A01H	
4330	71	#X OVL COKE+AMP		1B078E	1B078E	1B078E	A01H	
4340	72	#X OVL COKE+QUA		1B078F	1B078F	1B078F	A01H	
4350	72	#X OVL COKE+BRB		1B078G	1B078G	1B078G	A01H	
4360	72	#X OVL COKE+TRN		1B078H	1B078H	1B078H	A01H	
4370	72	COKE EXPERIMENT	1A149A	1B079A	1B079A	1B079A	A06A	
4380	72	COKE RELAX	1A149B	1B079B	1B079B	1B079B	A06A	
4390	72	COKE GET HIGH	1A149C	1B079C	1B079C	1B079C	A06A	
4400	72	COKE SK INSIGHT	1A149D	1B079D	1B079D	1B079D	A06A	
4410	72	COKE GD TM FRND	1A149E	1B079E	1B079E	1B079E	A06A	
4420	72	COKE FIT IN GRP	1A149F	1B079F	1B079F	1B079F	A06A	
4430	72	COKE GT AWY PRB	1A149G	1B079G	1B079G	1B079G	A06A	
4440	72	COKE BOREDOM	1A149H	1B079H	1B079H	1B079H	A06A	
4450	72	COKE ANGR&FRSTN	1A149I	1B079I	1B079I	1B079I	A06A	
4460	72	COKE GT THRU DA	1A149K	1B079J	1B079J	1B079J	A06A	
4470	72	COKE INCR EF DR	1A149L	1B079K	1B079K	1B079K	A06A	

ITEM REFERENCE NUMBER	PAGE LOCATION (IN THIS VOLUME)	ITEM DESCRIPTION (ABBREVIATED)	QUESTIONNAIRE LOCATION BY YEAR (FORM, SECTION, AND QUESTION NUMBER)				SUBJECT AREA	
			1975	1976	1977	1978	A	B C D E F G H I J K L M N O P Q R S
4480	72	COKE DCRS EF DR	1A149M	1B079L	1B079L	1B079L	A06A	
4490	72	COKE STAY AWAKE		1B079M	1B079M	1B079M	A06A	
4500	72	COKE GET>ENERGY	1A149N	1B079N	1B079N	1B079N	A06A	
4510	72	COKE I AM HOOKD	1A149O	1B079O	1B079O	1B079O	A06A	
4520	72	COK,GET VERY HI	1A150	1B080	1B080	1B080	A01E	
4530	73	COK,HIGH 24+ HR	1A151	1B081	1B081	1B081	A01F	
4540	73	*TRY STP COK&FL	1A152	1B082	1B082	1B082	A01I	
4550	73	MTHD COKE SNORT	1A153A	1B083A	1B083A	1B083A	A05D	
4560	73	MTHD COKE-SMOKE	1A153B	1B083B	1B083B	1B083B	A05D	
4570	73	MTHD COKE-INJCT	1A153C	1B083C	1B083C	1B083C	A05D	
4580	73	MTHD COKE-MOUTH	1A153D	1B083D	1B083D	1B083D	A05D	
4590	73	MTHD COKE-OTHER	1A153E	1B083E	1B083E	1B083E	A05D	
4600	73	NO COKE IN 5YR	1A154	1B084	1B084	1B084	A04A	
4610	74	#X/YR HER ALONE		1B086A	1B086A	1B086A	A05A	
4620	74	#X/YR HER-2 PPL		1B086B	1B086B	1B086B	A05B	
4630	74	#X/YR HER@PARTY		1B086C	1B086C	1B086C	A05C	
4640	74	#X/YR HER-DA/SP		1B086D	1B086D	1B086D	A05B	
4650	74	#X/YR HER-ADULT		1B086E	1B086E	1B086E	A05B	
4660	75	#X/YR HER-DATIM		1B086F	1B086F	1B086F	A05C	
4670	75	#X/YR HER@HOME		1B086G	1B086G	1B086G	A05C	
4680	75	#X/YR HER@SCHL		1B086H	1B086H	1B086H	A05C	
4700	75	#X/YR HER@CAR		1B086I	1B086I	1B086I	A05C	
4710	75	#X OVL HER +ALC		1B087A	1B087A	1B087A	A01H	
4720	75	#X OVL HER +MJ		1B087B	1B087B	1B087B	A01H	
4730	76	#X OVL HER +LSD		1B087C	1B087C	1B087C	A01H	
4740	76	#X OVL HER +PSY		1B087D	1B087D	1B087D	A01H	
4750	76	#X OVL HER +AMP		1B087E	1B087E	1B087E	A01H	
4760	76	#X OVL HER +QUA		1B087F	1B087F	1B087F	A01H	
4770	76	#X OVL HER +BRB		1B087G	1B087G	1B087G	A01H	
4780	76	#X OVL HER +TRN		1B087H	1B087H	1B087H	A01H	
4790	76	#X OVL HER +COK		1B087I	1B087I	1B087I	A01H	
4800	77	HERIN EXPERMENT	1A163A	1B088A	1B088A	1B088A	A06A	
4810	77	HERIN RELAX	1A163B	1B088B	1B088B	1B088B	A06A	
4820	77	HERIN GET HIGH	1A163C	1B088C	1B088C	1B088C	A06A	
4830	77	HERIN SK INSIGT	1A163D	1B088D	1B088D	1B088D	A06A	
4840	77	HERIN GD TM FRN	1A163E	1B088E	1B088E	1B088E	A06A	
4850	77	HERIN FT IN GRP	1A163F	1B088F	1B088F	1B088F	A06A	
4860	77	HERIN GT AWY PB	1A163G	1B088G	1B088G	1B088G	A06A	
4870	77	HERIN BOREDOM	1A163H	1B088H	1B088H	1B088H	A06A	
4880	77	HERIN ANGR&FRST	1A163I	1B088I	1B088I	1B088I	A06A	
4890	77	HERIN GT THR DA	1A163K	1B088J	1B088J	1B088J	A06A	
4900	77	HERIN INC EF DG	1A163L	1B088K	1B088K	1B088K	A06A	
4910	77	HERIN DEC EF DG	1A163M	1B088L	1B088L	1B088L	A06A	
4920	77	HERIN I AM HOOK	1A163N	1B088M	1B088M	1B088M	A06A	
4930	77	HER,GT VERY HI	1A164	1B089	1B089	1B089	A01E	
4940	77	HER,HI 24+ HRS	1A165	1B090	1B090	1B090	A01F	
4950	77	TRY STP HER& FL	1A166	1B091	1B091	1B091	A01I	
4960	77	METHD HRN SNORT	1A167A	1B092A	1B092A	1B092A	A05D	
4970	77	METHD HRN-SMOKE	1A167B	1B092B	1B092B	1B092B	A05D	
4980	77	METHD HRN-INJCT	1A167C	1B092C	1B092C	1B092C	A05D	
4990	77	METHD HRN-MOUTH	1A167D	1B092D	1B092D	1B092D	A05D	
5000	77	METHD HRN-OTHER	1A167E	1B092E	1B092E	1B092E	A05D	
5010	78	NO HER IN 5 YR	1A168	1B093	1B093	1B093	A04A	
5020	78	DR TOLD TK NARC	1A171	1B094	1B094	1B094	A01J	
5030	79	#X/YR NARC ALNE		1B096A	1B096A	1B096A	A05A	
5040	79	#X/YR NARC-2PPL		1B096B	1B096B	1B096B	A05B	
5050	79	#X/YR NARC@PRTY		1B096C	1B096C	1B096C	A05C	
5060	79	#X/YR NARC-DT/S		1B096D	1B096D	1B096D	A05B	
5070	79	#X/YR NARC-ADLT		1B096E	1B096E	1B096E	A05B	
5080	80	#X/YR NARC-DATM		1B096F	1B096F	1B096F	A05C	
5090	80	#X/YR NARC@HOME		1B096G	1B096G	1B096G	A05C	
5100	80	#X/YR NARC@SCHL		1B096H	1B096H	1B096H	A05C	
5120	80	#X/YR NARC @CAR		1B096I	1B096I	1B096I	A05C	
5130	80	#X OVL NARC+ALC		1B097A	1B097A	1B097A	A01H	
5140	80	#X OVL NARC+MJ		1B097B	1B097B	1B097B	A01H	
5150	81	#X OVL NARC+LSD		1B097C	1B097C	1B097C	A01H	

ITEM REFERENCE NUMBER	PAGE LOCATION (IN THIS VOLUME)	ITEM DESCRIPTION (ABBREVIATED)	QUESTIONNAIRE LOCATION BY YEAR (FORM, SECTION, AND QUESTION NUMBER)				SUBJECT AREA	
			1975	1976	1977	1978	A	B C D E F G H I J K L M N O P Q R S
5160	81	#X OVL NARC+PSY		1B097D	1B097D	1B097D	A01H	
5170	81	#X OVL NARC+AMP		1B097E	1B097E	1B097E	A01H	
5180	81	#X OVL NARC+QUA		1B097F	1B097F	1B097F	A01H	
5190	81	#X OVL NARC+BRB		1B097G	1B097G	1B097G	A01H	
5200	81	#X OVL NARC+TRN		1B097H	1B097H	1B097H	A01H	
5210	81	#X OVL NARC+COK		1B097I	1B097I	1B097I	A01H	
5220	82	#X OVL NARC+HER		1B097J	1B097J	1B097J	A01H	
5230	82	NARC EXPERIMENT	1A178A	1B098A	1B098A	1B098A	A06A	
5240	82	NARC RELAX	1A178B	1B098B	1B098B	1B098B	A06A	
5250	82	NARC GET HIGH	1A178C	1B098C	1B098C	1B098C	A06A	
5260	82	NARC SK INSIGTS	1A178D	1B098D	1B098D	1B098D	A06A	
5270	82	NARC GD TM FRND	1A178E	1B098E	1B098E	1B098E	A06A	
5280	82	NARC FIT IN GRP	1A178F	1B098F	1B098F	1B098F	A06A	
5290	82	NARC GT AWY PBM	1A178G	1B098G	1B098G	1B098G	A06A	
5300	82	NARC BOREDOM	1A178H	1B098H	1B098H	1B098H	A06A	
5310	82	NARC ANGR&FRSTN	1A178I	1B098I	1B098I	1B098I	A06A	
5320	82	NARC GT THRU DA	1A178K	1B098J	1B098J	1B098J	A06A	
5330	82	NARC INC EF DG	1A178L	1B098K	1B098K	1B098K	A06A	
5340	82	NARC DEC EF DG	1A178M	1B098L	1B098L	1B098L	A06A	
5350	82	NARC GET SLEEP		1B098M	1B098M	1B098M	A06A	
5360	82	NARC SBST HERIN	1A178O	1B098N	1B098N	1B098N	A06A	
5363		NARC RLV PHYS PN				1B098O	A06A	
5366		NARC RLV COUGHNG				1B098P	A06A	
5370	82	NARC I AM HOOKD	1A178N	1B098O	1B098O	1B098Q	A06A	
5380	82	NARC,GT VERY HI	1A179	1B099	1B099	1B099	A01E	
5390	82	NARC,HI 24+ HRS	1A180	1B100	1B100	1B100	A01F	
5400	82	NARC TKN MTHDNE	1A181A	1B101A	1B101A	1B101A	A01L	
5410	82	NARC TKN OPIUM	1A181B	1B101B	1B101B	1B101B	A01L	
5420	82	NARC TKN MRPHNE	1A181C	1B101C	1B101C	1B101C	A01L	
5430	82	NARC TKN CODEIN	1A181D	1B101D	1B101D	1B101D	A01L	
5440	82	NARC TKN DEMROL	1A181E	1B101E	1B101E	1B101E	A01L	
5450	82	NARC TKN PARGRC	1A181F	1B101F	1B101F	1B101F	A01L	
5460	82	NARC TKN TALWIN	1A181G	1B101G	1B101G	1B101G	A01L	
5470	82	NARC TKN LDANUM	1A181H	1B101H	1B101H	1B101H	A01L	
5480	82	NARC TKN OTHER	1A181I	1B101I	1B101I	1B101I	A01L	
5490	82	NARC TKN DNT KN	1A181J	1B101J	1B101J	1B101J	A01L	
5500	83	TRY STP NARC&FL	1A182	1B102	1B102	1B102	A01I	
5510	83	METH NARC SNORT	1A183A	1B103A	1B103A	1B103A	A05D	
5520	83	METH NARC SMOKE	1A183B	1B103B	1B103B	1B103B	A05D	
5530	83	METH NARC INJCT	1A183C	1B103C	1B103C	1B103C	A05D	
5540	83	METH NARC MOUTH	1A183D	1B103D	1B103D	1B103D	A05D	
5550	83	METH NARC OTHER	1A183E	1B103E	1B103E	1B103E	A05D	
5560	83	NO NARC IN 5YR	1A184	1B104	1B104	1B104	A04A	
5570	83	GR 1ST SMOK DLY	1A019	1B105A	1B105A / 3E12A	1B105A / 3E12A	A01G / A01G	
5580	83	GR 1ST TRY ALC	1A027	1B105B	1B105B / 3E12B	1B105B / 3E12B	A01G / A01G	
5590	83	GR 1ST TRY MJ	1A043	1B105C	1B105C / 3E12C	1B105C / 3E12C	A01G / A01G	
5600	84	GR 1ST TRY LSD	1A056	1B105D	1B105D / 3E12D	1B105D / 3E12D	A01G / A01G	
5610	84	GR 1ST TRY PSY	1A070	1B105E	1B105E / 3E12E	1B105E / 3E12E	A01G / A01G	
5620	84	GR 1ST TRY AMP	1A086	1B105F	1B105F / 3E12F	1B105F / 3E12F	A01G / A01G	
5630	84	GR 1ST TRY QUA	1A101	1B105G	1B105G / 3E12G	1B105G / 3E12G	A01G / A01G	
5640	84	GR 1ST TRY BRB	1A115	1B105H	1B105H / 3E12H	1B105H / 3E12H	A01G / A01G	
5650	84	GR 1ST TRY TRN	1A130	1B105I	1B105I / 3E12I	1B105I / 3E12I	A01G / A01G	
5660	85	GR 1ST TRY COK	1A143	1B105J	1B105J / 3E12J	1B105J / 3E12J	A01G / A01G	
5670	85	GR 1ST TRY HER	1A157	1B105K	1B105K / 3E12K	1B105K / 3E12K	A01G / A01G	
5680	85	GR 1ST TRY NRC	1A172	1B105L	1B105L	1B105L	A01G	

ITEM REFERENCE NUMBER	PAGE LOCATION (IN THIS VOLUME)	ITEM DESCRIPTION (ABBREVIATED)	QUESTIONNAIRE LOCATION BY YEAR (FORM, SECTION, AND QUESTION NUMBER)				SUBJECT AREA	
			1975	1976	1977	1978	A	B C D E F G H I J K L M N O P Q R S
					3E12L	3E12L	A01G	
5685		GR 1ST TRY INHAL				3E12M	A01G	
5690	98	US GO WAR FR OTH	2A38B	2A18B	2A18B	2A18B		H L
5700	85	*SC WRK NVR MNG		1D002	1D002	1D002		B
5710	85	*MST COUR V DUL		1D003	1D003	1D003		B
5720	86	*LRN SCH NT IMPT		1D004	1D004	1D004		B
5730	86	LOT CMPTN GRADE		1D005	1D005	1D005		B
5740	86	STDTS DSLK CHTG		1D006	1D006	1D006		B
5750	86	ST -LK PROV TCH		1D007	1D007	1D007		B
5760	86	FRD NCG/TCH -LK		1D008	1D008	1D008		B
5770	86	R IN WK-STDY PG		1D009	1D009	1D009		B C
5780	87	#X/YR COUNS IND		1D010	1D010	1D010		B M
5790	87	#X/YR COUNS GRP		1D011	1D011	1D011		B M
5800	87	R LK C COUNS MR		1D012	1D012	1D012		B M
5810	87	CSLNG VRY HLPFL		(1D013)	1D013	1D013		B M
5820	88	DALY WATCH TV		2A02A	2A02A	2A02A		B C
5830	88	DALY GO TO MOVIE		2A02B	2A02B	2A02B		B C
5840	88	DALY ART,MSC,PLA		2A02C	2A02C	2A02C		B C
5850		DALY RIDE FORFUN			2A02D	2A02D		C
5860	88	DALY CMNTY AFFRS		2A02E	2A02E	2A02E		C O
5870	89	DALY PLA MSC,SNG		2A02F	2A02F	2A02F		C
5880	89	DALY CREAT WRTNG		2A02G	2A02G	2A02G		C
5890	89	DALY ACTV SPORTS		2A02H	2A02H	2A02H		C
5900	89	DALY ART/CRAFTS		2A02I	2A02I	2A02I		C
5910	89	DALY WRK HSE,CAR		2A02J	2A02J	2A02J		C
5920	89	DALY VIST W/FRDS		2A02K	2A02K	2A02K		C M
5930	89	DALY GO SHOPPING		2A02L	2A02L	2A02L		C F
5940	90	DALY ALONE LEISR		(2A02M)	2A02M	2A02M		C
5950	90	DALY READ BK,MAG		2A02N	2A02N	2A02N		B C
5960	90	DALY GO TO BARS		2A02O	2A02O	2A02O		C
5970	90	DALY GO TO PARTY		2A02P	2A02P	2A02P		C
5980	88	DALY GO CHURCH		2A02D				C G
5990	90	US 2 MUCH PROFIT	2A23J	2A03A	2A03A	2A03A		F O
6000	90	2MUCH CNCRN MTRL	2A23K	2A03B	2A03B	2A03B		F
6010	91	ENCOURG PPL BUY>	2A23L	2A03C	2A03C	2A03C		F
6020	91	-WRNG ADVERTISNG	2A23M	2A03D	2A03D	2A03D		F
6030	91	MOR SHORTGS FUTR	2A23N	2A03E	2A03E	2A03E		F
6040	91	APRV PETITIONS	2A21A	2A04A	2A04A	2A04A		H I
6050	91	APRV BOYCOTT	2A21B	2A04B	2A04B	2A04B		H I
6060	91	APRV LWFL DMSTN	2A21C	2A04C	2A04C	2A04C		H I
6070	92	APRV OCCUPY BLDG	2A21D	2A04D	2A04D	2A04D		H I
6080	92	APRV WLDCAT STRK	2A21E	2A04E	2A04E	2A04E		H I
6090	92	APRV BLK TRAFFIC	2A21F	2A04F	2A04F	2A04F		H I
6100	92	APRV DAMAG THING	2A21G	2A04G	2A04G	2A04G		H I
6110	92	APRV PSNL VIOLNC	2A21H	2A04H	2A04H	2A04H		H I
6120	92	DFNTLY PRFR MATE	2A10	2A05	2A05	2A05		D
6130	92	THINK WILL MARRY	2A11	2A06	2A06	2A06		D
6140	93	LIKLY STAY MARRD	2A12A	2A07A	2A07A	2A07A		D
6150	93	LIKLY HAVE KIDS	2A12B	2A07B	2A07B	2A07B		D E
6160	93	-CHL,HB WK1.,W=0	2A15A	2A08A	2A08A	2A08A		C D
6170	93	-CHL,HB WK1.,W.5	2A15B	2A08B	2A08B	2A08B		C D
6180	93	-CHL,HB&WF WK 1.	2A15C	2A08C	2A08C	2A08C		C D
6190	94	-CHL,HB&WF WK .5	2A15D	2A08D	2A08D	2A08D		C D
6200	94	-CHL,W WK 1.,H.5	2A15E	2A08E	2A08E	2A08E		C D
6210	94	-CHL,W WK 1.,H=0	2A15F	2A08F	2A08F	2A08F		C D
6220	94	PSCH,HB WK1.,W=0	2A16A	2A09A	2A09A	2A09A		C D
6230	94	PSCH,HB WK1.,W.5	2A16B	2A09B	2A09B	2A09B		C D
6240	94	PSCH,HB&WF WK 1.	2A16C	2A09C	2A09C	2A09C		C D
6250	94	PSCH,HB&WF WK .5	2A16D	2A09D	2A09D	2A09D		C D
6260	95	PSCH,WF WK1.,H.5	2A16E	2A09E	2A09E	2A09E		C D
6270	95	PSCH,WF WK1.,H=0	2A16F	2A09F	2A09F	2A09F		C D
6280	95	H WK,W -WK,W CCR	2A17A	2A10A	2A10A	2A10A		D
6290	95	H WK,W -WK,W>CCR	2A17B	2A10B	2A10B	2A10B		D
6300	95	H WK,W -WK,=CHCR	2A17C	2A10C	2A10C	2A10C		D
6310	95	H WK,W -WK,H>CCR	2A17D	2A10D	2A10D	2A10D		D
6320	95	H WK,W -WK,H CCR	2A17E	2A10E	2A10E	2A10E		D

ITEM REFERENCE NUMBER	PAGE LOCATION (IN THIS VOLUME)	ITEM DESCRIPTION (ABBREVIATED)	QUESTIONNAIRE LOCATION BY YEAR (FORM, SECTION, AND QUESTION NUMBER)				SUBJECT AREA																		
			1975	1976	1977	1978	A	B	C	D	E	F	G	H	I	J	K	L	M	N	O	P	Q	R	S
6330	96	INTEREST IN GOVT	2A31	2A11	2A11	2A11									H									Q		
	136		4A29	3E01	3E01	3E01									H									Q		
	152		5A40	4A18	4A18	4A18									H									Q		
	177			5A19	5A19	5A19									H									Q		
6340	96	GOVT PPL -DSHNST	2A32	2A12	2A12	2A12									H			K								
6350	96	GOVT DSNT WASTE$	2A33	2A13	2A13	2A13									H			K								
6360	96	NEVER TRUST GOVT	2A34	2A14	2A14	2A14									H			K								
6370	96	GVT PPL DK DOING	2A35	2A15	2A15	2A15									H			K								
6380	97	GOVT RUN FOR PPL	2A36	2A16	2A16	2A16									H			K								
6390	97	DO OR PLN VOTE	2A37A	2A17A	2A17A	2A17A									H	I										
6400	97	DO OR PLN WRITE	2A37B	2A17B	2A17B	2A17B									H	I										
6410	97	DO OR PLN GIVE $	2A37C	2A17C	2A17C	2A17C									H	I										
6420	97	DO OR PLN WK CPG	2A37D	2A17D	2A17D	2A17D									H	I										
6430	97	DO OR PLN DEMNST	2A37E	2A17E	2A17E	2A17E									H	I										
6440	97	DO OR PLN BOYCOT	2A37F	2A17F	2A17F	2A17F									H	I										
6450	98	US SHD DISARM	2A38A	2A18A	2A18A	2A18A									H				L							
6460	98	US WAR PRTCT ECN	2A38C	2A18C	2A18C	2A18C									H				L							
6470	98	US ONLY WAR DFNS	2A38D	2A18D	2A18D	2A18D									H				L							
6480	98	-US MIL PWR>USSR	2A38E	2A18E	2A18E	2A18E									H				L							
6490	98	US NEED>PWR OTHS	2A38F	2A18F	2A18F	2A18F									H				L							
6500	99	US FRN PLCY NRRW	2A38G	2A18G	2A18G	2A18G									H				L							
6510	99	SRVCMEN SHD OBEY	2A38H	2A18H	2A18H	2A18H													L							
6520	99	FRQ FIGHT PARNTS	2A39A	2A19A	2A19A	2A19A														M						S
6530	99	FRQ HIT SUPRVISR	2A39B	2A19B	2A19B	2A19B														M						S
6540	99	FRQ FGT WRK/SCHL	2A39C	2A19C	2A19C	2A19C		B	C																	S
6550	99	FRQ GANG FIGHT	2A39D	2A19D	2A19D	2A19D																				S
6560	100	FRQ HURT SM1 BAD	2A39E	2A19E	2A19E	2A19E																				S
6570	100	FRQ THREAT WEAPN	2A39F	2A19F	2A19F	2A19F																				S
6580	100	FRQ STEAL <$50	2A39G	2A19G	2A19G	2A19G																				S
6590	100	FRQ STEAL >$50	2A39H	2A19H	2A19H	2A19H																				S
6600	100	FRQ SHOPLIFT	2A39I	2A19I	2A19I	2A19I																				S
6610	100	FRQ CAR THEFT	2A39J	2A19J	2A19J	2A19J																				S
6620	101	FRQ STEAL CAR PT	2A39K	2A19K	2A19K	2A19K																				S
6630	101	FRQ TRESPAS BLDG	2A39L	2A19L	2A19L	2A19L																				S
6640	101	FRQ ARSON	2A39M	2A19M	2A19M	2A19M																				S
6650	101	FRQ DMG SCH PPTY	2A39N	2A19N	2A19N	2A19N		B																		S
6660	101	FRQ DMG WK PRPTY	2A39O	2A19O	2A19O	2A19O			C																	S
6670	101	FRQ TRUBL POLICE	2A39P	2A19P	2A19P	2A19P																				S
6680	102	SM1 ROB YRS <$50		2A20A	2A20A	2A20A																			R	S
6690	102	SM1 ROB YRS >$50		2A20B	2A20B	2A20B																			R	S
6700	102	SM1 DMG YR PRPTY		2A20C	2A20C	2A20C																			R	S
6710	102	SM1 INJR U W/WPN		2A20D	2A20D	2A20D																			R	S
6720	102	SM1 THRTN U W/WP		2A20E	2A20E	2A20E																			R	S
6730	102	SM1 INJR YU -WPN		2A20F	2A20F	2A20F																			R	S
6740	102	SM1 THRT U W/INJ		2A20G	2A20G	2A20G																			R	S
6750	103	EASY GT MARIJUAN	2A40A	2A21A	2A21A	2A21A	A03A																			
6760	103	EASY GT LSD	2A40B	2A21B	2A21B	2A21B	A03A																			
6770	103	EASY GT PSYDELIC	2A40C	2A21C	2A21C	2A21C	A03A																			
6780	103	EASY GT AMPHTMNS	2A40D	2A21D	2A21D	2A21D	A03A																			
6790	103	EASY GT BBTUATES	2A40F	2A21E	2A21E	2A21E	A03A																			
6800	103	EASY GT TRANQLIZ	2A40G	2A21F	2A21F	2A21F	A03A																			
6810	104	EASY GT COCAINE	2A40H	2A21G	2A21G	2A21G	A03A																			
6820	104	EASY GT HEROIN	2A40I	2A21H	2A21H	2A21H	A03A																			
6830	104	EASY GT NARCOTIC	2A40J	2A21I	2A21I	2A21I	A03A																			
6840	104	CMP SATFD W/LIFE		2D01	2D01	2D01																	P	Q	R	
	132			3D01	3D01	3D01																	P	Q	R	
	156			4D01	4D01	4D01																	P	Q	R	
	178			5A21	5A21	5A21																	P	Q	R	
6850	104	HOW GD AS SPOUSE	2A19A	2D02A	2D02A	2D02A				D														Q		
6860	104	HOW GD AS PARENT	2A19B	2D02B	2D02B	2D02B				D														Q		
6870	105	HOW GD AS WORKER	2A19C	2D02C	2D02C	2D02C			C															Q		
6880	105	THK ABT SOC ISSU	*A06	2D03	2D03	2D03											J							Q		
	118			3A02	3A02	3A02											J							Q		
	142			4A05	4A05	4A05											J							Q		
	168			5A02	5A02	5A02											J							Q		
6890	105	DHNSTY LARG CORP	2A20A	2D04A	2D04A	2D04A												K								

ITEM REFERENCE NUMBER	PAGE LOCATION (IN THIS VOLUME)	ITEM DESCRIPTION (ABBREVIATED)	1975	1976	1977	1978	A	B C D E F G H I J K L M N O P Q R S
6900	105	DHNSTY LBR UNION	2A20B	2D04B	2D04B	2D04B		K
6910	105	DHNSTY COLL&UNIV	2A20C	2D04C	2D04C	2D04C		B ... K
6920	105	DHNSTY PBLC SCHL	2A20D	2D04D	2D04D	2D04D		B ... K
6930	106	DHNSTY CHURCHES	2A20E	2D04E	2D04E	2D04E		G ... K
6940	106	DHNSTY NEWS MDIA	2A20F	2D04F	2D04F	2D04F		B ... K
6950	106	DHNSTY PRES&ADMN	2A20G	2D04G	2D04G	2D04G		H ... K
6960	106	DHNSTY CONGRESS	2A20H	2D04H	2D04H	2D04H		H K
6970	106	DHNSTY SUPRM CRT	2A20I	2D04I	2D04I	2D04I		H K
6980	106	DHNSTY JUSTC SYS	2A20J	2D04J	2D04J	2D04J		H K
6990	107	DHNSTY POLICE	2A20K	2D04K	2D04K	2D04K		K
7000	107	DHNSTY MILITARY	2A20L	2D04L	2D04L	2D04L		K L
7010	107	2MCH COMPTN SCTY	2A23C	2D05A	2D05A	2D05A		Q
7020	107	2MANY YNG SLOPPY	2A23H	2D05B	2D05B	2D05B		Q
7030	107	2MUCH HARD ROCK	2A23I	2D05C	2D05C	2D05C		Q
7040	107	SHD DO OWN THING	2A23A	2D05D	2D05D	2D05D		Q
7050	108	KICK DO DANGR TH		2D05E	2D05E	2D05E		Q
7060	108	LIKE RISK SOME X		2D05F	2D05F	2D05F		Q
7070	108	ALL FRD SMK CIGS	2A41A	2D06A	2D06A	2D06A	A02A	
7080	108	ALL FRD SMK MARJ	2A41B	2D06B	2D06B	2D06B	A02A	
7090	108	ALL FRD TAKE LSD	2A41C	2D06C	2D06C	2D06C	A02A	
7100	108	ALL FRD TK PSYDL	2A41D	2D06D	2D06D	2D06D	A02A	
7110	109	ALL FRD TK AMPH	2A41E	2D06E	2D06E	2D06E	A02A	
7120	109	ALL FRD TK QUALD	2A41F	2D06F	2D06F	2D06F	A02A	
7130	109	ALL FRD TK BARBT	2A41G	2D06G	2D06G	2D06G	A02A	
7140	109	ALL FRD TK TRNQL	2A41H	2D06H	2D06H	2D06H	A02A	
7150	109	ALL FRD TK COKE	2A41I	2D06I	2D06I	2D06I	A02A	
7160	109	ALL FRD TK HERON	2A41J	2D06J	2D06J	2D06J	A02A	
7170	109	ALL FRD TK NARC	2A41K	2D06K	2D06K	2D06K	A02A	
7180	110	ALL FRD TK INHL	2A41L	2D06L	2D06L	2D06L	A02A	
7190	110	ALL FRD DRK ALCL	2A41M	2D06M	2D06M	2D06M	A02A	
7200	110	ALL FRD GT DRUNK	2A41N	2D06N	2D06N	2D06N	A02A	
7210		FBD CHLD CIG RGL			2E01A		A11C	
7220		FBD CHLD MJ OCCS			2E01B		A11C	
7230		FBD CHLD MJ RGLY			2E01C		A11C	
7240		FBD CHLD LSD OCC			2E01D		A11C	
7250		FBD CHLD AMPH OC			2E01E		A11C	
7260		FBD CHLD BARB OC			2E01F		A11C	
7270		FBD CHLD COKE OC			2E01G		A11C	
7280		FBD CHLD HRN OCC			2E01H		A11C	
7290		FBD CHLD DRNK OC			2E01I		A11C	
7300		FBD CHLD DRNK RG			2E01J		A11C	
7310		FBD CHLD DRUNKOC			2E01K		A11C	
7320	110	RSK/OT CIG1+PK/D		2E01A			A14B	
7330	110	RSK/OT MJ 1-2 X		2E01B			A14B	
7340	110	RSK/OT MJ OCSNLY		2E01C			A14B	
7350	111	RSK/OT MJ REGLY		2E01D			A14B	
7360	111	RSK/OT LSD 1-2 X		2E01E			A14B	
7370	111	RSK/OT LSD REGLY		2E01F			A14B	
7380	111	RSK/OT 'H' 1-2 X		2E01G			A14B	
7390	111	RSK/OT 'H' OCSNL		2E01H			A14B	
7400	111	RSK/OT 'H' REGLY		2E01I			A14B	
7410	111	RSK/OT BARB 1-2X		2E01J			A14B	
7420	112	RSK/OT BARB REGY		2E01K			A14B	
7430	112	RSK/OT AMPH 1-2X		2E01L			A14B	
7440	112	RSK/OT AMPH REG		2E01M			A14B	
7450	112	RSK/OT COKE 1-2X		2E01N			A14B	
7460	112	RSK/OT COKE REG		2E01O			A14B	
7470	112	RSK/OT 1-2 DRINK		2E01P			A14B	
7480	112	RSK/OT 1-2 DR/DA		2E01Q			A14B	
7490	113	RSK/OT 4-5 DR/DA		2E01R			A14B	
7500	113	RSK/OT 5+DR/WKND		2E01S			A14B	
7510		PRNT THK U DRINK			2E02	2E01	A09A	
7520		PRNT THK U SM MJ			2E03	2E02	A09A	
7530		PRNT THK USE DRG			2E04	2E03	A09A	
7540		TRN FA/MO DRG HP			2E05A		A08A	
7550		TRN SR/BR DRG HP			2E05B		A08A	

ITEM REFERENCE NUMBER	PAGE LOCATION (IN THIS VOLUME)	ITEM DESCRIPTION (ABBREVIATED)	1975	1976	1977	1978	A	B	C	D	E	F	G	H	I	J	K	L	M	N	O	P	Q	R	S
7560		TRN RLTVS DRG HP			2E05C		A08A																			
7570		TRN FRND DRG HP			2E05D		A08A																			
7580		TRN DOCTR DRG HP			2E05E		A08A																			
7590		TRN CLINC DRG HP			2E05F		A08A																			
7600		TRN CNSLR DRG HP			2E05G		A08A																			
7610		TRN TCHR DRG HP			2E05H		A08A																			
7620		TRN MNSTR DRG HP			2E05I		A08A																			
7630	85	R LIKES SCHOOL		1D001	1D001	1D001		B															Q		
	113			2E02	2E06	2E06		B															Q		
	139			3E08	3E07	3E07		B															Q		
	166			4E10	5E05	5E05		B															Q		
	191			5E04				B															Q		
7640	113	HRS/WK SPND HMWK		2E03	2E07	2E07		B																	
7650	113	PRCL INFL SCL RN		2E04A	2E08A	2E08A		B																	
7660	113	TCHR INFL SCL RN		2E04B	2E08B	2E08B		B																	
7670	114	STDS INFL SCL RN		2E04C	2E08C	2E08C		B																	
7680	114	PRTS INFL SCL RN		2E04D	2E08D	2E08D		B																	
7690	114	HAD DRUG EDUCATN		2E05	2E09	2E09	A10A																			
7700	115	NOW OWN HAIR DRY		2E09A								F													R	
7710	115	NOW OWN WT/S SKI		2E09B								F													R	
7720	115	NOW OWN CAMERA		2E09C								F													R	
7730	115	NOW OWN WATCH		2E09D								F													R	
7740	115	NOW OWN HKG BKPK		2E09E								F													R	
7750	115	NOW OWN CK RADIO		2E09F								F													R	
7760	115	NOW OWN EL SHAVR		2E09G								F													R	
7770	115	NOW OWN TENIS RQ		2E09H								F													R	
7780	115	NOW OWN TV SET		2E09I								F													R	
7790	115	NOW OWN BICYCLE		2E09J								F													R	
7800	115	NOW OWN CAR		2E09K								F													R	
7810	115	NOW OWN TAPE REC		2E09L								F													R	
7820	115	NOW OWN ELT CALC		2E09M								F													R	
7830	115	NOW OWN BT/SNMBL		2E09N								F													R	
7840	114	DG ED,>DG INTRST		2E06	2E10	2E10	A10A																			
7850	114	DG ED,SPC COURSE		2E07A	2E11A	2E11A	A10A																			
7860	114	DG ED,IN REG CRS		2E07B	2E11B	2E11B	A10A																			
7870	114	DG ED,NT REG CRS		2E07C	2E11C	2E11C	A10A																			
7880	114	DG ED,SPC DISCUS		2E07D	2E11D	2E11D	A10A																			
7890	114	DG ED,GRT VALUE		2E08	2E12	2E12	A10A																			
7900		16YR+,TEST->DIPL			2E13A	2E13A		B																	
7910		14YR+,TEST->DIPL			2E13B	2E13B		B																	
7920		ALL STD H.S.TEST			2E13C	2E13C		B																	
7930	118	MEN&WOMN/=$,=WRK	3A17A	3A03A	3A03A	3A03A			C	D															
7940	118	CNSDR WMN/HI JOB	3A17B	3A03B	3A03B	3A03B				D				H											
7950	118	WMN SHD =JOB OPP	3A17C	3A03C	3A03C	3A03C			C	D															
7960	118	WMN SHD =ED OPP	3A17D	3A03D	3A03D	3A03D		B		D															
7970	119	MN=ACHV/WMN=HOME	3A17H	3A03E	3A03E	3A03E				D															
7980	119	CHL SUFF W WK MO	3A17I	3A03F	3A03F	3A03F				D															
7990	119	WK MO AS WRM REL	3A17J	3A03G	3A03G	3A03G			C	D															
8000	119	POLLUT INCREASED	3A31A	3A04A	3A04A	3A04A						F													
8010	119	GOVT DEAL ENV PR	3A31D	3A04B	3A04B	3A04B						F		H											
8020	119	MR$ FR LASTG THG	3A31E	3A04C	3A04C	3A04C						F													
8030	120	USE BYC/MAS TRAN	3A31F	3A04D	3A04D	3A04D						F													
8040	120	EAT DIF->FD STRV	3A31G	3A04E	3A04E	3A04E						F									O				
8050	120	LIK WRK CAN FRGT	3A08D	3A05A	3A05A	3A05A			C																
8060	120	WRK=ONLY MK LVNG	3A08E	3A05B	3A05B	3A05B			C																
8070	120	WRK CNTRL PRT LF	3A08G	3A05C	3A05C	3A05C			C																
8080	120	OVTM 2DO BST JOB	3A08H	3A05D	3A05D	3A05D			C																
8090	121	SAME JOB MST LIF	3A08I	3A05E	3A05E	3A05E			C																
8100	121	ENUF$,NT WNT WRK	3A10	3A06	3A06	3A06			C																
	150		4A09A	4A14	4A14	4A14			C																
	171		5A11	5A06	5A06	5A06			C																
8110	121	DES FRND OTH RC	3A19A	3A07A	3A07A	3A07A														N					
8120	121	DES SUPVR DIF RC	3A19B	3A07B	3A07B	3A07B			C											N					
8130	121	DES FAM NX DF RC	3A19C	3A07C	3A07C	3A07C														N					
8140	122	DES CHL FD SM RC	3A19D	3A07D	3A07D	3A07D														N					
8150	122	DES CHL FD OT RC	3A19E	3A07E	3A07E	3A07E														N					

ITEM REFERENCE NUMBER	PAGE LOCATION (IN THIS VOLUME)	ITEM DESCRIPTION (ABBREVIATED)	QUESTIONNAIRE LOCATION BY YEAR (FORM, SECTION, AND QUESTION NUMBER)				SUBJECT AREA	
			1975	1976	1977	1978	A	B C D E F G H I J K L M N O P Q R S
8160	122	DES AL WKS SM RC	3A19F	3A08A	3A08A	3A08A		C N
8170	122	DES SO WKS DF RC	3A19G	3A08B	3A08B	3A08B		C N
8180	122	DES MS WKS DF RC	3A19H	3A08C	3A08C	3A08C		C N
8190	122	DES AL NGB SM RC	3A19I	3A09A	3A09A	3A09A		N
8200	122	DES SO NGB OT RC	3A19J	3A09B	3A09B	3A09B		N
8210	123	DES MS NGB OT RC	3A19K	3A09C	3A09C	3A09C		N
8220	123	DES AL CHL SM RC	3A19L	3A10A	3A10A	3A10A		B N
8230	123	DES SM CHL OT RC	3A19M	3A10B	3A10B	3A10B		B N
8240	123	DES MS CHL OT RC	3A19N	3A10C	3A10C	3A10C		B N
8250	123	FRNDS AL OT RC	3A22	3A11	3A11	3A11		N R
8260	123	NGBHD AL OT RC	3A23	3A12	3A12	3A12		N R
8270	123	ELEMSCH AL OT RC	3A21	3A13	3A13	3A13		N R
8280	124	HISCH AL OT RC	3A20	3A14	3A14	3A14		N R
8290	124	WRKRS AL OT RC		3A15	3A15	3A15		N
8300	124	DO LOT THG OT RC	3A24	3A16	3A16	3A16		N
8310	124	VRY GD EXP OT RC	3A25	3A17	3A17	3A17		N
8320	124	MARRD OR ENGAGED	3A41	3A18	3A18	3A18		E R
8330	124	WHN WANT GT MARR	3A42	3A19	3A19	3A19		E
8340	125	THGT LOT HAV CHL	3A43	3A20	3A20	3A20		E
8350	125	# CHLDN WANT(6+)	3A44	3A21	3A21	3A21		E
8360	125	IF -POP, MR CHLD	3A45	3A22	3A22	3A22		E
8370	125	WHN 1ST CHL(5+Y)	3A46	3A23	3A23	3A23		E M
8380	125	GD JB LARG CORPS	3A27A	3A24A	3A24A	3A24A		K
8390	126	GD JB LBR UNIONS	3A27B	3A24B	3A24B	3A24B		K
8400	126	GD JB COLLG&UNIV	3A27C	3A24C	3A24C	3A24C		B K
8410	126	GD JB PBLC SCHOL	3A27D	3A24D	3A24D	3A24D		B K
8420	126	GD JB CHURCHES	3A27E	3A24E	3A24E	3A24E		G K
8430	126	GD JB NEWS MEDIA	3A27F	3A24F	3A24F	3A24F		B K
8440	126	GD JB PRES&ADMIN	3A27G	3A24G	3A24G	3A24G		H K
8450	127	GD JB CONGRESS	3A27H	3A24H	3A24H	3A24H		H K
8460	127	GD JB SUPRM CRT	3A27I	3A24I	3A24I	3A24I		H K
8470	127	GD JB JUSTC SYST	3A27J	3A24J	3A24J	3A24J		H K
8480	127	GD JB POLICE	3A27K	3A24K	3A24K	3A24K		K
8490	127	GD JB MILITARY	3A27L	3A24L	3A24L	3A24L		K L
8500	127	MIL TOO MCH INFL	3A28	3A25	3A25	3A25		L
8510	128	US TOO MCH$ MILT	3A29	3A26	3A26	3A26		L
8520	128	12MO,#OCC PAINRF	3A48A	3A27A	3A27A	3A27A	A01B	
8530	128	12MO,#OCC SLP PL	3A48B	3A27B	3A27B	3A27B	A01B	
8540	128	12MO,#OCC AWK PL	3A48C	3A27C	3A27C	3A27C	A01B	
8550	128	12MO,#OCC CALM P	3A48D	3A27D	3A27D	3A27D	A01B	
8560	129	DAP SMK 1PCK CIG	(3A53A)	3A28A	3A28A	3A28A	A11A	
8570	129	DAP TRY MRJ 1-2T	(3A53B)	3A28B	3A28B	3A28B	A11A	
8580	129	DAP SMK MRJ OCCS	(3A53C)	3A28C	3A28C	3A28C	A11A	
8590	129	DAP SMK MRJ REGL	(3A53D)	3A28D	3A28D	3A28D	A11A	
8600	129	DAP TRY LSD 1-2T	(3A53E)	3A28E	3A28E	3A28E	A11A	
8610	129	DAP TKG LSD REGL	(3A53F)	3A28F	3A28F	3A28F	A11A	
8620	129	DAP TRY HRN 1-2T	(3A53G)	3A28G	3A28G	3A28G	A11A	
8630	129	DAP TKG HRN OCCS	(3A53H)	3A28H	3A28H	3A28H	A11A	
8640	130	DAP TKG HRN REGL	(3A53I)	3A28I	3A28I	3A28I	A11A	
8650	130	DAP TRY BRB 1-2T	(3A53J)	3A28J	3A28J	3A28J	A11A	
8660	130	DAP TKG BRB REGL	(3A53K)	3A28K	3A28K	3A28K	A11A	
8670	130	DAP TRY AMP 1-2T	(3A53L)	3A28L	3A28L	3A28L	A11A	
8680	130	DAP TKG AMP REGL	(3A53M)	3A28M	3A28M	3A28M	A11A	
8690	130	DAP TRY COC 1-2T	(3A53N)	3A28N	3A28N	3A28N	A11A	
8700	130	DAP TKG COC REGL	(3A53O)	3A28O	3A28O	3A28O	A11A	
8710	130	DAP TRY DRK ALCL	(3A53P)	3A28P	3A28P	3A28P	A11A	
8720	131	DAP 1-2 DRK/DAY	(3A53Q)	3A28Q	3A28Q	3A28Q	A11A	
8730	131	DAP 4-5 DRK/DAY	(3A53R)	3A28R	3A28R	3A28R	A11A	
8740	131	DAP 5+ DRK WKNDS	(3A53S)	3A28S	3A28S	3A28S	A11A	
8750	192	OFT W PL TK MARJ	3A55A	5E07A	5E08A	5E08A	A02B	
8760	193	OFT W PL TK LSD	3A55B	5E07B	5E08B	5E08B	A02B	
8770	193	OFT W PL TK PSYC	3A55C	5E07C	5E08C	5E08C	A02B	
8780	193	OFT W PL TK QUAL	3A55D	5E07D	5E08D	5E08D	A02B	
8790	193	OFT W PL TK BARB	3A55E	5E07E	5E08E	5E08E	A02B	
8800	193	OFT W PL TK TRQL	3A55F	5E07F	5E08F	5E08F	A02B	
8810	193	OFT W PL TK COKE	3A55G	5E07G	5E08G	5E08G	A02B	

ITEM REFERENCE NUMBER	PAGE LOCATION (IN THIS VOLUME)	ITEM DESCRIPTION (ABBREVIATED)	1975	1976	1977	1978	A	B	C	D	E	F	G	H	I	J	K	L	M	N	O	P	Q	R	S
8820	193	OFT W PL TK HRN	3A55H	5E07H	5E08H	5E08H	A02B																		
8830	193	OFT W PL TK NARC	3A55I	5E07I	5E08I	5E08I	A02B																		
8835	194	OFT W PL TK INHL	3A55J	5E07J	5E08J	5E08J	A02B																		
8840	194	OFT W PL TK ALCL	3A55K	5E07K	5E08K	5E08K	A02B																		
8850	133	OFTN SHRTNS BRTH		(3D02A)	3D02A	3D02A																	Q		
8860	133	OFTN HEART BEATG		(3D02B)	3D02B	3D02B																	Q		
8870	133	OFTN SPLLS DZZNS		(3D02C)	3D02C	3D02C																	Q		
8880	133	OFTN HNDS TRMBLE		(3D02D)	3D02D	3D02D																	Q		
8890	133	OFTN HNDS SWEATG		(3D02E)	3D02E	3D02E																	Q		
8900	133	OFTN CDNT GT GNG		(3D02F)	3D02F	3D02F																	Q		
8910	134	12MO REDUCE ALCL		3D03A	3D03A	3D03A	A01I																		
8920	134	12MO REDUCE CIG		3D03B	3D03B	3D03B	A01I																		
8930	134	12MO REDUCE MARJ		3D03C	3D03C	3D03C	A01I																		
8940	134	12MO REDUCE PSYC		3D03D	3D03D	3D03D	A01I																		
8950	134	12MO REDUCE AMPH		3D03E	3D03E	3D03E	A01I																		
8960	134	12MO REDUCE QUAL		3D03F	3D03F	3D03F	A01I																		
8970	134	12MO REDUCE BARB		3D03G	3D03G	3D03G	A01I																		
8980	134	12MO REDUCE COKE		3D03H	3D03H	3D03H	A01I																		
8990	134	12MO REDUCE HRN		3D03I	3D03I	3D03I	A01I																		
9000	135	12MO REDUCE NARC		3D03J	3D03J	3D03J	A01I																		
9010		NXT 12MOS USE MJ			3D04	3D04	A01B																		
9020	135	CNCRN PSYCH DAMG		3D04A	3D04A	3D04A	A06A																		
9030	135	CNCRN PHYSCL DMG		3D04B	3D04B	3D04B	A06A																		
9040	135	CNCRN GT ARRESTD		3D04C	3D04C	3D04C	A06A																		
9050	135	CNCRN BECOM ADCT		3D04D	3D04D	3D04D	A06A																		
9060	135	AGST MY BELIEFS		3D04E	3D04E	3D04E	A06A																		
9070	135	CNCRN LEGY&AMBTN		3D04F	3D04F	3D04F	A06A																		
9080	135	CNCRN LOSS CNTRL		3D04G	3D04G	3D04G	A06A																		
9090	135	MJ ->STRNGR DRGS		3D04H	3D04H	3D04H	A06A																		
9100	135	MJ NOT ENJOYABLE		3D04I	3D04I	3D04I	A06A																		
9110	135	PRNTS DISAPPROVE		3D04J	3D04J	3D04J	A06A																		
9120	135	HS/WF DISAPPROVE		3D04K	3D04K	3D04K	A06A																		
9130	135	DONT LIKE USERS		3D04L	3D04L	3D04L	A06A																		
9140	135	FRNDS DNT USE IT		3D04M	3D04M	3D04M	A06A																		
9150	135	PSSBLY BAD TRIP		3D04N	3D04N	3D04N	A06A																		
9160		TOO EXPENSIVE			3D04O	3D04O	A06A																		
9170		NOT AVAILABLE			3D04P	3D04P	A06A																		
9180		NOT WNT GET HIGH			3D04Q	3D04Q	A06A																		
9190	135	AL CS BEHV REGRT		3D05A	3D05A	3D05A	A07A																		
9200	135	AL HURT REL PRNT		3D05A	3D05A	3D05A	A07A																		
9210	135	AL HURT REL SPSE		3D05A	3D05A	3D05A	A07A																		
9220	135	AL HURT REL FRND		3D05A	3D05A	3D05A	A07A																		
9230	135	AL HURT REL TCHR		3D05A	3D05A	3D05A	A07A																		
9240	135	AL INV PL BD INF		3D05A	3D05A	3D05A	A07A																		
9250	135	AL HURT PERF JOB		3D05A	3D05A	3D05A	A07A																		
9260	135	AL CAUS<INTERSTD		3D05A	3D05A	3D05A	A07A																		
9270	135	AL CS<STABL EMTN		3D05A	3D05A	3D05A	A07A																		
9280	135	AL CS HAV<ENERGY		3D05A	3D05A	3D05A	A07A																		
9290	135	AL INTF THNK CLR		3D05A	3D05A	3D05A	A07A																		
9300	135	AL BD PSYCH EFCT		3D05A	3D05A	3D05A	A07A																		
9310	135	AL CS HEALTH BAD		3D05A	3D05A	3D05A	A07A																		
9320	135	AL CS DRIV UNSAF		3D05A	3D05A	3D05A	A07A																		
9330	135	AL GT TRBL W POL		3D05A	3D05A	3D05A	A07A																		
9340		AL CS NO PROBLEM			3D05A	3D05A	A07A																		
9350		AL NEVER USED DG			3D05A	3D05A	A07A																		
9360	135	MJ CS BEHV REGRT		3D05M	3D05M	3D05M	A07A																		
9370	135	MJ HURT REL PRNT		3D05M	3D05M	3D05M	A07A																		
9380	135	MJ HURT REL SPSE		3D05M	3D05M	3D05M	A07A																		
9390	135	MJ HURT REL FRND		3D05M	3D05M	3D05M	A07A																		
9400	135	MJ HURT REL TCHR		3D05M	3D05M	3D05M	A07A																		
9410	135	MJ INV PL BD INF		3D05M	3D05M	3D05M	A07A																		
9420	135	MJ HURT PERF JOB		3D05M	3D05M	3D05M	A07A																		
9430	135	MJ CAUS<INTERSTD		3D05M	3D05M	3D05M	A07A																		
9440	135	MJ CS<STABL EMTN		3D05M	3D05M	3D05M	A07A																		
9450	135	MJ CS HAV<ENERGY		3D05M	3D05M	3D05M	A07A																		
9460	135	MJ INTF THNK CLR		3D05M	3D05M	3D05M	A07A																		

ITEM REFERENCE NUMBER	PAGE LOCATION (IN THIS VOLUME)	ITEM DESCRIPTION (ABBREVIATED)	QUESTIONNAIRE LOCATION BY YEAR (FORM, SECTION, AND QUESTION NUMBER)				SUBJECT AREA																		
			1975	1976	1977	1978	A	B	C	D	E	F	G	H	I	J	K	L	M	N	O	P	Q	R	S
9470	135	MJ BD PSYCH EFCT		3D05M	3D05M	3D05M	A07A																		
9480	135	MJ CS HEALTH BAD		3D05M	3D05M	3D05M	A07A																		
9490	135	MJ CS DRIV UNSAF		3D05M	3D05M	3D05M	A07A																		
9500	135	MJ GT TRBL W POL		3D05M	3D05M	3D05M	A07A																		
9510		MJ CS NO PROBLEM			3D05M	3D05M	A07A																		
9520		MJ NEVER USED DG			3D05M	3D05M	A07A																		
9530	136	OT CS BEHV REGRT		3D05O	3D05O	3D05O	A07A																		
9540	136	OT HURT REL PRNT		3D05O	3D05O	3D05O	A07A																		
9550	136	OT HURT REL SPSE		3D05O	3D05O	3D05O	A07A																		
9560	136	OT HURT REL FRND		3D05O	3D05O	3D05O	A07A																		
9570	136	OT HURT REL TCHR		3D05O	3D05O	3D05O	A07A																		
9580	136	OT INV PL BD INF		3D05O	3D05O	3D05O	A07A																		
9590	136	OT HURT PERF JOB		3D05O	3D05O	3D05O	A07A																		
9600	136	OT CAUS<INTERSTD		3D05O	3D05O	3D05O	A07A																		
9610	136	OT CS<STABL EMTN		3D05O	3D05O	3D05O	A07A																		
9620	136	OT CS HAV<ENERGY		3D05O	3D05O	3D05O	A07A																		
9630	136	OT INTF THNK CLR		3D05O	3D05O	3D05O	A07A																		
9640	136	OT BD PSYCH EFCT		3D05O	3D05O	3D05O	A07A																		
9650	136	OT CS HEALTH BAD		3D05O	3D05O	3D05O	A07A																		
9660	136	OT CS DRIV UNSAF		3D05O	3D05O	3D05O	A07A																		
9670	136	OT GT TRBL W POL		3D05O	3D05O	3D05O	A07A																		
9680		OT CS NO PROBLEM			3D05O	3D05O	A07A																		
9690		OT NEVER USED DG			3D05O	3D05O	A07A																		
9700	136	PRVNT POL TOO >$		3E02A	3E02A	3E02A						F													
9710	136	PRVNT POL CST JB		3E02B	3E02B	3E02B						F													
9720	136	PRVNT POL PPL DK		3E02C	3E02C	3E02C						F													
9730	136	PRVNT POL -ENUF		3E02D	3E02D	3E02D						F													
9740	137	PRVNT POL USELSS		3E02E	3E02E	3E02E						F													
9750	137	FUTR,HAV2 CNSUM<		3E03	3E03	3E03						F													
9760	137	GOV HP PRB POPL	3A32N	3E04A	3E04A	3E04A					E			H											
9770	137	GOV NO POP PLCY	3A32A	3E04B	3E04B	3E04B					E			H											
9780	137	STR OVPOP,LMT FM	3A32B	3E04C	3E04C	3E04C					E														
9790	137	PRV OVPOP,NO CHL	3A32C	3E04D	3E04D	3E04D					E														
9800	138	HISCH INS BRTH C	3A32E	3E04E	3E04E	3E04E		B			E														
9810	138	BRTH CNT IMMORAL	3A32I	3E04F	3E04F	3E04F					E														
9820	138	GOV BRTHC NO CST	3A32M	3E04G	3E04G	3E04G					E			H											
9830	138	US POP SZ LRGER	3A34	3E06	3E05	3E05					E														
9840	138	GVNG FOOD O CNTY	3A33	3E05							E										O				
9850	138	WRLD POP SZ LRGR	3A35	3E07	3E06	3E06					E														
9860	139	HAD SEX ED IN HS		3E09	3E08	3E08				D	E														
9870	139	STUDY BC IN HS		3E10	3E09	3E09				D	E														
9871	166	SM1 SCL ROB <$50		4E11A	3E10A	3E10A																			R	S
9872	166	SM1 SCL ROB >$50		4E11B	3E10B	3E10B																			R	S
9873	166	SM1 SCL DMG PRTY		4E11C	3E10C	3E10C																			R	S
9874	166	SM1 SCL IN U W/W		4E11D	3E10D	3E10D																			R	S
9875	166	SM1 SCL TH U W/W		4E11E	3E10E	3E10E																			R	S
9876	167	SM1 SCL IN U -WP		4E11F	3E10F	3E10F																			R	S
9877	167	SM1 SCL TH U W/I		4E11G	3E10G	3E10G																			R	S
9880		DK DO W LEISR TM			3E11A				C																
9890		TM QUIK/LEIS HRS			3E11B				C																
9900		WASTE LEIS TIME			3E11C				C																
9910		ENUF TIME FR THG			3E11D				C																
9920	139	R WL VOTE IN '76		3E11										H											
9940	142	FUTR CNTRY WORSE	4A01	4A02	4A02	4A02									I										
9950	142	FUTR WORLD WORSE	4A02	4A03	4A03	4A03									I										
9960	142	FUTR R LIFE WRSE	4A03	4A04	4A04	4A04									I										
9970	142	PLLTN INCR IN US	4A22A	4A06A	4A06A	4A06A						F													
9980	143	PLLTN NT SO DANG	4A22B	4A06B	4A06B	4A06B						F													
9990	143	PLLTN NEC 4 GRTH	4A22C	4A06C	4A06C	4A06C						F													
10000	143	INDVL RESP 4 ENV	4A22D	4A06D	4A06D	4A06D						F													
10010	143	GOVT RESP 4 ENV	4A22E	4A06E	4A06E	4A06E						F		H											
10020	143	GOVT TAX PLLTRS	4A22F	4A06F	4A06F	4A06F						F		H											
10030	143	GOVT BAN DSPSBLE	4A22G	4A06G	4A06G	4A06G						F		H											
10040	144	TV COMM CRT NDS	4A22H	4A06H	4A06H	4A06H		B				F													
10050	144	TV COMMRCLS GOOD	4A22I	4A06I	4A06I	4A06I		B				F													
10060	144	FAM BUYS THG -ND	4A22L	4A06J	4A06J	4A06J						F													

Item Reference Number	Page Location (In This Volume)	Item Description (Abbreviated)	1975	1976	1977	1978	A	B	C	D	E	F	G	H	I	J	K	L	M	N	O	P	Q	R	S
	176			5A18I	5A18I	5A18I						F													
10070	144	POL SLVD BY 2000	4A22M	4A06K	4A06K	4A06K						F													
10080	144	R EFRT 2 HLP ENV	4A23	4A07	4A07	4A07						F													
10090	145	JOB IMPC SE RSLT	4A08A	4A08A	4A08A	4A08A			C																
10100	145	JOB IMPC STATUS	4A08B	4A08B	4A08B	4A08B			C																
10110	145	JOB IMPC INTRSTG	4A08C	4A08C	4A08C	4A08C			C																
10120	145	JOB IMPC ADVNCMT	4A08D	4A08D	4A08D	4A08D			C																
10130	145	JOB IMPC HLP OTH	4A08E	4A08E	4A08E	4A08E			C												O				
10140	145	JOB IMPC EARN $	4A08F	4A08F	4A08F	4A08F			C			F													
10150	145	JOB IMPC CREATVY	4A08G	4A08G	4A08G	4A08G			C																
10160	146	JOB IMPC UTILITY	4A08H	4A08H	4A08H	4A08H			C																
10170	146	JOB IMPC MK FRND	4A08I	4A08I	4A08I	4A08I			C										M						
10180	146	JOB IMPC USE SKL	4A08J	4A08J	4A08J	4A08J			C																
10190	146	JOB IMPC WRTHWLE	4A08K	4A08K	4A08K	4A08K			C												O				
10200	146	JOB IMPC VACATN	4A08L	4A08L	4A08L	4A08L			C																
10210	146	JOB IMPC MK DCSN	4A08M	4A08M	4A08M	4A08M			C																
10220	146	JOB IMPC FRE TIM		4A08N	4A08N	4A08N			C																
10230	147	JOB IMPC NO MVNG	4A08O	4A08O	4A08O	4A08O			C																
10240	147	JOB IMPC NO SPRV	4A08P	4A08P	4A08P	4A08P			C																
10250	147	JOB IMPC SECURTY	4A08Q	4A08Q	4A08Q	4A08Q			C																
10260	147	JOB IMPC LRNING	4A08R	4A08R	4A08R	4A08R		B	C																
10270	147	JOB IMPC BE SELF	4A08S	4A08S	4A08S	4A08S			C																
10280	147	JOB IMPC RESPECT	4A08T	4A08T	4A08T	4A08T			C																
10290	147	JOB IMPC CNTC PL	4A08U	4A08U	4A08U	4A08U			C										M						
10300	148	JOB IMPC EZ PACE		4A08V	4A08V	4A08V			C																
10310	148	JOB IMPC HRD PRB		4A08W	4A08W	4A08W			C																
10320	148	KIND OF WORK @30	4A09	4A09	4A09	4A09			C																
10330	149	R SURE GT THS WK		4A10	4A10	4A10			C																
10340	149	R SURE WK GD CHC		4A11	4A11	4A11			C																
10350	149	R THNK WK BE SAT		4A12	4A12	4A12			C													P			
10360	149	JOB OBSTC RELGN		4A13A	4A13A	4A13A			C				G												
10370	149	JOB OBSTC SEX		4A13B	4A13B	4A13B			C	D															
10380	149	JOB OBSTC RACE		4A13C	4A13C	4A13C			C											N					
10390	149	JOB OBSTC BKGRND		4A13D	4A13D	4A13D			C															R	
10400	150	JOB OBSTC POL VW		4A13E	4A13E	4A13E			C					H											
10410	150	JOB OBSTC EDUCTN		4A13F	4A13F	4A13F		B	C																
10420	150	JOB OBSTC -VOC T		4A13G	4A13G	4A13G			C																
10430	150	JOB OBSTC -ABLTY		4A13H	4A13H	4A13H			C															R	
10440	150	JOB OBSTC - PULL		4A13I	4A13I	4A13I			C															R	
10450	150	JOB OBSTC -WK HD		4A13J	4A13J	4A13J			C														Q		
10460	150	JOB OBSTC -CONFM		4A13K	4A13K	4A13K			C														Q		
10470	151	FEW GD MAR, ? IT	4A11A	4A15A	4A15A	4A15A				D															
10480	151	GD LIV TG BF MRG	4A11B	4A15B	4A15B	4A15B				D	E														
10490	151	1 PRTNR=RSTRCTVE	4A11C	4A15C	4A15C	4A15C				D	E														
10500	151	JB INTFR REL HBD	4A11E	4A15D	4A15D	4A15D			C	D															
10510	151	JB DVLP WF PERSN	4A11G	4A15E	4A15E	4A15E			C	D															
10520	151	RS CHLD + FR MAN	4A11H	4A15F	4A15F	4A15F				D															
10530	152	MO SH B W CHL>TM	4A11I	4A15G	4A15G	4A15G				D															
10540	152	WF WK,HBD SHD>HW	4A11K	4A15H	4A15H	4A15H			C	D															
10550	152	#HRS TV/DAY/5+		4A16	4A16	4A16		B																	
10560	152	#BKS LAST YR/10+		4A17	4A17	4A17		B																	
10570	153	>INFLC LARG CORP	4A14A	4A19A	4A19A	4A19A											K								
10580	153	>INFLC LBR UNION	4A14B	4A19B	4A19B	4A19B											K								
10590	153	>INFLC CHURCHES	4A14C	4A19C	4A19C	4A19C							G				K								
10600	153	>INFLC NEWS MDIA	4A14D	4A19D	4A19D	4A19D		B									K								
10610	153	>INFLC PRES&ADMN	4A14E	4A19E	4A19E	4A19E								H			K								
10620	153	>INFLC CONGRESS	4A14F	4A19F	4A19F	4A19F								H			K								
10630	154	>INFLC SUPRM CRT	4A14G	4A19G	4A19G	4A19G								H			K								
10640	154	>INFLC JUSTC SYS	4A14H	4A19H	4A19H	4A19H								H			K								
10650	154	>INFLC POLICE	4A14I	4A19I	4A19I	4A19I											K								
10660	154	>INFLC MILITARY	4A14J	4A19J	4A19J	4A19J											K	L							
10760		LAW 4 SMK TOBPUB			4A20K	4A20K	A13A																			
10770	154	ILGL AD SMK CIG		4A20A			A13A																			
10780	154	ILGL AD MRJ PRIV		4A20B	4A20A	4A20A	A13A																			
10790	155	ILGL AD MRJ PUBL		4A20C	4A20B	4A20B	A13A																			
10800	155	ILGL AD LSD PRIV		4A20D	4A20C	4A20C	A13A																			

ITEM REFERENCE NUMBER	PAGE LOCATION (IN THIS VOLUME)	ITEM DESCRIPTION (ABBREVIATED)	QUESTIONNAIRE LOCATION BY YEAR (FORM, SECTION, AND QUESTION NUMBER)				SUBJECT AREA																		
			1975	1976	1977	1978	A	B	C	D	E	F	G	H	I	J	K	L	M	N	O	P	Q	R	S
10810	155	ILGL AD LSD PUBL		4A20E	4A20D	4A20D	A13A																		
10820	155	ILGL AD AMP PRIV		4A20F	4A20E	4A20E	A13A																		
10830	155	ILGL AD AMP PUBL		4A20G	4A20F	4A20F	A13A																		
10840	155	ILGL AD HRN PRIV		4A20H	4A20G	4A20G	A13A																		
10850	155	ILGL AD HRN PUBL		4A20I	4A20H	4A20H	A13A																		
10860	155	ILGL AD DRNK PRV		4A20J	4A20I	4A20I	A13A																		
10870	156	ILGL AD DRNK PBL		4A20K	4A20J	4A20J	A13A																		
10880	156	CRIME 2 USE MARJ	4A32	4A21	4A21	4A21	A13C																		
10890	156	LEGAL 2 SELL MRJ	4A33	4A22	4A22	4A22	A13C																		
10900	156	USE<MJ IF LEGAL	4A34	4A23	4A23	4A23	A13C																		
10910	156	CMP SATFD W/JOB		4D02	4D02	4D02			C														P			
10920	157	I CNT CHNG WORLD	4A28A	4D03A	4D03A	4D03A									I	J							Q		
10930	157	SOCTY WONT LAST	4A28B	4D03B	4D03B	4D03B						F				J									
10940	157	THG TUF,TCHN SLV	4A28C	4D03C	4D03C	4D03C									I	J							Q		
10950	157	NO HOPE 4 WORLD	4A28D	4D03D	4D03D	4D03D										J							Q		
10960	157	WNDR PURPS 2 LIF	4A28E	4D03E	4D03E	4D03E										J							Q		
10970	157	WRLD UPHVL 10 YR	4A28F	4D03F	4D03F	4D03F										J							Q		
10980	158	ANNIHLTN IN LFTM	4A28G	4D03G	4D03G	4D03G										J							Q		
10990	158	HMN RCE RSILIENT	4A28H	4D03H	4D03H	4D03H										J							Q		
11000	158	#X BEER/LIFETIME		4D04A	4D04A	4D04A	A01A																		
11010	158	#X BEER/LAST12MO		4D04B	4D04B	4D04B	A01B																		
11020	158	#X BEER/LAST30DA		4D04C	4D04C	4D04C	A01C																		
11030	158	5+BR/LST2WK,10+X		4D05	4D05	4D05	A01D																		
11040	159	#X WINE/LIFETIME		4D06A	4D06A	4D06A	A01A																		
11050	159	#X WINE/LAST12MO		4D06B	4D06B	4D06B	A01B																		
11060	159	#X WINE/LAST30DA		4D06C	4D06C	4D06C	A01C																		
11070	159	#X 20OZ+ WN/2 WK		4D07	4D07	4D07	A01D																		
11080	159	#X LIQR/LIFETIME		4D08A	4D08A	4D08A	A01A																		
11090	160	#X LIQR/LAST12MO		4D08B	4D08B	4D08B	A01B																		
11100	160	#X LIQR/LAST30DA		4D08C	4D08C	4D08C	A01C																		
11110	160	#X 5+LIQ/LST 2WK		4D09	4D09	4D09	A01D																		
11120	160	MLTRY GET AHEAD		4E01A	4E01A	4E01A												L							
11130	160	MLTRY MORE ED		4E01B	4E01B	4E01B		B										L							
11140	160	MLTRY ADVNC RESP		4E01C	4E01C	4E01C												L							
11150	161	MLTRY >FLFLLG JB		4E01D	4E01D	4E01D			C									L							
11160	161	MLTRY IDEAS HERD		4E01E	4E01E	4E01E												L							
11170	161	EXTNT MLTRY JSTC		4E02	4E02	4E02												L							
11180	161	MLTRY DSCRM WOMN		4E03	4E03	4E03				D								L							
11190	161	MLTRY DSCRM BLKS		4E04	4E04	4E04												L		N					
11200	161	>FAIR MLTRY CVLN		4E05	4E05	4E05												L							
11210	162	-MLTRY COUP U.S.		4E06	4E06										H			L							
11220	162	NT VOL 4 NEC WAR		4E07	4E07	4E06												L							
11230	162	P'IDEA OF DO LIF	4A27A	4E08A	4E08A	4E07A													M						
11240	162	P'IDEA OF LSR TM	4A27B	4E08B	4E08B	4E07B			C										M						
11250	162	P'IDEA OF CLTHES	4A27C	4E08C	4E08C	4E07C													M						
11260	163	P'IDEA OF SPND $	4A27D	4E08D	4E08D	4E07D													M						
11270	163	P'IDEA OF DATE	4A27E	4E08E	4E08E	4E07E													M						
11280	163	P'IDEA OF OK DRK	4A27F	4E08F	4E08F	4E07F													M						
11290	163	P'IDEA OF OK MRJ	4A27G	4E08G	4E08G	4E07G													M						
11300	163	P'IDEA OF OK DRG	4A27H	4E08H	4E08H	4E07H													M						
11310	163	P'IDEA OF VALUES	4A27I	4E08I	4E08I	4E07I													M						
11320	163	P'IDEA OF EDUC	4A27J	4E08J	4E08J	4E07J		B											M						
11330	164	P'IDEA OF SX RLS	4A27K	4E08K	4E08K	4E07K				D									M						
11340	164	P'IDEA OF ECLOGY	4A27L	4E08L	4E08L	4E07L						F							M						
11350	164	P'IDEA OF RCL IS	4A27M	4E08M	4E08M	4E07M													M	N					
11360	164	P'IDEA OF RLGION	4A27N	4E08N	4E08N	4E07N							G						M						
11370	164	P'IDEA OF PLTICS	4A27O	4E08O	4E08O	4E07O								H					M						
11380	164	PRNT DAP CIGS	4A35A	4E09A	4E09A	4E08A	A12A																		
11390	165	PRNT DAP TRY MRJ	4A35B	4E09B	4E09B	4E08B	A12A																		
11400	165	PRNT DAP MJ OCC	4A35C	4E09C	4E09C	4E08C	A12A																		
11410	165	PRNT DAP MJ REG	4A35D	4E09D	4E09D	4E08D	A12A																		
11420	165	PRNT DAP TRY LSD	4A35E	4E09E	4E09E	4E08E	A12A																		
11430	165	PRNT DAP TRY AMP	4A35F	4E09F	4E09F	4E08F	A12A																		
11440	165	PRNT DAP 1-2DR/D	4A35G	4E09G	4E09G	4E08G	A12A																		
11450	165	PRNT DAP 4-5DR/D	4A35H	4E09H	4E09H	4E08H	A12A																		
11460	165	PRNT DAP 5+DR/WE	4A35I	4E09I	4E09I	4E08I	A12A																		

ITEM REFERENCE NUMBER	PAGE LOCATION (IN THIS VOLUME)	ITEM DESCRIPTION (ABBREVIATED)	QUESTIONNAIRE LOCATION BY YEAR (FORM, SECTION, AND QUESTION NUMBER)				SUBJECT AREA																		
			1975	1976	1977	1978	A	B	C	D	E	F	G	H	I	J	K	L	M	N	O	P	Q	R	S
11470		FRD DAP CIGS			4E10A		A12B																			
11480		FRD DAP TRY MARJ			4E10B		A12B																			
11490		FRD DAP MJ OCC			4E10C		A12B																			
11500		FRD DAP MJ REG			4E10D		A12B																			
11510		FRD DAP TRY LSD			4E10E		A12B																			
11520		FRD DAP TRY AMP			4E10F		A12B																			
11530		FRD DAP 1-2DR/DA			4E10G		A12B																			
11540		FRD DAP 4-5DR/DA			4E10H		A12B																			
11550		FRD DAP 5+DR/WKD			4E10I		A12B																			
11560		H&W WK,WF AL HWK			4E11A	4E10A				D																
11570		H&W WK,WF MS HWK			4E11B	4E10B				D																
11580		H&W WK,DO = HWRK			4E11C	4E10C				D																
11590		H&W WK,HB MS HWK			4E11D	4E10D				D																
11600		H&W WK,HB AL HWK			4E11E	4E10E				D																
11610		H&W WK+CH,W CHCR			4E12A	4E11A				D																
11620		H&W WK+CH,W>CHCR			4E12B	4E11B				D																
11630		H&W WK+CH,=CHCAR			4E12C	4E11C				D																
11640		H&W WK+CH,H>CHCR			4E12D	4E11D				D																
11650		H&W WK+CH,H CHCR			4E12E	4E11E				D																
11660	168	WR/NT NUCLER WAR	5A04A	5A03A	5A03A	5A03A											J									
11670	168	WR/NT POP GROWTH	5A04B	5A03B	5A03B	5A03B					E					J										
11680	168	WR/NT CRIME&VLNC	5A04C	5A03C	5A03C	5A03C											J									
11690	168	WR/NT POLLUTION	5A04D	5A03D	5A03D	5A03D						F					J									
11700	168	WR/NT ENRGY SHRT	5A04E	5A03E	5A03E	5A03E						F					J									
11710	169	WR/NT RACE RELTN	5A04F	5A03F	5A03F	5A03F											J				N					
11720	169	WR/NT HNGR&PVRTY	5A04G	5A03G	5A03G	5A03G						F					J									
11730	169	WR/NT USE OPN LD	5A04H	5A03H	5A03H	5A03H						F					J									
11740	169	WR/NT URBN DECAY	5A04I	5A03I	5A03I	5A03I											J									
11750	169	WR/NT ECON PRBLM	5A04J	5A03J	5A03J	5A03J											J									
11760	169	WR/NT DRUG ABUSE	5A04K	5A03K	5A03K	5A03K											J									
11770	169	XPRC MK R GD SPS		5A04A	5A04A	5A04A				D																
11780	170	XPRC MK R GD PRT		5A04B	5A04B	5A04B				D																
11790	170	XPRC MK R GD WKR		5A04C	5A04C	5A04C			C																	
11800	170	PLC WRK LG CORPN	5A09A	5A05A	5A05A	5A05A			C																	
11810	170	PLC WRK SM BSNSS	5A09B	5A05B	5A05B	5A05B			C																	
11820	170	PLC WRK GVT AGCY	5A09C	5A05C	5A05C	5A05C			C					H											
11830	170	PLC WRK MLTY SVC	5A09D	5A05D	5A05D	5A05D			C										L							
11840	170	PLC WRK SCH/UNIV	5A09E	5A05E	5A05E	5A05E		B	C																	
11850	171	PLC WRK PLC DEPT	5A09F	5A05F	5A05F	5A05F			C																	
11860	171	PLC WRK SOC SVCS	5A09G	5A05G	5A05G	5A05G			C													O				
11870	171	PLC WRK SML GRP	5A09H	5A05H	5A05H	5A05H			C																	
11880	171	PLC WRK SLF EMPL	5A09I	5A05I	5A05I	5A05I			C																	
11890	171	RCL CNTCT SCHOOL		5A07A	5A07A	5A07A		B													N					
11900	171	RCL CNTCT NGHBHD		5A07B	5A07B	5A07B															N					
11910	172	RCL CNTCT CHURCH		5A07C	5A07C	5A07C							G								N					
11920	172	RCL CNTCT SPORTS		5A07D	5A07D	5A07D															N					
11930	172	RCL CNTCT CLUBS		5A07E	5A07E	5A07E															N					
11940	172	RCL CNTCT JOB		5A07F	5A07F	5A07F			C												N					
11950	172	B/W RLTNS WRSE	5A15	5A08	5A08	5A08															N					
11960	172	DNT HV DRVR LCNS	5A22	5A09	5A09	5A09						F														
11970	172	DONT OWN CAR	5A23	5A10	5A10	5A10						F														
11980	173	NEVR USE OTHS CR	5A24	5A11	5A11	5A11						F														
11990	173	R CUT DRIVING		5A12	5A12	5A12						F														
12000	173	R CUT ELECTRICTY		5A13	5A13	5A13						F														
12010	173	RDCE HEAT R'S HM		5A14	5A14	5A14						F														
12020	173	ENJOY SHOPPING	5A35A	5A15A	5A15A	5A15A						F														
12030	173	CARE LATST FASHN	5A35B	5A15B	5A15B	5A15B						F														
12040	174	CR FAM HV NBR HV	5A35C	5A15C	5A15C	5A15C						F														
12050	174	XPCT 2 OWN>PRNTS	5A36	5A16	5A16	5A16						F														
12060	174	LST CNT OWN>PRNT	5A37	5A17	5A17	5A17						F														
12070	174	WRRY ABT OW CTRY	5A19A	5A18A	5A18A	5A18A																O				
12080	174	BTTR IF CTZ WRLD	5A19C	5A18B	5A18B	5A18B																O				
12090	175	-SYMP TWD STARVG	5A19E	5A18C	5A18C	5A18C						F										O				
12100	175	MNRTY NT MY BSNS	5A19F	5A18D	5A18D	5A18D															N	O				
12110	175	UPST PL TR -FAIR	5A19G	5A18E	5A18E	5A18E																O				
12120	175	HELP POOR W MY $	5A19I	5A18F	5A18F	5A18F																O				

ITEM REFERENCE NUMBER	PAGE LOCATION (IN THIS VOLUME)	ITEM DESCRIPTION (ABBREVIATED)	1975	1976	1977	1978	A	B	C	D	E	F	G	H	I	J	K	L	M	N	O	P	Q	R	S
12130	175	-MY PRB OT ND HP	5A19K	5A18G	5A18G	5A18G																O				
12140	175	RB CHNG ETG HABT		5A18H	5A18H	5A18H						F										O				
12150	176	FULLR LVS IF MRY	5A12A	5A18J	5A18J	5A18J				D																
12160	176	ENCRG=INDP DT/SN	5A12B	5A18K	5A18K	5A18K				D																
12170	176	BNG MOTH V FULFL	5A12D	5A18L	5A18L	5A18L				D																
12180	176	FTHR>TIME W CHLD	5A12G	5A18M	5A18M	5A18M				D																
12190	176	HSB MAK IMP DCSN	5A12H	5A18N	5A18N	5A18N				D																
12200	177	CTB TO UNTD FUND	5A20A	5A20A	5A20A	5A20A																O				
12210	177	CTB TO INTL RELF	5A20B	5A20B	5A20B	5A20B																O				
12220	177	CTB TO MNRTY GRP	5A20C	5A20C	5A20C	5A20C															N	O				
12230	177	CTB TO RELGS ORG	5A20D	5A20D	5A20D	5A20D							G									O				
12240	178	CTB TO PLTCL PTY	5A20E	5A20E	5A20E	5A20E								H								O				
12250	178	CTB TO CTZN LBBY	5A20F	5A20F	5A20F	5A20F								H	I							O				
12260	178	CTB TO VS DISEAS	5A20G	5A20G	5A20G	5A20G																O				
12270	178	CTB TO POP PRBMS	5A20H	5A20H	5A20H	5A20H					E											O				
12280	178	CTB TO ENVIR PBM	5A20I	5A20I	5A20I	5A20I						F										O				
12290	179	DSCM WN COLLG ED	5A21A	5A22A	5A22A	5A22A		B		D																
12300	179	DSCM WN LDRSHP	5A21B	5A22B	5A22B	5A22B				D																
12310	179	DSCM WN EXEC/BSN	5A21C	5A22C	5A22C	5A22C			C	D																
12320	179	DSCM WN TOP/PRFN	5A21D	5A22D	5A22D	5A22D			C	D																
12330	179	DSCM WN SKL LABR	5A21E	5A22E	5A22E	5A22E			C	D																
12340	179	DSCM WN PLTCL OF	5A21F	5A22F	5A22F	5A22F				D				H												
12350	180	DSCM WN=PAY=WK	5A21G	5A22G	5A22G	5A22G			C	D																
12360	180	RSK OF CIG1+PK/D	5A41A	5A23A	5A23A	5A23A	A14A																			
12370	180	RSK OF MJ 1-2 X	5A41B	5A23B	5A23B	5A23B	A14A																			
12380	180	RSK OF MJ OCSNLY	5A41C	5A23C	5A23C	5A23C	A14A																			
12390	180	RSK OF MJ REGLY	5A41D	5A23D	5A23D	5A23D	A14A																			
12400	180	RSK OF LSD 1-2 X	5A41E	5A23E	5A23E	5A23E	A14A																			
12410	181	RSK OF LSD REGLY	5A41F	5A23F	5A23F	5A23F	A14A																			
12420	181	RSK OF 'H' 1-2 X	5A41G	5A23G	5A23G	5A23G	A14A																			
12430	181	RSK OF 'H' OCSNL	5A41H	5A23H	5A23H	5A23H	A14A																			
12440	181	RSK OF 'H' REGLY	5A41I	5A23I	5A23I	5A23I	A14A																			
12450	181	RSK OF BARB 1-2X	5A41J	5A23J	5A23J	5A23J	A14A																			
12460	181	RSK OF BARB REGY	5A41K	5A23K	5A23K	5A23K	A14A																			
12470	181	RSK OF AMPH 1-2X	5A41L	5A23L	5A23L	5A23L	A14A																			
12480	182	RSK OF AMPH REG	5A41M	5A23M	5A23M	5A23M	A14A																			
12490	182	RSK OF COKE 1-2X	5A41N	5A23N	5A23N	5A23N	A14A																			
12500	182	RSK OF COKE REG	5A41O	5A23O	5A23O	5A23O	A14A																			
12510	182	RSK OF 1-2 DRINK	5A41P	5A23P	5A23P	5A23P	A14A																			
12520	182	RSK OF 1-2 DR/DA	5A41Q	5A23Q	5A23Q	5A23Q	A14A																			
12530	182	RSK OF 4-5 DR/DA	5A41R	5A23R	5A23R	5A23R	A14A																			
12540	182	RSK OF 5+DR/WKND	5A41S	5A23S	5A23S	5A23S	A14A																			
12550	183	POS ATT TWD SELF	5A39A	5D01A	5D01A	5D01A																		Q		
12560	183	LUCK>IMP HRD WRK	5A39B	5D01B	5D01B	5D01B																		Q		
12570	183	AM PRSN OF WORTH	5A39C	5D01C	5D01C	5D01C																		Q		
12580	183	DO WELL AS OTHRS	5A39D	5D01D	5D01D	5D01D																		Q		
12590	183	TRY GT AHD,STOPD	5A39E	5D01E	5D01E	5D01E																		Q		
12600	183	PLNNG MKS UNHPPY	5A39F	5D01F	5D01F	5D01F																		Q		
12610	184	ACPT LIFE->HAPPR	5A39G	5D01G	5D01G	5D01G																		Q		
12620	184	SATISFD W MYSELF	5A39H	5D01H	5D01H	5D01H																	P	Q		
12630	184	PPL LK ME -CHANC	5A39I	5D01I	5D01I	5D01I																		Q		
12640		MY PLANS DO WORK			5D01J	5D01J																		Q		
12650		OFTN FEEL LONELY			5D01K	5D01K														M				Q		
12660		-MUCH TO B PROUD			5D01L	5D01L																		Q		
12670		ALWYS SM1 HELP R			5D01M	5D01M														M				Q		
12680		I AM NO GOOD			5D01N	5D01N																		Q		
12690		OFTN FL LEFT OUT			5D01O	5D01O														M				Q		
12700		PPL MASTER FATE			5D01P	5D01P																		Q		
12710		USLY SM1 TALK TO			5D01Q	5D01Q														M				Q		
12720		I DO WRONG THING			5D01R	5D01R																		Q		
12730		OFT WSH MOR FRND			5D01S	5D01S														M				Q		
12740		PLANS->BTR RSLTS			5D01T	5D01T																		Q		
12750		MY LIFE NT USEFL			5D01U	5D01U																		Q		
12760		USLY FRDS BE WTH			5D01V	5D01V														M				Q		
12770	187	LV TGTH=BD MRLTY		5D05	5D02	5D02				D																
12780	184	PSN TKG MJ/AMBTS		5D02A			A12D																			

ITEM REFERENCE NUMBER	PAGE LOCATION (IN THIS VOLUME)	ITEM DESCRIPTION (ABBREVIATED)	1975	1976	1977	1978	A	B C D E F G H I J K L M N O P Q R S
12790	184	PSN TKG MJ/-SOCL		5D02B			A12D	
12800	184	PSN TKG MJ/CNFMG		5D02C			A12D	
12810	185	PSN TKG MJ/CRMNL		5D02D			A12D	
12820	185	PSN TKG MJ/-STBL		5D02E			A12D	
12830	185	PSN TKG MJ/INTRS		5D02F			A12D	
12840	185	PSN TKG MJ/RBLS		5D02G			A12D	
12850	185	PSN TKG MJ/SNSBL		5D02H			A12D	
12860	185	PSN TKG MJ/SX PR		5D02I			A12D	
12870	185	PSN TKG MJ/WKWLD		5D02J			A12D	
12880	188	FAM-MAR=BD MRLTY		5D06	5D03	5D03		D
12890	186	PSN TKG DG/AMBTS		5D03A			A12D	
12900	186	PSN TKG DG/-SOCL		5D03B			A12D	
12910	186	PSN TKG DG/CNFMG		5D03C			A12D	
12920	186	PSN TKG DG/CRMNL		5D03D			A12D	
12930	186	PSN TKG DG/-STBL		5D03E			A12D	
12940	186	PSN TKG DG/INTRS		5D03F			A12D	
12950	186	PSN TKG DG/RBLS		5D03G			A12D	
12960	187	PSN TKG DG/SNSBL		5D03H			A12D	
12970	187	PSN TKG DG/SX PR		5D03I			A12D	
12980	187	PSN TKG DG/WKWLD		5D03J			A12D	
12990		I HAVE ENOUGH $			5D04A	5D04A		C
13000		I LACK $ FR BILL			5D04B	5D04B		C
13010		I WRY @-FINDG JOB			5D04C	5D04C		C
13020		I CAN FIND JOB			5D04D	5D04D		C
13030		I CAN KEEP MYJOB			5D04E	5D04E		C
13040		I WRY @LOSS MYJOB			5D04F	5D04F		C
13050	187	R'S STATE LAW/MJ		5D04	5D05	5D05	A13D	
13060		I/MJ USR,>CREATV			5E01A	5E01A	A11D	
13070		I/MJ USR,<SENSBL			5E01B	5E01B	A11D	
13080		I/MJ USR,>INTRST			5E01C	5E01C	A11D	
13090		I/MJ USR,<HRDWKG			5E01D	5E01D	A11D	
13100		I/MJ USR,>INDPND			5E01E	5E01E	A11D	
13110		I/MJ USR,>UNSTBL			5E01F	5E01F	A11D	
13120		I/MJ USR,>CNCRND			5E01G	5E01G	A11D	
13130		I/MJ USR,>WKWLD			5E01H	5E01H	A11D	
13140		I/MJ USR,>CRMNL			5E01I	5E01I	A11D	
13150	188	FAM+REL GD/CHILD		5E01A				D M
13160	188	FAM+REL GD/PARNT		5E01B				D M
13170	188	FAM+REL GD/GRPNT		5E01C				D M
13180	188	FAM+REL,R LIK/PT		5E01D				D M
13190		PPL/MJUSR>CREATV			5E02A	5E02A	A12D	
13200		PPL/MJUSR<SENSBL			5E02B	5E02B	A12D	
13210		PPL/MJUSR>INTRST			5E02C	5E02C	A12D	
13220		PPL/MJUSR<HRDWKG			5E02D	5E02D	A12D	
13230		PPL/MJUSR>INDPND			5E02E	5E02E	A12D	
13240		PPL/MJUSR>UNSTBL			5E02F	5E02F	A12D	
13250		PPL/MJUSR>CNCRND			5E02G	5E02G	A12D	
13260		PPL/MJUSR>WKWLD			5E02H	5E02H	A12D	
13270		PPL/MJUSR>CRMNL			5E02I	5E02I	A12D	
13280	189	FAM+CPL GD/CHILD		5E02A				D
13290	189	FAM+CPL GD/PARNT		5E02B				D
13300	189	FAM+CPL GD/GRPNT		5E02C				D
13310	189	FAM+CPL,LIK/PRNT		5E02D				D
13320	189	FAM+CPL,LIK/-CHD		5E02E				D
13330		I/DG USR,>CREATV			5E03A	5E03A	A11D	
13340		I/DG USR,<SENSBL			5E03B	5E03B	A11D	
13350		I/DG USR,>INTRST			5E03C	5E03C	A11D	
13360		I/DG USR,<HRDWKG			5E03D	5E03D	A11D	
13370		I/DG USR,>INDPND			5E03E	5E03E	A11D	
13380		I/DG USR,>UNSTBL			5E03F	5E03F	A11D	
13390		I/DG USR,>CNCRND			5E03G	5E03G	A11D	
13400		I/DG USR,>WKWLD			5E03H	5E03H	A11D	
13410		I/DG USR,>CRMNL			5E03I	5E03I	A11D	
13420	190	CPL+OTH +CHD MAR		5E03A				D
13430	190	CPL+OTH +CHD DVC		5E03B				D
13440	190	CPL+OTH +MAR CPL		5E03C				D

ITEM REFERENCE NUMBER	PAGE LOCATION (IN THIS VOLUME)	ITEM DESCRIPTION (ABBREVIATED)	QUESTIONNAIRE LOCATION BY YEAR (FORM, SECTION, AND QUESTION NUMBER)				SUBJECT AREA																	
			1975	1976	1977	1978	A	B	C	D	E	F	G	H	I	J	K	L	M	N	O	P	Q	R	S
13450	190	CPL+OTH+DIV PRT		5E03D						D															
13460	190	CPL+OTH+UNMARRD		5E03E						D															
13470	190	CPL+OTH,LK,MR PT		5E03F						D															
13480	191	CPL+OTH,LK,DVC P		5E03G						D															
13490		PPL/DGUSR>CREATV			5E04A	5E04A	A12D																		
13500		PPL/DGUSR<SENSBL			5E04B	5E04B	A12D																		
13510		PPL/DGUSR>INTRST			5E04C	5E04C	A12D																		
13520		PPL/DGUSR<HRDWKG			5E04D	5E04D	A12D																		
13530		PPL/DGUSR>INDPND			5E04E	5E04E	A12D																		
13540		PPL/DGUSR>UNSTBL			5E04F	5E04F	A12D																		
13550		PPL/DGUSR>CNCRND			5E04G	5E04G	A12D																		
13560		PPL/DGUSR>WKWLD			5E04H	5E04H	A12D																		
13570		PPL/DGUSR>CRMNL			5E04I	5E04I	A12D																		
13580	191	STS SCH RT FAMLY		5E05A	5E06A	5E06A		B																R	
13590	191	STS SCH LDS STU		5E05B	5E06B	5E06B		B											M						
13600	191	STS SCH NIC CAR		5E05C	5E06C	5E06C		B				F													
13610	191	STS SCH HI GRDE		5E05D	5E06D	5E06D		B																	
13620	192	STS SCH GD ATHLT		5E05E	5E06E	5E06E		B																	
13630	192	STS SCH INTLCTL		5E05F	5E06F	5E06F		B																	
13640	192	STS SCH PLN CLG		5E05G	5E06G	5E06G		B																	
13650	192	DRG USE+,MAJ STD		5E06A	5E07A	5E07A	A12C																		
13660	192	DRG USE+,MY FRND		5E06B	5E07B	5E07B	A12B																		
13670		DRG USE+,MY FLGS			5E07C	5E07C	A11D																		
08780	193	OFT W PL TK QUAL		5E07D	5E08D	5E08D	A02B																		
08835	194	OFT W PL TK INHL		5E07J	5E08J	5E08J	A02B																		
13700	115	BY SOON HAIR DRY		2E10A								F													
13710	115	BY SOON WT/S SKI		2E10B								F													
13720	115	BY SOON CAMERA		2E10C								F													
13730	115	BY SOON WATCH		2E10D								F													
13740	116	BY SOON HKG BKPK		2E10E								F													
13750	116	BY SOON CK RADIO		2E10F								F													
13760	116	BY SOON EL SHAVR		2E10G								F													
13770	116	BY SOON TENIS RQ		2E10H								F													
13780	116	BY SOON TV SET		2E10I								F													
13790	116	BY SOON BICYCLE		2E10J								F													
13800	116	BY SOON CAR		2E10K								F													
13810	117	BY SOON TAPE REC		2E10L								F													
13820	117	BY SOON ELT CALC		2E10M								F													
13830	117	BY SOON BT/SNMBL		2E10N								F													
13835	139	IMP HAV 1 CAR		3E12A		3E11A						F													
13840	139	IMP HAV 2 CARS		3E12B		3E11B						F													
13850	140	IMP HAV LARG CAR		3E12C		3E11C						F													
13860	140	IMP HAV NW CR OF		3E12D		3E11D						F													
13870	140	IMP HAV NW CLTHS		3E12E		3E11E						F													
13880	140	IMP HAV OWN HSE		3E12F		3E11F						F													
13890	140	IMP HAV BIG YARD		3E12G		3E11G						F													
13900	140	IMP HAV NEAT LWN		3E12H		3E11H						F													
13910	140	IMP HAV APPLINCS		3E12I		3E11I						F													
13920	140	IMP HAV G STEREO		3E12J		3E11J						F													
13930	141	IMP HAV VAC HSE		3E12K		3E11K						F													
13940	141	IMP HAV REC VEH		3E12L		3E11L						F													
16320		EFCTV WRIT OFCLS				2E04A								H	I										
16330		EFCTV WRK PL CPN				2E04B								H	I										
16340		EFCTV VOTING				2E04C								H	I										
16350		EFCTV PETITIONS				2E04D								H	I										
16360		EFCTV BOYCOTT				2E04E								H	I										
16370		EFCTV LWFL DMSTN				2E04F								H	I										
16380		EFCTV OCPY BLDGS				2E04G								H	I										
16390		EFCTV WLDCT STRK				2E04H								H	I										
16400		EFCTV BLK TRAFIC				2E04I								H	I										
16410		EFCTV DAMAG THNG				2E04J								H	I										
16420		EFCTV PSNL VLNC				2E04K								H	I										
16430		SAT EVB CAR POOL				2E05A						F									O				
16440		SAT EAT<BEEF>GRN				2E05B						F									O				
16450		SAT TAX FR ECLGY				2E05C						F													
17860		DESRD LVG RURAL				4E09A						F													

ITEM REFERENCE NUMBER	PAGE LOCATION (IN THIS VOLUME)	ITEM DESCRIPTION (ABBREVIATED)	QUESTIONNAIRE LOCATION BY YEAR (FORM, SECTION, AND QUESTION NUMBER)				SUBJECT AREA	
			1975	1976	1977	1978	A	B C D E F G H I J K L M N O P Q R S
17870		DESRD LVG SM TWN				4E09B		F
17880		DESRD LVG SM CTY				4E09C		F
17890		DESRD LVG SUBURB				4E09D		F
17900		DESRD LVG LG CTY				4E09E		F
17910		DSRD HSG 1 FAMLY				4E09F		F
17920		DSRD HSG 2 FAMLY				4E09G		F
17930		DSRD HSG CNDMINM				4E09H		F
17940		DSRD HSG APT BLD				4E09I		F
17950		DSRD HSG HI RISE				4E09J		F
20590	131	12MO NR OTH MARJ		3A29A	3A29A	3A29A	A02B	
20600	131	12MO NR OTH LSD		3A29B	3A29B	3A29B	A02B	
20610	131	12MO NR OTH PSYC		3A29C	3A29C	3A29C	A02B	
20620	131	12MO NR OTH AMPH		3A29D	3A29D	3A29D	A02B	
20630	132	12MO NR OTH BARB		3A29E	3A29E	3A29E	A02B	
20640	132	12MO NR OTH TRQL		3A29F	3A29F	3A29F	A02B	
20650	132	12MO NR OTH COKE		3A29G	3A29G	3A29G	A02B	
20660	132	12MO NR OTH HRN		3A29H	3A29H	3A29H	A02B	
20670	132	12MO NR OTH NARC		3A29I	3A29I	3A29I	A02B	
20680	132	12MO NR OTH ALCL		3A29J	3A29J	3A29J	A02B	

Appendix A
Sampling Error Estimates and Tables

All of the percentages reported in this volume are really *estimates* of the response percentages that would have been obtained if, instead of using a sample survey, we had asked all high schools throughout the United States to participate, and in all schools that agreed to participate we had invited the whole senior class to fill out the questionnaires. The question naturally arises: How accurate are the present percentage estimates based on a limited number of schools and seniors? For any particular percentage resulting from a sample survey we cannot know exactly how much error has resulted from sampling, but we can make reasonably good estimates of "confidence intervals" — ranges within which the "true" population value is very likely to fall. The word "true" in this context is defined quite narrowly; it refers only to the value that would be found if we had set out to survey the total population — all high school seniors in the United States. Thus this concept of "true" population value does *not* take account of biases that might occur due to refusals, distortion of responses, faulty question wording, and other factors. Each of these sources of possible error is discussed in the "Representativeness and Validity" section of the Introduction to this volume. The reader is urged to review this material and take it into account along with the sampling error estimates included in this appendix.

The estimation of confidence intervals in surveys involving complex samples can be a highly complicated combination of statistical science plus informed judgment. It is an area in which there is no single "right answer" or "best approach." We suspect that many of those using this volume will not be especially interested in *how* we have chosen to solve the problems involved in estimating confidence intervals, so long as we provide guidelines

that can be applied in a fairly simple and straightforward manner. This appendix is designed to accomplish that. Appendix B provides a more extensive discussion of how we obtained the confidence intervals shown here, and it also provides guidelines for computing specific confidence intervals for a wider range of possible applications than can be covered in the tables provided in this appendix.

A very rough example of a confidence interval can be stated in these terms: For percentages based on the total sample (all five questionnaire forms), the "true" values are rarely more than 1.5 percent higher or lower than the percentage estimates reported in this volume. How rarely? The chances are much lower than 1 in 20. Indeed, many of the percentages reported for the total sample are accurate to within one percent.

Of course, most of the data reported here are based on items included only in one or another of the five questionnaire forms. Since such percentages are based on only one-fifth of the total sample, they are somewhat less accurate. The loss in accuracy is less than might be imagined, however, for reasons spelled out in Appendix B. For present purposes, it is enough to say that percentages based on 3,000 or more seniors responding to one questionnaire form are rarely (less than 1 in 20) farther than 2.4 percent away from the "true" value.

We have thus far provided two very rough illustrations of confidence intervals — a range of ±1.5 percent for percentages based on the total sample, and a range of ±2.4 percent for percentages based on the number of seniors responding to one questionnaire form. While these two intervals provide some notion of the overall range of accuracy of the sample, they fall short of our needs in a number of respects. We need to be able to assign confidence intervals for subgroups such as males, females, those who plan to complete college, and so forth, all of which involve smaller numbers of cases and thus some reduction in accuracy. We also need to take account of the fact that, other things equal, confidence intervals grow smaller when one moves from the middle of the scale (percentages near 50 percent) to the extremes (e.g., 4 percent or 96 percent). Further, we need to provide guidelines for evaluating the *difference* between two percentages; for example, we may wish to know whether the difference between male and female percentages in response to a particular question is large enough so that it is not likely to be merely the result of sampling error. Another type of difference of considerable interest is that between percentages from two different years; for example, we may wish to know whether an increase in the percentage of daily marijuana users from one year to the next is large enough to be considered a statistically significant change.

Each of the requirements mentioned above is taken into account in the tables of confidence intervals which follow.

Confidence Intervals for Single Percentages

Table A-1 provides confidence intervals for single percentages that are reasonably good approximations for most *variables* and for most *subgroups* (as well as for the total sample). The table entries slightly underestimate the confidence intervals for regional subgroups and for blacks. These underestimates can be corrected reasonably well by multiplying the entries in Table A-1 by a factor of 1.1 for data based on a single form and by a factor of 1.33 for data based on all five forms. A more serious problem is that the table entries substantially underestimate the confidence intervals for certain variables which tend to be somewhat homogeneous within schools, as well as other factors likely to show clustering according to geographical area or socioeconomic level. A discussion of some of these variables is provided at the end of this appendix.

Table A-1 accommodates various numbers of cases (presented as different columns in the table), and various percentages (presented as different rows in the table). The table entries, when added to and subtracted from the observed percentage, establish the 95 percent confidence interval (calculated as 1.96 sampling errors). Thus, for example, to determine the accuracy of a result of 67.4 percent based on a sample of 1,632 cases, one should first look for the closest values in the table (in this case, about 70 percent and a number of cases approximately equal to 1,500); next determine the values to be added to and subtracted from

the observed percentage (in this case the values would be +2.8 percent and -2.9 percent); and then compute the confidence interval around the observed percentage of 67.4 percent (in this case an interval ranging from 64.5 percent to 70.2 percent). This procedure yields an interval such that, for most variables, the chances are 95 in 100 that if all high school seniors in the country had been asked to participate in the survey the resulting percentage would fall within the interval.

Confidence Intervals for Differences between Two Percentages

Table A-2 provides confidence intervals for differences between certain percentages. Specifically, the table can be used for *comparisons* between males and females, between those who do and do not plan to complete four years of college, and between those falling into different categories of the five-level index of drug usage. The above comparisons are appropriate for data from any single year (e.g., male seniors in 1976 compared with female seniors in 1976, or the "marijuana only" seniors in 1977 compared with the "no illicit drugs" seniors in 1977). Table A-2 is also useful in assessing *one-year* trends for any of the above subgroups as well as for the total sample. For example, one may be interested in a confidence interval (or significance level) for the difference between the percentage of female seniors in 1977 who used marijuana and the percentage of female seniors in 1978 who did so. The values in Table A-2 are appropriate for confidence intervals across adjacent years (e.g., 1976 compared with 1977), provided the same subgroup (e.g., females) is being considered both years. The confidence intervals for comparisons across non-adjacent years (e.g., 1976 compared with 1978), are slightly larger.

With appropriate corrections, the entries in Table A-2 can be used for trends covering more than one year and for trends or comparisons involving regional subgroups and blacks. Each of these applications requires some upward adjustment of the table entries; guidelines for such adjustments are provided in the notes accompanying Table A-2.

For information on the derivation of Table A-2 and for guidelines to be used in computing confidence intervals not covered in that table, the reader is referred to Appendix B.

In order to find the appropriate confidence interval in Table A-2, one must first locate that portion of the table which deals with percentage values closest to the two percentages being compared (for example, if one wished to compare a value of 28.1 percent with one of 35.4 percent, the "p = 30 percent or 70 percent" portion of the table would be closest). The next step is to locate the specific table entry which corresponds most closely to the numbers of cases involved in the two percentages being compared (e.g., if those numbers were 1,478 and 1,563 for 28.1 percent and 35.4 percent, the correct table entry would be 3.9 percent). That table entry, when added to and subtracted from the difference between the two percentages, yields the 95 percent confidence interval for the difference. (In the above illustration that would be 7.3 percent ±3.9 percent or an interval from 3.4 percent to 11.2 percent.) The chances are only 1 in 20 that the "true" difference between two percentages lies outside of this interval.

Another use of Table A-2 is to test whether a difference between two percentages is "statistically significant." If the table entry is smaller than the difference between the two percentages (as is true in the above illustration), then the difference is statistically significant at the 95 percent level (sometimes indicated as p<.05).

Some Cautions

The tables provided here are based on averages of large numbers of sampling errors computed across a wide range of the variables which appear in this volume, as well as across all of the subgroups for which data are reported here. We are confident that the values in the tables are reasonably accurate for most purposes, but we must repeat the caution that the tables slightly underestimate confidence intervals for the following groups and comparisons:

Blacks
Regions (Northeast, North Central, South, West)
Comparisons among regions
Comparisons across non-adjacent years (e.g., 1976 vs. 1978)

A more important problem is that the tables substantially underestimate the confidence intervals for certain variables that, for various reasons, show greater than average homogeneity within schools. After an extensive, but by no means exhaustive, sampling of the kinds of variables which might show such clustering by school, we can provide the following examples of the kinds of variables for which Tables A-1 and A-2 substantially underestimate the confidence intervals.

Variables Related to Educational Background and Aspirations. The questionnaire items dealing with father's education, mother's education, high school curriculum (college preparatory versus all other), and plans for completing four years of col-

lege, all show an appreciable amount of clustering by school. Accordingly, for such variables the confidence intervals provided in the tables should be doubled.

Other items dealing with plans for technical/vocational schooling, a two-year college program, or graduate/professional study, also require adjustment. The confidence intervals in the tables should be multiplied by a factor of 1.5 in order to be applicable to these variables.

It seems clear that the common factor underlying these particular variables is the tendency for family socioeconomic level to be somewhat homogeneous within school districts — some schools serve wealthier populations than others. That makes the form of sampling we use somewhat less efficient for measuring those variables (like those listed above) which are closely associated with family socioeconomic level. Therefore, we urge the reader to treat with caution any variables which are likely to be strongly linked to socioeconomic factors. In the absence of more specific computations of sampling errors, a good rule of thumb for dealing with such variables would be to double the confidence intervals provided in Tables A-1 and A-2.

Variables Related to Geographic Location. Another category of variables which are somewhat homogeneous within schools and school districts consists of those things which reflect differences in region and/or urbanicity. An obvious example is a background question asking where the respondent grew up; the response category "on a farm" shows a very high degree of clustering within schools. One would have to more than double the confidence intervals in the tables to deal with such a measure. Similarly high clustering was found for some responses about religious preference; for example, those whose preference is Baptist are located primarily in the South (and probably heavily in rural areas), whereas those whose preference is Jewish are located primarily in the Northeast (especially in larger cities). The confidence intervals in Tables A-1 and A-2 should be multiplied by a factor as large as 3 in order to be applicable to such variables.

Other variables which show some greater than average homogeneity within schools include such ideologically related dimensions as frequency of attending religious services, importance of religion, and political preference. Still other variables showing high homogeneity, probably because of their association with urbanicity, include driving (percentage who usually do not drive at all), working (percentage with no job), and household composition (percentage with father not living in the home). For each of the variables mentioned in this paragraph, the confidence intervals shown in Tables A-1 and A-2 should be multipled by a factor of about 1.5.

Variables Involving Use of Alcohol and Marijuana. Extensive work has been done to compute sampling errors and confidence intervals for the drug use measures included in this volume (see Johnston, Bachman, and O'Malley, 1977, 1979, especially Appendix B). Most drug use variables show sampling errors which lie within the range of those provided in Tables A-1 and A-2. Usage levels for alcohol and marijuana, however, show some

degree of homogeneity within schools, thus requiring that the table levels be adjusted. For items dealing with alcohol use, the table entries should be multiplied by a factor of 1.6; for items dealing with marijuana use, the correction factor is 1.35.

As noted earlier, this appendix has presented guidelines for using the tables of confidence intervals provided herein. Those readers interested in learning more about the rationale underlying such tables, the procedures used to derive the particular tables presented here, and guidelines for further computations of confidence intervals may consult Appendix B of this volume.

Notes to Table A-1

Caution: The entries in this table systematically underestimate confidence intervals for regional subgroups and for blacks. In order to correct these underestimates, the table entries should be multiplied by a factor of 1.10 for data from a single form and by a factor of 1.33 for data based on five forms. Further cautions and corrections are required for some specific variables which relate to educational background and aspirations, geographic location,

and the use of alcohol and marijuana (see discussion in the final sections of Appendix A).

The values in this table, when added to and subtracted from an observed percentage, establish the 95 percent confidence interval around that percentage, incorporating a design effect. Table values were calculated using the following formula (adapted from Hays, 1973, p. 379):

$$\text{lower limit} = p - \frac{2N'p + (1.96)^2 - 1.96\sqrt{4N'p(1-p) + (1.96)^2}}{2[N' + (1.96)^2]}$$

$$\text{upper limit} = \frac{2N'p + (1.96)^2 + 1.96\sqrt{4N'p(1-p) + (1.96)^2}}{2[N' + (1.96)^2]} - p$$

where p = the percentage, and N' is the "effective N," $N' = N/(1.3 + .00015N)$. (See Appendix B for a discussion of the concept of "effective N.")

Table A-1

Confidence Intervals (95% Level) around Percentage Values

Number of Cases

	100	200	300	400	500	700	1000	1500	2000	2500	3000	3500	4000	5000	7000	10000	15000	20000
99% +	0.9	0.8	0.7	0.7	0.6	0.6	0.5	0.5	0.4	0.4	0.4	0.4	0.3	0.3	0.3	0.3	0.3	0.2
−	5.6	3.2	2.4	1.9	1.7	1.3	1.1	0.8	0.7	0.6	0.6	0.6	0.5	0.5	0.4	0.4	0.3	0.3
97% +	2.1	1.8	1.6	1.4	1.3	1.2	1.0	0.9	0.8	0.8	0.7	0.7	0.6	0.6	0.6	0.5	0.5	0.5
−	6.6	4.1	3.2	2.6	2.3	1.9	1.6	1.3	1.1	1.0	0.9	0.9	0.8	0.8	0.7	0.6	0.6	0.5
95% +	3.1	2.5	2.2	2.0	1.8	1.6	1.4	1.2	1.1	1.0	0.9	0.9	0.9	0.8	0.7	0.7	0.6	0.6
−	7.4	4.7	3.7	3.1	2.7	2.3	1.9	1.5	1.4	1.2	1.1	1.1	1.0	0.9	0.8	0.8	0.7	0.7
90% +	4.9	3.8	3.3	2.9	2.7	2.3	2.0	1.7	1.5	1.4	1.3	1.3	1.2	1.1	1.0	0.9	0.9	0.8
−	8.8	5.8	4.6	4.0	3.5	2.9	2.5	2.0	1.8	1.6	1.5	1.4	1.4	1.3	1.1	1.0	0.9	0.9
85% +	6.6	4.8	4.1	3.6	3.3	2.9	2.5	2.1	1.9	1.7	1.6	1.5	1.5	1.4	1.2	1.1	1.0	1.0
−	9.7	6.6	5.3	4.5	4.0	3.4	2.9	2.4	2.1	1.9	1.8	1.7	1.6	1.5	1.3	1.2	1.1	1.1
80% +	7.4	5.6	4.7	4.2	3.8	3.3	2.8	2.4	2.1	2.0	1.8	1.7	1.7	1.5	1.4	1.3	1.2	1.1
−	10.3	7.1	5.7	4.9	4.4	3.7	3.1	2.6	2.3	2.1	2.0	1.8	1.8	1.6	1.5	1.3	1.2	1.2
70% +	9.1	6.8	5.6	5.0	4.5	3.9	3.3	2.8	2.5	2.3	2.1	2.0	1.9	1.8	1.6	1.5	1.4	1.3
−	11.1	7.7	6.3	5.5	4.9	4.2	3.5	2.9	2.6	2.4	2.2	2.1	2.0	1.8	1.7	1.5	1.4	1.3
50% +	11.0	7.9	6.5	5.7	5.1	4.4	3.7	3.1	2.8	2.5	2.4	2.2	2.1	2.0	1.8	1.6	1.5	1.4
−	11.0	7.9	6.5	5.7	5.1	4.4	3.7	3.1	2.8	2.5	2.4	2.2	2.1	2.0	1.8	1.6	1.5	1.4
30% +	11.1	7.7	6.3	5.5	4.9	4.2	3.5	2.9	2.6	2.4	2.2	2.1	2.0	1.8	1.7	1.5	1.4	1.3
−	9.1	6.8	5.6	5.0	4.5	3.9	3.3	2.8	2.5	2.3	2.1	2.0	1.9	1.8	1.6	1.5	1.4	1.3
20% +	10.3	7.1	5.7	4.9	4.4	3.7	3.1	2.6	2.3	2.1	2.0	1.8	1.8	1.6	1.5	1.3	1.2	1.2
−	7.4	5.6	4.7	4.2	3.8	3.3	2.8	2.4	2.1	2.0	1.6	1.7	1.7	1.5	1.4	1.3	1.2	1.1
15% +	9.7	6.6	5.3	4.5	4.0	3.4	2.9	2.4	2.1	1.9	1.8	1.7	1.6	1.5	1.3	1.2	1.1	1.1
−	6.3	4.8	4.1	3.6	3.3	2.9	2.5	2.1	1.9	1.7	1.6	1.5	1.5	1.4	1.2	1.1	1.0	1.0
10% +	8.8	5.8	4.6	4.0	3.5	2.9	2.5	2.0	1.8	1.6	1.5	1.4	1.4	1.3	1.1	1.0	0.9	0.9
−	4.9	3.8	3.3	2.9	2.7	2.3	2.0	1.7	1.5	1.4	1.3	1.3	1.2	1.1	1.0	0.9	0.9	0.8
5% +	7.4	4.7	3.7	3.1	2.7	2.3	1.9	1.5	1.4	1.2	1.1	1.1	1.0	0.9	0.8	0.8	0.7	0.7
−	3.1	2.5	2.2	2.0	1.8	1.6	1.4	1.2	1.1	1.0	0.9	0.9	0.9	0.8	0.7	0.7	0.6	0.6
3% +	6.6	4.1	3.2	2.6	2.3	1.9	1.6	1.3	1.1	1.0	0.9	0.9	0.8	0.8	0.7	0.6	0.6	0.5
−	2.1	1.8	1.6	1.4	1.3	1.2	1.0	0.9	0.8	0.8	0.7	0.7	0.6	0.6	0.6	0.5	0.5	0.5
1% +	5.6	3.2	2.4	1.9	1.7	1.3	1.1	0.8	0.7	0.6	0.6	0.6	0.5	0.5	0.4	0.4	0.3	0.3
−	0.9	0.8	0.7	0.7	0.6	0.6	0.5	0.5	0.4	0.4	0.4	0.4	0.3	0.3	0.3	0.3	0.3	0.2

Notes to Table A-2

The entries in this table (which appear on the next two pages) are appropriate for *comparisons* between (a) males and females, (b) those who do and do not plan four years of college, and (c) those falling into different categories of the five-level index of drug usage. The table entries are also appropriate for *one-year trends* for the total sample and any of the subgroups except region. Most other trends and subgroup comparisons require that the table entries be multiplied by an adjustment factor, given below.

Outline of Steps to Follow (see text of appendix for illustrations)

1. Locate the portion of the table with "p" values closest to the two percentages being compared.

2. Locate the specific entry closest to the weighted Ns for the two percentages.

3. Multiply that entry by any necessary adjustment factor (see below).

4. That table value (or adjusted table value), when added to and subtracted from the difference between the two percentages, yields the 95 percent confidence interval for the difference.

5. Also, if the table value (or adjusted table value) is smaller than the difference between the two percentages, then the difference may be described as "statistically significant at the 95 percent level."

	Adjustment Factor (to be multiplied by table entry)
Adjustment Factors	
For comparisons between blacks and whites	
based on single form data	*
based on five form data	1.25
For comparisons between any two regions	
based on single form data	1.15
based on five form data	1.50
For one-year trends involving any region	
based on single form data	*
based on five form data	1.25
For trends over two or more years involving any region	
based on single form data	*
based on five form data	1.35
For trends over two or more years involving all other groups	
based on single form data	*
based on five form data	1.15

*indicates that no adjustment is necessary for category shown

NOTE: The table entries were calculated using the following formula: $1.96\sqrt{p(1-p)\ \dfrac{1}{N'_1} + \dfrac{1}{N'_2}}$

where $N'_1 = N_1/DEFF$, and $N'_2 = N_2/DEFF$, $DEFF = 1.3 + .000075\left[\dfrac{N_1 N_2}{N_1 + N_2}\right]$

Table A-2

Confidence Intervals (95% Confidence Level) for Differences Between Two Percentages

	$N_1=100$	200	300	400	500	700	1000	1500	2000	3000	4000	5000	7000	10000	15000	20000
$N_2=100$	3.2															
200	2.7	2.2														
300	2.6	2.0	1.8													
400	2.5	1.9	1.7	1.6												
500	2.4	1.9	1.6	1.5	1.4											
700	2.4	1.8	1.6	1.4	1.3	1.2										
1000	2.3	1.7	1.5	1.3	1.2	1.1	1.0									
1500	2.3	1.7	1.4	1.3	1.2	1.0	0.9	0.8								
2000	2.3	1.7	1.4	1.2	1.1	1.0	0.9	0.8	0.7							
3000	2.3	1.6	1.4	1.2	1.1	1.0	0.8	0.7	0.7	0.6						
4000	2.3	1.6	1.4	1.2	1.1	0.9	0.8	0.7	0.7	0.6	0.6					
5000	2.3	1.6	1.3	1.2	1.1	0.9	0.8	0.7	0.6	0.6	0.5	0.5				
7000	2.3	1.6	1.3	1.2	1.1	0.9	0.8	0.7	0.6	0.5	0.5	0.5	0.4			
10000	2.2	1.6	1.3	1.2	1.0	0.9	0.8	0.7	0.6	0.5	0.5	0.5	0.4	0.4		
15000	2.2	1.6	1.3	1.2	1.0	0.9	0.8	0.6	0.6	0.5	0.5	0.4	0.4	0.4	0.4	
20000	2.2	1.6	1.3	1.1	1.0	0.9	0.8	0.6	0.6	0.5	0.5	0.4	0.4	0.4	0.3	0.3

p = 1% or 99%

	$N_1=100$	200	300	400	500	700	1000	1500	2000	3000	4000	5000	7000	10000	15000	20000
$N_2=100$	5.4															
200	4.7	3.8														
300	4.4	3.5	3.1													
400	4.3	3.3	2.9	2.7												
500	4.2	3.2	2.8	2.6	2.4											
700	4.1	3.1	2.7	2.4	2.3	2.1										
1000	4.0	3.0	2.5	2.3	2.1	1.9	1.8									
1500	4.0	2.9	2.4	2.2	2.0	1.8	1.6	1.5								
2000	3.9	2.9	2.4	2.1	1.9	1.7	1.5	1.4	1.3							
3000	3.9	2.8	2.3	2.1	1.9	1.7	1.5	1.3	1.2	1.1						
4000	3.9	2.8	2.3	2.0	1.9	1.6	1.4	1.2	1.1	1.0	0.9					
5000	3.9	2.8	2.3	2.0	1.8	1.6	1.4	1.2	1.1	1.0	0.9	0.9				
7000	3.9	2.8	2.3	2.0	1.8	1.6	1.4	1.2	1.0	0.9	0.9	0.8	0.8			
10000	3.9	2.8	2.3	2.0	1.8	1.5	1.3	1.1	1.0	0.9	0.8	0.8	0.7	0.7		
15000	3.8	2.7	2.3	2.0	1.8	1.5	1.3	1.1	1.0	0.9	0.8	0.7	0.7	0.6	0.6	
20000	3.8	2.7	2.3	2.0	1.8	1.5	1.3	1.1	1.0	0.9	0.8	0.7	0.7	0.6	0.6	0.6

p = 3% or 97%

Table A-2 (continued)

$N_1 =$	100	200	300	400	500	700	1000	1500	2000	3000	4000	5000	7000	10000	15000	20000
$N_2 = 100$	6.9															
200	6.0	4.9														
300	5.6	4.5	4.0													
400	5.5	4.3	3.8	3.5												
500	5.4	4.1	3.6	3.3	3.1											
700	5.2	3.9	3.4	3.1	2.9	2.7										
1000	5.1	3.8	3.2	2.9	2.7	2.5	2.2									
1500	5.1	3.7	3.1	2.8	2.6	2.3	2.1	1.9								
2000	5.0	3.6	3.1	2.7	2.5	2.2	2.0	1.7	1.6							
3000	5.0	3.6	3.0	2.6	2.4	2.1	1.9	1.6	1.5	1.4						
4000	5.0	3.6	3.0	2.6	2.4	2.1	1.8	1.6	1.4	1.3	1.2					
5000	4.9	3.6	2.9	2.6	2.3	2.0	1.8	1.5	1.4	1.2	1.2	1.1				
7000	4.9	3.5	2.9	2.6	2.3	2.0	1.7	1.5	1.3	1.2	1.1	1.0	1.0			
10000	4.9	3.5	2.9	2.5	2.3	2.0	1.7	1.4	1.3	1.1	1.1	1.0	0.9	0.9		
15000	4.9	3.5	2.9	2.5	2.3	2.0	1.7	1.4	1.3	1.1	1.0	1.0	0.9	0.8	0.8	
20000	4.9	3.5	2.9	2.5	2.3	1.9	1.7	1.4	1.3	1.1	1.0	0.9	0.9	0.8	0.7	0.7

p = 5% or 95%

$N_1 =$	100	200	300	400	500	700	1000	1500	2000	3000	4000	5000	7000	10000	15000	20000
$N_2 = 100$	9.5															
200	8.2	6.7														
300	7.8	6.2	5.5													
400	7.5	5.9	5.2	4.8												
500	7.4	5.7	4.9	4.6	4.3											
700	7.2	5.4	4.7	4.3	4.0	3.7										
1000	7.1	5.2	4.5	4.0	3.7	3.4	3.1									
1500	7.0	5.1	4.3	3.8	3.5	3.2	2.8	2.6								
2000	6.9	5.0	4.2	3.7	3.4	3.0	2.7	2.4	2.2							
3000	6.9	4.9	4.1	3.6	3.3	2.9	2.6	2.2	2.1	1.9						
4000	6.8	4.9	4.1	3.6	3.3	2.8	2.5	2.2	2.0	1.8	1.7					
5000	6.8	4.9	4.0	3.6	3.2	2.8	2.4	2.1	1.9	1.7	1.6	1.5				
7000	6.8	4.9	4.0	3.5	3.2	2.8	2.4	2.0	1.8	1.6	1.5	1.4	1.3			
10000	6.8	4.8	4.0	3.5	3.2	2.7	2.3	2.0	1.8	1.6	1.4	1.4	1.3	1.2		
15000	6.8	4.8	4.0	3.5	3.1	2.7	2.3	2.0	1.8	1.5	1.4	1.3	1.2	1.1	1.1	
20000	6.8	4.8	4.0	3.5	3.1	2.7	2.3	1.9	1.7	1.5	1.4	1.3	1.2	1.1	1.0	1.0

p = 10% or 90%

Table A-2 (continued)

$N_1 =$	100	200	300	400	500	700	1000	1500	2000	3000	4000	5000	7000	10000	15000	20000
$N_2 = 100$	11.3															
200	9.8	8.0														
300	9.3	7.3	6.6													
400	9.0	7.0	6.2	5.7												
500	8.8	6.7	5.9	5.4	5.1											
700	8.6	6.5	5.6	5.1	4.8	4.4										
1000	8.4	6.2	5.3	4.8	4.5	4.0	3.7									
1500	8.3	6.1	5.1	4.6	4.2	3.8	3.4	3.0								
2000	8.2	6.0	5.0	4.5	4.1	3.6	3.2	2.9	2.7							
3000	8.2	5.9	4.9	4.3	3.9	3.5	3.0	2.7	2.5	2.2						
4000	8.1	5.8	4.9	4.3	3.9	3.4	2.9	2.6	2.3	2.1	2.0					
5000	8.1	5.8	4.8	4.2	3.8	3.3	2.9	2.5	2.3	2.0	1.9	1.8				
7000	8.1	5.8	4.8	4.2	3.8	3.3	2.8	2.4	2.2	1.9	1.8	1.7	1.6			
10000	8.1	5.8	4.8	4.2	3.8	3.2	2.8	2.4	2.1	1.9	1.7	1.6	1.5	1.4		
15000	8.1	5.7	4.7	4.1	3.7	3.2	2.7	2.3	2.1	1.8	1.7	1.6	1.4	1.3	1.3	
20000	8.0	5.7	4.7	4.1	3.7	3.2	2.7	2.3	2.1	1.8	1.6	1.5	1.4	1.3	1.2	1.2

$p = 15\%$ or 85%

$N_1 =$	100	200	300	400	500	700	1000	1500	2000	3000	4000	5000	7000	10000	15000	20000
$N_2 = 100$	12.7															
200	11.0	9.0														
300	10.4	8.2	7.4													
400	10.0	7.8	6.9	6.4												
500	9.8	7.5	6.6	6.1	5.7											
700	9.6	7.2	6.2	5.7	5.3	4.9										
1000	9.4	7.0	6.0	5.4	5.0	4.5	4.1									
1500	9.3	6.8	5.7	5.1	4.7	4.2	3.8	3.4								
2000	9.2	6.7	5.6	5.0	4.6	4.0	3.6	3.2	3.0							
3000	9.1	6.6	5.5	4.9	4.4	3.9	3.4	3.0	2.8	2.5						
4000	9.1	6.5	5.4	4.8	4.3	3.8	3.3	2.9	2.6	2.4	2.2					
5000	9.1	6.5	5.4	4.7	4.3	3.7	3.2	2.8	2.6	2.3	2.1	2.0				
7000	9.1	6.5	5.4	4.7	4.2	3.7	3.2	2.7	2.5	2.2	2.0	1.9	1.8			
10000	9.0	6.5	5.3	4.7	4.2	3.6	3.1	2.7	2.4	2.1	1.9	1.8	1.7	1.6		
15000	9.0	6.4	5.3	4.6	4.2	3.6	3.1	2.6	2.3	2.0	1.9	1.7	1.6	1.5	1.4	
20000	9.0	6.4	5.3	4.6	4.2	3.6	3.1	2.6	2.3	2.0	1.8	1.7	1.6	1.5	1.4	1.3

$p = 20\%$ or 80%

Table A-2 (continued)

p = 30% or 70%

N_1=	100	200	300	400	500	700	1000	1500	2000	3000	4000	5000	7000	10000	15000	20000
N_2= 100	14.5															
200	12.6	10.3														
300	11.9	9.4	8.4													
400	11.5	8.9	7.9	7.3												
500	11.3	8.6	7.6	7.0	6.6											
700	11.0	8.3	7.2	6.5	6.1	5.6										
1000	10.8	8.0	6.8	6.2	5.7	5.2	4.7									
1500	10.6	7.8	6.6	5.9	5.4	4.8	4.3	3.9								
2000	10.6	7.7	6.4	5.7	5.2	4.6	4.1	3.7	3.4							
3000	10.5	7.6	6.3	5.6	5.1	4.4	3.9	3.4	3.2	2.9						
4000	10.4	7.5	6.2	5.5	5.0	4.3	3.8	3.3	3.0	2.7	2.5					
5000	10.4	7.5	6.2	5.4	4.9	4.3	3.7	3.2	2.9	2.6	2.4	2.3				
7000	10.4	7.4	6.1	5.4	4.9	4.2	3.6	3.1	2.8	2.5	2.3	2.2	2.1			
10000	10.4	7.4	6.1	5.3	4.8	4.2	3.6	3.0	2.7	2.4	2.2	2.1	1.9	1.8		
15000	10.3	7.4	6.1	5.3	4.8	4.1	3.5	3.0	2.7	2.3	2.1	2.0	1.8	1.7	1.6	
20000	10.3	7.4	6.1	5.3	4.8	4.1	3.5	3.0	2.6	2.3	2.1	2.0	1.8	1.7	1.6	1.5

p = 35% to 65%

N_1=	100	200	300	400	500	700	1000	1500	2000	3000	4000	5000	7000	10000	15000	20000
N_2= 100	15.8															
200	13.7	11.2														
300	13.0	10.3	9.2													
400	12.6	9.8	8.6	8.0												
500	12.3	9.4	8.2	7.6	7.2											
700	12.0	9.0	7.8	7.1	6.7	6.1										
1000	11.8	8.7	7.5	6.7	6.2	5.6	5.1									
1500	11.6	8.5	7.2	6.4	5.9	5.3	4.7	4.3								
2000	11.5	8.4	7.0	6.2	5.7	5.1	4.5	4.0	3.7							
3000	11.4	8.2	6.9	6.1	5.5	4.8	4.3	3.7	3.4	3.1						
4000	11.4	8.2	6.8	6.0	5.4	4.7	4.1	3.6	3.3	3.0	2.8					
5000	11.3	8.1	6.7	5.9	5.4	4.7	4.1	3.5	3.2	2.8	2.7	2.5				
7000	11.3	8.1	6.7	5.9	5.3	4.6	4.0	3.4	3.1	2.7	2.5	2.4	2.2			
10000	11.3	8.1	6.7	5.8	5.3	4.5	3.9	3.3	3.0	2.6	2.4	2.3	2.1	2.0		
15000	11.3	8.0	6.6	5.8	5.2	4.5	3.8	3.3	2.9	2.5	2.3	2.2	2.0	1.9	1.8	
20000	11.3	8.0	6.6	5.8	5.2	4.5	3.8	3.2	2.9	2.5	2.3	2.1	2.0	1.8	1.7	1.6

Appendix B
Procedures Used to Derive Design Effects and Sampling Errors

Appendix A provided a very brief and relatively nontechnical explanation of sampling error estimates, accompanied by two tables of confidence intervals which can be used to ascertain the accuracy of most percentages reported in this volume. The present appendix is intended to provide some background concerning the strategy and rationale involved in computing these confidence intervals. It also offers guidance for those wishing to make sampling computations beyond those contained in Appendix A.

This appendix, like the first, is intended to be readable and usable by the nonstatistician. For that reason, we take the time to outline (albeit briefly) a number of relatively elementary factors involved in estimating confidence intervals.

Factors Influencing the Size of Confidence Intervals

The most straightforward types of samples, from a statistical standpoint at least, are simple random samples. In such samples the confidence limits for a proportion are influenced by the size of the sample or subgroups being considered and also by the size of the proportion. For example, the 95 percent confidence interval for a proportion p based on a simple random sample of N cases is approximated by: $p \pm 1.96 \sqrt{p(1-p)/N}$. In a complex probability sample such as the present one, there are a number of other factors which influence the size of confidence limits. This section lists all of the factors which have been taken into account in calculating confidence intervals for use with the data in this volume, beginning with the most simple factors and then proceeding to the more complex.

Number of Cases (N). Other things equal, the larger a sample (or subgroup within a sample), the smaller or more precise will be the confidence interval for a percentage based on that sample. One of the factors determining the size of the confidence interval is $1/\sqrt{N}$. Thus, for example, if all other things were equal, a sample of 400 would have confidence intervals half as large (or twice as precise) as a sample of 100, because $1/\sqrt{400}$ is half as large as $1/\sqrt{100}$.

Size of Percentage. Other things equal, percentage values around 50 percent have larger confidence intervals than higher or lower percentage values. This is because another of the factors determining the size of the confidence interval is $\sqrt{p(1-p)}$ where p is a proportion ranging from 0 to 1.0 (or, to put it in percentage terms, the factor is $\sqrt{x\%(100-x\%)}$). Thus, for example, a proportion of either .1 or .9 (a percentage of either 10 percent or 90 percent) will have a confidence interval only three-fifths as large as the confidence interval around a proportion of .5 (or 50 percent), because $\sqrt{.1(1-.1)}$ is three-fifths as large as $\sqrt{.5(1-.5)}$.

Design Effects in Complex Samples. Under conditions of simple random sampling, a confidence interval can be determined solely on the basis of the number of cases and the percentage value involved. More complex samples such as the one used in the present study make use of stratification and clustering and often differential weighting of respondent scores, and these all influence sampling error. While stratification tends to heighten the precision of a sample, the effects of clustering and weighting reduce precision (compared with a simple random sample of the same size). Therefore, it is not appropriate to apply the standard, simple random sampling formulas to such complex samples in order to obtain estimates of sampling errors, because they would almost always underestimate the actual sampling errors.

Methods exist for correcting for this underestimation, however. Kish (1965, p. 258) defines a correction term called the design effect (DEFF), where:

$$\text{DEFF} = \frac{\text{actual sampling variance}}{\begin{array}{c}\text{expected sampling variance}\\\text{from a simple random sample}\\\text{with same number of elements}\end{array}}$$

Thus, if the actual sampling variance in a complex sample is four times as large as the expected sampling variance from a simple random sample with the same number of cases, the DEFF is 4.0. Since confidence intervals are proportionate to the square root of variance, the confidence intervals for such a sample would be twice as large (because the square root of 4 is 2) as the confidence interval for a simple random sample with the same number of cases. A fairly simple and straightforward way of applying the concept of design effect may be to note that an increase in design effect has the same impact on precision as a reduction in the number of cases in a simple random sample. For example, a sample of 16,000 cases with a design effect of 4.0 would have the same degree of precision (the same size confidence intervals around various percentages) as a simple random sample of 4,000.

In principle, every different statistic resulting from a complex sample can have its own design effect, and different statistics in the same sample may have quite different design effects. However, it is not feasible to compute every design effect, nor would it be feasible to report every one. Thus, in practice, design effects are averaged across a number of statistics and these average values are used to estimate the design effects for other statistics based on the same sample. Sometimes a single design effect is applied to all statistics of a given type (e.g., percentages) for a given sample. In the present study, however, a rather extensive exploration of design effects revealed a number of systematic differences. These systematic differences have to do with the particular measures being examined, the subgroups involved, and the question of whether a trend over time is being considered. The most consistent difference involves the number of cases in the group or subgroup for which the design effect is computed.

The Relationship between Subgroup Size and Design Effects. Kish et al. (1976) have observed that design effects tend to be smaller for subgroups than for total samples; moreover, the smaller the subgroup the smaller the design effect is likely to be. The explanation for this widespread phenomenon is that the average number of cases in each sampling cluster is an important factor in determining the size of the design effect, and as subgroup size decreases so does this average number of cases per cluster. This point is illustrated by several subgroups treated in the present volume — males, females, those planning four years of college, and those not planning four years of college. All (or virtually all) of the schools in the sample have both male and female students, as well as some students who plan four years of college and others who do not. Thus, each of these four subgroups is spread more or less evenly across the full number of clusters (schools). Since each of these subgroups includes roughly half of the total sample, the average number of cases per cluster is about half as large as for the total sample, and this leads to a smaller design effect than is found for the total sample. Other subgroups involving different patterns of drug use are also distributed more or less evenly across all clusters and thus are subject to the same phenomenon of smaller design effects because of the smaller number of cases per cluster.

One very important exception to the pattern of smaller design effects for subgroups involves the four geographic region subgroups presented in this volume. These subgroups do not cut across all clusters; instead, regions have been described as "segregated" subgroups, in contrast to the "cross-class" subgroups discussed above. For such segregated subgroups the average number of cases per cluster is about the same as is found in the total sample, and thus the design effects are not lower than those for the total sample (Kish et al., 1976). Another subgroup which is in some respects similar to regional subgroups is the category of blacks. Black respondents are not found equally across high schools throughout the United States. There are, of course, regional differences in proportions of blacks, and these contribute substantially to this lack of equal distribution. In addition, there are patterns of segregation in housing which continue to be reflected in the unequal distribution of blacks in high schools. The net effect of these several factors is that the black subgroup in our sample is "partially segregated" in a sampling sense as well as in the more usual usage of that word. For that reason, the design effects for blacks are somewhat larger than for other subgroups of approximately similar size.

Because the subgroups consisting of blacks and the four regional groups all have larger design effects than other subgroups of the same size, it is necessary to adjust the confidence intervals for these subgroups as indicated in Appendix A. (At a later point in the present appendix we will say more about these adjustment factors.)

One other kind of "subgroup" must be noted in this discussion of the relationship beteen subgroup size and design effects. One-fifth of the total sample filled out each of the five separate questionnaire forms, and thus the respondents to each of these forms may be viewed as a "cross-class" subgroup of the total sample. The average cluster size for a single form is exactly 20 percent of the average cluster size for the total sample. That means, of course, that the single form samples (which are the basis for the large majority of the data presented in this volume) are distinctly more "efficient" than the sample based on all five forms. Accordingly, single form data have much smaller design effects (as displayed later in this appendix).

Design Effects for Comparisons between Subgroups. We noted above that a number of subgroups treated in this volume can be described as "cross-class" subgroups, meaning that members of the subgroup are distributed more or less evenly across sampling clusters. For these kinds of subgroups, it turns out that *comparisons* are relatively efficient, from a sampling standpoint. The technical explanation for this phenomenon is that there is a higher degree of covariance between such subgroup pairs than would be the case in a comparison of independent subgroups. Now let us offer a fairly nontechnical illustration to indicate why this is so. Suppose that a researcher interested in use of marijuana during the senior year of high school obtained data from five high schools concerning female seniors' marijuana use and data from five other high schools concerning male seniors' marijuana use. Suppose that the percentage values for marijuana use during senior year were as follows:

Female seniors (five schools): 60%, 20%, 65%, 30%, 50%

Male seniors (five other schools): 40%, 80%, 25%, 70%, 60%

Even though there is a difference of ten percentage points between males and females (if the five schools in each case are averaged), there is still so much variability among schools that one would not conclude with very much confidence that females in general are less likely than males to use marijuana during the senior year of high school. Suppose, on the other hand, that the researcher had obtained data from a total of only five schools and had obtained data concerning both male and female seniors in each school as follows:

	Females	Males
School A	60%	70%
School B	20%	25%
School C	65%	80%
School D	30%	40%
School E	50%	60%

The same group of percentages, this time based on five pairings of males and females rather than independent observations, are much more strongly suggestive of systematic differences between the sexes.

A process analogous to that illustrated above is involved when "cross-class" subgroups are compared, and the increased accuracy or sampling efficiency is reflected in relatively small sampling errors and design effects.

Design Effects for Trends. Thus far this discussion of factors influencing design effects and confidence intervals has focused only on groups and subgroups within a single year. But one of the central purposes of the Monitoring the Future project is to monitor trends over time; indeed, the study procedures have been standardized across years insofar as possible in order to provide the opportunity for sensitive measurement of change. One of the factors designed to produce an added degree of consistency from one year to the next is the use of each school for two data collections, which means that for any two successive years half of the sample of schools is the same. This, plus the fact that the other half of the school sample in a given year is from the same primary sampling units as the half sample it replaced, means that there is a good deal of consistency in the sampling and clustering of the sample from one year to the next. As a result, when cross-year comparisons are made (say, between 1976 and 1977), the design effects are appreciably smaller (i.e., the efficiency is greater) than if completely independent samples of schools had been drawn each year. In other words, the 1976 and 1977 samples are not independent; on the contrary, there is a considerable degree of covariance between them. A similar level of covariance occurs between any pair of adjacent-year samples (e.g., 1977 and 1978), because about half of the schools in both samples were the same. This covariance, or partial "matching," reduces the design effect for differences observed between adjacent years, compared to what they would have been with totally independent samples.

It follows from the discussion above that a trend over an interval greater than one year (e.g., a comparison between 1976 and 1978 which involves totally non-overlapping school samples) is likely to have a design effect which is larger than that for a comparison between adjacent-year samples.

Variables with Unusually Large Design Effects. Kish et al. (1976) stress the importance of computing sampling errors for many kinds of variables, and they point out that they have found "very wide ranges in values of sampling errors (standard errors and design effects) between diverse variables within the same survey" (p. 21). Our own experience has been that, among most variables, the variation in sampling errors and design effects seems more random than consistent, and thus we are reasonably comfortable with the use of averaging procedures (described below) in order to derive a set of general purpose tables. There are some important exceptions to the above generalization, however. Variables which are likely to be grouped according to geographical area (region and/or urbanicity), as well as variables that may differ systematically from one school to another, show much higher than usual amounts of homogeneity within sample clusters. It follows necessarily that such variables also have much higher than usual design effects. The variables in the Monitoring the Future study which seem most likely to show such high design effects tend to be grouped into the questionnaire segment dealing with background factors and educational aspirations (Section C of all questionnaire forms). These variables were excluded from the process of computing overall design effects and the confidence intervals provided in Tables A-1 and A-2. Appendix A provides a further discussion of some of these variables and offers some suggestions for adjusting the confidence interval tables to deal with them.

Procedures Used in Deriving Design Effects and Tables of Confidence Intervals

Having taken some pains to review the several factors which can influence design effects and confidence intervals, it is now a fairly simple matter for us to summarize the steps followed to compute the tables of confidence intervals shown in Appendix A. We were heavily influenced in this effort by the work of Kish and his colleagues (Kish, 1965; Kish et al., 1976) in two ways. First, we followed their recommendation that sampling errors be computed and averaged across a goodly number of variables and subgroups. Second, we paid particular attention to their observation that design effects tend to be smaller for subgroups than for total samples (a point discussed earlier in this appendix).

Confidence Intervals for Single Percentages. Our procedure was to compute sampling errors and design effects for most of the variables which are common to all five forms (those in the C sections of all questionnaires, and those in the B sections of Forms 2 through 5), and for every twentieth varia-

ble in the A, D, and E sections of Forms 2 through 5. (Form 1 was omitted because most of this form is comprised of drug-related items, and such items involve high proportions of missing data because respondents are instructed to skip over many questions which are not applicable to them). Design effects were computed for each of the subgroups reported in this volume, as well as for the total sample. Design effects for each subgroup and for the total were averaged across variables for the C section material (all five forms), the B section material (drug use measures, all five forms), and the sampling of variables from the A, D, and E sections (single form data). As noted earlier, the variables which showed unusually high levels of homogeneity within sample clusters were excluded from the C section variables when they were averaged. The 1977 data were used for this analysis. Later replication using 1976 data provided nearly identical values.

The averaging process consisted of taking a mean of the *square roots* of the design effects. Kish and his colleagues (1976) refer to the design effect as DEFF, and to the square root of the design effect as DEFT; thus, $\sqrt{\text{DEFF}}$ = DEFT. We will find it useful to use this terminology in what follows. The rationale for computing means of DEFT rather than DEFF is that the former value is directly proportionate to the size of confidence intervals. A further reason for doing so is that the values of DEFT approximate a normal distribution much more closely than the values of DEFF, which are skewed upward. (A comparison of mean DEFTs and median DEFTs showed them to be quite similar, something which certainly is not true of mean and median DEFFs).

Bearing in mind that design effects tend to be smaller for subgroups than for total samples, and bearing in mind also that confidence intervals are directly proportionate to DEFT and to $\sqrt{N}$, we plotted the mean DEFT values for the total sample and for all subgroups, in each case relating DEFT to $\sqrt{N}$. The results are shown in Figure B-1. Note that distinctions are made between "cross-class" and "segregated" subgroups, and between mean DEFTs based on five forms and those based on single forms (the $\sqrt{N}$ values for the latter are, of course, much smaller).*

Setting aside the "segregated" subgroups (regions and blacks) for the moment, it is clear that the rest of the mean DEFTs in Figure B-1 show a very clear and consistent pattern: the higher the value $\sqrt{N}$ the higher the mean DEFT. It turns out that these mean DEFT values are very closely approximated by the function DEFT =

*The five form data consisted of C section material, excluding those variables related to region, urbanicity, and/or socio-economic level.

Figure B-1
Design Effects for Single Percentages

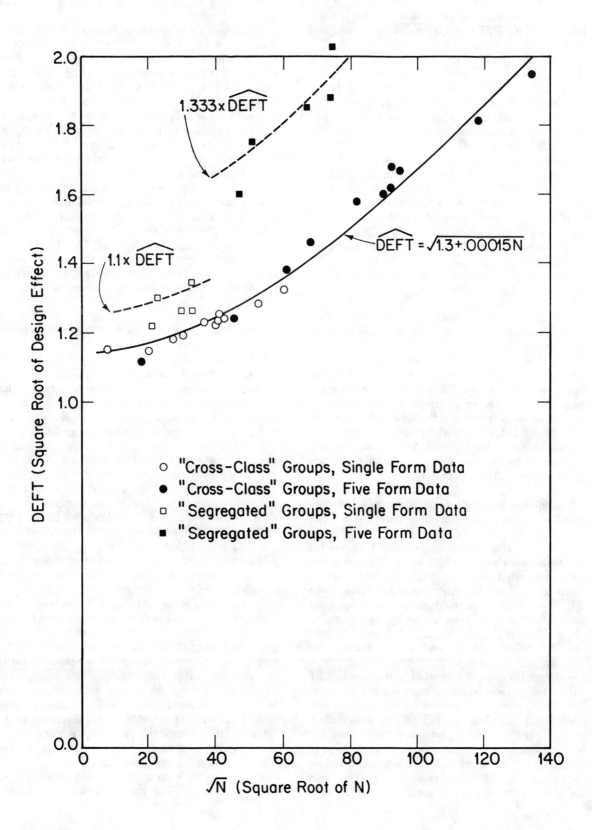

$$\widehat{DEFT} = \sqrt{1.3 + .00015N}$$

1.333 × $\widehat{DEFT}$

1.1 × $\widehat{DEFT}$

DEFT (Square Root of Design Effect)

○ "Cross–Class" Groups, Single Form Data
● "Cross–Class" Groups, Five Form Data
□ "Segregated" Groups, Single Form Data
■ "Segregated" Groups, Five Form Data

$\sqrt{N}$ (Square Root of N)

$\sqrt{1.3\ +\ .00015N}$, as shown by the solid line in the figure. (The function can also be stated as DEFF = 1.3 + .00015N.) The particular parameters in that function were derived empirically, but the basic function (i.e., DEFF = $\sqrt{a\ +\ bN}$) was adapted directly from the work of Kish et al. (1976).

Given the above function that fitted the mean DEFT values for the total sample and the "cross-class" subgroups, we returned to the problem of assigning DEFT values for the "segregated" subgroups. The simplest solution was to select two adjustment factors which could be multiplied by the confidence interval values in Table A-1. These adjustment factors are shown by the dashed lines in Figure B-1; they correspond to multiplying the "standard" DEFT (solid line) by a factor of 1.1 for single form data and by a factor of 1.33 for five form data. These adjustments, which were selected on empirical grounds, yield design effects for the "segregated" subgroups which are approximately equal to the design effects for the total sample (treating single form and five form data separately, of course). This is reassuring, since Kish et al. (1976) have reported that "segregated" subgroups can in general be expected to show design effects approximately equivalent to the design effects for the total sample.

After the data in Figure B-1 were plotted and the form of the main function (indicated by the solid line) was determined, DEFT values for drug use measures (material in Section B of all forms) were checked. It was found that the DEFTs for only two drug categories, alcohol and marijuana, exceeded the values indicated by the function; accordingly, adjustment factors were developed for these two drugs (1.6 and 1.35, respectively).

Confidence Intervals for Differences between Two Percentages. Our procedure here was directly parallel to that followed in determining confidence intervals for single percentages. DEFT values for the differences between 1977 and 1976 percentages were computed using virtually the same set of items as used earlier. Also computed were mean DEFT values for comparisons in the same year between subgroups such as males and females, those who did and did not plan to complete four years of college, blacks and whites, pairings of regions, and pairings of drug use groups. It was found that, for any given level of N, the mean DEFT values for subgroup comparisons were quite similar to the mean DEFT values for one-year trends; accordingly, all of these mean DEFTs were included in Figure B-2, which plots mean DEFTs for differences between percentages. In this figure, as in Figure B-1, the strong relationship was evident between mean DEFTs and the numbers of cases in the two groups being compared. This relationship

can be verly closely approximated by the function DEFT = $\sqrt{1.3\ +\ .000075N}$ (which can also be stated DEFF = 1.3 + .000075N), where N = $2N_1N_2/N_1\ +\ N_2$.

It was expected on grounds of sampling theory that as we found earlier, the function which fit most differences between percentages would not fit differences involving regions and differences involving blacks. In fact, the data indicated that some adjustment is necessary for black-white comparisons using data from all five forms, and also for comparisons as well as trends involving any region. We have not tried to show those adjustments in Figure B-2, but the several values involved are shown in the guidelines to Table A-2.

It was also expected on the grounds of sampling theory that trends across an interval of two or more years would show somewhat higher values of DEFT than one-year trends. It turned out that this was true only for data from all five forms; data based on one form only did not show significantly higher values. The adjustment factors for trends involving five forms over two or more years are shown in Table A-2.

Use of Weighted Numbers of Cases in Entering Confidence Interval Tables. We should mention in passing that the recommendations for using the tables in Appendix A indicate that *weighted* N values should be used. The computer program which generated our design effect statistics makes use of weights in calculating percentages and actual sampling variances. But in computing the DEFF ratio, defined as the actual sampling variance divided by the expected sampling variance from a simple random sample with the same number of elements, the program makes use of the *unweighted* numbers of cases to determine "the same number of elements." Since the mean weights used in the 1975, 1976, and 1977 data tables are slightly lower than 1.0, this means that when entering the tables in Appendix A with weighted data from those years, one is being very slightly "conservative" (slightly reduced risk of a Type 1 error, slightly increased risk of a Type 2 error). It is important to realize that if one took the trouble to make corrections for this "conservatism," the correction would rarely be as great as multiplying the Table A-1 and Table A-2 entries by a factor of .95; and in the large majority of cases the correction would involve multiplying by a factor of about .98. We find such discrepancies to be trivially small, particularly when compared with what Kish et al. (1976, p. 12) describe as the "heroic simplifications" required in some of the steps leading to general purpose tables of design effects and confidence intervals.

Before the 1978 data tables were produced we had come to realize the advantages in having

Figure B-2
Design Effects for Differences Between Percentages

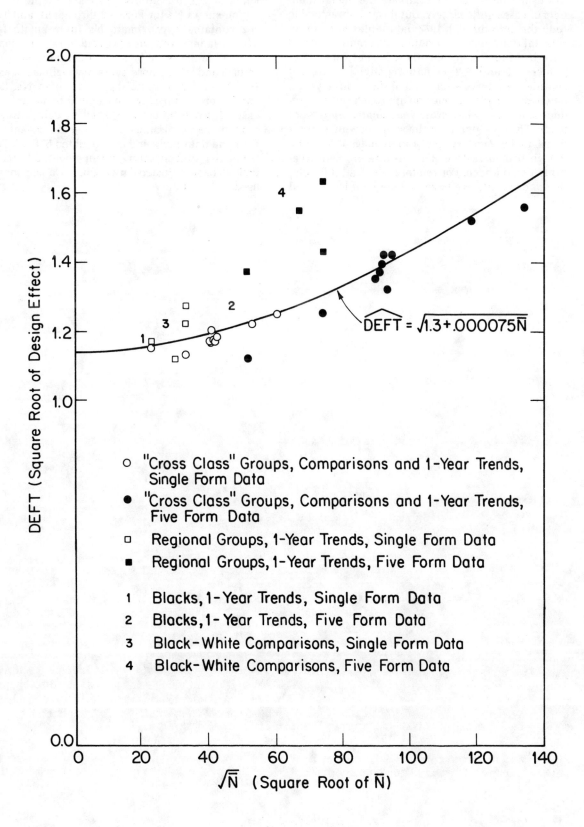

DEFT (Square Root of Design Effect)

$$\widehat{DEFT} = \sqrt{1.3 + .000075\overline{N}}$$

○   "Cross Class" Groups, Comparisons and 1-Year Trends, Single Form Data

●   "Cross Class" Groups, Comparisons and 1-Year Trends, Five Form Data

□   Regional Groups, 1-Year Trends, Single Form Data

■   Regional Groups, 1-Year Trends, Five Form Data

1   Blacks, 1-Year Trends, Single Form Data
2   Blacks, 1-Year Trends, Five Form Data
3   Black-White Comparisons, Single Form Data
4   Black-White Comparisons, Five Form Data

$\sqrt{\overline{N}}$ (Square Root of $\overline{N}$)

weighted values which averaged 1.0; accordingly, beginning with the 1978 data, the weighted N values in the tables do approximate the actual numbers of cases quite closely. But it was impractical to redo the 1975 through 1977 data tables to incorporate this refinement. Another alternative would have been to employ slightly different versions of Tables A-1 and A-2, containing slightly different confidence intervals for each of those three years; however, we felt that such an approach could introduce confusion when cross-year comparisons were made. Thus, we opted for the solution which seems to us to be most simple and manageable, even though it involves the slight degree of "conservatism" noted above. For readers who find this solution undesirable, we have included Tables B-1 and

B-2, which present weighted and unweighted Ns for the various subgroups for each year. Table B-1 contains Ns for all five forms (except for 1975 which shows Ns for Forms 2 through 5), and Table B-2 contains approximate Ns for a single form. Thus, readers who wish to avoid the slight "conservatism" (and also to be more precise for subgroups in 1978 and later whose average weight is not exactly 1.0) may determine the unweighted Ns. Some correction for missing data should be made in this case; this can be accomplished by calculating the percentage of missing data (using the weighted Ns from the data table and the weighted N from Table B-1 or B-2) and adjusting the unweighted N accordingly. These adjusted unweighted Ns can then be used in Appendix A.

Table B-1

Sample Sizes (Unweighted and Weighted) in Subgroups by Year

Number of Cases

	Class of 1975[a]		Class of 1976		Class of 1977		Class of 1978	
	Unwtd.	Wtd.	Unwtd.	Wtd.	Unwtd.	Wtd.	Unwtd.	Wtd.
Total Sample	12627	12108	16678	15138	18436	15830	18924	18916
Sex:								
Male	5799	5571	7999	7241	8449	7358	8603	8779
Female	6371	6100	7924	7257	9188	7850	9416	9266
Race:								
White	b	b	12933	11796	13818	12240	14663	14847
Black	b	b	1806	1716	2500	1938	2205	2096
Region:								
Northeast	3014	2695	4034	3570	4760	3959	4841	4607
North Central	3951	3832	5098	4687	5697	4758	5576	5411
South	3366	3857	4177	4597	4908	4820	5566	6292
West	2296	1724	3369	2284	3071	2294	2941	2605
College Plans:								
Complete 4 yrs	b	b	7963	6994	8933	7407	9264	8844
None or under 4 yrs	b	b	7179	6877	7764	7048	7857	8413
Illicit Drug Use:								
None	4329	4400	6532	6091	6672	5878	6400	6595
Marijuana Only	2044	1894	3950	3457	4955	4050	5354	5214
Few Pills	1163	1113	1942	1736	2173	1813	2329	2304
More Pills	2157	1989	3427	2987	3857	3266	3906	3885
Any Heroin	231	216	319	268	321	280	289	302

[a] The number of cases shown for 1975 is based on Forms 2 through 5 only, because the data from Form 1 are intentionally not included in tabulations based on drug and demographic items which appeared in all forms.

[b] Missing data problems were severe for race and college plans in 1975; accordingly, these data have been excluded from all tables in the 1975 report.

Table B-2

Sample Sizes (Unweighted and Weighted) in Subgroups by Year
for Questions on a Single Form

	Number of Cases							
	Class of 1975		Class of 1976		Class of 1977		Class of 1978	
	Unwtd.	Wtd.	Unwtd.	Wtd.	Unwtd.	Wtd.	Unwtd.	Wtd.
Total Sample	3157	3027	3336	3028	3687	3166	3785	3783
Sex:								
Male	1450	1393	1600	1488	1690	1472	1721	1756
Female	1371	1525	1505	1451	1838	1570	1883	1853
Race:								
White	a	a	2587	2359	2764	2448	2933	2969
Black	a	a	361	343	500	388	441	419
Region:								
Northeast	754	674	807	714	952	792	968	921
North Central	988	958	1020	937	1139	952	1115	1082
South	842	964	835	919	982	964	1113	1258
West	574	431	674	457	614	459	588	521
College Plans:								
Complete 4 yrs	a	a	1593	1399	1787	1481	1853	1769
None or under 4 yrs	a	a	1436	1375	1553	1410	1571	1683
Illicit Drug Use:								
None	1082	1100	1306	1218	1334	1176	1280	1319
Marijuana Only	511	474	790	691	991	810	1071	1043
Few Pills	291	278	388	347	435	363	466	461
More Pills	539	497	685	597	771	653	781	777
Any Heroin	58	54	64	54	64	56	58	60

[a] Missing data problems were severe for race and college plans in 1975; accordingly, these data have been excluded from all tables in the 1975 report.

Further Applications of these Design Effects and Sampling Errors

One of the reasons for providing the above review of the factors influencing design effects and confidence intervals, and the procedures used in computing our confidence interval tables, is to provide sufficient background and data to permit the interested reader to go beyond the material provided in Appendix A. In this section we consider two specific extensions, the calculation of levels of "statistical significance" higher than 95 percent and the computation of means and their confidence intervals.

Calculating Confidence Intervals for Higher Levels of Statistical Significance. The entries contained in Tables A-1 and A-2 provide the 95 percent confidence level (also referred to as the .05 level of significance). These entries were computed by multiplying the standard error (square root of sample variance) by a factor of 1.96. The 99 percent confidence interval (.01 level of significance) uses a factor of 2.58 standard errors, and the 99.9 percent confidence interval (.001 level of significance) uses a factor of 3.29 standard errors. To convert the entries in Tables A-1 and A-2 to these higher levels, it is necessary only to multiply the entries by the appropriate constant shown below (keeping in mind that any other adjustments required in the tables must also be applied):

Confidence Interval	Significance Level	Multiply entries in Tables A-1 and A-2 by the following:
99%	.01	2.58/1.96 = 1.32
99.9%	.001	3.29/1.96 = 1.68

Computing Means and Their Confidence Intervals. Many of the questionnaire items included in this volume have ordinal response scales (e.g., agree, agree mostly, neither, disagree mostly, disagree), and it is often the case that a survey analyst will be willing to treat such scales as if they involved equal intervals. In such cases, means and standard deviations are more "efficient" in their use of information than are dichotomies which yield a single percentage or a pair of percentages (e.g., those who respond "agree" or "agree mostly," versus all others). It is a relatively straightforward matter to compute means and standard deviations for the total sample or any of the subgroups treated in this volume. The problem, then, is to be able to

specify confidence intervals for the means, or for the differences between pairs of means. In the case of simple random samples, one needs only the means, standard deviations (or variances), and numbers of cases in order to compute confidence intervals. But in complex samples such as the present one, it is also necessary to take account of design effects. If an estimate of design effect is available, one of the simplest procedures to follow is to divide the actual numbers of cases by the design effect (thereby "depreciating" the actual number to its equivalent value in simple random sample terms) and then employ the standard statistical procedures which have been developed for application to simple random samples. Thus, for example, if the design effect (DEFF) for a sample of 18,000 were 4.0, then one could divide the 18,000 by 4.0 and the result, 4,500, could be entered as the value of "N" in statistical tables and formulas designed for use with simple random samples. To take another example, if one were comparing means based on two subgroups, each involving about 9,000 cases, and if DEFF (for both subgroups) was 2.0, then one could compute the significance of the difference between the two means as if the N for each group were 4,500 (i.e., 9,000 divided by 2.0)

In short, the strategy involves dividing the actual number of cases by the appropriate DEFF in order to get a "simple random sampling equivalent N" or, more simply, an "effective N" for use in statistical procedures designed for random samples.

Design Effects for Use in Computing "Effective Ns." In order to employ the strategy outlined above, one must have estimates of design effects which are judged to be appropriate for one's purposes. In the case of means based on the percentages reported in this volume, we are confident (based on personal communications with Kish) that it is appropriate to use the same DEFF values as were used in developing Tables A-1 and A-2. For other, more complex statistics, we cannot make the same assertion, although it is generally the case that design effects for such statistics are not larger than those for means and percentages (Kish and Frankel, 1970; Frankel, 1971).

In Table B-3 we provide guidelines for computing DEFF values for single percentages (or means) and for differences between two percentages (or means). For reasons discussed elsewhere in this appendix, we must provide for different (and somewhat higher) DEFFs for "segregated" subgroups (regional subgroups and sometimes also blacks), and for trends over two or more years (in contrast to one-year trends). And in all instances, of course, the DEFF values are very much influenced by the average size of sampling clusters, which is always dependent on the number of cases

Table B-3
Guidelines for Computing Design Effects (DEFFs) for Percentages
and Means Derived from Monitoring the Future Samples

DEFINITIONS

$$\text{DEFF (design effect)} = \frac{\text{(estimated) sampling variance}}{\begin{array}{c}\text{expected sampling variance from simple}\\ \text{random sample with same number of elements}\end{array}}$$

N = number of respondents on whom a single percentage or mean is based

$\overline{N} = 2N_1 N_2 / (N_1 + N_2)$, for use in comparisons of two percentages or means, based on two groups of sizes N_1 and N_2.

DESIGN EFFECT FORMULAS

1. For single percentages or means involving . . .
   a. regional subgroups or blacks
      DEFF for single form data .... $(1.3 + .00015N) (1.21)$
      DEFF for five form data .... $(1.3 + .00015N) (1.78)$

   b. all other subgroups or total sample
      DEFF for single form *or* five form data .... $1.3 + .00015N$

2. For comparisons between . . .
   a. any two regions
      DEFF for single form data .... $(1.3 + .000075\overline{N}) (1.32)$
      DEFF for five form data .... $(1.3 + .000075\overline{N}) (2.25)$

   b. blacks and whites
      DEFF for single form data .... $1.3 + .000075\overline{N}$
      DEFF for five form data .... $(1.3 + .000075\overline{N}) (1.56)$

   c. genders, college plans groups, or any two "drug use" subgroups
      DEFF for single form *or* five form data .... $1.3 + .000075\overline{N}$

3. For one-year trends involving . . .
   a. any region
      DEFF for single form data .... $1.3 + .000075\overline{N}$
      DEFF for five form data .... $(1.3 + .000075\overline{N}) (1.56)$
   b. all other subgroups or total sample
      DEFF for single form or five form data .... $1.3 + .000075\overline{N}$

4. For trends over two or more years involving . . .
   a. any region
      DEFF for single form data .... $1.3 + .000075\overline{N}$
      DEFF for five form data .... $(1.3 + .000075\overline{N}) (1.82)$
   b. all other subgroups or total sample
      DEFF for single form data .... $1.3 + .000075\overline{N}$
      DEFF for five form data .... $(1.3 + .000075\overline{N}) (1.32)$

(N). Accordingly, all of the design effect formulas in Table B-3 require computations which take account of N. (It should also be noted that the formulas in Table B-3 correspond exactly to the values of design effects and adjustment factors used in Tables A-1 and A-2 in Appendix A.)

A Concluding Note. In their very useful paper dealing with sampling errors for fertility surveys, Kish et al. (1976) commented that some of the methods they used ". . . emerged after several false starts." They went on to say that the volume and diversity of the data they were dealing with ". . . presented new challenges and opportunities." And they added, "Our methods are subject to further developments and modifications, and we invite participation and suggestions" (p. 10). Our own attempts to apply the methods of Kish and his colleagues to the data reported in this volume have been challenged by the diversity of the data, have involved several false starts, and we hope are subject to further developments and modifications. We invite readers to offer their suggestions, and we also encourage readers to inquire about further work that we and/or others may carry out during the coming months and years.

Appendix C
Questionnaire Covers, Instructions, and Sample Page

monitoring **the future**

a continuing study of the lifestyles and values of youth

This questionnaire is part of a nationwide study of high school seniors, conducted each year by the University of Michigan's Institute for Social Research. The questions ask your opinions about a number of things--the way things are now and the way you think they ought to be in the future. In a sense, many of your answers on this questionnaire will count as "votes" on a wide range of important issues.

If this study is to be helpful, it is important that you answer each question as thoughtfully and frankly as possible. All your answers will be kept strictly confidential, and will never be seen by anyone who knows you.

This study is completely voluntary. If there is any question that you or your parents would find objectionable for any reason, just leave it blank.

In a few months, we would like to mail each of you a summary of the nationwide results from this study. Also, in about a year we would like to mail another questionnaire to some of you, asking about how your plans have worked out and what's happening in your lives.

In order to include you in these mailings, we ask for your name and address on a special form at the end of this questionnaire. This form is to be torn out and handed in separately. Once the address form and the questionnaire have been separated, there is no way they can be matched again, except by using a special computer tape at the University of Michigan. The only purpose for that tape is to match a follow-up questionnaire with this one.

Other seniors have said that these questionnaires are very interesting and that they enjoy filling them out. We hope you will too. Be sure to read the instructions on the other side of this cover page before you begin to answer. Thank you very much for being an important part of this project.

INSTITUTE FOR SOCIAL RESEARCH
THE UNIVERSITY OF MICHIGAN
ANN ARBOR, MICHIGAN

INSTRUCTIONS

1. This is not a test, so there are no right or wrong answers; we would
    like you to work fairly quickly, so that you can finish.

2. All of the questions should be answered by marking one of the answer spaces.
    If you don't always find an answer that fits exactly, use the one that comes
    closest. If any question does not apply to you, or you are not sure of what it
    means, just leave it blank.

3. Your answers will be read automatically by a machine called an optical mark
    reader. Please follow these instructions carefully:

    • Use only the black lead pencil you have been given.

    • Make heavy black marks inside the circles.

    • Erase cleanly any answer you wish to change.

    • Make no other markings or comments on the
      answer pages, since they interfere with the
      automatic reading. (If you want to add a
      comment about any question, please use the
      space provided below.)

These kinds of markings
will work: ● ◖ ⬤

These kinds of markings
will NOT work: ⊙ ⬤ ○

(THIS SPACE FOR WRITTEN COMMENTS)

WHY YOUR NAME AND ADDRESS?

As we told you earlier, we'd like to send you a summary of the nationwide results of the present study, and in about a year we want to mail a shorter questionnaire to some of you. In order to include you in these follow-ups, we would like to have an address where information will be sure to reach you during the coming year.

HOW IS CONFIDENTIALITY PROTECTED?

- The information on this page will be used ONLY for mailing, and will always be kept separate from your answers. A special Grant of Confidentiality from the U.S. government protects all information gathered in this research project.

- The questionnaire and address pages will be collected separately, sealed immediately in separate envelopes, and sent to two different cities for processing.

- Once a questionnaire and address page have been separated, there is no way they can be matched, except by using a special computer tape at the University of Michigan. That tape contains the two DIFFERENT numbers that appear on the back of this address page and on the back of the questionnaire. These numbers will be used ONLY to match a follow-up questionnaire with this one.

Before filling out this address page, please separate it from the rest of the questionnaire by FOLDING ALONG THE PERFORATED LINE AND TEARING CAREFULLY.

Please **PRINT** your name and the address where you can most likely be reached during the coming year.

Mr.
Miss
Ms. _____
Mrs.   FIRST NAME   INITIAL   LAST NAME

STREET _____

CITY _____

STATE _____ ZIP _____

TELEPHONE NO.   (   ) — _____
                     AREA

In case we should have trouble getting mail to you, if you move, please **PRINT** the name and address of one other person (with a different address than your own) who will know where to reach you in the future. (Examples of such a person: aunt or uncle, older sister or brother, or close friend.)

Mr.
Miss
Ms. _____
Mrs.   FIRST NAME   INITIAL   LAST NAME

STREET _____

CITY _____

STATE _____ ZIP _____

TELEPHONE NO.   (   ) — _____
                     AREA

THANK YOU AGAIN FOR YOUR HELP

PART A

* **BEFORE BEGINNING BE SURE YOU HAVE READ THE INSTRUCTIONS ON THE COVER.**

1. Taking all things together, how would you say things are these days--would you say you're very happy, pretty happy, or not too happy these days?

   ○ Very happy
   ○ Pretty happy
   ○ Not too happy

2. Some people think a lot about the social problems of the nation and the world, and about how they might be solved. Others spend little time thinking about these issues. How much do you think about such things?

   ① Never
   ② Seldom
   ③ Sometimes
   ④ Quite often
   ⑤ A great deal

3. Of all the problems facing the nation today, how often do you worry about each of the following? (Mark one circle for each line.)

	Never	Seldom	Sometimes	Often
a. Chance of nuclear war	①	②	③	④
b. Population growth	①	②	③	④
c. Crime and violence	①	②	③	④
d. Pollution	①	②	③	④
e. Energy shortages	①	②	③	④
f. Race relations	①	②	③	④
g. Hunger and poverty	①	②	③	④
h. Using open land for housing or industry	①	②	③	④
i. Urban decay	①	②	③	④
j. Economic problems	①	②	③	④
k. Drug abuse	①	②	③	④

4. How well do you think your experiences and training (at home, school, work, etc.) have prepared you to be a good. . .

	Poorly	Not So Well	Fairly Well	Well	Very Well
a. ...husband or wife?	①	②	③	④	⑤
b. ...parent?	①	②	③	④	⑤
c. ...worker on a job?	①	②	③	④	⑤

5. Apart from the particular kind of work you want to do, how would you rate each of the following settings as a place to work? (Mark one circle for each line.)

	Not At All Acceptable	Somewhat Acceptable	Acceptable	Desirable
a. Working in a large corporation	①	②	③	④
b. Working in a small business	①	②	③	④
c. Working in a government agency	①	②	③	④
d. Working in the military service	①	②	③	④
e. Working in a school or university	①	②	③	④
f. Working in a police department or police agency	①	②	③	④
g. Working in a social service organization	①	②	③	④
h. Working with a small group of partners	①	②	③	④
i. Working on your own (self-employed)	①	②	③	④

6. If you were to get enough money to live as comfortably as you'd like for the rest of your life, would you want to work?

   ① I would want to work
   ② I would not want to work

—1—

(Base Year & Follow-up: Form 5—Part A)

References

Adelson, J. "What Generation Gap?" *New York Times Magazine*. January 18, 1970, pp. 1-11.

Adelson, J. "Adolescence and the Generation Gap." *Psychology Today*, September 1979, pp. 33-37.

Bachman, J.G.; O'Malley, P.M.; and Johnston, J. Youth in Transition, Volume VI: *Adolescence to Adulthood — A Study of Change and Stability in the Lives of Young Men*. Ann Arbor: Institute for Social Research, 1978.

Bachman, J. G., and Johnston, L. D. *The Monitoring the Future Project Design and Procedures*. Ann Arbor: Institute for Social Research, 1978.

Frankel, M. R. *Inference from Survey Samples: An Empirical Investigation*. Ann Arbor: Institute for Social Research, 1971.

Golladay, M. *The Condition of Education*. National Center for Education Statistics, Washington, D.C.: U.S. Government Printing Office, 1976.

Golladay, M. *The Condition of Education*. National Center for Education Statistics, *Volume 3, Part 1*. Washington, D.C.: U.S. Government Printing Office, 1977.

Hays, William L. *Statistics for the Social Sciences* (2nd ed.). New York: Holt, Rinehart, & Winston, 1973.

Johnston, L. D. *Drugs and American Youth*. Ann Arbor: Institute for Social Research, 1973.

Johnston, L. D.; Bachman, J. G.; and O'Malley, P. M. *Drug Use Among American High School Students 1975-1977* (National Institute on Drug Abuse). Washington, D.C.: U.S. Government Printing Office, 1977.

Johnston, L. D.; Bachman, J. G.; and O'Malley, P. M. *Drugs and the Class of 1978: Behaviors, Attitudes, and Recent National Trends* (National Institute on Drug Abuse). Washington, D.C.: U.S. Government Printing Office, 1979.

Johnston, L. D.; O'Malley, P. M.; and Eveland, L. K. *Some Preliminary Results from Drugs and American Youth II: A Longitudinal Resurvey*. (Interim report to the National Institute on Drug Abuse.) Ann Arbor: Institute for Social Research, 1975.

Kish, L., and Frankel, M. R. "Balanced Repeated Replication for Standard Errors." *Journal of the American Statistical Association, 65 (1970): 1071-1094*.

Kish, L.; Groves R.M.; and Krotki, K.P. *Sampling Errors for Fertility Surveys* (Occasional Papers Series No. 17). Voorburg, Netherlands: International Statistical Institute, 1976.

U. S. Bureau of the Census. *Current Population Reports*, Series P-20, No. 319. School enrollment — social and economic characteristics of students: October 1976. Washington, D.C.: U.S. Government Printing Office, 1978.